*To All of the Students
who have participated in my
Investigating Culture class
in one version or another,
Thank You*

Carol
Delaney

INVESTIGATING

CULTURE

An
Experiential
Introduction
to
Anthropology

Blackwell
Publishing

BLACKWELL PUBLISHING
350 Main Street, Malden, MA 02148-5020, USA
9600 Garsington Road, Oxford OX4 2DQ, UK
550 Swanston Street, Carlton, Victoria 3053, Australia

First published 2004 by Blackwell Publishing Ltd

5   2006

Library of Congress Cataloging-in-Publication Data

Delaney, Carol Lowery, 1940–
   Investigating culture : an experiential introduction to anthropology /
Carol Delaney.
      p. cm.
   Includes bibliographical references and index.
   ISBN 0-631-22236-7 (alk. paper) – ISBN 0-631-22237-5 (alk. paper)
1. Anthropology. I. Title.

GN25.D45 2004
301–dc21

                                          2003012131

ISBN-13: 978-0-631-22236-1 (alk. paper) – ISBN-13: 978-0-631-22237-8 (alk. paper)

A catalogue record for this title is available from the British Library.

Set in 10/12.5 pt Dante
by SNP Best-set Typesetter Ltd, Hong Kong
Printed and bound in Singapore
by Markono Print Media Pte Ltd

The publisher's policy is to use permanent paper from mills that operate a sustainable forestry policy, and which has been manufactured from pulp processed using acid-free and elementary chlorine-free practices. Furthermore, the publisher ensures that the text paper and cover board used have met acceptable environmental accreditation standards.

For further information on
Blackwell Publishing, visit our website:
www.blackwellpublishing.com

Contents

Acknowledgments

The course on which this book is based emerged as a result of "trial by fire" when I had to offer a course – to start in two weeks' time – in cultural anthropology and comparative religion to a small group of freshmen at a large East coast university. I had very little time to prepare and decided to use the class as an experiment, that is, to use the experience of entering the university as an analogy to think about what it was like for anthropologists to go elsewhere. It worked. It was exciting. We had a great time and learned a lot. However, the course and the book are not just for freshmen: it can be, and has been, used at any time and place during the typical four-year college education. I continue to hear from the students who took that first course long ago (1986) who feel it set them on a path of discovery which is what an undergraduate education ought to be. Over the years the course has changed considerably, in part because of the insights and critiques of my students.

In addition, however, I have been fortunate to get research funds to hire some of them as research assistants. Not only have they made trips to the library while I was writing, and looked up material on the Internet, at which they are far more proficient than I am, but also they have served as "guinea pigs" telling me when the tone was all wrong or that a particular example was passé (so blame them if it doesn't grab you!). They have also suggested topics and then gone and found material to address them. I would, therefore, like to acknowledge the help of Alisha Niehaus (my first student research assistant), who was indefatigable in locating interesting material and telling me when I was "off." Sam Gellman and Andrea Christensen helped during the summer of 2001 and Andrea, along with Katie Cueva, assisted during the final phases in the summer of 2002. Theirs was a tough job: they had to do a lot of research on new topics and they served as editors, reading and rereading the chapters. At the final stage, doctoral student Kevin O'Neill chased down the missing references. To all of you I extend heartfelt thanks; the book is a better product because of your input and I am deeply grateful for your help.

But I must also acknowledge the initial interest and enthusiasm of Jane Huber, my editor at Blackwell Publishing. Without her ongoing support my energy might have flagged; in addition, she suggested material and perspectives when my focus had narrowed. My daughter, Elizabeth Quarartiello, and colleagues Miyako Inoue (Stanford) and Don Brenneis (University of California, Santa Cruz) read and made suggestions for the language chapter. Steve Piker, a professor at Swarthmore, was brave enough to try out the penultimate draft on his students at the same time I was using it with mine, and the response has been gratifying. I hope the future users of this book find inspiration, new perspectives, and ways of making connections between things they never thought were related.

Carol Delaney

The author and publishers gratefully acknowledge the following for permission to reproduce copyright material:

1   Bohannan, Laura. "Shakespeare in the Bush." *Natural History* (Aug–Sept 1966): 28–33. © Laura Bohannan.
2   Beckham, Sue Bridwell. "The American Front Porch: Women's Liminal Space." From *Making the American Home: Middle-Class Women and Material Culture, 1840–1940*, ed. Marilyn Ferris Motz and Pat Browne. Bowling Green: Bowling Green State University Press, 1988, pp. 69–78, 82–9. © 1988. Reprinted by permission of The University of Wisconsin Press.
3   Goodman, Ellen. "Time is for Savoring." *Boston Globe*, October 1977. Copyright 1977 by Globe Newspaper Co (MA). Reproduced with permission of Globe Newspaper Co (MA) via Copyright Clearance Center.
4   Sahlins, Marshall. "The Original Affluent Society." From *Stone Age Economics*. Chicago: Aldine-Atherton, London Routledge, 1972, pp. 1–39, 316–19, 321–4, 326–7, 329–31, 333–6.
5   LeGuin, Ursula. "She Unnames Them." From *Buffalo Gals and Other Animal Presences*. New York: Plume Books, 1987, pp. 194–6. © 1985 by Ursula Le Guin, first appeared in the *New Yorker*; reprinted by permission of the author and the author's agent, the Virginia Kidd Agency, Inc.
6   Dundes, Alan. "Seeing is Believing." *Natural History Magazine* (May 1972): 8–12, 86–7. Reprinted by permission of Natural History Magazine.
7   Eckert, Penelope. "Symbols of Category Membership." From *Jocks and Burnouts: Social Categories and Identity in the High School*. New York: Teachers College Press, 1989, pp. 49–72, 185–8.
8   Hocart, A. M. "Kinship Systems." From *The Life-Giving Myth*. London: Tavistock Publishers, 1973 / Royal Anthropological Society, pp. 173–84.
9   Miner, Horace. "Body Ritual Among the Nacirema." *American Anthropologist*, 58 (1956): 503–7.

10 Dubisch, Jill. "You Are What You Eat: Religious Aspects of the Health Food Movement." From *The American Dimension: Culture Myths and Social Realities*, 2nd ed., ed. Susan P. Montague and W. Arens. Palo Alto, CA: Mayfield Publishing Company, 1981, pp. 115–27. Reprinted by permission of Jill Dubisch and The McGraw-Hill Companies Inc.

11 Ribeyro, Julio Ramón. "Alienation." From *Marginal Voices: Selected Stories*, translated by Dianne Douglas © 1993. By permission of the University of Texas Press.

12 Geertz, Clifford. "The Impact of the Concept of Culture on the Concept of Man." From *The Interpretation of Cultures: Selected Essays by Clifford Geertz*. Basic Books, 1973, pp. 33–54. With permission from Clifford Geertz.

13 Easter, Mary. Poem: "Sitting on the Porch." From *Absorb the Colors: Poems by Northfield Women Poets*, ed. Beverly Voldseth and Karen Herseth Wee. Northfield, MN: privately published, 1986. Reproduction with permission from Mary Easter.

14 Atwood, Margaret. "An Encyclopedia of Lost Practices: The Saturday Night Date." *New York Times Magazine* (December 5, 1999). Late Edition – Final, Section 6, p. 148, column 1.

15 Erica Jong. "Is Life the Incurable Disease?" From *At the Edge of the Body*. New York: Holt, Rinehart and Winston, p. 17. © 1979, 1991 Erica Mann Jong. Used by permission of Erica Jong.

16 Leviticus 11. Herbert G. May and Bruce M. Metzger (editors). From *Revised Standard Version of the Bible* © 1946, 1952, 1971 by the Division of Christian Education of the National Council of Churches of Christ in the USA. Used by permission. All rights reserved.

17 Shell, Ellen Ruppel. "An International School Lunch Tour." *New York Times*, Op-Ed (February 1, 2003). Late Edition – Final, Section A, p. 19, column 1.

18 Morris, Bob. "Precious Cargo." *New York Times Magazine*. Style (October 11, 1998). Sunday, Late Edition – Final, Section 6, p. 63, column 1.

19 Delaney, Carol. "Let's Send All Our Missiles to the Sun." *New York Times* (December 30, 1991). © 1991 Carol Delaney.

20 Lowell, Robert. From "Hawthorne." In *For the Union Dead*. Farrar, Straus & Giroux, Inc., and Faber & Faber, Ltd., 1964, p. 39. © 1959 by Robert Lowell. Copyright renewed 1987 by Harriet Lowell, Caroline Lowell, and Sheridan Lowell. Reprinted by permission of Farrar, Straus and Giroux LLC and Faber and Faber Ltd.

Table Credits

Table 3.1   "Mean daily consumption as percentage of recommended allowances." From Margaret McArthur, "Food Consumption and Dietary Levels of Groups of Aborigines Living on Naturally Occurring Foods." In *Records of the Australian-American Scientific Expedition to Arnhem Land, Volume 2: Anthropology and Nutrition*, ed. C. P. Mountford. Melbourne: Melbourne University Press, 1960. In Mountford volume as Figure 3.5.

Table 3.2   "Daytime rest and sleep, Fish Creek group." From Frederick D. McCarthy and Margaret McArthur. "The Food Quest and the Time Factor in Aboriginal Economic Life." In *Records of the Australian-American Scientific Expedition to Arnhem Land, Volume 2: Anthropology and Nutrition*, ed. C. P. Mountford. Melbourne: Melbourne University Press, 1960. In Mountford volume as Figure 3.5.

Table 3.3   "Daytime rest and sleep, Hemple Bay group." From Frederick D. McCarthy and Margaret McArthur. "The Food Quest and the Time Factor in Aboriginal Economic Life." In *Records of the Australian-American Scientific Expedition to Arnhem Land, Volume 2: Anthropology and Nutrition*, ed. C. P. Mountford. Melbourne: Melbourne University Press, 1960. In Mountford volume as Figure 3.5.

Table 3.4   "Summary of Dobe Bushmen work diary." From Richard Lee, "!Kung Bushman Subsistence: An Input–Output Analysis." In *Environment and Cultural Behavior*, ed. A. Vayda. Garden City, NY: Natural History Press, 1969. Reprinted with permission from Natural History Press 1969.

Every effort has been made to trace copyright holders and to obtain their permission for the use of copyright material. The author and publishers will gladly receive any information enabling them to rectify any error or omission in subsequent editions.

1

Disorientation and Orientation

Introduction; how culture provides orientation in the world; what is culture and how do anthropologists investigate it? Learning to think anthropologically.

Disorientation and Orientation

Introduction

A number of years ago I was asked to teach a course on anthropology and comparative religion to incoming freshmen at a large urban university on the East coast. I was intrigued because anthropology is not usually taught to freshmen, at least not in the United States. Furthermore, the course was to begin in two weeks, leaving me very little time to prepare a syllabus and order books. Consequently, I decided to take a bold approach. Rather than trying to do a typical survey course, beginning with human origins and moving on to hunters and gatherers, and then peasants, to modern urban society, I decided to treat the course as an anthropological experience. I wanted students to imagine themselves as anthropologists coming to study another culture, for, although they wouldn't think of it that way, that was a part of what they were doing when they entered college. I wanted them to learn not only *about* anthropology, but also about what it is to *be* an anthropologist.

That original course was an adventure for all of us and it was a great success. However, when I first came to Stanford, I was not able to teach it as a freshman course because freshmen were being tracked into a number of prescribed large lecture courses. Instead, I taught somewhat revised forms for upperclassmen, for students planning to go abroad for a time, and at the Stanford campus in Berlin. Other professors borrowed it, modified it, and taught it at Stanford campuses in Spain and Italy. When the university instituted a "freshman seminar" program a few years ago I was able, once again, to teach this course to entering freshmen. While the course can, obviously, be taught in a number of contexts, I still think it works best for freshmen as they enter college or university, not because the material is simplified, but because their experience is fresh.

The course is an innovative way to introduce students to anthropology, and because it has been a success, I was asked by the publisher to write a textbook based on it so that it might become available to students elsewhere. Although each chapter is devoted to one of the topics I discuss in class, such as space or time or food, it is not meant to be an exhaustive analysis of any one of them. Otherwise, each chapter could easily have become a book on its own. Even less is this book meant to be an in-depth analysis of American, British, or any other culture, even as it is intended for use in the United States and Britain. I juxtapose a range of material – classical anthropological material about a variety of cultures, contemporary items drawn from the newspaper or the Web, from Stanford, and from my own fieldwork in Turkey – for the purpose of generating ideas and indicating the range of areas for further exploration.

My goal is not to teach *about* other cultures. That is the normal pedagogical approach adopted in schools, but it is passive and distanced learning. I believe that people learn best when they are actively involved in the process. You will learn about anthropology and about culture by learning how to think like an anthropologist, that is, by becoming amateur anthropologists. Not everyone is able to go to another culture to gain this experience, but it is possible to simulate it. As I illustrate below, you will learn to draw analogies between your own experience of entering and becoming acclimated to college life and the experience of anthropologists who go to study another culture. Both can be quite disorienting, at least initially. Hold on to the disorientation for a while because it provides some mental space from which you can grasp, as they occur, aspects of the new culture you have entered and how these aspects relate to each other. Even while the focus must be on your own environment, the aim is not to illuminate merely the "culture" of your particular school, but to explore the way those particular aspects connect to and represent concepts, values, and structures of the wider culture. Indeed, I think the use of the word "culture" in that restricted sense is inappropriate.

Clifford Geertz, probably the most famous American anthropologist alive today, made the point very clear: "[T]he locus of study is not the object of study. Anthropologists don't study villages (tribes, towns, neighborhoods . . .); they study *in* villages" (1973: 22). Substitute "college" for village and you will see what I mean. Although I conducted my fieldwork in a village in central Turkey, my aim was to try to understand something about Turkish culture and how it was inflected in that one place. Analogously, the object of your study is the culture of your country even as you investigate it in your particular locale. My goal is to get you to learn *experientially*, to get you to adopt an anthropological approach that you can use to investigate any social or cultural phenomenon in any culture. Prerequisite is a mind open to new ways of thinking about things; it requires that you take nothing for granted. Anything is available for inspection, including the most ordinary, mundane items and events such as a McDonald's hamburger, a pair of blue jeans, a birthday, or New Year's Eve and so forth. These items and events are *clues* you can use to investigate your sociocultural system. Each of them provides a window into an entire system of beliefs, power relations, and values. For example, what would you make of a culture that celebrates death days rather than birthdays? How might that fact relate to other facets of that society? What other kinds of questions would you need to ask to begin to understand not just that practice but the culture in which it occurs?

Disorientation

The experience of beginning college can be exhilarating, anxiety-producing, and disorienting. This is magnified for those who come from other parts of the country or from foreign countries. Even when the language is familiar and you have not moved from your home town or city, college life is different from high school. It *is* like entering a new world. You don't know where anything is or how to find it; you don't understand the time schedule or how to manage your time; you don't know the lingo – the insider abbreviations and acronyms; and you don't know the code of dress or behavior. For those who go away to college, it might be the first time you are away from home, alone. It might be the first time you share a room with someone or have a room of your own. It might be the first time you have to schedule your own time.

Listen to the echoes of your experience when you read what is one of the most famous and oft-quoted sentences in anthropology. It was written by Bronislaw Malinowski, who is credited with inventing the anthropological method of intensive fieldwork. This is what he said at the beginning of his work in the Trobriand Islands in the South Pacific, where he was interned during World War I:

> Imagine yourself suddenly set down surrounded by all your gear, alone on a tropical beach close to a native village, while the launch or dinghy which has brought you sails away out of sight. ([1922] 1961: 4)

An analogous translation might be something like:

> "Imagine yourself suddenly set down surrounded by all your gear, alone in your room but with unfamiliar people nearby, while the car that brought you drives away out of sight."

Many students, just like many anthropologists, get a feeling of panic at that moment. "What am I doing here?" "Why didn't I go to X?" "I want to go home." Anthropologists call this feeling of panic "culture shock." The term is credited to Ruth Benedict, but Cora Du Bois defines it as a "syndrome precipitated by the anxiety that results from losing all your familiar cues" (cited in Golde [1970] 1986: 11); in short, you become disoriented. Culture shock is not confined to that initial moment but can resurface at various times at the beginning of any new adventure. Nor is it confined only to anthropologists or to students, but can occur at other life-changing moments, for example, when you take a new job or move to a new city. Anthropologists who have studied the phenomenon of "culture shock" have noted the following telltale signs: "frustration, repressed or expressed aggression against the source of discomfort, an irrational fervor for the familiar and comforting, and disproportionate anger at trivial interferences" (Golde, [1970] 1986: 11).[1] It is useful to keep this in mind during the first few weeks of college life.

As an example, let me tell you about something that happened to me when I began my fieldwork in Turkey. I was excited to be there and ready to begin my fieldwork but I didn't know how I was supposed to go about it or where to start. I recall that I got a craving for vanilla yogurt. This was a very trivial thing and I was never even that fond of yogurt at home, but in Turkey I had to have vanilla yogurt. Now you have to realize that Turkey is full of yogurt, it is one of their basic foods. Yogurt, yogurt everywhere, but no vanilla to be found anywhere. I was frustrated and angry: how could they not have vanilla? What kind of people are they anyway? I began a frantic search, feeling that I would not be happy until I found it; vanilla yogurt would be my comfort food, my little piece of home. I eventually found a few desiccated pods of vanilla in a spice shop and ground my own. After that I was prepared for anything.

In order to avoid severe culture shock and to overcome students' initial disorientation, it is no wonder colleges set aside some time, often several days, for "Orientation."

Orientation

An orientation program is, obviously, intended to help you get oriented in the new environment. Often you are told something about the history, the resources, and the rules of the school, you are shown where to go for class, for books, for food, for exercise, and for help if you get sick. Such a program helps you to get your bearings – literally and figuratively.

The purpose of orientation programs is to help you feel at home and become acclimated to your new environment. It can also be viewed quite productively as an *initiation* ritual, for it does initiate you into your new status – that of undergraduate. Initiation rituals are one type of *rites de passage* first analyzed by a Flemish anthropologist, Arnold Van Gennep, in 1909. Although there are a number of rites of passage, rites that mark transitions from one life stage to another, such as at birth, puberty, marriage, and death, Van Gennep focused primarily on initiation rites that occur around the time of puberty in a number of small-scale, kinship-based, hunter-gatherer societies, namely those societies we have so condescendingly called "primitive."[2] Initiation rites are the rituals that transform youths/adolescents into adults; during the rituals they are initiated by tribal elders into the lore of the tribe and into adult responsibilities. In some places the rites occur over a number of weeks or months, but in others they have been known to last several years. Among Australian aborigines, for example, the initiation rites traditionally took about four years, exactly equivalent to a typical American college education.

According to Van Gennep's schema, most *rites de passage* have three stages: (1) rites of separation, when the person is detached from his or her group or family; (2) rites that characterize the *liminal* period, which is *the* transitional stage. Victor

Turner, a famous British anthropologist who developed Van Gennep's schema in his own studies of ritual, characterized this stage as "betwixt and between" fixed statuses when a boy, for example, is no longer a child but not yet a man with adult responsibilities (1967: 93–111). The last stage (3) includes the rites of reaggregation when the transformed person is inserted back into society.

You will have to analyze your own orientation programs for some of these features. The example that follows, from my university, is meant to be used for comparative purposes; it is not held up as the norm or as an ideal, I use it because it is my locale. While some of the particulars vary from year to year, the orientation program follows quite closely the pattern laid down by Van Gennep. It is primarily for freshmen and it lasts for three days, a weekend, *before* the other students arrive. Students leave their homes, their familiar surroundings and friends. This is the beginning of the "separation" phase. On Friday the freshmen arrive, often with their parents, siblings, and sometimes friends in tow. Some come by car, others arrive by plane, train, or bus. They are taken to their living quarters and introduced to their roommates and the resident heads. After a few activities that include parents, there is an announced time when parents (and friends) are supposed to leave. This truly marks the "separation" phase, though at this point the separation is often more traumatic for the parents. Students then have their first dinner with their assembled dormmates.

Saturday resembles the "liminal" phase of the rite when initiates are expected to undergo a number of *ordeals*. At Stanford, these can vary from being led around campus in the dead of night not knowing where you are or where you are going, to being awakened at dawn and dragged out of bed to participate in a scavenger hunt. Later in the day students sit for hours and take placement exams that will determine what level of what classes they will be permitted to enroll in. They also must consider what other classes they will take and activities they would like to participate in. At least for a while, their choices will have an impact on their academic and social direction (or orientation). Other parts of the *ordeal* can include being quizzed on the names of other students, residence heads, the local jargon that they should have memorized, and so forth. In the evening they are sometimes required to participate in a race and gender sensitivity-training program, which can be unsettling for a number of students who must confront their prejudices. Then they are taught some of the new rules for academic and personal behavior – what is acceptable and what is not.

Culminating the orientation weekend is a football game, where the freshmen go *en masse* and sit in a special area reserved for them. Many alumni attend this game and faculty are given free passes. The freshmen are being made into Stanfordites; they are shown the school symbols, they hear the school songs and cheers for the first time, and they are being caught up in the school spirit, routing for *their* team against the opponents. This could be imagined as the *reaggregation* ritual, for symbolically, they are being incorporated into the Stanford community.

You could also easily imagine the entire four years of college as a prolonged initiation ritual; for during that time, you are separated from the rest of society. You are no longer a child, but are not yet a fully functioning adult. You have a special, liminal, "student" status that is socially recognized; you receive certain benefits –

discounts on buses, airplanes, movies, etc. and a wide berth for some types of disruptive behavior. During the college years students are freer than they ever will be again to "discover who they are," to try on various identities, and to prepare themselves for their adult roles in society. In this latter task, they are aided by the wisdom of the elders – professors and counselors – just as in initiation rites among traditional societies.

For some students, the liminal phase is more interesting or even comforting than what awaits them "outside" in the "real world" and they desire to stay on as long as possible. Eventually, however, most of them pass through the initiation and come out ready to be reinserted, as adults, into society. This achievement is marked by the graduation ceremony, which, with ironic connotations, is called "Commencement," no doubt to indicate that this is the *beginning* of the rest of your life, as a newly fledged person.

Anthropology

The foregoing may not be *at all* your image of what anthropology is. Most people think it has to do with *elsewhere* but not here, and think it has to do with "stones and bones." This is a very common assumption that I hear in the responses of people when I tell them that I am an anthropologist. They often launch into an account of some program they have seen on television about an ancient site or a recent bone find. They are thinking of archaeology (the "stones") and physical anthropology (the "bones"). Yet, these are only two of the traditional four subfields of anthropology. Linguistics is the third subfield. Other people sometimes think of Margaret Mead and realize that anthropology can also be about psychology and human behavior; the kinds of studies she conducted fall in the major "subfield" of the discipline – social and cultural anthropology. Many anthropologists today, myself included, no longer subscribe to the four-field division of the discipline but feel, instead, that the defining element is not so much what one studies but the *theoretical* stance one takes toward the material one studies. The difference has to do with the way people define or, at least, imagine human nature and culture (see Segal and Yanagisako 2004).

Nature/Culture

To give you some sense of what this means in practice, think about some of the ways you have tended to account for differences between *peoples*: environment, race, genetics, religion, economy, technology and development. Often these differences are collapsed into broader categories of *nature* vs. *culture*, with race and genetics put in the nature or biology box while religion, economy, and technology are put in the culture box. Yet the two categories can overlap since there has been an underlying assumption that those with the most advanced culture are also "better" naturally, that is, they have the best natural endowment (genes, intelligence, strength).

But who was making these judgments about "advanced" vs. "primitive," and whose scale was being used as the standard? Advanced in what sense? If kinship was the focus, then the system of the Australian aborigines was/is one of the most complex, as are, arguably, their religious concepts. If one takes technology of loco-motion as an index, then some of the Western nations are more advanced, and if one takes meditative practices, then Hindus or Zen Buddhists might be the most sophisticated. In the nineteenth century, social theorists ranked peoples of the world on an evolutionary, progressive, unilinear, and universal scale of culture that ended, not coincidentally, with themselves at the top. It was simply assumed that all peoples necessarily tread the same path to civilization. There was only one scale and one orientation – up and West.

A very popular notion about anthropology is that it is the search for human universals with the corollary that whatever is universal must, *ipso facto*, be natural. People want to know what is natural to the human species and often try to make analogies from animal behavior to human behavior, believing that the overlap indicates what is natural about human nature. For a long time it was believed that *homo sapiens* developed to their modern form first (two-legged stance, opposable thumb, large brain), and *then* invented culture. Instead, it is now generally accepted not just that *homo sapiens* developed from their ape-ical ancestors to their modern form but also, more importantly, that culture was part of that development. Clifford Geertz informs us that "the greater part of human cortical expansion has *followed*, not pre-ceded, the 'beginning' of culture" (1973: 64, emphasis mine). In other words, "cul-tural resources are ingredient, not accessory, to human thought" (Geertz 1973: 83).

Nevertheless, scientists continue to see in animal behavior (not so) faint echoes of our own. They persist in drawing analogies *from* animal *to* human, but really what they are doing is using concepts and beliefs drawn from human society, imposing them on animals, and then reading back again to human society. Curiously, Marx was the first to notice this sleight-of-hand movement: "It is remarkable how Darwin recognizes among beasts and plants his English society with its division of labour, competi-tion, opening of new markets, 'inventions,' and the Malthusian 'struggle for existence'" (cited in Sahlins 1976: 53). Engels continued:

> The whole Darwinian teaching of the struggle for existence is simply a trans-ference from society to living nature of Hobbes's doctrine of *"bellum omnium contra omnes"* and of the bourgeois-economic doctrine of competition together with Malthus's theory of population. When this conjurer's trick has been performed . . . the same theories are transferred back again from organic nature into history and it is now claimed that their validity as eternal laws of human society has been proved. (Cited in Sahlins 1976: 54)

In no way is this meant to detract from the general notion of human phys-ical evolution outlined by Darwin, but it does question some of the

"The war of all against all," or everyone out for himself. Hobbes believed that in a state of nature, humans would be at each other's throats. This assumption, at the heart of his philosophy, is behind much of economic rationality. However, *humans were never in a state of nature; humans developed in society and with culture.* That means that people are always affiliated with some group, such as a kinship group, where there are social ties that bind them to each other and rules that mitigate such actions. In addition, war is caused for all kinds of reasons; it is not the result of some innate human aggression.

This awareness is attributed to Franz Boas, the founder of American anthropology, by one of his famous students, Ruth Benedict. She believed that his fieldwork in Baffinland among people who could see different colors of sea water when he could not led him to the conclusion that the seeing eye is "not a mere physical organ but a means of perception conditioned by the tradition in which its possessor has been reared" (cited in Stocking, 1968: 146). There is a story that this experience is what converted Boas from a career in physics to one in anthropology. However, George Stocking, a leading historian of anthropology, has read Boas's letters and diary and thinks the story apocryphal, that the awareness was much more gradual.

assumptions he made about what motivates the process and the ease with which the animal–human equation is drawn when it comes to "society" or "social relations."[3]

A sense of the difference between those who assume they can "read" directly from animal behavior to human behavior and those who argue that there can be no unmediated account, that human culture must be considered, can readily be grasped from a film series produced by the BBC called *A Planet for the Taking*. In one of the films, identical sequences of animal behavior are shown but with different voice-over narratives; one about male dominance and aggression, the other about grooming behavior and bonding. It was easy to *see* the behavior in either scenario – another instance of the idea that we see what we are culturally trained to see, that the "seeing eye is the organ of tradition."

In a short but insightful article, "Seeing is Believing," Alan Dundes "shows how American culture affects the way Americans experience their world" (1972: 14; see chapter 4); especially illuminating is his discussion of the way we use sight metaphorically in describing the acquisition of knowledge (see my three examples in this sentence).[4] A blind student in my Fall 2001 class made us all aware of the extent to which Americans depend on sight, and not just the metaphor of it, as the primary means of cultural knowledge. For instance, think how quickly you make judgments about people based solely on how they look or the clothes they wear. Nevertheless, the *judgments* are made not because of sight but because of the meanings and values supplied by the culture.

While the capacity for culture is a human universal, that doesn't explain why cultures are so different. The fact that "everywhere people mate and produce children, have some sense of mine and thine and protect themselves in one fashion or another from rain and sun are neither false nor, from some points of view, unimportant" (Geertz 1973: 40), but it is questionable, Geertz says, "whether a lowest-common-denominator view of humanity is what we want anyway . . . it may be in the cultural particularities of people – in their oddities – that some of the most instructive revelations of what it is to be generically human are to be found" (p. 43).

It is not only that humans developed along with culture in the generic sense, but we are always within culture in the particular sense. Humans cannot exist outside of culture, the tales of "wolf boys" – children reared by wolves or other animals –

Stylites were hermit-like monks (fifth to seventh centuries in what is now Syria and Turkey) who sat on top of pillars to separate themselves from society and devote themselves to prayer. The most famous is St. Simon.

notwithstanding. Hermits or stylites – people who deliberately isolate themselves from society – are a different matter; they have already been reared in that society and, even when totally alone, carry on silent dialogue with it. People "unmodified by the customs of particular places do not in fact exist, have never existed, and most important, could not in the very nature of the case exist" (Geertz 1973: 35).

What Geertz and others argue is that there is no backstage, no place outside of culture in both the generic and particular senses, where you can go to study the so-called "naked ape" stripped of his or her culture. People are molded by culture from the moment of birth, and probably even before that due to the cultural prescriptions for pregnancy and birth and the expectations that people have about the child.

For a very long time, however, a major assumption in the humanities has been that there *is* a constant human nature and that the differences are only superficial. Such an assumption implies that a Shakespeare play, for example, could be understood by all people (once it was translated) because people everywhere would have the same concepts, emotions, and motivations. Indeed, Shakespeare's genius, like that of any great artist, is supposed to rest on his ability to appeal to universal emotions and circumstances. But others have asked whether a people's emotions and responses are instead conditioned by the particularities of the culture they live in. Anthropologist Laura Bohannan put these different positions to the test when she told the story of Hamlet to a group of Africans with whom she was living and conducting her anthropological fieldwork. A major difficulty arose with the translation – not just the words, but the concepts. Was it possible to translate the concepts and emotions from Shakespeare's world into the African language and context to render the story understandable to them, or did the translation totally alter it? Her famous article is included with this chapter.

To understand people and cultures, you have to get into the particulars, in the details. That is where you pick up the clues. This is anthropology in a new key;[5] it does not dismiss human universals, but discovering them is not its primary goal since they help us very little in understanding why different peoples do things differently. In short, although universals give us the common human denominator, they do not tell us very much about specific cultures. What, then, is this "culture" that we should be mindful of it?

Because I think it is important for you to come to your own understanding of culture, I do not intend to give it a specific definition, although, in the next section, I will briefly discuss some general ideas that have been put forth by a variety of theorists who have dealt with the concept. Before reading this section, it would be useful to stop here and define "culture" for yourself and then see how your understanding of it changes as you read further in the book.

Culture

Culture is, admittedly, a slippery concept, difficult to grasp. According to British social theorist Raymond Williams:

> Culture is one of the two or three most complicated words in the English language. This is so partly because of its intricate historical development, in several European languages, but mainly because it has now come to be used for important concepts in several distinct intellectual disciplines and in several distinct and *incompatible* systems of thought. (Williams [1976] 1983: 87, emphasis mine)

Culture has become such a contested word that some anthropologists think we should drop it. Since I have used the word in the title of this book, it is clear that I do not agree. To get some sense of the approach taken in this book it is helpful, I think, to examine some of the meanings of the word. I begin with the historical etymology worked out by Williams in his helpful book, *Keywords: A Vocabulary of Culture and Society* ([1976] 1983).

According to Williams, "[c]ulture in all its early uses was a noun of process: the tending *of* something, basically crops or animals." This is the sense behind such words as hortic*ulture*; vini/vitic*ulture*, and agric*ulture*. Beginning in the eighteenth century, the idea of *cultivation* was transferred to humans and with it was born the notion of a *cultivated* person. This had distinct class overtones and was closely related to the idea of *civilization*. That idea has not completely died out, for culture is still often associated with "great works" that are housed in libraries and museums or performed on stage. Poetry and literature, painting and sculpture, symphony and opera, theater and dance – these were, and still are to a large extent, what most people think of when they think of culture. Not so long ago, these were the things you went to college to learn about. To be a cultured person you had to know about them and know how to appreciate them. In addition, especially among the upper classes, it was thought essential that students complete their education with a European tour to absorb the great works of Western culture. Moreover, Western culture was held to be the epitome of civilization. When combined with a belief that culture is an evolutionary, unidirectional, and progressive phenomenon that all peoples are striving for, one can sense the way assumptions about class and race and gender were reinforced by such a tour.

In the twentieth century, many anthropologists have dropped this framework with the realization that different cultures are just different. And while cultures are conditioned by the global network of power and resources in which they are embedded, they nevertheless spring from different premises about what life is all about, and they have different goals and values. This idea stems from Johann Gottfried von Herder, an eighteenth-century German historian, who thought that every people, *volk*, had their own values, language, and *geist* or spirit. He also argued against the presumptions of European superiority:

> Men of all the quarters of the globe, who have perished over the ages, you have not lived solely to manure the earth with your ashes, so that at the end of time your posterity should be made happy by European culture. The very thought of a superior European culture is a blatant insult to the majesty of Nature. (Cited in Williams [1976] 1983: 89)

It is from Herder that the notion of culture in the plural derives, and it is in this sense that the concept entered anthropology, notably through Franz Boas. Boas is credited with being the founder of American anthropology even though he was German and trained in the German intellectual tradition. In New York at Columbia University he established the first department of anthropology in the United States. Boas was also a major player in championing *nurture* over *nature*, a debate that did then and still has racial underpinnings and implications, for if your nature (now read "genes") is responsible for your lowly position, nothing can be done. But if that position can be attributed to (the lack of) nurture, here meaning not only food and nutriments but also cultural and social resources, then social measures can be instituted to ameliorate it.

Raymond Williams claims that "in archaeology and in *cultural anthropology* the reference to culture or a culture is primarily to *material* production, while in history and *cultural studies* the reference is primarily to *signifying* or *symbolic* systems" (p. 91). While that may be true in the British context, it is not so in the American. Culture, among American anthropologists, generally refers to signifying or symbolic systems, as we shall see. (More proof of George Bernard Shaw's dictum that England and the United States are two countries divided by a common language.) No wonder some anthropologists wish to abandon the term culture altogether. But Williams's take on this issue is, I believe, related to another important difference between British and American anthropology. As he notes, the adjective *cultural* came into prominence at the end of the nineteenth and early twentieth centuries with the emergence of anthropology. This usage develops in relation, and often in contrast, to the adjective *social*.

Social and Cultural Anthropology

Within the major (sub)field of social and cultural anthropology (see p. 8 above), there is yet another division around which some of the most contentious debates revolve. British anthropologists tend to emphasize the "social," while American anthropologists tend to put a greater emphasis on the "cultural." This is a gross generalization, since most anthropologists on both sides of the Atlantic try to do both, yet it helps to give a sense of the different orientations. Those who emphasize the social system tend to argue that it is social organization that determines the culture, often assuming that there are given or universal social domains (such as kinship, economy, and religion), instantiated in institutions, that can be compared cross-culturally. Those who emphasize the cultural system tend to argue that culture greatly influences the types of social organization found "on the ground," and do not assume, *a priori*, that there are distinct universal domains (kinship etc.) that can be analyzed separately from the rest of the culture. They believe the domains of each culture must be arrived at by empirical investigation.

Each position stems from a different intellectual lineage – the American lineage draws, to a large extent, on the German tradition beginning with Herder through Boas, as noted above, while the British were heavily influenced by the French theorist Emile Durkheim and by utilitarianism, a socioeconomic theory developed by philosophers Hobbes and Locke and economists Malthus and Smith. Utilitarianism is an individualistic theory based on the rational pursuit of self-interest that assumes wants are *given* rather than produced by culture and society.[6]

Ideas about social evolution were also prominent in the works of British (as well as some American) social theorists like E. B. Tylor and Herbert Spencer, who might be considered the "founders" of British social anthropology. Durkheim, too, was influenced by evolutionary theory. But his major contribution to anthropology was his belief that society is something *sui generis* (of its own kind, unique); this means that the functioning of society cannot be reduced to, or explained in terms of, psychology, and even less to biology. Society, for Durkheim, is greater than the parts it is composed of, and it has its own laws which the sociologist must discover. Society cannot be grasped except in its *collective representations*, which are essentially the shared categories (and the images and symbols) through which a society represents itself to itself. Some American anthropologists think these representations are analogous to culture. For Durkheim they are religious in origin: "If religion has given birth to all that is essential in society, it is because the idea of society is the soul of religion" ([1915] 1965: 466); what he means is that there is an integration between a particular society and its elementary religious concepts. Social anthropologists seem to have overlooked this aspect since they continue to treat religion as a separate domain.

An example of what is at stake in the debate between social and cultural anthropologists can be illustrated by material from two British social anthropologists, Peter Worsley and Meyer Fortes, as critiqued by an American, Marshall Sahlins. According to Sahlins, Worsley contends that among the Talensi, an African group he studied:

> the jural or ritual relationship between a Tale father and son depends on their relationship in production (pp. 41–49, 62). Yet it is evident that their relationship in production also depends on the authority of the father in a patrilineal structure and the ritual piety of the son (Fortes, 1949, p. 204). But the basic dilemma in this, as throughout the analysis, is that one cannot determine the kinship properties of the relation by the economic coordinates of the interaction. Nothing in the material conditions or the economic interests specifies the quality of kinship as such. (Sahlins 1976: 9)

For Sahlins, therefore, one cannot assume there is a kinship relationship separate from an economic relationship or a ritual/religious one; first one needs to understand the domains and categories of that society rather than impose those from our own.

That idea, too, is reflected in the position taken by David Schneider, who believed that culture is a system of symbols and meanings.

> By symbols and meanings I mean the basic premises which a culture posits for life; what its units consist in; how those units are defined and differentiated; how they form an integrated order or classification; how the world is structured; in what parts it consists and on what premises it is conceived to exist, the categories and classifications of the various domains of the world of man and how they relate one with another, and the world that man sees himself living in. (Schneider 1972: 38)

"Culture," for Schneider, "concerns the stage, the stage setting, and the cast of characters; the normative system consists in the stage directions for the actors and how the actors should play their parts on the stage that is so set" (1972: 38). By "normative system" he meant the norms or rules of behavior in a society. Schneider believed that one needed first to learn how the X divide up the world, to see what their major categories and domains are, before imposing our own as if they were natural, given, and universal. He objected to the piecemeal comparisons that result from attempts to compare "kinship systems," for example, across different cultures, a method he felt was analogous to comparing apples and oranges, which similarly distorted the particular flavor of each culture.

Clifford Geertz, a former colleague of Schneider at the University of Chicago, took a similar approach. The following is one of Geertz's most frequently quoted statements:

> The concept of culture I espouse is essentially a semiotic one. Believing with Max Weber, that man is an animal suspended in webs of significance he himself has spun, I take culture to be those webs, and the analysis of it to be therefore not an experimental science in search of law but an interpretive one in search of meaning. (Geertz 1973: 5)

The difference between an explanatory science and an interpretative science is also a feature that tends to distinguish between the social and the cultural anthropologists. However, the differences between them need not be so rigidly defined, as people who concentrate on social organization, social phenomena "on the ground," must also pay attention to culture and, conversely, those whose primary interest is "culture" – the symbols and meanings – must investigate the way they are expressed and embedded in social activity.

Marxist theory, which imagined culture as *superstructure* that reflects more basic economic realities, was taken up by some anthropologists and reworked into a variety of forms, notably "structural Marxism" and "political economy," that deal with ideology, and the influence of capitalism on the world system.[7] More sophisticated versions, called "praxis theory" and first developed by Pierre Bourdieu ([1972] 1977), attempt to understand how individual agency both reproduces and changes the "system." Rather than singling out particular domains, especially "modes of production," or prominent rituals of society, practice theorists, according to Sherry Ortner, pay more attention to:

> the little routines people enact, again and again, in working, eating, sleeping, and relaxing, as well as the little scenarios of etiquette they play out again and again in social interaction. All of these routines and scenarios are predicated upon, and embody within themselves, the fundamental notions of temporal, spatial, and social ordering that underlie and organize the system as a whole. In enacting these routines, actors not only continue to be shaped by the underlying organizational principles involved, but continually re-endorse those principles in the world of public observation and discourse. (Ortner 1984: 154)

It seems to me that cultural anthropologists have been doing just that for quite some time. Another intellectual trend that uses the notion of culture is *cultural studies*, which spans a number of disciplines, particularly literary fields and anthropology. A cultural studies approach is concerned not only with the products of culture and their meanings, but also with the processes of production and the ways that certain meanings or works become valorized. Those who use a cultural studies approach

The concept of *hegemony* is attributed to Italian political intellectual Antonio Gramsci. He was interested in the way certain groups were able to dominate society not by coercion but by the power of their ideas and discourses to create widespread social consent and support.

attempt to expose the *hegemonic* order by which the dominant classes impose their values and meanings on the masses.

As we go about *investigating culture* in this book, I try to use insights from all of these theoretical approaches without becoming dogmatic about any of them. However, I wish to make it clear that my own training and inclination is oriented more toward *culture*, as its inclusion in the title suggests. I am, after all, an American, trained in the American cultural anthropological tradition, and include as my teachers and mentors David Schneider, Marshall Sahlins, and Clifford Geertz, the very theorists that British anthropologist Adam Kuper attacks in his book *Culture: The Anthropologists' Account* (1999). (Is it *the* anthropologists' account or *an* anthropologist's account?)

Subculture/Boundless Culture

In recent years, in the United States anyway, the idea of an "American" culture has been challenged; in a country with so many different ethnic groups, how can there be an overarching national culture? Instead, the word "culture" has come to be more often associated with ethnicity, as in "Latino culture," or "African American culture," part of the contested arena of identity politics in a multi*cultural* society. I am not yet ready to throw out the idea of a mainstream or hegemonic culture, for it seems to me that the various subcultures define themselves against it or in relation to it while simultaneously incorporating many of its concepts and values. But I do feel

I intended to include public schooling until one of my students reminded me that she was home-schooled, and that a lot of people in the United States are engaged in alternative forms of education. Then, too, there is no nationwide curriculum as in France or the United Kingdom; instead, each county in each state determines what will be taught and what books will be ordered. Nevertheless, for a time there was considerable overlap. President Bush's program of school vouchers will further fragment the educational system and, thus, the people.

that the use of the term *culture* in phrases such as "corporate culture," "X school culture," or the "culture of the Boy Scouts" is much too narrow and urge that it be dropped in those senses. What these uses seem to be alluding to is the ambience or spirit of a place or group. Generally, discussions of culture in these restricted uses fail to relate the particular cases to the prevailing system of beliefs and values. So, for example, when you conduct your ethnographic research at your own school, you will, no doubt, reveal some unique features of that place, but do not stop your analysis there. Pick up the thread and follow it as it weaves into the concepts, values, and constraints of the broader cultural system.

Since the United States *is* multicultural, is there any sense in which we can speak of an "American" culture? Is there anything we share? Actually, I think there is quite a lot we share – television, movies, news, politics and voting, laws, rights, notions of freedom, independence, opportunity, and a host of other things – albeit in different degrees and from very different standpoints. For example, the notion and value of freedom will be very differently inflected in the life of a billionaire like Bill Gates and in the life of a welfare mother. Even the arch-intellectualist Claude Lévi-Strauss noted: "one has to be very naive or dishonest to imagine that men choose their beliefs independently of their situation" ([1955] 1975: 148). A cultural analysis should make explicit the particular positionality of the person doing the analyzing as well as that of the people being analyzed, and more importantly, account for the differentials of power and inequality between people and between groups. However, as my colleague Sylvia Yanagisako and I argued in our co-edited volume, *Naturalizing Power*, it is important to recognize that these "differentials of power (often) come already embedded in culture . . . (so that) power appears natural, inevitable, even god-given" (Yanagisako and Delaney 1995: 1). Despite all these differences, however, many of the peoples who make up this nation came here precisely because of what "America" symbolizes – the land of opportunity, for example – regardless of what that may mean or how it may work out in practice. Investigating exactly what "America" does mean to its diverse citizens would make an excellent and important research project.

The whole issue of *a* national culture that is bounded and discrete has also recently been challenged. The challengers argue that the concept of culture has too often been equated with "nation" in the sense of nation-state with territorial boundaries. When it was realized that "nations," especially as nation-states, were relatively recent constructions, that idea of a national culture began to break down. "Nation," however, did not always have that meaning; instead it referred to a "people" bound by language, religion, and birth (from the Latin word *natio*, which comes from the verb to be born). The Ottoman Empire, for example, was composed of many nations – the Jewish nation, the (Greek) Orthodox nation, the Armenian nation, and the Muslim nation. These were different "confessional" groups where religion, language, and ethnicity went together. In addition, the borders of the Empire were not so distinct. Although Mustafa Kemal Atatürk, the founder of the Republic of Turkey, wanted to create a nation-state on the model of European nations, he also wanted to create a national identity different from the ethnic identities of the Ottoman Empire. Turkish identity would be based on language and civilization; different groups would be assimilated by means of education. "Turk," during the Ottoman period, meant a country bumpkin and referred to the peasantry; it was not an ethnic designation even though Europeans called the people Turks. Unfortunately, the choice of Turkey rather than Anatolia as the name of the new nation had the result of perpetuating ethnic identities and divisions.

> Anatolia, or *Anadolu* in Turkish, is the traditional name for all of the land mass on the Asian "side," that is, the majority of the land, and where most of the peasants lived. Situating the capital in Ankara instead of Istanbul was another way Atatürk indicated that the new country was of, and for, the people.

In my view, the concept of culture need not be co-extensive with nation-state. For example, Turks living in Europe bring along many of the concepts, beliefs, values, feelings, foods, modes of social interaction, dress and aesthetics that were inculcated in Turkey. Surely this becomes diluted in the second and third generations born outside of Turkey, but it is not entirely wiped out. Turkish culture exceeds the boundaries of the nation of Turkey. If one thinks of culture not only as material items but as a system of symbols and meanings, then there is nothing that confines it to a specific place. At the same time, it is extremely important to investigate the ways in which power, aggression, repression, and exploitation have had an important influence on the development and expression of culture. Turks in Europe have many restrictions placed on their cultural expression and they are often the targets of state repression and private aggression. Their example helps to expose the processes of cultural production – who gets to make culture and how is it transmitted – as well as the creative ways that cultural expressions and productions persist and flourish in an often hostile environment. For example, by modifying their traditional *döner kebab* to suit German tastes, Turks have been extremely successful in creating a very popular fast food snack in Germany. You can now find them being sold on almost every street corner and at every train station, and Germans have taken to them with gusto.

The Personal is Political

This discussion about culture and its many senses has been theoretical, but how you think about it affects your personal life. When you enter college or university, most of you will encounter some people very different from yourselves, people who come from different places, who have different values, different styles of interacting and of clothing, and different tastes in food and music. How do you interpret these differences?

Do you simply dismiss them with the thought "they are just different" and then seek out those similar to yourself? Do you dismiss them by assigning the differences to race or ethnicity, different religious backgrounds, the region of the country they are from, their socioeconomic class, or their upbringing and values? Or do you simply accept that they have different natural talents and endowments – intellectual, physical, and artistic?

At a small conference in 1993, Sylvia Yanagisako made an eloquent defense of retaining the concept of culture. "(W)e need to explore and refine explanations of difference other than what I call the three R's: Race, Religion, and Reason or Rationality. These three R's were the forms of explanation of social difference . . . in the 19th century" (n.d.: 9); they incorporated hierarchical and unidirectional notions of progress and advancement but they end by putting the beliefs and values of white, Christian, Euro-American males at the top.

The concept of culture should be retained, she said, because it "is the conceptual and discursive space we reserve to struggle to refine our understandings of social differences and similarities. It is that elusive abstraction we find it impossible to agree upon but one that we find it equally impossible to live without" (p. 10). The main features of this elusive concept, Yanagisako noted, have been with us since the 1920s. Perhaps we know what this concept isn't better than we are able to grasp what it is. Culture is "learned not inherited [i.e., it is not biological]; it is shared and not idiosyncratic [i.e., it is not psychological]; and it is particular and not universal [i.e., it is not a matter of philosophy]" (p. 10).

The social differences noted above are important and need to be taken into our anthropological accounts. Rather than avoiding them, we need to become more aware of the ways these social differences and their *meanings* emerge in a particular cultural context. They are *culturally constituted*; that means they emerge in relation to interlocking patterns of meaning that are constructed by and struggled over by people who occupy different social positions that incorporate differentials of power. Some of these meanings we inherit (in the sense of being *socially*, not genetically, transmitted) from previous generations, some we can affect and change, and some we can even invent – but only in relation to what went before.

Investigating

So, how does one go about investigating such an elusive thing as culture? Where is it and how do you find it? I find it helpful to think of culture as a big *mystery* and the anthropologist as a *detective*. To me, the primary anthropological question is: Why are things the way they are and not some other way? Do you think the way things are is natural, inevitable, and maybe even necessary? How do you feel when you realize that people elsewhere do things differently – that your way is just one among a number of possibilities? Do you assume your way is best or does the realization create doubt about your way? If the specter of doubt does not become too unsettling, it can be the goad to anthropological investigation. However, it does make some students nervous. That is how it should be. It is an indication of why anthropology is a very different enterprise from other disciplines. It is a critical discipline; it calls into question conventional knowledge and taken-for-granted truths.

Claude Lévi-Strauss, the French anthropologist known for his structuralist theories, felt that anthropological fieldwork was the nursemaid of doubt: "This anthropological doubt consists not merely in knowing that one knows nothing, but in resolutely exposing what one knows, even one's own ignorance, to the insults and denials inflicted on one's dearest ideas and habits by those ideas and habits which may contradict them to the highest degree" (cited in Sontag 1966: 188–9). While it is hard to imagine this most cerebral of anthropologists exposing his ignorance, that *is* what happens in fieldwork and it can induce a kind of psychological vertigo.

As an example, I will relate one of my more humiliating experiences during fieldwork in the Turkish village. Most of the time, except for breakfast, I ate at other people's houses because there was no store in the village and, without fields and animals of my own, it was difficult to procure food. One day a fish vendor came to the village and I bought some to cook on my own. I was in the midst of steaming them with herbs and spices when several of my neighbors walked in. "That is no way to cook fish," they said. "The only way is to fry them in oil." I was becoming defensive; not only did they think my way was barbaric, they were also insulting my intelligence. I testily replied, "Well, I've been cooking for over twenty years and this is one of the ways I prepare fish" (so there!). They left without trying any, shaking their heads at my strange ways and scoffing at my lack of expertise; I was unnerved. Through this and other such trials I learned much about the rules and beliefs in that culture. These experiences also made me question the way "we" do things. I began to live teetering between two worlds – that is where the vertigo comes in – my old world no longer seemed so stable, so resolutely obvious.

When anthropologists conduct "fieldwork," what they are really doing is collecting *clues* to help solve the mystery of culture: why do these people do things the way they do? What are their motivations and goals? How are they constrained by the cultural definitions of their race, gender, age, class, etc.? Where do you find the clues? I believe you can begin anywhere, there is no privileged place to begin the investigation. When a detective is investigating a murder, there may be obvious clues such as a gun tossed in a trash bin – it might have fingerprints on it or, alternatively, the type of gun can be traced. But other clues are less obvious and may seem irrelevant at first, yet end up more significant. The analogy, of course, goes only so far – culture is not a crime! However, it is mysterious. Part of training to become a perspicacious observer is training yourself to look at things anew, to take nothing for granted, and to try not to let your preconceptions (or theory) dictate what you will see and include as evidence. Pick any aspect or item of culture and begin to ask questions about it. Who uses it? Where does it fit in the system of classifications? What resources are needed to make it, and how are these socially mobilized?

In Turkey, for example, children have to memorize vast quantities of knowledge. Education was not a "drawing out" as the etymology of the English word means, but was a "putting in." (See also Eickelman 1978.) This was the mode of teaching in the secular schools, yet the pedagogical precedent can be found in the religious schools where memorization is very important. There are even illiterate villagers who can recite the entire Qur'an from memory in Arabic, a language totally unrelated to Turkish. They memorize in Arabic because it is held to be God's literal word communicated through the angel Gabriel. A translation is not the same, merely an interpretation.

Take your classroom, for example. When I asked my graduate students to do a cultural analysis of our classroom, they were totally stumped. The freshmen got it much faster. You might begin by considering just who is sitting there. Only a certain segment of the population, a relatively privileged segment, is there. In order to be there, you must have completed high school or its equivalent and passed the rigorous entrance exams, and you or your parents must be able to pay for it whether in full or by a combination of scholarship and loans. Because you (or your parents) are willing to sacrifice a lot of money for a college education, you must think it is a worthwhile endeavor. Then you would need to contrast those who are sitting in the classroom with segments of the population who are not. How would you account for that? That should lead you to consider issues of class, race, gender, and social inequality. You could also begin by observing how the classroom is arranged spatially. Is the teacher in front and the desks set in rows facing him or her? Or do you sit around a big table? What different ideas and values are expressed just by this arrangement of space? One set-up implies a lecture format with the teacher talking and conveying knowledge, while the other implies a discussion group where the ideas are tossed back and forth and argued over. Both types are in use in most colleges, but they are constructed from different theories of education and perhaps are intended for different types of students – freshmen vs. upperclass or graduate students. Different theories of education relate to different theories of child development and other cultural values. How quickly one gets from such an ordinary thing as a classroom to much deeper theories and values in a culture. By following the threads where they lead, you are pulling on the fabric of culture. You begin to understand that nothing in culture stands alone; each item is woven into a vast, interconnected web that no one person can ever really grasp in its entirety. That is the mystery and the challenge.

Fieldwork and Ethnography

Fieldwork is one of the things that sets anthropology apart from other academic disciplines – anthropologists must leave the library, the classroom, and their offices and go out and live for extended periods of time among the people they study. An ethnography is what anthropologists write up after completing their fieldwork. However, it is not just a *description* of a particular society and culture (the X do it like this), but an *analysis* that tries to get at the question of why. In writing ethnographies, anthropologists utilize the theories and jargon of the discipline at the time of writing and hope to contribute new theoretical insights and knowledge. The practice of fieldwork has been discussed theoretically and there exist a number of descriptions *about* the experience of fieldwork,[8] but nothing captures the experience itself as much as the ethnographic novel *Return to Laughter*, by Elenore Smith Bowen, the pseudonym for Laura Bohannan. For novels take us into the world they portray, and immerse us in that world for the period of reading.

Her novel is set in Africa where Bohannan actually conducted fieldwork. It was written in 1954, yet despite the outdated style and the problematics of doing fieldwork in an African nation under British colonial rule, it takes you into her *experience* of going to another culture and of how she gradually got oriented in it. She vividly describes the feeling of panic when she first arrived in the village where she was to live for a year; she lets us in on how and when she learned things, the ethical problems she encountered, the humiliating but illuminating incidents she endured, and she confesses her feelings and prejudices about some of their ways and her rising doubts about some of her own society's ways.

As David Riesman, a former Harvard sociologist, notes in his foreword to the 1964 edition of the book, it "focusses less on the West African tribe . . . and more on her own emotional hegira as a neophyte anthropologist" (Bowen 1964: x). I generally assign the book in the first week of my class; it forms a common experience we use as we begin to conduct our own fieldwork and we refer back to it throughout the course.

Riesman was curious about why Bohannan decided to use a pseudonym for this book. Although she claimed it was to protect the tribe, he felt that she might also be afraid "that the book might hurt her reputation as a competent and objective ethnographer" (p. xvi). That was probably an accurate assessment of the times, but he went on to say that "as a work of ethnography, and as a primer of anthropological method, *Return to Laughter* can stand on its own feet" (p. xvi). Fieldwork is messy and it contradicts the image most people have of scientific research; one cannot perform experiments on a living group, nor can one submit them to detached observation as a slide under a microscope. But that, too, was the image of science at the time. Today there is more awareness that even the "hard" physical sciences are not as objective as they were assumed to be; that the frameworks and theories of science are themselves human constructions that depend on all kinds of "subjective" features that include the personal concerns of the scientists and the particular social and political milieu that determines, through networks of support, what to study and how to study it.[9]

For several decades now, anthropologists have been discussing the very craft of writing an ethnography. It is a *construction* made from their experience in the field. What, then, is the difference between an ethnographic novel and a "scientific" ethnography? If fieldwork is *one and the same* experience for the anthropologist, what is it that gets converted into "fact" in a standard monograph and into "fiction" in an ethnographic novel? What is the difference between creating composite characters or events, and writing up "marriage rules" or "kinship structures?" These questions also raise the issue of truth – what kind of truth and for what purpose?

Orientation to the Book

As I noted earlier, this book is not intended to be a compendium of knowledge about anthropology or about any particular culture. Nor does it make pronouncements about universals of human behavior or human nature because, as should be clear by now, I feel these are strongly inflected by particular cultures and the ways in which power is encoded and enacted. The purpose of the book and the course is, first, to sensitize you to the *culturally specific* ways that humans orient themselves – in space and time, by means of language and social relations, with the body, food, and clothes, by the structures of everyday life, and in terms of the symbols and frameworks provided by public myth, religion, and ritual. The book is not organized to focus on specific institutions or domains such as kinship, the economy, or religion. Instead, these are discussed as they relate to the topics dealt with in each chapter.

Second, the goal is to get you to dig deeper and analyze both the particular meanings embodied in these phenomena and the ways they are interconnected. Aspects of power and economy are integrated into the discussion of each topic and attention is paid to the way all of these are experienced differently depending on race, class, and gender. Examples are drawn from a number of different cultures, and throughout I will insert material from my own fieldwork in Turkey.[10]

It is expected that this book will be used in conjunction with other readings; a bibliography is appended at the end of each chapter from which you or your teacher can select additional material. Drawing on the readings, class discussions are meant to compare and contrast classic anthropological works with contemporary articles whether these are academic papers, newspaper articles, or material on the Web. At the end of each chapter are ethnographic exercises where you will conduct your own research and get a chance to use what you have learned. (Sometimes I find that it is more exciting to conduct the research *before* the reading assignment.) With this textbook, the supplementary readings, the ethnographic exercises, and the class discussions, my expectation is that you will become aware that (each) culture is neither inevitable nor natural, but constructed by humans struggling to make meaning of their lives. As a constructed phenomenon, culture is available to the investigation of its explicit forms and implicit premises.

The next chapter takes up the topic of space in order to give you some metaphorical grounding, since space is the widest cosmological framework within which humans live. From there we move to time, another extremely important coordinate of human life, and take up the question of whether people perceive of, and categorize, time in the same way everywhere. If not, what are the consequences? Language is, of course, the major way we communicate with each other, but as you will see in chapter 4, it is also instrumental in constructing the world conceptually.

Humans are social animals, so the fifth chapter is devoted to social relations. We are also physical beings and chapter 6 takes up notions of the body, while chapters 7 and 8 discuss what we put into and onto our bodies, that is, food and clothes. Finally, the last substantive chapter looks at significant cultural icons – places, people, and events – that both grasp the imaginations of the majority of the population and symbolize important cultural values.

Most people have the idea that anthropologists have to work in faraway places, whether to study ancient archaeological sites or exotic "primitive" peoples. While that was true, to a large extent, during the period when anthropology was becoming a distinctive discipline, it is only partially so today. While some anthropologists still go off to cultures very different from their own, more and more are turning their focus to modern, industrial societies, including their own. In either case, it is an adventure in which you learn as much about yourself as about the culture you are studying.

Notes

1   See also the introduction to Lewis and Jungman (1986).
2   Because of the pejorative connotations that have become attached to the word *primitive*, some anthropologists refuse to use it. For a defense of the term and the virtues of primitive society, see Stanley Diamond's *In Search of the Primitive* (1974), which is also a scathing critique of so-called modern, industrial society.
3   For those who wish to explore this issue further, you might begin with Haraway (1989, 1991) and Marks (1995).
4   "insightful," "illuminating," and "see."
5   This is an allusion to Suzanne Langer's book *Philosophy in a New Key* (1942), which Geertz acknowledges as being influential in bringing to scholarly attention the role and importance of the symbolic function in human life (1973: 3).
6   To get a more complete definition of utilitarianism consult the *International Encyclopedia of the Social Sciences*. It is an excellent reference work that also includes articles on major theorists such as Durkheim, Spencer, Hobbes, etc.
7   For structural Marxism, see the work of Meillassoux, Althusser, Godelier, and for political economy look at the work of Eric Wolf and Sidney Mintz, who utilize theories from Immanuel Wallerstein, *The Modern World-System: Capitalist Agriculture and the Origins of the European World-Economy in the Sixteenth Century* (New York: Academic Press, 1976). For some problems with these theories, see Ortner (1984).
8   For example: Andre Beteille and T. N. Madan, *Encounter and Experience: Personal Accounts of Fieldwork* (1974); Jean Briggs, *Never in Anger: Portrait of an Eskimo Family* (1970); Manda Cesara, *Reflections of a Woman Anthropologist: No Hiding Place* (1982); Peggy Golde, ed., *Women in the Field: Anthropological Experiences* (1970); Bronislaw Malinowski, *A Diary in the Strict Sense of the Term* (1967); David Maybury-Lewis, *The Savage and the Innocent* (1965); Paul Rabinow, *Reflections on Fieldwork in Morocco* (1977); M. N. Srinivas, A. M. Shah, E. A. Ramaswamy, eds., *The Fieldworker and the Field: Problems and Challenges in Sociological Investigation* (1979); and Paul Stoller and Cheryl Olkes, *In Sorcery's Shadow: A Memoir of Apprenticeship among the Songhay of Niger* (1987), to name just a few.
9   One early and accessible presentation of this idea can be found in the first section of Suzanne Langer's *Philosophy in a New Key* (1942). See also Donna Haraway's "Animal

Sociology and a Natural Economy of the Body," Parts 1 and 2, in *Signs*, 4 (1978): 21–36, 37–60, "Situated Knowledge: The Science Question in Feminism as a Site of Discourse on the Privilege of Partial Perspective," in *Feminist Studies*, 14 (1988): 575–99, and *Primate Visions* (1989); Sandra Harding, *The Science Question in Feminism* (1986); and Stefan Helmreich, *Silicon Second Nature: Culturing Artificial Life in a Digital World* (1998).

10   For a fuller account of that work, see Delaney (1991).

Bibliography

Bohannan, Laura (1966) "Shakespeare in the Bush." *Natural History* (August–September): 28–33.

Bourdieu, Pierre ([1972] 1977) *Outline of a Theory of Practice*. Trans. Richard Nice. Cambridge: Cambridge University Press.

Bowen, Elenore Smith (1954) *Return to Laughter: An Anthropological Novel*. New York: Harper & Brothers; 1964 Doubleday.

Delaney, Carol (1991) *The Seed and the Soil: Gender and Cosmology in Turkish Village Society*. Berkeley: University of California Press.

Diamond, Stanley (1974) *In Search of the Primitive: A Critique of Civilization*. New Brunswick, NJ, and London: Transaction Books.

Dundes, Alan (1972) "Seeing is Believing." *Natural History* (May 1972): 8–12, 86–7.

Durkheim, Emile ([1915] 1965) *The Elementary Forms of Religious Life*. Trans. Joseph Ward Swain. New York: Free Press.

Eickelman, Dale (1978) "The Art of Memory, Islamic Education and its Social Reproduction." *Comparative Studies in Society and History*, 20 (4): 485–516.

Geertz, Clifford (1973) *Interpretation of Cultures*. New York: Basic Books.

Golde, Peggy, ed. ([1970] 1986) *Women in the Field: Anthropological Experiences*. Berkeley: University of California Press.

Haraway, Donna (1989) *Primate Visions: Gender, Race, and Nature in the World of Modern Science*. New York: Routledge.

Haraway, Donna (1991) *Simians, Cyborgs, and Women: The Reinvention of Nature*. New York: Routledge.

Kuper, Adam (1999) *Culture: The Anthropologists' Account*. Cambridge, MA: Harvard University Press.

Langer, Suzanne ([1942] 1979) *Philosophy in a New Key: A Study in the Symbolism of Reason, Rite, and Art*. Cambridge, MA: Harvard University Press.

Lévi-Strauss, Claude ([1955] 1975) *Tristes Tropiques*. Trans. John and Doreen Weightman. New York: Atheneum.

Lewis, Tom J. and Jungman, Robert E., eds. (1986) *On Being Foreign: Culture Shock in Short Fiction. An International Anthology*. Yarmouth, ME: Intercultural Press.

Malinowski, Bronislaw ([1922] 1961) *Argonauts of the Western Pacific*. New York: E. P. Dutton.

Marks, Jonathan (1995) *Human Biodiversity: Genes, Race, and History*. New York: Aldine de Gruyter.

Ortner, Sherry (1984) "Theory in Anthropology since the Sixties." *Comparative Studies in Society and History*, 26 (1): 126–65.

Sahlins, Marshall (1976) *Culture and Practical Reason*. Chicago: University of Chicago Press.

Schneider, David (1972) "What is Kinship All About?" In *Kinship Studies in the Morgan Centennial Year*, ed. P. Reining. Washington, DC: Anthropological Society, pp. 32–63.

Segal, Dan and Yanagisako, Sylvia, eds. (2004) *Unwrapping the Sacred Bundle: Reflections on the Disciplining of Anthropology*. Durham, NC: Duke University Press, forthcoming.

Sontag, Susan (1966) "The Anthropologist as Hero." In *Against Interpretation*. New York: Farrar, Straus & Giroux.

Stocking, George W., Jr. (1968) *Race, Culture, and Evolution: Essays in the History of Anthropology*. New York: Free Press.

Turner, Victor (1967) "Betwixt and Between: The Liminal Period in *Rites de Passage*." In *The Forest of Symbols: Aspects of Ndembu Ritual*. Ithaca: Cornell University Press, pp. 93–111.

Van Gennep, Arnold ([1909] 1960) *Rites de Passage*. Trans. Monika B. Vizedom and Gabrielle L. Caffee. Chicago: University of Chicago Press.

Williams, Raymond ([1976] 1983) *Keywords: A Vocabulary of Culture and Society*. New York: Oxford University Press.

Yanagisako, Sylvia (n.d.) "Defining Culture." Paper presented at a mini-conference held at Stanford University, 1993.

Yanagisako, Sylvia and Delaney, Carol (1995) *Naturalizing Power: Essays in Feminist Cultural Analysis*. New York and London: Routledge.

Shakespeare in the Bush
Laura Bohannan

Just before I left Oxford for the Tiv in West Africa, conversation turned to the season at Stratford. "You Americans," said a friend, "often have difficulty with Shakespeare. He was, after all, a very English poet, and one can easily misinterpret the universal by misunderstanding the particular."

I protested that human nature is pretty much the same the whole world over; at least the general plot and motivation of the greater tragedies would always be clear – everywhere – although some details of custom might have to be explained and difficulties of translation might produce other slight changes. To end an argument we could not conclude, my friend gave me a copy of *Hamlet* to study in the African bush: it would, he hoped, lift my mind above its primitive surroundings, and possibly I might, by prolonged meditation, achieve the grace of correct interpretation.

It was my second field trip to that African tribe, and I thought myself ready to live in one of its remote sections – an area difficult to cross even on foot. I eventually settled on the hillock of a very knowledgeable old man, the head of a homestead of some hundred and forty people, all of whom were either his close relatives or their wives and children.

Like the other elders of the vicinity, the old man spent most of his time performing ceremonies seldom seen these days in the more accessible parts of the tribe. I was delighted. Soon there would be three months of enforced isolation and leisure, between the harvest that takes place just before the rising of the swamps and the clearing of new farms when the water goes down. Then, I thought, they would have even more time to perform ceremonies and explain them to me.

I was quite mistaken. Most of the ceremonies demanded the presence of elders from several homesteads. As the swamps rose, the old men found it too difficult to walk from one homestead to the next, and the ceremonies gradually ceased. As the swamps rose even higher, all activities but one came to an end. The women brewed beer from maize and millet. Men, women, and children sat on their hillocks and drank it.

People began to drink at dawn. By midmorning the whole homestead was singing, dancing, and drumming. When it rained, people had to sit inside their huts: there they drank and sang or they drank and told stories. In any case, by noon or before, I either had to join the party or retire to my own hut and my books. "One does not discuss serious matters when there is beer. Come, drink with us." Since I lacked their capacity for the thick native beer, I spent more and more time with *Hamlet*. Before the end of the second month, grace descended on me. I was quite sure that *Hamlet* had only one possible interpretation, and that one universally obvious.

Early every morning, in the hope of having some serious talk before the beer party, I used to call on the old man at his reception hut – a circle of posts supporting a thatched roof above a low mud wall to keep out wind and rain. One day I crawled through the low doorway and found most of the men of the homestead sitting huddled in their ragged cloths on stools, low plank beds, and reclining chairs, warming themselves against the chill of the rain around a smoky fire. In the center were three pots of beer. The party had started.

The old man greeted me cordially. "Sit down and drink." I accepted a large calabash full of beer, poured some into a small drinking gourd, and tossed it down. Then I poured some more into the same gourd for the man second in seniority to my host before I handed my calabash over to a young man for further distribution. Important people shouldn't ladle beer themselves.

"It is better like this," the old man said, looking at me approvingly and plucking at the thatch that had caught in my hair. "You should sit and drink with us more often. Your servants tell me that when you are not with us, you sit inside your hut looking at a paper."

The old man was acquainted with four kinds of "papers": tax receipts, bride price receipts, court fee receipts, and letters. The messenger who brought him letters from the chief used them mainly as a badge of office, for he always knew what was in them and told the old man. Personal letters for the few who had relatives in the government or mission stations were kept until someone went to a large market where there was a letter writer and reader. Since my arrival, letters were brought to me to be read. A few men also brought me bride price receipts, privately, with requests to change the figures to a higher sum. I found moral arguments were of no avail, since in-laws are fair game, and the technical hazards of forgery difficult to explain to an illiterate people. I did not wish them to think me silly enough to look at any such papers for days on end, and I hastily explained that my "paper" was one of the "things of long ago" of my country.

"Ah," said the old man. "Tell us."

I protested that I was not a storyteller. Storytelling is a skilled art among them; their standards are high, and the audiences critical – and vocal in their criticism. I protested in vain. This morning they wanted to hear a story while they drank. They threatened to tell me no more stories until I told them one of mine. Finally, the old man promised that no one would criticize my style "for we know you are struggling with our language." "But," put in one of the elders, "you must explain what we do not understand, as we do when we tell you our stories." Realizing that here was my chance to prove *Hamlet* universally intelligible, I agreed.

The old man handed me some more beer to help me on with my storytelling. Men filled their long wooden pipes and knocked coals from the fire to place in the pipe bowels; then, puffing contentedly, they sat back to listen. I began in the proper style, "Not yesterday, not yesterday, but long ago, a thing occurred. One night three men were keeping watch outside the homestead of the great chief, when suddenly they saw the former chief approach them."

"Why was he no longer their chief?"

"He was dead," I explained. "That is why they were troubled and afraid when they saw him."

"Impossible," began one of the elders, handing his pipe on to his neighbor, who interrupted, "Of course it wasn't the dead chief. It was an omen sent by a witch. Go on."

Slightly shaken, I continued. "One of these three was a man who knew things" – the closest translation for scholar, but unfortunately it also meant witch. The second elder looked triumphantly at the first. "So he spoke to the dead chief saying, 'Tell us what we must do so you may rest in your grave,' but the dead chief did not answer. He vanished, and they could see him no more. Then the man who knew things – his name was Horatio – said this event was the affair of the dead chief's son, Hamlet."

There was a general shaking of heads round the circle. "Had the dead chief no living brothers? Or was this son the chief?"

"No," I replied. "That is, he had one living brother who became the chief when the elder brother died."

The old men muttered: such omens were matters for chiefs and elders, not for youngsters; no good could come of going behind a chief's back; clearly Horatio was not a man who knew things.

"Yes, he was," I insisted, shooing a chicken away from my beer. "In our country the son is next to the father. The dead chief's younger brother had become the great chief. He had also married his elder brother's widow only about a month after the funeral."

"He did well," the old man beamed and announced to the others, "I told you that if we knew more about Europeans, we would find they really were very like us. In our country also," he added to me, "the younger brother marries the elder brother's widow and becomes the father of his children. Now, if your uncle, who married your widowed mother, is your father's full brother, then he will be a real father to you. Did Hamlet's father and uncle have one mother?"

His question barely penetrated my mind: I was too upset and thrown too far off balance by having one of the most important elements of *Hamlet* knocked straight out of the picture. Rather uncertainly I said that I thought they had the same mother, but I wasn't sure – the story didn't say. The old man told me severely that these genealogical details made all the difference and that when I got home I must ask the elders about it. He shouted out the door to one of his younger wives to bring his goatskin bag.

Determined to save what I could of the mother motif, I took a deep breath and began again. "The son Hamlet was very sad because his mother had married again so quickly. There was no need for her to do so, and it is our custom for a widow not to go to her next husband until she has mourned for two years."

"Two years is too long," objected the wife, who had appeared with the old man's battered goatskin bag. "Who will hoe your farms for you while you have no husband?"

"Hamlet," I retorted without thinking, "was old enough to hoe his mother's farms himself. There was no need for her to remarry." No one looked convinced. I gave up. "His mother and the great chief told Hamlet not to be sad, for the great chief himself would be a father to Hamlet. Furthermore, Hamlet would be the next chief: therefore he must stay to learn the things of a chief. Hamlet agreed to remain, and all the rest went off to drink beer."

While I paused, perplexed at how to render Hamlet's disgusted soliloquy to an audience convinced that Claudius and Gertrude had behaved in the best possible manner, one of the younger men asked me who had married the other wives of the dead chief.

"He had no other wives," I told him.

"But a chief must have many wives! How else can he brew beer and prepare food for all his guests?"

I said firmly that in our country even chiefs had only one wife, that they had servants to do their work, and that they paid them from tax money.

It was better, they returned, for a chief to have many wives and sons who would help him hoe his farms and feed his people: then everyone loved the chief who gave much and took nothing – taxes were a bad thing.

I agreed with the last comment, but for the rest fell back on their favorite way of fobbing off my questions: "That is the way it is done, so that is how we do it."

I decided to skip the soliloquy. Even if Claudius was here thought quite right to marry his brother's widow, there remained the poison motif, and I knew they would disapprove of fratricide. More hopefully I resumed. "That night Hamlet kept watch with the three who had seen his dead father. The dead chief again appeared, and although the others were afraid, Hamlet followed his dead father off to one side. When they were alone, Hamlet's dead father spoke."

"Omens can't talk!" The old man was emphatic.

"Hamlet's dead father wasn't an omen. Seeing him might have been an omen, but he was not." My audience looked as confused as I sounded. "It *was* Hamlet's dead father. It was a thing we call a 'ghost.'" I had to use the English word, for unlike many of the neighboring tribes, these people didn't believe in the survival after death of any individuating part of the personality.

"What is a 'ghost?' An omen?"

"No, a 'ghost' is someone who is dead but who walks around and can talk, and people can hear him and see him but not touch him."

They objected. "One can touch zombis."

"No, no! It was not a dead body the witches had animated to sacrifice and eat. No one else made Hamlet's dead father walk. He did it himself."

"Dead men can't walk," protested my audience as one man.

I was quite willing to compromise. "A 'ghost' is the dead man's shadow."

But again they objected. "Dead men cast no shadows."

"They do in my country," I snapped.

The old man quelled the babble of disbelief that arose immediately and told me with that insincere, but courteous, agreement one extends to the fancies of the young, ignorant, and superstitious. "No doubt in your country the dead can also walk without being zombis." From the depths of his bag he produced a withered fragment of kola nut, bit off one end to show it wasn't poisoned, and handed me the rest as a peace offering.

"Anyhow," I resumed, "Hamlet's dead father said that his own brother, the one who became chief, had poisoned him. He wanted Hamlet to avenge him. Hamlet believed this in his heart, for he did not like his father's brother." I took another swallow of beer. "In the country of the great chief, living in the same homestead, for it was a very large one, was an important elder who was often with the chief to advise and help him. His name was Polonius. Hamlet was courting his daughter, but her father and her brother . . . [I cast hastily about for some tribal analogy] warned her not to let Hamlet visit her when she was alone on her farm, for he would be a great chief and so could not marry her."

"Why not?" asked the wife, who had settled down on the edge of the old man's chair. He frowned at her for asking stupid questions and growled, "They lived in the same homestead."

"That was not the reason," I informed them. "Polonius was a stranger who lived in the homestead because he helped the chief, not because he was a relative."

"Then why couldn't Hamlet marry her?"

"He could have," I explained, "but Polonius didn't think he would. After all, Hamlet was a man of great importance who ought to marry a chief's daughter, for in his country a man could have only one wife. Polonius was afraid that if Hamlet made love to his daughter, then no one else would give a high price for her."

"That might be true," remarked one of the shrewder elders, "but a chief's son would give his mistress's father enough presents and patronage to more than make up the difference. Polonius sounds like a fool to me."

"Many people think he was," I agreed. "Meanwhile Polonius sent his son Laertes off to Paris to learn the things of that country, for it was the homestead of a very great chief indeed. Because he was afraid that Laertes might waste a lot of money on beer and women and gambling, or get into trouble by fighting, he sent one of his servants to Paris secretly, to spy out what Laertes was doing. One day Hamlet came upon Polonius's daughter Ophelia. He behaved so oddly he frightened her. Indeed" – I was fumbling for words to express the dubious quality of Hamlet's madness – "the chief and many others had also noticed that when Hamlet talked one could understand the words but not what they meant. Many people thought that he had become mad." My audience suddenly became much more attentive. "The great chief wanted to know what was wrong with Hamlet, so he sent for two of Hamlet's age mates [school friends would have taken long explanation] to talk to Hamlet and find out what troubled his heart. Hamlet, seeing that they had been bribed by the chief to betray him, told them nothing. Polonius, however, insisted that Hamlet was mad because he had been forbidden to see Ophelia, whom he loved."

"Why," inquired a bewildered voice, "should anyone bewitch Hamlet on that account?"

"Bewitch him?"

"Yes, only witchcraft can make anyone mad, unless, of course, one sees the beings that lurk in the forest."

I stopped being a storyteller, took out my notebook and demanded to be told more about these two causes of madness. Even while they spoke and I jotted notes, I tried to calculate the effect of this new factor on the plot. Hamlet had not been exposed to the beings that lurk in the forests. Only his relatives in the male line could bewitch him. Barring relatives not mentioned by Shakespeare, it had to be Claudius who was attempting to harm him. And, of course, it was.

For the moment I staved off questions by saying that the great chief also refused to believe that Hamlet was mad for the love of Ophelia and nothing else. "He was sure that something much more important was troubling Hamlet's heart."

"Now Hamlet's age mates," I continued, "had brought with them a famous storyteller. Hamlet decided to have this man tell the chief and all his homestead a story about a man who had poisoned his brother because he desired his brother's wife and wished to be chief himself. Hamlet was sure the great chief could not hear the story without making a sign if he was indeed guilty, and then he would discover whether his dead father had told him the truth."

The old man interrupted, with deep cunning, "Why should a father lie to his son?" he asked.

I hedged: "Hamlet wasn't sure that it really was his dead father." It was impossible to say anything, in that language, about devil-inspired visions.

"You mean," he said, "it actually was an omen, and he knew witches sometimes send false ones. Hamlet was a fool not to go to one skilled in reading omens and divining the truth in the first place. A man-who-sees-the-truth could have told him how his father died, if he really had been poisoned, and if there was witchcraft in it; then Hamlet could have called the elders to settle the matter."

The shrewd elder ventured to disagree. "Because his father's brother was a great chief, one-who-sees-the-truth might therefore have been afraid to tell it. I think it was for that reason that a friend of Hamlet's father – a witch and an elder – sent an omen so his friend's son would know. Was the omen true?"

"Yes," I said, abandoning ghosts and the devil; a witch-sent omen it would have to be. "It was true, for when the storyteller was telling his tale before all the homestead, the great chief rose in fear. Afraid that Hamlet knew his secret he planned to have him killed."

The stage set of the next bit presented some difficulties of translation. I began cautiously. "The great chief told Hamlet's mother to find out from her son what he knew. But because a woman's children are always first in her heart, he had the important elder Polonius hide behind a cloth that hung against the wall of Hamlet's mother's sleeping hut.

Hamlet started to scold his mother for what she had done."

There was a shocked murmur from everyone. A man should never scold his mother.

"She called out in fear, and Polonius moved behind the cloth. Shouting, 'A rat!' Hamlet took his machete and slashed through the cloth." I paused for dramatic effect. "He had killed Polonius!"

The old men looked at each other in supreme disgust. "That Polonius truly was a fool and a man who knew nothing! What child would not know enough to shout, 'It's me!'" With a pang, I remembered that these people are ardent hunters, always armed with bow, arrow, and machete; at the first rustle in the grass an arrow is aimed and ready, and the hunter shouts "Game!" If no human voice answers immediately, the arrow speeds on its way. Like a good hunter Hamlet had shouted, "A rat!"

I rushed in to save Polonius's reputation. "Polonius did speak. Hamlet heard him. But he thought it was the chief and wished to kill him to avenge his father. He had meant to kill him earlier that evening. . . ." I broke down, unable to describe to these pagans, who had no belief in individual afterlife, the difference between dying at one's prayers and dying "unhousell'd, disappointed, unaneled."

This time I had shocked my audience seriously. "For a man to raise his hand against his father's brother and the one who has become his father – that is a terrible thing. The elders ought to let such a man be bewitched."

I nibbled at my kola nut in some perplexity, then pointed out that after all the man had killed Hamlet's father.

"No," pronounced the old man, speaking less to me than to the young men sitting behind the elders. "If your father's brother has killed your father, you must appeal to your father's age mates; *they* may avenge him. No man may use violence against his senior relatives." Another thought struck him. "But if his father's brother had indeed been wicked enough to bewitch Hamlet and make him mad that would be a good story indeed, for it would be his fault that Hamlet, being mad, no longer had any sense and thus was ready to kill his father's brother."

There was a murmur of applause. *Hamlet* was again a good story to them, but it no longer seemed quite the same story to me. As I thought over the coming complications of plot and motive, I lost courage and decided to skim over dangerous ground quickly.

"The great chief," I went on, "was not sorry that Hamlet had killed Polonius. It gave him a reason to send Hamlet away, with his two treacherous age mates, with letters to a chief of a far country, saying that Hamlet should be killed. But Hamlet changed the writing on their papers, so that the chief killed his age mates instead." I encountered a reproachful glare from one of the men whom I had told undetectable forgery was not merely immoral but beyond human skill. I looked the other way.

"Before Hamlet could return, Laertes came back for his father's funeral. The great chief told him Hamlet had killed Polonius. Laertes swore to kill Hamlet because of this, and because his sister Ophelia, hearing her father had been killed by the man she loved, went mad and drowned in the river."

"Have you already forgotten what we told you?" The old man was reproachful. "One cannot take vengeance on a madman: Hamlet killed Polonius in his madness. As for the girl, she not only went mad, she was drowned. Only witches can make people drown. Water itself can't hurt anything. It is merely something one drinks and bathes in."

I began to get cross. "If you don't like the story, I'll stop."

The old man made soothing noises and himself poured me some more beer. "You tell the story well, and we are listening. But it is clear that the elders of your country have never told you what the story really means. No, don't interrupt! We believe you when you say your marriage customs are different, or your clothes and weapons. But people are the same everywhere; therefore, there are always witches and it is we, the elders, who know how witches work. We told you it was the great chief who wished to kill Hamlet, and now your own words have proved us right. Who were Ophelia's male relatives?"

"There were only her father and her brother." Hamlet was clearly out of my hands.

"There must have been many more; this also you must ask of your elders when you get back to your country. From what you tell us, since Polonius was dead, it must have been Laertes who killed Ophelia, although I do not see the reason for it."

We had emptied one pot of beer, and the old men argued the point with slightly tipsy interest. Finally one of them demanded of me, "What did the servant of Polonius say on his return?"

With difficulty I recollected Reynaldo and his mission. "I don't think he did return before Polonius was killed."

"Listen," said the elder, "and I will tell you how it was and how your story will go, then you may tell me if I am right. Polonius knew his son would get into trouble, and so he did. He had many fines to pay for fighting, and debts from gambling. But he had only two ways of getting money quickly. One was to marry off his sister at once, but it is difficult to find a man who will marry a woman desired by the son of a chief. For if the chief's heir commits adultery with your wife, what can you do? Only a fool calls a case against a man who will someday be his judge. Therefore Laertes had to take the second way: he killed his sister by witchcraft, drowning her so he could secretly sell her body to the witches."

I raised an objection. "They found her body and buried it. Indeed Laertes jumped into the grave to see his sister once more – so, you see, the body was truly there. Hamlet, who had just come back, jumped in after him."

"What did I tell you?" The elder appealed to the others. "Laertes was up to no good with his sister's body. Hamlet prevented him, because the chief's heir, like a chief, does not wish any other man to grow rich and powerful. Laertes would be angry, because he would have killed his sister without benefit to himself. In our country he would try to kill Hamlet for that reason. Is this not what happened?"

"More or less," I admitted. "When the great chief found Hamlet was still alive, he encouraged Laertes to try to kill Hamlet and arranged a fight with machetes between them. In the fight both the young men were wounded to death. Hamlet's mother drank the poisoned beer that the chief meant for Hamlet in case he won the fight. When he saw his mother die of poison, Hamlet, dying, managed to kill his father's brother with his machete."

"You see, I was right!" exclaimed the elder.

"That was a very good story," added the old man, "and you told it with very few mistakes. There was just one more error, at the very end. The poison Hamlet's mother drank was obviously meant for the survivor of the fight, whichever it was. If Laertes had won, the great chief would have poisoned him, for no one would know that he arranged Hamlet's death. Then, too, he need not fear Laertes' witchcraft; it takes a strong heart to kill one's only sister by witchcraft."

"Sometime," concluded the old man, gathering his ragged toga about him, "you must tell us some more stories of your country. We, who are elders, will instruct you in their true meaning, so that when you return to your own land your elders will see that you have not been sitting in the bush, but among those who know things and who have taught you wisdom."

1   You are about to leave for another culture (you may specify the one you are going to or would like to go to) for a stay of at least 6 months.
   • What do you think you will need to take?
   • What do you think will sustain you while you are there – here you may think of favorite books or other items as well as certain psychological capacities.

2   When you were planning to leave home for college or university, what did you think you would need to bring?
   • What did you bring? Why?
   • What do you think will prove to be important? Unnecessary?
   • What do you wish you *had* brought?
   • What has been the most difficult thing to get used to since you arrived? How is it different from your former life?

E
X
E
R
C
I
S
E
S

2

Spatial Locations

How do we situate or locate ourselves in space? Are notions of space "universal" or are they shaped by culture? This chapter explores these questions from macro to micro contexts, including discussion of maps, nations, segregation, public spaces, invisible spaces, and that space that is no place: cyberspace.

Spatial Locations

Space is, perhaps, our primary means of orientation in the world – physically, socially, and cosmologically. The need for spatial orientation is universal among humans, but the meanings of space are not. Space is neither empty nor neutral, it is filled with things and with meanings. Why is it, for example, that even when the physical distance is the same, it seems shorter when you go to visit a friend than when you have to run an odious errand? Physical space is rarely only that; it also encodes social meanings and values. In *Return to Laughter* (noted in chapter 1), Elenore Smith Bowen describes this very well:

> Some walks overtaxed my own strength. . . . One "not far" excursion put me to bed for a couple of days after a twenty-five-mile round trip without food or water, where-after I set out on a "far" journey equipped with lunch and water, only to find it less than four miles in all. At first I thought their use of these words was incontrovertible evidence that they had no idea of distance. Then I figured out that "far" referred not only to space, but to time and social distance as well. (1964: 52)

What does it mean if someone says: "Give me space!" What would or should your reaction be? Or, in a relationship, how do you feel if you are on the receiving end of a comment such as "I need some space"? Does it mean that the person needs a bigger room or a few acres to plant vegetables? No! It usually implies that the other person is feeling emotionally caged in, trapped, perhaps a little claustrophobic. Does it mean you are being too possessive? Personal space is also very much a matter of culture.

Americans tend to stand quite far apart when talking. If someone gets too close to us, we tend to take a step backward. We feel they are invading our "bubble" of private space – that pocket of air surrounding our body. Whereas in other cultures, speakers get so close you can feel as well as smell their breath. To many Americans, this would be offensive except in intimate situations or with an infant.

In this chapter we will explore a number of different levels of spatial organization and their effects on everyday life. Providing some ground under our conceptual feet, we will first look at spatial coordinates on earth and then briefly move to their wider cosmological moorings before coming back to earth to discuss the spatial divisions of nations and regions, the public spaces of work and leisure, and the more personal spaces of home and the very rooms we occupy. Finally, we will take a look at the new space that is no place, cyberspace, and consider the implications for rearrangements of space in the future.

Maps

When we enter another culture we enter another world – not totally, of course, but to a greater or lesser extent. This is true even if it is another regional culture or the culture of a different ethnic group in one's own country. We need to orient ourselves and get our bearings. We need maps and guidebooks to tell us *what* is there and the *significance* of what we are seeing. It is difficult to get your bearings in a new city or new country without a map, even more so if you do not know the language, and especially if you do not know the writing system and, therefore, cannot even read the signs. For example, as an English speaker you could recognize the letters in French or German and could ask someone for a particular street address; but what if the signs were in Arabic or Chinese and you did not know those languages? You couldn't even read the signs to be able to ask someone. In many of the cultures that anthropologists have studied, maps and guidebooks are scanty or non-existent, and no one hands anthropologists an orientation packet. Each of us has to make our own mental map.

Even with a map it can be difficult if the orientation is different from what is familiar. Conventionally, north is at the top of contemporary maps, but on the map of the Stanford University campus, north is at the bottom. No wonder people get lost! But why is north conventionally at the top? Who decided that, and what are the consequences? From the standpoint of outer space there is no north. It depends on perspective, but whose? Ali Mazrui, Kenyan-born professor at both the University of Michigan and the University of Jos in Nigeria, and host of a nine-part television series on Africa, asked: "Is Europe *north* of Africa? Is Europe *up* and Africa *down* in geographical location, as well as in income, power, and global status? Of course, the maps say Europe is north of Africa (and therefore *up*). But that decision was arbitrary and made primarily by European mapmakers" (quoted in *Dial*, September 1986: 21–2). European mapmakers also distorted the size of continents. The Mercator map, which in various versions has been in common use since the sixteenth century, has had insidious consequences. Mazrui comments: "The visual memories of millions of children across generations have carried distorted ideas about the comparative physical scale of northern continents in relation to southern

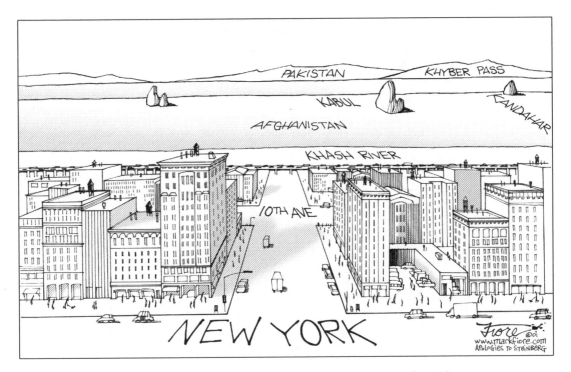

Figure 2.1   Post-9/11 version of Saul Steinberg's *View of the World from 9th Avenue*, by Mark Fiore. Published in *San Francisco Chronicle* (September 30, 2001). © Mark Fiore.

ones" (p. 22). For on that map North America is shown to be one and a half times the size of Africa whereas Africa is three and a half times the size of North America! He suggests that every class ought to experiment with turning the world upside down.

Similar things can be said about east and west, because what is east to one is west to another. I spent most of my life on the East coast of the United States; to me "large body of water" (the Atlantic) was east and west always meant the Wild West – the high mountains of Colorado and Wyoming. When I moved to California I got very disoriented. If someone gave me directions to go east, I naturally headed in the direction of "large body of water," i.e., the Pacific, and when they told me to go west, I headed inland in the direction of Wyoming and Colorado. In my own mental map I had never really considered California part of the west – it was beyond the pale, another place altogether. Once our mental maps are ingrained, they are very difficult to dislodge. The artist Steinberg expressed this visually in his humorous map of the world from the perspective of a New Yorker where known places beyond the Hudson River were few and their locale vague. Others, such as Mark Fiore, have made their own versions (see figure 2.1).

Now, living in California, I have to go west to get to the Far East. Somewhere over the Pacific a line was drawn determining our spatial and temporal coordinates, so that in crossing the Pacific, you not only enter the "East," you also enter a new day; it is also where we entered the new millennium. The placing of that line was/is arbitrary; it was made not just by human decision but by the decision of a few people. Maps, then, are not just physical guides but also ideological. Think of the meanings we have invested in "East" and "West," "Western culture," "the Orient," the "Middle East." These meanings have become incorporated in our notions of the way the world *is*. Yet we need to ask why is the area that is now occupied by Israel and a number of Arab nations called the "Middle East," or the "Near East"? For whom is it "near" or "middle"? Whose view of the world is being imposed, and what are the implications? (Cf. Said 1979: 19 for a detailed discussion.)

Cosmology

Such meanings may be more obvious in medieval maps of the world, *mappae mundi* as they are called. On these maps, heavily influenced by a Christian worldview and often made by monks, east, not north, was generally at the top because that is where Paradise (the Garden of Eden) was presumed to be. In that worldview there were only three continents, those that were to be populated by the descendants of the three sons of Noah after the Flood (Genesis 9: 18–19), that is, Shem, Ham, and Japhet, or Asia, Africa, and Europe. It was maps like these that miraculously guided Christopher Columbus to the New World, and it was into that framework that he fitted his discoveries.

Humans everywhere have cosmic concepts. They are oriented not only on the earth but in a universe or cosmos, although maybe even the notion of *uni*-verse is not universal since it implies one world organized by the same principles. We speak of four directions, four cardinal points, four *corners* of the globe. But there can be no corners on a round earth. Unlike any generation before ours, we have seen what our planet looks like from outer space. In the photographs taken by astronauts our planet looks blue and is swathed in clouds and floating in space. This space is imagined as relatively empty, not layered as in ancient and medieval worldviews. Empty also implies devoid of meaning. We think of the planet as physical material that can be explored scientifically, an idea we think came from the Greeks, yet it also derives from the biblical worldview. It was precisely the belief in the separation of the Creator from Creation, the simplification of power to one dynamic principle, and the lawful organization of matter that allowed early modern scientists to think they were investigating God's laws embedded in the material (nature) he supposedly created. The scientific notion of nature is, thus, intimately involved with a biblical worldview. In this worldview, there is a distinction between the divine and the material (supernatural vs. natural); not only do they stand in hierarchical relation, but there is also felt to be no divine *in* nature and vice versa. This is not the case in other cosmologies, other worldviews. While the cosmos can be explored scientifically, it depends upon a *prior* notion of cosmos that is, itself, derived from a religious worldview. The separation of divine from physical is peculiarly Western and has all kinds of implications for the way we imagine our lives and our place in the world. It has implications for our exploitation of resources and the disdain that we often exhibit toward people with very different cosmologies.

Cosmic concepts are not dependent on what is personally seen or experienced. Instead, by symbolic means, humans construct and live in spatially coordinated worlds that transcend personal or individual experience. Today people talk with ease about "outer space," even though only a few have ever been there and they not very far. And there are competing theories about how it is shaped and how far it extends, and these theories are first and foremost based on mental images – images that by and large have been constructed in a particular cultural milieu. By planting the American flag on the moon, were the astronauts staking a claim to that territory? Some people think they can colonize "outer space," that they can create boundaries and shields that will keep certain things in and other things out. But by what right? Still others have begun to think about creating other worlds to inhabit once we have destroyed this one, an idea no doubt that influenced and was popularized by *Star Trek*.

In the medieval Christian worldview the Garden of Eden and Heaven and Hell were imagined as if they existed in physical space. Some people still hold this view. Regardless, no one except Adam and Eve (if you believe they existed) has ever seen or experienced the Garden of Eden, yet some people are looking for the archaeological remains of it, which they believe is in modern-day Bahrain. Hell, as a physical place, has surely fired the imaginations of millions of people and helped to keep them on the straight and narrow path – a moral concept that is, nevertheless, spatially expressed.

Cosmology, then, is not just the science of the stars but, as I use it, is also a term for worldview in its widest cultural meaning. It gives us a sense of where we are and what kind of world we live in. Conversely, cultural notions of what kind of world it is also influence the mental images that scientific cosmologists turn into theories. It is a two-way exchange.

Nations and Regions

Between "outer space" and "inner space" there is a whole range of spatial concepts that order and organize our lives – from the nation and region, to public spaces, parks, buildings, houses, and rooms. First, let us think about the nation. We take it for granted that nations are the natural, obvious way to divide up the world – but only because we have been born into a world that is divided into nations. The notion of a nation as a *bounded territory* is a very Western and relatively modern idea; *nation* used to mean a people identified by language and religion rather than a specific piece of land.

Arabs, too, have had a very different notion of land. Borders were not important, maybe non-existent. This made perfect sense in an area that was mostly desert, a space that needed to be crossed in order to get someplace – to the oases and to water and people. So they did not have borders around their territories. The lines drawn in the sand, literally, by the British at the end of World War I created the nations of Iraq, Lebanon, Syria, and Palestine. These bounded territories had little to do with the inhabitants' notions of land. Not surprisingly, the lines have been contentious ever since. The one drawn between Iraq and Kuwait, for example, divided what had been basically one territory under the control of the Ottomans. Not only that, it created tensions over the land bordering the Arabian Gulf – especially when it transected the oil fields and left Iraq a tiny exit to the sea. The Gulf War of 1991 was fought to maintain the line. Another line, drawn after World War II, has been a continuous source of friction that portends to draw not just the Middle East but the whole world into a conflagration – that is, the line that created the state of Israel from Palestinian land.

Other people, too, have very different notions of land and territory. Some think it a very strange idea that individuals can *own* a piece of the planet and enclose it for their own use and even defend it at gunpoint. They think of land as a resource for all humans. You might have usufruct in it but never own it. Even if you own land, how far down does that ownership go? In the United States, owning property was what entitled you to a vote, in a sense giving you status as a real person. Today, owning property gives tax benefits that homeless people and renters (arguably those who need them most) do not get.

Nomadic peoples also do not accept the notion of bounded territory. They are accustomed to traverse a wide area in search of pasture for their animals. While they often visit the same places in their yearlong cycle, they do not have a permanent residence. When the land they were accustomed to crossing became divided between different nations, the issue of the border became volatile, and measures have been taken to force them to become sedentary. Gypsies also roam far and wide, not so much to pasture animals as to trade and do odd jobs. They, too, make "nations" very nervous since they cross borders and do not give allegiance to any nation in particular. Migrant workers also move across land in search of work. They, too, confound a system that assumes permanent residence and a permanent place of work, making it difficult for them to get health and social security benefits or be able to enroll their children in school. All of these groups are examples of what British anthropologist Mary Douglas calls "matter out of place." In her book *Purity and Danger* (1966), she argues that anything that confounds a particular system of order is "matter out of place." Because the boundaries or lines of the system have been sullied, the offending matter is culturally perceived as polluting, as dirt.

Even more than migrants, nomads, or gypsies, the homeless confound the social order. With no place to call their own, they are forced to live "on the street," most spectacularly exemplifying Mary Douglas's notion of "matter out of place." No wonder they are so often considered polluting. City officials try to move them, to get them out of sight. People walking down the street often turn their heads away, pretending not to see them; do they think they will be contaminated? Or is it that the homeless threaten our complacency, making us uncomfortably aware that we, too, could end up there? The real question is why, in one of the richest countries in the world, are there homeless people living on the streets and in public parks? While the stereotypic image is the drug-addicted man or woman, more than a quarter of a million (300,000) children under 10 are homeless (Leach 1994: 173). They are hardly recognized in life and when they die many of them are buried in an unmarked grave in a ditch at a place called Potter's Field. Potter's Field is New York City's public burial ground, it's on an island in Long Island Sound, it's part of a prison colony. The children are brought there from hospital morgues and buried by prison inmates. No ceremony memorializes their existence. Their mothers can't attend their burial, and that may be just as well. It wouldn't be consoling. Half the people buried in Potter's Field since 1981 are infants. A lot of them the children of the homeless. (Kozol, 1989: 13)

What has happened to the social contract? Penelope Leach, a British psychologist and pediatrician, has written eloquently about this in her ground-breaking book, *Children First: What Our Society Must Do – And Is Not Doing – For Our Children Today* (1994). She believes that the "principal problems of rich societies . . . are not a shortage of money but of political will" (p. 174).

Spatial Segregation

Australian aborigines, tenants on that continent for 40,000 years, had a very unusual notion of their land. Their land is fairly barren; to our eyes there are few distinguishing markers to take directions from. But for them it was filled with signs and these were related to their cosmological beliefs. This is a complicated issue that is beyond the scope of this chapter, but one of the results was their belief that the Ancestors had traveled across the vast territory *singing* about the sites, thereby naming them. These "songlines," then, "created ways of communication between the most far-flung groups. . . . A 'song' . . . was both map and direction-finder. Providing you knew the song, you could always find your way across the country . . . (for) the distance between two . . . sites can be measured as a stretch of song" (Chatwin 1987: 13). The late Bruce Chatwin was a travel writer, not an anthropologist, yet, after the time he spent with the aborigines, he was able to convey their notion of space and land better than many of the anthropologists. The aborigines, he said, "could not imagine territory as a block of land hemmed in by frontiers: but rather as an interlocking network of 'lines' or 'ways through'" (p. 56), i.e., the songlines. This is not to say they were, therefore, landless or had no system of ownership. He explained:

> everyone inherited, as his or her private property, a stretch of the Ancestor's song and the stretch of country over which the song passed. A man's verses were his title deeds to territory. He could lend them to others. He could borrow other verses in return. The one thing he couldn't do was sell or get rid of them. (p. 57)

When the British arrived they took over the aborigines' land, put them on reservations or sent them to work on cattle ranches. The indigenous population was decimated by European diseases, and by the despondency created as their way of life and their identity were destroyed. Recently, however, some groups are attempting to restore their culture and reclaim certain specific sites.

Similar things happened to the aboriginal population of the Americas. Estimates about the island population in the Caribbean before the encounter that began with Columbus number between 1 and 8 million, with more recent estimates at the higher end (cf. Sales 1990: 160–1). Twenty years later, approximately only 28,000 remained, slaughtered when they resisted or dead because of the ravaging diseases brought with the Europeans. In either case, this "is more than decimation, it is a carnage . . . closer to genocide" (p. 161). To my mind, it *is* genocide. In North America, things were not so different. The settlers (invaders) seemed to assume they had a divine right to the land, it was their "manifest destiny." They were bringing true religion and civilization to the "naked" savages, often justifying their actions with biblical quotes. "Ask of me, and I shall give thee, the heathen for thine inheritance, and the uttermost parts of the earth for thy possession" (Psalm 2: 8), or Romans 13: 2: "Whosoever therefore resisteth the power, resisteth the ordinance of God: and they that resist shall receive to themselves damnation" (cited in Zinn [1980] 1990: 14). The number of Native Americans who perished has been subject to considerable research but, according to recent scholarship, the "data reveal the actual rate of extermination pertaining to Native North America during the period of conquest as having been between 98 to 99 percent overall. . . . [This] vastly exceed[s] that experienced by the Jews of Europe under the Nazis, it represents a scale and scope of genocide without parallel in recorded human history" (Jaime 1992: 7). Those who survived often had their land taken by broken treaties or by being "relocated" onto reservations that, not surprisingly, had the least arable land. The social problems that have resulted from this devastation have too often been blamed on the victims. The pattern of disinheriting Native Americans continues to the present day. The most recent example concerns Yucca Mountain in Nevada. This mountain, which is sacred to both Western Shoshone and Paiute groups, is located on Western Shoshone land that is supposedly guaranteed by treaty. Yet in 2002, President Bush pushed through legislation that designated it as the dump site for nuclear waste, thereby abrogating the treaty. Native Americans have been fighting back to regain some of their lands or the benefits from the land, but it is too early to tell whether they will be able to stop this project.

The removal of Native Americans to reservations was one form of racial/spatial segregation. So, too, was *apartheid* in South Africa. Although that system has been dismantled, lines are still drawn that keep blacks separate from whites. Providing them with inferior education, making housing costs formidable, and keeping them from certain jobs contributes to the separation. The same institutionalized segregation was and is practiced in the United States. Until relatively recently, there were separate places for blacks and whites – bathrooms, lunch counters, neighborhoods, churches, schools – the space of the South divided up between different groups of people. The inner-city ghettos in the North are another outcome of that legacy as blacks escaped from the confines of the South.

But spatial divisions do not always divide people who are racially or linguistically different. The "Berlin Wall," first erected during the night of August 12–13, 1961, eventually extended not only 28 miles through Berlin but also an additional 75 miles around West Berlin, effectively making it an island in the middle of East Germany. The Wall divided people who considered themselves a nation in the sense of a people of the same "stock" (another term that means something very similar to race), language, and religion. The Wall was a structure that not only separated East from West, but became a major source of orientation both spatially and temporally for all Berliners, albeit from two different perspectives. It provided a physical frame for the construction of different narratives within which the individuals on either side constructed and made sense of their lives. The physical division into two countries for almost 30 years created two different peoples with different histories; they lived with different ideologies that permeated their life experiences. The assumption that they were really the same people (race, ethnic group) created problems during the so-called "unification" after the Wall came down in the fall of 1989, and the problems continue. Sameness of "blood" clearly does not translate as cultural sameness. I find it very disturbing to see a similar kind of wall being erected to separate ethnic groups from each other – this time in Israel, by people who had, themselves, been ghettoized. It makes me wonder whether we really learn any lessons from history.

Ghetto used to refer to sections in European cities set aside for Jews; it has become generalized to refer to an area in cities where poor people or minorities live. The *barrios* in Brazil and the *gecekondu* in Turkey are similar phenomena. But there are ghettos at the opposite extreme. I live in what is called "the faculty ghetto" at Stanford because it is a place on the campus where *only* faculty can live. It used to be a facetious and somewhat derogatory name because of all the gorgeous homes there. Now, because of the enormous increase in housing costs in the surrounding Silicon Valley, it is about the only place most faculty can afford to live. The recent development of "gated communities" is, perhaps, a better example. These are "ghettos" of the rich; they keep out "unwanted elements" and keep in "desirable" people like themselves. Some of these communities make further distinctions when they are designed expressly for singles or for retired people.

We have seen how spaces are divided by race, ethnicity, and income, but they are also divided by gender, age, occupation, and habit. In a book called *Women and Space: Ground Rules and Social Maps*, the editor Shirley Ardener notes that

> any restricted area such as a club, theatre or nation-state has rules determining its boundary, how it shall be crossed, who can occupy that space. In order to do so one must meet certain kinds of criteria (become a member, buy a ticket, get a visa, pass a citizenship test) and each has a gate-keeper whether that is a porter, usher, or Immigration Officer. (Ardener, 1981: 11)

It is important to become more aware of how space keeps certain people in and out – prisons and mental hospitals are obvious examples, but so too do courts, churches, offices, government buildings, and even public parks regulate who can enter. Who has freedom of movement? In a classroom, who can walk about? In an office, what people are "chained to their desks"? Who feels safe walking in a city at night or in a large park alone? A number of years ago when I was living in Cambridge, Massachusetts, the mayor put a curfew on women after dark because there had been an increase in the number of attacks and rapes. I called and asked why not put the curfew on men since they were the ones creating the problem. Why not let women, for once, have free use of the streets? (My request was not instituted.) The same idea seems to have inspired the "Take Back the Night" events that began in England in the late 1970s but quickly became international in scope, although organized by local communities. Women, men, and children march to protest violence against women and families and to make it safe to walk at night. Very few men, I think, understand the restricted spaces in which women can move easily and freely and the effects of this on their lives (cf. Massey 1994).

In many places in the world there are spaces divided by gender – the "men's house," for example, in a number of cultures we label "primitive." But the same is true for certain places in the so-called civilized, industrial world; in Turkey, men can sip tea in the *çayhane* but women are excluded, and there have been (and still are) men's clubs in Britain and the United States. Silvia Rodgers (1981) compared the Iatmul men's house in New Guinea with the British House of Commons, with striking results. Throughout most of its history, the House of Commons *was* a men's house. "The classification of physical space," Rodgers claims, "derives from the cultural map of political power" (1981: 53). The Speaker of the House sits at the front, and members of the party currently in power sit in front of him on his right, the opposition on the left. After his ceremonial entry, the Speaker's prayers both open the session and make a direct link to the sacred power of the church. "A member's entry and exit into the chamber is marked by a bow towards the Chair" (p. 53). Since all of these positions have traditionally been held by men, it is not too surprising that it was very difficult for them to accept women in their midst, they appear to be "matter out of place." Since 1919, women have been able to be elected to Parliament, yet there are still very few female members, in part because of the pervasive atmosphere and veiled hostility. One seemingly trivial way they were "told" they did not belong concerned the bathrooms. The women's bathroom was clearly marked: "Private, Lady Members Only," while the men's room had emblazoned on the door, "Members Only." "Does this demonstrate the implicit assumption that in the symbolic ordering of the British political system the members of the House are men?" (p. 55). No doubt very similar things could be said about the United States Congress, especially the Senate where there are so few women.

Spaces in Cities

Primary, of course, is a source and control of water and a system to provision inhabitants with food; both of these imply political organization, consolidation of power, and thus hierarchy. In addition, there must be certain kinds of building materials and styles of housing that can accommodate large numbers of people in a smaller space.

Cities developed in the ancient Near East around 4000 BC – Erech and Ur in Sumer, now Iraq, are thought to be the oldest cities. Although cities are a very efficient way to consolidate power, they are extremely dependent on those outside it, unlike peasant villages or nomadic encampments, which are much more self-sufficient. Think of what is necessary in order for a city to come into being and to maintain itself. Regardless of the needs of cities, those needs do not dictate the design of a city, that is an artifact of culture.

Edward Hall has noted that in Europe there are two major systems for patterning space. One of these, found primarily in France and Spain, is the "radiating star," while the other is the grid that traveled from Asia Minor (ancient Turkey) with Caesar to England (Hall 1966: 137). The contrast becomes obvious if you compare the Place de la Concorde in Paris with the numbered streets in New York, Chicago, or San Francisco. Hall claims that the "French-Spanish system connects all points and functions . . . [while] the grid system separates activities by stringing them out" (p. 137). It is something worth pondering, especially his further claim that the former is sociopetal while the other is sociofugal; these neologisms mean, I suppose, that one brings people together while the other tends to disperse them.

Cities are also generally divided up into a variety of sections by activity – business or financial section, shopping section, and theater district, for example, and also by ethnic group and income category.[1] Look around your city or the one closest to you and try to figure out who does what where and when and who lives where. In the not too distant past, cities were the major places to shop. Even if you lived outside the city, you had to go to the city, indeed "downtown," to shop for a new dress, a coat, or a pair of shoes. It was an outing, a special occasion. Downtown areas in cities, and Main Streets in towns, began to decline in the 1960s as a very different phenomenon began to appear – the shopping mall. A mall is set outside the city and even outside the town. At first, people wondered who would go there. There is nothing there! Today, that is probably where most people do their shopping. Shopping malls are thought to provide the variety of the city with the convenience of the country since it is much easier to park the car at a mall than "downtown." They are also self-contained worlds – not only are there department-type stores, but numerous specialty shops featuring items such as shoes, jewelry, toys, children's clothes, sporting goods, and evening wear. Many also have flower shops and grocery stores as well as coffee shops, restaurants, beauty parlors, spas, movie theaters, video-game halls, and even places to leave the children for a couple of hours while you shop. It is a totally artificial environment, not rooted to any place in particular, although there are variations and differences related to the wealth of the communities around them. But it is this environment that has become especially popular as a "meeting place" with young people among whom a whole "mall culture" has sprung up. Investigations of this phenomenon have begun to yield insights not just about adolescents but also about the effect of space on notions of self and consumer vs. citizen.

It is also interesting to consider the difference between an American mall and the shopping areas in Middle Eastern cities. In the Middle East, each shopping area has numerous shops selling the same kind of things rather than a variety of things in one place. That means that in one area or street you will find only leather goods, in another kitchenware, or carpets, or wedding clothes, or goldsellers. Each shop has the very same kind of items, for example, gold bracelets, earrings, and necklaces; there may be a slight variation in styles but basically the same items are sold in each shop. This arrangement may have the unintended consequence of keeping the shopkeepers relatively honest, because if one of them began to charge exorbitant prices, he could lose customers to his neighbors who are not. The reasons you patronize one rather than another is not so much because of the difference in the items sold as because of social connections, because it is run by a relative or a friend, or it was recommended by one. Generally, each shopping excursion has a specific purpose in mind. There are exceptions, of course. For example, in some Middle Eastern cities there are "passages" – spaces between buildings or underground where a variety of small shops coexist. This is also true in the Grand Bazaar (*Kapılı Çarsı* – Covered Bazaar) in Istanbul, perhaps the world's first shopping mall, established soon after the Muslim conquest of the city in 1453. Today, there are about 4,000 tiny shops selling a variety of goods under its roof. Nevertheless, they are still arranged in different "streets" according to the type of item sold, for example, "the goldsellers street."

Public Places

All cities, towns, and even villages have public places where numbers of people can gather, not only for ceremonial displays or protests but also where more informal meetings can take place. There are public squares such as Red Square in Moscow, Trafalgar Square in London, or Times Square in New York, as well as parks and green spaces – the Mall in Washington, DC, Hyde Park in London, and Central Park in New York. While parks such as these also serve as major public gathering places, they are used more informally as well – for reading the newspaper, for picnics, for pushing the baby carriage, or for jogging. Not only do they break up the monotony and oppressiveness of buildings, they also provide a breathing space for the city's inhabitants. Nevertheless, different cultures have very different ideas about what a park is and what it should look like. In Paris, for instance, the parks are very well manicured and are often filled with formal gardens, fountains, statuary, and artificial pools of water. People keep to the graveled paths and sit on park benches. The whole thing is extremely decorous. In contrast, in Berlin, there are many parks scattered all over the city and some of them are quite wild – lots of woods and bushes and natural ponds. People ride their bikes and even horses on the paths and sit or lie down on the grass or ground. It gives Berliners a feeling they have been able to get into the countryside even in the heart of the city. I taught in Berlin for a semester, and at first I was quite wary of going into these parks alone because of my enculturation in the United States, where entering such a place can be extremely risky for women. But this does not seem to be the case in Berlin; I never heard of any assaults against women in parks. This is not to say they did not or never happen, but it would be an unusual event, and I saw many women walking alone, sitting and reading alone, and even sunbathing topless alone. They seemed to have the feeling that they had as much right to the use of the parks as men – at any time. More importantly, the men did not seem to feel this as an infringement on *their* space. What do you think accounts for this difference (cf. Massey 1994)? More important, what do you think is necessary to make it safe for women to walk in parks day or night? What other ways do you think the space of the city is felt and used differently according to gender?

In the United States, at the other end of the spectrum from city or town parks are State Parks and National Parks. These are away from cities and towns and demand a more extended excursion. They are not just a place to stroll at lunchtime or after the evening meal. Although they are public, they are usually not free but require an entrance or use fee. State Parks are meant primarily as recreational spaces for their citizens; they are designed for family activities – swimming, boating, games, and some camping. State Parks tend to be more domesticated while National Parks were designed to protect "wilderness" areas from human traffic. "In wildness is the preservation of the world," said Henry David Thoreau,[2] who not only gave expression to a vigorous but suppressed religious belief in the effects of nature (cf. Albanese 1990), but also, unknowingly, gave inspiration for a movement to preserve America's wilderness areas for posterity.

Yet, despite the image of wilderness, National Parks are well controlled. There are designated places for tourists, normally on the periphery, so they might get some sense of the natural beauty; but except for these places there are few domestic amenities in National Parks. Those who wish to enter the "wild" must usually get permission and enter at their own risk. These parks provide a space for wild animals and dwindling numbers of endangered species. While it is also a place for some people to escape, for a brief period of time, the intrusions, especially the noise, of modern life, the park often displaced the people who had been living there. National Parks are also often the site where certain people play out the cultural myths of "returning to nature," often with dire consequences. An especially poignant story is told in *Into the Wild*, by Jon Krakauer (1996).

Other Public Spaces

Sporting arenas and museums can also be considered public spaces since generally anyone who can afford a ticket can enter that space. And they are also considered public because they are often, but not always, supported by public taxes. Further along this continuum are such places as movie theaters, cafés, and pubs. These are privately owned, sometimes by corporations, but public insofar as anyone who can pay the price of admission or is of the appropriate age can enter.

Restaurants, too, are other semi-public spaces. Some are extremely exclusive due to prohibitive cost, others attract only a young boisterous crowd; women have tended to feel "out of place" if they go alone, and sometimes are made to feel that way; whereas the lone male diner rarely encounters the same stigma. Some restaurants have "family sections." In the United States it generally means that families, mainly the babies and children, should be kept away from adults who wish to dine by themselves. What cultural messages are being communicated? In Turkey, at least in some towns, it is felt to be inappropriate for women unaccompanied by men to be seen in restaurants, so "family restaurant" means a place where women can eat, with or without their children.

Almost every restaurant now has a smoking section, segregating people by their habit, and recently, some restaurants have, thankfully, set aside separate sections for cell phone users. What other kinds of sections or divisions do you find? A restaurant is a good place to examine social divisions. Look closely at who is occupying which spaces. Who is working behind the scene? Who is in the dining area? While it is true that these very same people might change places in another location, or at another restaurant, the social divisions still remain.

Let us return, briefly, to the subject of bathrooms. In the United States, bathrooms in public places are generally segregated by sex. If there is just one bathroom, each sex would use it separately. That is not what I found in what I considered staid Belgium. There the toilets are often unisex, which means that both men and women use the same bathroom at the same time. I found it a bit disconcerting. In American public bathrooms there are now often tiny places for changing baby diapers – but they are generally only in the women's bathrooms, a subtle indication that American culture views diaper-changing a woman's job. In Scandinavian countries, in contrast, there are such areas in both men's and women's bathrooms. What different notions of gender are being expressed?

Work Space

When you enter a large office, aren't you immediately aware of the status of the person sitting at the desk? Or at least make assumptions about it. The status is not just communicated by the plush carpets, the view, the furnishings, but from the sheer size of the office. The size of an office, even if the difference is only a few square feet, can create all kinds of personnel issues and conflicts. In academia, which is the place I know best, there is a pecking order for who gets what office and it would be an insult if you were more senior but got a smaller office than a new assistant professor. In Turkey, professors generally have to share offices. Meanwhile, in France, professors generally do not have offices at all! They work at home and meet students in cafés. How do you think status would be communicated there? In American business, a president, vice president, or chief executive officer will normally have a large office with a view, often on a different, usually higher, floor altogether. But even the head of a particular department will have a private office – often in a corner or place somewhat away from the other workers. By contrast, "the man in charge of a French office can often be found in the middle – with his minions placed like satellites on strings radiating outward from him" (Hall 1966: 138). In Britain, the members of Parliament have no offices but apparently "conduct their business on the terrace overlooking the Thames" (p. 130)! How do you think American Congress(wo)men would react to that?

We spend a great deal of our time working, therefore work space is important for how we feel about ourselves. Different occupations demand different kinds of spaces: scientists need laboratories; architects need large tables, chefs need kitchens, etc. But if the space is designed only for efficiency without taking into consideration workers' needs, they will probably not be very efficient. In factories, priority is given over to machines; how do you think that affects how workers view themselves and their work, especially when a foreman is watching from a platform above the workfloor? When you visit a business, observe how the space is arranged. Where do the clerical staff sit, and what kind of space are they allotted? Who has an office?

Are there separate spaces for eating, for recreation, and for child care? What can you tell about the business just by the spatial arrangements?

Houses and Rooms

Forms of shelter, or what I shall call "houses" for purposes of simplification, are enormously varied – not just across the world, but across time and region. This is a huge and interesting subject that we can only touch upon. Houses express who we are, both as individuals and as peoples. They vary not just in the materials used but in square footage, in layout and design – in other words, their use of space. In an extraordinary book, *The Material World* (Menzel 1994), a photographer set about the task of making portraits of people and their possessions in different parts of the world. He was interested to get a "representative" family, that is, a family that represented the statistical average. In Mali, for instance, a family of seven live in an adobe (mudbrick) house that is 540 sq. ft.; the same number of people live in a cement block house of 400 sq. ft. in South Africa. In Mongolia, a family of six live in a *yurt* (a one-room round tent) that is only 200 sq. ft., while a family of the same size in Kuwait has 4,850 sq. ft. to move around in. The average in the United States was a family of four living in 1,600 sq. ft. In all of these countries, there is obviously a wide variation in wealth, family size, and house size, but the averages, nevertheless, tell a great deal about the "normal" lifestyle and spatial values in that culture.

I thought a lot about this when I spent a year in the Groot Begijnhof in Leuven, Belgium. Established in AD 1230 for a group of *béguines* (pious lay women) who devoted themselves to charitable work, it was taken over by the Katholieke Universiteit te Leuven in 1962 as a residence for faculty and visiting scholars. The Begijnhof was a beautiful, quiet place cut off from the traffic and noise of the city by a surrounding wall. There were streams and tiny footbridges connecting different parts of it; the houses were of brick and half-timber – the size and scale depending on each woman's circumstance – and each one had a tiny garden and a view. What really struck me, however, was the exquisite and careful design. In that tiny enclosed space, even though houses were right next to or across from each other, you could not see into your neighbor's house.

Turkish example

Turkish living space varies considerably from city to village. In the cities, and even now in towns, very few people live in houses anymore. Most people live in apartment buildings of four to eight stories. While there are significant differences regarding luxury, especially size and materials, most are fairly similar in design: generally, each apartment has three to four bedrooms, and there are only four apartments on each floor – each commanding a corner. It is assumed that people have children and even newly married people generally live with their parents until they can afford to buy their own flat. The few people who live in separate houses are either the very rich who, for example, live in villas along the Bosphorus in Istanbul, or the very poor who live in makeshift houses in the *gecekondu* (literally, built in a night) areas on the outskirts of the city, or in villages.

In the village where I conducted my fieldwork, most of the people lived with their extended family in traditional houses made of mudbrick. Today, many villagers are constructing houses of cement block, which are considered "modern." However, cement blocks do not provide as good insulation as mudbrick, which stays warm in the winter and cool in the summer. There was also a fairly standard design for the living space, called *karnıyarık*, which means "split womb." Such a house is meant to accommodate several families: ideally of brothers, but often including their parents. The house I lived in was only half a *karnıyarık*; but the other example shows two typical *karnıyarık* designs and also a half (see figures 2.2 and 2.3). In the middle house there is a central hallway, called *hayat*, which means life. Each room is, in theory, considered to be an entire house (perhaps evoking memories of the Turks' nomadic past when they lived in tents), though today some rooms are distinguished by function, i.e., bedroom, kitchen, sitting room. Often, however, the sitting room is multifunctional: people sleep there, cook there, eat there, bathe there, sew and knit and card wool there. I once even saw the carcass of a whole cow being cut up for various forms of meat. Divans are placed against the walls all around the room and possessions are stored underneath. Rarely is there a table or chairs. The major large piece of furniture is a cupboard in which the television is placed and other important mementos such as photographs or postcards. A relatively small room in a Turkish village house can easily accommodate 20–50 people for dancing during wedding activities, for example. In the same size room, most Americans would begin to feel uncomfortable if there were more than five people occupying that space – so filled are our rooms with large pieces of furniture. Today, however, when young Turkish villagers get married, they are requesting living room, dining room, and bedroom "sets" that represent to them a more "modern" lifestyle.

In the village, people generally live on the second story of their houses; the ground floor is for animals, machinery, storage space for food, and often the place where bread and cheese are made. Animals are typically sheltered beneath the living quarters so that their warmth also warms the house. The house complex is surrounded by a wall, part of which actually is a house wall. A gate, however flimsy, marks a very important boundary – it signifies that the house area is private. Anyone who enters must call out. Women are freer to enter houses because the house is the woman's place. An unrelated man must wait at the gate or just inside the entrance to the courtyard. Not surprisingly, *thresholds* carry symbolic importance – the entrance not only to the complex, but also to the house proper. Before entering a house, people must remove their shoes.

Inside the house the space is not neutral but is meaningfully (culturally) coded. Every child knows implicitly what the *seating arrangements* are. Old men sit on the divan near the window and farthest from the door. Other men sit next to them; women on the floor or on other divans. A person's rank and relative value are expressed in these arrangements. When a group gathered, I formed a boundary between male and female. I was in a "liminal" space, "betwixt and between" the categories of honored guest and woman (an honorary man in some instances).

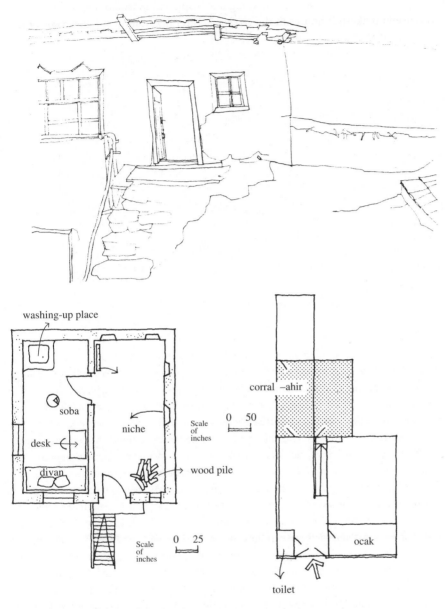

Figure 2.2 Plan of "my" house – half a *karnıyarık*. Drawn by Oya Aksoy.

Once outside the house, the space is also coded. Because the lanes and paths between houses are considered public, and therefore dirty, people throw their garbage there. It is expected that the dogs, goats, and other animals that pass by will eat it. As the house is the primary preserve of women, the streets are men's space, and women are not as free to move around there. In the village a woman needed permission from her father or husband to visit another woman in the village, even if she lived just across the street, and normally she had to be accompanied. Although

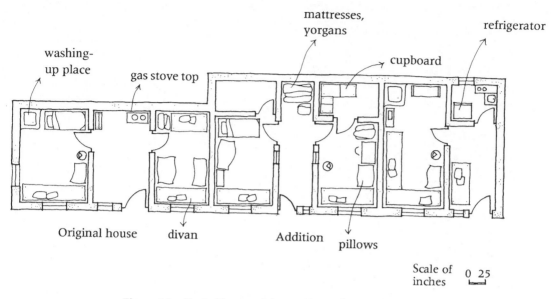

Figure 2.3   Typical *karnıyarık* layout. Drawn by Oya Aksoy.

it took less than 10 minutes to walk from one end of the village to the other, women did not walk around alone. To leave the village was impossible without permission and, besides, everyone would see you. Moreover, there were miles of "wild" space between the village and the nearest town (40 kilometers away), and that space was for shepherds, their flocks, and the vicious dogs who are trained to attack intruders. Young men did not need permission to walk around the village – that was their domain – but they did need it to leave the village in order to go to town.

You can understand how my relatively free movements were unsettling for the villagers. They often asked me: "Who gave you permission to come to our village?" "Was it your father, your university, or your government?" It became an issue every time I left the village – to get supplies or to visit friends in the city and pick up my mail. Since the teachers and the midwife (who were outsiders) needed to have government permission to leave, didn't I? I solved this problem by informing the *muhtar* (headman) every time I was planning to leave and when I was planning to return so that he could answer their inquiries and not have his honor called into question.

The inside–outside dichotomy was replicated at other levels of structure. Inside and outside the village had many of the same meanings as the inside and outside of the house. Villagers thought of their village as *kapalı* (closed), which is the same word used to refer to women who cover their hair. The headscarf symbolizes that the women are *kapalı*, closed, off limits.[3] They are enclosed by the honor and protection of their menfolk. Although there was no wall around the village, there might just as well have been. Outsiders could be seen approaching the village and would

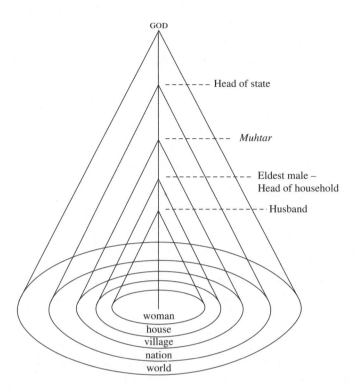

Figure 2.4   The structure of traditional Turkish authority relations as they are symbolically gendered (Delaney 1991). The female symbolizes the physical, unregenerate aspects of cultural entities – the house, the village, the nation, and the world. The male encloses, represents, and forms the generative relations between them. In this role he stands in line with the divine.

be scrutinized. For insiders, entering the village felt similar to entering a home, you felt as if you were entering a place of refuge and protection.

Inside and outside the nation carries similar connotations. At the collapse of the Ottoman Empire, Atatürk was able to rally the people to the nation's honor that had been defiled by the capitulations the Ottomans made to outside powers. He felt called upon to establish the borders of the nation, to keep outsiders out and fellow citizens in. For Muslim Turks, the whole world should be under the protection of God; they think of non-Muslims as living in Dar el Harb (The Place / Space of War), while they themselves live in Dar es Islam (The Abode of the Muslims, i.e., those who *submit* to God).

What is not often noticed is that these physical places are symbolically coded as female; men are go-betweens – men rule over and represent the household in public records and gatherings; the elected headman of the village ruled the village and represented it to the government; a man has always been president (there has been one female prime minister, Tansu Çiller) who rules over and represents the nation to the rest of the world. And ultimately, God rules over all (see figure 2.4).

"The American home"

Because the United States has always been multi-ethnic or multicultural, and because it is such a huge country with a number of very different regions, there is no such thing as the typical American house (cf. Foley 1980). The differences tell us a lot about the concepts and values of the different regions and ethnic groups. At the same time, there are overlaps by means of which they draw upon and express wider American values or different sides of them. There are certain styles of house that one associates with New England, "Saltbox colonial," for example. When you see such a house in California, you would say "there's a New England-style house." However, it is unlikely you would find an adobe-style New Mexico house in Vermont. The different styles do not derive merely from the materials available or even the weather, but express different cultural meanings.

Unlike the Turkish village where all the houses are together and the fields and land surround the village, the American dream has been for each family to have its own house set in the middle of its own land – at least since the days of the pioneers. This is as true in the farming country of the midwest, where houses are few and far between, as it is in suburbia, where each house is set on a tiny plot of land. We are said to value our individualism and our privacy; we don't want neighbors peering in our windows or overhearing our arguments. In a Turkish village, however, that very proximity creates a brake on domestic violence. In the past, especially on the East coast, houses normally had several stories and there were separate rooms for separate functions, each with a door. And that was the case not just for the rich but also for the working class.

In the 1950s a new trend toward more open space swept across the nation – rooms without boundaries, rooms that were multifunctional or at least blended one into another. Dining room and kitchen or dining room and living room, or kitchen and living room; bathroom and bedroom or sleeping loft; study and guest room or television room or "family room"; even hallways became more open as they often were combined with stairs on split levels. "Ranch houses" became popular. Not modeled on any real ranch house, the term referred to a house built all on one sprawling level.

In the past a "house was thought of as the repository of a family's history"; it was a place where family heirlooms and other memories were displayed (Carol Vogel, *New York Times Magazine*, June 28, 1987). Research conducted by the Joint Center for Housing Studies (at MIT and Harvard) indicates that that image of a house is long gone and instead it is viewed more as an investment. And what people are "interested in purchasing [is] a life style, with all the modern conveniences of affluent urban life – such as security and maintenance services – minus the crime and dirt" (ibid.).

Although house size has increased with middle-class affluence, the two-income couples who live there hardly have any time left to spend in them since they are generally working (more than) full-time. No wonder they desire "bringing some semblance of resort living into [their] everyday lives" (ibid.), referring to the desire for swimming pools, hot tubs, tennis or squash courts and even golf courses in their planned communities. The emphasis is no longer on unique individual houses but on luxury and comfort in the upscale housing developments that cater to this kind of lifestyle.

"Good fences make good neighbors"

So said Robert Frost in a poem about neighborliness (or lack thereof) in rural New Hampshire. A neighbor insisted on rebuilding a wall even though there was no ostensible need. Frost quips:

> Before I built a wall I'd ask to know
> What I was walling in or walling out,
> And to whom I was like to give offense.

Yet Americans seem to love fences – picket or ranch, chain link, tall filigreed iron, or stockade; fences are another expression of the desire for privacy and possession. They announce: this is my property, my castle, however humble; keep off until or unless invited in. Fences like these create a kind of buffer zone between the privacy of the house and the public area of the street or sidewalk. The distance seems similar to the distance we like to keep between ourselves and the person we are speaking to.

> It is true that some people build a fence to keep in the dog or the children, or to keep out deer from a vegetable garden; these fences are functional and are not what I am talking about.

Porches used to perform the function of "buffer zone," according to Sue Beckham in "The American Front Porch: Women's Liminal Space" (1988). The author associates the porch mania that flourished in the century between 1840 and 1940 with the rise of the industrial revolution and the era (at least among the middle classes) when men went off to work in a factory or business and women were increasingly confined to the home. During this time, the home came to be regarded as a sanctuary and identified as women's space. But the porch became a symbol of women's resourcefulness in overcoming the isolation they were experiencing (p. 88) – it was "betwixt and between" the private inside of the house and the public arena dominated by men.

> For women, kept at home by children in need of care and the labor necessary to keep a household going, the porch functioned as a social place – their own space – at home yet not inside – a space simultaneously work place and salon – where they could visit, keep track of neighborhood activities and exchange news flashes from passers by while they watched their children and performed the more portable and sedentary chores. (p. 74)

My mother, who as an adolescent lived in Brooklyn, New York, during the 1920s, described how she and her mother would "freshen up" to sit out on the porch after the evening meal and the dishes were done. It was a place not just to cool off but to visit with the neighbors as they walked by or came up to sit with them for a while. This was a place young men could court the girls, for the rules were more relaxed

Figure 2.5   An American porch, 1945. Photo Irene Jordan/Detroit News.

on the porch than in the parlor. Porches were often equipped with swings and hammocks and rocking chairs – adding to the languid atmosphere of the place. The custom has not vanished completely. My daughter and her husband recently bought an old house in the Boston area with a small open front porch. When they and the children are out there, the neighbors do drop by to chat.

I also recall spending many happy hours on the wraparound porch of a farm in New York state where we spent several summers. Not only was it the place where the grownups sat and smoked or did their mending, it was also the place where we children shelled peas, shucked corn, and snapped beans in preparation for canning. Today instead, people tend to prefer patios and decks, generally situated at the back, and more private side, of the house. But what is lost when we shift to the back or when we enclose porches with screens or glass or move inside where it is air-conditioned?

Perhaps dogs perform some of the same functions in neighborhoods today as porches did half a century and more ago. Walking your dog around your neighborhood allows you to talk to the neighbors and exchange news and gossip without having to invite them into your house. We think of dogs as members of the family and, like children, they permit us to talk to people, even strangers, on the street. They, too, provide that "liminal" space "betwixt and between" the privacy of our homes and the public place of work. At the same time, according to Constance Perin in *Belonging in America: Reading Between the Lines* (1988), dogs can also destroy the sense of community in a neighborhood by their digging up gardens, despoiling sidewalks, continually barking, and occasionally biting. And they can also be used to create barriers – "Keep Out: Guard Dog."

Rooms and Spatial Arrangements

The size of rooms, like house size, varies tremendously. Arabs, apparently, like huge rooms with ceilings so high they do not "impinge on the visual field; and in addition there must be an unobstructed view" (Hall 1966: 162). In conversations with Arabs, Edward Hall said that the "term 'tomb' kept cropping up in conjunction with enclosed space. . . . [They] don't mind being crowded by people but hate to be hemmed in by walls" (p. 162). Furniture is generally placed on the periphery, leaving the center of the room empty. Americans, he noted, felt very uncomfortable in such rooms, accustomed as we are to filling them with furniture.

Victorian houses had parlors or sitting rooms where guests were received. Guests did not go wandering around the house and only on occasion would they be invited to the dining room. Wealthy people who had servants also had hidden corridors and stairways so that they would not be found in the same spaces with the family or the guests – two almost entirely separate groups of people occupied the same house.[4] Social differences once again are marked by spatial arrangements.

From the 1950s on, the "family room" took over the functions of the living room so much that many people hardly ever use their living rooms except on formal occasions. The family room was the place to watch television and to promote family "togetherness." In the new millennium this may be a thing of the past, gone the way of gathering for the family meal, since it is far more likely that each family member watches his or her favorite programs on his or her own television. Kitchen counters with stools or "breakfast nooks" are, today, more likely to be the places where people eat rather than dining rooms. Even though fewer and fewer people are doing much cooking, kitchens among the affluent have, nevertheless, become large and equipped with all the latest appliances. They give a semblance of the ideal American family but are more symbolic than real. "Houses don't always reflect the way we really live, often they represent fantasies of the way we'd like to live" (Vogel, *New York Times Magazine*, June 28, 1987, quoting New York architect Robert Stern).

Spatial arrangement does not just refer to the size and layout of stove, sink, refrigerator, etc. but also to where each person decides to put things. Have you ever noticed, when you are trying to use another person's kitchen, how difficult it can be to find anything? Everything is in its place but clearly that place is different from the one that you would assign. Each of us has our own sense of order. Nevertheless, this sense has been influenced by our culture and by the region we grew up in, the ethnic, educational, and economic background of our parents, and by the times we live in.

No doubt everyone of you has had some experience in moving furniture around. Many of you have moved from one house or apartment to another, some many times. No doubt you have become aware of how different spaces demand different arrangements, even different types of furniture. But even if you have lived in the same place all your life, you have probably changed your room as you moved out of childhood into adolescence. Not only different furniture or colors are desired but also a different arrangement of your space. Even if your own room is a mess with piles of clothes and books scattered about, can't you tell if someone has been in it? Something will be out of place; even the slightest movement of an object will signal trespass.

Americans are brought up to think that each child ideally needs his or her own room right from birth, but other people think it is cruel to put an infant in a room by itself. In most cultures, babies sleep with their parents, not only in the same room, but in the same bed. While a "room of one's own" is the American ideal, many of us share rooms with siblings. However, some ethnic groups in the United States are used to having the whole family sleeping in the same room, and this has created a controversy among housing authorities and rental agents (Pader 1994). In other words, the cultural ideal has social consequences.

If you are boarding at college you have been assigned a room and probably a roommate. Was one of your first conversations about the use of space? Who would have which bed, which side? Or did you think of making bunk beds to create extra space? A number of my students have confided to me that when they first arrive as freshmen, they wanted to duplicate as closely as possible their room at home. They filled it with the same things; but when they returned as sophomores they wanted their rooms to be entirely different. Why do you think that is? I also heard of a very creative and unusual arrangement that would probably not be allowed in some places. A group of six students, male and female, who had a three-room suite decided to use one room for communal sleeping, another for study, and the third for a living room! In many colleges and universities today, dormitories are co-ed, something that was simply unimaginable when I went to college. Men could visit in the parlor only on certain days and times; never were they permitted on our floors, let alone in our rooms.

Each of us has an idea about our spatial arrangements, but rarely do we try to analyze our underlying assumptions. In some cultures, however, spatial arrangements are a matter of explicit and extended discourse. "In the West, we are taught to perceive and to react to the arrangements of objects and to think of space as 'empty' [whereas] . . . the Japanese are trained to perceive the shape and arrangements of spaces" (Hall 1966: 153). They even have a word for this, *ma*, which means interval, and "it is a basic building block in all Japanese spatial experience. It is functional not only in flower arrangements but apparently is a hidden consideration in the layout of all other spaces" (p. 153). One need only think of Japanese rock gardens, which are merely the arrangement of a few rocks on sand or gravel, but the effect can be stunning. Space as a meaningful and integral part of the overall design is also reflected in their paintings in the term *yohaku*, which means "white space." The background space was as important a part of the overall effect as the brush strokes.

Ancient Chinese philosopher Lao Tzu also captured this idea in chapter eleven in the *Tao Te Ching*:

> Thirty spokes converge on a single hub,
> but it is in the space where there is nothing
> that the usefulness of the cart lies.
> Clay is molded to make a pot,
> but it is in the space where there is nothing
> that the usefulness of the clay pot lies.
> Cut out doors and windows to make a room,
> but it is in the space where there is nothing
> that the usefulness of the room lies.

Therefore,

> Benefit may be derived from something,
> but it is in nothing that we find usefulness.
>   (Lao Tzu 1990: 70)

> Lao Tzu is thought to have lived ca. sixth century BC; his wise sayings may have been transmitted orally and written down sometime in the third century BC.

Invisible Spaces

So far we have discussed spaces for living – macro and micro. Yet there are other spaces we often do not think about unless, or until, we have to go there. These are spaces that are somewhat hidden from normal daily life – hospitals, nursing homes, mental institutions, prisons, and cemeteries – places for the ill, the criminal, the dying and the dead, the things we do not like to think about or be reminded of. Hospitals are the most conspicuous and located not too far from living areas. Still, they are places we do not like to go unless we have to. Perhaps that is why "hospital space is at a premium," there never seem to be enough "beds." But beds don't take up very much room, and in the grand scheme of things they are not expensive! It is a way of talking about other things, about social values and priorities – the fact that medical schools restrict the number of MDs they produce, that the greed of managed care companies not only reduces the number of nurses and other support staff, but also ensures that they are not paid enough.

Most of us are generally not familiar with nursing homes, mental institutions, and prisons unless we work there or know someone who is in one. Not only are they often hidden from the spaces and places of routine daily life, but also the people in them become invisible, hidden from the view of the general public. What values about the old and the infirm are being expressed by their spatial location? Why are they as invisible as criminals? What message is conveyed? Even here, because of the

Feng Shui

Feng Shui is the Chinese art of "auspicious placement" of houses, rooms, furniture, and other objects in order to create a balance between the lived environment and the natural world. The goal is to let the *chi*, the life energy that animates all things, flow without obstruction. According to this art, the house is like a second body and so it is very important to get both in "sync." Feng Shui has become very popular in the United States in recent years, as witnessed by the numerous books available, consultants and workshops, but it is often detached from the wider philosophy/cosmology/worldview to which it is deeply connected. Nevertheless, it has created more awareness of the use and meaning of space.

limitations on space (!), they will not get the attention they deserve, but it is important to include them so that they will not be left out of our account of space.

In stark contrast to all the living places, including even prisons and nursing homes, is the space for the dead. Cemeteries are places-spaces that house the dead. They can be huge, fairly impersonal places, or small, intimate, very local places; they can be places of national mourning and ritual, such as Arlington National Cemetery, or they can be sites of pilgrimage for family members and for devotees. For example, rock music lovers visit the Cimetière du Père Lachaise in Paris where Jim Morrison, the lead singer of the Doors, is buried, and thousands have gone to view the burial place of Princess Diana. Interestingly, Princess Margaret chose to be cremated. In India, Hindus are cremated while Muslims must be buried: how might each group view the practices of the other? Cremation was anathema for the Turkish villagers I knew, and they told me they would not fly in an airplane in case it crashed and their bodies burned. Turkish workers who die abroad have their bodies returned to their native soil, normally to the town or village where they were born.

Space that is No Place: Cyberspace

We cannot leave this discussion of space without talking about *cyberspace*.[5] According to science writer Margaret Wertheim, we are witnessing a new creation, and just like the "Big Bang" that scientific cosmologists talk about, cyberspace is expanding exponentially. "In the early eighties few people outside the military and the academic field of computer science . . . were even aware that 'cyberspace' existed" (Wertheim 1999: 225). By the end of the twentieth century, however, "the World Wide Web (the most public component of the Internet) has over 300 million pages . . . and is currently growing by a million pages a day" (pp. 226, 228). It is "the fastest-growing 'territory' in history" (p. 228). More surprising and mind-bending is that it is not like any space that physicists and cosmologists have been thinking about or looking for; it came "out of the blue," "out of left field," it is "beyond the space that physics describes . . . *it is not subject to the laws of physics*, and hence it is not bound by the limitations of those laws" (p. 228). It is, in effect, a non-material space even as it may depend on a material base, and this phenomenon "is of profound psycho-social significance" that has the possibility of changing notions not just of the world, but also of society and of ourselves.

Already cyberspace is a place that more and more people are inhabiting – some spending many hours of their lives there not just in search of information, but also chatting with friends, meeting new ones, creating new personas and experiencing other aspects of oneself, playing games, and buying everything from food and cloth-ing to airline tickets and vacations. But, asks William J. Mitchell, Dean of the School of Architecture at MIT and author of *e-topia*, how will this affect social life and community?

> Where will we get together? What sorts of meeting places, forums, and markets will emerge in the electronically mediated world? What will be the twenty-first-century equivalents of the gathering at the well, the water cooler, the Greek agora, the Roman forum, the village green, the town square, Main Street and the mall? (1999: 85)

His view, while enthusiastic, is more cautious. He worries, for instance, about the way that the Web can reinforce "sociocultural boundaries and categorical identities . . . [for it] typically provides efficient means for linking up like-minded people rather than for confronting differences" – in this way creating new types of gated com-munities. And there are already guards at the gates of "cyberturf" (p. 94), trying to keep some people out or preventing them from contacting those inside. At the same time, he is aware that it opens up new avenues for political organization and mobilization, as became obvious during the Tiananmen Square struggle and the Zapatista rebellion.

Nevertheless, we should not forget the gap between those who have access and the millions who do not. Although there are now "Internet cafés" scattered through-out the Third World, giving the impression that it is available to all, access is still affected by cultural mores. For example, in dirt-road small towns in Turkey, one can find an "Internet café" but the only people in them are adolescent boys. The gender gap is likely to remain critical as long as there is gender segregation and discrim-ination. Similarly, old people have mostly been left out of the "digital revolution," yet the Web could ease their loneliness and provide an interesting use of their time if they were brought "on-line."

Because Mitchell feels that the virtual and physical communities are somewhat co-dependent, he is more positive about the Internet's effect on local communities. As the digital revolution puts back together what the industrial revolution sundered, that is, joins work and home, he thinks people will become more, not less, con-cerned about their local environment. Unlike the commuters who leave their bedroom communities behind when they go to work, the cybercommuters will pre-sumably become more involved in the communities they live *and* work in. Beauti-ful, historic cities that were economically sidelined, like Venice, Bath, and Savannah, can again become vital because work will no longer require one to live near the centers of industry and finance (p. 77). As an architect, Mitchell is aware that this new kind of space that is no place will have an enormous impact on the design of living spaces, both domestic and public; however, at this point in time, it is too early to tell just how.

Returning to where we began this chapter, it is clear that cyberspace will also have an enormous impact on cosmology and perceptions of the world. Wertheim is perhaps an avatar, for she claims that "with each shift in our conception of space also comes a commensurate shift in our conception of our universe – and hence of our own place and role within that universe. . . . In a very real sense, we are the products of our spatial schemes" (1999: 308). What will be the personal, social, and cosmological consequences of cyberspace? What notion of the self, of society, and of the universe will emerge? She thinks that we are

> in a similar position to Europeans of the sixteenth century who were just becoming aware of the physical space of the stars, a space quite outside their prior conception of reality. Like Copernicus, we are privileged to witness the dawning of a new kind of space. What history will make of this space, appropriately enough, only time will tell. (p. 308)

What better place to turn to an investigation of time and the way it informs and is informed by culture.

Notes

1   See the work being done by Saskia Sassen and Manuel Castells about the way the global economy is affecting different groups living in the city.
2   It is also the title of a Sierra Club book with photographs by Eliot Porter, 1962.
3   That is, spatial boundaries are projected onto bodies. See Douglas (1966) and Boddy (1982, 1989).
4   The British television series *Upstairs, Downstairs*, as well as the film *Gosford Park*, give good portrayals of this.
5   The term was coined in 1984 by William Gibson in his novel *Neuromancer*.

Bibliography

Albanese, Catherine (1990) *Nature Religion in America: From the Algonkian Indians to the New Age*. Chicago: University of Chicago Press.
Ardener, Shirley, ed. (1981) *Women and Space: Ground Rules and Social Maps*. New York: St. Martin's Press.
Beckham, Sue (1988) "The American Front Porch: Women's Liminal Space." In *Making the American Home: Middle-Class Women and Domestic Material Culture, 1840–1940*, ed. Marilyn F. Motz and Pat Browne. Bowling Green: Popular Press.
Boddy, Janice (1982) "Womb as Oasis: The Symbolic Context of Pharaonic Circumcision in Rural Northern Sudan." *American Ethnologist*, 15 (1): 4–27.

Boddy, Janice (1989) *Wombs and Alien Spirits: Women, Men, and the Zar Cults in Northern Sudan*. Madison, WI: University of Wisconsin Press.

Carroll, Raymonde (1988) "Home." In *Cultural Misunderstandings: The French-American Experience*. Chicago: University of Chicago Press.

Carsten, Janet and Hugh-Jones, Stephen (1995) *About the House: Lévi-Strauss and Beyond*. Cambridge: Cambridge University Press.

Castells, Manuel (1989) *The Informational City: Information, Technology, Economic Restructuring, and the Urban-Regional Process*. Oxford and Cambridge, MA: Blackwell.

Chatwin, Bruce (1987) *The Songlines*. London: Jonathan Cape.

Douglas, Mary (1966) *Purity and Danger: An Analysis of the Concepts of Pollution and Taboo*. London: Routledge & Kegan Paul.

Foley, Mary Mix (1980) *The American House*. New York: Harper & Row.

Hall, Edward (1966) *The Hidden Dimension*. Garden City, NY: Doubleday.

Hall, Edward (1983) *The Dance of Life*. Garden City, NY: Doubleday.

Hallowell, A. Irving (1977) "Cultural Factors in Spatial Orientations." In *Symbolic Anthropology: A Reader in the Study of Symbols and Meanings*, ed. Janet Dolgin, David S. Kemnitzer, and David Schneider. New York: Columbia University Press.

Jaime, M. Annette, ed. (1992) *The State of Native America: Genocide, Colonization, and Resistance*. Boston: South End Press.

Kozol, Jonathan (1989) "Adrift in America." *Texas Observer*, February 24, pp. 10–14.

Krakauer, Jon (1996) *Into the Wild*. New York: Villard Books.

Lao Tzu (1990) *Tao Te Ching*. Trans. Victor H. Mair. New York: Bantam Books.

Leach, Penelope (1994) *Children First: What Our Society Must Do – And Is Not Doing – For Our Children Today*. New York: Alfred A. Knopf.

Massey, Doreen (1994) *Space, Place, and Gender*. Minneapolis: University of Minnesota Press.

Menzel, Peter (1994) *Material World: A Global Family Portrait*. Text by Charles Mann, introduction by Paul Kennedy. San Francisco: Sierra Club Books.

Mitchell, William J. (1999) *e-topia*. Cambridge, MA: MIT Press.

Motz, Marilyn F. and Browne, Pat, eds. (1988) *Making the American Home: Middle-Class Women and Domestic Material Culture, 1840–1940*. Bowling Green: Popular Press.

Pader, Ellen-J. (1994) "Spatial Relations and Housing Policy: Regulations that Discriminate Against Mexican-Origin Households." *Journal of Planning Education and Research*, 13 (2): 119–35.

Perin, Constance (1988) *Belonging in America: Reading Between the Lines*. Madison: University of Wisconsin Press.

Rodgers, Silvia (1981) "Women's Space in a Men's House: The British House of Commons." In *Women and Space: Ground Rules and Social Maps*, ed. Shirley Ardener. New York: St. Martin's Press.

Said, Edward (1979) *Orientalism*. New York: Vintage Books.

Sales, Kirkpatrick (1990) *The Conquest of Paradise*. New York: Alfred A. Knopf.

Sassen, Saskia (1995) "Analytic Borderlands: Race, Gender and Representation in the New City." In *Re-Presenting the City: Ethnicity, Capital and Culture in the Twenty-First Metropolis*, ed. Anthony D. King. London: Macmillan.

Sobel, Dava (1995) *Longitude*. New York: Penguin.

Wertheim, Margaret (1999) *The Pearly Gates of Cyberspace: A History of Space from Dante to the Internet*. New York: W. W. Norton.

Zinn, Howard ([1980] 1990) *A People's History of the United States: 1492–Present*. New York: HarperCollins.

The American Front Porch: Women's Liminal Space

Sue Bridwell Beckham

Sitting on the Porch
An event, in those days
for which one freshened up.
The houses were close to the street
and to sit on the porch
meant to be accessible
to visit, to chat and receive,
to be public and on display.
My grandmother did not
sit on the porch
before four o'clock
but sometimes stayed there
through sweet summer evenings.
And when I was with her
I thought of it as
an occasion. (Easter 15)

Every evening of a summer, after supper dishes were done, my mother-in-law insisted that the whole household gather on the front porch to "cool off." The ritual made good sense before her husband persuaded her to let him install air conditioners in their Mississippi home, but long after the house was kept at a comfortable 70 degrees, Ms. Beckham continued to insist that we all troop out on the porch after supper to cool off. Whenever I tried to beg off because I wished to read a book or watch a television show, the lady was convinced that nothing less than a rift with some family member would keep anybody indoors. And she was equally certain that whatever pique there was would disappear once I occupied a rocker on the front porch and communed with the group. Clearly, her faith in the ministry of the porch went deeper than relief from the heat. The porch for my mother-in-law was, as it was for Mary Easter, author of the poem above, and her grandmother, a ritual space. For those women, it was a space which met certain largely female needs, a space which, like a church, required compliance with certain forms for maximum benefit – and also, like a church, permitted the casting off of other social forms in order to realize a largely hidden self.

While virtually all American porches owe their architectural being to forms developed in other cultures, the American front porch is a peculiarly American institution. The earliest porches in recorded history were ceremonial. Porticoes on Greek temples and on the ceremonial buildings of America's Mississippian Indians alike blurred boundaries between the populace outside and the high priests performing their rituals in the inner sanctum. They were bridges between the sacred and the profane from which the highly revered could speak with the lowly and on which they could perform public rites for untutored – or unsanctified – audiences on the outside. It is far in space and times from Greek temples and pre-Columbian Indians to the porches on American houses and yet, unless the function were somewhat similar, my mother-in-law would not have placed so much faith in her porch and its restorative power. Nor would Mary Easter have recalled the ritual of freshening up at the appropriate time of day for the "occasion" of sitting on the porch.

Those authors, particularly women, who write of the American experience have long been aware that a ritual significance attaches to the front porch; the absence of direct allusion to that significance, however, suggests the realization to have been subconscious. In *The Ballad of the Sad Cafe*, for example, Carson McCullers recounts the peculiar use her protagonist, Miss Amelia Evans, made of her porch. Having lost her mother in early childhood and her father at the vulnerable age of nineteen, Miss Amelia, six feet tall and utterly masculine in build, had not learned – or chose to acknowledge – the womanly virtues, but implicitly she understood the proprieties of a woman living alone. In the daytime, she admitted men to the store on the ground floor of her house where they bought necessities such as feed, fertilizer and snuff. In the evening, when male visitors inside would have been improper, she sold men her moonshine through the kitchen door –

liquor she would never permit to be consumed in her house or her store.

Miss Amelia did, however, permit the men to drink her liquor on her front porch. The porch was Miss Amelia's property, readers are told, but this intensely possessive woman "did not regard [it] as her premises; the premises began at the front door and took in the entire inside of the building" (118). Clearly Miss Amelia understood the porch to be neither her home nor public property. She allowed the men to consume her liquor on the porch and to enjoy a certain amount of social interchange, but all the time she remained standing in the doorway guarding the inner sanctum and presiding over the proceedings. For this woman and for the town in which she lived, the porch was a space "betwixt and between" private and public, and once we consider the special properties attributed to the liquor consumed there, it becomes a place for ritual communion as well:

> For the liquor of Miss Amelia has a special quality of its own. It is clean and sharp on the tongue, but once it is down a man it glows inside him for a long time afterward. And that is not all. It is known that if a message is written with lemon juice on a clean sheet of paper there will be no sign of it. But if the paper is held for a moment to the fire then the letters turn brown and the meaning becomes clear. Imagine that the whisky is the fire and that the message is that which is known only in the soul of a man – then the worth of Miss Amelia's liquor can be understood. (107)

It was night on the front porch when, after consuming the liquor of self knowledge, Miss Amelia first encountered love and did the most ill advised and spiritually significant act of her life: She shared the liquor with a total stranger and *invited him into her house*. The fictional Miss Amelia and her creator Carson McCullers clearly sensed the front porch as a space of ritual significance. So did Russell Baker. In his autobiography, *Growing Up*, Baker's grandmother Ida Rebecca, had a very different ritual use for her porch.

In the 1920s, women of rural towns were generally proscribed from the exercise of public power. Despite feminist movements that thrived in the cities, the heady power of getting the vote waned, and the reprieve from domesticity provided by

World War I was history. The majority of women were once again housebound, and their accepted authority was only over furniture and children. Women, however, found socially acceptable ways to circumvent their public limitations. Whatever the mores of her time, Ida Rebecca, mother of twelve strapping sons and one daughter, was the acknowledged head of "a sprawling empire" and the unacknowledged ruler of the small Virginia town of Morrisonville. Baker's earliest and most vivid memories of his grandmother reveal her "sitting in state in the front porch rocker that served as her throne." Whether she was waiting for a son to bring home a prospective bride, presiding over the mandatory Sunday family gatherings, or surveying her domain, Baker recalls her sitting in that rocker, on that porch situated on a rise that put her at one end of and a few feet above the rest of Morrisonville. And in Morrisonville, "everybody said, 'It's her way or *no way*'" (28–32).

Whether or not Ida Rebecca thought of her porch as a mystic space from which she as high priest would preside, that is certainly the way it impressed young Russell and the citizens of Morrisonville. And why not? Forbidden by her motherhood to run for public office or to engage in business enterprises as Miss Amelia did, forbidden by custom and, as we have recently learned, by fearful male clergy, to seek the ministry, forbidden then to have an official office or temple, Ida Rebecca devised her own space from which to rule, and if we are to believe her grandson, she did it with aplomb. For Ida Rebecca, then, the front porch must have been a space betwixt and between the dwelling to which she had been condemned and the public arena in which she was forbidden to function, between the sanctity of the home and the profanity of the marketplace.

The porch for Miss Amelia and Ida Rebecca – and for millions of women from the mid-nineteenth century to the mid-twentieth – was a sort of "liminal space." Anthropologist Victor Turner speaks of a "liminal state" which occurs in those more primitive cultures studied by anthropologists – a time when the participants in a ritual are "betwixt and between" two cultural states – neither completely inside the culture nor yet outside it since their position is a transitional one.[1] Among those Turner describes as liminal are stone age peoples undergoing puberty rituals and medieval squires practicing the rites preparatory to knighthood. Two comparatively modern female liminal states are experienced by women who have declared their availability for marriage but who have not yet been claimed (debutantes, for example) and engaged women – both betwixt and between the protection of their parents and that of their husbands.

During their liminal period, such people are neither children nor adults, neither aspiring nor fully achieving. Using Tuner's model, the front porch becomes a liminal space – neither sanctified as the hearth nor public as the road. One must be *invited* to sit on the porch, but, on the other hand, one has the right to *expect* that invitation because a person sitting on the porch has declared herself "to be accessible/to visit, to chat and receive/to be public and on display." Occupants of a porch are betwixt and between because they are neither fully sheltered from the elements nor fully exposed to them – neither fully a part of the workings of the public sphere nor fully excluded from them.

Although every structural feature of the porch is borrowed from another culture, the domestic front porch is an American institution – owing its origin to the Southeastern climate and gradually spreading into the fabric of American life in all geographic regions. While it was English settlers and African slaves who conceived of and built the first American front porches early in the seventeenth century, they borrowed concepts from the Indian bungalow, the Haitian "shotgun" house, and the French side and back "galleries."[2] Later, wealthier English stock tempered the practical porch with majestic columns and ornate porticoes borrowed from the ancient Greeks. While those formal porches testify to the architectural genius of such men as George Washington and Thomas Jefferson, and ever the more humble porches of the common people were usually conceived and built by men, one suspects that women had something to do with their proliferation and their pervasiveness by the mid-nineteenth century.

The widespread use of the domestic front porch in the United States came at a time when the functions of male heads of households and of their female counterparts were being redefined. Late in the eighteenth century and early in the nineteenth, the industrial revolution for the first time made

working away from home the order of the day for great numbers of people. Before that, soldiers and adventurers left home for months on end, hunters for shorter periods. Wealthy Europeans, perhaps, maintained multiple dwellings and moved freely among them as they do today. But the masses of the earth's people lived and worked together in exceedingly small geographic areas. While their chores were often delineated by sex, both men and women were involved in work in or near the dwelling – even when, as with nomads, home itself moved seasonally. Families and groups of families could count on social intercourse and highly valued work. In the western world of the nineteenth century, however, all that would change. Particularly in the United States, the industrial revolution and unbridled capitalism brought about for all classes a departure from traditional ways of life. And it brought about corresponding changes in domestic architecture. One historian of American domestic architecture characterizes the new culture of the American mid-nineteenth century this way:

> The dynamics of this entire era was nothing less than the industrialization of America. . . . Life itself was harder and more cynical. The old Jeffersonian vision of an agrarian democracy, of independent men, rooted in the security of their own land or their own handicraft skills, had become more dream than actuality. The ruptures, dislocations, and insecurities of wage work and absentee ownership were increasingly the realities of American life.
>
> But with these miseries came also the optimism that was part of a period of phenomenal growth. It was the opening of an age of untrammeled *laissez-faire* capitalism, of rugged individualism, of unparalleled opportunity. . . . America felt herself to be the inheritor of all the riches of the historic past and scientific present, claiming furthermore an inalienable right to do with her inheritance exactly as she wished. This was true no less in architecture than in the mining, lumbering, and marketing conquest of a continent. (Foley 163)

American men may certainly have enjoyed that sense of unparalleled opportunity and the inalienable right to do with their political inheritance exactly as they wished. Women, however, are notably absent from that female writer's concept – and with good reason. With the industrial revolution and the rise of the middle class in European and American societies, it became possible for large numbers of families to "enjoy the luxury" of sending their men out to earn a living while the women stayed home and "enjoyed" the pleasures of domestic life. Wealthy women, of course, still could employ servants to handle domestic chores and carriages to move about in society. At the other end of the spectrum, every able bodied member of less fortunate families was required to work for wages just to keep food on the table.

But increasingly, the class which could neither afford servants nor needed the proceeds of every member's work to survive became the dominant class. What developed was a caste of women whose roles kept them largely indoors and solitary during the day. These women were to engineer domestic bliss, "influence" the children in Christian virtue, and act as moral guides to their men. Much has been written about the stress and frustration women suffered in this period because of their isolation and the gradual devaluation of their work. And much has already been written about ways they devised to deal with it. But one strategy women used to maintain contact with the community remains unconsidered.

The author of the quote above who celebrated the unparalleled opportunity for American men and the accompanying effervescence in domestic architecture of the period includes in her book dozens of drawings of representative American houses built between 1860 and 1941. And virtually every one of those examples has a front porch of some sort. And yet, like the women of the period she celebrates, the porches seem to be invisible. As in most other histories of American architecture, porches are virtually unmentioned in this book and, while architecture is seen as indicative of the consciousness which spawned it, no quarter is given to implications of ubiquitous porches.

It is probably impossible to prove that women had any direct influence on the porch mania that swept America from this period through the early 1940s. But it is a notable coincidence that, in the era in which the house became woman's domain and man exited to the market place, porches blossomed with an unprecedented abandon and pervasiveness. Before that time, American porches were confined to the Southeast where climate demanded the

indoor–outdoor space. Beginning in the 1850s, however, virtually every domestic structure was built with a porch. And to those whose builders failed to catch on to the trend soon enough, porches were sure to be added. A careful look at older residential sections of almost any American community reveals a healthy sprinkling of appended porches among the more common houses on which the porches are integral.

Whether or not women were responsible for the explosion of porches spanning three generations, there can be no doubt that indoor/outdoor living space became for them a way of countering domestic isolation, at least during the warm months. For women, kept at home by children in need of care and the labor necessary to keep a household going, the porch functioned as a social place – their own space – at home yet not inside – a space simultaneously work place and salon – where they could visit, keep track of neighborhood activities and exchange news flashes with passers by while they watched their children and performed their more portable and sedentary chores. Middle-class women could – and did – sit on the porch swing to prepare vegetables and fruits for cooking, even for preservation. Shelling peas, peeling apples and peaches, snapping beans, shucking corn – all were acceptable porch activities. So were hand sewing, endless mending, knitting in preparation for the colder indoor months and the more leisurely "fancy work." And while women performed those chores, they could keep an eye on the children – those middle-aged people who today remember the porch as partially sheltered playground.

The more fortunate women who had a back porch as well could do their more strenuous and less presentable chores in the back. Their poorer sisters, however, often actually canned those peeled apples and shelled peas on the front porch. The cramped kitchen would have been just too hot. The porch also served as summer laundry room. Today, adults from the South especially recall playing the familiar automobile game of "counting washing machines on the front porch" in the late thirties, the forties and into the fifties. Those washing machines had replaced earlier boilers and washtubs.

Porches did make heavy chores more pleasant in hot weather, and they did offer the opportunity to take quieter tasks into the semi-public, but the most liberating use women found for the porch, one imagines, was social. On the porch, the casual visitor, the maid separated from the family by class and caste, the family itself experienced "communitas." One characteristic Turner ascribes to people in a liminal state is "communitas" – the temporary but vital attachment that only people caught between cultural states can establish. Communitas, according to Turner, is "undirected, equalitarian, direct, non-rational, existential." Thus behavior in the liminal space is "spontaneous, immediate, concrete." The rules that apply to relationships and behavior in the structured environment on either side of the liminal space do not apply within it. So it is with the porch. There, betwixt and between absolute private and absolute public, relationships that would be impossible elsewhere can flourish for however brief a time – and they can be spontaneous. Thus, bashful and protected youth in the first flush of intimacy are free to experiment with new relationships; thus, caste and class can be suspended and commonality explored; thus the boundary between friend and stranger breaks down; thus, the powerless are empowered; and thus, established relationships are freed from the constraints and tensions of business on the outside and busy-ness indoors to commune and, if my mother-in-law is to be taken seriously, to heal.

The communitas established on the porch has contributed to the transmission of culture from generation to generation. In the evening, when whole families gathered on porches, family lore was passed in the guise of stories of old times. On my grandfather's porch, in the long televisionless summer evenings, I learned family history – and family legend. But in the day, with my grandmother, I learned my proper place. The turn-of-the-century girl child in the illustration learns from a female family retainer how to sweep a porch – and the importance of keeping it swept. At the turn of the century, at the height of Jim Crow, she also learned that it was sometimes socially acceptable for blacks to sit with whites – at least with white children – on porches, but never in living rooms. On some porches white female employers could indulge the friendships they formed with black employees without public censorship. It was my mother-in-law's custom

to invite her maid for a mid-morning Coke on the screened part of the front porch – and again in the mid-afternoon. Ida Rebecca Baker's realm was more strict. Her black maid and lifelong friend Annie was permitted the sanctity of a porch rocker only in times of sickness or death and then only, like the woman in the illustration, in the company of children. (Baker 42) It was a reward for service rendered.

The porch also provided a setting within which blacks could maintain social relationships with whites. A white woman who would never have entered her black friend's living room unless it was to impart some matriarchal service could sit on the black woman's porch with impunity. When he filmed *The Color Purple*, Stephen Spielberg retained Alice Walker to advise him on cultural mores with which he was unfamiliar. In the film he illustrated proper decorum for whites visiting blacks. When Sophia's white employer brought Sophia to spend the day with her relatives, she could not start the car to return home. One of Sophia's sisters, eager not to have her celebratory dinner interrupted while her menfolks ministered to the white woman's car, offered to fix her a plate of food and serve it on the porch. While the white woman refused the proffered gift, it is clear that eating "colored" food on the porch was permissible. The liminal porch was clearly a place where the color barrier could be weakened if not destroyed.

The sex barrier was also weakened on the front porch. In literature and the popular arts, as in life, the porch was the place for innocent courting. Young men have always been more or less able to come and go as they please. Not so young women. Traditionally, they must wait for men to come along, men to make the first move toward courtship, men to suggest marriage.

Most of us know that while women did often initiate acceleration of a relationship, the myth of the male initiator was a charade that had to be maintained, and it was maintained with the help of the porch. Since it was inappropriate for women to go into the public arena in search of potential mates, they needed a way to shop and to sample before making a selection – while all the time seeming to acquiesce in a male decision. Thus the porch, betwixt indoors and out, between public and private, became a sexual market place where the woman seemed to be on display but where she actually sampled wares presented before her.

The nineteenth century was a time, it must be remembered, when peddlers sold house to house, when dressmakers brought their bolts and patterns to the consumer, when fruits and vegetables were delivered to the back door. So it was with men. While Amanda Wingfield in Tennessee Williams' semi-autobiographical *The Glass Menagerie* does not mention her front porch, we are rather certain her living room would not have contained the seventeen gentlemen callers who visited her one fateful Sunday afternoon. And both Margaret Mitchell and David O. Selznik opened *Gone With the Wind* with Scarlett surveying masculine wares on the front veranda. Incidentally, Selznik was at least subconsciously aware of the ritual significance of a porch. While Scarlett is at her feminine best, the veranda is intact. When she returns to Tara to take over the man's job of running the place and even working in the fields, the porch is gone. We are led to believe that Yankees destroyed it, but the subtext is that a gritty female farmer has no use for the accoutrements of a girl whose only responsibility was to snare a husband.

It was for good reason that the porch was the place to entertain gentlemen callers. Inside the rules of propriety and chaperonage were restrictive. On the porch, neither in the parents' parlor nor in the forbidden public arena, certain rules could be broken. A girl on her mother's porch was properly chaperoned, but so long as her mother was inside, she could steal a touch or even a kiss and, in the cover of night, she could talk of subjects inappropriate indoors.

Conversely, while the porch offered relative freedom for the protected young lady, for unchaperoned women it was itself protection from men who thought *they* were doing the shopping. In the movie *Judge Priest*, set sometime around 1910, the principal female character was an orphan condemned to live alone in her inherited house. While she could never invite gentlemen callers indoors, this young woman could entertain the occasional male guest on her porch secure in the knowledge that, were he to get out of line – and one did – she was in the hearing of Judge Priest next door. And she could hardly have

become the subject of gossip when she entertained in full view of the street.

Not only had women the right to expect such protection from male neighbors – their virtue was the responsibility of such neighbors. An incident that Amory, Mississippi, residents would almost as soon forget illustrates the extremes to which that obligation extended. Early one sweltering summer eve in the 1920s, dentist and respected Amory citizen Dr. I. W. Beauchamp (pronounced Bee-chum) sat on the porch of his ornate Victorian house on Amory's Fifth Street with his wife and his two visiting and virginal nieces. Dr. Beauchamp was secure in the knowledge that his young charges would witness nothing unseemly from the sanctity of his porch, but that particular steamy evening as the women and the man sat decorously fanning, chatting, and observing events on Fifth Street – usually few and commonplace – the unspeakable and the anti-social happened. Across the street in the less stately home at 105 S. Fifth Street lived the Frashes, a large family with several adult married sons. All of the Frash boys including one "Billy" known to be "not quite right" and his brother "Jim" worked for the Frisco Railroad maintaining engines.

Having guests the Beauchamps probably sat on the porch later than usual. On the other hand the working men across the street had to be up with the sun and opted for an early bedtime. Billy went to his room to prepare for bed as usual – except this time he veered from the norm. He forgot to lower the shade over the large front window to his bedroom! The japonica that now provides a degree of privacy even for forgetful people had not yet reached window level. The result was the virginal nieces learned more about male anatomy than was ever customary before marriage. The nieces may have secretly been delighted, but Dr. Beauchamp was enraged. He was entitled to entertain female guests in his outdoor sitting room confident that their innocence would not be violated. The willing compromise to privacy one accepts by sitting on the porch in full view of the street does not extend to being forced to witness indecent exposure.

In the humid dawn of the next day, after what was probably a night of trying in vain to sleep on sticky sheets in a ninety degree plus bedroom, Dr. Beauchamp made his angry way to the roundhouse in search of his neighbors. Unfortunately, the first Frash he came upon was Jim – entirely innocent of all wrong doing. Equally unfortunately, Jim bore a strong family resemblance to his forgetful brother. Thinking he had found his man, Dr. Beauchamp collared his prey, threw him against the wall and shot Jim – not Billy – dead. And he was never brought to trial![3]

The incident makes a good story – amusing, shocking and tragic, even gothic – but its real significance is what it reveals about the culture of porches. Nobody today remembers much about the legal proceedings following the shooting. What they know, however, is what Dr. Beauchamp and the Mississippi legal system knew then – that young women had the right to sit on porches and expect the community to protect their virtue. That right, in fact, was so sacred that men were justified in going to any extreme to assure that it was maintained – even to the point of shooting the wrong man.

While Dr. Beauchamp could avenge his nieces' loss of innocence if he could not protect them from it, the dead parents of the protagonist in Bobbie Ann Mason's short story "Residents and Transients" were entirely helpless to protect her from her own instincts. Mason creates an entirely 1980s version of the liminal nature of porch entertaining when Mary Sue, left at loose ends while her husband is away on extended business obligations, relies on her inherited porch, and perhaps the spirits of her parents, to protect her from her own darker desires. Bored and confused about her place in her culture and her marriage, Mary Ann is surprised one afternoon when her *dentist*, seeing her on her porch, stops for a friendly chat. Nothing unseemly in that – except that the porch is the back porch! Since hers is a farmhouse, the back porch faces the road and functions as front porches usually do, but for Mason the fact that it is a back porch offers the chance for ambiguous messages. While no taboos forbid men to visit women on front porches, back porches, with their suggestion of privacy and even secrecy, are something else again. Thus, the character herself is in the ambiguous position of not knowing whether she is being unfaithful or merely friendly.

The dentist's first visit grows into a custom with which Mary Sue can live – so long as they are visible from the road, the couple have not done anything

technically anti-social. The crucial step in the relationship is not taken until the dentist crosses the threshold into the inner sanctum of the house. Then, just as when Miss Amelia took the stranger into her house after dark, an irreversible and fateful step has been taken. It is Mason's custom not to make reading her stories easy for the reader by resolving them, but the reader knows that once the visitor is inside, Mary Sue can no longer refrain from confronting her own ambiguities.

Mary Sue's dilemma is definitely a twentieth-century problem with well-articulated options once she interprets her own feelings. In earlier decades women confused about their place in the world had no clearly delineated choices. But they did have porches, understood – subconsciously at least – as places where rules could be suspended. In *The Awakening*, when Kate Chopin's protagonist, Edna Pontellier, begins to awaken to the limiting nature of her role as a Creole wife, much of the action takes place on the porch of her summer cabin. Vacations are suggested by Turner to be liminal periods when the vacationers temporarily move outside the expectations of their culture. Resorts, then, must be themselves liminal spaces. Thus Edna, summering at a vacation spot where many of her daily routines are suspended, is outside her culture enough to examine her lifestyle. And she doesn't like what she sees.

Edna's culture, however, has not taught her fulfilling alternatives. Even so, timidly at first, she begins to experiment. One experiment she tries is flirtation. At the resort, that is entirely acceptable. When she entertains her chosen gentleman friend on her own porch, her husband remarks how pleased he is that she has the young man to keep her amused while he is away during the week attending to business. It is only when, back in the city in colder weather, Edna invites her guests *indoors* in her husband's absence that family and friends perceive something untoward in her search for self.

But receiving gentleman callers is not the most significant indication that Edna – and Chopin – perceive the front porch to be a liminal space. On the night that Edna first awakens to her intense dissatisfaction with her life, the night that she begins a long campaign to declare her independence, she does it on the porch. Edna is accustomed to honoring her husband's every nighttime whim whether it be for a sexual encounter or to leave her bed to check on children who are obviously sleeping peacefully. On this particular night, however, she refuses to come in from the porch when her spouse announces it is time for bed. Throughout the night, she continues to reject any ruses her husband devises to attract her indoors where his rule is supreme. Subconsciously, at least, she realizes that, on the porch, she is subject neither to the rules that govern her performance in her husband's house and nor to those of the public domain.

Edna, of course, becomes acutely aware that her life thus far has been a series of command performances. In *The Presentation of Self in Everyday Life*, Erving Goffman outlined his now classic contention that in their everyday lives virtually all people present themselves to others in full-fledged performances that include costume, setting and, most of all, acting. Thus, the place where people act becomes a stage and the witnesses an audience. Preparation for such a performance, of course, demands a backstage. In his chapter on "Regions and Regional Behavior," Goffman discusses "front places" and "back places" (106–40). A front place is where performances are staged. A back place, on the other hand, is not only where the actor prepares for performance, but where she can be herself. For women and their porches, a strange reversal of back and front sometimes occurs. We have already seen that for Edna Pontellier, the front porch in full view of friends and neighbors – the audience – is where she feels most free to try being herself. Indoors, in the bedroom, one of the most back places for Goffman, with only her husband for audience, Edna must act the role of perfect wife and mother.

In *Their Eyes Were Watching God*, Zora Neale Hurston suggests a variation on the reversal theme when her protagonist Janie tries to free herself from the restrictions of her role as wife. In earlier times, before the advent of air conditioning, businesses were often equipped with porches, but these public porches were gathering places for men. Women were unwelcome. So it was with the store Janie ran with her husband. Janie was expected to mind the store for the occasional customer when groups of men – and sometimes unattached women – gathered on the store porch. To Janie, excluded in the dark store – merely a spectator to the camaraderie in front,

> When the people sat around on the porch and passed around the pictures of their thoughts for the others to look at and see, it was nice. The fact that the thought pictures were always crayon enlargements of life made it even nicer to listen to. (81)

When Janie moved to join the tempting revelry on the porch, her husband told her in no uncertain terms that her place was inside, and when finally, in defiance, she engaged her husband in a game of insults on the porch, it was an act of rebellion that was to destroy the marriage. A wife sharing his porch with him was not part of the role Janie's husband wanted to play. That happened in the middle of Janie's story. After taking the reader with Janie on a strenuous journey into genuine love and self knowledge, Hurston involves her protagonist and the reader in another porch scene. Having learned that she need not conform to society's artificial rules for her, Janie exchanges pictures of her spiritual journey with her bosom friend on the porch of her own house. The porch for Janie was symbolic of both her limitations and her freedom. While the store porch was a front place for Janie's husband, for her it had been a back place from which she was excluded. In the store, she acted the role of dutiful wife; on the porch she broke the rules and learned something about herself. And on the house porch, another back place located on the front, Janie experienced communitas with her female friend.

Goffman, writing in the 1950s, had an interesting view of women – a view possible only in a patriarchy. While in his examples, drawn primarily from the workplace, women have roles every bit as important as men, he sees the places where women get together alone as "back places" – no concept that they might perform for each other since he seems to consider women alone as "back people." With some accuracy he cites Simone de Beauvoir to bolster his position. What both he and de Beauvoir miss is that in the same chapter from which he quotes, de Beauvoir mentions situations in which women present themselves for women.[4] Surely when women decorated their houses, collected china, glassware and other paraphernalia for entertaining, they did not do it to impress men. And surely, when they decorate their porches they do it neither purely for personal satisfaction nor to impress some all-male world.

Nineteenth- and early twentieth-century women seem to have been more free to be themselves on porches than any place else. They could enjoy the communion of passers by and chance visitors on the porch while they watched children and did some of their more portable chores. And they could keep up with community news via casual exchanges with people on the street. As a matter of fact those people on the street were very important in building a porch culture. The porch served a dual role as stage and orchestra for Goffmanesque performances. As Mary Easter indicates, sitting on the porch at certain times of day, was "an occasion." People planned it; people freshened up for it. Women retired to their porches after demands of the protestant work ethic had been met to see and be seen. From their perch above the street, they could look down on passers by, wave, greet, and, after the passer had gone, comment. Each new event on the street was occasion for new stories or for dragging out old ones. And at the same time, those who walked by were audience for the performance on the porch.

Except at resorts and vacation cottages, the stage function of the porch seems to have been the only part of women's porch culture to survive into the 1980s. True, people do still sit on porches – when they have them – in the spring and fall, but it seems usually to be a sentimental harkening to days gone by. When it gets really hot, they huddle indoors with their air conditioning. Women, equipped with cars and telephones, no longer need to sit outdoors to maintain social contact. Television supplies continuous undemanding entertainment for those who are bored. And most women of the eighties are too busy performing the superwoman roles today's society has assigned them to have time to sit outdoors to greet and be greeted. In our frenetic society, a new need for "privacy" demands that what serious outdoor activity remains be relegated to decks at the rear of newer homes. And houses are seldom built with porches any more.

At the end of *The Ballad of the Sad Cafe*, Miss Amelia, bereft of the love who appeared one night on her front porch, waits three years on the same porch for his return, but no longer is there any com-

munion on that porch, and finally she shuts herself inside – away from all society. So it seems in the American summertime as row upon row of tightly shut-up air-conditioned houses suggest that communion is unwelcome, that the pedestrian is an intruder. Many of the porches that remain have been enclosed to provide indoor living space. Like Miss Amelia, female residents in these houses have shut themselves inside away from communion with their neighbors. And the porches that remain outdoors have often been partially enclosed with unsightly screens – allowing occupants to be indoors and outdoors at the same time but denying access to passers by. Traces of the porch as stage remain, however, to show that women reluctantly relinquish the liminality of the porch.

In the South, where porches provided indoor/outdoor living space for most of the year, new houses are built with rudimentary vestiges of the once grand veranda. With spindly columns and scarcely three feet of width, these so called porches are furnished as carefully as the living room within, but not as if to be used. Women spend hours scouting to find the correct antique mammy's bench, wickerwork cradle or hand caned rocker to suggest that any minute now a woman in hoop skirts, baby in hand, will come out to sip iced tea and wave at the neighbors. Untold thousands are spent on wrought iron furniture never intended for the derriere to suggest gracious living in a time just past. Blossoming plants tended as the babies once were extend the garden a little closer to the seldom used front door – people today enter through the attached garage, never seeing the outdoors as they emerge from their air-conditioned cars. Those fortunate enough to own older homes, north and south, furnish their porches with comfortable traditional swings and rocking chairs, but often they reveal the merely decorative nature of the furniture by placing them so close to the walls that rocking or swinging would be disastrous.

Those remembrances of community past are amusing and often even attractive. Other porches, however, seem almost tragic in the longing they reveal for a time of greater neighborliness. Women deprived of self actualization, not by today's mores but by their age and the era in which they grew, sometimes decorate their porches as if they were their last mute contact with other people. It is not unusual to find a single porch sporting wind chimes, all-season wreaths, plastic flora and fauna, concrete plant urns and [. . .] even a wine bottle or two. Even more heart rending for me, however, are the houses with no porch at all.

Once air conditioning made porches expendable, people for whom home ownership itself must have been a dream come true put the money that might once have gone for a porch into window units. The result was what I call a "mean little house" – mean in the sense of stingy, giving only what must be given, begrudging even that. These unadorned dwellings seem often to occupy lots with few or no trees, and equally often they seem to house older people – people who were once part of porch culture. And in front of or beside these houses, older women can often be seen huddled under the eave on a kitchen chair, or in the car port, knowing, regardless of an air-cooled interior, the need to "cool off" on the porch just as my mother-in-law did.

Last summer I visited my home town in Kentucky to show my children where I grew up and, incidentally, to photograph porches. As we strolled by one of the grandest houses from my day – the house of the federal judge – I was telling my children how excited I had been when the judge's granddaughter invited me to play with paper dolls on that very porch when we noticed in the corner of that great front porch, a tiny, shriveled-up woman. Her live-in companion confirmed that the woman on the porch was the judge's wife and grandmother of my childhood friend and invited me to speak with her, warning me she wouldn't know me. True, she did not recognize me, but she would never forget the ritual of the porch. Strapped in her chair so that she wouldn't fall, bereft of most of the knowledge she had accumulated in ninety-odd years, she greeted me as she had hundreds of other visitors to her porch over all those years – as if it were once again 1951, and she had yet to have a car of her own, the only air conditioning was to be found in movie houses, televiewing was relegated to those who had a stomach for professional wrestling, and the ritual of the porch had never ended. She had freshened up to sit on the porch, she was "assessable, receiving," and I was a neighbor who passed on the street and stopped to chat.

Women of her era, often foggy about the present, have no difficulty recalling the porch's meaning for women for over a century of American history. For her, for me, and for countless other women the front porch will remain an artifactual testimony to the isolation women once experienced and the resourcefulness with which they overcame it.

Notes

1 All information on Turner's liminality and communitas is drawn from Victor Turner, *Dramas, Fields and Metaphors: Symbolic Action in Human Society*, Chapters 1 and 7, although he has written of the concepts in many of his writings.

2 Material on the actual history of porches is difficult to find, and most of what is available is impressionistic – as is this article. The most serious scholarship on the front porch as significant domestic architecture to date is a mere two pages by John Michael Vlach. In *The Afro-American Tradition in Decorative Arts*, Vlach has carefully documented the African and Caribbean origins of the traditional American front porch (136–8). In "The North Carolina Porch: A Climactic and Cultural Buffer," Ruth Little-Stokes reported the same origins but her essay is primarily interpretive. Davida Rochlin's essay, "The Front Porch," reports the social significance of American porches but eschews history. In his classic history of architecture, Sir Bannister Fletcher acknowledges the ancient European origins of the "grand porticoes" and galleries of the early American Southeast, but porches *per se* are beneath his concern. Other sources have undoubtedly mentioned perfunctorily the appendages on American houses, but the architectural history of porches is most significant for its invisibility.

3 This story, very difficult if not impossible to track down through newspapers of the day, was related by T. H. Beckham, 86-year-old lifetime resident of Amory and Beauchamp's neighbor after 1940 when he bought and moved into the house at 105 S. Fifth Street.

4 Goffman quotes de Beauvoir when he quite accurately demonstrates that women alone are often freed from the restraints of social performance (125). In *The Second Sex*, a startling new book when Goffman wrote *The Presentation of Self in Everyday Life*, Simone de Beauvoir also shows that women perform for other women as well as for men although she appears unaware that she is describing performers when she

describes women's behavior among themselves (528–45).

Works Cited

Baker, Russell, *Growing Up*. New York: Congdon and Weed, 1982.

de Beauvoir, Simone, *The Second Sex*. New York: Alfred A. Knopf, 1953.

Easter, Mary, "Sitting on the Porch." *Absorb the Colors: Poems by Northfield Women Poets*. Ed. Beverly Voldseth and Karen Herseth Wee. Northfield, Minnesota: privately published, 1986.

Fletcher, Sir Bannister, *A History of Architecture*, 17th ed. New York: Charles Scribner's Sons, 1983.

Foley, Mary Mix, *The American House*. New York: Harper and Row, 1980.

Goffman, Erving, *The Presentation of Self in Everyday Life*. Garden City, NY: Doubleday, 1959.

Hurston, Zora Neale, *Their Eyes Were Watching God*. 1937. Urbana, Illinois: University of Illinois Press, 1980.

Little-Stokes, Ruth, "The North Carolina Porch: A Climactic and Cultural Buffer." *Carolina Dwelling*. Ed. Douglas Swaim.

Mason, Bobbie Ann. "Residents and Transients." *Shiloh and Other Stories*. New York: Harper, 1983, pp. 121–31.

McCullers, Carson. *The Ballad of the Sad Cafe*. *Seven Contemporary Short Novels*. 3rd ed. Ed. Charles Clerc and Louis Leiter. Glenview, Illinois: Scott, Foresman and Company, 1982.

Rochlin, Davida, "The Front Porch." *Home Sweet Home: American Domestic Vernacular Architecture*. New York: Rizzoli, 1983.

Turner, Victor, *Dramas, Fields and Metaphors: Symbolic Action in Human Society*. Ithaca: Cornell University Press, 1974.

Vlach, John Michael, *The Afro-American Tradition in Decorative Arts*. Cleveland, Ohio: The Cleveland Museum of Art, 1978.

E
X
E
R
C
I
S
E
S

Part I   Draw a map of your college or university from your own perspective (that expresses *your* perception of the space and your use of it). It may be sketched in broad strokes; it need not be very detailed.

boundary lines
North arrow

Part II   After completing your map, take a trip around campus – on foot or by bike, car, or bus (depending on which applies) and pay attention to the way space is organized. Write about two pages, addressing the following three questions.

1   What kinds of spatial divisions are noticeable? Hint: think about the differences between "town and gown," between study and leisure, etc.

2   How does the space relate to different categories of people, for example: male and female; children and elderly; faculty and students; clerical staff and other workers? Who has freedom of movement in these spaces, when and where?

3   In what ways are activities classified by space, for example, sleeping, eating, and so on. (They are also related to time, but that is another topic.)

Think about (but don't write about) the criteria by which you organized the space in your room. Did you discuss this with your roommate (if applicable)? Could you tell if someone had moved something of yours?

The purpose of this exercise is to get you to think more deeply about how these spatial arrangements order our everyday lives and at the same time incorporate cultural values.

In your notebook begin to keep track of spatial metaphors in everyday speech, for example: warm *up*, cool *down*, *high* society, *lower* class.

3

All We Have Is Time

Time is another major way we orient ourselves. What does it mean to be on time, out of time, or in time? This chapter discusses different cultural notions of time, the development of measuring time and clocks, the construction of the Western calendar and its rootedness in a sacred worldview, and birthdays and other markers of time.

All We Have Is Time

"Time is money."

With that simple statement Benjamin Franklin captured the spirit that would transform America. The quotation is a very condensed summary of what has been called the "Protestant Ethic." This ethic, according to Max Weber, is what really fueled the beginnings of capitalism in the sixteenth century. In *The Protestant Ethic and the Spirit of Capitalism*, Weber characterized the ethic as "this-worldly asceticism" in contrast to the more typical kind of asceticism that focuses on the next world. It was ascetic because it frowned upon luxury and consumption and encouraged thrift and saving in order to build up capital; the accumulation of wealth for its own sake should not be the motive, "but the attainment of it as a fruit of labour in a calling was a sign of God's blessing" (Weber [1904–5] 1958: 172). Today, this ethic, in an age of consumption and prodigal spending, seems very distant, especially its religious underpinnings, but it set the stage for widespread transformation of the way our lives would be conducted and our time used.

The Protestant ethic became more entrenched with the industrial revolution in Europe and the United States in the nineteenth century. While seemingly unrelated to Protestantism or to ethics, time was, nevertheless, part of both. People had to change their perception and relation to time. Time became a commodity to be used (well) rather than the medium in which life is lived. It had to be used for work, not pleasure; and any time spent not working meant less money. Work began to be strictly plotted against the clock so that workers were paid by the hour; thenceforth each hour became equivalent to a specific amount of money. So much is the equivalence taken for granted that the language we use for time is the same that we use

86,400 Seconds Per Day

Imagine there is a bank that credits your account each morning with $86,400. It carries over no balance from day to day. Every evening it deletes whatever part of the balance you failed to use during the day. What would you do? Draw out every cent, of course! Each of us has such a bank. Its name is TIME. Every morning, it credits you with 86,400 seconds. Every night it writes off, as lost, whatever of this you have failed to invest to good purpose. It carries over no balance. It allows no overdraft. Each day it opens a new account for you. Each night it burns the remains of the day. If you fail to use the day's deposits, the loss is yours. There is no going back. There is no drawing against "tomorrow." You must live in the present on today's deposits. Invest it so as to get from it the utmost in health, happiness, and success! The clock is running. Make the most of today.

To realize the value of ONE YEAR, ask a student who failed a grade.
To realize the value of ONE MONTH, ask a mother who gave birth to a premature baby.
To realize the value of ONE WEEK, ask the editor of a weekly newspaper.
To realize the value of ONE HOUR, ask the lovers who are waiting to meet.
To realize the value of ONE MINUTE, ask a person who missed the train.
To realize the value of ONE SECOND, ask a person who just avoided an accident.
To realize the value of ONE MILLISECOND, ask the person who won a silver medal in the Olympics.

Treasure every moment that you have. And treasure it more because you shared it with someone special, special enough to spend your time. And remember that time waits for no one. Yesterday is history. Tomorrow is mystery. Today is a gift. That's why it is called the present!

for money: we save it, we spend it, we borrow it, we waste it, and we budget it. This notion of time now seems so natural that it is difficult for most of us to imagine other ways of thinking about it. The idea that time is money also implies that it comes in different quantities, not nickels, dimes, quarters, but seconds, minutes, and hours. Time, thus imagined, is also like a ruler (in both senses of the term); not only does it reign over us, but it is calibrated like inches, feet, yards. Each of the time-segments is equal to all others in the same category; that is, each second is equal to every other second. Time is imagined as something outside of ourselves against which we measure our work and days. But what if time was considered a gift? What different metaphors would describe it? How might such a different conception of time affect your daily life?

Cosmological Time

Time, like space, is one of the major ways we orient ourselves in the world. Although we talk about it all the time, it is also something we take very much for granted. Time and space, we assume, are given in the human condition and, therefore, universal. While true, we must ask a further question. Paraphrasing linguist Benjamin Lee Whorf (1956: 138):

> Are our concepts of time and space and matter given in substantially the same form by experience to all people? Or are they conditioned by the particularities of language and culture?

Is the *experience* the same worldwide and then conceptually warped or channeled differently due to local custom? Or, is the very experience itself shaped and molded by culture? This chapter is not intended to provide answers but rather to raise awareness of the issues involved. In this first part, we will consider the widest, cosmological aspects of time – clocks and calendars. In the second part, we focus more on lived time, that is, the myriad ways time forms the context and parameters of our lives.

Relativity of time

Ever since Einstein, we have been taught that time is relative even if we do not understand his theories. Time is relative to space, neither is absolute, they are mutually constitutive; nor is there any independent standpoint for measurement. While the theory of relativity involves sophisticated mathematical knowledge and calculations, even a child becomes aware that time is relative to space as soon as he or she tries to call a grandparent living in another time zone.

Still, this is a different sense of the relativity of time from what I am getting at, namely that the concepts and experience of time are also relative. Surely even in your own lives you are aware of different experiences of time – sometimes it flies by, and at other times it drags and seems to stand still. We remember our childhoods as slow and seemingly endless; as we enter our forties and fifties time seems to speed up, the years begin to flip over very fast. Our clocks and calendars are unable to represent even this common experience.

What notions of time does Octavio Paz, the Mexican poet, capture in this excerpt from his poem "Hymn among the Ruins"?

Day, Round day
luminous orange in 24 sections
all filled with the same sunny sweetness . . .

Clearly, he had the roundness of the earth, the roundness of the sun, and the roundness of a clock dial in mind. Between them, he seems to say, a homology exists. The
poem was obviously composed before the invention of "digital" clocks. Although
the word "digital" refers to fingers, and thus evokes a "hand," making all clocks
"digital," it has come to refer to a very specific kind of clock or watch invented in
July of 1970. Digital clocks and watches became affordable and widespread in the
1980s. Until then clocks and watches were most commonly in the form of a circle
with hours 1–12 set around the dial. Two hands, one for the hour and one for the
minutes (and occasionally a third one to mark the seconds) moved "clockwise"
around the dial. On digital clocks and watches the exact time, for example 3:23,

Figure 3.1   Worldly Wit cartoon by Mike Scott © 1989 Cartoonists and Writers Syndicate.

flashes in the window. The numbers are alone, not set in the context of the round of hours, as on a clock face.

Today when I ask someone what time it is, I usually get an answer more exact than I want so that I have to pause to figure it out according to my time frame. I have a mental model of the round clock face and am used to hearing someone say "it's ten past four," not "4:11," or "quarter to six," not "5:48." Time has become linear in the extreme and calibrated to the second. Children today are being brought up not only with a much more linear view of time but also one timed to the precise moment. They are also being made more aware of time at an earlier age because of television, for they quickly learn that they will miss their favorite programs if they don't know how to tell time. Not only are they learning how to tell time, they are also being trained early to think of it as something external – as something against which to coordinate their activities. We do not yet know the long-term effects of this on their lives.

Some people think of time as a *RIVER* – it flows on and on – and Heraclitus, an ancient Greek philosopher, made the comment that you can never step into the same river twice. Other people think of time as a *PENDULUM* – back and forth, tick-tock, representing the alternation of night and day. Still others think of time as *CYCLICAL*, that it goes round and round, with the continual return of the seasons.

Our view of time is that it marches on relentlessly and impersonally. We live with a mechanical sense of time because our culture is so dominated by machines – the "clockwork universe." Yet there are other models of time. One former student imagined the following possibilities: agriculturalists and peasants, he thought, must live with a seasonal view of time, and people in fishing societies live with a tidal view of time. No doubt, surfers do too!

But these are not the only alternatives; some groups live by flower time – the Australian aborigines, who traditionally were hunters and gatherers, kept time by the type of flower in bloom and, thus, when to expect honey and certain kinds of fruit. And in *Return to Laughter* (see chapter 1), Bowen says something similar: "there was the season of yams, of guinea corn, and of millet" (1964: 69). Your grandparents surely had some sense of this because of the seasons when certain fruits and vegetables would be available, for example, spinach, Brussels sprouts, blueberries, tomatoes, grapefruit, and oranges. Do you know what seasons they traditionally appeared in? While it is wonderful to have all things available all the time (from someplace), do we lose that sense of anticipation? Is it possible our senses get blunted?

Time before clocks

> Time – the time that we know through clocks and calendars – was invented.
> *Encyclopedia Britannica* (www.britannica.com/clockworks/article.html)

Most of us think about time in terms of clocks; they are so pervasive in our lives it is difficult to think of life without them. But many people live and have lived their entire lives without clocks. They lived by the diurnal rhythms of the sun and the alternation of the seasons. Elenore Bowen (Laura Bohannan) well captured her own struggle with the time sense among the people she studied in Africa. After only 10 weeks "in the field," she said:

> already time had taken on a more individualistic and yet more seasonable aspect than I had been used to. Already the days of the week and the month were no more than a heading printed on my diary pages. I did try to keep count; old habit made me feel I ought to know the date. Yet, in July, when I went back to the station for supplies, I found I had lost three days. (1964: 68)

She went on to say that it was easier to give up the idea of "right time of day" and instead went on her own time zone. In order to maintain some kind of schedule, she decided that "dark and seven by the clock were to coincide. Every few weeks for the rest of my stay in the bush, I readjusted the clock."

> I learned to forget months and to live by moons: to anticipate the full moon for its dances and storytelling; to fear the dark of the moon when witches were abroad.
>
> Cutting through the moons was, for me, a complicated combination of weeks. First there was the cook's seven-day curry week, highlighting Saturdays. Then there was the five-day cycle of markets by which everyone made engagements. Finally there was the seven-day-beer-brewing week. . . . There was no year, merely a succession of seasons and agricultural activities uncorrelated with moons or markets. The rains began when it began to rain; when it began to rain people started to plant. One could say that a man had done his planting late, but not that the rains had come late. (p. 69)

Evans-Pritchard, a well-known British anthropologist, said something similar about the Nuer, a different African group he studied.

> The Nuer have no expression equivalent to "time" in our language, and they cannot, therefore, as we can, speak of time as though it were something actual, which passes, can be wasted, can be saved, and so forth. I do not think that they ever experience the same feeling of fighting against time or of having to co-ordinate activities with an abstract passage of time because their points of reference are mainly the activities themselves, which are generally of a leisurely character. Events follow a logical order, but they are not controlled by an abstract system, there being no autonomous points of reference to which activities have to conform with precision. ([1940] 1976: 103)

The Nuer, he concludes, are fortunate. For us time is the enemy, we are always fighting against it. Ultimately, of course, it is a battle we will lose. Might our conception of time have anything to do with the frantic pace and anxiety that have come to characterize our lives? Perhaps this anxiety is related to the current interest in

Eastern philosophies and techniques of relaxation and meditation. However, these practices, in the West, are taken out of context, unhinged from the worldview or cosmology that produced them.

Time's beginning and end

Where or when does time start and where or when will it end? Ali Mazrui, whom I discussed in chapter 2, also asked why it is that Greenwich in Britain is "the mean time for the alarm clocks of the human race. The clocks of the world have responded to that choice. Even when we say 'universal standard time' we are really predicating it on Greenwich mean time. A spot on the British Isles has changed the clocks and watches of the world" (quoted in *Dial*, September 1986: 21). He noted how that was a political act. It had to do with Britain's domination of the world, when it was an Empire over which the sun never set, that is, when it had a colony in every time zone.

Clocks were introduced beginning in the fourteenth century; at that time they were primarily installed in church towers and were used to ring out the time of *matins* and *vespers* – morning and evening prayers. But clocks were not very accurate and people continued to use sundials, even to set the clocks, in the seventeenth, eighteenth, and nineteenth centuries. Most towns ran on their own time, setting the clocks at high noon. The impetus for a *standard* for time was the railroad, and it was a Canadian, Sanford Fleming, who came up with the idea.[1]

Actually, the clocks of the world are no longer set according to Greenwich mean time. Since 1972 we have gone onto UTC (Coordinated Universal Time) calculated by the atomic clock(s) at the US Naval Observatory. Time is no longer "measured by the motion of the earth in space but by the oscillations at the atomic level of a rare, soft, bluish-grey metal called *cesium*" (Duncan 1998: 290). And it is based on the measure of a *second* rather than minutes, hours, or days. "Our second is now determined by the difference in energy state of the cesium-133 atom when its nucleus and outer electron spin in the same or opposite direction" (Barnett 1998: 167). There are officially 86,400 seconds in each day (see box on p. 80); however, every now and again "leap seconds" have to be added because there is a gap between the atomic clock and the earth's rotation! It is too perfect for this wobbly and flawed earth.

> In accordance with the theory of relativity, atomic clocks do not keep uniform time, but depend on the gravitational field where they happen to be placed. Their running also varies with the latitude of the place, the height above sea level, the distance of the earth from the sun, the distance of the moon, etc. But all of these variations can be calculated and allowed for, thus arriving at a suitable scale of time. (Fraser 1966: 411)

Suitable for whom? Fortunately, most of us do not yet need to calculate our lives according to nanoseconds or picoseconds but can get by with conventional clocks and watches.

The International Dateline

The idea for the international dateline came about when Greenwich mean time was accepted as the universal prime meridian, that is, the point from which longitude was calculated and world time was set. This was decided in 1884 at a conference in Washington, DC, attended by representatives of 25 nations but, at that time, was accepted by only 22. The international dateline, which set the time zones of the planet, was to be halfway round the world, at 180 degrees, in the mid-Pacific. Not all countries accepted this at first; the last two nations were Saudi Arabia, 1962, and Liberia, 1972.

Calendars

The word "calendar" comes from *calends,* the beginning of the month when religious leaders would announce that month's festal days.

Calendars, like clocks, help us keep track of time – they mark not the minutes and the hours but the days, weeks, months, and years. Most of us have calendars not only on our walls or on our desks and in our computers but also in our purses, bookbags, and briefcases – whether they are filofaxes or palm pilots. We carry them with us so we can schedule appointments and keep track of our activities. Calendars also help us to situate ourselves in the world and history, for we plot world events according to the calendar. We characterize history in terms of decades and centuries – the sixties, for example, or the nineteenth century. We know we are living in the twenty-first century and are poised to compare it with centuries past.

But our calendar, itself, relates to a specific history. The Western calendar, which for all intents and purposes has become the world calendar (more on that later), dates from the year of Christ's birth. It is – insert current year – AD (*Anno Domini* – in the year of Our Lord).[2] Some people have begun to use CE (common era) instead of AD as a more "politically correct" form. But just *whose* common era? Jews preceded Christians by at least a millennium and the two religions have surely not merged despite the hyphen in Judeo-Christian. I find CE a euphemism because the common era still begins with Christ's birth and, thus, conceals the political implications. For is it not a way that Jews are incorporated into the Christian time system and into their history?

Jews have their own calendar; at the Christian year 2000, the Jewish calendar recorded 5,760 years since the *world* began. The traditional Chinese calendar was lunar and the year 2000 was, for the Chinese, 4698. When Mao Zedong accepted the Gregorian calendar in 1949, the Chinese people lost 2,649 years! However, they continue with their 12-year cycles of animals (the year 2000 was the year of the Dragon). Muslims also have their own calendar; I will describe it in somewhat more detail since I know a little more about it and because it is unfamiliar to non-Muslim Westerners.

The Muslim calendar

Although Islam is one of the Abrahamic religions – because it goes back to the founding story of Abraham – and shares much with both Judaism and Christianity, its calendar is different from both. It is not dated from the beginning of the world as is the Jewish calendar, nor does it begin with the birth of Muhammad as the Christian calendar begins with the birth of Jesus. The calendar commemorates a specific event that was critical for the establishment of the new Muslim community. The Muslim calendar dates from Muhammad's migration (*Hijra*) from Mecca to Medina that occurred in the AD year 622; that was year 1 AH (After the *Hijra*).

The Muslim calendar is a lunar calendar whereas the calendar that dominates the West is a solar calendar. Between the two types of calendars there is a discrepancy of about 10 days; thus determining the Muslim year in relation to the Christian year involves a complicated calculation that takes into account that accumulated discrepancy over the years. The Muslim or lunar year consists of 354 or 355 days divided into 12 lunar months of alternately 29 and 30 days. Each month begins with the new moon, an important symbol of Islam, which is why it is found on the flags of Muslim nations.

A lunar calendar has little relation to seasons. Therefore the important Muslim holidays rotate around the seasonal year. This is in stark contrast to Christmas and Easter for Christians or Yom Kippur and Passover for Jews. Every year Muslim holidays fall about 10 days earlier than the previous year. The entire cycle makes a complete circuit every 33 years. For example, Ramazan/Ramadan, the month of fasting, will begin 10 days earlier this year than it did last year. One is supposed to fast from dawn (when you can distinguish a white thread from a black) to about an hour after sunset. During the time I was in Turkey, Ramazan fell at the worst possible times, August and July respectively – which meant that people fasted – ate nothing and drank nothing – for up to 18 hours every day.

This movement of the festivals through the year communicates a subtle message. Their lack of attachment to earthly seasons points *beyond them* to emphasize the distinction between the earthly and divine realms. It also helps to highlight the mutability and transitoriness of earthly life and the immutability and eternity of the divine realm. Thus the calendar, itself, incorporates meanings of cosmological and spiritual significance.

So, too, does the call to prayer (*ezan* in Turkish), which is intoned five times a day from a minaret, the slender tower adjacent to a mosque. Each *ezan* has a specific name and the intervals between them are not equal. The longest intervals are the ones between the late-night *ezan* and the one when first light appears, and between that *ezan* and the one at midday. In addition, the daily schedule changes from summer to winter since the timing and therefore the intervals depend on the hours of daylight. The intervals are shorter in winter and longer in summer. Regardless, five times a day Muslims are oriented toward Mecca – an unseen point on the horizon – which is the earthly symbol of their original and final destination. The call to prayer orients Muslims both temporally, spatially, and spiritually.

Calendar changes

We think of the calendar as a neutral kind of chronological record-keeping mechanism, but it is actually a highly political institution. For example, after the fall of the Ottoman Empire, Atatürk changed the country's calendar to coincide with that of the West. This was meant as a secularizing, modernizing, and Westernizing reform but it is, of course, also the Christian calendar. Not surprisingly, a number of devout Turks resent this change for, to them, it means living by the time of the infidels. However, Atatürk was not the first to change his country's calendar.

French revolutionary calendar

After the French Revolution, a new calendar was instituted. "The count of the years would begin with 1792; and the New Year's Day would be 22 September – the equinox" (Aveni 1989: 144). Anthony Aveni, an astronomer who became fascinated with anthropology, wrote a splendid book, *Empires of Time: Calendars, Clocks, and Cultures*, which gives a brief account of the French revolutionary calendar. It was to be very "rational" and designed to counteract the "irrational" elements inherent in religion, specifically to break the hold of Christianity over the people. The new calendar consisted of a 10-day week with three weeks to a month. Each day had 10 hours of 100 minutes each and each minute had 100 seconds. Each day was named numerically rather than after celestial bodies and the Norse gods that represented them, as are the English days: Sun day is obvious; Moon day = Monday; Tiw's day = Tuesday; Woden's day = Wednesday; Thor's day = Thursday; Fria's day = Friday; and Saturn day = Saturday. In the French revolutionary calendar, months were named after the kinds of weather characteristic of the time, for example, mist, frost, snow. The year had 360 days and the five or six extra were given special names and became days of festivity. Most of the people hated the new calendar because, after a while, it became difficult to know what day was Sunday and, thus, what day to go to church, make confession, take the sacrament, and receive blessing. It lasted only 14 years; the old (Gregorian) calendar was reinstated after Napoleon took power.

Soviet Union revolutionary calendar

Another attempt to change the calendar was made by Russian revolutionaries. In 1929 the Soviet Union embarked on a five-day continuous production week – four days for work and the fifth was free. There were six weeks in a month and, although the Gregorian names of the months were retained, the days of the week were numbered. Each worker was assigned to a particular day and each day had a particular color. Some people would begin their work-week on day one and work for four days then have a day off, others would begin on day two, work for four days and have a day off, still others would begin on day three, and so forth. That is what made it a *continuous production* week, but the social consequences were significant. First, only one-fifth of the population was off on any given day. It became very difficult to remember when various friends and relatives had their day off. Would their day off coincide with yours? Would you ever be able to go on an outing together? Since no more than a fifth of the population would be free at the same time, it became difficult for people to mobilize for protests and demonstrations. The calendar was, clearly, a measure of social control, but it, too, was implemented expressly to destroy "the opiate of the people," that is, their addiction to religion. Like the French revolutionary calendar before it, the Soviet version also faced strong resistance from the people. A number of changes were made but it was finally abandoned in 1940 when the Soviets, too, returned to the Gregorian calendar.

The Gregorian calendar

The Gregorian calendar itself marked a significant change from the Julian calendar that preceded it. The motive for change was that the Julian calendar was out of sync with the solar year and so Easter and other religious holy days were falling at the wrong times. So, "in 1582, Pope Gregory XIII officially revised the accepted length of the year to 365.2422 days, adjusted the leap-year rule, and lopped off the 10 extra days" (http://www.britannica.com/clockworks/article2.html)!

The week

So many of us take the seven-day week for granted that we probably assume it is "natural." Yet the Romans had an eight-day week, and other peoples have had "weeks" consisting of 3 to 10 days. But why bother with weeks? Couldn't we get along just fine with days, months, and years? British anthropologist Edmund Leach claims that people need to punctuate the seamless flow of time, to give order and rhythm to their lives.

> We talk of measuring time, as if time were a concrete thing waiting to be measured; but in fact we *create time* by creating intervals in social life. Until we have done this there is no time to be measured. (Leach 1961: 135)

Knowing what day it is is often the first thing we think of when we get up, because we do different things on different days. So says Eviatar Zerubavel, a sociologist who has written a fascinating book on the history and meaning of the week, *The Seven Day Circle* (1985). Ordinarily, there is an alternation between "sacred" time and "profane" time, one day is a holy day (holiday) or festival day or, as in the Soviet calendar, a day of rest breaking up the week of labor. You have different classes on different days; you have sports practice on Mondays, say, or theater group on Thursday mornings. Knowing what day it is is "indispensable for transcending our subjectivity and participating – at least mentally – in a social, rather than a merely personal world" (Zerubavel 1985: 2). Each day of the week also has its own distinct "feel." Friday afternoons, for example, have a very different feel than do Monday mornings (except if you happen to be a museum employee, since museums are usually closed on Mondays). Weekends, for most of us, are completely different from the work-week – a time for relaxation, for shopping, for sports, for a movie, or church. The differing meanings of the days become apparent to those who do not have a Satur-day night date or, at least, some alternative plan.

Some of you may never have thought about where our week comes from; others are probably well aware that it is intimately related to religion. It is the legacy of Genesis, the first book of the Bible, common to both Jews and Christians. In Genesis it is stated that God created the world in six days and rested on the seventh day. Our work-week, then, is a dim reflection of the work of Creation. This rhythm of days has been going on since the times of the ancient Hebrews:

> Six days shalt thou labor, and do all thy work but the seventh day is the sabbath of the Lord thy God; in it thou shalt not do any work – thou, nor thy son, nor thy daughter, thy manservant, nor thy maidservant, nor thy cattle, nor the stranger that is within thy gates. For in six days, the Lord made heaven and earth, the sea and all that is in them, and rested the seventh day: wherefore the Lord blessed the sabbath day and hal-lowed it. (Exodus 20: 8–11)

Even for non-believers, or for believers of other faiths, each week reenacts the bib-lical event. For those of you who think that religion is something private, a personal individual decision, it is important to realize how a religious tradition creates world-views and influences attitudes, values, and even notions of time and space that affect everyone regardless of their private, personal beliefs. We don't use the calendar we do because it is better. The use of a specific calendar is deeply political – the result of battles, of power and politics, and of the domination by one particular segment of the world's population.

Clearly, calendars can be changed – after all, they are arbitrary – but it is very dif-ficult because they have important meanings that people become very attached to and are conditioned by. The secular calendars have been resisted for a number of reasons, but the primary one was because they were seen as sacrilegious, they trans-gressed the sacred rhythm of days ordained by God and laid down in Genesis, at the beginning.

The year, as well as the week, also has a religious foundation – not from Genesis but from Christianity. What of the recent millennium? Whose millennium is it? It signifies 2,000 years of Christianity. What about people who do not or did not have a seven-day week or the same calendar? Do you think they should adopt it because the Christian calendar is better? More accurate? Or, do you think they have been forced to adopt it because of political domination? In my opinion, the millennium offered an opportunity to begin again. For, despite its Christian roots, the entire world did acknowledge and celebrate it. We could have started with year 0 to avoid the problems the Christian calendar created because it began with year 1. We could have called it Global Calendar or GC for short. Even though it would be built on the Christian calendar, it would quickly become separate from it since Christians could continue with their own calendar just as Jews, Muslims, Hindus, Chinese, and others already do, but a Global Calendar might gain worldwide consent as long as it was separate and distinct and used for secular, communicative, and business purposes.

Our notions of time, not just calendars, also have religious roots that are entangled with the concept of Creation. While this discussion may challenge or even offend those who believe strongly in the monotheistic God of Judaism, Christianity, or Islam, it is important to think about. Stephen Hawking, perhaps the most famous contemporary physicist-cosmologist, is well aware of the relation between religious concepts and time. In his book *A Brief History of Time* he said:

> So long as the universe had a beginning, we could suppose it had a Creator. But if the universe is really completely self-contained, having no boundary or edge, it would have neither beginning nor end; it would simply be. What place, then, for a Creator? (1988: 140–1)

While all peoples have myths of origin, not all stories of origin are stories of creation and, thus, not all have a notion of a creator. Some origin myths recount transformations of one thing into another, or describe emergences from underground, or even portray the world as dream or illusion. Some peoples may have a variety of origin myths to explain and account for the variety of phenomena. A culture influenced by monotheism has a tendency to search for monocausal explanations – for example, the current search by physicists for a "grand unified theory" – one theory to explain how the universe (and everything in it) came into being.

We tend to think of time as linear, universal, and quantifiable, yet we know this view is not universal. Our notion of time incorporates a specific teleology – the idea that there is a purpose, goal, or reason inherent in it; but that idea, itself, derives from a particular *mythos*, a legacy from the Judeo-Christian worldview. I quote Johannes Fabian, a Dutch anthropologist, from his book *Time and the Other*:

> In the Judeo-Christian tradition [and I would add Islamic tradition], Time has been conceived as the medium of a sacred history. Time was thought, but more often celebrated, as a sequence of specific events that befell a chosen people. Much has been said about the linear character of that conception as opposed to pagan, cyclical views of Time as an *eternal retour*. Yet such spatial metaphors of temporal thought tend to obscure something of more immediate significance. . . . Faith in a covenant between a Divinity and one people, trust in divine providence as it unfolds in a history of salvation centered on one Savior, make for sacred conceptions of Time. They stress the specificity of Time, its realization in a given cultural ecology – the Eastern Mediterranean, first, and the circum-Mediterranean with Rome at its hub, later. [For Muslims it is Mecca, and for all three religions, Jerusalem is a sacred city they fight over.] (Fabian 1983: 2; my remarks in square brackets)

Fabian continues:

> Decisive steps toward modernity, those that permitted the emergence of anthropological discourse, must be sought not in the invention of a linear conception, but in a succession of attempts to *secularize* Judeo-Christian Time by generalizing and universalizing it. (p. 2; my italics)

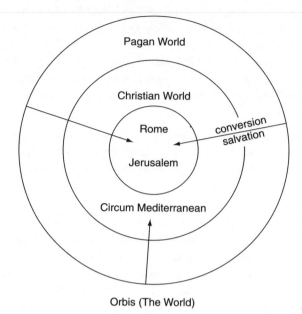

Figure 3.2   Premodern time/space: incorporation (Fabian 1983).

What he is saying is that *our* (Western) time became the time of all others. On the surface that sounds inclusive but, in fact, it denies or effaces other people's senses of time. Because of political power, our sense of time has become the truth and the way for understanding others.

The notion of Creation implies a beginning – not just of the universe but of time – symbolized in the Bible by the "Fall" when Adam and Eve left the Garden of Eden. We might easily imagine that the scientific theory of the "big bang" origin of the universe is a *secularization* of the notion of Creation at a specific moment, though cosmologists might take exception. The notion of a *beginning* to time also affects ideas about history which recounts events that unfold in time, and are not repeatable. This, too, is a legacy from a specific religious tradition.

> The early Christian writers stressed the importance of individual historical events that would not be repeated. History, they said, did not move in cycles. On the contrary, there had been a Creation at a particular point in time. Christ had died on the Cross but once, and had been resurrected from the dead on but one occasion. Finally, at some point in the future, God's plan would be completed, and He would – once and for all – bring the world to an end. (Morris 1984: 11)

From this perspective, one could not imagine, as some cultures do, time as a deep-layered phenomenon in which the present moment was not just the end result of all that preceded it but also contained all of what went before. "Past," in that view, is "co-present"; whereas for us past is past, over and done with. We are oriented toward the future. So much so that we send "time capsules" into the future so that

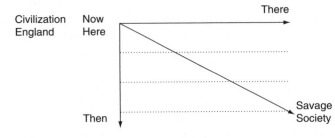

Figure 3.3   Modern time/space: distancing (Fabian 1983).

those who come after us might get some sense of what we were like. For example, each year at graduation, Stanford students place a time capsule under a pavement stone in the main quad that has the year's date engraved on it; it will be opened 100 years hence. At the same time, they dig one up from 100 years ago. Time capsules have been made elsewhere in the country, some intended to come due in 1,000, or even 5,000, years.

The linear view of time permitted the rise of notions of advancement and progress, and also of evolution. But it can also imply degeneration and collapse (entropy), and these ideas have figured prominently in theories and interpretations of human culture. In the nineteenth century when the issue of human evolution was first raised, theorists divided into two camps. *Monogenists* believed that modern humans all have the same origin. This basically recapitulates the Adam and Eve story in scientific dress. *Polygenists*, on the other hand, believed that there were different origins for the different races. According to this view, some of the peoples encountered might not be quite human. But the monogenist position also has racist implications. For, when theorists of monogenist persuasion encountered "primitives," they assumed they had degenerated from an earlier, more advanced, state and thus had to be recivilized.[3] Variants of these positions are still circulating.

Cultures inspired by religious traditions that are not monotheistic or even theistic do not, then, have a Creator god or gods who create the variety of things. They would have very different notions of time, of history, and the course and meaning of life.

The assumption of a general, universal, and secular time underpinned, and continues to underpin, the project to create a universal history which is, at the same time, imagined as a *natural history* rather than the particular Christian history of salvation. This was, in part, accomplished in the nineteenth century by the demise of Bishop Ussher's calculation, based on the genealogies in Genesis, that the world began in 4004 BC, and its replacement by theories of geological time. In the middle of the nineteenth century, according to anthropologist Thomas

There are other cultural implications from the notion of Creator–Creation. In the monotheistic religions (Judaism, Christianity, and Islam) there is a great gulf between the Creator and his Creation. It is not a monistic worldview such as that of certain Native American groups and Hindus. Instead, God and Creation are separate. Thus the very notion of *Nature* and the natural world is conditioned by its place in a cosmological/religious system. Such notions cannot, therefore, be universal (see chapter 2, p. 38). Even though Creator and Creation are separate, these entities are not equal; it is not a dualistic system but a hierarchical one and this has had enormous implications for the Western view of nature and gender.

Trautman, the bottom "door" of time dropped out, that is, it extended backwards not just by thousands but by millions of years. This radical transformation of Western notions of time and the rupture in the context of people's lives has hardly been appreciated. No longer was history divided into just ancient, medieval, and modern but a new category, "prehistory," was invented.

Prehistory came *before* ancient history; prehistory also implies non-literate. When Europeans encountered peoples without written texts, they dubbed them "pre-literate" and, therefore, "primitive," and placed them at the bottom of the evolutionary scale – implying that there is a teleology to literacy. These peoples were relegated to the rim of civilized space and the dawn of history. We refer to some of them as "Stone-*Age* peoples," and imply by such a term that they are like people who existed long *before* us in the very distant past. "Stone-*tool* peoples," focusing on their technology and way of life, is a better way of describing such people who are our contemporaries. We have imagined ourselves at the (advanced) center, they are at the edge, that is, earlier in time and peripheral in space. Time was not only naturalized, generalized, and secularized, it was also spatialized. People living *far* from the center of "civilization" were *lower* on the evolutionary ladder. The closer to the beginning, the *lower* on the evolutionary scale. No wonder we call them aborigines, from *ab origine* meaning at the origin. We have thought that these ways of looking at others are scientific, but perhaps we have not really understood the mythical foundation of some of our basic scientific concepts.

The notion of progress (perhaps the secular version of salvation) and the naturalization and secularization of time were essential for the emergence of theories of evolution. Social evolutionary theories, meaning that some people are more advanced than others, had been around long before Darwin, and it is important to remember that his theory is primarily about *biological* evolution. What happened, however, was that the theory of biological evolution became allied with theories of social evolution and their combination resulted in some very dangerous beliefs and projects, for example the eugenics movement in the early twentieth century and, more recently, sociobiology – both of these theories place emphasis on genetic endowment at the expense of culture and environment. Unlike Darwin, proponents of these theories give *natural selection* agency and a teleology. I believe this concept is a secularization of the Calvinist notion of "divine election" (Yanagisako and Delaney 1995: 5); in either case, the agency is imagined as beyond human control.

The transformation in time sense is also intimately related to the emergence of the academic disciplines of geology, archaeology, history, anthropology, economics, comparative religion, and probably others. They could not exist without these linear notions of time. My intention is not to disparage these intellectual accomplishments but to make you more aware that they have been achieved *within* the frame of a specific temporal-cosmological view. They have come with certain costs, most notably an inability to imagine otherwise. For example, we do not know what other theories and accomplishments might be made with different worldviews. This inability promotes a tendency to assume our way is the only way and is both right and true.

Lived Time

The American author Sinclair Lewis said in his novel *Main Street* (1920):

> The greatest mystery about a human being is not his reaction to sex or praise, but the
> manner in which he contrives to put in twenty-four hours a day. It is this which puzzles
> the longshoreman about the banker, and the Londoner about the bushman [and no
> doubt your professor about you, and vice versa!].

In other words, the experience of time is related to a particular form of life – occupation, gender, age, class, and race. That particular form, however, is not just something individual but also cultural – the particular forms are relative to and embedded in a particular culture with its particular history. In the previous section we discussed the cosmological concepts of time – notions of beginnings and endings, calendars and clocks, and their religious underpinnings. These notions form the widest context in which we live our lives. In this section we will focus on the ways particular understandings of time affect our daily lives – our work and leisure and our dreams and possibilities.

Think again about your time. The fact that you are in college or university means that you have spent time in the past studying so that you would get the grades necessary for admission. Decisions about how you spent your time were made long ago. You gave up some of your free time because you thought, or were told, that your future depended on it, that you could not get the job you want without a college education. Some of you may also have worked at odd jobs to earn spending money or to help support your family. That cut down on your study time and put you at a disadvantage to someone who did not have to work. Of course, a lot of young people from affluent families don't spend their time studying either, but they might be able to get a private tutor when it is necessary.

Class, then, affects how we are able to spend our time. It also affects how we think about it. For example, it affects how we think about our future. It is claimed that youth in the inner city get into so much trouble not just because of poverty but also because they do not have (an idea of) a *future*, a future that would be significantly different from their present. Similar statements have been made about young people who join terrorist groups. Without a sense of, and hope for, the future, people tend to see and use each day as if it might be their last, and for too many it is. In the United States, a 15- to 19-year-old is murdered every 5 hours (note how the statistics are correlated with time). This terrible statistic was part of a list of "Moments in America" published in 1991 by the Children's Defense Fund. Some of the other "moments" are: Every 35 seconds an infant is born into poverty; every 64 seconds an infant is born to a teenage mother; every 2 minutes an infant is born to a mother who received late or no prenatal care; every 14 minutes an infant dies in the first year of life; and every 14 hours a child younger than 5 is murdered (Sidel 1992: ix). Others *do time* – in jail. What exactly does that mean? Why do you think the overwhelming majority of them are minorities? Do you think there is something inherent *in* them that predisposes them to criminal activity? Or, do you think their rate of incarceration has to do with cultural assumptions about race, and the political and economic arrangements that reinforce them? What are some of the ways that class and race affect how you spend your time?

Family time

Another area in which the use of time is rapidly changing concerns the amount of time parents spend with their children. Most, if not all, children in the United States – whether rich or poor – have less time with their parents than did children in the past. Of course, wealthy parents can provide substitutes in the form of nannies and private tutors and time-filling activities such as piano (and other) lessons, while children of poor parents are often left alone, or with inadequate supervision, or on the streets. British pediatrician Penelope Leach says that parent–child time has decreased by 40 percent since 1975. Part of this can be attributed to the fact that in many families today, both parents are working – some because they cannot support a family on just one income, and others because both parents also want to engage in a fulfilling career. At the same time, the number of one-parent families is growing. In that case the parent, normally the mother, is doing the job of two, and too often she is working long hours at low wages with few, if any, benefits. With so many parents working, a likely time to spend with family would be dinner times. But that is not the case: in the United States, families eat together "one-third less often than in the mid-1970s" (*San Francisco Chronicle*, September 24, 2000). Many families never have the evening meal together; instead each family member is off doing his or her "own thing." How often did you (or do you) eat dinner with your family?

One of the students who helped me with some of the research for this book spent the year between high school and college in France. Living with a French family, she became very aware of different cultural patterns and values. One of the things she cherished about that experience was that the whole family (which at that time included her) ate dinner together every night. When she came back home she tried to institute it with her own family, but it was not possible. Everyone had his or her own schedule.

The decrease in the amount of time parents spend with their children is a social change that signifies a major change in values. In *Children First* (1994), Penelope Leach has written eloquently on the need for changing our priorities so that we might begin to change the way we work *and* care for children. Children are suffering from this lack of *time* with their parents. To make up for this deficit, psychologists introduced the concept of "quality time." The amount of time a parent spends with his or her child is held to be not as important as the "quality" or meaningfulness of the interaction. The concept sounds good but there is a major flaw: the time a parent has available may not coincide with the times the child really needs parental attention. Not only that, parents miss the chance to shape the child's values and leave that job to whoever is with the child most of the day. For values are instilled not just verbally, not just during the moments of "quality time," but subtly by actions and by modeling of behavior. No doubt the concept of "quality time" has helped to assuage the guilt of many working mothers. But why not of working fathers? Why is it *women's time* that is at issue? Here we encounter an example of the way that time is gendered. The old adage that "a woman's work is never done" is just as true now as ever, maybe more so as so many women are working what Arlie Hochschild calls "the second shift" of housework and childcare work after a full day at the office (Hochschild 1975).

Lifetime

Since we are talking about lived time, we should back up and start with a life*time*. We believe we "have one life to live," as the soap opera says, and thus we want to make the most of it. But how much time do we have and how shall it be filled? In the United States, and most industrialized countries, life expectancy has increased dramatically over the past century, even in the last 50 years. For example, in 1950 the average for all races and both genders was 68.2 years, whereas in 2001 it was 77.3 years (from US Department of Health and Human Services, in *Almanac and Book of Fact, 2002*). Of course, that doesn't mean all of us will reach those ages, but in general, people are living a longer time than in the past. In Third World countries there is more variation: in Kenya, for example, in 1950, life expectancy for both genders was 41 years, then it reached a high of around 60 in 1990, but has been declining ever since, so that in 2000 it was only 49 years (http://www.unstats.un.org). Meanwhile, in Turkey, which has been considered a Third World country, the increase has been from 43.6 in 1950 to more than 70 in 2000! The gender disparity is in favor of women in industrialized nations, but shifts in favor of men in the Third World. What, do you think, might be responsible for this difference?

Anthropologists have given considerable attention to lifecycle rituals, the *rites de passage* we spoke of in chapter 1. Such rituals focus on major events in the lifecycle, for example birth, adolescence, marriage, and death, which often, but not always, correlate with notions of a lifetime, for example when a child dies. Rather than discussing lifecycle rituals in a separate chapter or section, I discuss them in different chapters and in a variety of contexts. Instead, this section explores how we think about a lifetime. We do not think just of getting older and older, but break the time into a series of categories: infancy, childhood, youth, adolescence, young adulthood, adulthood, middle age, and elderly or just plain old. We see a lifetime as a curve ascending until maybe 40 or so and then it's "downhill all the way." People everywhere attach certain significance to particular dates (*times*). In the United States, for example, one such date is "sweet sixteen"; in many states, it is also the age at which you can legally drive. Other important ages are 18, when you can vote, buy lottery tickets or a gun, join the army and get legally married, and 21, when you can drink legally. What other ages do you consider milestones? What significance, if any, do you give to turning 30, 40, 50, 60? In the United States, 65 used to hold meaning when it was the mandatory age of retirement; but, citing ageism, the law was repealed and now people can work for as long as they want. Yet, under the aegis of ageism, there are many people who will feel guilty if they don't keep working. Perhaps it was better when the decision was out of individuals' hands and was the same for all.

Birthdays

In South Korea, the first birthday is the most important and is lavishly celebrated with special food and clothes.

Yearly birthday celebrations are especially important to children – it is their special day – and many would feel bereft if they did not have a party. Parties are normally made for children, though adults celebrate certain of them – 60 and 65 being fairly popular. For adults, especially women, each year passed is often not cause for celebration but for depression. Age is differently gendered: in American culture, and many others as well, an older man is still imagined as attractive and vital, but older women are imagined as "old crones," the butt of jokes, or ignored. Nevertheless, 75 and 100 seem to be birthdays worth celebrating for those who reach them. While we tend to mark and celebrate birthdays, people in many cultures do not. As noted in chapter 1, people in Turkey celebrate and mark death days, perhaps because that is the day a person is born into the next, and better, world. Those who have become westernized have picked up the custom of celebrating birthdays, but many villagers did not know their birthday, only the year in which they were born.

Death, of course, is the end of a lifetime; everywhere it is socially marked even though by some peoples more than others. The way it is conceptualized and dealt with, especially the way the body is disposed of, reveals a lot about cultural beliefs concerning the constitution of the human person. Does anything of the person persist after death? Is there a soul? If so, what happens to it? Americans tend to be in a state of "denial" about death;[4] as a culture we fear it, do not mention it, and do not set aside a time for mourning as is so common elsewhere. Maybe that is why we have so enthusiastically embraced birthdays.

It is even thought to be a major indication of culture. Some animals seem to have rituals after the death of one of their kind (e.g. elephants), thus raising the question of the origin of culture.

Sex, love, and marriage

Even though we are living longer, the age at which young people today have their first sexual experience is considerably younger than just a generation ago. They are claiming a sexual identity (heterosexual, bisexual, or homosexual) at an age when people of my generation didn't even know what these terms meant. Why is this, and what is the cultural significance? It used to be if you were female and weren't married by the time you were 21 you were "an old maid," and if you were male and still unmarried by the time you were 30 you were clearly a "bachelor." Today many people are choosing not to get married – some to remain single, others to live together. Still others wish they could marry someone of the same sex.

College has become a time to experiment with one's identity, including sexual identity. It is a time when many of you will meet the person with whom you intend to spend the rest of your life. Yet, it can also be a time of romantic disappointments. According to research conducted by Zick Rubin, Charles T. Hill, and Letitia Peplau, romantic relationships between college students tend to break up during May/June, September, or December/January, that is, during times before or after holidays when they might have been separated (http://www.trinity.edu/~mkearl/time-1.html).

There seems also to be a season for other major lifetime events. June, for instance, is the favored month for weddings. Births are thought to peak in late summer; deaths in northern countries tend to occur in the winter. More than half of all marriages end in divorce and, again, there seems to be a timing to that also – the highest percentage of divorce occurs before four years have passed.

School time

In most industrialized countries people must go to school until they are 16, but many go beyond that. They finish high school (usually by 18), and then go on to other kinds of schools – trade schools, art/music/dance schools, technical schools, colleges and universities, and then beyond to law school, business school, graduate school, or medical school. Some of you began school before you were 6, having attended infant day care or nursery school. Some of you will have been in school from the time you were 2 or 3 until you are over 30. That is a long time apprenticing, a long time waiting for and preparing for the future; the long apprenticeship is, however, premised on a belief in a long life. Of course we are living while we are preparing, but we often do not think of it that way; we say "when I begin real life" or "when I enter the real world."

Time is a major topic of thought and conversation among college students. Many freshmen have told me that learning to manage their own time was one of the most difficult things they encountered as college students. Up until then, you went to school in the morning, at 8 a.m. or so, and finished in the afternoon sometime around 3 p.m. Then you either went to work or went home. Time was managed for you. Even time for homework was often decreed by parents. Suddenly, at college, no one is monitoring your time; no one is checking to see if you go to class, do your homework, eat your meals, get enough sleep, or get your papers in on time. (You are probably not aware that the term *deadline* originally meant "a boundary line in prison that prisoners can cross only at the risk of being shot" [*American Heritage Dictionary*].) You are the one who has to decide *how to spend your time*. What are your priorities? Why? Where did they come from? What other activities besides schoolwork eat into your time? How do you spend your free time?

Holidays

Because we are in school so long, school time lays down a kind of rhythm to our days that in later life is difficult to erase. For me Labor Day still signals the end of what, in June, had seemed an endless summer, and the beginning of a new year. Today, many schools begin school before Labor Day, but I know that I would find that very difficult, and I feel sorry for my colleagues who must begin then.

An important indication of a nation's meaningful events, at least the official ones, can be gleaned from a study of its ritual or holiday calendar.[5] Punctuating the American year, for example, is a series of holidays

Labor Day is an American holiday that commemorates working people. It is celebrated on the first Monday in September (which makes a long weekend); traditionally the school year would begin on Wednesday of that week.

that provide the intervals between "sacred" and "profane" time (see Edmund Leach, above), yet not all are days off from school. Could it be that the most sacred days are truly holidays (holy days) that you have off from school and/or work? Beginning with the school year, the first holiday used to be Columbus Day (a federal holiday but not necessarily a public holiday); Veterans' Day is similar – it is a federal holiday but is not observed in certain businesses and schools – Halloween, then Thanksgiving, Christmas, and New Year's Day. In the new year, the first noteworthy day is Martin Luther King Day, then Valentine's Day and Washington's birthday, which has been renamed President's Day. Following along is St. Patrick's Day, Easter, Mother's Day, Memorial Day,[6] Father's Day, and then, in mid-summer, the Fourth of July, Independence Day. Some of these days are religious holidays (Christmas, Easter) or sacred to the nation (Memorial Day, Fourth of July, Thanksgiving, and President's Day). New Year's Day seems to be an anomaly; it is a holiday from work and school but seems to be neither religious nor strictly national. Indeed, at the turn of the millennium, it was celebrated worldwide. Rosh Hashanah, Yom Kippur, Hanukkah, Passover – religious holidays for Jews – and more recently the African American Kwanza, while often marked on the calendar, are not official holidays. This is a clear sign that the calendar in force in the United States is a Christian-influenced one.

> Some schools in England celebrate Hindu and Muslim holidays but they are not national holidays and children do not get the day off from school.

Another way of looking at the cycle of holidays is in terms of social solidarity, according to Caplow and Williamson: "National solidarity is celebrated on Independence Day, Memorial Day, and Washington's birthday; family solidarity on Thanksgiving, Mother's Day, and Father's Day, and (with a special nuance) Valentine's Day; neighborhood solidarity on Halloween and New Year's; and civic solidarity on Memorial Day" (1980: 222–3). Religious solidarity is implied by Christmas and Easter, though they argued that both holidays have considerable secular aspects. What is behind the more recent trend to name days, weeks, and months for certain causes such as World Peace Day, National Cheese Day, Women's History Month, Aids Awareness Day etc.? What social forces must be mobilized to steer these through legislation?

Work vs. leisure

We have yet to talk about one of the major distinctions of lived time – that is, the distinction between work and leisure. Most of us assume we will have to spend a certain amount of *time* working, a certain amount of our life*time* at work. The distinction between work and leisure is also spatialized; normally we work in one place and take our leisure in another place. But were these distinctions always like this? If not, how did they come about?

Anthropologists have long been puzzled over why hunters and gatherers would ever switch to agriculture since the former work, at most, about 20 hours a week to supply all their needs. In his article "The Original Affluent Society" (1972), Marshall Sahlins, a well-known anthropologist at the University of Chicago, turns upside down the conventional view that also drives Western economic theory. That view assumes that in "primitive" society there are scarce resources so the people must be working all the time just in order to survive. That was never the case; instead Sahlins shows that they worked fewer than 2–3 hours a day and that most of their time was spent in leisure, social activity, and ceremonies. He explains that affluence is a relation between wants and the means to satisfy them; hunter-gatherer wants were in *proportion* to their ability to satisfy them, thus they could feel affluent, and this was expressed in their behavior. Rather than hoarding goods because of scarcity, people were generous, even profligate. This behavior continually mystified the explorers and missionaries who came in contact with them. In contrast, our wants are out of proportion to our ability to satisfy them; they are unlimited and new ones are created every day. This imbalance intensifies the feeling of scarcity.

Agricultural labor is arduous, time-consuming, and risky, yet people still retain control over their time and the products of their labor. Agricultural work is also episodic, that is, there are times of intense labor (normally in the summer) and times of great leisure (generally in the winter). British social theorist E. P. Thompson noted that "[T]he work pattern was one of alternate bouts of intense labour and of idleness, wherever men were in control of their own working lives" (1967: 73). He goes on to say that this "pattern persists among some self-employed – artists, writers, small farmers, and perhaps also with students" and wonders if this is not a more "natural human work-rhythm." This was certainly my experience living in the Turkish village for two years (see p. 105), *and* as a student and professor, although neither of these have periods of idleness, instead just other non-academic activities.

In addition, "for an academic or artist, money is time," claimed anthropologist Lawrence Rosen, overturning the epithet that opened this chapter. In order to devote oneself to painting or writing one needs time, lots of it. The trick is to find a way to get the money to provide that time. Although artists and writers and some others devote many, many hours to their work and struggle over it, the time is often not *felt* as work. Not only that, work and leisure alternate more organically and many do not *go out* to work. This is definitely not the work-rhythm most of us experience.

Some people, of course, may prefer working outside the home from 9 a.m. to 5 p.m. and then have the rest of the time for themselves, for leisure. But we need to ask if this kind of work schedule is really necessary – why should anyone have to work like that? Why should life be so sliced up? What are we working for, and for whom?

People in our modern industrialized and post-industrial capitalist societies are working longer hours than ever before in human history. According to a report released by the International Labor Organization at the United Nations on Labor Day, 2001, Americans are working more today than 10 years ago; indeed, they are working more than people in other industrialized nations and have fewer vacation days than anywhere else. Just in the decade of the 1990s they have added an extra week of work. And that seems to have escalated: "According to the International Labor Organization, Americans now work 1,978 hours annually, a full 350 hours – nine weeks – more than Western Europeans" (de Graaf, *New York Times*, April 12, 2003). To point this out dramatically, John de Graaf

Germans, for example, get many more vacation days, at least a month, than Americans. In addition, most stores close at noon on Saturday and remain closed all day Sunday. The idea is to encourage more family time. However, it also assumes a stay-at-home housewife or, if she works, it puts an added burden on her since she would have to do the shopping during lunch hours or after work. The French, too, as of January 2000, have a 35-hour work-week and more than a month of holiday time.

has coordinated the national "Take Back Your Time Day" scheduled for October 24, 2003, exactly nine weeks before the end of the year!

Although the official hours of work each day and week have decreased over the past century, many people today are working more than the standard 8 hours per day. This is as true of professionals as it is of lower-income people working *overtime* or working two jobs (*New York Times*, September 3, 2001). With so-called "progress," shouldn't we be working less? What happened? How did we come to have the kind of work time we do?

E. P. Thompson claims that "the transition to mature industrial society entailed a severe restructuring of working habits" (1967: 57), which in turn involved a change in notions of time. Once clocks became available to individuals, not just churches and government offices, employers were able to use them to *discipline* workers, not in the sense of punishment but in the sense of regimentation. In order to get paid, workers had to check in *on time*; their work was *timed* according to the clock, and they were released at a specific *time*. Their time was no longer their own, it belonged to the employer. If they wanted to keep their jobs they had to conform to employers' schedules, they had to perform in relation to the external measure – the clock. It did not take much intelligence to realize that "time is money."

The industrial revolution in the nineteenth century changed the way we work. One of the biggest social consequences was the separation of work from home. No longer was work just part of sustaining the family as in farming communities, nor piecework taken into the home and paid for by the piece, nor a family business attached to the home. Instead, one went out to work for a certain period of time and then returned home for "leisure" time. Work and home became antinomies, opposites. And they were gendered. "Work" became identified with men and the "home" with women. Men were paid a "family wage" in order to be able to keep their wives at home to attend to children and housework. Not only did this rhetoric disguise the fact that many women did go out to work, thus ignoring the issues of race and class, it also made women's work in the home invisible.

But in middle-class families women became more and more confined to the home, where they were expected to provide the rest and respite from the working world their men went out to battle each day. Despite all the work women were actually doing, it was no longer conceptualized as work that contributed to the gross national product (see Folbre 1991 for fuller discussion), yet without it the whole edifice would collapse. Furthermore, they were no longer imagined as "helpmates" in keeping the household going. Is it any wonder that women have been rebelling ever since? The "cult of domesticity" or the "cult of true womanhood," as the phenomenon has been called, reemerged in full force in the 1950s after World War II but, at that time, women had even more problems. They had been out working while the men were at war,[7] and increasing numbers of them had also received college educations and wanted to do something more with their lives than housework or child care. Isolated in their new suburban homes for most of the day, with all the so-called "time-saving" devices, they were bored, and they became ill with "the problem that has no name," as Betty Friedan called it in *The Feminine Mystique*. The second wave of the women's movement, launched in the early 1960s, was

The first wave, for those who do not know, really took off at the Seneca Falls convention of 1848, where women gathered to protest slavery as well as marriage which, given the laws at the time, they theorized as another form of slavery.

the outcome. Time-saving devices lulled women into their new roles for a time, or at least the advertisements made it seem so. But, did these machines really save time or did they "merely allow us to do more in the same number of minutes, leaving us with full schedules and the need to find more ways to save time"? So asks syndicated columnist Ellen Goodman in "Time is for Savoring" (October 1977).

The latest "time-saving" device is the computer. It does everything so much faster than any human could ever do. It is supposed to save us time, but everything has speeded up. Can we ever keep up? Because of the computer we simply have more information to process and respond to. Not so long ago professors had secretaries; now each of us is expected to do all of our own correspondence and manuscript typing. This means hundreds of letters of recommendation in addition to our lectures, articles, books, book reviews, tenure evaluations, and so forth. More important, someone else has lost a job. Quite presciently, John Stuart Mill understood the deceptiveness of machines: "It is questionable," he said, "if all the mechanical inventions yet made have lightened the day's toil of any human being" ([1848] 1985: 90). Marx added that they may have lightened the toil of the rich.

Now, more and more women are working outside the home than ever before, but a major problem has not been resolved – who is going to care for the children, the sick, and the aged? The answer, it seems to me, is not to send women back home, nor to create even more institutionalized care such as day care centers, hospitals, and nursing homes, but to begin to change our notions of time, work, and life goals. One place to begin involves the very notion of a "career."

A career is a profession or occupation that has a trajectory that is measured against time. It is believed that intellectual achievements, like athletic ones, come relatively early in life. But they do not just happen; in order to achieve, you have to put in a lot of time. When people comment how few women "geniuses" there are, or composers, or artists, or whatever, they ignore the way in which time has been, and continues to be, gendered. In her article "Inside the Clock-Work of Male Careers" (1975), Arlie Hochschild examines the gendered timetable. Although her example is an academic career, the same holds true for most others. "The classic profile of the academic career is cut to the image of the traditional man with his traditional wife" (1975: 49). What she means is that if you want to become a full professor one day, you must begin by getting into the best graduate school possible, you must choose a topic early so that you do not *waste time*, and make your work your top priority so that you do not take too much *time* to finish. You must take the best job you can get, then spend what remains of your twenties and definitely your thirties writing articles and books, giving papers at conferences, getting your name known, getting tenure. Then you must write more articles and books so you can be advanced to full professor. Although Hochschild's article was written a quarter of a century ago, it rings (almost) as true today as then. What are some of the problems with this scenario?

To concentrate on your work with the zeal required, it surely helps if you have someone taking care of the housework, the cooking, the shopping, the laundry, and the cleaning, not to mention the children. Already

To be fair I must admit that my own case is an anomaly. I was 36 when I went to graduate school in 1976, the oldest person the department had ever admitted. Not only that, I had a child and was on welfare. I was told that the program was very rigorous, and was asked what I intended to do with my child while I was studying. I was also told that by the time I finished I would be ready to retire! Clearly, older students, especially women, were not taken very seriously. The burden to prove them wrong was heavy, and so it was with great glee I informed them about my job at Stanford.

you can see why this typical pattern, designed with men's lifetimes in mind, disadvantages women before they even start. In the past, women used to be told that if they wanted a career they better not marry. Today, instead, we hear women say: "I need a wife."

Hochschild concludes that "the very clockwork of a career system . . . seems to eliminate women not so much through malevolent disobedience to good rules, but through the making up rules to suit half the population in the first place" (p. 59). But why shouldn't we all have the opportunity to pursue a career and also enjoy the benefits of love, marriage, and children if we want? Why shouldn't everyone be required to spend part of their time caring for others – whether children, the sick, or the elderly, and regardless of whether they are one's own relatives or not? After all, we have all been cared for by others.

Some people see salvation in the computer for it enables more and more people to work at home and thus offers the possibility of, once again, combining work and leisure into a more organic life rhythm. Personally, I am doubtful; it seems more likely that home will be turned more and more into a work place, and work will begin to take over other times. What, then, will happen to social relations? Nevertheless, one of the interesting phenomena brought about by computers and the Internet/World Wide Web is what some analysts call "time-space compression." That is, for some purposes, time and space have collapsed; communication is instantaneous around the globe. Perhaps a totally new and unexpected sense of time – equivalent to "cyberspace" – will emerge. Then we might come close to experiencing Mark Twain's enigmatic statement: "Time is nature's way of preventing everything from happening all at once."

Village time

In the village, time was the most difficult thing for me to get accustomed to. I am not sure I ever got the hang of it. I could not incorporate (literally, to bring into my body, corpus) their tempo and daily rhythms, and that affected my speech, my behavior, and my style of movement. My *sense of timing* was off, I could feel my rough edges, and my gait was all wrong. One does not rush in the village, it is undignified.

Sometimes I would ask when we were going to do something and the answer would be: *şimdi* – which means now. But *now* could mean anywhere from immediately to a few minutes to a few hours, and sometimes was simply a way of letting the matter drop eventually. I could never really tell when something was going to start – a wedding, for example. For us such a major event is announced well in advance and the date and time are specified on the invitation. If you are late you will miss it completely. In the village, even when a wedding was announced formally (invitations were newly being introduced and had become a kind of status symbol) and the day and time specified, that information did not have much meaning. The wedding would begin when enough people had gathered. How many is enough? I don't know, and the number varied for each occasion. But on each occasion at a certain magical moment, everything would begin.

Visiting forms one of the major components of village life and hospitality is a primary virtue. Unlike Americans who often say "drop in anytime" but really don't mean it (cf. Varenne 1986), Turks would say its equivalent and *mean it*. People can and did drop in anytime. You are *honored* by a visit – at any time – and you are expected to drop whatever you are doing and welcome your guests. You cannot say, "I am really busy now, could you come back later?" Social life in the village presumes that someone (a woman) will be at home to receive visitors and to prepare the tea to refresh them.

In the village, work was integrated into daily activities and took place at a *leisurely* pace; there was no hurry and no time clock. Although the villagers complained that their work was hard, I had a difficult time trying to explain that for us it is also hard because of all the rushing and the pressure – determined not by our own rhythms and tasks to be done, but by external demands and external clocks. People do not work alone; there are always household members, friends, or relatives to help.

When I went to work in the fields, I always had the impression that if an outsider – whether an urban Turk or a foreigner – should see us, he or she would think we were involved in backbreaking peasant labor. It wasn't so. Just when I thought it was getting hard, it was time for a tea break (all the tea implements were carried to the fields, including a portable gas burner, glasses, and sugar). The work throughout the day was leisurely. I don't assume it was always like this or that it is like this in other parts of Turkey – but it did give me pause to reconsider certain assumptions I had.

Villagers kept commenting to me: *"Çok harcayorsun"* – you're exerting yourself too much. You're spending yourself, you're wasting energy. It is not *time* one spends or wastes, but oneself! Time had not yet been objectified, it had not yet become a commodity. Instead, the village experience of time was much more like what French anthropologist Pierre Bourdieu described in his article, "The Attitude of the Algerian Peasant Toward Time":

> Inwardly felt, as the very movement of life rather than as a constraining limit, time cannot be dissociated from the experience of activity and of the space in which that activity takes place. Duration and space are described by reference to the performance of a concrete task; e.g. the unit of duration is the time one needs to do a job, to work a piece of land. (1963: 60)

In Turkey the term that describes a parcel of land is a *dönem*. Today it is a specific measurement, but it derives from the amount of land a man was thought to be able to work in a day, that is, before tractors and mechanical plows were introduced. Space and time were not only related but equivalent and both were dimensions of a specific activity. This is called "task orientation," which, according to E. P. Thompson, has three major qualities: (1) "it is more humanly comprehensible than timed labour"; (2) there is "the least demarcation between 'work' and 'life'"; and (3) to outsiders who work under the clock, it "appears to be wasteful and lacking in urgency" (1967: 60), all of which fit my experience in the village.

While villagers complained about the heavy work, some who had tried working in town talked of how monotonous and boring most of it was. All day long one had to do the same kind of thing, whereas in the village they do many different kinds of tasks and see them through the whole process – such as building a house, which begins with gathering stones for the foundation and making mud bricks; caring for the fields and fruit trees, which involves planting, harvesting, and preserving their own food; and caring for animals and processing their meat, their milk, and their wool or (goat) hair.

Work in the village was an occasion for social activity and people were not alienated from their labor, that is, they saw the process from beginning to end and benefited from the end products. Many of you might not find this kind of life appealing because you want to develop and use other talents and capacities. But you should also keep in mind that in our industrial and post-industrial world, it is the fortunate few who are really able to work in a non-alienated way. You may not end up working in a factory (though millions do), but you may end up spending all day at an office at a desk in front of a computer.

Peasant labor is changed eradically when work is no longer primarily for subsistence but is geared toward production for the market. Given villagers' attitude to life and to work, it is not difficult to imagine the *ambivalence* generated by the shift from subsistence to production for the market. Machines have reduced the arduousness of some of the work and greatly increased the amount of land under cultivation. The extra cultivated land is not necessary for their own needs but is intended to produce the food to feed the urban population. The cash income generated from the surplus food nevertheless makes them indebted, especially for the machines but also for the additional seeds and fertilizer. They end up working more and their sociability is being destroyed. How do you think villagers were convinced to produce for the market? What forces might have been exerted? In what ways do you think their sense of time changed?

In Islam there is a belief that your lifetime is already determined at your birth but only God knows its length. While there were some fairly old people in the village, the average life expectancy was much lower than in the United States. They remarked on my age and the fact that although I had a child, I was still in school; "here we just keep having children, and then we die." It is very important to have children; that is what establishes you as an adult. Sons are especially important because it is through them that the family line will continue. But it is also important to have children because they are expected to take care of you in your old age in return for the care you gave them when they were young. As a person grows from child to adult there is a kind of backward look, toward the parents, whereas in the United States children are pointed always toward the future. Most Turks, rural or urban, frowned on the American habit of putting their parents in retirement homes or nursing homes.

Although there is a backward look to a life span, the goal is toward the "other world," which is your original, true, and final home. Mecca, believed to be the place where the first land appeared upon the waters, is felt to be the closest to the "other world" one can get in this life; it is the *axis mundi* (the navel of the world). Making the *hajj* (pilgrimage) to Mecca at least once in a lifetime, if at all possible, is incumbent upon Muslims. But rather than a going forth as exemplified in John Bunyan's *Pilgrim's Progress*, this pilgrimage is a return, back to the source. This, too, I believe, gives a very different feeling to time (and space) and a lifetime from that of people raised in a country dominated by Christianity.

A common wall hanging in villagers' homes included a saying attributed to the medieval Muslim scholar al-Ghazali. It went like this:

> What are you? Where do you come from? Where are you going? Whether your life span be short or long, the world is but a brief lodging (a guesthouse), so take care to make provisions for the eternal home.

Unlike the Protestant ethic with its focus on "this-worldly" asceticism, the Muslim ethic, at least in this saying, encourages an asceticism that focuses on the "other world." For while the reward in both cases is Heaven, Protestants were also encouraged to save in this world so that they could launch a thousand ships, gain capital for business, and bequeath the riches to their children. This does not mean that villagers went around in a pious state all the time, but they made a big distinction between "this world" and the "other world," and the "other world" was very real. For example, they would say "I have three children in this world, and two in the other world," meaning two children had died. Villagers were very much involved with life in this world and curious about material things. But there was also a sense in which they were not so identified with their things; they did not seem to depend on them as much as we do. With so few material possessions, you would think they would be more, not less, concerned about them, but that was not the case at all. They were very generous in sharing whatever they had and giving away a treasured possession was not uncommon. They also seemed to possess a sense of humor about the vicissitudes of life that I found unusual and refreshing (cf. Sahlins 1972) – perhaps because they were confident about the rewards awaiting them. Death, for the villagers, was the means to the second birth, not baptism as in Christianity. And the next life, especially for men, who will have anywhere from 7 to 70 *houris* (virginal maidens) waiting on them, is expected to be a life of ease and comfort.

Notes

1   For those interested in the story, I recommend Clark Blaise's *Time Lord: Sir Sanford Fleming and the Creation of Standard Time* (New York: Pantheon Books, 2001).
2   For an accessible investigation of the calendar see David Ewing Duncan's book, *Calendar: Humanity's Epic Struggle to Determine a True and Accurate Year*. He claims that the AD dating system was devised by Dionysius Exiguus ("Little Dennis") in the year AD 531, although how Dionysius decided that he was living 531 years after the birth of Christ is a mystery, especially since the date of "Christ's birth is unknown and a matter of immense controversy even today" (Duncan 1998: 91–2).
3   See Stocking (1968) and Gould (1981).
4   A scathing account was published by Jessica Mitford, *The American Way of Death* (1963).
5   For example, see Caplow and Williamson (1980).
6   For a classic analysis of Memorial Day, see Warner (1953).
7   See, for example, the film *Rosie the Riveter* (1980).

Bibliography

Aveni, Anthony F. (1989) *Empires of Time: Calendars, Clocks, and Cultures*. New York: Basic Books.

Barnett, Jo Ann (1998) *Time's Pendulum: The Quest to Capture Time – From Sundials to Atomic Clocks*. New York and London: Plenum.

Berger, John (1979) *Pig Earth*. New York: Pantheon.

Bourdieu, Pierre (1963) "The Attitude of the Algerian Peasant Toward Time." In *Mediterranean Countrymen*, ed. J. Pitt-Rivers. Paris: Mouton, pp. 55–72.

Campbell, Jeremy (1986) *Winston Churchill's Afternoon Nap: A Wide-Awake Inquiry into the Human Nature of Time*. New York: Simon & Schuster.

Caplow, Theodore and Williamson, Margaret Holmes (1980) "Decoding Middletown's Easter Bunny: A Study in American Iconography." *Semiotica*, 32 (3/4): 221–32.

Duncan, David Ewing (1998) *Calendar: Humanity's Epic Struggle to Determine a True and Accurate Year*. New York: Avon Books.

Evans-Pritchard ([1940] 1976) *The Nuer: A Description of the Modes of Livelihood and Political Institutions of a Nilotic People*. Oxford: Clarendon Press.

Fabian, Johannes (1983) *Time and the Other: How Anthropology Makes Its Object*. New York: Columbia University Press.

Folbre, Nancy (1991) "The Unproductive Housewife: Her Evolution in Nineteenth-Century Economic Thought." *Signs*, 16 (31): 463–84.

Fraser, J. T. (1966) *The Voices of Time: A Cooperative Survey of Man's Views of Time as Expressed by the Sciences and by the Humanities*. New York: George Braziller.

Gould, Stephen Jay (1981) *The Mismeasure of Man*. New York: Norton.

Hawking, Stephen (1988) *A Brief History of Time*. New York: Bantam Books.

Hochschild, Arlie (1975) "Inside the Clock-Work of Male Careers." In *Women and the Power to Change*, ed. Florence Howe. Sponsored by the Carnegie Commission on Higher Education, New York: McGraw-Hill.

Leach, Edmund (1961) "Two Essays Concerning the Symbolic Representation of Time." In *Rethinking Anthropology*. London: University of London, Athlone Press.

Leach, Penelope (1994) *Children First: What Our Society Must Do – And Is Not Doing – For Our Children Today*. New York: Alfred A. Knopf.

Mill, John Stuart ([1848] 1985) *Principles of Political Economy: With Some of their Applications to Social Philosophy, Books IV and V*. Ed. with an introduction by Donald Winch. Harmondsworth: Penguin.

Morris, Richard (1984) *Time's Arrows: Scientific Attitudes Toward Time*. New York: Simon & Schuster.

Sahlins, Marshall (1972) "The Original Affluent Society." In *Stone Age Economics*. Chicago: Aldine-Atherton.

Sidel, Ruth (1992) *Women and Children Last: The Plight of Poor Women in Affluent America*. New York and London: Penguin.

Steel, Duncan (2000) *Marking Time: The Epic Quest to Invent the Perfect Calendar*. New York: John Wiley.

Stocking, George W., Jr. (1968) *Race, Culture, and Evolution: Essays in the History of Anthropology*. New York: Free Press.

Thompson, E. P. (1967) "Time, Work-Discipline and Industrial Capitalism." *Past and Present*, 38: 56–97.

Varenne, Hervé (1986) " 'Drop in Anytime': Community and Authenticity in American Everyday Life." In *Symbolizing America*, ed. Hervé Varenne. Lincoln: University of Nebraska Press, pp. 209–28.

Warner, William L. (1953) "An American Sacred Ceremony." In *American Life*. Chicago: University of Chicago Press, pp. 1–26.

Weber, Max ([1904–5] 1958) *The Protestant Ethic and the Spirit of Capitalism*. Trans. Talcott Parsons. New York: Charles Scribner's Sons.

Whorf, Benjamin (1956) "The Relation of Habitual Thought and Behavior to Language." In *Language, Thought and Reality*. Cambridge, MA: MIT Press.

Yanagisako, Sylvia and Delaney, Carol (1995) *Naturalizing Power: Essays in Feminist Cultural Analysis*. New York and London: Routledge.

Zerubavel, Eviatar (1985) *The Seven Day Circle: The History and Meaning of the Week*. New York: Free Press.

Time is for Savoring

Ellen Goodman

A few months ago, when a preening French official descended from his Concorde into Washington, he bragged to Tip O'Neill that he saved four, count 'em, four hours traveling supersonically.

At that point the Speaker turned and asked him, benignly, what he had done with the four hours he'd saved. The official, as the story goes, was taken aback, right aback into silence. This exchange stuck in my mind, and not because I'm snooping into the Frenchman's activities. I'm not that sort of reporter.

But it occurred to me that O'Neill's response was a nice healthy challenge to the time-saving obsession of our lives. I guess the Concorde is as good a place to begin as any.

It has taken the accumulated wisdom of centuries to build this plane, and what have we got? For one thing, a noisier airplane which uses more fuel to carry fewer people in less comfort from one continent to the other at greater expense. We call this peculiar achievement "progress" for only one reason: It does all this absurd stuff in a shorter amount of time than a conventional plane.

Saving time, it seems, has a primacy that's too rarely examined. From the Concorde to the microwave oven to the Speed Reading class, we value saving time more than the way we spend it and

more than the values we may sacrifice to it. At times we behave like the efficiency expert in *Pajama Game* whose rationalization for his life was simple: "For a time-study man to waste time / is a crime."

We tell ourselves that we are all busy people. Our lives are geared to the school bells and alarm clocks and factory whistles outside of our control. But on the whole, the time-saving devices – both mechanical and personal – that are supposed to help us save time, don't. They merely allow us to do more in the same number of minutes, leaving us with full schedules and the need to find more ways to save time.

With the aid of the plane, the official and the businessman can turn a two-day trip into a one-day trip. But they are usually faced with two one-day trips. The people who learn to Speed Read don't spend less time reading; they just read more in the same time.

The machines that make it possible for us to do things that we could never do before – like cook a roast in a half hour – also make it more likely that we will do things we never would have done before. Like cook that roast.

These things don't save time, any more than the assembly line saves the worker time.

There is actually no way to bank our minutes

away. The best we can do, with the most sophisticated machinery products, is to redistribute those minutes. And, like the French official, we don't always do a good job of that. We have even become so addicted to saving time that we forget to differentiate between the things we like to do (dining with our families, for example) and the things we hate to do (cleaning the oven). We efficiently shorten them all.

At the end of a busy day, families often get dinner "down to a science": the science of convenience foods, mixes, and fifteen-minute "gourmet" recipes. In some houses, dinner goes from the refrigerator to the dishwasher in less than an hour. Then, having saved all these minutes, rather than spending them with each other, we drop them like quarters in a television slot machine.

Either we spend more and more energy processing ourselves through our days, doing more and more in the same amount of time, or we throw away our "free time" like Daddy Warbucks.

It's not that I want to go back to ox carts, let alone wooden washtubs, but it seems to me that we ought to make some personal judgments about the machines that are pushed on us in the name of the clock. We have to ask: Is it really going to save time? *My* time? Is it going to cut down unpleasant time, or pleasant time? And, as the Speaker would say, what am I going to do with the time I save?

Ultimately, time is all you have and the idea isn't to save it but to savor it. Like the man on the record, James Taylor, says, "The secret o' life is enjoying the passage of time."

The Original Affluent Society
Marshall Sahlins

If economics is the dismal science, the study of hunting and gathering economies must be its most advanced branch. Almost universally committed to the proposition that life was hard in the paleolithic, our textbooks compete to convey a sense of impending doom, leaving one to wonder not only how hunters managed to live, but whether, after all, this was living? The specter of starvation stalks the stalker through these pages. His technical incompetence is said to enjoin continuous work just to survive, affording him neither respite nor surplus, hence not even the "leisure" to "build culture." Even so, for all his efforts, the hunter pulls the lowest grades in thermodynamics – less energy/ capita/year than any other mode of production. And in treatises on economic development he is condemned to play the role of bad example: the so-called "subsistence economy."

The traditional wisdom is always refractory. One is forced to oppose it polemically, to phrase the necessary revisions dialectically: in fact, this was, when you come to examine it, the original affluent society. Paradoxical, that phrasing leads to another useful and unexpected conclusion. By the common understanding, *an affluent society is one in which all the people's material wants are easily satisfied.* To assert that the hunters are affluent is to deny then that the human condition is an ordained tragedy, with man the prisoner at hard labor of a perpetual disparity between his unlimited wants and his insufficient means.

For there are two possible courses to affluence. *Wants may be "easily satisfied" either by producing much or desiring little.* The familiar conception, the Galbraithean way, makes assumptions peculiarly appropriate to market economies: that man's wants are great, not to say infinite, whereas his means are limited, although improvable: thus, the gap between means and ends can be narrowed by industrial productivity, at least to the point that "urgent goods" become plentiful. But there is also a Zen road to affluence, departing from premises somewhat different from our own: that human material wants are finite and few, and technical means unchanging but on the whole adequate. Adopting the Zen strategy, *a people can enjoy an unparalleled material plenty – with a low standard of living.*

That, I think, describes the hunters. And it helps explain some of their more curious economic behavior: their "prodigality" for example – the inclination to consume at once all stocks on hand, as if they had it made. Free from market obsessions of scarcity, hunters' economic propensities may be more consistently predicated on abundance than our own. Destutt de Tracy, "fish-blooded bourgeois doctrinaire" though he might have been, at least compelled Marx's agreement on the observation that "in poor nations the people are comfortable," whereas in rich nations "they are generally poor."

This is not to deny that a preagricultural economy operates under serious constraints, but only to insist, on the evidence from modern hunters and gatherers, that a successful accommodation is usually made. After taking up the evidence, I shall return in the end to the real difficulties of hunting-gathering economy, none of which are correctly specified in current formulas of paleolithic poverty.

Sources of the Misconception

"Mere subsistence economy," "limited leisure save in exceptional circumstances," "incessant quest for food," "meagre and relatively unreliable" natural resources, "absence of an economic surplus," "maximum energy from a maximum number of people" – so runs the fair average anthropological opinion of hunting and gathering.

> The aboriginal Australians are a classic example of a people whose economic resources are of the scantiest. In many places their habitat is even more severe than that of the Bushmen, although this is perhaps not quite true in the northern portion. . . . A tabulation of the foodstuffs which the aborigines of northwest central Queensland extract from the country they inhabit is instructive. . . . The variety in this list is impressive, but we must not be deceived into thinking that variety indicates plenty, for the available quantities of each element in it are so slight that only the most intense application makes survival possible. (Herskovits, 1958, pp. 68–9)

Or again, in reference to South American hunters:

> The nomadic hunters and gatherers barely met minimum subsistence needs and often fell far short of them. Their population of 1 person to 10 or 20 square miles reflects this. Constantly on the move in search of food, they clearly lacked the leisure hours for nonsubsistence activities of any significance, and they could transport little of what they might manufacture in spare moments. To them, adequacy of production meant physical survival, and they rarely had surplus of either products or time. (Steward and Faron, 1959, p. 60; cf. Clark, 1953, pp. 27f; Haury, 1962, p. 113; Hoebel, 1958, p. 188; Redfield, 1953, p. 5; White, 1959)

But the traditional dismal view of the hunters' fix is also preanthropological and extra-anthropological, at once historical and referable to the larger economic context in which anthropology operates. It goes back to the time Adam Smith was writing, and probably to a time before anyone was writing.[1] Probably it was one of the first distinctly neolithic prejudices, an ideological appreciation of the hunter's capacity to exploit the earth's resources most congenial to the historic task of depriving him of the same. We must have inherited it with the seed of Jacob, which "spread abroad to the west, and to the east, and to the north," to the disadvantage of Esau who was the elder son and cunning hunter, but in a famous scene deprived of his birthright.

Current low opinions of the hunting-gathering economy need not be laid to neolithic ethnocentrism, however. Bourgeois ethnocentrism will do as well. The existing business economy, at every turn an ideological trap from which anthropological economics must escape, will promote the same dim conclusions about the hunting life.

Is it so paradoxical to contend that hunters have affluent economies, their absolute poverty notwithstanding? Modern capitalist societies, however richly endowed, dedicate themselves to the proposition of scarcity. Inadequacy of economic means is the first principle of the world's wealthiest peoples. The apparent material status of the economy seems to be no clue to its accomplishments; something has to be said for the mode of economic organization (cf. Polanyi, 1947, 1957, 1959; Dalton, 1961).

The market-industrial system institutes scarcity, in a manner completely unparalleled and to a degree nowhere else approximated. Where production and distribution are arranged through the behavior of prices, and all livelihoods depend on getting and spending, insufficiency of material means becomes the explicit, calculable starting point of all economic activity.[2] The entrepreneur is confronted with alternative investments of a finite capital, the worker (hopefully) with alternative choices of remunerative employ, and the consumer. . . . Consumption is a double tragedy: what begins in inadequacy will end in deprivation. Bringing together an international division of labor, the market makes available a dazzling array of products: all these Good Things within a man's reach – but never all within his grasp. Worse, in this game of consumer free choice, every acquisition is simultaneously a deprivation, for every purchase of something is a forgoing of something else, in general only marginally less desirable, and in some particulars more desirable, that could have been had instead. (The point is that if you buy one automobile, say a Plymouth, you cannot also have the Ford – and I judge from current television commercials that the deprivations entailed would be more than just material.)[3]

That sentence of "life at hard labor" was passed uniquely upon us. Scarcity is the judgment decreed by our economy – so also the axiom of our Economics: the application of scarce means against alternative ends to derive the most satisfaction possible under the circumstances. And it is precisely from this anxious vantage that we look back upon hunters. But if modern man, with all his technological advantages, still hasn't got the wherewithal, what chance has this naked savage with his puny bow and arrow? Having equipped the hunter with bourgeois impulses and paleolithic tools, we judge his situation hopeless in advance.[4]

Yet *scarcity is not an intrinsic property of technical means. It is a relation between means and ends.* We should entertain the empirical possibility that hunters are in business for their health, a finite objective, and that bow and arrow are adequate to that end.[5]

But still other ideas, these endemic in anthropological theory and ethnographic practice, have conspired to preclude any such understanding.

The anthropological disposition to exaggerate the economic inefficiency of hunters appears notably by way of invidious comparison with neolithic economies. Hunters, as Lowie put it blankly, "must work much harder in order to live than tillers and breeders" (1946, p. 13). On this point evolutionary anthropology in particular found it congenial, even necessary theoretically, to adopt the usual tone of reproach. Ethnologists and archaeologists had become neolithic revolutionaries, and in their enthusiasm for the Revolution spared nothing denouncing the Old (Stone Age) Regime. Including some very old scandal. It was not the first time philosophers would relegate the earliest stage of humanity rather to nature than to culture. ("A man who spends his whole life following animals just to kill them to eat, or moving from one berry patch to another, is really living just like an animal himself" [Braidwood, 1957, p. 122].) The hunters thus downgraded, anthropology was free to extol the Neolithic Great Leap Forward: a main technological advance that brought about a "general availability of leisure through release from purely food-getting pursuits" (Braidwood, 1952, p. 5; cf. Boas, 1940, p. 285).

In an influential essay on "Energy and the Evolution of Culture," Leslie White explained that the neolithic generated a "great advance in cultural development . . . as a consequence of the great increase in the amount of energy harnessed and controlled per capita per year by means of the agricultural and pastoral arts" (1949, p. 372). White further heightened the evolutionary contrast by specifying *human effort* as the principal energy source of paleolithic culture, as opposed to the *domesticated plant and animal resources* of neolithic culture. This determination of the energy sources at once permitted a precise low estimate of hunters' thermodynamic potential – that developed by the human body: "average power resources" of one-twentieth horsepower per capita (1949, p. 369) – even as, by eliminating human effort from the cultural enterprise of the neolithic, it appeared that people had been liberated by some labor-saving device (domesticated plants and animals). But White's problematic is obviously misconceived. The principal mechanical energy available to both paleolithic and neolithic culture is that supplied by human beings, as transformed in both cases from plant and animal sources, so that, with negligible exceptions (the occasional direct use of nonhuman power), the amount of energy harnessed per *capita* per year is the same in paleolithic and neolithic economies – and fairly constant in human history until the advent of the industrial revolution.[6]

Another specifically anthropological source of paleolithic discontent develops in the field itself, from the context of European observation of existing hunters and gatherers, such as the native Australians, the Bushmen, the Ona or the Yahgan. This ethnographic context tends to distort our understanding of the hunting-gathering economy in two ways.

First, it provides singular opportunities for naïveté. The remote and exotic environments that have become the cultural theater of modern hunters have an effect on Europeans most unfavorable to the latter's assessment of the former's plight. Marginal as the Australian or Kalahari desert is to agriculture, or to everyday European experience, it is a source of wonder to the untutored observer "how anybody could live in a place like this." The inference that the natives manage only to eke out a bare existence is apt to be reinforced by their marvelously varied diets (cf. Herskovits, 1958, quoted above). Ordinarily including objects deemed repulsive and inedible by Europeans, the local cuisine lends itself to the supposition that the people are starving to death. Such a conclusion, of course, is more likely met in earlier than in later accounts, and in the journals of explorers or missionaries than in the monographs of anthropologists; but precisely because the explorers' reports are older and closer to the aboriginal condition, one reserves for them a certain respect.

Such respect obviously has to be accorded with discretion. Greater attention should be paid a man such as Sir George Grey (1841), whose expeditions in the 1830s included some of the poorer districts of western Australia, but whose unusually close attention to the local people obliged him to debunk his colleagues' communications on just this point of economic desperation. It is a mistake very commonly made, Grey wrote, to suppose that the native Australians "have small means of subsistence, or are at times greatly pressed for want of food." Many and "almost ludicrous" are the errors travellers have fallen into in this regard: "They lament in their journals that the unfortunate Aborigines should be reduced by famine to the miserable necessity of subsisting on certain sorts of food, which they have found near their huts; whereas, in many instances, the articles thus quoted by them are those which the natives most prize, and are really neither deficient in flavour nor nutritious qualities." To render palpable "the ignorance that has prevailed with regard to the habits and customs of this people when in their wild

state," Grey provides one remarkable example, a citation from his fellow explorer, Captain Sturt, who, upon encountering a group of Aboriginals engaged in gathering large quantities of mimosa gum, deduced that the "'unfortunate creatures were reduced to the last extremity, and, being unable to procure any other nourishment, had been obliged to collect this mucilaginous.'" But, Sir George observes, the gum in question is a favorite article of food in the area, and when in season it affords the opportunity for large numbers of people to assemble and camp together, which otherwise they are unable to do. He concludes:

> Generally speaking, the natives live well; in some districts there may be at particular seasons of the year a deficiency of food, but if such is the case, these tracts are, at those times, deserted. It *is, however, utterly impossible for a traveller or even for a strange native to judge whether a district affords an abundance of food, or the contrary* . . . But in his own district a native is very differently situated; he knows exactly what it produces, the proper time at which the several articles are in season, and the readiest means of procuring them. According to these circumstances he regulates his visits to different portions of his hunting ground; *and I can only say that I have always found the greatest abundance in their huts.* (Grey, 1841, vol. 2, pp. 259–62, emphasis mine; cf. Eyre, 1845, vol. 2, pp. 244f.)[7]

In making this happy assessment, Sir George took special care to exclude the *lumpen-proletariat* aboriginals living in and about European towns (cf. Eyre, 1845, vol. 2, pp. 250, 254–5). The exception is instructive. It evokes a second source of ethnographic misconceptions: the anthropology of hunters is largely an anachronistic study of ex-savages – an inquest into the corpse of one society, Grey once said, presided over by members of another.

The surviving food collectors, as a class, are displaced persons. They represent the paleolithic disenfranchised, occupying marginal haunts untypical of the mode of production: sanctuaries of an era, places so beyond the range of main centers of cultural advance as to be allowed some respite from the planetary march of cultural evolution, because they were characteristically poor beyond the interest and competence of more advanced economies. Leave aside the favorably situated food collectors, such as Northwest Coast Indians, about whose (comparative) well-being there is no dispute. The remaining hunters, barred from the better parts of the earth, first by agriculture, later by industrial economies, enjoy ecological opportunities something less than the later-paleolithic average.[8] Moreover, the disruption accomplished in the past two centuries of European imperialism has been especially severe, to the extent that many of the ethnographic notices that constitute the anthropologist's stock in trade are adulterated culture goods. Even explorer and missionary accounts, apart from their ethnocentric misconstructions, may be speaking of afflicted economies (cf. Service, 1962). The hunters of eastern Canada of whom we read in the *Jesuit Relations* were committed to the fur trade in the early seventeenth century. The environments of others were selectively stripped by Europeans before reliable report could be made of indigenous production: the Eskimo we know no longer hunt whales, the Bushmen have been deprived of game, the Shoshoni's piñon has been timbered and his hunting grounds grazed out by cattle.[9] If such peoples are now described as poverty-stricken, their resources "meagre and unreliable," is this an indication of the aboriginal condition – or of the colonial duress?

The enormous implications (and problems) for evolutionary interpretation raised by this global retreat have only recently begun to evoke notice (Lee and DeVore, 1968). The point of present importance is this: rather than a fair test of hunters' productive capacities, their current circumstances pose something of a supreme test. All the more extraordinary, then, the following reports of their performance.

"A Kind of Material Plenty"

Considering the poverty in which hunters and gatherers live in theory, it comes as a surprise that Bushmen who live in the Kalahari enjoy "a kind of material plenty," at least in the realm of everyday useful things, apart from food and water:

As the !Kung come into more contact with Europeans – and this is already happening – they will feel sharply the lack of our things and will need and want more. It makes them feel inferior to be without clothes when they stand among strangers who are clothed. But in their own life and with their own artifacts *they were comparatively free from material pressures*. Except for food and water (important exceptions!) of which the Nyae Nyae !Kung have a sufficiency – but barely so, judging from the fact that all are thin though not emaciated – they all had what they needed or could make what they needed, for every man can and does make the things that men make and every woman the things that women make. . . . *They lived in a kind of material plenty* because they adapted the tools of their living to materials which lay in abundance around them and which were free for anyone to take (wood, reeds, bone for weapons and implements, fibers for cordage, grass for shelters), or to materials which were at least sufficient for the needs of the population. . . . The !Kung could always use more ostrich egg shells for beads to wear or trade with, but, as it is, enough are found for every woman to have a dozen or more shells for water containers – all she can carry – and a goodly number of bead ornaments. In their nomadic hunting-gathering life, travelling from one source of food to another through the seasons, always going back and forth between food and water, they carry their young children and their belongings. With plenty of most materials at hand to replace artifacts as required, the !Kung have not developed means of permanent storage and have not needed or wanted to encumber themselves with surpluses or duplicates. They do not even want to carry one of everything. They borrow what they do not own. With this ease, they have not hoarded, and the accumulation of objects has not become associated with status. (L. Marshall, 1961, pp. 243–4, emphasis mine)

Analysis of hunter-gatherer production is usefully divided into two spheres, as Mrs. Marshall has done. Food and water are certainly "important exceptions," best reserved for separate and extended treatment. For the rest, the nonsubsistence sector, what is here said of the Bushmen applies in general and in detail to hunters from the Kalahari to Labrador – or to Tièrra del Fuego, where Gusinde reports of the Yahgan that their disinclination to own more than one copy of utensils frequently needed is "an indication of self-confidence." "Our Fuegians," he writes, "procure and make their implements with little effort" (1961, p. 213).[10]

In the nonsubsistence sphere, the people's wants are generally easily satisfied. Such "material plenty" depends partly upon the ease of production, and that upon the simplicity of technology and democracy of property. Products are homespun: of stone, bone, wood, skin – materials such as "lay in abundance around them." As a rule, neither extraction of the raw material nor its working up take strenuous effort. Access to natural resources is typically direct – "free for anyone to take" – even as possession of the necessary tools is general and knowledge of the required skills common. The division of labor is likewise simple, predominantly a division of labor by sex. Add in the liberal customs of sharing, for which hunters are properly famous, and all the people can usually participate in the going prosperity, such as it is.

But, of course, "such as it is": this "prosperity" depends as well upon an objectively low standard of living. It is critical that the customary quota of consumables (as well as the number of consumers) be culturally set at a modest point. A few people are pleased to consider a few easily-made things their good fortune: some meagre pieces of clothing and rather fugitive housing in most climates;[11] plus a few ornaments, spare flints and sundry other items such as the "pieces of quartz, which native doctors have extracted from their patients" (Grey, 1841, vol. 2, p. 266); and, finally, the skin bags in which the faithful wife carries all this, "the wealth of the Australian savage" (p. 266).

For most hunters, such affluence without abundance in the nonsubsistence sphere need not be long debated. A more interesting question is why they are content with so few possessions – for it is with them a policy, a "matter of principle" as Gusinde says (1961, p. 2), and not a misfortune.

Want not, lack not. But are hunters so undemanding of material goods because they are themselves enslaved by a food quest "demanding maximum energy from a maximum number of people," so that no time or effort remains for the provision of other comforts? Some ethnographers testify to the contrary that the food quest is so successful that half the time the people seem not to know what to do with themselves. On the other hand, *movement* is a condition of this success, more movement in some cases than others, but always

enough to rapidly depreciate the satisfactions of property. Of the hunter it is truly said that his wealth is a burden. In his condition of life, goods can become "grievously oppressive," as Gusinde observes, and the more so the longer they are carried around. Certain food collectors do have canoes and a few have dog sleds, but most must carry themselves all the comforts they possess, and so only possess what they can comfortably carry themselves. Or perhaps only what the women can carry: the men are often left free to react to the sudden opportunity of the chase or the sudden necessity of defense. As Owen Lattimore wrote in a not too different context, "the pure nomad is the poor nomad." Mobility and property are in contradiction.

That wealth quickly becomes more of an encumbrance than a good thing is apparent even to the outsider. Laurens van der Post was caught in the contradiction as he prepared to make farewells to his wild Bushmen friends:

> This matter of presents gave us many an anxious moment. We were humiliated by the realization of how little there was we could give to the Bushmen. Almost everything seemed likely to make life more difficult for them by adding to the litter and weight of their daily round. They themselves had practically no possessions: a loin strap, a skin blanket and a leather satchel. There was nothing that they could not assemble in one minute, wrap up in their blankets and carry on their shoulders for a journey of a thousand miles. They had no sense of possession. (1958, p. 276)

A necessity so obvious to the casual visitor must be second nature to the people concerned. This modesty of material requirements is institutionalized: it becomes a positive cultural fact, expressed in a variety of economic arrangements. Lloyd Warner reports of the Murngin, for example, that portability is a decisive value in the local scheme of things. Small goods are in general better than big goods. In the final analysis "the relative ease of transportation of the article" will prevail, so far as determining its disposition, over its relative scarcity or labor cost. For the "ultimate value," Warner writes, "is freedom of movement." And to this "desire to be free from the burdens and responsibilities of objects which would interfere with the society's itinerant existence," Warner attributes the Murngin's "undeveloped sense of property," and their "lack of interest in developing their technological equipment" (1964, pp. 136–7).

Here then is another economic "peculiarity" – I will not say it is general, and perhaps it is explained as well by faulty toilet training as by a trained disinterest in material accumulation: some hunters, at least, display a notable tendency to be sloppy about their possessions. They have the kind of nonchalance that would be appropriate to a people who have mastered the problems of production, even as it is maddening to a European:

> They do not know how to take care of their belongings. No one dreams of putting them in order, folding them, drying or cleaning them, hanging them up, or putting them in a neat pile. If they are looking for some particular thing, they rummage carelessly through the hodgepodge of trifles in the little baskets. Larger objects that are piled up in a heap in the hut are dragged hither and yon with no regard for the damage that might be done them. The European observer has the impression that these [Yahgan] Indians place no value whatever on their utensils and that they have completely forgotten the effort it took to make them.[12] Actually, no one clings to his few goods and chattels which, as it is, are often and easily lost, but just as easily replaced. . . . The Indian does not even exercise care when he could conveniently do so. A European is likely to shake his head at the boundless indifference of these people who drag brand-new objects, precious clothing, fresh provisions, and valuable items through thick mud, or abandon them to their swift destruction by children and dogs. . . . Expensive things that are given them are treasured for a few hours, out of curiosity; after that they thoughtlessly let everything deteriorate in the mud and wet. The less they own, the more comfortable they can travel, and what is ruined they occasionally replace. Hence, they are completely indifferent to any material possessions. (Gusinde, 1961, pp. 86–7)

The hunter, one is tempted to say, is "uneconomic man." At least as concerns nonsubsistence goods, he is the reverse of that standard caricature immortalized in any *General Principles of Economics*, page one. His wants are scarce and his means (in relation) plentiful. Consequently he is "comparatively free of material pressures," has "no sense of possession," shows "an undeveloped sense of property," is "completely indifferent to any material pres-

sures," manifests a "lack of interest" in developing his technological equipment.

In this relation of hunters to worldly goods there is a neat and important point. From the internal perspective of the economy, it seems wrong to say that wants are "restricted," desires "restrained," or even that the notion of wealth is "limited." Such phrasings imply in advance an Economic Man and a struggle of the hunter against his own worse nature, which is finally then subdued by a cultural vow of poverty. The words imply the renunciation of an acquisitiveness that in reality was never developed, a suppression of desires that were never broached. Economic Man is a bourgeois construction – as Marcel Mauss said, "not behind us, but before, like the moral man." It is not that hunters and gatherers have curbed their materialistic "impulses"; they simply never made an institution of them. "Moreover, if it is a great blessing to be free from a great evil, our [Montagnais] Savages are happy; for the two tyrants who provide hell and torture for many of our Europeans, do not reign in their great forests, – I mean ambition and avarice . . . as they are contented with a mere living, not one of them gives himself to the Devil to acquire wealth" (LeJeune, 1897, p. 213).

We are inclined to think of hunters and gatherers as *poor* because they don't have anything; perhaps better to think of them for that reason as *free*. "Their extremely limited material possessions relieve them of all cares with regard to daily necessities and permit them to enjoy life" (Gusinde, 1961, p. 1).

Subsistence

When Herskovits was writing his *Economic Anthropology* (1958), it was common anthropological practice to take the Bushmen or the native Australians as "a classic illustration of a people whose economic resources are of the scantiest," so precariously situated that "only the most intense application makes survival possible." Today the "classic" understanding can be fairly reversed – on evidence largely from these two groups. A good case can be made that hunters and gatherers work less than we do; and, rather than a continuous travail, the food quest is intermittent, leisure abundant, and there is a greater

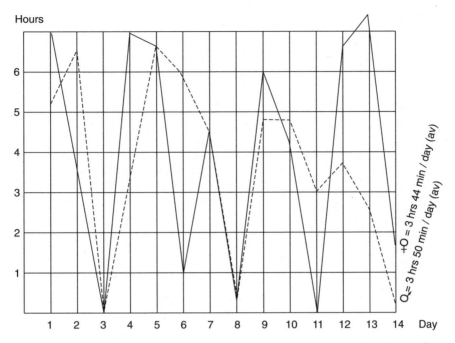

Figure 3.4   Hours per day in food-connected activities: Fish Creek Group (McCarthy and McArthur 1960).

amount of sleep in the daytime per capita per year than in any other condition of society.

Some of the substantiating evidence for Australia appears in early sources, but we are fortunate especially to have now the quantitative materials collected by the 1948 American-Australian Scientific Expedition to Arnhem Land. Published in 1960, these startling data must provoke some review of the Australian reportage going back for over a century, and perhaps revision of an even longer period of anthropological thought. The key research was a temporal study of hunting and gathering by McCarthy and McArthur (1960), coupled to McArthur's analysis of the nutritional outcome.

Figures 3.3 and 3.4 summarize the principal production studies. These were short-run observations taken during nonceremonial periods. The record for Fish Creek (14 days) is longer as well as more detailed than that for Hemple Bay (seven days). Only adults' work has been reported, so far as I can tell. The diagrams incorporate information on hunting, plant collecting, preparing foods, and repairing weapons, as tabulated by the ethnographers. The people in both camps were free-ranging native Australians, living outside mission or other settlements during the period of study, although such was not necessarily their permanent or even their ordinary circumstance.[13]

One must have serious reservations about drawing general or historical inferences from the Arnhem Land data alone. Not only was the context less than pristine and the time of study too brief, but certain elements of the modern situation may have raised productivity above aboriginal levels: metal tools, for example, or the reduction of local pressure on food resources by depopulation. And our uncertainty seems rather doubled than neutralized by other current circumstances that, conversely, would lower economic efficiency: these semi-independent hunters, for instance, are probably not as skilled as their ancestors. For the moment, let us consider the Arnhem Land conclusions as experimental, potentially credible in the measure they are supported by other ethnographic or historic accounts.

The most obvious, immediate conclusion is that the people do not work hard. The average length of

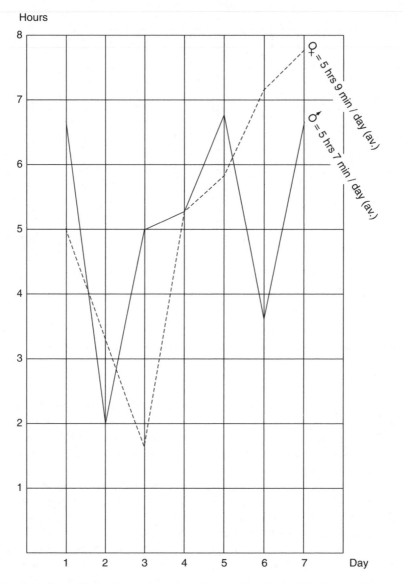

Figure 3.5 Hours per day in food-connected activities: Hemple Bay Group (McCarthy and McArthur 1960).

time per person per day put into the appropriation and preparation of food was four or five hours. Moreover, they do not work continuously. The subsistence quest was highly intermittent. It would stop for the time being when the people had procured enough for the time being, which left them plenty of time to spare. Clearly in subsistence as in other sectors of production, we have to do with an economy of specific, limited objectives. By hunting and gathering these objectives are apt to be irregularly accomplished, so the work pattern becomes correspondingly erratic.

In the event, a third characteristic of hunting and gathering unimagined by the received wisdom: rather than straining to the limits of available labor and disposable resources, these Australians seem to *underuse* their objective economic possibilities.

Table 3.1 Mean daily consumption as percentage of recommended allowances (from McArthur, 1960)

	Calories	Protein	Iron	Calcium	Ascorbic Acid
Hemple Bay	116	444	80	128	394
Fish Creek	104	544	33	355	47

The quantity of food gathered in one day by any of these groups could in every instance have been increased. Although the search for food was, for the women, a job that went on day after day without relief [but see our figures 3.3 and 3.4], they rested quite frequently, and did not spend all the hours of daylight searching for and preparing food. The nature of the men's food-gathering was more sporadic, and if they had a good catch one day they frequently rested the next. . . . Perhaps unconsciously they weigh the benefit of greater supplies of food against the effort involved in collecting it, perhaps they judge what they consider to be enough, and when that is collected they stop. (McArthur, 1960, p. 92)

It follows, fourthly, that the economy was not physically demanding. The investigators' daily journal indicates that the people pace themselves; only once is a hunter described as "utterly exhausted" (McCarthy and McArthur, 1960, pp. 150f.). Neither did the Arnhem Landers themselves consider the task of subsistence onerous. "They certainly did not approach it as an unpleasant job to be got over as soon as possible, nor as a necessary evil to be postponed as long as possible" (McArthur, 1960, p. 92).[14] In this connection, and also in relation to their underuse of economic resources, it is noteworthy that the Arnhem Land hunters seem not to have been content with a "bare existence." Like other Australians (cf. Worsley, 1961, p. 173), they become dissatisfied with an unvarying diet; some of their time appears to have gone into the provision of diversity over and above mere sufficiency (McCarthy and McArthur, 1960, p. 192).

In any case, the dietary intake of the Arnhem Land hunters was adequate – according to the standards of the National Research Council of America. Mean daily consumption per capita at Hemple Bay was 2,160 calories (only a four-day period of obser-

vation), and at Fish Creek 2,130 calories (11 days). Table 3.1 indicates the main daily consumption of various nutrients, calculated by McArthur in percentages of the NRCA recommended dietary allowances.

Finally, what does the Arnhem Land study say about the famous question of leisure? It seems that hunting and gathering can afford extraordinary relief from economic cares. The Fish Creek group maintained a virtually full-time craftsman, a man 35 or 40 years old, whose true specialty however seems to have been loafing:

He did not go out hunting at all with the men, but one day he netted fish most vigorously. He occasionally went into the bush to get wild bees' nests. *Wilira* was an expert craftsman who repaired the spears and spear-throwers, made smoking-pipes and drone-tubes, and hafted a stone axe (on request) in a skillful manner; apart from these occupations he spent most of his time talking, eating and sleeping. (McCarthy and McArthur, 1960, p. 148)

Wilira was not altogether exceptional. Much of the time spared by the Arnhem Land hunters was literally spare time, consumed in rest and sleep (see tables 3.2 and 3.3). The main alternative to work, changing off with it in a complementary way, was sleep:

Apart from the time (mostly between definitive activities and during cooking periods) spent in general social intercourse, chatting, gossiping and so on, some hours of the daylight were also spent resting and sleeping. On the average, if the men were in camp, they usually slept after lunch from an hour to an hour and a half, or sometimes even more. Also after returning from fishing or hunting they usually had a sleep, either immediately they arrived or whilst game was being

Table 3.2 Daytime rest and sleep, Fish Creek group (data from McCarthy and McArthur, 1960)

Day	♂ Average	♀ Average
1	2′15″	2′45″
2	1′30″	1′0″
3	Most of the day	
4	Intermittent	
5	Intermittent and most of late afternoon	
6	Most of the day	
7	Several hours	
8	2′0″	2′0″
9	50″	50″
10	Afternoon	
11	Afternoon	
12	Intermittent, afternoon	
13	–	–
14	3′15″	3′15″

Table 3.3 Daytime rest and sleep, Hemple Bay group (data from McCarthy and McArthur, 1960)

Day	♂ Average	♀ Average
1	–	45″
2	Most of the day	2′45″
3	1′0″	–
4	Intermittent	Intermittent
5	–	1′30″
6	Intermittent	Intermittent
7	Intermittent	Intermittent

cooked. At Hemple Bay the men slept if they returned early in the day but not if they reached camp after 4.00 p.m. When in camp all day they slept at odd times and always after lunch. The women, when out collecting in the forest, appeared to rest more frequently than the men. If in camp all day, they also slept at odd times, sometimes for long periods. (McCarthy and McArthur, 1960, p. 193)

The failure of Arnhem Landers to "build culture" is not strictly from want of time. It is from idle hands.

So much for the plight of hunters and gatherers in Arnhem Land. As for the Bushmen, economically likened to Australian hunters by Herskovits, two excellent recent reports by Richard Lee show their condition to be indeed the same (Lee, 1968, 1969). Lee's research merits a special hearing not only because it concerns Bushmen, but specifically the Dobe section of !Kung Bushmen, adjacent to the Nyae Nyae about whose subsistence – in a context otherwise of "material plenty" – Mrs. Marshall expressed important reservations. The Dobe occupy an area of Botswana where !Kung Bushmen have been living for at least a hundred years, but have only just begun to suffer dislocation pressures. (Metal, however, has been available to the Dobe since 1880–90.) An intensive study was made of the subsistence production of a dry season camp with a population (41 people) near the mean of such settlements. The observations extended over four weeks during July and August 1964, a period of transition from more to less favorable seasons of the year, hence fairly representative, it seems, of average subsistence difficulties.

Despite a low annual rainfall (6 to 10 inches), Lee found in the Dobe area a "surprising abundance of vegetation." Food resources were "both varied and abundant," particularly the energy-rich mangetti nut – "so abundant that millions of the nuts rotted on the ground each year for want of picking" (all references in Lee, 1969, p. 59).[15] His reports on time spent in food-getting are remarkably close to the Arnhem Land observations. Table 3.4 summarizes Lee's data.

The Bushman figures imply that one man's labor in hunting and gathering will support four or five people. Taken at face value, Bushman food collecting is more efficient than French farming in the period up to World War II, when more than 20 percent of the population were engaged in feeding the rest. Confessedly, the comparison is misleading, but not as misleading as it is astonishing. In the total population of free-ranging Bushmen contacted by Lee, 61.3 percent (152 of 248) were effective food producers; the remainder were too young or too old to contribute importantly. In the particular camp under scrutiny, 65 percent were "effectives." Thus the ratio of food producers to the general population is actually 3 : 5 or 2 : 3. *But*, these 65 percent of the people "worked 36 percent of the time, and 35 percent of the people did not work at all" (Lee, 1969, p. 67)!

Table 3.4 Summary of Dobe Bushmen work diary (from Lee, 1969)

Week	Mean group size[a]	Man-days of consumption[b]	Man-days of work	Days of work/ week/adult	Index of subsistence effort[c]
1	25.6	179	37	2.3	.21
(July 6–12)	(23–29)				
2	28.3	198	22	1.2	.11
(July 13–19)	(23–37)				
3	34.3	240	42	1.9	.18
(July 20–6)	(29–40)				
4	35.6	249	77	3.2	.31
(July 27–Aug. 2)	(32–40)				
4-week totals	30.9	866	178	2.2	.21
Adjusted totals[d]	31.8	668	156	2.5	.23

[a] Group size shown in average and range. There is considerable short-term population fluctuation in Bushmen camps.

[b] Includes both children and adults, to give a combined total of days of provisioning required/week.

[c] This index was constructed by Lee to illustrate the relation between consumption and the work required to produce it: $S = W/C$, where W = number of man-days of work, and C = man-days of consumption. Inverted, the formula would tell how many people could be supported by a day's work in subsistence.

[d] Week 2 was excluded from the final calculations because the investigator contributed some food to the camp on two days.

For each adult worker, this comes to about two and one-half days' labor per week. ("In other words, each productive individual supported herself or himself and dependents and still had 3-½ to 5-½ days available for other activities.") A "day's work" was about six hours; hence the Dobe work week is approximately 15 hours, or an average of 2 hours 9 minutes per day. Even lower than the Arnhem Land norms, this figure however excludes cooking and the preparation of implements. All things considered, Bushmen subsistence labors are probably very close to those of native Australians.

Also like the Australians, the time Bushmen do not work in subsistence they pass in leisure or leisurely activity. One detects again that characteristic paleolithic rhythm of a day or two on, a day or two off – the latter passed desultorily in camp. Although food collecting is the primary productive activity, Lee writes, "the majority of the people's time (four to five days per week) is spent in other pursuits, such as resting in camp or visiting other camps" (1969, p. 74):

A woman gathers on one day enough food to feed her family for three days, and spends the rest of her time resting in camp, doing embroidery, visiting other camps, or entertaining visitors from other camps. For each day at home, kitchen routines, such as cooking, nut cracking, collecting firewood, and fetching water, occupy one to three hours of her time. This rhythm of steady work and steady leisure is maintained throughout the year. The hunters tend to work more frequently than the women, but their schedule is uneven. It is not unusual for a man to hunt avidly for a week and then do no hunting at all for two or three weeks. Since hunting is an unpredictable business and subject to magical control, hunters sometimes experience a run of bad luck and stop hunting for a month or longer. During these periods, visiting, entertaining, and especially dancing are the primary activities of men. (1968, p. 37)

The daily per-capita subsistence yield for the Dobe Bushmen was 2,140 calories. However, taking into account body weight, normal activities, and the age-sex composition of the Dobe population, Lee estimates the people require only 1,975 calories per capita. Some of the surplus food probably went to the dogs, who ate what the people left over. "The conclusion can be drawn that the Bushmen do not lead a substandard existence on the edge of starvation as has been commonly supposed" (1969, p. 73).

Taken in isolation, the Arnhem Land and Bushmen reports mount a disconcerting if not decisive attack on the entrenched theoretical position. Artificial in construction, the former study in particular is reasonably considered equivocal. But the testimony of the Arnhem Land expedition is echoed at many points by observations made elsewhere in Australia, as well as elsewhere in the hunting-gathering world. Much of the Australian evidence goes back to the nineteenth century, some of it to quite acute observers careful to make exception of the aboriginal come into relation with Europeans, for "his food supply is restricted, and . . . he is in many cases warned off from the waterholes which are the centers of his best hunting grounds" (Spencer and Gillen, 1899, p. 50).

The case is altogether clear for the well-watered areas of southeastern Australia. There the Aboriginals were favored with a supply of fish so abundant and easily procured that one squatter on the Victorian scene of the 1840s had to wonder "how that sage people managed to pass their time before my party came and taught them to smoke" (Curr, 1965, p. 109). Smoking at least solved the economic problem – nothing to do: "That accomplishment fairly acquired . . . matters went on flowingly, their leisure hours being divided between putting the pipe to its legitimate purpose and begging my tobacco." Somewhat more seriously, the old squatter did attempt an estimate of the amount of time spent in hunting and gathering by the people of the then Port Phillip's District. The women were away from the camp on gathering expeditions about six hours a day, "half of that time being loitered away in the shade or by the fire"; the men left for the hunt shortly after the women quit camp and returned around the same time (p. 118). Curr found the food thus acquired of "indifferent quality" although

"readily procured," the six hours a day "abundantly sufficing" for that purpose; indeed the country "could have supported twice the number of Blacks we found in it" (p. 120). Very similar comments were made by another old-timer, Clement Hodgkinson, writing of an analogous environment in northeastern New South Wales. A few minutes fishing would provide enough to feed "the whole tribe" (Hodgkinson, 1845, p. 223; cf. Hiatt, 1965, pp. 103–104). "Indeed, throughout all the country along the eastern coast, the blacks have never suffered so much from scarcity of food as many commiserating writers have supposed" (Hodgkinson, 1845, p. 227).

But the people who occupied these more fertile sections of Australia, notably in the southeast, have not been incorporated in today's stereotype of an Aborigine. They were wiped out early.[16] The European's relation to such "Blackfellows" was one of conflict over the continent's riches; little time or inclination was spared from the process of destruction for the luxury of contemplation. In the event, ethnographic consciousness would only inherit the slim pickings: mainly interior groups, mainly desert people, mainly the Arunta. Not that the Arunta are all that bad off – ordinarily, "his life is by no means a miserable or a very hard one" (Spencer and Gillen, 1899, p. 7).[17] But the Central tribes should not be considered, in point of numbers or ecological adaptation, typical of native Australians (cf. Meggitt, 1964). The following tableau of the indigenous economy provided by John Edward Eyre, who had traversed the south coast and penetrated the Flinders range as well as sojourned in the richer Murray district, has the right to be acknowledged at least as representative:

Throughout the greater portion of New Holland, where there do not happen to be European settlers, and invariably when fresh water can be permanently procured upon the surface, the native experiences no difficulty whatever in procuring food in abundance all the year round. It is true that the character of his diet varies with the changing seasons, and the formation of the country he inhabits; but it rarely happens that any season of the year, or any description of country does not yield him both animal and vegetable food. . . . Of these [chief] articles [of food], many are not only procurable in abundance, but in such vast quantities at the proper seasons, as to afford for a considerable length of time an ample means of subsistence to many hundreds of natives congregated at one place. . . . On many parts of the coast, and in the larger inland rivers, fish are obtained of a very fine description, and in great abundance. At Lake Victoria . . . I have seen six hundred natives encamped together, all of whom were living at the time upon fish procured from the lake, with the addition, perhaps, of the leaves of the mesembryanthemum. When I went amongst them I never perceived any scarcity in their camps. . . . At Moorunde, when the Murray annually inundates the flats, fresh-water cray-fish make their way to the surface of the ground . . . in such vast numbers that I have seen four hundred natives live upon them for weeks together, whilst the numbers spoiled or thrown away would have sustained four hundred more. . . . An unlimited supply of fish is also procurable at the Murray about the beginning of December. . . . The number [of fish] procured . . . in a few hours is incredible. . . . Another very favourite article of food, and equally abundant at a particular season of the year, in the eastern portion of the continent, is a species of moth which the natives procure from the cavities and hollows of the mountains in certain localities. . . . The tops, leaves, and stalks of a kind of cress, gathered at the proper season of the year . . . furnish a favourite, and inexhaustible supply of food for an unlimited number of natives. . . . There are many other articles of food among the natives, equally abundant and valuable as those I have enumerated. (Eyre, 1845, vol. 2, pp. 250–4)

Both Eyre and Sir George Grey, whose sanguine view of the indigenous economy we have already noted ("I have always found the greatest abundance in their huts"), left specific assessments, in hours per day, of the Australians' subsistence labors. (This in Grey's case would include inhabitants of quite undesirable parts of western Australia.) The testimony of these gentlemen and explorers accords very closely with the Arnhem Land averages obtained by McCarthy and McArthur. "In all ordinary seasons," wrote Grey (that is, when the people are not confined to their huts by bad weather), "they can obtain, *in two or three hours* a sufficient supply of food for the day, but their usual custom is to roam indolently from spot to spot, lazily collecting it as they wander along" (1841, vol. 2, p. 263; emphasis mine). Similarly, Eyre states: "In almost every part of the continent which I have visited, where the presence of

Europeans, or their stock, has not limited, or destroyed their original means of subsistence, I have found that the natives could usually, *in three or four hours*, procure as much food as would last for the day, and that without fatigue or labour" (1845, pp. 254–5; emphasis mine).

The same discontinuity of subsistence of labor reported by McArthur and McCarthy, the pattern of alternating search and sleep, is repeated, furthermore, in early and late observations from all over the continent (Eyre, 1845, vol. 2, pp. 253–4; Bulmer, in Smyth, 1878, vol. 1, p. 142; Mathew, 1910, p. 84; Spencer and Gillen, 1899, p. 32; Hiatt, 1965, pp. 103–4). Basedow took it as the general custom of the Aboriginal: "When his affairs are working harmoniously, game secured, and water available, the aboriginal makes his life as easy as possible; and he might to the outsider even appear lazy" (1925, p. 116).[18]

Meanwhile, back in Africa the Hadza have been long enjoying a comparable ease, with a burden of subsistence occupations no more strenuous in hours per day than the Bushmen or the Australian Aboriginals (Woodburn, 1968). Living in an area of "exceptional abundance" of animals and regular supplies of vegetables (the vicinity of Lake Eyasi), Hadza men seem much more concerned with games of chance than with chances of game. During the long dry season especially, they pass the greater part of days on end in gambling, perhaps only to lose the metal-tipped arrows they need for big game hunting at other times. In any case, many men are "quite unprepared or unable to hunt big game even when they possess the necessary arrows." Only a small minority, Woodburn writes, are active hunters of large animals, and if women are generally more assiduous at their vegetable collecting, still it is at a leisurely pace and without prolonged labor (cf. p. 51; Woodburn, 1966). Despite this nonchalance, and an only limited economic cooperation, Hadza "nonetheless obtain sufficient food without undue effort." Woodburn offers this "very rough approximation" of subsistence-labor requirements: "Over the year as a whole probably an average of less than two hours a day is spent obtaining food" (Woodburn, 1968, p. 54).

Interesting that the Hadza, tutored by life and not by anthropology, reject the neolithic revolution in order to *keep* their leisure. Although surrounded by cultivators, they have until recently refused to take up agriculture themselves, "mainly on the grounds that this would involve too much hard work."[19] In this they are like the Bushmen, who respond to the neolithic question with another: "Why should we plant, when there are so many mongomongo nuts in the world?" (Lee, 1968, p. 33). Woodburn moreover did form the impression, although as yet unsubstantiated, that Hadza actually expend less energy, and probably less time, in obtaining subsistence than do neighboring cultivators of East Africa (1968, p. 54).[20] To change continents but not contents, the fitful economic commitment of the South American hunter, too, could seem to the European outsider an incurable "natural disposition":

> the Yamana are not capable of continuous, daily hard labor, much to the chagrin of European farmers and employers for whom they often work. Their work is more a matter of fits and starts, and in these occasional efforts they can develop considerable energy for a certain time. After that, however, they show a desire for an incalculably long rest period during which they lie about doing nothing, without showing great fatigue. . . . It is obvious that repeated irregularities of this kind make the European employer despair, but the Indian cannot help it. It is his natural disposition. (Gusinde, 1961, p. 27)[21]

The hunter's attitude towards farming introduces us, lastly, to a few particulars of the way they relate to the food quest. Once again we venture here into the internal realm of the economy, a realm sometimes subjective and always difficult to understand; where, moreover, hunters seem deliberately inclined to overtax our comprehension by customs so odd as to invite the extreme interpretation that either these people are fools or they really have nothing to worry about. The former would be a true logical deduction from the hunter's nonchalance, on the premise that his economic condition is truly exigent. On the other hand, if a livelihood is usually easily procured, if one can usually expect to succeed, then the people's seeming imprudence can no longer appear as such. Speaking to unique developments of the market economy, to its institutionalization of scarcity, Karl Polanyi said that our "animal dependence upon food has been bared and the

naked fear of starvation permitted to run loose. Our humiliating enslavement to the material, which all human culture is designed to mitigate, was deliberately made more rigorous" (1947, p. 115). But our problems are not theirs, the hunters and gatherers. Rather, a pristine affluence colors their economic arrangements, a trust in the abundance of nature's resources rather than despair at the inadequacy of human means. My point is that otherwise curious heathen devices become understandable by the people's confidence, a confidence which is the reasonable human attribute of a generally successful economy.[22]

Consider the hunter's chronic movements from camp to camp. This nomadism, often taken by us as a sign of a certain harassment, is undertaken by them with a certain abandon. The Aboriginals of Victoria, Smyth recounts, are as a rule "lazy travellers. *They have no motive to induce them to hasten their movements*. It is generally late in the morning before they start on their journey, and there are many interruptions by the way" (1878, vol. 1, p. 125; emphasis mine). The good *Père* Biard in his *Relation* of 1616, after a glowing description of the foods available in their season to the Micmac ("Never had Solomon his mansion better regulated and provided with food"), goes on in the same tone:

> In order to thoroughly enjoy this, their lot, our foresters start off to their different places with as much pleasure as if they were going on a stroll or an excursion; they do this easily through the skillful use and great convenience of canoes . . . so rapidly sculled that, without any effort, in good weather you can make thirty or forty leagues a day; nevertheless we scarcely see these Savages posting along at this rate, for their days are all nothing but pastime. They are never in a hurry. Quite different from us, who can never do anything without hurry and worry. (Biard, 1897, pp. 84–5)

Certainly, hunters quit camp because food resources have given out in the vicinity. But to see in this nomadism merely a flight from starvation only perceives the half of it; one ignores the possibility that the people's expectations of greener pastures elsewhere are not usually disappointed. Consequently their wandering, rather than anxious, take on all the qualities of a picnic outing on the Thames.

A more serious issue is presented by the frequent and exasperated observation of a certain "lack of foresight" among hunters and gatherers. Oriented forever in the present, without "the slightest thought of, or care for, what the morrow may bring" (Spencer and Gillen, 1899, p. 53), the hunter seems unwilling to husband supplies, incapable of a planned response to the doom surely awaiting him. He adopts instead a studied unconcern, which expresses itself in two complementary economic inclinations.

The first, prodigality: the propensity to eat right through all the food in the camp, even during objectively difficult times, "as if," LeJeune said of the Montagnais, "the game they were to hunt was shut up in a stable." Basedow wrote of native Australians, their motto "might be interpreted in words to the effect that while there is plenty for today never care about tomorrow. On this account an Aboriginal is inclined to make one feast of his supplies, in preference to a modest meal now and another by and by" (1925, p. 116). LeJeune even saw his Montagnais carry such extravagance to the edge of disaster:

> In the famine through which we passed, if my host took two, three, or four Beavers, immediately, whether it was day or night, they had a feast for all neighboring Savages. And if those people had captured something, they had one also at the same time; so that, on emerging from one feast, you went to another, and sometimes even to a third and a fourth. I told them that they did not manage well, and that it would be better to reserve these feasts for future days, and in doing this they would not be so pressed with hunger. They laughed at me. "Tomorrow" (they said) "we shall make another feast with what we shall capture." Yes, but more often they capture only cold and wind. (LeJeune, 1807, pp. 281–3)

Sympathetic writers have tried to rationalize the apparent impracticality. Perhaps the people have been carried beyond reason by hunger: they are apt to gorge themselves on a kill because they have gone so long without meat – and for all they know they are likely to soon do so again. Or perhaps in making one feast of his supplies a man is responding to binding social obligations, to important imperatives of sharing. LeJeune's experience would confirm either view, but it also suggests a third. Or rather, the

Montagnais have their own explanation. They are not worried by what the morrow may bring because as far as they are concerned it will bring more of the same: "another feast." Whatever the value of other interpretations, such self-confidence must be brought to bear on the supposed prodigality of hunters. More, it must have some objective basis, for if hunters and gatherers really favored gluttony over economic good sense, they would never have lived to become the prophets of this new religion.

A second and complementary inclination is merely prodigality's negative side: the failure to put by food surpluses, to develop food storage. For many hunters and gatherers, it appears, food storage cannot be proved technically impossible, nor is it certain that the people are unaware of the possibility (cf. Woodburn, 1968, p. 53). One must investigate instead what in the situation precludes the attempt. Gusinde asked this question, and for the Yahgan found the answer in the selfsame justifiable optimism. Storage would be "superfluous,"

> because throughout the entire year and with almost limitless generosity the sea puts all kinds of animals at the disposal of the man who hunts and the woman who gathers. Storm or accident will deprive a family of these things for no more than a few days. Generally no one need reckon with the danger of hunger, and everyone almost anywhere finds an abundance of what he needs. Why then should anyone worry about food for the future! . . . Basically our Fuegians know that they need not fear for the future, hence they do not pile up supplies. Year in and year out they can look forward to the next day, free of care. (Gusinde, 1961, pp. 336, 339)

Gusinde's explanation is probably good as far as it goes, but probably incomplete. A more complex and subtle economic calculus seems in play – realized however by a social arithmetic exceedingly simple. The advantages of food storage should be considered against the diminishing returns to collection within the compass of a confined locale. An uncontrollable tendency to lower the local carrying capacity is for hunters *au fond des choses*: a basic condition of their production and main cause of their movement. The potential drawback of storage is exactly that it engages the contradiction between wealth and mobility. It would anchor the camp to an area soon depleted of natural food supplies. Thus immobilized by their accumulated stocks, the people may suffer by comparison with a little hunting and gathering elsewhere, where nature has, so to speak, done considerable storage of her own – of foods possibly more desirable in diversity as well as amount than men can put by. But this fine calculation – in any event probably symbolically impossible (cf. Codere, 1968) – would be worked out in a much simpler binary opposition, set in social terms such as "love" and "hate." For as Richard Lee observes (1969, p. 75), the technically neutral activity of food accumulation or storage is morally something else again, "hoarding." The efficient hunter who would accumulate supplies succeeds at the cost of his own esteem, or else he gives them away at the cost of his (superfluous) effort. As it works out, an attempt to stock up food may only reduce the overall output of a hunting band, for the have-nots will content themselves with staying in camp and living off the wherewithal amassed by the more prudent. Food storage, then, may be technically feasible, yet economically undesirable, and socially unachievable.

If food storage remains limited among hunters, their economic confidence, born of the ordinary times when all the people's wants are easily satisfied, becomes a permanent condition, carrying them laughing through periods that would try even a Jesuit's soul and worry him so that – as the Indians warn – he could become sick:

> I saw them, in their hardships and in their labors, suffer with cheerfulness. . . . I found myself, with them, threatened with great suffering; they said to me, "We shall be sometimes two days, sometimes three, without eating, for lack of food; take courage, *Chihiné*, let thy soul be strong to endure suffering and hardship; keep thyself from being sad, otherwise thou wilt be sick; see how we do not cease to laugh, although we have little to eat." (LeJeune, 1897, p. 283; cf. Needham, 1954, p. 230)

Rethinking Hunters and Gatherers

> Constantly under pressure of want, and yet, by travelling, easily able to supply their wants, their lives lack neither excitement or pleasure. (Smyth, 1878, vol. 1, p. 123)

Clearly, the hunting-gathering economy has to be revaluated, both as to its true accomplishments and its true limitations. The procedural fault of the received wisdom was to read from the material circumstances to the economic structure, deducing the absolute difficulty of such a life from its absolute poverty. But always the cultural design improvises dialectics on its relationship to nature. Without escaping the ecological constraints, culture would negate them, so that at once the system shows the impress of natural conditions and the originality of a social response – in their poverty, abundance.

What are the real handicaps of the hunting-gathering *praxis*? Not "low productivity of labor," if existing examples mean anything. But the economy is seriously afflicted by the *imminence of diminishing returns*. Beginning in subsistence and spreading from there to every sector, an initial success seems only to develop the probability that further efforts will yield smaller benefits. This describes the typical curve of food-getting within a particular locale. A modest number of people usually sooner than later reduce the food resources within convenient range of camp. Thereafter, they may stay on only by absorbing an increase in real costs or a decline in real returns: rise in costs if the people choose to search farther and farther afield, decline in returns if they are satisfied to live on the shorter supplies or inferior foods in easier reach. The solution, of course, is to go somewhere else. Thus the first and decisive contingency of hunting-gathering: it requires movement to maintain production on advantageous terms.

But this movement, more or less frequent in different circumstances, more or less distant, merely transposes to other spheres of production the same diminishing returns of which it is born. The manufacture of tools, clothing, utensils, or ornaments, however easily done, becomes senseless when these begin to be more of a burden than a comfort. Utility falls quickly at the margin of portability. The construction of substantial houses likewise becomes absurd if they must soon be abandoned. Hence the hunter's very ascetic conceptions of material welfare: an interest only in minimal equipment, if that; a valuation of smaller things over bigger; a disinterest in acquiring two or more of most goods; and the like. Ecological pressure assumes a rare form of concreteness when it has to be shouldered. If the gross product is trimmed down in comparison with other economies, it is not the hunter's productivity that is at fault, but his mobility.

Almost the same thing can be said of the demographic constraints of hunting-gathering. The same policy of *débarrassement* is in play on the level of people, describable in similar terms and ascribable to similar causes. The terms are, cold-bloodedly: diminishing returns at the margin of portability, minimum necessary equipment, elimination of duplicates, and so forth – that is to say, infanticide, senilicide, sexual continence for the duration of the nursing period, etc., practices for which many food-collecting peoples are well known. The presumption that such devices are due to an inability to support more people is probably true – if "support" is understood in the sense of carrying them rather than feeding them. The people eliminated, as hunters sometimes sadly tell, are precisely those who cannot effectively transport themselves, who would hinder the movement of family and camp. Hunters may be obliged to handle people and goods in parallel ways, the draconic population policy an expression of the same ecology as the ascetic economy. More, these tactics of demographic restraint again form part of a larger policy for counteracting diminishing returns in subsistence. A local group becomes vulnerable to diminishing returns – so to a greater velocity of movement, or else to fission – in proportion to its size (other things equal). Insofar as the people would keep the advantage in local production, and maintain a certain physical and social stability, their Malthusian practices are just cruelly consistent. Modern hunters and gatherers, working their notably inferior environments, pass most of the year in very small groups widely spaced out. But rather than the sign of underproduction, the wages of poverty, this demographic pattern is better understood as the cost of living well.

Hunting and gathering has all the strengths of its weaknesses. Periodic movement and restraint in wealth and population are at once imperatives of the economic practice and creative adaptations, the kinds of necessities of which virtues are made. Precisely in such a framework, affluence becomes possible. Mobility and moderation put hunters' ends within range of their technical means. An undevel-oped mode of production is thus rendered highly effective. The hunter's life is not as difficult as it looks from the outside. In some ways the economy reflects dire ecology, but it is also a complete inversion.

Reports on hunters and gatherers of the ethno-logical present – specifically on those in marginal environments – suggest a mean of three to five hours per adult worker per day in food production. Hunters keep banker's hours, notably less than modern industrial workers (unionized), who would surely settle for a 21–35 hour week. An interesting comparison is also posed by recent studies of labor costs among agriculturalists of neolithic type. For example, the average adult Hanunoo, man or woman, spends 1,200 hours per year in swidden cul-tivation (Conklin, 1957, p. 151); which is to say, a mean of three hours twenty minutes per day. Yet this figure does not include food gathering, animal raising, cooking and other direct subsistence efforts of these Philippine tribesmen. Comparable data are beginning to appear in reports on other primitive agriculturalists from many parts of the world. The conclusion is put conservatively when put nega-tively: hunters and gatherers need not work longer getting food than do primitive cultivators. Extrapo-lating from ethnography to prehistory, one may say as much for the neolithic as John Stuart Mill said of all labor-saving devices, that never was one invented that saved anyone a minute's labor. The neolithic saw no particular improvement over the paleolithic in the amount of time required per capita for the production of subsistence; probably, with the advent of agriculture, people had to work harder.

There is nothing either to the convention that hunters and gatherers can enjoy little leisure from tasks of sheer survival. By this, the evolutionary inadequacies of the paleolithic are customarily explained, while for the provision of leisure the neolithic is roundly congratulated. But the tradi-tional formulas might be truer if reversed: the amount of work (per capita) increases with the evolution of culture, and the amount of leisure decreases. Hunters' subsistence labors are charac-teristically intermittent, a day on and a day off, and modern hunters at least tend to employ their time off in such activities as daytime sleep. In the tropical habitats occupied by many of these existing hunters, plant collecting is more reliable than hunting itself. Therefore, the women, who do the collecting, work rather more regularly than the men, and provide the greater part of the food supply. Man's work is often done. On the other hand, it is likely to be highly erratic, unpredictably required; if men lack leisure, it is then in the Enlightenment sense rather than the literal. When Condorcet attributed the hunter's unprogressive condition to want of "the leisure in which he can indulge in thought and enrich his understanding with new combinations of ideas," he also recognized that the economy was a "necessary cycle of extreme activity and total idleness." Apparently what the hunter needed was the *assured* leisure of an aristocratic *philosophe*.

Hunters and gatherers maintain a sanguine view of their economic state despite the hardships they sometimes know. It may be that they sometimes know hardships because of the sanguine views they maintain of their economic state. Perhaps their confidence only encourages prodigality to the extent the camp falls casualty to the first untoward circumstance. In alleging this is an affluent economy, therefore, I do not deny that certain hunters have moments of difficulty. Some do find it "almost inconceivable" for a man to die of hunger, or even to fail to satisfy his hunger for more than a day or two (Woodburn, 1968, p. 52). But others, especially certain very peripheral hunters spread out in small groups across an environment of extremes, are exposed periodically to the kind of inclemency that interdicts travel or access to game. They suffer – although perhaps only fractionally, the shortage affecting particular immobilized families rather than the society as a whole (cf. Gusinde, 1961, pp. 306–7).

Still, granting this vulnerability, and allowing the most poorly situated modern hunters into comparison, it would be difficult to prove that privation is distinctly characteristic of the hunter-gatherers. Food shortage is not the indicative property of this mode of production as opposed to others; it does not mark off hunters and gatherers as a class or a general evolutionary stage. Lowie asks:

But what of the herders on a simple plane whose maintenance is periodically jeopardized by plagues – who, like some Lapp bands of the nineteenth century were obliged to fall back on fishing? What of the primitive peasants who clear and till without compensation of the soil, exhaust one plot and pass on to the next, and are threatened with famine at every drought? Are they any more in control of misfortune caused by natural conditions than the hunter-gatherer? (1938, p. 286)

Above all, what about the world today? One-third to one-half of humanity are said to go to bed hungry every night. In the Old Stone Age the fraction must have been much smaller. *This* is the era of hunger unprecedented. Now, in the time of the greatest technical power, is starvation an institution. Reverse another venerable formula: the amount of hunger increases relatively and absolutely with the evolution of culture.

This paradox is my whole point. Hunters and gatherers have by force of circumstances an objectively low standard of living. But taken as their *objective*, and given their adequate means of production, all the people's material wants usually can be easily satisfied. The evolution of economy has known, then, two contradictory movements: enriching but at the same time impoverishing, appropriating in relation to nature but expropriating in relation to man. The progressive aspect is, of course, technological. It has been celebrated in many ways: as an increase in the amount of need-serving goods and services, an increase in the amount of energy harnessed to the service of culture, an increase in productivity, an increase in division of labor, and increased freedom from environmental control. Taken in a certain sense, the last is especially useful for understanding the earliest stages of technical advance. Agriculture not only raised society above the distribution of natural food resources, it allowed neolithic communities to maintain high degrees of social order where the requirements of human existence were absent from the natural order. Enough food could be harvested in some seasons to sustain the people while no food would grow at all; the consequent stability of social life was critical for its material enlargement. Culture went on then from triumph to triumph, in a kind of progressive contravention of the biological law of the minimum, until it proved it could support human life in outer space – where even gravity and oxygen were naturally lacking.

Other men were dying of hunger in the market places of Asia. It has been an evolution of structures as well as technologies, and in that respect like the mythical road where for every step the traveller advances his destination recedes by two. The structures have been political as well as economic, of power as well as property. They developed first within societies, increasingly now between societies. No doubt these structures have been functional, necessary organizations of the technical development, but within the communities they have thus helped to enrich they would discriminate in the distribution of wealth and differentiate in the style of life. The world's most primitive people have few possessions, *but they are not poor.* Poverty is not a certain small amount of goods, nor is it just a relation between means and ends; above all it is a relation between people. Poverty is a social status. As such it is the invention of civilization. It has grown with civilization, at once as an invidious distinction between classes and more importantly as a tributary relation – that can render agrarian peasants more susceptible to natural catastrophes than any winter camp of Alaskan Eskimo.

All the preceding discussion takes the liberty of reading modern hunters historically, as an evolutionary base line. This liberty should not be lightly granted. Are marginal hunters such as the Bushmen of the Kalahari any more representative of the paleolithic condition than the Indians of California or the Northwest Coast? Perhaps not. Perhaps also Bushmen of the Kalahari are not even representative of marginal hunters. The great majority of surviving hunter-gatherers lead a life curiously decapitated and extremely lazy by comparison with the other few. The other few are very different. The Murngin, for example: "The first impression that any stranger must receive in a fully functioning group in Eastern Arnhem Land is of industry. . . . "And he must be impressed with the fact that with the exception of very young children . . . there is no idleness" (Thomson, 1949a, pp. 33–4). There is nothing to indicate that the problems of livelihood are more difficult for these people than for other hunters (cf. Thomson, 1949b). The incentives of their unusual industry lie elsewhere: in "an elaborate and exacting ceremonial life," specifically in an elaborate ceremonial exchange cycle that bestows prestige on craftsmanship and trade (Thomson, 1949a, pp. 26, 28, 34f,. 87 passim). Most other hunters have no such concerns. Their existence is comparatively colorless, fixed singularly on eating with gusto and digesting at leisure. The cultural orientation is not Dionysian or Apollonian, but "gastric," as Julian Steward said of the Shoshoni. Then again it may be Dionysian, that is, Bacchanalian: "Eating among the Savages is like drinking among the drunkards of Europe. Those dry and ever-thirsty souls would willingly end their lives in a tub of malmsey, and the Savages in a pot full of meat; those over there tale only of drinking, and these here only of eating" (LeJeune, 1897, p. 249).

It is as if the superstructures of these societies had been eroded, leaving only the bare subsistence rock, and since production itself is readily accomplished, the people have plenty of time to perch there and talk about it. I must raise the possibility that the ethnography of hunters and gatherers is largely a record of incomplete cultures. Fragile cycles of ritual and exchange may have disappeared without trace, lost in the earliest stages of colonialism, when the intergroup relations they mediated were attacked and confounded. If so, the "original" affluent society will have to be rethought again for its originality, and the evolutionary schemes once more revised. Still this much history can always be rescued from existing hunters: the "economic problem" is easily solvable by paleolithic techniques. But then, it was not until culture neared the height of its material achievements that it erected a shrine to the Unattainable: *Infinite Needs.*

Notes

1 At least to the time Lucretius was writing (Harris, 1968, pp. 26–7).
2 On the historically particular requisites of such calculation, see Codere, 1968 (especially pp. 574–5).
3 For the complementary institutionalization of "scarcity" in the conditions of capitalist production, see Gorz, 1967, pp. 37–8.
4 It deserves mention that contemporary European-Marxist theory is often in accord with bourgeois economics on the poverty of the primitive. Cf. Boukharine, 1967; Mandel, 1962, vol. 1; and the economic history manual used at Lumumba University (listed in bibliography as "Anonymous, n.d.").

5   Elman Service for a very long time almost alone among ethnologists stood out against the traditional view of the penury of hunters. The present paper owes great inspiration to his remarks on the leisure of the Arunta (1963, p. 9), as well as to personal conversations with him.

6   The evident fault of White's evolutionary law is the use of "per capita" measures. Neolithic societies in the main harness a *greater total amount of energy* than preagricultural communities, because of the greater number of energy-delivering humans sustained by domestication. This overall rise in the social product, however, is not necessarily effected by an increased productivity of labor – which in White's view also accompanied the neolithic revolution. Ethnological data now in hand (see text *infra*) raise the possibility that simple agricultural regimes are not more efficient thermodynamically than hunting and gathering – that is, in energy yield per unit of human labor. In the same vein, some archaeology in recent years has tended to privilege stability of settlement over productivity of labor in explanation of the neolithic advance (cf. Braidwood and Wiley, 1962).

7   For a similar comment, referring to missionary misinterpretation of curing by blood consumption in eastern Australia, see Hodgkinson, 1845, p. 227.

8   Conditions of primitive hunting peoples must not be judged, as Carl Sauer notes, " 'from their modern survivors, now restricted to the most meagre regions of the earth, such as the interior of Australia, the American Great Basin, and the Arctic tundra and taiga. The areas of early occupation were abounding in food' " (cited in Clark and Haswell, 1964, p. 23).

9   Through the prison of acculturation one glimpses what hunting and gathering might have been like in a decent environment from Alexander Henry's account of his bountiful sojourn as a Chippewa in northern Michigan: see Quimby, 1962.

10 Turnbull similarly notes of Congo Pygmies: "The materials for the making of shelter, clothing, and all other necessary items of material culture are all at hand at a moment's notice." And he has no reservations either about subsistence: "Throughout the year, without fail, there is an abundant supply of game and vegetable foods" (1965, p. 18).

11 Certain food collectors not lately known for their architectural achievements seem to have built more substantial dwellings before being put on the run by Europeans. See Smyth, 1871, vol. 1. pp. 125–8.

12 But recall Gusinde's comment: "Our Fuegians procure and make their implements with little effort" (1961, p. 213).

13 Fish Creek was an inland camp in western Arnhem Land consisting of six adult males and three adult females. Hemple Bay was a coastal occupation on Groote Eylandt; there were four adult males, four adult females, and five juveniles and infants in the camp. Fish Creek was investigated at the end of the dry season, when the supply of vegetable foods was low; kangaroo hunting was rewarding, although the animals became increasingly wary under steady stalking. At Hemple Bay, vegetable foods were plentiful; the fishing was variable but on the whole good by comparison with other coastal camps visited by the expedition. The resource base at Hemple Bay was richer than at Fish Creek. The greater time put into food-getting at Hemple Bay may reflect, then, the support of five children. On the other hand, the Fish Creek group did maintain a virtually full-time specialist, and part of the difference in hours worked may represent a normal coastal-inland variation. In inland hunting, good things often come in large packages; hence, one day's work may yield two day's sustenance. A fishing-gathering regime perhaps produces smaller if steadier returns, enjoining somewhat longer and more regular efforts.

14 At least some Australians, the Yir-Yiront, make no linguistic differentiation between work and play (Sharp, 1958, p. 6).

15 This appreciation of local resources is all the more remarkable considering that Lee's ethnographic work was done in the second and third years of "one of the most severe droughts in South Africa's history" (1968, p. 39; 1969, p. 73n.).

16 As were the Tasmanians, of whom Bonwick wrote: "The Aborigines were never in want of food; though Mrs. Somerville has ventured to say of them in her 'Physical Geography' that they were 'truly miserable in a country where the means of existence were so scanty.' Dr. Jeannent, once Protector, writes: 'They must have been superabundantly supplied, and have required little exertion or industry to support themselves' "(Bonwick, 1870, p. 14).

17 This by way of contrast to other tribes deeper in the Central Australian Desert, and specifically under "ordinary circumstances," not the times of long-continued drought when "he has to suffer privation" (Spencer and Gillen, 1899, p. 7).

18 Basedow goes on to excuse the people's idleness on the grounds of overeating, then to excuse the overeating on the grounds of the periods of hunger natives, suffer, which he further explains by the droughts Australia is heir to, the effects of which have been exacerbated by the white man's exploitation of the country.

19   This phrase appears in a paper by Woodburn distrib-
     uted to the Wenner-Gren symposium on "Man the
     Hunter," although it is only elliptically repeated
     in the published account (1968, p. 55). I hope I do
     not commit an indiscretion or an inaccuracy citing it
     here.

20   "Agriculture is in fact the first example of servile labor
     in the history of man. According to biblical tradition,
     the first criminal, Cain, is a farmer" (Lafargue, 1911
     [1883] p. 11n.)

     It is notable too that the agricultural neighbors
     of both Bushmen and Hadza are quick to resort to
     the more dependable hunting-gathering life come
     drought and threat of famine (Woodburn, 1968, p.
     54; Lee, 1968, pp. 39–40).

21   This common distaste for prolonged labor manifested
     by recently primitive peoples under European
     employ, a distaste not restricted to ex-hunters, might
     have alerted anthropology to the fact that the tradi-
     tional economy had known only modest objectives,
     so within reach as to allow an extraordinary disen-
     gagement, considerable "relief from the mere
     problem of getting a living."

     The hunting economy may also be commonly
     underrated for its presumed inability to support spe-
     cialist production. Cf. Sharp, 1934–5, p. 37; Radcliffe-
     Brown, 1948, p. 43; Spencer, 1959, pp. 155, 196, 251;
     Lothrup, 1928, p. 71; Steward, 1938, p. 44. If there is
     not specialization, at any rate it is clearly for lack of
     a "market," not for lack of time.

22   At the same time that the bourgeois ideology of
     scarcity was let loose, with the inevitable effect of
     downgrading an earlier culture, it searched and found
     in nature the ideal model to follow if man (or at least
     the workingman) was ever to better his unhappy lot:
     the ant, the industrious ant. In this the ideology may
     have been as mistaken as in its view of hunters. The
     following appeared in the *Ann Arbor News*, January 27,
     1971, under the head, "Two Scientists Claim Ants a
     little Lazy": Palm Springs, Calif. (AP) – "Ants aren't
     all they are reported [reputed?] to be," say Drs.
     George and Jeanette Wheeler.

     The husband–wife researchers have devoted years
     to studying the creatures, heroes of fables on
     industriousness.

     "Whenever we view an anthill we get the impres-
     sion of a tremendous amount of activity, but that is
     merely because there are so many ants and they all
     look alike," the Wheelers concluded.

     "The individual ants spend a great deal of time
     just loafing. And, worse than that, the worker ants
     who are all females, spend a lot of time primping."

Bibliography

Anonymous (n.d.) *Aperçu d'histoire et d'économie: Vol. 1, Formations précapitalistes*. Moscow: Editions du Progrès.

Basedow, Herbert (1925) *The Australian Aboriginal*. Adelaide: Preece.

Biard, le Père Pierre (1897) "Relation of New France, of its Lands, Nature of the Country, and of its Inhabitants . . ." In R. G. Thwaites (ed.), *The Jesuit Relations and Allied Documents*, vol. 3. Cleveland: Burrows. (First French edition, 1616.)

Boas, Franz (1940) *Race, Language and Culture*. New York: Free Press.

Bonwick, James (1870) *Daily Life and Origin of the Tasmanians*. London: Low and Merston.

Boukharine, N. (1967) *La Théorie du matérialisme historique*. Paris: Editions Anthropos. (First Russian edition, 1921.)

Braidwood, Robert J. (1952) *The Near East and the Foundations for Civilization*. Eugene: Oregon State System of Higher Education.

Braidwood, Robert J. (1957) *Prehistoric Men*, 3rd ed. Chicago Natural History Museum Popular Series, Anthropology, Number 37.

Braidwood, Robert J. and Willey, Gordon R. (eds.) (1962) *Courses Toward Urban Life*. Chicago: Aldine.

Clark, Colin and Haswell, Margaret (1964) *The Economics of Subsistence Agriculture*. London: Macmillan.

Clark, Graham (1953) *From Savagery to Civilization*. New York: Schuman.

Codere, Helen (1968) "Money-Exchange Systems and a Theory of Money." *Man* (n.s.), 3: 557–77.

Conklin, Harold C. (1957) *Hanunoo Agriculture*. Rome: Food and Agriculture Organization of the United Nations.

Curr, E. M. (1965) *Recollections of Squatting in Victoria, then Called the Port Phillip District, from 1841–1851*. Melbourne: Melbourne University Press. (First edition, 1883.)

Dalton, George (1961) "Economic Theory and Primitive Society." *American Anthropologist*, 63: 1–25.

Eyre, Edward John (1845) *Journals of Expeditions of Discovery into Central Australia, and Overland from Adelaide to King George's Sound, in the Years 1840–41*. 2 vols. London: Boone.

Gorz, Andre (1967) *Le Socialisme difficile*. Paris: Seuil.

Grey, Sir George (1841) *Journals of Two Expeditions of Discovery in North-West and Western Australia, During the Years 1837, 38, and 39. . . . 2* vols. London: Boone.

Grinnell, George Bird (1923) *The Cheyenne Indians*. New Haven, CT: Yale University Press.

Gusinde, Martin (1961) *The Yamana*, 5 vols. New Haven, Conn.: Human relations Area Files. (German edition 1931.)

Harris, Marvin (1968) *The Rise of Anthropological Theory*. New York: Thomas Y. Crowell.

Haury, Emil W. (1962) "The Greater American Southwest." In J. Braidwood and G. R. Willey (eds.), *Courses toward Urban Life*. Chicago: Aldine.

Herskovits, Melville J. (1958) *Economic Anthropology*. New York: Knopf.

Hiatt, L. (1965) *Kinship and Conflict*. Canberra: Australian National University.

Hodgkinson, Clement (1845) *Australia, from Post Macquarie to Moreton Bay, with Descriptions of the Natives*. London: Boone.

Hoebel, E. Adamson (1958) *Man in the Primitive World*, 2nd ed. New York: McGraw-Hill.

Lafargue, Paul (1911) *The Right to be Lazy*. Chicago: Kerr. (First French edition 1883.)

Lee, Richard (1968) "What Hunters Do for a Living, or, How to Make Out on Scarce Resources." In R. Lee and I. DeVore (eds.), *Man the Hunter*. Chicago: Aldine.

Lee, Richard (1969) "!Kung Bushman Subsistence: An Input–Output Analysis." In A. Vayda (ed.), *Environment and Cultural Behavior*. Garden City, NY: Natural History Press.

Lee, Richard B. and DeVore Irven (eds.) (1968) *Man the Hunter*. Chicago: Aldine.

LeJeune, le Père Paul (1897) "Relation of What Occurred in New France in the Year 1634." In R. G. Thwaites (ed.), *The Jesuit Relations and Allied Documents*, vol. 6. Cleveland: Burrows. (First French edition, 1635.)

Lothrup, Samuel K. (1928) *The Indians of Tierra del Fuego*. New York: Museum of the American Indian, Heye Foundation.

Lowie, Robert H. (1938) "Subsistence." In F. Boas (ed.), *General Anthropology*. Boston: Heath.

Lowie, Robert H. (1946) *An Introduction to Cultural Anthropology*, 2nd ed. New York: Rinehart.

McArthur, Margaret (1960) "Food Consumption and Dietary Levels of Groups of Aborigines Living on Naturally Occurring Foods." In C. P. Mountford (ed.), *Records of the Australian-American Scientific Expedition to Arnhem Land, Vol. 2: Anthropology and Nutrition*. Melbourne: Melbourne University Press.

McCarthy, Frederick D. and McArthur, Margaret (1960) "The Food Quest and the Time Factor in Aboriginal Economic Life." In C. P. Mountford (ed.), *Records of the Australian-American Scientific Expedition to Arnhem Land, Vol. 2: Anthropology and Nutrition*. Melbourne: Melbourne University Press.

Mandel, Ernest (1962) *Traité d'économie marxiste*. 2 vols. Paris: Julliard.

Marshall, Lorna (1961) "Sharing, Talking, and Giving: Relief of Social Tensions Among !Kung Bushmen," *Africa*, 31: 231–49.

Mathew, John (1910) *Two Representative Tribes of Queensland*. London: Unwin.

Meggitt, Mervyn (1964) "Indigenous Forms of Government Among the Australian Aborigines." *Bijdragen tot de Taal- Land- en Volkenkunde*, 120: 163–80.

Needham, Rodney (1954) "Siriono and Penan: A Test of Some Hypotheses." *Southwestern Journal of Anthropology*, 10: 228–32.

Polanyi, Karl (1947) "Our Obsolete Market Mentality." *Commentary*, 3: 109–17.

Polanyi, Karl (1957) "The Economy as Instituted Process." In K. Polanyi, C. Arensberg, and H. Pearson (eds.), *Trade and Market in the Early Empires*. Glencoe: Free Press.

Polanyi, Karl (1959) "Anthropology and Economic Theory," in M. Fried (ed.), *Readings in Anthropology*, vol. 2. New York: Crowell.

Quimby, George I. (1962) "A Year with a Chippewa Family, 1763–1764." *Ethnohistory*, 9: 217–39.

Radcliffe-Brown, A. R. (1948) *The Andaman Islanders*. Glencoe: Free Press. (First edition 1922.)

Redfield, Robert (1953) *The Primitive World and its Transformations*. Ithaca, NY: Cornell University Press.

Service, Elman R. (1962) *Primitive Social Organization*. New York: Random House.

Service, Elman R. (1963) *Profiles in Ethnology*. New York: Harper & Row.

Sharp, Lauriston (1934–5) "Ritual Life and Economics of the Yir-Yiront of Cape York Peninsula." *Oceania*, 5: 19–42.

Sharp, Lauriston (1958) "People without Politics." In V. F. Ray (ed.), *Systems of Political Control and Bureaucracy in Human Societies*. American Ethnological Society. Seattle: University of Washington Press.

Smyth, R. Brough (1871, 1878) *The Aborigines of Victoria*, 2 vols. Melbourne: Government Printer.

Spencer, Baldwin and Gillen, F. J. (1899) *The Native Tribes of Central Australia*. London: Macmillan.

Spencer, Robert F. (1959) *The North Alaskan Eskimo: A Study in Ecology and Society*. Smithsonian Institution Bureau of American Ethnology Bulletin 171. Washington, DC: US Government Printing Office.

Steward, Julian (1938) *Basin-Plateau Aboriginal Sociopolitical Groups*. Smithsonian Institution Bureau of American Ethnology Bulletin 120. Washington, DC: US Government Printing Office.

Steward, Julian H. and Faron, Louis C. (1959) *Native Peoples of South America*. New York: McGraw-Hill.

Thomson, Donald F. (1949a) *Economic Structure and the Ceremonial Exchange Cycle in Arnhem Land*. Melbourne: Macmillan.

Thomson, Donald F. (1949b) "Arnhem Land: Explorations Among an Unknown People." *The Geographical Journal*, 113: 1–8; 114: 54–67.

Turnbull, Colin (1965) *Wayward Servants*. Garden City, NY: Natural History Press.

Van der Post, Laurens (1958) *The Lost World of the Kalahari*. New York: Morrow.

Warner, W. Lloyd (1964) *A Black Civilization*. New York: Harper & Row. (Harper "Torchback" from the edition of 1958; first edition 1937.)

White, Leslie A. (1949) *The Science of Culture*. New York: Farrar, Stauss.

White, Leslie A. (1959) *The Evolution of Culture*. New York: McGraw-Hill.

Woodburn, James (1968) "An Introduction to Hadza Ecology." In R. Lee and I. DeVore (eds.), *Man the Hunter*. Chicago: Aldine.

Woodburn, James (director) (1966) "The Hadza" (film available from the anthropological director, Department of Anthropology, London School of Economics).

Worsley, Peter M. (1961) "The Utilization of Food Resources by an Australian Aboriginal Tribe." *Acta Ethnographica*, 10: 153–90.

1   Make a list of all the ways we are reminded of time in our daily lives. Try to have at least 15 different ways.

2   What would it mean to say "time is a gift"? How different is "time as a gift" from "time as money"? How might such a view change our lives? Can you think of any negative aspects to this view of time?

3   Talk to a student with a cultural background different from your own. Ask him or her what they have noticed about Americans' view (or British or the normative view wherever you find yourself using this book) or approach to time. How is it different (or similar) to the approach with which they are familiar?

   OR If you are from another cultural background than most of the students around you, briefly describe any differences or similarities you notice between your own notion and approach to time and those that are dominant here.

EXERCISES

4

Language: We Are What We Speak

Is language quintessentially human or do some other animals possess it? Communication versus language. Writing. The symbolic function and metaphor: different languages, different worlds? The social function: what information do you obtain from a person's speech? How are race, class, and gender inflected in language?

Language: We Are What We Speak

We are what we speak in more ways than one. Speech is what makes us human; no other species speaks. When you hear someone speak and have no visual clues, such as on the telephone, think of all the things you can immediately grasp, or at least infer, about that person. Gender, nationality or ethnicity, region of origin, age, emotional attitude (anger, fear, sadness, elation), mental state (confident, anxious, confused), physical state (just waking up, cold, drunk), class, education, and often relationship to the hearer. All of this information is perceived almost without thinking but it predisposes you to respond in a certain way. The way this information is evaluated – the meaning given to it – is, of course, heavily influenced by your culture.

There is yet another way we are what we speak. Edward Sapir, a famous American linguist, captured it well:

> Human beings do not live in the objective world alone, nor alone in the world of social activity as ordinarily understood, but are very much at the mercy of the particular language which has become the medium of expression for their society. It is quite an illusion to imagine that one adjusts to reality essentially without the use of language and that language is merely an incidental means of solving specific problems of communication or reflection. The fact of the matter is that the "real world" is to a large extent unconsciously built up on the language habits of the group. No two languages are ever sufficiently similar to be considered as representing the same social reality. *The worlds in which different societies live are distinct worlds, not merely the same world with different labels attached.* (Sapir 1949: 69; emphasis mine)

This idea may be startling to you, for most of us are brought up believing that the "real world" is quite separate and distinct from language; we simply assume that language merely *reflects* that world. Language, in that view, presumes a kind of transparency or direct connection between words and things. This commonsense assumption has been called the "Adamic" view of language because that is how the biblical Adam in Genesis went around giving names to things.

> And out of the ground the Lord God formed every beast of the field, and every fowl of the air; and brought *them* unto Adam to see what he would call them: and what-soever Adam called every living creature, that *was* the name thereof. And Adam gave names to all cattle, and to the fowl of the air, and to every beast of the field. (Genesis 2: 19–20)

In this "Adamic" view of language, names or words are like labels hung onto things (whether those "things" are concrete objects or "feelings"). For a pointed but amusing attack on this view, see the short story by Ursula LeGuin (daughter of American anthropologist Albert Kroeber) included with this chapter. In addition, words are assumed to refer to things, thus all we need to do is to point to something and we will get the name for it. This view is reinforced because it appears to us that that is the way babies learn language. René Magritte, the surrealist painter, poked fun at this simplistic notion of language in his paintings where he tried to disrupt the association of word and thing, noting that "an object is never so closely attached to its name that another cannot be found that suits it better."[1] Michel Foucault picked up this theme in his book *This Is Not a Pipe* (1982), titled after one of Magritte's paintings. Learning a language is far more complicated than learning the names for things, as those of you who have tried to learn another language are keenly aware. Knowing the words for things does not allow you to speak properly or to get the sense of what someone is saying.

The commonsense view of language is that it is both a reflection *of* reality and that it *refers* primarily *to* reality. Since most of us assume that language is a transparent medium primarily for the purpose of communication, it is difficult to accept the idea that our thoughts, feelings, and descriptions are conditioned, even shaped, by the possibilities of our language. Yet the bilingual (or trilingual or more) among you know that no two languages are really equivalent; not only does each have a different feeling and tone, but the structures are different (some have no verb tenses, others put the subject at the end of the sentence), the vocabulary is different, and there are some things you simply cannot say in some languages. Translation, therefore, is not just a matter of finding the corresponding words in the other language, since sometimes there are no equivalents, but of trying to convey the sense and meaning. This can be exceedingly difficult. For example, you cannot say "I had a lot of fun" in Russian, because there is no word that translates as "fun." In addition, "Russian has a single word for 'happiness' and 'luck,' suggesting that happiness is more a matter of good fortune than an inalienable right" (Lourie and Mikhalev 1989). Nor is it possible to say something like "Starting one's own business can be quite a challenge," since there is no word that translates "challenge" in that sense. The authors believe the transformation of the Russian economy will provide ample opportunity for the invention of such a word.

Translation has often been a metaphor for what anthropologists do – they are thought to translate one culture into the terms of another, i.e., the anthropologist's

Figure 4.1   René Magritte, *Personnage marchant vers l'horizon* (1928–9). Collection of Staats-galerie Stuttgart, Stuttgart. © ADAGP, Paris and DACS, London 2004.

own. While accurate in a very broad sense, it also assumes that culture is like a text, "out there," and readily available for translation.[2] Yet, it is important to realize that the construction of a cultural text derives from the anthropologist's own experience of interaction and collaboration with the people among whom he or she is living.

This chapter, like the preceding ones, is divided roughly into two parts. In the first part we will examine theories of language and, although I will indicate some of the ways they have been used by anthropologists to develop models for thinking about culture, you should be able to make some analogies on your own. In the second part, we will move into the area of "sociolinguistics" – basically, how people use language. This division coincides to some degree with the distinction made by Ferdinand de Saussure, an enormously influential French linguist who had a signifi-cant impact on anthropology, particularly through the *structuralism* as developed by Claude Lévi-Strauss. Language, according to Saussure, is divided into *langue* and *parole*; *langue* is the systematic aspect of language, but it exists only in individual speaking acts, *parole*. Unlike other linguists of his era and before, he was not concerned with origins, grammar, or etymology; instead he was fascinated by the systematic aspects of language.

Theories of Language

Saussure was the first to realize that "language is a system of interdependent terms in which the value of each term results solely from the simultaneous presence of the others" (1959: 114). It must be a system, otherwise our speaking would make no sense. However, the system as a whole is not accessible; it does not exist some-*place*, instead we must infer it from individual acts of speaking. It is the job of the linguist or analyst to make the system more explicit. By analogy, this is how some people have come to think about culture. Culture, like language, does not exist some*place*, but must be inferred from non-verbal behavior as well as speech, other-wise social life would be incomprehensible.

Language is a symbolic system

Each of us inherits a language; we learn it as babies, which is why our native lan-guage is often called our "mother tongue." "No society, in fact, knows or has ever known language other than as a product inherited from preceding generations" (Saussure 1959: 71). It is through and through a *social* invention and a social institu-tion – no one person invented it. An artificial language such as Esperanto has not been fully adopted by any society, and if it were put into circula-tion it would be "transmitted according to laws which have nothing in common with those of its logical creation. . . . [It] would be borne along, willy-nilly, by the current that engulfs all languages" (p. 76). Computer "languages" are also artificial languages; they are not at all like natural lan-guages because their significations are fixed.

> Esperanto, meaning hopeful, was invented in 1887 by Ludwik L. Zamenhof, a Polish physician and oculist. Although there are alleged to be about 100,000 speakers in 83 countries, it has not really taken off as a worldwide language (*Encyclopedia Britannica*).

Language is not just a system, it is a completely *symbolic* system. There is no necessary connection between a sound (word) and the concept sig-nified; different languages have different words for the same concepts. This means that the relation is arbitrary and symbolic; each word *represents* a concept. Rather than representing or reflecting the world, each language represents a conceptual scheme. The origins of language lie in the misty past and may never be known; but what has become clear is that the capacity for symbolic thought was a major ingredient in the transformation of *homo sapiens* from its hominid ances-tors. According to philosopher Suzanne Langer, "it is not the essential act of thought that is symbolization, but an act *essential to thought*, and prior to it" ([1942] 1979: 41). Humans are symbol-making creatures. We did not first arrive at a fully complete, large-brained, and erect human body, and then create language and culture, they were an essential part of our *physical* evolution (see Geertz 1973).

Furthermore, contrary to popular belief, language appears to have developed not for practical reasons – not so humans could bring things to their hand or mouth – but "to bring things *into their minds*" (Langer [1942] 1979: 121), and to be able to ruminate about them *in absentia*. Langer gave the example of Helen Keller, a deaf and blind young woman who finally learned language not when she *needed* some-thing, like water, but when she realized that "water" symbolized or stood for the cool liquid flowing over her hands. Language is what allows us to think. "Real thinking is possible only in the light of genuine language" (p. 63).

Thinking is done with concepts or ideas. But ideas do not exist ready made before words – the words and the concepts coincide. Words unite "not a *thing* and a name, but a concept and a sound-image" (Saussure 1959: 66). Not only does this challenge our commonsense belief that words *mean* things, but it should also remind us that words are composed not of letters but of sounds. Writing comes much later and will be discussed shortly. A word, or *sign* in Saussure's usage, is like a sheet of paper. One side is the sound and the other the concept. Clearly, this relationship is arbitrary – there is no intrinsic reason to relate a specific slice of sound with a specific concept.

However, and maybe even more important, the meaning of that particular sign does not exist by itself but emerges *only* in relation to all the other signs, not the external world. Words are defined by other words; that is what a dictionary does. *Meaning*, therefore, is a function of an environment of signs, according to Saussure. Meaning, as we shall see later, is also a function of *context*. To get an idea of what Saussure meant, think about the nuances and differences between the words *afraid*, *fear*, *terrified*, and *dread*. We can distinguish between a present fear, in different degrees (*afraid*, *terrified*), and an anticipated fear (*dread*). The relation between *afraid* and the other two is one of intensity and that would be removed if there was no word *afraid*; the meaning would have to be divided between the other two. Think also of words for edibility – *appetizing, tasty, delicious, juicy, luscious, succulent*. They mutually condition each other and have slight variations in meaning that would be absent if we had only one word. (Why is it that all of these words can also be used to describe women? Does it mean that women are edible? We shall get to this kind of metaphoric transfer in a moment.) The issue here is that each word evokes and is conditioned by the range of synonyms and antonyms. Theories of language are a complicated subject but, for our purposes, the main points are:

1   language is a symbolic system;
2   there is no transparent relationship between words and things;
3   meaning is not the same as reference; and
4   the system is relatively arbitrary.

How does this change your thinking about language? Can you see the implications for theories of culture?

If there are no preexisting concepts but these are constructed simultaneously with language, then it is somewhat easier to understand why no two languages are exact equivalents. One important example is that some languages do not have abstract nouns for things like "time," but have a number of different words that characterize different qualities of what we call "time." Our language allows us to talk about time as if it is a concrete thing, as we discussed in the previous chapter. How could one philosophize about "the good, the true, and the beautiful" if there were no abstract nouns to symbolize these concepts? This, clearly, has major implications for philosophy, the practice of which is conducted, to a very large extent, in abstract terms and assumes a kind of universality to its thought. Yet different social groups have conceptualized things differently even though there might be considerable overlap between some of them. As a child, you learn the conceptual structure of the language you are taught. This doesn't mean that you can't learn other languages, but your native language will always remain your ground.

Communication vs. language

There are no simple or incomplete languages. Languages that do not have abstract nouns (see above) are not more rudimentary, they are just different. Hunters and gatherers have as grammatical and complete languages as do people living in contemporary New York. But "[b]etween the clearest animal call of love or warning or anger, and a man's least, trivial *word*, there lies a whole day of Creation – or in modern phrase, a whole chapter of evolution" (Langer [1942] 1979: 103). This is not to say that animals don't communicate, they do. Some of them can understand some language; for example, my cat seems to know her name and comes when I call her, and she responds to a number of other questions, commands, and terms of endearment.

There is a great deal of communication that goes on between humans and other animals. But communication is not the same thing as possessing language. The major questions about whether some animals have language concern the difference between (1) comprehension and performance, (2) sign-using and symbol-using, and (3) being able to communicate and being able to express a worldview. *Sign* in this instance does not have the same meaning that Saussure gave it; here it means something more like signal. (The confusion has to do with the difference between French and English.)

Linguist Emile Benveniste takes up the issue of "Animal Communication and Human Language" (1971) in his article of that title. His example is bees rather than hominids, whom we will discuss momentarily, for it has long been noticed that bees have some form of communication between each other. If one bee finds honey, it can go back to the hive and apparently "tell" the others. That bee does not have to lead them to the honey; the directions, communicated by means of some kind of dance, are sufficient. "The message passed on contains three items of information . . . the existence of a source of food, its distance, and its direction" (1971: 52). This is clearly a significant form of communication. But what it lacks, according to Benveniste, are the following: the message is relayed without voice, there is no dialogue or reply, and the message cannot be reproduced by another bee that has not seen whatever the first one saw. It is a "signal code," highly sophisticated, but not a language.

Perhaps the most striking thing that differentiates bee communication from human language is that bees cannot sit around discoursing about honey as "nectar of the gods," or use it as a term of endearment. Bee communication lacks the metaphorical possibilities of language. The difference, in Suzanne Langer's terms, is the mind. The mind is not just a transmitter – not just a switchboard to relay messages – but a transformer. The process of symbolization enables us to express a conception of life and of the world. Some symbolic ability seems also to be true of some of our nearest hominid neighbors.

Apes and language

Experiments teaching language to different kinds of hominids have included Koko, a gorilla, Washoe and Lana, chimpanzees, and Kanzi, a bonobo chimpanzee, to name only a few of the most famous. Not only do they understand some language but they can also communicate with some level of symbolic performance. They have been taught Ameslan (American Sign Language), a sign language for the deaf, and appear to be using it "in many of the ways that humans use it – to construct a world, to obtain desirables, and to regulate the behavior of others" (Hill 1980: 337). Hill, who summarized the findings of a number of experiments, said that some of these hominids have also creatively elaborated the signs that they know. For example, "Washoe produced 'water-bird' on first seeing ducks; . . . Lana used 'coke which is orange' for Fanta orange drink . . . and Koko signed 'finger bracelet' for ring, 'white tiger' for zebra" (p. 140). Koko has also been able to report on "her inner states of happiness, sadness, fear, and shame" (p. 341, citing Koko's trainer).

As of the year 2000, Koko was about 30 years old and appeared to have an understanding of, and ability to use, about 1,000 words according to the people who work with her, but the process has been extremely time-consuming and demanded incredible patience. A baby understands quite a lot of words before he or she is a year old and often talks in sentences by the age of 2. Due to the lack of vocal equipment that enables humans to speak, Koko, for all her remarkable achievements, cannot talk, and she does not appear to be able to transmit her facility with language to her offspring.

Since Hill's report, more recent work has been conducted with bonobo chimpanzees, and the results are even more haunting. Sue Savage-Rumbaugh, who has been working with some of these animals since 1980, developed a keyboard with a variety of signs for words. The chimps learned the meanings and could press the keys to "talk" to her and her assistants. Her primary subject was Matata, an adult female. Even after Matata gave birth to Kanzi, Savage-Rumbaugh continued to focus her teaching on Matata with the idea that she would start with Kanzi when he was about 2. However, it turned out that Kanzi was learning all along simply by listening and watching, just as human children do. One day, his mother was taken away for mating purposes; Savage-Rumbaugh expected to use that time to "begin more systematic instruction with Kanzi, making certain that he could both use and understand symbols" (Savage-Rumbaugh, Shanker, and Taylor 1998: 23). But to their astonishment, his secret skill erupted. On the first day after his mother left, Kanzi "produced 120 separate utterances" (p. 22) and used them correctly. Nor was it simply an accident, for he continued to "talk" and expand his knowledge and ability. As Savage-Rumbaugh noted:

> I was in a state of disbelief. It was several weeks before I and others working with Kanzi began to accept the fact that he had really learned to talk even though we had not been attempting to teach him. . . . It was not just that I had successfully taught him how to use symbols to stand for things. . . . I had not intentionally taught Kanzi anything, nor had I been able to teach his mother what he had somehow learned, even though I had been trying to do so for two years. (p. 25)

This remarkable achievement threw a wrench into her theories about teaching chimps to "talk" and forced her to develop new ones. From that time on she "decided to abandon all instruction and focus attention instead on what was *said to Kanzi* rather than on what we could teach him to say" (p. 27).

These examples are truly poignant signs of simian intelligence which should give pause to those who so easily kill these animals or put them in cages to be gawked at. Or, in Hill's words, "it seems clear that the experiments, while holding out the possibility of apes as particularly refined human surrogates, at the same time cast serious doubts on the ethics of using them in that role" (1980: 351).

The exception to this definition is, obviously, sign language, which is a fully human language even though it is not sound. This may be a place where the line between human and animal communication becomes blurred. In both cases, however, sign language must be *seen*; communication must be conducted face to face or perhaps, with new technology, by long-distance video.

In spite of the strides in these experiments with hominid language, many linguists still have doubts, believing that the animals are merely imitating their human trainers, or that the trainers are imagining hand signs when they do not exist. The recent studies using computers and/or keyboards with symbols and icons representing things and concepts raise questions about whether the animals have simply been taught to respond to certain cues without really using language. Savage-Rumbaugh, Shanker, and Taylor think part of the reluctance of linguists to accept animal language is because they have reified language and taken it out of the social contexts in which it is embedded. This is possible in literate societies where written language is separable from such contexts (Savage-Rumbaugh et al. 1998: 195). Clearly, the argument about whether some animals possess, or can be taught, language will continue, and the verdict is still open. The one thing the animals are *not* doing is speaking, and that is surely one of the first definitions of language – that it is primarily sound.

Orality vs. literacy

When we think of language, we generally think of the written word. When we learn a new language, we generally start with a textbook. Yet, as noted above, language is primarily an oral and aural phenomenon, that is, it is composed of intelligible *sounds*. Living, as we do, in a primarily print culture, we too easily forget this essential fact. Through the work of Walter J. Ong, specifically his book *Orality and Literacy: The Technologizing of the Word* ([1982] 1999), we will look briefly at some of the features of oral cultures and the social implications of literacy.

It is extremely difficult, says Ong, for us to put ourselves in the place of someone in a primary oral culture – "a culture where no one has ever 'looked up' anything" (Ong [1982] 1999: 31). If you were brought up in an oral culture you could not look up a word, nor could you *see* it in the mind's eye; a word would not be a visual thing. Speaking is an *event* and one that is evanescent. "Sound exists only when it is going out of existence. . . . [T]here is no way to stop sound and have sound. . . . [I]f I stop the movement of sound, I have nothing – only silence" (p. 32). There are no texts, so there can be no document to contradict a spoken statement or claim. At the same time, there are ways to aid memory in oral cultures:

In primary oral culture, to solve effectively the problem of retaining and retrieving carefully articulated thought, you have to do your thinking in mnemonic patterns, shaped for ready oral recurrence. Your thought must come into being in heavily rhythmic, balanced patterns, in repetitions or antitheses, in alliterations and assonances. (p. 34)

Knowledge of the world and the history of the group are communicated in poetic, narrative, and aphoristic form but are very much contextualized and communal. Generally, you speak *to* someone or a group of people. Speaking, therefore, assumes a response, what Ong calls an *agonistic* quality; there is an interaction between speaker and hearer. "Oral communication unites people in groups. Writing and reading are solitary activities" (p. 69). Writing distances and objectifies. It is writing that fosters the notion that words are merely labels hung onto things.

Writing

People were speaking for thousands of years before the invention of writing. And it is an invention; it is completely artificial and it is neither necessary nor inevitable. Therefore Ong suggests we ought not to call oral cultures illiterate, because of the pejorative sense of the term, nor pre-literate, which suggests an evolutionary trajectory, but simply "oral cultures." Writing was first invented sometime around 3500 BC by the Sumerians in ancient Mesopotamia. The impetus seems to have been urbanization and the need to control people, collect taxes, and plan projects, that is, for some kind of record keeping (see Schmandt-Besserat 1986).

The first writing, called *cuneiform*, was iconic, that is, it employed pictographs that had some resemblance to what was represented. Gradually these signs became more symbolic and abstract (see figure 4.2). But a "script in the sense of true writing . . . does not consist of mere pictures, of representations of things, but is a representation of an *utterance*, of words that someone says or is imagined to say" (Ong [1982] 1999: 84). Ong goes on to say that writing "was and is the most momentous of all human technological inventions. It is not a mere appendage to speech. Because it moves speech from the oral-aural to a new sensory world, that of vision, it transforms speech and *thought* as well" (p. 85; emphasis mine). In other words, it has transformed human consciousness. He claims we could not think as we do, particularly long, involved analytic formulations, without writing. Our thought patterns and our speech patterns have now been conditioned by the technique of writing. Writing is, to a certain extent, context-free; it need not have a present interlocutor or audience even though one must be imagined. But it is surely context-dependent in terms of culture and era, and the age, ethnicity, gender, education, and religious background of the writer.

Writing was further enhanced by the invention of the alphabet and then by print. "The most remarkable fact about the alphabet no doubt

A vast number of cuneiform tablets, some shaped like biscuits that included "envelopes," were stolen or destroyed when the Iraqi Museum in Baghdad was vandalized in April 2003 during the war. These tablets contained not just business records but the Epic of Gilgamesh and many stories reminiscent of those in the first part of Genesis. Many had never been photographed or deciphered. The loss is irreparable, and not just for Iraq or the Middle East. It is of world historical significance.

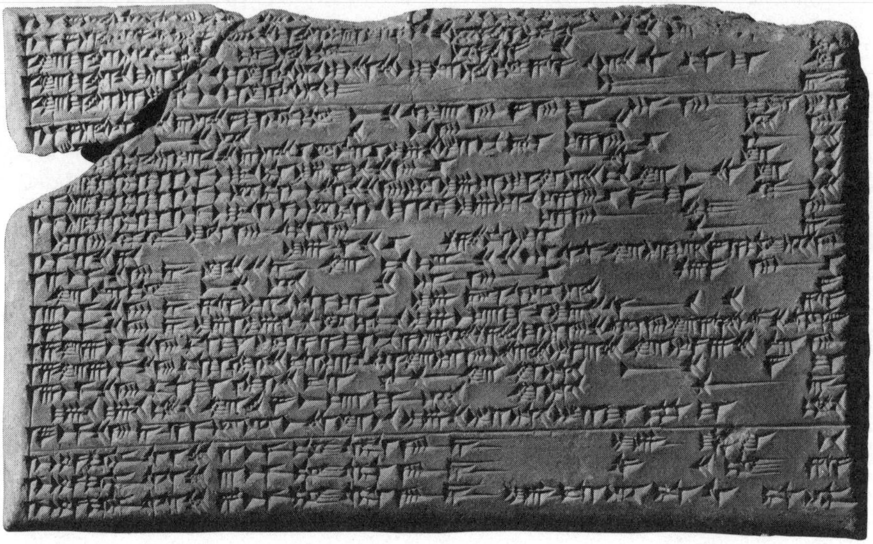

Figure 4.2 Cuneiform writing on a clay tablet, astronomical forecasts derived from obser-vations of the sun. 7th century BC, from Nineveh. British Museum, London. Photo Michael Holford.

is that it was invented only once. It was worked up by a Semitic people or Semitic peoples around the year 1500 BC, in the same general geographic area where the first of all scripts appeared, the cuneiform, but two millennia later than the cuneiform" (Ong [1982] 1999: 89). The Egyptians had used symbols for sounds but mixed them up with pictographs; it was the people living in the Levant who are believed to have invented the alphabet. Then the Phoenicians carried it to the Greeks who added vowels, and from them all modern alphabets derive. The phonetic alphabet makes writing much easier to learn and thus more democratic than it had been. Some writing systems such as Chinese are not alphabetic but have elaborate characters representing words, concepts, even whole phrases, and take many years to master.

The invention of moveable print type by Johann Gütenberg in the fifteenth century further enhanced the possibilities of the written word. No longer were manuscripts copied by hand by elite scribes but could be mass produced for a mass reading public. The Bible was not only the first book to appear in print, but it was printed in vernacular languages and no longer in the Learned Latin that had been the possession of the elite. People could finally read and interpret the Bible for themselves rather than having it mediated by priests, and this was a major factor contributing to the Protestant Revolution now known as the Reformation.

In Europe, Learned Latin had been the language not just of the church but of school and of international exchange. It was also a language of men. Although it had once been a mother tongue, "for well over a thousand years, it was sex-linked, a language written and spoken only by males, learned outside the home in a tribal

setting which was in effect a male puberty rite setting . . . it had no direct connection with anyone's unconscious of the sort that mother tongues, learned in infancy,
always have" (Ong [1982] 1999: 113). Latin was isolating and exclusive and, thus,
extremely powerful. Only certain privileged males were initiated; most of the great
scientists and philosophers did their thinking and writing in Latin. Although some
women learned to read and write, they were excluded from this kind of education;
when some of them began to put their thoughts on paper, they wrote in the vernacular and tended to focus on events and relationships in the domestic sphere to
which they were generally confined. Ong believes that women's very different life
experience led to the invention of the novel.

Writing was suspect when first invented, especially since it was the preserve of
the elite. But there were other reasons. In *Phaedrus*, Plato has Thamus, the King of
Egypt, say the following to Theuth, the god who invented letters:

> this invention will produce forgetfulness in the minds of those who learn to use it,
> because they will not practice their memory. Their trust in writing, produced by ex-
> ternal characters which are no part of themselves, will discourage the use of their own
> memory within them. You have invented an elixir not of memory, but of reminding;
> and you offer your pupils the appearance of wisdom, not true wisdom, for they will
> read many things without instruction and will therefore seem to know many things,
> when they are for the most part ignorant and hard to get along with, since they are
> not wise, but only appear wise.[3]

Not dissimilar criticism has been leveled at the use of computers. People already
complain that with the avalanche of email and other electronic information, they
cannot remember things. In addition to datebooks or palm pilots for keeping track
of meetings and appointments, many people now depend on the computer *memory*
to store what they need to know, assuming they can retrieve it at will. Like writing,
computers have also transformed the way we think. I know very well that I write
quite differently if I sit down with a pad of paper and a pencil than if I sit in front
of the computer screen. It is also far different from a typewriter, even an electric
one, because I can revise, erase, and move sentences around at will: sometimes,
when I do that, I notice that I lose track of the meaning.

Children are now often learning to type on the computer keyboard before they
can write; indeed, one wonders whether the art (or technique) of writing will soon
disappear. Perhaps, in the near future, we may revert to oral composition. Computers and telephones, for example, have "voice recognition." Very soon, I believe,
someone will speak into the computer and it will either transfer the message into
print or forward it by voice. Clearly this will be a boon to millions of non-literate
people around the world, but what will be the effect on literate cultures? Will writing
and print become a quaint artifact of the past?

Language, culture, and reality

We assume everyone sees the same things, that perception is, itself, the apparatus
that permits us to see. Yet, we see what we are trained to see, what we are

socialized to see. Each of us is born into a particular culture and language, as well as into a particular family, birth order, sex, class, ethnic group, and religion. Our parents or parental surrogates who guide our interactions and interpretations, and hence our experience, socialize us. They tell us what is there, what to look for, how to look for it, how to feel about it, what to think about it – in short, what it means. Language (and culture) is what mediates between us and the world or "reality," in other words, perception is not direct but always mediated. This is as true of what are called the "empirical sciences" as it is for ordinary everyday perception.

> Observation has become almost entirely indirect; and *readings* take the place of genuine witness. The sense-data on which the propositions of modern science rest are, for the most part, little photographic spots and blurs, or inky curved lines on paper. These data are empirical enough, but of course they are not themselves the phenomenon in question; the actual phenomena stand behind them as their supposed causes. Instead of watching the process that interests us, that is to be verified – say, a course of celestial events . . . – we really see only the fluctuations of a tiny arrow . . . and *calculate to the "facts" of our science*. What is directly observable is only a sign of the "physical fact"; it requires interpretation to yield scientific propositions. Not simply seeing is believing, but *seeing and calculating, seeing and translating*. (Langer [1942] 1979: 20)

These "facts" are through and through symbolic, for "facts" exist only in relation to a (conceptual, and therefore language-based) theory. Langer goes on to say that "the triumph of empiricism in science is jeopardized by the surprising truth that *our sense-data are primarily symbols*," indeed, "the edifice of human knowledge stands before us, not as a vast collection of sense reports, but as a structure of *facts that are symbols* and *laws that are their meanings*" (p. 21). If sense perception is guided by language, then it should be becoming clearer that we live in symbolically constructed worlds – a situation I have heard described as "an inverted pyramid in which only one block rests on the ground"![4]

If this is somewhat difficult to accept, let's try another tack. Benjamin Whorf who, along with Sapir, became one of the most famous linguists of the twentieth century, began his career as an investigator for a fire insurance company. What ignited his interest in linguistics was his observation that people acted on the basis of linguistic cues. One of his most memorable examples involved "empty" gasoline drums. Workers assumed the drums were not dangerous because they were empty, so they smoked and threw their cigarette butts around, and were surprised when there was an explosion. Most of us today now realize that vapor from "empty" gasoline drums is just as dangerous, perhaps more so, than containers full of gasoline.

Such examples in which just one word seemed to trigger behavior led Whorf to wonder about the full extent of a given language to model behavior. Like anthropologists who usually study other cultures before turning to their own, Whorf felt that the "best approach [to the study of language] is through an exotic language, for in its study we are at long last pushed willy-nilly out of our ruts. Then we find that the exotic language is a mirror held up to our own" (1956: 138). Consequently, he went on to study Native American languages, particularly Hopi. Almost at once he noticed important differences between Hopi and what he called Standard Average European (SAE).

One of the first things that struck him was the different representations of time in the Hopi language. In English we can say "ten men" and "ten days" as if they are somehow similar, standing in a row. Our language objectifies or quantifies time. In Hopi one cannot say "ten days" but only something like "he left on the eleventh day." We make nouns out of temporal phenomena and then assume that these are somehow objective units that we can stand in a row. In Hopi, summer or morning are not nouns but something like adverbs, "when it is the morning phase," or "when conditions are hot." But nothing influences our thought about time more than the "three-tense system of SAE verbs" (1956: 143). Whorf says that if "we inspect consciousness we find no past, present, future . . . [instead] everything is in consciousness," what we call the "present" is really the sensuous aspect – seeing, hearing, touching; what we call the "past" is the non-sensuous aspect of memory, while the future is the non-sensuous aspect of belief, intuition, and uncertainty (pp. 143–4). What we do experience is that everything gets later and later, but we lose this sense because of the way our language predisposes us to think about time. Quite a few languages have only two verb tenses – "earlier" and "later," and some have no verb tenses at all but express these aspects of time with other linguistic modifiers.

We objectify time and assume it is a kind of "thing" divisible into measurable units – it is another example of the way our language persuades us to think in terms of formless matter and form: a *glass* of water, a *cup* of coffee, a *moment* or *hour* of time. At the same time (!), Whorf notes that our "objectified view of time is, however, favorable to historicity and to everything connected with the keeping of records," whether these are diaries, histories, calendars, or projections. Whereas, for the Hopi, for whom "everything that ever happened still is [presumably in consciousness] . . . there is less incentive to study the 'past'" (p. 153).

In effect, we *spatialize* time or duration as well as other modalities. "All languages," says Whorf, "need to express durations, intensities, and tendencies" but "it is characteristic of SAE . . . to express them metaphorically. The metaphors are those of spatial extension, i.e., of size, number (plurality), position, shape, and motion" (p. 145). For example, Whorf says we

> express duration by long, short, great, much, quick, slow, etc.; intensity by large, great, much, heavy, light, high, low, sharp, faint, etc.; tendency by more, increase, grow, turn, get, approach, go, come, rise, fall, stop, smooth, even, rapid, slow; and so on through an almost inexhaustible list of metaphors that we hardly recognize as such, since they are virtually the only linguistic media available. (p. 145)

In other words, peoples with SAE languages tend to spatialize even the most non-spatial situations and we do not recognize this tendency as metaphoric and imaginary. Think, for example, of such common phrases as: *high* society, *lower* class, that's *deep*, getting *high*, warm *up*, cool *down*, *far out*, *shallow*, *uppity*, *down*town, *up*town, fooling *around*, hang *out*, the *in* crowd, etc. To most of us, these seem to characterize the situation as it *is*, we think these are normal, hardly metaphoric, statements.

The idea, proposed by both Sapir and Whorf, that language massively influences culture became known as the "Sapir–Whorf hypothesis." While there have been a number of critiques and most linguists and anthropologists no longer accept it *in toto*, it has, nevertheless, been extremely productive. Their primary focus was the *structure* of languages rather than the characteristic *ways* of saying things in each particular language. It is quite difficult to prove that there is a correlation between language structure and culture. But the idea that each language is a different conceptual system, and that there are characteristic ways of interpreting and expressing things, "fashions of speaking" in Whorf's terminology, that have an impact on culture, is a correlation that holds up very well. Perhaps it is not in the structure of language but in the metaphors utilized in each culture that habitual ways of thought, behavior, and worldview are best glimpsed.

Metaphor

George Lakoff and Mark Johnson imply the importance of metaphor in our lives by the title of their book, *Metaphors We Live By*. "If our conceptual system is largely metaphorical then the way we think, what we experience, and what we do every day is very much a matter of metaphor" (1980: 3). This was recognized long ago by Aristotle, who claimed: "The greatest thing by far is to be master of metaphor" (Aristotle, *Poetics*, 1459a). So too did Rousseau: "As man's first motives for speaking were of the passions, his first expressions were tropes. Figurative language was the first to be born" (*Essay on the Origin of Language*, in Moran and Gode 1967: 12). Suzanne Langer, whose influential theories about language and symbolization affected symbolic anthropology, felt keenly the constructive power of metaphor:

> The use of metaphor can hardly be called a conscious device. It is the power whereby language, even with a small vocabulary, manages to embrace a multimillion things; whereby new words are born and merely analogical meanings become stereotyped into literal definitions. . . . [S]peech becomes increasingly discursive, practical, prosaic, until human beings can actually believe that it was invented as a utility, and was later embellished with metaphors for the sake of a cultural product called poetry. (Langer [1942] 1979: 141–2)

She calls attention to the popular view that language is primarily for utilitarian communication rather than for expression (of a worldview). However, her discussion of Helen Keller and of dreams, ritual, and artistic creation challenges that view, and suggests that language enables the creation of a world to live in, that is, a culture.

Nevertheless, despite these advocates of the power and importance of metaphor, it has not fared very well in modern times. Instead, it is more commonly regarded as the "fancy dress of language" that covers up the "real, true, bones" of whatever is at issue. As Lakoff and Johnson state in the first paragraph of their book,

> Metaphor is for most people a device of the poetic imagination and the rhetorical flourish – a matter of extraordinary rather than ordinary language. Moreover, metaphor is typically viewed as a characteristic of language alone, a matter of words rather than thought or action. For this reason, most people think they can get along perfectly well without metaphor. We have found, on the contrary, that metaphor is pervasive in everyday life. (1980: 3)

The first example they use to illustrate their point is that we tend to think about argument as war. They say

> we don't just *talk* about arguments in terms of war. We can actually win or lose arguments. We see the person we are arguing with as an opponent. We attack his positions and we defend our own. We gain and lose ground. We plan and use strategies. If we find a position indefensible, we can abandon it and take a new line of attack. Many of the things we *do* in arguing are partially structured by the concept of war. Though there is no physical battle, there is a verbal battle, and the structure of an argument – attack, defense, counterattack, etc. – reflects this. It is in this sense that the ARGUMENT IS WAR metaphor is one that we live by in this culture; it structures the actions we perform in arguing. (p. 4)[5]

The authors ask the reader to imagine a culture in which "arguing" took the form of a dance. The structure would be different and so would the outcome, so much so that we would not see what they were doing as "argument." Lakoff and Johnson go on to stress that it is not just the words that are metaphoric, but the concept of what an argument, in essence, *is*. In this case, as in many others, the metaphors are not some cover-up or "fancy dress" but constitute reality for us.

In "Anthropological Aspects of Language: Animal Categories and Verbal Abuse," British anthropologist Edmund Leach analyzes the metaphoric construction of terms of abuse. "Why," he asks, "should expressions like 'you son of a bitch' or 'you swine' carry the connotations that they do, when 'you son of a kangaroo' or 'you polar bear' have no meaning whatsoever?" (1964: 29). What is the relationship between animal categories and terms of abuse? His answer, quite ingenious and somewhat complicated, depends on the widespread association between eating and sexual intercourse, even though what is eaten and who is an appropriate sexual partner can vary cross-culturally. Leach shows how the British classification of animals, in terms of distance from oneself, is homologous with a classification of both living environments and kinship relationships. Starting with the self and proceeding outward, Europeans and Americans classify kin in the following manner: (1) the closest are the nuclear family – the people with whom sexual relations, except for the married couple, are taboo; (2) next are kin but not as close – the category of first cousins – with whom marriage is forbidden or strongly disapproved, yet it is still permitted in 26 of the United States (*New York Times*, April 4, 2002; cf. Ottenheimer 1996) and is also practiced in parts of the Middle East, including Turkey; (3) neighbors (friends) who are not kin but potential affines (in-laws), the category from which one might expect to obtain a husband or wife; and finally, (4) distant strangers – people known to exist but with whom no social relations exist.

Analogously, the English, Leach claimed, "put most of their animals into four very comparable categories: (1) those who are very close, i.e., pets; you do not eat your pet dog; he is almost one of the family, and "man's best friend"; (2) those who are tame but not very close, i.e., farm animals who are edible if immature or castrated; (3) field animals, i.e., "game" – animals who live under human protection but are not tame – and who are edible only at certain set times of the year; and finally (4) remote wild animals deemed inedible. Terms of abuse derive from animals that are closest to us, and so too do terms of endearment, for example, we can say "you bitch" or "lamb"; furthermore, some of them "serve as near obscene euphemisms for unmentionable parts of the human anatomy" (cock, ass, pussy) (pp. 49–50). While the homology is not exact, and Leach did not answer the question of why the terms for female animals are the ones most commonly used as terms of abuse, the exercise revealed a number of important cultural beliefs.

Sexual metaphors

In my own work I have discovered that sexuality, particularly related to procreation, forms a massive metaphorical area that influences the way we think not only of men and women, but also of such seemingly unrelated areas as education and cosmology, whether scientific or religious. For thousands of years, the dominant *folk* theory of procreation in the West is what I have called the "seed-soil" theory (Delaney 1986, 1991). This theory is inscribed in some of our most influential texts: the Bible, the work of Plato and Aristotle, the writings of early and medieval Christian theologians, and Freud's work, for example, and persists even today on television, in popular songs, poems, and in turns of phrase. In this theory, the male is imagined as the one to plant the seed (*inseminate* literally means to put the seed in), which renders the woman analogous to the nurturant, or possibly barren, *soil*. This

These meanings might also make understandable the Catholic Church's position on birth control, abortion, and homosexuality. In a major document about human sexuality, *Humanae Vitae*, promulgated in 1968, the church stated that each marriage act (read heterosexual intercourse) must be open to the *transmission* of life, recapitulating the ancient idea that that life (or soul) is transmitted via semen. Yet life is not transmitted at all; it is a process that begins when ovum and sperm merge and mitosis begins – a process that normally takes place *inside* the woman's body (or today, occasionally on a petri dish). Homosexual acts (or masturbation) were imagined as "spilling of seed," and therefore seen as sinful, the loss of potential life.

seemingly simple and innocuous agricultural metaphor is a very important example of what Sylvia Yanagisako and I mean by "naturalizing power" (1995), because it attributes the creative, engendering, identity-giving role to the male; he *begets*. The child, in essence, is in the seed. The female is not imagined as co-creator, she *bears*. Her role is secondary and supportive; she merely nurtures the seed-child and brings it forth. The folk theory of procreation symbolically allies men with the creative, life-giving ability of God, and women with what was created *by* God (Nature). This analogy constitutes a metaphoric (and hierarchical) relationship between cosmology and humans.

Think of the different images and meanings evoked by the phrases "to father" and "to mother," paternity and maternity, and patrimony and matrimony. These images and meanings were established long ago, long before the science of genetics emerged whereby we now believe that both male and female, through sperm (from *sperma*, meaning seed) and ova, provide half the genetic endowment, half the *seed*, so to speak, to each child. In addition, of course, the woman also continues the nurturing role while the child is in the womb and after it is born. Until very recently that is the role that defined "mother," yet a mother's role has now been fragmented into birth mother, surrogate mother, genetic mother.

We think of the process of procreation as *reproduction*, a word that was not introduced to refer to the process until mid-nineteenth century and, at the time, was considered a quaint metaphor. Until then the biblical *begetting* and *bearing*, or *generation*, or *procreation* were used. To my mind, *reproduction* is not an improvement for it conjures images of churning out copies, like a Xerox machine. Because our gender definitions are so deep and independent from scientific theory, it is very difficult to change them unless conscious effort is expended to do so, and that will involve developing different metaphors and images.

The relation between the theory of procreation and the monotheistic view of Creation seems quite clear. But that is religion, what does it have to do with science? Yet scientific cosmologists have been searching for the grand unified theory (i.e., *one* "mono-theory" to explain the coming into being of the universe), and also to conceptualize the origin of the universe as a "single seed smaller than an atom" yet "so potent it blossomed into everything there is" – the single seed that exploded in the Big Bang?[6] Do you think people with different cosmologies and different theories of procreation would come to the same conclusions?

The same theory of procreation is carried into the area of education. Why do we have *fields* of study, *bodies* of knowledge? I believe that the *body* of knowledge is symbolically female because women have been associated with nature, that which is to be explored, subdued, penetrated, and exploited.[7] The explorer, scientist, "knower" is symbolically male, while that which is explored and known is symbolically female; this may derive from the biblical notion that to have sex was "to know." Similarly, the word *conceive* can refer to both intellectual and physical conceptions. *Seminal* ideas are defined as original and creative; women can have them, but the language suggests that creative thought is masculine in character. We do not hear of *ovulul* ideas, and *pregnant* ones, while auspicious, are merely potential. Because high-quality thinking is characterized as seminal and penetrating, do you think there might be some correlation to why women thinkers and scholars have not been taken as seriously as their male counterparts? What about the gendering of the "hard" vs. "soft" sciences, or more basic – the sciences vs. the humanities? Can you think of other gendered metaphors pertaining to the acquisition of knowledge?

The sexual metaphors have also shaped the image of the anthropologist in doing *field*work. Clifford Geertz characterized anthropological work as follows: "In the study of culture, analysis penetrates into the very body of the object" (1973: 15). Why must analysis "penetrate"? Why is culture imagined as a body? What kind of body? Why is the body passive and inert, an object (to be penetrated) rather than an active, living, participant, subject? Regardless of the *sex* of the analyst, the *gender* is masculine. The question is: are these merely words or do they shape the way we think and go about our studies? Philosopher Paul Ricoeur, who has written extensively on metaphor, considers it to be the supreme creative act, which carries cognitive import and expands knowledge, like Aristotle before him and anthropologist Marilyn Strathern[8] after him. Yet Ricoeur also perpetuates the sexual connotations for, to him, "metaphor is an idyll with a new partner who resists while giving in" (1976: 56).

Language in Use

The previous section has briefly introduced you to theory about language and its consequences; in this section I would like to shift to the more "sociolinguistic" aspects of language. Sociolinguistics is the study of the social uses of language – or language in use. Scholars interested in this side of language tend to study not just slang and regional variations of speaking but also the way gender, race, and class are indexed, which is closely related to the ways power and dominance are enacted linguistically. Since my own work has focused more on gender, that will get somewhat more attention here.

Language and gender

The word *gender* was first and foremost a linguistic term, referring to the way some languages classify words according to sex. For example, the articles *le* and *la* in French both mean *the*, but *le* modifies masculine nouns, as in *le soleil* (the sun), while *la* modifies feminine nouns, as in *la lune* (the moon). The gender of the noun also determines the indefinite article ("a"), as in *un* and *une*.

The use of the word *gender* to refer to the social and cultural meanings of male and female developed in the 1970s. Until then, most people simply assumed, and were socially encouraged to think, following Freud, that "biology is destiny." This meant that your biological sex, defined in relation to your role in reproduction, determined your social role.[9] However, if that is true, then you would expect that sex roles and definitions would be the same worldwide. But anthropologists had long known that the definitions of male and female, and the social roles they were expected to perform, varied considerably cross-culturally (e.g. Mead 1928, 1935, 1949). By the early 1970s, feminist anthropologists adopted the word *gender* to highlight that awareness and to utilize ethnographic knowledge to challenge mainstream Euro-American definitions of masculinity and femininity.[10] While sex and gender are surely related in some way, exactly how has not yet been conclusively determined. Instead, it has become clearer that gender is inextricably entwined with cosmology, religion, language, culture, economics, and kinship, as well as with sex and biology.

Once the anthropological concept of gender was invented, it was adopted and elaborated by scholars in a number of different fields, and it should be obvious that it does not apply just to women! The concept of gender has also helped men to question stereotypical definitions and roles of masculinity, and opened up a wider discussion that includes issues of homosexuality and transgender (see chapters 5 and 8). However, the word (and the concept) *gender* does not exist in many languages. It does not exist in French, for example, and French feminists have not tried to adopt it; instead, their strategy is to use only *sex* but try to show that it is not just about biology. For all their sophistication on the topic, particularly the relation between sex and language, the use of "sex" continues to plague their analyses.[11] "Gender" does not exist in Turkish either, and I was forced to use the word for "sex" (*cinsiyet*) in the Turkish translation of my book, *The Seed and the Soil: Gender and Cosmology in Turkish Village Society*, thus undermining my intention.

Pronouns

One of the first linguistic issues concerning gender had to do with pronouns, namely the use of *he* to stand for both *she* and *he* similar to the way that the generic *man* is intended to stand for both men and women, or what Wendy Martyna, among others, calls "He/Man" language (1980). Although we assume that men and women are covered by the general pronoun, it is not immediately obvious. Sometimes it does include both, but just as often it is intended to refer only to *males*. The US Constitution says: "All men are created equal," but women were not necessarily, or always, included, otherwise there would be no need for the Equal Rights Amendment which, to this day, has still not passed. Once you are sensitized to the question of inclusiveness of pronouns, reading can become difficult as you try to ascertain in each instance whether or not you are included. Through the consciousness-raising movements of the late 1960s and early 1970s, women began to hear themselves excluded in the very language around them, for example when a teacher said to a mother of a daughter, "every student must do *his* own homework," or when a politician said that "every voter must follow *his* own conscience in the stance *he* takes on the transportation bond issue" (Morton 1972: 181–2; emphasis mine). Nelle Morton, one of the first to write about this phenomenon, commented: "The prevalence of male terminology in the common speech appeared insignificant and even funny at first. Everybody knew that everybody did not mean literally male and that was that: *Then there came a time when it ceased to be funny.* Women began hearing themselves shut out of their own traditions" (p. 182). At first many people thought the issue of pronouns was silly; indeed, in 1971

> the linguistics faculty of Harvard criticized an attempt by a theology class to eliminate sexist language from its discussions: The fact that the masculine gender is the unmarked gender in English . . . is simply a feature of grammar . . . there is really no cause for anxiety or pronoun-envy on the part of those seeking such changes. (Martyna 1980: 483)

They would soon have to eat those words, for it became more and more obvious that the language was pervasively sexist. It is worth noting that the language issue became politicized first in religion and theology classes, in this case at Harvard Divinity School, which during the 1970s exploded with feminist critiques of theological language. (I know because I was there!) The critiques began with language but did not stop there; they went on to criticize the institutional structure and personnel of the organized religions, and then launched a wider critique of the society influenced by the monotheistic religions. In this, they echoed the first "wave" of the women's movement in the mid-nineteenth century, the spokeswomen of which critiqued the gendered language in the Bible, rewrote some biblical stories, and published them as *The Woman's Bible* (1898). It was quickly banned and not republished until 1974.

The problems hit close when we turn to the law: "Where a statute imposed duties or penalties on persons, where the masculine form was used it was asserted that women were included. . . . Yet where a statute imposed privileges or benefits upon persons, the opposite was the case: courts held that women were not intended to be included" (Hamilton, Hunter, and Stuart-Smith 1992: 341). It is quite disturbing to think that the law which is assumed to be impartial can be so selectively used.

The "pseudogeneric" *he*, as Debora Schweikart calls it, has not always been prescriptively used in the law, but only became so in the past 150 years. In Britain it was mandated in an Act of Parliament in 1850. The idea was first proposed by J. Kirkby in 1746, but perhaps reached its most explicit form in the following statement of grammarian Goold Brown:

> The gender of words, in many instances, is to be determined by the following principle of universal grammar. Those terms which are equally applicable to both sexes (if they are not expressly applied to females), and those plurals which are known to include both sexes, should be called masculine in parsing; for, *in all languages, the masculine gender is considered the most worthy*,† and is generally employed when both sexes are included under one common term. Thus *parents* is always masculine.
>
> † The Supreme Being (*God*, . . .) is, in all languages, masculine; in as much as the masculine sex is the superior and more excellent; and as He is the Creator of all, the Father of gods and men. (Schweikart 1998: 2, citing Brown, 1851; first emphasis mine)

It is clear that Brown did not know many languages or cultures for not all languages have gender, and surely not all religions have a masculine god, or even a god at all, as in the case of Buddhism and numerous others. But the statement is very telling about the relationship between gender, religion, and societies influenced by the Abrahamic religions (Judaism, Christianity, and Islam).

The issue of the pronoun can have serious consequences, as a number of legal scholars have begun to point out. For example, Hamilton, Hunter, and Stuart-Smith, in an article about jury instructions, ask "Can a woman claim self-defense when 'he' is threatened?" (1992: 340). In the language of the court, it actually becomes difficult to determine just who is the assailant and who the victim. In a case where a woman killed someone, allegedly in self-defense, these were part of the verbatim instructions to the jury (gendered pronoun italicized):

> when there is no reasonable ground for the person attacked to believe that *his* person is in imminent danger of death or great bodily harm, and it appears to *him* that only an ordinary battery is intended and is all that *he* has reasonable grounds to fear from *his* assailant, *he* has a right to stand *his* ground and repel such an assault. But *he* has *no right* to repel a threatened assault by the use of bare hands or a deadly weapon, unless *he* believes, and has reasonable grounds to believe, that *he* is in imminent danger of death or great bodily harm. (p. 342)

One begins to think that the assailant was the victim of the attack. This case was used in a study to determine the effect of the masculine generic *he* in comparison with *he and she*, or just *she*, as would have been appropriate in this case, and concluded that the results of the study "indicate that the most important decisions before the jury in many murder trials, the decision concerning self-defense, might potentially be affected by the pronoun used in jury instructions" (p. 346). That is serious business. Part of the problem has to do with the idea and ideal of the "reasonable man," that is, what would a reasonable man do in similar circumstances? But in situations of physical threat, it is not reasonable to compare women's behavior with men's.

The linguistic changes wrought by the twentieth-century women's movement have been far reaching and have become embedded in "normal" language, so much so that those of you reading this in the twenty-first century must think it all very odd and antiquated. For my part it is difficult to communicate the intensity of discussions about pronouns that took place in the media, academia, and across the kitchen table, let alone in the bedroom, during that not so long ago time.

Along with the discussion of pronouns came the awareness that a woman's marital status, but not a man's, was linguistically indicated. Two forms of address, *Miss* and *Mrs.*, contrast with just one, *Mr.*, for men. In order to change this unequal treatment, women campaigned for *Ms.* to apply to all women, but it has met with only limited success. In addition, married women's identity is further erased when they are addressed as Mrs. John Smith. Other words distinguish gender in English, for example, actor-actress; waiter-waitress; poet-poetess, etc.

Gendered language, even something as seemingly neutral as a pronoun, creates images in the mind that are difficult to supplant. They affect the way we imagine things to be and that affects the way we respond. What happens to girls when the books they read use only the male pronoun to refer to doctors, lawyers, archaeologists, or professors, and the female pronoun only in reference to nurses, teachers, or librarians? In addition, gendered language affects the way we imagine, reconstruct, and display the past, for example in theories of "Man the Hunter," or exhibits in museums of natural history, where men are portrayed as the actors (see, for example, Hager 1997; Haraway 1989; Landau 1991; Zihlman 1991). The gender critique of language did not stop with pronouns and forms of address.

Gendered talk

Other scholars were interested in the way language is used by each gender, noticing that "gender hierarchies display themselves in all domains of social behavior, not the least of which is talk" (Ochs 1992: 336). Girls are socialized to talk differently than boys. As a result, women's talk is more tentative and does not command the same attention as men's speech, in part because of rising intonation (at the end of sentences that are not questions), "hedges" (as in "I kind of wanted to go"), qualifiers ("that was so very, very nice of you"), phrases ("Oh dear, I dropped the house keys"), and tag questions ("that looks okay, doesn't it?") vs. direct commands (see Robin Lakoff's *Language and Woman's Place*, 1975). Others such as Deborah Tannen (1990) suggest that women speak to maintain connections, give support, preserve intimacy, and avoid isolation whereas men speak to preserve independence, negotiate hierarchy, give information, and avoid failure. It has been claimed that children recognize gendered language by the time they reach first grade (Edelsky 1976).

In a study that contrasted the white middle-class American style of mothering with that of Samoan women, Elinor Ochs concluded that the verbal strategies used by American mothers helped to "construct a low image of themselves" (1992: 347). They did this by prioritizing the child's point of view and excluding their own participation in helping a child accomplish certain tasks. "Mother," Ochs says, "is underrated because she does not socialize children to acknowledge her participation in accomplishments. 'Mother' is ignored because through her own language behavior, 'mother' has become invisible" (p. 355). The devaluation of motherhood in American society is not solely dependent on mothers' *language*, but Ochs's study does indicate that American mothers are complicit in devaluing their status by their linguistic style. At the same time, we should not forget that mothers, too, have been socialized by their culture and childcare experts in communicating with babies and young children.

At college, it has been noticed that men tend to dominate classroom discussions, or perhaps professors tend to pay more attention to them. No doubt this relates to the discussion above that women's mode of talking does not command the same kind of attention as men's, but it might also have something to do with the way "the knower," knowledge, and the pursuit of knowledge are characterized. Do these dynamics hold in your classes? What about outside of class?

Language and race

It is not necessary to repeat all the horrible epithets that have been used to put down people on the basis of race – whether the people in question are black, Jewish, Asian, Irish, Hispanic, Italian, or some other. You might have noticed that not all of the categories mentioned are what are normally counted as "racial," instead some refer to "ethnic" groups. Nevertheless, members of these groups have all been the butt of the same kind of linguistic behavior. As children we are taught that "sticks and stones will break my bones, but words will never hurt me." But they do.

Anthropologists have long argued that there is no such thing as race, that the overlap between people whose surface physiognomy appears different is so great as to make the category "race" meaningless. Recent breakthroughs in genetics, DNA, and the Human Genome only confirm this. We are all one human race; in fact, we are 98 percent chimpanzee – we share 98 percent of our DNA with chimps.[12]

Although there is overwhelming biological and anthropological evidence that race as a *natural* category does not exist, it nevertheless exists as a *social* category – one that wields enormous power and causes enormous strife and suffering. The concept of race is created by people as a way to draw boundaries between a "we" and a "they." Rather than dismiss the notion of race, as the biological and genetic data would dictate, it is important to investigate its construction. As a social category race "denotes a particular way in which communal differences come to be constructed and therefore it cannot be erased from the analytical map" (Anthias and Yuval-Davis 1992: 2). In their book *Racialized Boundaries*, Anthias and Yuval-Davis suggest that we understand "racisms as modes of exclusion, inferiorization, subordination and exploitation that present specific and different characters in different social and historical contexts" (p. 2). That is, racism is not just one thing but takes different forms in different times and places. Their analytical framework includes the overlapping but somewhat different category of ethnicity and its corollaries, nation and nationalism; in addition they suggest that the way in which racism operates on both gender and class also needs to be investigated. In *Orientalism* (1979), Edward Said examined the racist attitudes of Europeans toward Orientals (who, in that context, were Middle Eastern Arabs). What he did not show was the sexist metaphors in which this construction was made, that is, the Orient was imagined as veiled, seductive, and sexual, and in need of "mastery" by the white Europeans who were symbolically, and often literally, male. How did these images prefigure encounters with Arabs, and how did they affect Arab women and men?

It is not the purpose of this chapter or this book to attempt an account of the construction of race or of racism; however, we will briefly look at a couple of ways race and racism are expressed and enacted linguistically. One simple, or seemingly simple, way involves the label that gets attached to a particular group, for example in the linguistic nomenclature that extends from Negro to black to African American. "Negro" now appears to belong to discredited racial theories; "black," in contrast, became a label of self-definition during the 1960s with the Black Power movement, while African American is seen as an ethnic designation similar to Italian American or Irish American that focuses on one's cultural heritage. One can say black British but it is far more difficult to say African British or African German. Linguistically, "American" does not carry the same racial-ethnic load that either "British" or "German" do, though in practice it does. In Britain some South Asians (from India) have identified themselves with the category "black" as a political state-ment (cf. Baumann 1996).

As another example, ethnicity is also indexed by the labels attached to Spanish-speaking people in the United States, especially in the Southwest. "Speakers of Spanish, regardless of geographical origin or citizenship, were traditionally called 'Mexicans' by Anglos. In the 1960s many Americans of Mexican heritage adopted 'Chicano', but the term remains controversial among Spanish speakers in the region" (Hill 1993: 169 n. 1). Hill goes on to say that some prefer 'Latino' while others feel that term "applies only to Spanish speakers from the Caribbean. 'His-panic' is . . . essentially a 'race' term introduced by the US Justice Department to include Puerto Ricans, Cubans, Spaniards, Mexicans, Salvadorenos, Colombians, etc." (p. 169 n. 1).

In her article "Hasta La Vista, Baby," Hill discusses the way the misuse of Spanish words and phrases by Anglos is one method that racism is enacted linguistically. The title is a good example of what she is getting at; the phrase "hasta la vista" means "until we meet again" and is a "rather formal farewell, uttered sincerely to express hope for the pleasure of a future meeting" (p. 145). When Arnold Schwarzenegger used the phrase, adding "baby," in *Terminator 2*, it was a parody, and became an expression of contempt as "he blows the bad terminator away forever (he thinks)" (p. 145).

Another example of a possible linguistic "put-down" presented itself as Hill had breakfast in a hotel restaurant. All of the employees were Hispanic, but the place-mat that greeted her said *Buenas Dias* rather than *Buenos Dias*. A simple mistake, but it could so easily have been avoided. Did the owner of the restaurant check the spelling? Did the workers notice the misspelling? If so, how did they feel about it? By itself, this may seem an insignificant example, but added up, they can create a hostile work environment. Hill argues that in the Southwest, Anglo uses of Spanish are strategic, that they are part of the construction of a "regional political economy based on racial hierarchy, that requires Anglos to produce and reproduce the sub-ordination of Spanish-speaking and Native American populations who have a prior claim to the resources of the region," reducing them to "a profound marginality from which recovery is only just beginning" (p. 147). A good bilingual education for both Spanish speakers and English speakers might help in this recovery.

Bilingual education

Bilingual education, however, is a hotly debated issue in the United States, where, next to English, Spanish is the most widely spoken language. Nevertheless, the bilingual education issue is not just about Spanish, nor did it begin with it. In 1974, the United States Supreme Court decided that the San Francisco School Department had violated the civil rights of a Chinese American student to obtain a public education. The court determined that this child, and other students like him with limited proficiency in English, were denied access to equal public education because they could not understand the language of instruction. This case, *Lau v. Nichols*, would turn out to be the landmark case in bilingual education. After the decision in support of Lau, Congress passed the Equal Education Opportunity Act, and school districts across the country scrambled to come up with programs for children who did not speak English.

> But what is San Francisco supposed to do when there are over 90 different languages spoken by its primary grade schoolchildren?

Bilingual education is not a uniform system by any stretch of the imagination. Inextricably linked to race and class, it has come to mean different things in different states, school districts, and parts of the country. In some school districts, students with limited English proficiency ("LEP" in educational parlance) must take English as a Second Language before being "mainstreamed" with native speakers at their grade level. In others, students participate in "double-immersion" or "two-way" programs that provide English speakers with an opportunity to learn a second language while ensuring that speakers of the other language (such as Spanish or Cantonese) learn English. In others, it means students receive most of their instruction in their native language (perhaps French or Korean) while learning English at a slower pace; this is the method most people associate with "bilingual education."

Advocates of bilingual education argue that children should have at least some of their classes in their primary language because they will more quickly gain knowledge and literacy in that language. Once you learn to read – in any language – it is apparently easier to learn to read in another language, thus the transition to English may be smoother. In addition, becoming literate in one's native language and gaining knowledge through that language would also give these children the confidence to succeed in school.

Opponents of bilingual education, including some native Spanish speakers (e.g. Richard Rodriguez), say that such a policy holds children back and prevents them from achieving success in the English-speaking world. They argue that the best, if not the only, way to teach a language is total immersion, and that the only language that really matters in the United States is English. They argue that many LEP students end up languishing in bilingual classrooms for years without ever learning enough English to be "mainstreamed."

Today, bilingual education is a hot button topic. Ballot initiatives funded by California millionaire Ron Unz asked voters in California, Arizona, Massachusetts, and Colorado to overturn decades of bilingual education policy and submit all children to the "sink or swim" approach. The initiatives passed in all states but Colorado. Massachusetts voters approved the most draconian initiative of all, which included a provision stating that teachers could be sued for using a child's native language. This hit close to home since my oldest grandson began his education in a bilingual public school that opened for the first time in fall of 1999. Half of his class were native Spanish speakers, the other half were native English speakers, and classroom time was spent equally in Spanish and English.

From my own observations and from anecdotal evidence, it seems to be working very well for the Spanish-speaking kids but not as well for the English-speaking kids. After all, English is the ambient language; the native Spanish speakers hear it in the stores, on television, and in the gym and lunchroom. Nonetheless, it is the English speakers who gain cultural capital by learning "another" language; it is not really necessary that they do so. But to succeed in school and the workplace in the United States Spanish speakers, like speakers of Chinese or Vietnamese, *need* English. Beyond this, however, is a much bigger philosophical issue to consider: the way in which language is tied up with the nation-state and nationalism. Why should there be only one national language? Wouldn't it be better if all of us could speak at least two if not more languages as many people in Europe already do? And aren't bilingual employees more sought after than those who speak only one language?

Ebonics

Ebonics, or African American Vernacular English, is spoken by vast numbers of African American youngsters. There are many people who think it is merely slang, a lazy or defective language, and this affects how they think about those who speak it. Linguist John Rickford, and others, argue that it is a structured, systematic, grammatical, and rule-governed language like any other, and for many African American children it is their primary language. Rickford and other like-minded linguists were able to persuade the Linguistics Society of America to recognize it as such. In January 1997, the Society passed a resolution to that effect and also pronounced the Oakland school board's decision to take it into account in teaching Standard English "linguistically and pedagogically sound" (Rickford 1998/9). While it could be considered a dialect of English, it is important to realize that the distinction between a dialect and a language is made on social and political grounds, not linguistic ones. Rickford gives the example of Norwegian and Swedish, which are considered two separate languages although speakers can understand each other, whereas speakers of a variety of Chinese dialects cannot. While there is not a move to *teach* Ebonics, the recognition of it as a legitimate language helps make the teaching of Standard English easier. On this issue the controversy over Ebonics is clearly intertwined with that about bilingualism.

> It was in Oakland, California, where the debate over Ebonics erupted and where pressure mounted for it to be taken seriously in schools.

Language and class

Class has to do with differences in status, power, and birth, not just wealth. Members of traditional upper classes can tell immediately who is *"nouveau riche"* by his or her pronunciation, grammar, and vocabulary. "Bankers clearly do not talk the same as busboys, and professors don't sound like plumbers. They signal the social differences between them by features of the phonology, grammar, and lexical choice, just as they do extralinguistically by their choices in clothing, cars, and so on" (Guy 1988: 37). People are judged by the way they speak, and the judgments determine how others will respond, if at all.

American Tongues is an excellent film that demonstrates the range of regional differences in American English and raises the question of why certain ways of speaking – a Brooklyn or South Boston accent – are disparaged. Speaking voice and perfect grammar are expected of mainstream, prime-time newscasters – maybe it is part of the job description. Why do you think there is no one with a deep Southern drawl as host of a major network news program? What other ways do you think your manner of speaking might affect your social life and job possibilities?[13]

While the speaking voice is a marker of class, so too is grammar. In recent years I have noticed an increase in grammatical mistakes even among educated people. One of the most glaring mistakes is the confusion over when to use "I" and when to use "me." I frequently hear statements like the following: "She brought the video to Tim and I" rather than "She brought the video to Tim and me," or "Do you want to go to the movies with Jane and I?" rather than "Do you want to go to the movies with Jane and me?" Are children no longer being taught the different parts of speech in grammar school? Do they not know the difference between the subjective and objective cases, or that prepositions such as *at, in, to, from,* and *with* always take the objective case? Do they even know what a preposition is? Another mistake is using "good" when it should be "well," as in "I am good, thanks," rather than "I am well, thank you," or "real" when it should be "really," as in "that was a real good dinner" instead of "that was a really good dinner." A third type of mistake is mispronunciation of words – saying "nukular" instead of "nuclear" (this apparently began with President Jimmy Carter but George W. Bush also mispronounces it regularly), or "breakfrist" for "breakfast." The use of "like" not as a comparative but in constructions such as "like, you know?" or "he was, like, cool," or "she, like, completely ignored me" is becoming widespread. This "filler" word seems to indicate an inability on the part of speakers to express what they mean.[14] Additionally, many people are using "whatever" as a way of being noncommittal, of deferring a decision, such as when someone asks whether you want to go to the movies or rollerblading and you answer "whatever." It is also used when one's facts or logic are challenged; using "whatever," said Theodore Roszak, "means not even arguing the point because truth is beside the point" (*San Francisco Chronicle*, July 16, 2000); it is a weary response that seems to say "who cares?" It is also another instance of the dumbing down of America to the lowest common denominator rather than encouraging all to speak well.

What does it mean when the American editors of the Harry Potter books changed not only the spelling of many words but the words themselves? For example, they substituted gray for grey, color for colour, flavor for flavour and changed lorry to truck, post to mail, Hoover to vacuum, fortnight to two weeks, and crumpets to English muffins. "Are we afraid that when presented with new vocabulary, children will shrink away?" asks Peter Gleick in a *New York Times* op ed piece (July 10, 2000). Isn't it more interesting for children to read about English children having tea and crumpets instead of English muffins? Wouldn't that stir their curiosity and spur them to ask, "what are crumpets?" or, heaven forbid, to consult a dictionary (!) and thus expand their cultural horizons? "By insisting that everything be Americanized," Gleick argues, "we dumb down our own society rather than enrich it." "Dumbing down" also involves the issue of class. Did the editors think that no one would understand the English words or did they think that the words sounded too pretentious and uppity?

Language is, clearly, about much more than communication. Recall the passage from Sapir:

> No two languages are ever sufficiently similar to be considered representing the same social reality. The worlds in which different societies live are distinct worlds, not merely the same world with different labels attached. (1949: 69)

Thus, we live in different worlds, and it behooves all of us to get some sense of them. Language is an extremely important means for investigating culture; you cannot possibly understand a culture without knowing the language. At the same time, it is very important to realize that language and culture are not necessarily isomorphic, that is, "language, culture, and race do not form a single package but, rather, each element pursues a different historical trajectory" (Briggs 2002: 483). After all, people of different ethnicities can learn the same language, and people of the same ethnicity can learn different languages, just as they can learn other cultures, and learn to function in them.

Nevertheless, it is important to become more aware of the way the language you use conditions what you think and what you perceive. That is the anthropological legacy from Sapir. Another aspect of language, however, concerns how people use language to influence others and achieve power. That is the anthropological legacy from sociolinguistics.

Turkish

Turkish is a very unusual language. It is not related to any of the major language groups such as Indo-European or Semitic. Consequently, you will probably not find any cognates unless they have been directly borrowed. Some scholars think Turkish is related to Uralic-Altaic languages or to Finnish, others say that the structure, although not the words, is similar to Japanese. In part it is an agglutinative language, which means that significant aspects (tense, negation, interrogative) of a word occur within or are attached to the word rather than, as in English, simply multiplying the number of words. For example: "I am going" = *gidiyorum*; "I am not going" = *gitmiyorum*. The "I" is not a separate word but is the *-um* ending, and the negative "not" is the tiny part in the middle, *-mi-*. Direct and indirect objects are indicated by the endings that are attached to the nouns or pronoun. *Pre*positions in English, that is, words like "with," "to," "from," "at," "in," are *post*positions in Turkish, and are attached at the end of the noun, e.g. *Ankara'ya* = to Ankara, *Ankara'da* = in or at Ankara.

The verb and subject come at the end of the sentence preceded by all kinds of phrases and modifiers. Consequently, you learn about the context and conditions before you know *who* is involved or affected. Similarly, you cannot say in Turkish "I am hungry" but rather *karnım aç* – my stomach is open; not "I have a headache" but *kafam ağrıyor* – my head aches. It is not "I" who desires food or complains of pain, but the particular body part involved. I am not clear to what extent this may help relieve one of responsibility for one's desires or dissociate oneself from pain. In the village, pregnant women who craved certain sweets were generally indulged because it was thought to be the baby who required and desired them; and no one would deny a baby.

Turkish is also a vowel-harmonic language, which means that all the vowels in a word have to agree, that is, if one is a front vowel, the other vowels must also be front vowels, and if one is a back vowel, then all must be. During the Ottoman period Turkish was written in Arabic script even though Turkish is not at all related to Arabic. In addition, Arabic script was totally unsuited to Turkish since Arabic, like Hebrew, does not indicate vowels in its script! Because of this, Turkish, or *Osmanlıcı* (Ottoman) as it was called, was extremely difficult to read or write and most of the people were illiterate.

When Mustafa Kemal Atatürk established the Republic of Turkey at the end of World War I and the collapse of the Ottoman Empire, one of his first major reforms was language. He decreed that Turkish would no longer be written in Arabic script but would switch to Latin letters. Newspapers were given only a few weeks to make the switch, one that many thought would or should take years. Atatürk himself went around the country with a blackboard instructing the people in the new script. With this sweeping reform, millions of people were able to learn to read and to write their own language. Nevertheless, this change angered devout Muslims who believed that Arabic (and Arabic script) was sacred since the Qur'an was delivered from God to Muhammad in Arabic. They believed that Atatürk had switched to the language of the infidels.

Although the people were able to read and write more easily, the change also cut them off from their history. Today if a Turk wishes to read Ottoman documents, he or she must take courses in Ottoman in order to do so; it is, apparently, like learning a foreign language. But even Turkish written in Latin letters has changed since the 1920s, as substantially as the difference between Chaucerian English and modern English (Henze 1982)!

Another part of Atatürk's language reform was to establish the Turkish Language Association. This association was mandated to study the history of the Turkish language, which Atatürk believed was the original Ur language. He also wanted to purge Turkish of foreign loan words, especially Persian, Arabic, and French, and requested the Association to seek Turkish replacements. Every few years the Association has published numerous lexicons of the new words. Although they are referred to as *Öz Türkçe* or real, true Turkish, they are actually new compositions created from Turkish roots.

Turkish, as it is spoken in Turkey today, is one form of a number of Turkic languages that are spoken in Mongolia and some of the former provinces of the Soviet Union. Within Turkey itself, there are regional variations in pronunciation and some differences in form, for example villagers use slightly different forms from those used by the urban educated elite. But they have no trouble understanding each other. Turkish spoken in Istanbul is held to be the standard as a Northeast accent is the standard in the United States, the standard used for radio and television news reporters. But there is a difference by gender; elite Istanbul women speak in a distinct style that includes a particularly high pitch of the voice and the use of exceptionally polite forms much like Japanese women do (cf. Inoue 2002).

Because Turkish is not widely studied outside of Turkey, many Turks also learn English, French, or German throughout school so they can converse with their European neighbors and American visitors. Some use these linguistic skills when they continue their education abroad, but even at a number of (the most prestigious) universities in Turkey, English is the language of instruction. And most professors write in English, as well as in Turkish, so that their work will reach an international audience. But it is hardly only the well educated who are bi- or trilingual; many taxi drivers, restaurant owners, and rug merchants speak very passable English and/or German.

The dominance of English around the world surely makes it easier for Americans abroad, but it is not because it is an easy language. Think about how and why English has come to dominate the linguistic world. Do you think English *should* become the world language? Why? Why is it that Americans are so bad at learning languages, and why does the study of foreign languages have such a low priority in schools? Do you think endangered languages should be preserved? Is the loss of them equivalent to the loss of endangered species? What might it mean for life on the planet?

Notes

1   Attributed to Magritte, *La Révolution Surréaliste* (1929), but cited at an exhibition of his work at the San Francisco Museum of Modern Art, 2000.
2   E.g. Bruner (1984); Clifford and Marcus (1986); Rabinow and Sullivan (1979).
3   Plato, *Phaedrus*, trans. Harold North Fowler (Loeb Classical Library; Cambridge, MA: Harvard University Press, 1960), p. 563.
4   It seems likely that this image was provided by Langer, Sapir, or Whorf, but it could have been said by my teachers Sahlins or Schneider. I have scoured their works and cannot find it. I don't think I invented it, but if so, it captures the import of what they are saying.
5   George Lakoff wrote and circulated a paper on the Internet during the Gulf War, entitled "Metaphor and War: The Metaphor System Used to Justify War in the Gulf."
6   These quotes are taken from a film, *Creation of the Universe*, in which scientific cosmologists, including several Nobel Prize winners, are discussing the origin of the universe. It was shown for the first time on PBS November 20, 1985. The narrator is Timothy Ferris, a science writer and professor at the University of Southern California.
7   Brian Easlea examines some of the precursors of this idea, especially Francis Bacon's "The Masculine Birth of Time," and the fearful implications in the manufacture of nuclear weapons in his *Fathering the Unthinkable: Masculinity, Scientists, and the Nuclear Arms Race* (London: Pluto Press, 1983). See also Carol Cohn's "Sex and Death in the Rational World of Defense Intellectuals," *Signs* 12, 4 (1987): 687–719.

8   In an article on the use of certain metaphors to discuss NPRs (new reproductive tech-
     nologies), Marilyn Strathern claims that "Culture consists in the way analogies are drawn
     between things, in the way certain thoughts are used to think others" (1992: 33).

9   In the 1950s–1970s, women who rejected or rebelled against their sex role were made
     to feel that there was something wrong with them. They were sent to psychiatrists and
     psychologists for therapy, and were also prescribed tranquilizers to help them accept and
     adjust to their role. See Betty Friedan's *The Feminine Mystique* (1963) for a description of
     those times.

10   See, for example, the trailblazing volumes *Women, Culture, and Society*, ed. Michelle
     Rosaldo and Louise Lamphere (1974), *The Anthropology of Women*, ed. Rayna Reiter
     (1975), and *Nature, Culture, and Gender*, ed. Carol MacCormack and Marilyn Strathern
     (1980).

11   Most French feminist discussions of language and sex draw upon the work of Jacques
     Lacan, a Freudian psychoanalyst, and focus on the *phallus* as a key signifier but reject the
     idea that it has anything to do with the penis. Instead, I would argue that it has every-
     thing to do with what the penis has meant, namely, that it was imagined as the organ
     through which *life* was transmitted, via seed. See the work of Julia Kristeva, Luce Iri-
     garay, Hélène Cixous, and Monique Wittig.

12   See *What It Means to Be 98% Chimpanzee: Apes, People, and their Genes* (Berkeley: Univer-
     sity of California Press, 2002) by biologist Jonathan Marks.

13   Penny Eckert's book *Jocks and Burnouts: Social Categories and Identity in the High School*
     (New York and London: Teachers College Press, 1989) is a lively ethnography of the
     ways in which class among high school students is expressed and reinforced not just by
     clothing, drug use, and activities, but by the difference in linguistic use.

14   Linguists make a distinction between "prescriptive" and "descriptive" grammar, the first
     having to do with the prestige variety of a language while the second is the study and
     analysis of language in use. Don Brenneis, a linguistic anthropologist, also explained to
     me that some of what I call "mispronunciations" may reflect regional dialect differences
     (see also Macaulay 1994, 1997).

Bibliography

Anthias, Floya and Yuval-Davis, Nira, in association with Harried Cain (1992) *Racialized
    Boundaries: Race, Nation, Gender, Colour and Class and the Anti-Racist Struggle*. London:
    Routledge.

Baumann, Gerd (1996) *Contesting Culture: Discourses of Identity in Multicultural London*.
    Cambridge: Cambridge University Press.

Benedict, Ruth ([1946] 1976) *Chrysanthemum and the Sword: Patterns of Japanese Culture*. New
    York: Meridian, New American Library.

Benveniste, Emile (1971) "Animal Communication and Human Language." In *Problems in
    General Linguistics*. Coral Gables, FL: University of Miami Press.

Briggs, Charles L. (2002) "Linguistic Magic Bullets in the Making of a Modernist Anthropo-
    logy." *American Anthropologist*, 104 (2): 481–98.

Bruner, Edward M., ed. (1984) *Text, Play, and Story: The Construction and Reconstruction of Self
    and Society*. Prospect Heights, IL: Waveland Press.

Clifford, James and Marcus, George, eds. (1986) *Writing Culture: The Poetics and Politics of
    Ethnography*. Berkeley: University of California Press.

Delaney, Carol (1986) "The Meaning of Paternity and the Virgin Birth Debate." *Man*, 21 (3):
    494–513.

Delaney, Carol (1991) *The Seed and the Soil: Gender and Cosmology in Turkish Village Society*. Berkeley: University of California Press.

Dolgin, Janet, Kemnitzer, David S., and Schneider, David, eds. (1977) *Symbolic Anthropology: A Reader in the Study of Symbols and Meanings*. New York: Columbia University Press.

Douglas, Mary (1966) "The Abominations of Leviticus." In *Purity and Danger: An Analysis of the Concepts of Pollution and Taboo*. London: Routledge & Kegan Paul.

Eckert, Penny (1989) *Jocks and Burnouts: Social Categories and Identity in the High School*. New York and London: Teachers College Press.

Edelsky, Carole (1976) "The Acquisition of Communicative Competence: A Recognition of Linguistic Correlates of Sex Roles." *Merrill-Palmer Quarterly*, 22 (1): 47–59.

Foucault, Michel (1982) *This Is Not a Pipe*. Berkeley: University of California Press.

Geertz, Clifford (1973) *Interpretation of Cultures*. New York: Basic Books.

Guy, Gregory (1988) "Language and Social Class." In *Linguistics: The Cambridge Survey*, vol. 6, ed. Fredrick J. Newmeyer. Cambridge: Cambridge University Press, pp. 37–63.

Hager, Lori (1997) *Women in Human Evolution*. New York: Routledge.

Hamilton, Mykol C., Hunter, Barbara, and Stuart-Smith, Shannon (1992) "Jury Instructions Worded in the Masculine Generic: Can a Woman Claim Self-Defense when "He" is Threatened?" In *New Directions in Feminist Psychology*, ed. Joan C. Chrisler and Doris Howard. New York: Springer, pp. 340–7.

Haraway, Donna (1989) *Primate Visions: Gender, Race, and Nation in the World of Modern Science*. New York: Routledge.

Henze, Paul (1982) "Turkey: On the Rebound." *Wilson Quarterly* 6 (5): 108–25.

Hill, Jane (1980) "Apes and Language." In *Speaking of Apes: A Critical Anthology of Two-Way Communication with Man*, ed. Thomas A. Sebeok and Jean Umiker-Sebeok. New York: Plenum, pp. 331–51.

Hill, Jane (1993) "Hasta La Vista, Baby." *Critique of Anthropology*, 13 (2): 145–76.

Inoue, Miyako (2002) "Gender, Language, and Modernity: Toward an Effective History of Japanese Women's Language." *American Ethnologist*, 29 (2): 392–422.

Lakoff, George and Johnson, Mark (1980) *Metaphors We Live By*. Chicago: University of Chicago Press.

Lakoff, Robin (1975) *Language and Woman's Place*. New York: Harper and Row.

Landau, Misia (1991) *Narratives of Human Evolution*. New Haven: Yale University Press.

Langer, Suzanne ([1942] 1979) *Philosophy in a New Key: A Study in the Symbolism of Reason, Rite, and Art*. Cambridge, MA: Harvard University Press.

Leach, Edmund (1964) "Anthropological Aspects of Language: Animal Categories and Verbal Abuse." In *New Directions in the Study of Language*, ed. Eric Lenneberg. Cambridge, MA: MIT Press, pp. 23–63.

Le Guin, Ursula (1987) "She Unnames Them." In *Buffalo Gals and Other Animal Presences*. New York: Plume Books.

Lourie, Richard and Mikhalev, Aleksei (1989) "Why You'll Never Have Fun in Russia." *New York Times*, June 18.

Macaulay, Ronald K. S. (1994) *The Social Art: Language and Its Uses*. New York: Oxford University Press.

Macaulay, Ronald K. S. (1997) *Standards and Variations in Urban Speech: Examples from Lowland Scots*. Philadelphia: John Benjamins.

Martyna, Wendy (1980) "Beyond the 'He/Man' Approach: The Case for Nonsexist Language." *Signs: Journal of Women in Culture and Society*, 5 (3): 482–93.

Mead, Margaret (1928) *Coming of Age in Samoa: A Psychological Study of Primitive Youth for Western Civilization*. New York: William Morrow.

Mead, Margaret (1935) *Sex and Temperament in Three Primitive Societies*. New York: William Morrow.

Mead, Margaret (1949) *Male and Female: A Study of the Sexes in a Changing World*. New York: William Morrow.

Moran, John H. and Gode, Alexander, trans. (1967) *On the Origin of Language: Jean-Jacques Rousseau, Essay on the Origin of Language; Johan Gottfried Herder, Essay on the Origin of Language*. New York: F. Ungar.

Morton, Nelle (1972) "The Rising Women's Consciousness in a Male Language Structure." *Andover-Newton Quarterly*, 12: 177–90.

Ochs, Elinor (1992) "Indexing Gender." In *Rethinking Context*, ed. A. Duranti and C. Goodwin. New York: Cambridge University Press, pp. 335–58.

Ong, Walter J., S.J. ([1982] 1999) *Orality and Literacy: The Technologizing of the Word*. New York: Routledge.

Ottenheimer, Martin (1996) *Forbidden Relatives: The American Myth of Cousin Marriage*. Urbana and Chicago: University of Illinois Press.

Rabinow, Paul and Sullivan, William M., eds. (1979) *Interpretative Social Science*. Berkeley: University of California Press.

Rickford, John (1998/9) "Using the Vernacular to Teach the Standard." From California State University Long Beach Conference on Ebonics, March 25, 1998, available at http://www.stanford.edu/~rickford/papers/VernacularToTeachStandard.html

Ricoeur, Paul (1976) *Interpretation Theory: Discourse and the Surplus of Meaning*. Fort Worth: Texas Christian University Press.

Ricoeur, Paul (1977) *The Rule of Metaphor: Multidisciplinary Studies of the Creation of Meaning in Language*. Toronto: University of Toronto Press.

Said, Edward (1979) *Orientalism*. New York: Vintage Books.

Sapir, Edward (1949) *Culture, Language, and Personality*. Berkeley: University of California Press.

Saussure, Ferdinand de (1959) *Course in General Linguistics*. New York: McGraw-Hill.

Savage-Rumbaugh, Sue, Shanker, Stuart G., and Taylor, Talbot J. (1998) *Apes, Language, and the Human Mind*. Oxford: Oxford University Press.

Schmandt-Besserat, Denise (1986) "An Ancient Token System: The Precursor to Numerals and Writing." *Archaeology*, 39 (6): 32–9.

Schweikart, Debora (1998) "The Gender Neutral Pronoun Redefined." *Women's Rights Law Reporter*, 20 (Fall–Winter): 1–9.

Singer, Milton (1984) *Man's Glassy Essence: Explorations in Semiotic Anthropology*. Bloomington: Indiana University Press.

Stanton, Elizabeth Cady et al. (1898) *The Woman's Bible*. New York: European Publishing Company. Republished by Seattle Coalition on Women and Religion, 1974.

Strathern, Marilyn (1992) *Reproducing the Future: Essays on Anthropology, Kinship, and the New Reproductive Technologies*. Manchester: Manchester University Press.

Tannen, Deborah (1990) *You Just Don't Understand: Women and Men in Conversation*. New York: Morrow.

Whorf, Benjamin (1956) *Language, Thought and Reality*. Cambridge, MA: MIT Press.

Yanagisako, Sylvia and Delaney, Carol (1995) *Naturalizing Power: Essays in Feminist Cultural Analysis*. New York and London: Routledge.

Zihlman, Adrienne (1991) "Mechanism and Meaning of Reproduction: Myths of Paternity, Realities of Maternity." Paper prepared for Wenner-Gren Symposium.

She Unnames Them

Ursula LeGuin

Most of them accepted namelessness with the perfect indifference with which they had so long accepted and ignored their names. Whales and dolphins, seals and sea otters consented with particular grace and alacrity, sliding into anonymity as into their element. A faction of yaks, however, protested. They said that "yak" sounded right, and that almost everyone who knew they existed called them that. Unlike the ubiquitous creatures such as rats or fleas who had been called by hundreds or thousands of different names since Babel, the yaks could truly say, they said, that they had *a name*. They discussed the matter all summer. The councils of the elderly females finally agreed that though the name might be useful to others, it was so redundant from the yak point of view that they never spoke it themselves, and hence might as well dispense with it. After they presented the argument in this light to their bulls, a full consensus was delayed only by the onset of severe early blizzards. Soon after the beginning of the thaw their agreement was reached and the designation "yak" was returned to the donor.

Among the domestic animals, few horses had cared what anybody called them since the failure of Dean Swift's attempt to name them from their own vocabulary. Cattle, sheep, swine, asses, mules, and goats, along with chickens, geese, and turkeys, all agreed enthusiastically to give their names back to the people to whom – as they put it – they belonged.

A couple of problems did come up with pets. The cats of course steadfastly denied ever having had any name other than those self-given, unspoken, effa-nineffably personal names which, as the poet named Eliot said, they spend long hours daily contemplating – though none of the contemplators has ever admitted that what they contemplate is in fact their name, and some onlookers have wondered if the object of that meditative gaze might not in fact be the Perfect, or Platonic, Mouse. In any case it is a moot point now. It was with the dogs, and with some parrots, lovebirds, ravens, and mynahs that the trouble arose. These verbally talented individuals insisted that their names were important to them, and flatly refused to part with them. But as soon as they understood that the issue was precisely one of individual choice, and that anybody who wanted to be called Rover, or Froufrou, or Polly, or even Birdie in the personal sense, was perfectly free to do so, not one of them had the least objection to parting with the lower case (or, as regards German creatures, uppercase) generic appellations poodle, parrot, dog, or bird, and all the Linnaean qualifiers that had trailed along behind them for two hundred years like tin cans tied to a tail.

The insects parted with their names in vast clouds and swarms of ephemeral syllables buzzing and stinging and humming and flitting and crawling and tunneling away.

As for the fish of the sea, their names dispersed from them in silence throughout the oceans like faint, dark blurs of cuttlefish ink, and drifted off on the currents without a trace.

None were left now to unname, and yet how close I felt to them when I saw one of them swim or fly or trot or crawl across my way or over my skin, or stalk me in the night, or go along beside me for a while in the day. They seemed far closer than when their names had stood between myself and them like a clear barrier: so close that my fear of them and their fear of me became one same fear. And the attraction that many of us felt, the desire to smell one another's smells, feel or rub or caress one another's scales or skin or feathers or fur, taste one another's blood or flesh, keep one another warm, – that attraction was now all one with the fear, and the hunter could not be told from the hunted, nor the eater from the food.

This was more or less the effect I had been after. It was somewhat more powerful than I had anticipated, but I could not now, in all conscience, make an exception for myself. I resolutely put anxiety away, went to Adam, and said, "You and your father lent me this – gave it to me, actually. It's been really useful, but it doesn't exactly seem to fit very well lately. But thanks very much! It's really been very useful."

It is hard to give back a gift without sounding peevish or ungrateful, and I did not want to leave him with that impression of me. He was not paying much attention, as it happened, and said only, "Put it down over there, OK?" and went on with what he was doing.

One of my reasons for doing what I did was that talk was getting us nowhere; but all the same I felt a little let down. I had been prepared to defend my decision. And I thought that perhaps when he did notice he might be upset and want to talk. I put some things away and fiddled around a little, but he continued to do what he was doing and to take no notice of anything else. At last I said, "Well, goodbye, dear. I hope the garden key turns up."

He was fitting parts together, and said without looking around, "OK, fine, dear. When's dinner?"

"I'm not sure," I said. "I'm going now. With the –" I hesitated, and finally said, "With them, you know," and went on. In fact I had only just then realized how hard it would have been to explain myself. I could not chatter away as I used to do, taking it all for granted. My words now must be as slow, as new, as single, as tentative as the steps I took going down the path away from the house, between the dark-branched, tall dancers motionless against the winter shining.

Seeing is Believing

Alan Dundes

Whether from early memories of playing "peek-a-boo," "showing and telling" in school, or learning the opening phrase of the national anthem – "Oh, say can you see" – the primacy of vision in American culture is affirmed again and again as infants grow to adulthood. Americans are conditioned from childhood to believe that "what you see is what you get."

There is more to such a phenomenon than immediately meets the eye. That Americans rely more on vision than on other senses doesn't mean that they are aware of it. Nor does it mean that it is a peculiarly American trait. People everywhere rely on their senses to perceive their world and order their experiences, but since my data are derived from American folk speech, I cannot speak about others. In any case, because I have been taught to mistrust hearsay, I have decided to take a look at the evidence for a visual bias and to see for myself.

In Western thought, a distinction has commonly been made between sensory perception and reasoning. The power of reason is presumably the superior of the two. According to Aristotle, there are five senses – sight, hearing, smell, taste, and touch – which provide data generally deemed less trustworthy or, at least, frequently illusory, compared to the information that is provided by the faculties of rational thought. Subjective versus objective and body versus mind are other expressions of this distinction between the sensory and the rational. If we assume, however, that reasoning cannot take place without some reference to metaphor, then it is certainly possible that much American logic and reasoning is closely tied to metaphor in general and to visual metaphor in particular.

The allegedly inferior sensory experiences seem to be ranked according to how effective or reliable a given sense is assumed to be. In American culture, the sense of sight is normally the first of the five senses to be listed. However, whether sight is actually more useful or crucial for perception than the other senses is a moot question and, in fact, does not require an answer to show that a cultural bias for the sense of sight really exists. In the present context, it is not the literal meaning of sight that is important, but the metaphorical. I believe that, metaphorically speaking, Americans tend to *see* the world around them, rather than hear, feel, smell, or taste it. It may be no accident that Americans *observe* laws and holidays.

American speech provides persuasive evidence to support the notion that "vision" is used as a metaphor for "understanding." Consider, for example, the classic punning proverb, "'I see,' said the blind man, as he picked up his hammer and saw." The oppositional structure in this text is produced by the juxtaposition of sight and blindness. Here is a clear distinction between literal and metaphorical seeing. Literally a blind man cannot see, but figuratively he certainly can.

Americans consistently speak of "seeing" the point of an argument when, in fact, an argument is not really seen but comprehended. Intellectual positions, or "perspectives," are frequently referred to as points of *view*. When articulated, they may be introduced by such formulas as, "As I see it" or "It all depends on how you look at it."

American culture is pronouncedly concerned with empiricism, and this empiricism is explicitly visual. "Seeing is believing" and "I'm from Missouri" (which means "you've got to show me") are indications of the emphasis on seeing something for oneself and the tendency to distrust anyone else's report of a given event. "I saw it with my own (two) eyes" is a common authenticating formula, as is the invitation to "see for yourself."

Without sight, there may be disbelief or lack of faith: "I'll believe it when I see it," "That I've got to see," or "I can't picture that." Even though the reliability of vision may be questioned – "There's more to this than meets the eye" – in general, people tend to believe what they see. Thus, when something is really out of the ordinary, we say, "I couldn't believe my eyes." Something that is incredible or unbelievable is termed "out of sight," a phrase dating from before the end of the nineteenth century.

Imagination is sometimes called "the mind's eye," but why should the mind have an eye? Probably for the same reason that patients want doctors "to see them." Telephone conversations or other purely oral–aural channels are not considered entirely satisfactory. Actually, the patient is probably relieved by *his* seeing the doctor. Seeing the doctor, in turn, is part of the widespread cultural insistence upon interviews. Literally, the word *interview* refers to A seeing B and B seeing A.

Consider the nature of American tourist philosophy – sightseeing. To "see the sights" is a common goal of tourists, a goal also reflected in the mania for snapping pictures as permanent records of what was seen. Typical travel boasting consists of inflicting an evening of slide viewing on unwary friends so that they may see what their hosts saw.

This is surely a strange way of defining tourism. Visiting a foreign locale certainly involves all of the sensory apparatus. There are exotic smells and tastes, and the opportunity to savor new foods and experience the "feel" of a foreign setting is as important in understanding a country and its people as seeing them. One reason Americans frequently fail to enjoy touring as much as they might may be their almost compulsive tendency to see as many sights as possible. The seeing of many sights is, of course, consistent with a tendency to quantify living, and, specifically, with the desire to get one's money's worth.

When shopping, whether in foreign countries or at home, Americans are reluctant to buy anything "sight unseen." They prefer "to look something over," "to walk into something with their eyes open." A thorough inspection theoretically allows one to "see through" a pretense or fake. And obviously, a product can only "catch a person's eye" if he sees it.

Public "images," too, are part of the visual pattern. But why, after all, should a person have to be depicted in a term such as image? Even though looks may be deceiving ("Never judge a book by its cover"), it seems clear that packaging that appeals to visual esthetics is equally effective whether one is hawking cigarettes or automobiles or selling political candidates.

The reduction of persons or events to purely visual terms is also evident in the use of the popular slang phrase for a detective: "private eye." By the same token, sleep is commonly referred to as "shuteye," which obviously singles out only one aspect of the dormant state. Furthermore, this suggestion that sleep is shut-eye also implies that the waking state is marked chiefly by having one's eyes open.

As I collected examples of folk speech, I soon found that comparison of vision with the other senses reaffirmed the superiority of sight. That a "seer" can make predictions by gazing into a crystal ball, for example, suggests that vision is more effective than the other senses in fore*seeing* future events.

The same bias in favor of the visual is found in American greeting and leave-taking formulas. Examples include: "See you around," "I'll be seeing you," or "I haven't seen so-and-so in ages." Greetings may also be couched in visual terms. "It's good to see you," Americans say, rather than, "It's good to hear, smell, or feel you."

There seem to be relatively few complimentary references to hearers, smellers, talkers, and touchers. "Look, but don't touch" hints at a delight in gawking (girl-watching), and possibly at a cultural distaste for body contact. Someone who is "touchy" is not pleasant to have around. A "soft touch," which sounds as if it should have a positive connotation, is a slang term for a dupe or easy mark.

One of the most interesting pieces of evidence supporting the notion of visual superiority over the other senses is that the original version of "Seeing's believing" was presumably "Seeing's believing, but feeling's the truth." That most Americans have dropped the second portion of the proverb does not seem to be an accident. Rather, it reflects a definite penchant for the visual in contrast to the tactual. Originally, the proverb denigrated "seeing" in favor of "feeling."

Comparisons between the visual and the aural are the most common, however, with hearing considered second best. Consider "Believe nothing of what you hear and only half of what you see." Although caution is urged against believing everything one sees, seeing is surely depicted as being more reliable and trustworthy than hearing. Compare the following two statements: "I hear that X has just moved to Miami," and "I see that X has just moved to Miami." The first statement is possibly true, possibly not true: there is an element of doubt. The second, in contrast, seems to be a statement of fact.

Other instances are found in legal parlance. Although judges hear cases, there is no doubt that *hearsay*, that is, aural–oral, evidence is not in the same league as that offered by an eyewitness. Actually, the word *witness* indicates that the person was physically present during an event and saw with his own eyes the activities in question. If so, then the term *eyewitness* is redundant. Strangely enough, at *hearings* there is an insistence that *hearsay* evidence be rejected and that only *eyewitness* testimony be accepted. On the other hand, it is interesting to recall that Justice is depicted as being blind. Justice cannot see and presumably blindness guarantees fairness. But of course, sometimes even an innocent man may be guilty "in the eyes of the law."

The eye is also more powerful than the ear insofar as it is regarded as an active rather than a passive agent. The eye looks, peers, or gazes. There is seductive power in the eye, as in "giving a girl the eye," and the malevolent power of the eye is manifested in "the evil eye." The ear, by contrast, is a passive receptacle. There is little evidence of evil ears. Remember also that "big brother is watching you," not listening to you, although bugging rooms with microphones makes listening more likely than watching. Note also that voyeurs, such as Peeping Toms, are considered to be worse than eavesdroppers. The active versus passive with respect to seeing and hearing may also be implied by the connotative differences between "spectators" and "audience."

Marshall McLuhan and his followers have suggested that the oral–aural channels of preliterate, or rather, nonliterate man may be enjoying a renaissance. According to this view, as man becomes literate, written language – which must be seen to be read – takes priority over the oral. Recently, however, radio and television have created postliterate man, whose world is once more primarily oral–aural. Many Americans learn the news of the day by hearing it on the radio rather than by reading it in newspapers. Even on television, the argument says, the news is mainly told, not shown. Then, too, telephone conversations are replacing letter writing more and more.

One can contend, however, that television has replaced radio, and thus the visual still supersedes the purely aural. Americans still prefer to get agreements in writing rather than to trust a gentleman's handshake (a tactile sign) or take someone's word or say-so (oral sign) for a contract. Once an agreement is down in black and white, Americans watch out for, and read, the small print, with an "eye" toward avoiding an unfavorable set of conditions.

If Americans do have a deep-seated penchant for the visual sense, as I have tried to suggest by examining American folk speech, the question of what it means remains to be answered. It is not just a matter of being able to see more clearly why Americans tend to look for men of vision to lead them. Much more important is the influence of folk metaphors on scientific thought. American science is not culture-free, no matter how devoutly American scientists wish that it were or think that it is.

As an anthropologist, I am struck by the fact that American anthropologists insist upon being participant observers (no voyeurs!) when they go into the field so as to gain insight into the world-views of other cultures. Why "insight"? Do all examples of problem solving by insight actually involve visual perception? And why world-view?

Anthropologists do not always agree whether man is active or passive with regard to world-view. Bronislaw Malinowski, for example, tended to consider man passive: he depicted man as being molded by the impress of a culturally patterned, cookie cutter kind of world-view, which imposed its structure upon human minds. "What interests me really in the study of the native," Malinowski said, "is his outlook on things, his *Weltanschauung*. Every human culture gives its members a definite vision of the world." In contrast, Robert Redfield, by defining world-view as "the way a people characteristically look outward upon the universe," suggested that man was a more active participant. In any case, whether man passively accepts a culturally determined world-view or actively creates a world-view system, the visual bias in the very search by anthropologists for world-view is evident.

It has been observed that for Americans the universe is essentially something they can draw a picture or diagram of. But surely a person's world is felt, smelled, tasted, and heard as well. This propensity for visual metaphorical categories may produce distortion in attempts to describe facets of American culture. It is unlikely that such distortion would even be noticed, since the distortion, like beauty, is strictly in the subjective eye of the beholder. But what happens when Americans or American scientists seek to describe features of other cultures or the features of the natural world?

It is at least possible that by looking for the world-view of other peoples, we run the risk of imposing our own rank-ordering of the senses upon data that may not be perceived in the same way by the people whose cultures are being described. If we are truly interested in understanding how other peoples perceive reality, we must recognize their cognitive categories and try to escape the confines of our own.

The history of man is full of instances of one group's conscious or unconscious attempts to impose its particular set of cognitive categories upon another group. The imposing group typically claims that its categories represent the true nature of reality (as opposed to the categories of the victimized group, which are deemed odd at best and false at worst). Whether it is nineteenth-century American linguists searching in vain for Latin cases (for example, the dative or accusative) in American Indian languages, or a modern Western physician, imbued with the number three, trying to persuade an American Indian, who believes in the sacredness of the number four, that only three doses or inoculations are sufficient (as in a series of three polio shots), the issue is the same.

This is why it is essential for Americans (and for other peoples as well) to become aware of their dependence upon cognitive categories such as the visual metaphorical mode I have been talking about. Armed with this awareness, it is possible to appreciate more fully the aptness of the visual metaphor Ruth Benedict used to explain why so many social theorists failed to notice custom or culture: "We do not see the lens through which we look." A conscious recognition of our visual bias may help make the lens visible. We must never forget the possible relativity of our own sensory perception categories.

Inventories of the same or similar sense categories found in other cultures may help. Clifford Geertz reports, for example, that the Javanese have five senses (seeing, hearing, *talking*, smelling, and feeling), which do not coincide exactly with our five. The delineation of such differences may teach us just how culture-bound or culture-specific our own observations of nature may be. We tend to delude ourselves into thinking we are studying the nature of nature, foolishly forgetting that we cannot observe raw or pure nature. We can perceive nature only through the mediation of culture, with its panoply of culturally relative cognitive categories.

Much of the study of "natural history" often turns out to be "cultural history" in disguise. Theories and ideas about the natural world are invariably couched in terms of a specific human language and are based upon data obtained from human observation. With human observation expressed in human language, one simply cannot avoid cultural bias.

Searching for culture-free descriptions of nature may be a worthwhile goal, and perhaps man will one day succeed in achieving it. In the meantime, we must be wary of mistaking relatives for absolutes, of mistaking culture for nature. Cross-cultural comparisons of sense categories may not only reveal critical differences in the specific senses, but also whether or not the apparent priority of vision over the other senses is a human universal. For the moment, we can do little more than wait and *see*.

E X E R C I S E S

1   You were asked to keep track of spatial metaphors (e.g. "warm up") that occur in everyday speech. List at least 20 of such phrases and give a short definition.

2   Select three or four of the above. Following the point made by Sapir (see below), what do these metaphors say about our culture? What values are encoded? How do they structure and influence the way we perceive reality?

It is quite an illusion to imagine that one adjusts to reality essentially without the use of language and that language is merely an incidental means of solving specific problems of communication or reflection. The fact of the matter is that the "real world" is to a large extent unconsciously built up on the language habits of the group. . . . We see and hear and otherwise *experience* very largely as we do because the language habits of our community predispose certain choices of interpretation. (Sapir 1949: 69)

5

Relatives and Relations

Notions of kinship and kinship theory: to whom are we related and how? Is there any truth to the idea that "blood is thicker than water"? What constitutes a family? This chapter also discusses different meanings of friendship, romantic relationships, and parent–child relationships.

Relatives and Relations

Social relationships are at the heart of anthropology, just as they are at the heart of life. We are social beings; we exist in a web of social relationships that shape who we are. In this chapter we will look at a variety of relationships we experience and how we define them. We will also explore the way in which cultural meanings are expressed in and through our relations with others. When you hear the word *relationship* you probably first think about romance, as in "they're in (or having) a relationship." Romantic relationships are a very important kind of relationship, especially among people of college age, for that is the socially sanctioned time for young people to explore their identity, sexual and otherwise. College is also the place where young people expect, or are expected, to find a mate. We will, therefore, start with courtship and romantic relationships before moving to a discussion of "kinship," which was for a long time a major focus of anthropology.

Courtship

Ideas and practices of courtship vary considerably around the world. In the West there is a long romantic tradition that there exists only one person ideally suited to you – a "soulmate." This concept is thought to have emerged in the medieval period, but it may have originated with Plato's idea that each person seeks his or her other half. In this cultural scenario, you may meet this "other half" by chance or you may have to overcome obstacles for true love to flower. Romantic novels, poems, songs, and movies express these formulaic themes. These ideas about romance color our expectations of a romantic relationship, even among those who believe the expectations are unrealistic.

Although the background assumptions about romantic relationships in the United States have remained relatively unchanged, courtship rituals have altered a great deal since the middle of the last century. Then, as now, young people met primarily at school and work, but parents and friends took a much larger role in introducing them to each other. Social elites devised what were called "coming out parties," intended to introduce young women to "society," which meant basically to the eligible young men. In many places, this traditional "rite of passage" is fast disappearing, yet in others it is being revived, for example among the Filipino community in San Francisco. In an analogous ritual, the *quinceanera*, 15-year-old Hispanic girls are presented to the rest of the community. The ritual is a way to announce that a girl has reached sexual maturity and is, theoretically, eligible for marriage. Apparently, getting tattooed used to perform a similar function for girls and boys from Samoa, Hawaii, and Tahiti (*San Francisco Chronicle*, December 30, 2001).

College, for the group who is able to attend, has long been considered the primary place for finding a mate, but the means have changed since the early 1960s when I was in college. Then, women's dormitories had what were called "parietals," which meant that women had to be in the dorm by a certain hour at night, usually around 10 p.m. on weekdays and midnight on Saturday. You had to sign out, giving the name of the person you were with and where you were going, and when you returned, you had to sign in, otherwise an administrative official would go in search of you. As far as I know, men did not have parietals and had much more freedom than women. It was expected that a man would call a woman for a date at least a week in advance. They could not just drop by, they could visit the dorm only on certain days and had to remain in the sitting room. Women could not go away for the weekend without parental permission. The school, in other words, was acting *in loco parentis* (in place of parents) by taking on the responsibility for their female children. If this sounds like the dark ages, it was in the 1960s, just before everything changed. I know because I was expelled in 1961 for staying out beyond the curfew. By the mid-1960s many colleges abandoned parietals and began to allow men to visit in the dorms and even in rooms.

We would never have dreamed that a few decades later, there would be co-ed dorms and even co-ed floors and bathrooms. But that is probably the context in which many of you are living. Clearly, there are ample opportunities for men and women to meet each other. Ironically, however, co-ed dorm living has had the effect of diminishing romance rather than fostering it. You get to see each other's habits – messy rooms, wet towels on the floor, hair in rollers etc. – rather than the public *persona*. Dormmates apparently become more like siblings than possible partners; indeed, I have heard the term "dormcest" to refer to a romantic relationship that springs up between dormmates. While dormmates often go out together as friends or in groups, they must seek elsewhere for someone to date.

What is a date?

A *date* is a focal point for romantic relationships. The concept of a date is so commonplace that probably few of you have thought about defining it. Everyone simply knows what it is. As budding anthropologists, however, you need to step back a bit and ask about these most commonplace, taken-for-granted items of your culture, for that is how you will begin to discover the cultural values embedded in them. Following are just a few of the questions you will need to ask in order to find out what a date is: Does the word *date* refer to the person or the event, or both? How many people are involved in a date? Is it assumed they are heterosexual or can they be homosexual, and if so, why? How is going out on a date different from going out with a friend or friends? How is it different from other kinds of appointments? Answers to these questions help to highlight the meaning of the concept *date* and at the same time illuminate the classification of different categories of people. The concept of a date also relates to different categories of time, since dates most normally occur in the evenings, with Saturday night being a primary date time.

The concept of a date, let alone going on one, would be unknown to a huge portion of the world's youth. So, then, what makes the date possible? At the minimum, it requires the means to contact the person you wish to ask for a date, usually a telephone, or today, often a computer with email. Second, it requires a certain degree of independence and freedom of the two parties, who generally do not need parental permission but decide themselves both whom to ask and whether to accept an invitation. This, in turn, involves a specific notion of individual autonomy and responsibility. Third, it requires that the individuals have at least a small amount of their own money so they can go to the movies, take the subway, or go for a coffee or dinner. Fourth, and perhaps most important, it requires a culture which assumes that romantic relationships between young people are desirable or expected, one that permits young people of opposite sexes to be in public together, and offers places where they can go. Without these social underpinnings, would a date be possible?

> Most cultures expect that young people of the same sex do pal around together, so that even if they are in a romantic relationship, being seen together does not raise the same kinds of concerns.

Besides the framework of a date, what are the expectations? What is a date supposed to accomplish? What is its social function? A date is just a date, you might say, it is something to do – for fun. But it is also the means by which young people discover themselves and what they seek in a relationship. Physical attraction plays a large part, at least initially, in "coupling." But people also stress feeling comfortable and being able to talk to the other person. One student told me that finding someone you can talk to is the most important thing in a relationship: "What often begins a relationship is that the two of you discover you can talk to each other, that you have some interests or ideas in common, and you end up staying up late, sometimes all night, just talking." Talking together is the primary way we feel we get to know another person. We learn what they believe in, what they value, and their personal and political goals.

If you were Apache, however, you would not speak to your girlfriend or boyfriend for weeks or months, even as you might go out to events holding hands.

The Saturday Night Date by Margaret Atwood

Ten years ago, I had a girl of 15 ask me: *what was your social life like when you were my age?*

I counted back: that would have been the 50's. "Well," I said, "first the boy would call you up ahead of time and ask you for a date."

Really? she said. (Young people her age did not go on dates by that time. They traveled in schools, like fish, on the spur of the moment.)

"Then he would ring the doorbell, wearing a shirt and tie – *Really?* – and you would ask him in and introduce him to your parents, who were usually your actual biological mother and father – *No kidding!* – and they would all make nervous conversation while you put the finishing touches on your hair." (The hair part was understood.)

What did you wear?

"If you were going to a formal dance, you might have a strapless gown – two melons made of wire, and a skirt that looked like a varnished lettuce. If it was to the drive-in – *The what?* – you'd wear a circle skirt with a crinoline, a cinch belt and white buck shoes with triple-rolled white cotton socks (these all needed explanations), but if it was a more formal occasion, then high-heeled shoes, nylons with seams and a panty girdle. *A what?*

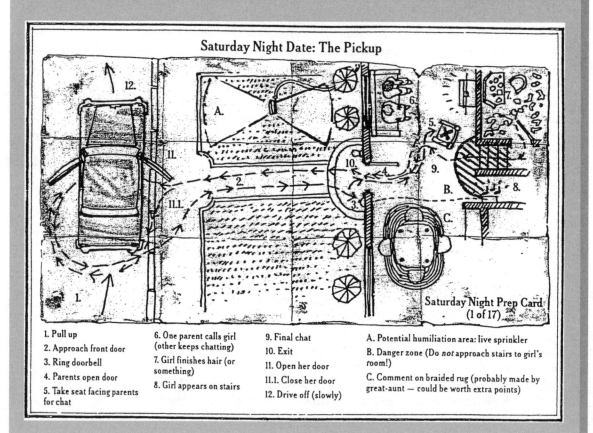

Saturday Night Date: The Pickup

Saturday Night Prep Card (1 of 17)

1. Pull up
2. Approach front door
3. Ring doorbell
4. Parents open door
5. Take seat facing parents for chat
6. One parent calls girl (other keeps chatting)
7. Girl finishes hair (or something)
8. Girl appears on stairs
9. Final chat
10. Exit
11. Open her door
11.1. Close her door
12. Drive off (slowly)

A. Potential humiliation area: live sprinkler
B. Danger zone (Do *not* approach stairs to girl's room!)
C. Comment on braided rug (probably made by great-aunt — could be worth extra points)

("I remember those," said a male friend of my vintage. "The rubber ones. It was steamy in there, like a Turkish bath – and once you got your hand in, you couldn't get it out.")

"Then," I continued, "the boy would escort you to the car, open the door and assist you into it – *ohmigawd!* – and he would park, and extract you from the car, and you would go to the movie, and he would pay." *Really?*

There were many never-stated but well-understood rules for what went on after the movie – a set of complex handholds and bodily movements as stylized as judo, incarnating at least 4,000 years of assumptions about men and women and how they should behave when so entangled – but I didn't go into those, teenagers being notoriously prudish.

We're all flies in amber. Up to the minute, out of date, flavor of the month – these are the pins that fix us into place, and also into time. What a difference a day makes, not to mention a thousand years! Will you – dear readers, inheritors of the future – be able to understand a single word of this? Not if you are giant cockroaches, as some predict. But even if you're still human, you'll have trouble. There's one page of the Talmud that is entirely commentary on a single word of text. And so it is with the Saturday Night Date. A small thing in itself, but what a once-living, now-drowned universe it bodies forth.

According to anthropologist Keith Basso (1970), Apache are sparing of words and feel that "there are types of situations" in which, as one of his consultants commented, "it is right to give up on words" (1970: 217). Typical situations are when someone is a stranger and you are encountering him or her for the first time, another is courtship. Basso described a work group in which one of the members was an outsider. No one spoke to him until they had ample time to observe what kind of man he was. He notes that their "verbal reticence with strangers is directly related to the conviction that the establishment of social relationships is a serious matter that calls for caution, careful judgement, and plenty of time" (p. 217). This is quite different from typical mainstream American practice of engaging strangers in conversation, for example in the check-out line at the supermarket. But given the Apache attitude toward social relations, it is not surprising that words are not risked in courtship in the initial stages. Said one boy of 17:

> It's hard to talk with your sweetheart at first. She doesn't know you and won't know what to say . . . you get very bashful . . . so you just go around together and don't talk. At first, it's better that way. Then after a while, when you know each other, you aren't shy anymore and can talk. (p. 219)

Some of you might wonder, how *do* they get to know each other? And what do they learn about each other while keeping silent? You might want to give it a try. Although Basso's research was conducted in the 1960s, making it quite likely that the situation, or at least aspects of it, have changed since then, it still provides a very interesting contrast to typical American notions of how to conduct a (courtship) relationship.

In the United States, people expect compatibility – sexually, intellectually, and emotionally – with another person *before* they would even consider a committed relationship. How different from Turkish youth in the village where I worked. There it was assumed that compatibility and love would develop *after* marriage! Women wanted a husband who did not swear or drink and who would be a good provider; men wanted a wife who was a virgin, a good worker, and one who would get along with his mother. Physical attraction was rarely mentioned as a prerequisite for a marriage relationship, although a pleasant personality was desired. Most of the marriages were "arranged," that is, they are initiated by the parents of the boy who discuss it with the parents of the girl. When presented with the offer, the young women usually, but not always, had veto power. In many ways this manner of contracting a marriage makes sense in a society where the woman usually moves into the home of her husband's family and would have to get along with his mother, with whom she would be sharing the work of the household.

Urban, elite Turkish youth tend to follow American-European modes of relationship and dating. They go out together – in couples and in groups – to clubs and movies, to malls and snack shops, to sports events and concerts. Their style is quite sophisticated, especially in Istanbul. Yet there are millions of Turks who live in the urban environment but follow village custom. These Turks are poor and have often recently migrated from rural parts of Turkey; some are nominally Muslim, others are quite fundamentalist and do not allow young men and women to mix socially together.

In the United States we expect young people to find their own mates. While Americans extol the notion of *free choice*, our practice also has its costs. Many young people do not find a partner before they enter intense careers where there is little time left over for that kind of activity. There was more leeway in the 1960s, when college graduates at least did not have to rush immediately into career-oriented jobs. The economy was such that people could work part-time and still pay rent and live decently, leaving them more time to explore. Because everything has become more expensive and some things, like rent, have gotten out of proportion with income, it now often takes a full-time salary to just keep afloat. With so little time to find and explore relationships, it is no wonder that myriad dating services and "Personals" in the newspaper and on the Internet have sprung up. Resorting to such services would never have been considered 20 or 30 years ago. Formalized courtship rituals have the benefit that everyone knows the rules and how to play the game; in the absence of such rituals, conflicting ideas and expectations can lead to painful misunderstandings and sometimes to violence.

Couples

Dating sometimes leads to the formation of a "couple," when two people decide to be together in some form of a committed or exclusive relationship. While most of you are probably aware that dating and mating rituals vary cross-culturally, you probably also assume that there are some qualities that are universally expected in a couple relationship, or at least among our European contemporaries. Yet,

Raymonde Carroll, a French woman married to an American man, both of whom are anthropologists, feels quite differently. In her book *Cultural Misunderstandings: The French-American Experience* (1988), she discusses a number of important differences expected in the behavior of couples.

In France, if a couple joins a group of friends, for example, it is expected that "the group has priority over the couple and does not admit an exclusive relationship . . . the group must make sure (often by playing little games or tricks on the lesser known partner) that my couple relationship does not affect or threaten my other relationships" (1988: 63). In addition, she claims, French couples show with words rather than with their bodies and gestures that they are a couple. Often this includes banter that would make many Americans uncomfortable. Carroll reported a typical response:

> when we are with others, in the presence of friends, my partner and I can gently poke fun at each other. . . . [W]e can contradict each other, have "violent" discussions, or take opposing sides on an issue. We can "intervene" (Wouldn't you be better off not having another drink?) . . .; we can become exasperated with each other . . . and even get angry without worrying our friends in the least. . . . In fact, I would go so far as to say that one would probably be wary of a couple who always seemed to be in perfect agreement. (pp. 63–4)

She believes this type of behavior would be unacceptable among most American couples.

American couples, she claims, show that they are a couple visibly – by standing close to each other, holding hands, and other physical contact. Furthermore,

> the ideal American couple always agrees. No contradictions, and especially no "corrections" . . . no admonition, no intervention, no advice, no disagreement, no radically different opinions, no fighting, no frowns, no disapproving silences, no reproaches, no anger, and especially, no yelling. All conflict, all threat of conflict or suggestion of conflict, is a bad sign: the couple has problems and probably will not last. (p. 65)

This is somewhat of an exaggeration but it does, I believe, capture some major differences in what people expect in a couple relationship. But why do these differences exist? Carroll outlines what she believes are the *cultural* premises that underpin the differences.

1   *French*: "The stability of the couple is created by the possibility (the freedom) to be myself, to be accepted as I am with my faults as well as my strong points" (p. 68).
    American: "The stability of the couple is created by the fact that my partner encourages me to be as I would like to be. . . . [C]riticism, reproach, disagreement, and contradiction are therefore, by definition, destructive" (p. 69).
2   *French*: "Our affective ties and our conduct are separate; one is not necessarily the reflection of the other. Thus, we can easily accept that a couple may spend their time fighting but that this doesn't prevent them from loving each other. . . . Affective ties are not necessarily synonymous with harmony" (p. 68).

American: "Affective bonds and behavior reflect each other. . . . Affective bonds are the equivalent of harmony" (p. 69).

3   *French*: A "couple's relationship is considered to be a relationship of equality or, rather, of equilibrium in its complementarity" (p. 69). Except for the sexual aspect, she feels it resembles more the relationship between siblings.

American: Because "each person needs the other to satisfy his or her desires (encouragement, sympathy, support), the couple's relationship can only be a relationship of interdependency, or of alternating dependency" (pp. 69–70). Again, except for the sexual aspect, Carroll feels that American couple relationships are modeled more on parent–child relationships, especially because we do not expect the ideal parent to criticize, correct or humiliate us in public but to encourage and support (p. 70).

Whether or not you agree completely with these characterizations, Carroll does point to some major areas of difference in couples' expectations of each individual in a committed relationship. Any of you who have been involved in a heterocultural relationship no doubt have your own examples of how these implicit, unvocalized assumptions can cause puzzlement, anger, resentment, and hurt. Unless they are confronted and analyzed, the relationship will probably not last.

Greeting and leave taking

Couple behavior is often quite distinct from that between friends or family. How can you tell who is greeting whom? Try to imagine the kinds of behaviors that are expressed when a lover is greeting or leaving a lover, a parent is greeting or leaving a child, a male friend is greeting or leaving a male friend/female friend, a host is greeting a guest or a guest is leaving the host, etc. Then, as an exercise in observation, you might go out to some busy meeting place and observe greeting and leave-taking behaviors.

This is just what a group of social psychologists at the University of California at Davis did when they conducted a study of couple behavior at airports (Aproberts, *San Francisco Chronicle*, C-6, December 12, 1999). Some of the couples were asked to answer a questionnaire about their relationship, others were simply observed. Airports are ideal places to observe all kinds of emotional dramas, for they highlight in a very concrete way the more mundane activities of greetings and goodbyes, reunions and leave taking. The researchers observed numerous reunions and partings and began to categorize behaviors, such as "the goodbye hug," "contact seeking" (various forms of stroking, hand holding, leaning heads on shoulders), and "grooming behavior" where a man might smooth a woman's hair or a woman might pick lint off a man's jacket, that the couples engaged in. Soon they were able to surmise something about the type and quality of the relationship by the kinds of behaviors exhibited.

But such a study does not stop with mere description. Analysis begins when you start to ask *why* certain kinds of behaviors occur with different kinds of persons. In answering that question you would also need to consider notions of personhood, gender, relationship, age-related behavior, power and authority, and respect and deference. How are these notions given visible form? Are there definite cultural and ethnic differences in expression? In France friends generally kiss each other on both cheeks when they meet and when they part; in Belgium this is extended to three kisses – left, right, left again! In Turkey women embrace and kiss women, and men embrace and kiss men when they meet, but, except among the urban elite, such behavior is not acceptable *between* the sexes. In the United States friends merely wave, give a "high-five," or possibly shake hands. A student from Iowa – a place that seemed as exotic to many of my students as New Guinea – said that a typical wave in greeting is two fingers off the steering wheel as you pass each other on the road. Some women in the United States, but rarely men, do embrace when greeting or leaving each other. Greeting and leave taking are emotionally charged events (after all, we do not know if or when we will see that person again); we recognize this by the various rituals that, ironically, because they are ritualized, seemingly minimize their importance.

Marriage

Until fairly recently, the expected outcome of a couple relationship was marriage; before moving on to other options, let us think for a moment about how marriage is typically handled in the United States and other Western nations. It very closely follows Van Gennep's three-part schema for rites of passage discussed in chapter 1. When you marry you *separate* yourself from your friends, at least to some extent. You are meant to "cleave only unto" your spouse. The formation of a new social unit is what, in part, the wedding ceremony accomplishes. The *liminal* period is, for those who can afford it, the "honeymoon" – a trip away from family and friends that allows you to adjust to each other and the new state of being married. Upon return you take up residence together, often in a new home, and are *reintegrated* back into society as a new entity – a married couple. The public recognition through public rituals is what formalizes and gives legitimacy to the new social state, which may be one reason gays and lesbians want to be able to legally marry.

> Many people spend inordinate amounts of money, and often go deeply into debt, for this one day – money for a wedding gown, for flowers, for food and a wedding cake, and presents for the attendants of the bride and groom.

Most societies recognize a period of time – sometimes only a night, more often several days or weeks – necessary for the couple to become a social entity. In the Turkish village on the morning of the wedding, the bride is surrounded by her family and girlfriends getting prepared (elaborate bath, hair braiding, and getting dressed). Once she is ready, she is taken from her home, heavily veiled, to the home of her husband and his parents. There she sits "in state" all day, not speaking to the friends and relatives of her husband's family who come to view her. After the marriage is formalized by the *imam*, the couple can retreat to their own room. Although they wake up in the husband's household, there is a period of 40 days people acknowledge as a liminal period, at the end of which they take up their roles and chores as a couple in the village.[1]

Today, in Europe and in the United States, there are a number of other options for couple behavior. Children in grade and high school "go steady" and begin to engage in sexual relationships much earlier than previous generations. Couple relations such as these are not expected to end in marriage, they are experiments or trials, although often they are emotionally costly. In some regions of the United States, notably large cities in the Northeast and West coast, young couples can "live together" more freely than in the past. They do not have to get married; indeed, the reason to do so is often to receive benefits such as health care, social security, inheritance, etc. (One would think that a great affluent nation like the United States might be able to figure a way to insure that all its citizens were entitled to, and able to receive, such benefits regardless of marital status.)

Among all groups and nations there are restrictions on whom one can marry, yet the rules vary considerably. Almost everywhere marriage is forbidden with the closest relatives, but sexual relations with them are not that unusual, for example father–daughter incest (Herman 1981; McKinnon 1995). In some places, notably parts of the Middle East, marriage with a first cousin is the preferred type of marriage, especially between the children of two brothers. In the village in Turkey where I did my fieldwork, half of the marriages contracted while I was there were between relatives, of which one quarter were between first cousins on either the mother's or father's side (Delaney 1991: 108).

In the United States, cousin marriages were fairly common in the eighteenth and nineteenth centuries, especially in Boston and New York. Lewis Henry Morgan, who was a lawyer in upstate New York in the nineteenth century and is considered the "founder" of kinship studies, married his first cousin. Perhaps that contributed to his interest in kinship. We will discuss his kinship work shortly. Even today, marriage with a first cousin is permitted, with certain restrictions, in 26 states including New York, California, and Massachusetts, according to a report in the *New York Times* (April 4, 2002). Martin Ottenheimer's *Forbidden Relatives* (1996) discusses the issue at length.

Among Australian aborigines, people are assigned to "marriage groups" at birth. There are a number of these, but for purposes of exposition let us look at an 8-"class" system shown in table 5.1. This is the way it works: If you are a male *Panunga* you must marry a female in the *Purula* group, and your children (male or female) will be *Appungerta*. But if you are a male *Purula* you must marry a female in the *Panunga* group and then your children (male or female) will be *Kumara*. An *Appungerta* must marry an *Umbitchana*; if male, the children will be in the *Panunga* group; if female, they will be assigned to the *Panunga* group.[2] All that you need to know is which group you belong to and which group you must take a partner from.

Table 5.1   Australian aboriginal marriage groups

I	II	III	IV
Panunga	Purula	Appungerta	Kumara
Uknaria	Ungalla	Bulthara	Umbitchana
Bulthara	Kumara	Uknaria	Purula
Appungerta	Umbitchana	Panunga	Ungalla

All of the foregoing, whether Australian or American, has assumed and related to heterosexual couples; Carroll notes that in France, at least, "couple" refers to a heterosexual couple. It would be interesting to explore cultural differences in homosexual couple relationships. Do they follow the same patterns as heterosexuals in each culture or are there distinct differences within each culture? Why, for example, do homosexual couples in the United States seek marriage? Is it primarily for the benefits just mentioned or because it is the culturally approved way to legitimate and recognize a committed relationship? Why have so few states allowed it? What does that say about the meaning of the word *marriage*? Do homosexual couples in other cultures seek to marry?

> From his fieldwork in Indonesia, anthropologist Tom Boellstorff writes that there are lots of people there who do not see homosexual identity and heterosexual marriage as incompatible, a practice that calls into question assumptions about sexuality and lifestyle held by many people in Western societies.

Marriage is, itself, a culturally specific term. Just because we find conjugal relationships between men and women and family-type relationships all around the world doesn't mean that *marriage* is universal or that *family* means the same thing everywhere. The notion of marriage in the West derives primarily from a Christian heritage that prescribes heterosexuality; according to the biblical text, male and female were created for each other and for the purpose of procreation. For these reasons the church has been loath to accept homosexuality, and has considered it a sin. Secondly, Christianity understands the conjugal relation as a *union* of a man and a woman – "and the two shall become one" – the couple forms one entity (with the male as head). That is hardly the case among numerous other peoples. Turkish villagers, for example, were adamant that marriage was not a union. It was a contractual relationship for economic and sexual benefits; the two individuals remained distinct and valued that separateness.

I discovered that one of the unexpected benefits of an arranged marriage, at least for the woman, is that she is not identified with her husband. This leaves her psychologically and emotionally much freer than her American contemporaries who, from my observation, often tend to become merged with the identity of their husbands. Since the choice and decision to marry a particular man were hers, she is affected by his behavior. In the Turkish village, if a husband does something stupid it does not reflect on the woman; his behavior has nothing to do with her. On the other hand, her behavior does seriously reflect on him; she can tarnish his *honor* if she raises suspicions that she has looked at or talked with another man. This has the result that her freedom to move about is quite circumscribed. In American culture where individual freedom and choice are quintessential values, the institution of arranged marriages would not have a chance. Yet I cannot say that Turkish village marriages are any less "happy" than American marriages.

Because Americans expect so much more from a marriage than do Turkish villagers, perhaps it is not so surprising that about half end in divorce. Or is this high percentage because Americans have very little idea of what marriage *is*, and have little instruction about it? The conventional idea and romantic notion is that marriage is expected to last "until death us do part." This is a Christian notion – part of the marriage vows – and is, obviously, not a universal belief or expectation; indeed, many Americans no longer believe or expect this kind of commitment. Thus it is important to try to understand what is going on that so many marriages end in divorce. Why is it, for instance, that most divorces occur after the birth of a first child? Many couples do not have a clue about what to expect as they move from being a couple to being a family. As one person told my daughter and her husband as they were expecting their first child: "It is as if a bomb fell on your marriage." That turned out to be good advice for it warned them that dramatic changes were about to occur.

Single fathers – men who get custody of the children – do not experience the same kind of hardship. First, they typically earn more money than the wife did, they tend to remarry fairly quickly whereas divorced women do not, and, because their situation is seen as unusual, they find sympathetic women to help with child care.

If you do not weather that storm and you split up, the usual result is that a man's standard of living rises and the woman's plummets. "When a couple with children breaks up, frequently the man becomes single, while the woman becomes a single parent" (Pearce 1990: 267). And that usually means considerable hardship. "For most women and children divorce means precipitous downward mobility – both economically and socially" (Okin 1989: 161).

Divorce exposes the reality that marriage is not, and cannot be, an equal partnership. While many young couples today say they want to share child-rearing and domestic tasks, that is rarely possible, because their choices are already socially constrained. If marriage is to become an equal partnership, then wider societal changes are necessary, including variable work times and job sharing, notions of career (see chapter 3), and the provision of more widespread and accessible child care and health care.[3] Instead, what often happens is that women end up working the "second shift" (Hochschild with Machtung 1989) of housework and child care in addition to their wage-earning jobs. Political scientist Susan Okin, among others, has addressed this issue in a chapter titled "Vulnerability in Marriage" in her book *Justice, Gender, and the Family* (1989):

> The division of labor within marriage (except in rare cases) makes wives far more likely than husbands to be exploited both within the marriage relationship and in the world of work outside the home. To a great extent and in numerous ways, contemporary women in our society are *made* vulnerable by marriage itself. They are first set up for vulnerability during their developing years by their personal (and socially reinforced) expectations that they will be the primary caretakers of children, and that in fulfilling this role they will need to try to attract and to keep the economic support of a man, to whose work life they will be expected to give priority. They are rendered vulnerable by the actual division of labor within almost all current marriages. They are disadvantaged at work by the fact that the world of wage work, including the professions, is still largely structured around the assumption that "workers" have wives at home. They are rendered far more vulnerable if they become the primary caretakers of children, and their vulnerability peaks if their marriages dissolve and they become single parents. (1989: 138–9)

I have first-hand experience of this. When I got divorced and became a single parent, my daughter was only a year old. I received minimal child support payments for about a year and then they stopped. It was difficult to collect the payments as the courts were, and still are, ill-equipped to deal with the demand. I was able to earn only slightly more than I had to pay a babysitter (there was no day care then, but it wouldn't have helped since day care is also extremely expensive, often taking half of a woman's take-home pay).

The realization of my vulnerability radicalized me. I realized that no matter how much I worked, I would be unable to pay the babysitter *and* also the rent, the food, medical bills, clothes, let alone some toys and entertainment. This realization inspired me to investigate our cultural assumptions about gender and family. Even though I was divorced, I was still a mother and I wanted very much to be involved with my daughter's care and upbringing. Is it more socially valuable to have all single mothers of young children working full-time, or would it be better for the children and for society if they spent at least part of their time *with* their children?

At that time, the only option for me was to go on welfare, for which I was very thankful; it allowed me to give up the futile attempts to collect child support, to spend more time with my daughter, and try to get on with my life. However, welfare in the United States is an extremely stigmatized and punitive program. Out of 17 industrialized nations, the United States ranks as one of the lowest in its "family support" program, only Israel and Ireland being lower.[4] The stereotypes of welfare mothers are not only erroneous but also racist (for further information see Delaney 1998: 241–7 and notes). We need to become a nation more friendly to families whether these are two-parent, single-parent, heterosexual or homosexual. Many scholars agree that providing adequate support for all children in the United States is economically possible; indeed, it could alter the welfare of all children in the world. What is lacking is the social will to do so (Katz 1986: 272; Leach 1994: 174). This state of affairs is even more appalling when you realize that welfare was and is only a tiny fraction of the military budget.

Beyond that girls need to be raised to think they will have to support themselves and possibly a family; instead, however, the old "romance" tales continue to fire girls' imaginations and condition their prospects. In the United States, romance novels such as the Harlequin books are read by more than 20 million people, mostly girls and women. A study done in 1981 showed that Harlequins accounted for about 12 percent of the paperback market in the United States, and 28 percent in Canada (Jensen 1984: 15). Apparently, they meet a need for both excitement and security. "The basic plot is that the hero and heroine meet and fall in love but there is an obstacle to their love," thus providing the excitement. "The barriers are removed in the last chapter and the hero and heroine are allowed to unite" and live happily ever after. "Any variation unfolds itself within this structure" (p. 76), thus making readers secure in the knowledge that love conquers all. Through novels like these and other social influences, girls are conditioned to become sexually attractive to some male who will fall in love with them and support them. While the realities do not support this script, parents, guidance counselors, and other authority figures perpetuate this scenario.

Women's work and careers are often thought to be secondary, merely supplementary to the main *breadwinner's* job and income. Men's higher salaries reflect this antiquated idea that men should be the supports of families and therefore should be paid a higher, "family" wage; the discrepancy in male–female wages has remained despite the fact that more women are working today and many of them are supporting families (see also chapter 3, p. 103). Women's work *in* the home, whether cooking and cleaning, or the "dependency work" (Young 1995) of caring for children, the sick, and the elderly, is not considered work; instead, it is considered a "labor of love." Yet men could not work as they do and become "breadwinners" without all this subsidiary labor (cooking, laundry, cleaning, child or elderly care, etc.). To the extent that men have been *exempt* from dependency work, they are dependent on the women who do it, but this is almost never acknowledged. A very interesting report on the value of women's traditional work can be found in *If Women Counted* (Waring 1990).

Just so you don't think this is purely a woman's point of view, I cite two male sociologists who go even further. Carl Degler, a Stanford social historian, has written:

> One might want to question the term "the historic family" as if that was a universal stable entity throughout time; see discussion following.

The historic family has depended for its existence and character on women's subordination . . . meaning that a woman will subordinate her individual interests to those of others – the members of the family. . . . [T]he equality of women and the institution of the family have long been at odds with each other. (Degler 1980: vi–viii)

In addition, the well-known black social theorist at Harvard, William Julius Wilson, agrees. He said: "Historically, stable marriage systems have rested upon coercion, overt or veiled, and on inequality. . . . Without coercion, divorce and single motherhood rates will remain high" (Wilson, cited in Stacey 1996: 68). I am not sure what Degler means by the "historic family" since family forms have not remained the same since time immemorial; nevertheless, the statements do seem to apply to families since the industrial revolution. The choice facing the United States (and other highly industrialized nations) is whether to coerce women into the "traditional" family and prevent their full personhood or to develop creative, supportive, alternative ways to foster fulfilling work for women *and* nurturing care for children, the ill, and the elderly.

Family

Family, like marriage, is another of those terms we use freely, assuming it is a self-evident, natural entity necessary to the survival of the human race. As a natural entity we further assume it is universal. However, it is precisely these seemingly natural, self-evident concepts and social forms that should be scrutinized. Just because humans generally live in domestic household groups doesn't mean that the *family* is universal. Once again it is useful to investigate the meaning of the word. Etymologically, it has a very particular meaning and history in the West. Derived from the Latin *familia* and *famulus*, it meant all those dependent on a male head. It included not just wife and children but also slaves and servants. That is where the word comes from, but the idea of a male-headed family also has biblical roots. The male is the established head of the family; he is really the one who *has* a family. This becomes obvious when one becomes aware of the reluctance of government officials, among others, to consider single parents with children as families and why they are most often referred to as *female-headed households* or possibly *broken families*.

If they were considered families, there would be less stigma and more social support and concern for them. Because so many marriages end in divorce and many women are raising children as single parents, perhaps it is time to rethink the entire notion of family.

Traditionally, the notion of family has assumed a heterosexual couple and their biological children; sometimes it included grandparents, especially if they were living under the same roof. Today, however, in addition to single parents, there are heterosexual couples raising non-biological, adopted children, and gay couples raising children. In the first instance there is no "blood" connection between the parents and the child, but the "proper" family form is affirmed especially if the adopted child is of the same race or ethnic group. That family can easily be assimilated to the "normal" family form. But interracial and transnational adoptions present even more of a challenge to the biological notions of family and these can provoke hostility from the surrounding community. My second grandson was adopted from Korea; he does not look like his parents or his brothers. My daughter reported one nasty encounter at the supermarket when a woman walked up to her and in front of her son said "he is not your *real* son, is he?" Then, "he's Chinese, isn't he?" When she said, "no, he is from Korea," the woman replied, "oh, it's all the same thing anyway!" Some Native American groups do not want *their* children to be adopted outside of the community, and some countries will not permit transnational adoptions for fear the children will be used for their organs.[5] Gays and lesbians are able to adopt children in some states. In some lesbian couples, one of the women will opt to have the baby by sperm donation. Often her partner will not be allowed to adopt the child, that is, to become its other parent. But while there is a "blood" connection with one of the parents, the family form challenges the norm.

In her book *Families We Choose: Lesbians, Gays, Kinship* (1990), anthropologist Kath Weston writes about the way gays and lesbians go about constructing families, especially when their own "blood" relatives shun them. For many of them, family doesn't necessarily include children. Should all of these different groupings be considered *family*, or should the term be restricted to its traditional sense?

This familial topic is provocatively addressed in an article titled "Is There a Family?" by anthropologists Collier, Rosaldo, and Yanagisako, who raised the question of whether the family is, indeed, universal. Reviewing the anthropological literature on the family, they pointed out how its universality was simply assumed, and how the logic for that assumption was circular. The "logic of the argument is that because people need nurturance, and people get nurtured in The Family, then people need The Family" (1992: 41). But nurturance could be provided in a number of ways and by people other than family. They show that when the idea of "nurturance" is scrutinized, it becomes clear that it means more than

> the provision of food, clothing, and shelter required for biological survival. What is evoked by the word *nurturance* is a certain kind of relationship: a relationship that entails affection and love, that is based on cooperation as opposed to competition, that is enduring rather than temporary, that is noncontingent rather than contingent upon performance, and that is governed by feeling and morality instead of law and contract. (p. 42)

The family represents to many of us the place of refuge, the place where people love you no matter what, the place where you will be taken care of. This idealized conception of the family operates to create expectations and longings that persist throughout our lives. The reality, for many people, however, is just the reverse; the family may not be a place that provides support and nurturance, indeed it may be a place of terrible emotional and physical violence. Because the family is sacrosanct and the ultimate *private* sphere, it has been off bounds for the law; police and child welfare workers are hesitant to interfere and thus serious problems often go undetected for a long time.

Collier, Rosaldo, and Yanagisako argue that the idealized view of the family emerged historically as industry was separating from the home; "what gives shape to much of our conception of The Family is its symbolic opposition to work and business, in other words, to the market relations of capitalism" (1992: 42). In discussing and analyzing the family, theorists often assume that it is a unity that stands as a distinct and separate entity, particularly when facing the world. Inside the family, however, there are often very conflicting goals and desires. For example, there may be conflicts over the way the household money is spent, the way chores are allocated, or who has the burden of housework and child care.

This brief discussion has, I hope, convinced you that it is extremely important to try to understand the definitions and meanings of various social groupings and relationships from, as anthropologists often say, "the native's point of view." This assertion also carries through to the next section. Kinship was, and continues to be, a major focus of study in anthropology and a major contribution to the social sciences.

Kinship: Relatives and Relations

Kinship is a vast area of social relations that has occupied anthropologists from the beginning; kinship and religion were the major topics of study when the field of anthropology emerged in the nineteenth century. Kinship concerns *kin* or people we call *relatives* – those people to whom we are related by blood or marriage, or, in anthropological jargon, by *consanguinity* (blood) and *affinity* (affines, relatives by marriage). What forcefully struck some of the early anthropologists was their discovery that there existed significant differences between the *kinship systems* of different societies. It became the task of these anthropologists to investigate and explain these differences.

Lewis Henry Morgan

Lewis Henry Morgan, considered the "founding father" of kinship studies, noticed that the Iroquois near whom he lived in upper New York state had a kinship *system* very different from the English-American one. For example, where we have two different words to demarcate the people we think of as *father* and *father's brother* (uncle in English), or *mother* and her sister (aunt in English), the Iroquois use the same word. That is, if you were Iroquois, you would use the same word to refer to your mother as to her sister, your aunt. The children of both your mother's sister and your father's brother would be called by you *"brother"* and *"sister,"* although the children of your mother's brother or your father's sister would be called the equivalent of *"cousin."* Notice that in this instance, the only difference is the sex of the parent's sibling. If you had been Morgan, what would you make of this? How would you resolve it?

> I put these words in quotes because they are not really equivalents, but to use the Iroquois terms would not help either. At least this way you will know from your/our system who is referred to.

The more Morgan came to know the Iroquois, the more he became fascinated as well as perplexed. Wasn't it obvious that family relations must be the same everywhere since they rest on the same biological facts of sex and reproduction? What was the reason for this very different system? He began to wonder if all Native American groups had a similar system. He devised a questionnaire that he took when he visited other Native American groups. He then wondered about the variety of kinship systems around the world, and sent the questionnaire out with missionaries, explorers, and government officials to all parts of the globe. Morgan thought that the completed questionnaires might provide a clue to the relationship between different groups of people and their diffusion across the globe. He assumed, for example, that if the Native American kinship system was the same as that prevailing in India, there must be a historical connection between the two groups of people.

He asked the missionaries, explorers, etc. to fill in the blanks giving the correct native word that corresponded to our relationship of mother, father, sister, brother, aunt, uncle, cousin, grandmother, etc. All of this material, along with his discussion and theorizing of it, was compiled and included in the largest and most expensive book the Smithsonian had ever published, *Systems of Consanguinity and Affinity in the Human Family* (1871). Morgan's questions and the survey seem straightforward and fairly simple, but they turned out to be extremely complicated. What kind of problems do you think were encountered? How would you go about finding out who is related to whom?

In order to be able to ask such questions, one first needs to know the language of each culture studied. But if there is no word to distinguish someone's father from his brother, how can one ask someone who is his/her father? It is, clearly, not just a matter of language and translation, although that is obviously very important. An investigator would surely need to have fairly intimate knowledge of the society and the existing personal relationships, something the early anthropologists, explorers, and colonial officials rarely had.

Nevertheless, after collecting and comparing thousands of charts from different parts of the world, Morgan discerned two primary types of kinship systems, each with myriad variations. The two major types he called *classificatory* and *descriptive*; consult the charts in figures 5.1–5.4 for examples. For those of you who have not seen a kinship chart, *Ego* is you and the relations and terms are from your perspective. Triangles are the symbols for men and circles for women; the equal sign means marriage, horizontal lines link sibling groups, and vertical lines show the children from each parental couple.

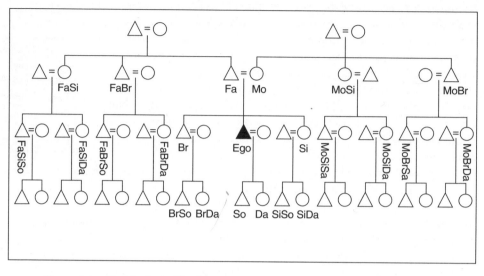

Figure 5.1   Kinship chart: The descriptive system.

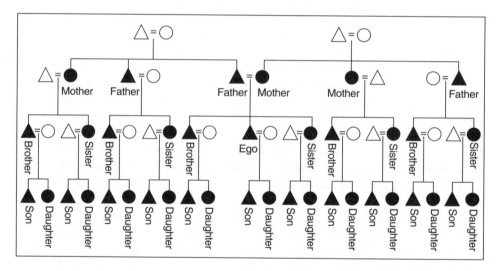

Figure 5.2   Kinship chart: Classificatory system.

1   The *classificatory* type of system was called such because it classifies a whole group of relatives by the same term. For example, all the men of the generation above you (men of your "father's" generation) on your "father's," or male, side would be called by the same term, let's say *tama*, and the males on your mother's, or female, side would be called *vungo*. The same idea (but with different terms) would be used to categorize or classify all the women in that generation. In some systems, such as the "Hawaiian," all of the men in each generation (above yours, yours, and after yours) would be called by the same terms, i.e., not distinguished by male or female side.

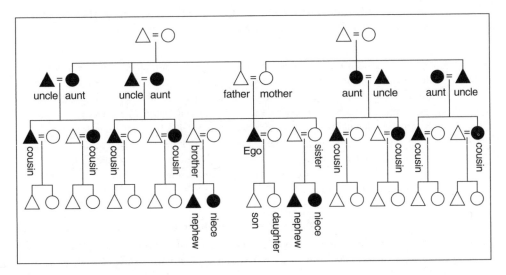

Figure 5.3   Kinship chart: American Eskimo system.

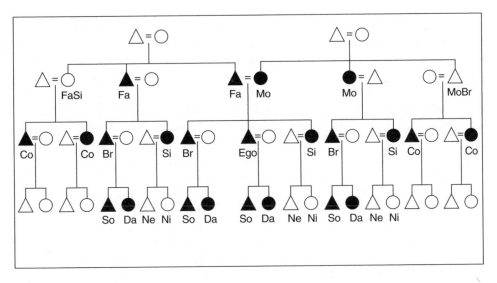

Figure 5.4   Kinship chart: Iroquois system.

2   A *descriptive* system would have separate words for each distinct relationship. The Euro-American system is a modified form of a descriptive system since the same word (e.g. *aunt*) is used to denote a father's sister and a mother's sister. Other systems, the Turkish for example, is more descriptive because it has different words for each of those relations: *teyze* (mother's sister) and *hala* (father's

sister). For Morgan, the descriptive system was the epitome, the true and correct system. Here is his famous definition:

> As a system it is based upon a true and logical appreciation of the natural outflow of the streams of blood, of the distinctiveness and perpetual divergence of these several streams, and of the difference in degree, numerically, and by lines of descent, of the relationship of each and every person to the central *Ego*. It is, therefore, a natural system, founded upon the nature of descents, and it may be supposed to have been of spontaneous growth. But it manifestly proceeds upon the assumption of the existence of marriage between single pairs, and of the certainty of parentage through this marriage relation. Hence it must have come into existence after the establishment of marriage between single pairs. (1871: 468–9)

Morgan assumed the differences related to the stage of evolution each group had reached. From the simplest, most "primitive" type of classificatory system up to the supposedly more advanced descriptive system, Morgan arranged each culture in evolutionary sequence depending on the type of kinship system in use. Not surprisingly, European/American culture was the epitome and the standard because they used the descriptive system, although, as noted, it was not the most descriptive.

Morgan's evolutionary model of kinship and cultures was worked out primarily in *Ancient Society*, published in 1877. Morgan's theories were picked up by Marx and Engels as the basis for their theories of the *Origin of the Family, Private Property and the State* (1884). Morgan believed that the motive for the change from a classificatory to a descriptive kinship system was the development of private property, which he believed would just *naturally* be in the hands of men, who, just as naturally, would want to pass it down to their "legitimate" heirs. Morgan's theories remained the basis of Soviet social science until the collapse of the Soviet Union.

There are several things that demand clarification here. When Morgan first encountered the classificatory system he assumed that people were not pair-bonding, that they were engaging in promiscuous intercourse and group marriage; that was the only way he could imagine that the kinship terms made sense. However, behind this was another assumption that was not articulated, namely, that always and everywhere kinship terms *reflect* biological relations, specifically the "streams of blood" as they flow from one generation to the next. In other words, he, like most other theorists of his time and like most people in the United States and Europe today, believed that kinship was/is a matter of sex, reproduction, and biology, reflecting knowledge of the "facts of life." Thus, he naturally assumed that people with classificatory systems were unaware of the biology of reproduction.

Before moving on to the issue of what kin terms mean, it is worthwhile to note that there were a couple of other voices on the topic of kinship. A contemporary of Morgan, John McLennan, a Scotsman, suggested that kinship terminological systems were merely forms of address and did not necessarily indicate blood relationships. He hypothesized that the kinship system was a means to incorporate and be able to address everyone in the group. It was a way of indicating who was in the group and who was a stranger. Nevertheless, for McLennan, just as for Morgan, real, true kinship was a matter of sex, blood, and biology; their only difference concerned the nature of the kin *terms*.[6]

Later, other kinship theorists concerned themselves with issues of *descent*, which focused mainly on *lineages* whether patrilineal or matrilineal, or with *alliance*, where the focus was on the bonds created between affines. Alliance theory depended on the idea that marriages between members of different groups were a deterrence to intertribal warfare, no doubt influenced by E. B. Tylor's famous suggestion that one must "marry out or be killed out" (1889: 267). Mostly these theories were worked out from the study of groups in Africa, and generally the anthropologists continued to believe that kinship was a matter of blood, sex, and biology.

In the 1970s a few new voices began to challenge these biological assumptions. A. M. Hocart, in a very short but influential article titled "Kinship Systems" (1973), brought the question of translation to the forefront. He noted that if you ask a Melanesian man: "Who is your *tama*?" he will often point to his "father." So the anthropologists duly wrote down "father" as the meaning of *tama*. "It was soon noticed, however, that other men besides the father are called *tama*. By all rules the first translation should have been dropped, and a new one found to cover all the different *tamas*, and thus express the essence of *tama*-ship" (1973: 173). Instead what happened is that anthropologists accepted the first meaning and then *extended* it to cover the others. "That expression implies that the meaning father is primary and that all other uses result from extending the term to an ever-widening circle of kinsmen" (p. 174), but that is simply wrong, since "these terms do not express consanguinity, as we have unfortunately been accustomed by Morgan to believe, but they fix the place of any relative according to generation and side" (p. 175). We might have learned a great deal more about kinship and kinship systems had we turned the issue around and asked what "fatherhood" might look like through the lens of *tama*-ship.

While *we* want to know nearest of kin, the Melanesian wants to know what generation (basically, age-set) and side (male line or female line) a person belongs to. "All our difficulties spring from a preconceived idea that kinship terms everywhere try to express the same thing as they do in Aryan and Semitic languages, and that in those languages they show the place on the family tree" (p. 176). Not only have we totally misunderstood other people's notions of kin, we have also very seriously misunderstood our own.

David Schneider, an anthropologist at the University of Chicago, began in the 1970s to undermine Western, and especially anthropologists', ingrained ideas about kinship. He first became aware of differences in thinking about kinship when he did fieldwork on the Pacific island of Yap, but he also realized that many Americans among whom he conducted fieldwork included their pets or roommates as "part of the family" but excluded some of those clearly related by blood.

Although we believe that "blood is thicker than water," Schneider noted, in an oft-quoted statement, how difficult it is "at times to convince an American that blood as a fluid has nothing in it which *causes* ties to be deep and strong" (1972: 48; emphasis mine), except insofar as our culturally informed thinking makes us believe so. Following Schneider's point to its logical conclusion, one has to realize that, indeed, blood does not constitute, but *symbolizes*, relations of kinship among

Euro-Americans and numerous, but not all, others. This is not because of the fact that even members of the same family may not have the same blood type, but rather, that blood (in general) is the symbol for biogenetic relationship. In investigating kinship relations anywhere, one must first understand the cultural categories and symbols inherent in the society. The kinship system is part of the cultural whole and, thus, cannot be easily separated out and compared with "kinship systems" elsewhere, as had been done until then. For Schneider, as noted in chapter 1, the cultural system is an interconnected system of symbols and meanings that includes its background notions about the world and how it came to be, in other words, a society's "cosmology." One place to investigate these notions is to examine a society's origin myths – those foundational narratives that shape a culture's identity and destiny.

In the West, the primary origin narrative has been Genesis. Regardless of whether one is a believer, it is extremely useful to know something about this narrative in studying the West. Notions of how humans come into being are expressed in Genesis and are, I believe, symbolically related to notions of Creation – how the world and all the other things come into existence. We have already discussed this relationship a little in chapter 3, but it becomes very relevant in the context of kinship.

Even our ideas about the biological, sexual foundation of kinship are not as obvious as it might first appear. We associate reproduction primarily with women – with pregnancy and childbirth – and feel that reproduction is what allies us most closely with animals. We do what comes "naturally." These assumptions led Simone de Beauvoir in *The Second Sex* to claim that women are devalued because they merely reproduce the species while men produce monuments of culture. In other words, she equated women with *nature* and men with *culture*. Anthropologist Sherry Ortner took exception to the belief in a (now) famous article, "Is Female to Male as Nature is to Culture?" (1974). The cause of women's secondary status, she believed, is not rooted *in* nature but rather that in all cultures women are more closely *associated* with nature and that culture's project is to subordinate nature. Reproduction, we have assumed, is a matter of nature and is therefore universal; it is devalued both because it is associated with nature not culture, and with women rather than men.

Marilyn Strathern, a British anthropologist, challenged this widely held view. In "No Nature, No Culture: The Hagen Case" (1980) she demonstrated that the nature–culture dichotomy, long held to be universal, was not the way the Hagen of New Guinea conceptualized their world. They advocate a major division between the "wild" and "domesticated," and while this dichotomy is related to their ideas about gender, they do not easily map onto Western views.

The Western notion of nature, I believe, is deeply embedded in our views about the cosmos that originally derived from the Bible. In Genesis, nature was created by God; it was material and dependent. It was governed by divinely inscribed laws, a view that prompted early modern scientists to investigate the natural world. In modern scientific culture, God (and divine law) has dropped out of the picture, yet the notion that nature is law-governed is a biblical legacy. As it rests on specific cultural (religious) texts, this notion of nature cannot, therefore, be universal. Since different peoples have different cosmologies, their concept of "nature" will also be different.

Westerners think of reproduction as self-evidently natural, but that view was itself historically and culturally constructed. The word "reproduction" was not used to refer to the production of human beings until well into the nineteenth century; prior to that people talked about the process of "generation," or "procreation," thus associating it with "Creation." They might also just use the biblical phrases "begetting" and "bearing." But note the very different meanings. Today, the very word "reproduction" evokes association to Xerox machines rather than to the creation of unique, sentient individuals on whom people in the West have placed incredible value. I began to wonder whether it was really the process of "reproduction" that caused the devaluation of women or the way we *thought* about it.

The theory of procreation in Genesis and the rest of the Bible (and influential Greek texts as well as the Qur'an) is what I have called the "seed-soil" theory (Delaney 1986, 1991, 1998). In this theory, which still continues in popular imagination and language, the man was/is imagined to create the child (with God's help) – to *beget* via his *seed* – while the woman's role was to nurture that *seed*-child in the womb, give birth, and nurture it after birth. In the Qur'an, for example, men are told: "Women are given to you as fields; go therein and sow your seed" (Sura 2: 223). In this view, the male is *the* procreator; his power to engender symbolically allied him with the Creator. In monotheistic religious cosmology, there is not a God and Goddess who, together, bring forth the world; instead, the male-imaged God created without a partner. What he created, namely the earth, became symbolically female; it was dependent on, and in a hierarchical relation to, the Creator. So, too, the human mother was not (and is not) imagined as the co-creator; the male was/is thought to plant the seed while the woman was/is imagined as the "soil" that nurtures it. She is either fertile or barren – words that further associate her with soil, the earth. There are more references to the word/concept *seed* in Genesis than anywhere else in the Bible; however, you will not find the word seed in some editions such as the New Revised Version. In an attempt to use more gender-neutral language, *seed* was changed to *progeny*, as if the words and their meanings had little import beyond that context.

What all of this is meant to demonstrate is that our terms "father" and "mother" do not just reflect or represent "natural biological" roles but are culturally constructed notions of male and female roles. And the words are not equivalent, as male and female parent, but have different meanings and, most important, different values; just think of the very different images and thoughts evoked by the terms "to father" vs. "to mother." Our words, images, metaphors, laws, and social arrangements have not yet caught up with the changed theory of procreation. Today we have a duo-genetic theory of procreation – both the male and the female contribute the same kind of material to the embryo, namely genes. In addition, of course, women contribute nurture both inside and outside the womb and the labor of childbirth, i.e., those very aspects that have traditionally defined the word *mother*. It is very important to realize that the terms "mother" and "father" were developed long before scientific theory and thus do not change along with changes in scientific theory; they depend on deeply rooted cultural notions that relate to far more than simply the process of reproduction. Therefore, to use the terms "father" and "mother" as equivalents for kinship terms in other cultures surely distorts other people's notions of relatedness as it continues to obscure our own notions of relationships from ourselves.

New forms of kinship and kinship studies

The study of kinship continues to be an important part of the anthropological enterprise, but in recent years the focus has shifted dramatically. Feminist anthropologists have pointed out that conventional kinship studies were based on assumptions about gender. While anthropologists had long been aware that *male* and *female* are defined differently in different societies and also that their roles differ, they did not follow through with this realization. It took feminist anthropologists like Jane Collier and Sylvia Yanagisako to

> argue that gender and kinship have been defined as fields of study by our folk conception of the same thing, namely, the biological facts of sexual reproduction. Consequently, what have been conceptualized as two discrete fields of study constitute a single field that has not succeeded in freeing itself from notions about natural differences between people. (1989: 15)

They do not deny

> that men and women are different, just as individuals differ, generations differ, races differ, and so forth. Rather, we question whether the particular biological difference in reproductive function that our culture defines as the basis of difference between males and females, and so treats as the basis of their relationship, is used by other societies to constitute the cultural categories of male and female. (p. 48)

Perhaps somewhere gender differences are defined by the differential distribution of hair on the body or by breasts or lack of them! But even if procreation is a salient area, it is clear from the foregoing that different cultures, including our own, have understood this process very differently. It matters whether the male is seen as *the* progenitor, *the* engenderer, or whether the woman is; or whether the entire process is imagined to be in the hands of ancestral spirits and not in those of the two persons intimately involved.

The work of Collier and Yanagisako was primarily a critique of past and prevailing theories of kinship with suggestions about how future studies of gender and kinship should be unified. Other voices working on that edge have begun to be heard: (1) gays and lesbians who question the heterosexual basis/bias of kinship and gender studies; (2) groups of people who feel a kinship bond because they have the same genetic disease, thus raising the question of whether blood is the defining issue (indeed, blood generally symbolizes genetic relationship); (3) groups formed of people with adopted children, who would argue that kinship is not about sex and blood, but about care and nurturance; and (4) those who have used the new reproductive technologies (NRTs) which fragment the roles, e.g. sperm donor, egg donor, biological mother, surrogate mother, birth mother, etc.[7] All of these people have been challenging the taken-for-granted notions of kinship and forging new defini-

tions that we are only beginning to understand and accommodate socially and culturally. One thing is clear: kinship is not and never has been stable; it is not something given "in the nature of things" but is constructed in particular cultures in
particular ways around particular notions of person and cosmos.

Friends

How do we define a friend? Often people become friends because they live in the
same neighborhood or go to the same school.[8] They discover they share similar
interests or responses to things. Among girls and young women, telling secrets to
each other is the seal of a friendship, and betraying those secrets usually signals the
end of the friendship. What is friendship, and how is it similar to or different from
love?

Raymonde Carroll was forced to rethink her beliefs about friendship after an
experience that occurred when she was doing her initial fieldwork on the Pacific
atoll of Nukuoro. She elected to stay "at home" while the villagers had gone out
sailing. She looked forward to a period of quiet, of not having to concentrate on
the language, and just being alone. That was not to be the case. Very soon she was
visited by a village woman who, once she noticed that Raymonde was staying
behind, decided to come keep her company so she wouldn't be alone! The woman
refused to abandon Raymonde despite her subtle hints that she actually wanted to
be alone. In addition, the local woman declared herself a *friend*, and said that friends
brought each other gifts (she had brought a coconut) and that, as a friend, she would
teach and correct Raymonde's use of the language. Raymonde wrote:

> What seems particularly important to me is the shock that this incident brought to
> my concept of friendship. This woman declared herself my friend point blank, without
> even asking me, in a way that I guessed would be irrevocable. What is more, she
> seemed to be according me an extraordinary favor. Where I come from, dear lady, I
> thought to myself, one does not unilaterally declare oneself someone's friend. One
> "becomes" a friend, and this is based on mutual (though tacit) agreement. (Carroll
> 1988: 72)

Something very similar happened to me early during my fieldwork in the Turkish
village. The midwife with whom I stayed the first week or so asked: "do you love
me?" I was shocked and wondered, at first, if this was some kind of lesbian over-
ture. Then she asked if I would be her friend. I was just as surprised as Raymonde
Carroll and thought to myself, "I don't even know you! She doesn't understand what
it means to be a friend, and moreover, I don't want to be her friend, I don't particularly like her." But when I asked a sophisticated, well-educated, urban Turk, he said
it is quite similar in Turkey. He said, "Once the declaration has been made, you will
become friends. It is a relationship that is taken seriously and often lasts throughout
one's life and it doesn't matter if you are very different." Most Americans, I think,
want their friends to be like them, to confirm their feelings and agree with their
views.

The issue becomes, perhaps, even more difficult when friendship occurs between people who come from what we so easily assume are similar cultures, for example France and the United States. Raymonde Carroll notes, in fact, that at the descriptive level, the conception of friendship in the two countries is almost identical. But, she says, "it is not the category that proves to be the source of cultural misunderstanding but rather the presuppositions that enter into this category, which can be very different" (p. 78). Friends, she says, are the people who understand us; but what they *do* to show how much they understand us will be very different. Not unlike her characterization of couples, Americans tend to seek friends who are supportive, who, when you do something stupid, will try to make you "feel better by finding extenuating circumstances, by reminding" you of your good qualities. A French friend, in contrast, will help you see more clearly the stupid thing you did and help you "find a means to patch things up. . . . This means that my friend understands me because he or she is another me, . . . in the sense that he or she is the half of me that remains reasonable" (p. 79). She claims that such friends can show you what you did wrong without judging you and still remain your friend.

In Turkey, France, and many other places, it is normal for women friends or men friends to walk arm in arm. This behavior does not signal a homosexual relationship but merely friendship. But in the United States it is rarely done. Why do Americans have such a phobia about touching, particularly between people of the same sex? A personal experience may be illustrative. When my daughter was in eighth grade (and about 13), she was about as tall as I am. We got along very well and sometimes when we were walking around Cambridge, Massachusetts, where we lived at the time, I used to take her arm. She didn't like it, it simply wasn't done. Not only would it make it seem that we were not mother and daughter – a distinction she wanted to be obvious since many people took us for sisters; furthermore, she didn't want people to think we were lesbians. When she was 16 she visited me in Turkey, and then we fell quite easily into this habit. It seemed natural there since everyone else was doing it and it was a pleasant way to walk and talk. Later, when I returned to Cambridge, and she was in college, we again took up the practice – just strolling around walking and talking. People made rude remarks that surprised us both. But by that time she let them pass over her; the experience in another culture made her aware that there was nothing intrinsic about the behavior that gave it meaning but rather the way it signified specific things in a specific culture. And by this time, she didn't care what such people thought.

In Praise of Manners

Social relations are made smooth because of conventional, ritualized practices of interaction and behavior. These practices are sometimes referred to in terms of manners or as etiquette. From an early age, children are inducted into the society's rules of etiquette. This training was often supplemented by books on the topic. I remember a truly horrid children's etiquette book called *Slovenly Peter* that told of terrible things that would befall you if you neglected your manners. In addition, such books answered questions about situations that were outside of everyday experience, or that occurred rarely in one's own life such as weddings, funerals, etc. Today, however, books of etiquette and manners seem to be going the way of white gloves and crinolines. People tend to think manners are unnecessary or pretentious; however, they are socially important. We can't actually escape the issue for "no manners" are a form of them. The lack of manners expresses a view of society where individualism has gone awry, where people feel there is no need to conform to social norms, no need to smooth social relations. It is a society that has lost the awareness that people live in and through society, that people are shaped *in* and *by* society, that no one exists outside of society. In the United States, the limits of social behavior are being pushed, for if everyone really "did their own thing" we would be in chaos, but, as of this writing, "doing one's own thing" is still socially recognizable; it is (just) within the parameters of the society's norms, otherwise it would not make sense, it would be viewed as insane.

> The *New York Times*, April 4, 2002, as well as Peter Jennings's ABC news the same night, reported that a study of manners in the United States concluded that Americans' manners have deteriorated considerably since the 1950s.

Having socially accepted and widely known forms of etiquette actually make social life easier; everyone knows what is expected in particular circumstances. Manners are primarily the responsibility of parents; it is up to them to teach and train their children. Other adults such as grandparents and other relatives, teachers, counselors, and coaches can also help, especially as a child grows, but the major responsibility belongs to parents.

Parents' responsibilities

Please and thank-you

In past generations, according to my mother-in-law, children were taught to say please and thank-you at very young ages; sometimes they were the first words a child was taught. This conveyed, very early on, a sense that there were others out there to consider and to respect. From my observations of parents and children in the United States today, it appears that children are no longer being taught these simple but important phrases. Children do seem ruder and more selfish. They are not being taught to consider others, let alone have any respect for authority, including their parents. Instead, from this observer's point of view, it seems they are being taught to fight for themselves, individually. Has our world really become so Hobbesian? Has our world become so individualistic? Perhaps it ought not to be so surprising that theories of utilitarianism, social Darwinism, and its latest form – sociobiology – have all emerged in English-American societies. This is not the way it is in France, according to Raymonde Carroll.

> As soon as I become a parent in France, I must answer to society for my behavior toward the child. As a parent, my role is to transform this "malleable, innocent, impressionable, and irresponsible" creature into a social being, a responsible member of the society. . . . [T]his means that on becoming a parent, it is first and foremost to the society that I incur an obligation, a debt, rather than to my child, who comes second. If I give priority to my child, I isolate myself from this society. (1988: 47)

She goes on to say that to

> understand the American situation, one need only in a sense reverse all the signs. When I (an American) become a parent, I incur an obligation to my children rather than to society, which comes second. My obligation is not to teach my children the rules and practices of society, but above all to give them every possible chance to discover and develop their "natural qualities," to exploit their gifts, and to blossom. (p. 49)

No doubt, these are somewhat exaggerated stereotypes, but nevertheless they do indicate very different ideas about society and its value.

Not surprisingly, France was the home of the great social thinker Emile Durkheim, who was the first really to think of society as something *sui generis*, that is, not just the sum of all the individuals in it but something with its own characteristics and momentum. His insights provided the basis for the field of sociology. In the United States, in contrast, our behavior expresses a deep belief and adherence to notions of individualism and individual freedom to pursue our own desires and goals. Our social policy, too, tends to perpetuate this; we have much less of a safety net for people than does France or any other European nation. In the United States, you sink or swim on your own.

Table manners

It is obvious that table manners vary from time to time and place to place. Europeans tend to use their knives and forks differently from Americans. They cut their meat the same way Americans do, but they raise it to their mouths on an overturned fork held in the left hand; Americans generally put the knife down, switch the fork back into the right hand, and use it right side up.

In America and Europe, dinner conversation is expected, but in the Turkish village people were not expected to carry on conversation when eating; that was reserved for after dinner when people sat upon the divans and drank tea. While different cultures have different norms for table manners, in each particular culture there are still norms or rules of behavior and, with training, these become habitual. These habits allow the dinner to proceed without incident. But what happens if someone goes against the norms? All attention is turned to that person; his or her behavior disrupts the dinner and makes people uncomfortable. Although I have heard young people in the United States say they should be able to eat as they wish, "it's a free country," they do not realize that their behavior is really an attention-grabbing maneuver. It also communicates the message that they do not care what other people think. In turn, the other people might then decide that person is not worth caring about. All of this goes on without one word being spoken, but such behavior can have serious consequences both in terms of romance and careers. When everyone is taught how to eat, how to cut their meat, which fork or knife to use for which items, then social life proceeds smoothly, one can concentrate on the food, on one's dinner partners, and on the conversation rather than on someone's execrable manners.

Ms. Manners, Ann Landers, etc.

In a country where there are so few widely accepted notions of manners and etiquette, it becomes understandable why news columns such as Ann Landers and Ms. Manners or advice talk shows on radio and television are so popular. People, quite often, simply do not know how to act in certain situations and do not know what to expect from others; they can, therefore, offend the very people they are trying to please and get offended and hurt by actions which they do not understand. They need to get advice from experts. But experts in what? Etiquette and manners, of course! They are performing the function that the etiquette books used to perform; they let brides know they have to send thank-you letters for gifts received or whether they can exchange wedding gifts; they tell parents when it is appropriate to intrude and interfere with their children's choice of friends or their marriages and when it is not; they tell some people what forks or soup bowls to use and when you can dispense with them; they tell what kinds of sexual actions are inappropriate for what ages, and whether you have the right to say no; they tell people how to respond to their mothers- or fathers-in-law; and what to wear to a funeral, and so on.

Americans are often proud that we have so few social rules, they think "anything goes" here, but it doesn't, as too many learn the hard way. Regardless of whatever help Ann Landers and Ms. Manners may give to the writers or callers, they point to a lack of consensus of social mores and behavior or, perhaps, to lack of transmission from one generation to the next, creating holes in the American social fabric. And so, these holes become an important site for cultural investigation. Where are they? Why? What values are implied in the responses? What kind of society is imagined?

Turkish social relations

From more than 25 years of acquaintance with Turks and Turkish society, I feel I can say that Turks, in general, are extremely gracious and hospitable people; indeed, hospitality is a national value and a primary virtue. This is as true among peasant villagers as among the urban elite, perhaps more so. They possess a kind of civility and grace that contradict the image of the fierce and warlike Turk, for so long promulgated in European literature and imagination. They do not appear as suspicious of strangers as are most Americans, for example, and I have often seen them invite total strangers into their homes and give them tea and some food.

The majority of parents in the United States are child-directed, that is, their focus is the child and his or her future. They try to push and promote the child forward, and provide whatever support and help they can to launch him or her into the world. In Turkey, parents surely care deeply for their children, but children are brought up to consider and respect their parents in a way that is generally lacking in the United States. Turkish youth assume they will have to take care of their parents in their old age. In the village, women's nursing of their infants establishes "milk rights," they can expect their child to nurture them in their old age as they nurtured the child in infancy.

Young men did not smoke in front of their parents, especially their father; it was considered an affront to his dignity and authority. In the village, they needed their father's permission to leave and go to town; young women needed it simply to visit a friend at the other side of the village. Both needed parental permission to continue school beyond the then mandatory requirement of fifth grade. (Currently, children are required to complete junior high school or eighth grade.)

Not only did children do what they were told, they did it without complaining as is so common among American children, especially teenagers. I remember very vividly one occasion when many villagers were going to a wedding in the next village. This was greeted as a special outing, a time to meet new people and just get out of the village. My next-door neighbors were planning to go; but at the last minute the husband-father decided he did not want to go. He could not stay home alone – who would fix his meals! So a teenage daughter was told she had to remain at home. She did so without a murmur. I asked her if she wasn't disappointed, she smilingly said she had to care for her father. He was hardly a typical patriarch, but her acquiescence clearly demonstrated submission to patriarchal ideology. At the same time, she also knew she had much to thank him for since he gave permission for her to attend the middle school in the village (she was one of only three girls to do so).

> Later, when she again finished at the top of her class, he permitted her to attend high school. However, then it required that she leave the village and live with relatives in town.

Notes

1   For a full description of Turkish marriage and wedding practices, see Delaney (1991).

2   This information is taken from W. B. Spencer and F. J. Gillen, *The Native Tribes of Central Australia* (London: Macmillan, 1899), p. 72.

3   See Hochschild (1975). Despite the date, the material in the article is just as relevant today.

4   This was reported in the *New York Times*, August 14, 1995, citing the Luxembourg Income Study. See also the Carnegie Foundation, "Starting Points: Meeting the Needs of Our Youngest Children" (1994); Handler (1995); Kamerman (1984); Kamerman and Kahn (1984, 1989); Katz (1986); Leach (1994); and Sidel ([1986] 1992, 1996).

5   For excellent work on these topics see Gailey (2000); Howell (2001); Modell (1994); and Strong (2001).

6   For "McLennan as well as for Morgan, 'kinship' was about marriage, about the facts of procreation and conception, about blood-ties and genetic relationships as they could be known or were knowable, about the ties that arise out of the biological facts of human reproduction; for McLennan, rights and duties, succession and estates followed blood-ties, not kinship terms" (Schneider 1972: 35).

7   All of these issues are taken up in Franklin and McKinnon (2001). For further references, see their bibliography.

8   Penny Eckert, a linguistic anthropologist, studied the way young people begin to classify each other – a process that began in junior high school but continued into high school – and how these identifications affect the rest of the students' lives. I have included a chapter from her book *Jocks and Burnouts: Social Categories and Identity in the High School* (1989). While "jock" or "burnout" might not be the lingo you used during that time of your life, you will be able to make analogies.

Bibliography

Basso, Keith (1970) "To Give Up On Words: Silence in Western Apache Culture." *Southwest Journal of Anthropology*, 26 (3): 213–30.

Carroll, Raymonde (1988) *Cultural Misunderstandings: The French-American Experience*. Chicago: University of Chicago Press.

Collier, Jane and Yanagisako, Sylvia (1989) *Gender and Kinship: Toward a Unified Analysis*. Stanford: Stanford University Press.

Collier, Jane, Rosaldo, Michelle, and Yanagisako, Sylvia (1992) "Is There a Family?" In *Rethinking the Family: Some Feminist Questions*, ed. Barrie Thorne and Marilyn Yalom. Boston: Northeastern University Press.

Degler, Carl (1980) *At Odds: Women and the Family in America from the Revolution to the Present*. New York: Oxford University Press.

Delaney, Carol (1986) "The Meaning of Paternity and the Virgin Birth Debate." *Man*, 21 (3): 494–513.

Delaney, Carol (1991) *The Seed and the Soil: Gender and Cosmology in Turkish Village Society*. Berkeley: University of California Press.

Delaney, Carol (1998) *Abraham on Trial: The Social Legacy of Biblical Myth*. Princeton: Princeton University Press.

Franklin, Sarah and McKinnon, Susan, eds. (2001) *Relative Values: Reconfiguring Kinship Studies*. Raleigh, NC: Duke University Press.

Gailey, Christine Ward (2000) "Race, Class and Gender in Intercountry Adoption in the U.S." In *Intercountry Adoption: Developments, Trends, and Perspectives*, ed. Peter Selman. London: Skyline House/British Agencies for Adoption and Fostering.

Handler, Joel (1995) *The Poverty of Welfare Reform*. New Haven: Yale University Press.

Herman, Judith Lewis (1981) *Father–Daughter Incest*. Cambridge, MA: Harvard University Press.

Hocart, A. M. (1973) "Kinship Systems." In *The Life-Giving Myth*. London: Tavistock.

Hochschild, Arlie (1975) "Inside the Clock-Work of Male Careers." In *Women and the Power to Change*, ed. Florence Howe. Sponsored by the Carnegie Commission on Higher Education, New York: McGraw-Hill.

Hochschild, Arlie, with Machtung, Anne (1989) *The Second Shift*. New York: Avon Books.

Howell, Signe (2001) "Self-Conscious Kinship: Some Contested Values in Norwegian Transnational Adoption." In *Relative Values: Reconfiguring Kinship Studies*, ed. Sarah Franklin and Susan McKinnon. Raleigh, NC: Duke University Press.

Jensen, Margaret Ann (1984) *Love's Sweet Return: The Harlequin Story*. Toronto: Women's Press.

Kamerman, Sheila (1984) "Women, Children, and Poverty: Public Policies and Female-Headed Families in Industrialized Countries." *Journal of Women in Culture and Society*, 10 (21).

Kamerman, Sheila and Kahn, Alfred (1984) "Social Policy and Forms of Family in Europe." *International Social Security Review*, 47 (3–4).

Kamerman, Sheila and Kahn, Alfred (1989) "Single-Parent, Female-Headed Families in Western Europe: Social Change and Response." *International Social Security Review* (January).

Katz, Michael (1986) *In the Shadow of the Poorhouse*. New York: Basic Books.

Leach, Penelope (1994) *Children First: What Our Society Must Do – And Is Not Doing – For Our Children Today*. New York: Alfred A. Knopf.

Lévi-Strauss, Claude ([1949] 1969) *The Elementary Structures of Kinship*. Boston: Beacon Press.

McKinnon, Susan (1995) "American Kinship/American Incest: Asymmetries in a Scientific

Discourse." In *Naturalizing Power: Essays in Feminist Cultural Analysis*, ed. Carol Delaney and Sylvia Yanagisako. New York: Routlege, pp. 25–46.

Marx, Karl and Engels, Frederick ([1884] 1972) *Origin of the Family, Private Property and the State*. Ed. with an Introduction by Eleanor Burke Leacock. New York: International Publishers.

Modell, Judith (1994) *Kinship with Strangers: Adoption and Interpretations of Kinship in American Culture*. Berkeley: University of California Press.

Morgan, Lewis Henry (1871) *Systems of Consanguinity and Affinity in the Human Family*. Washington, DC: Smithsonian Contributions to Knowledge, No. 17.

Morgan, Lewis Henry (1877) *Ancient Society*. New York: Henry Holt.

Okin, Susan Moller (1989) *Justice, Gender, and the Family*. New York: Basic Books.

Ortner, Sherry (1974) "Is Female to Male as Nature is to Culture?" In *Women, Culture, and Society*, ed. Michelle Rosaldo and Louise Lamphere. Stanford: Stanford University Press.

Ottenheimer, Martin (1996) *Forbidden Relatives: The American Myth of Cousin Marriage*. Urbana and Chicago: University of Illinois Press.

Payne, Kay E. (2001) *Different But Equal: Communication Between the Sexes*. Westport, CT: Praeger.

Pearce, Diana (1990) "Welfare is Not *For* Women: Why the War on Poverty Cannot Conquer the Feminization of Poverty." In *Women, the State, and Welfare*, ed. Linda Gordon. Madison: University of Wisconsin Press.

Schneider, David (1968) *American Kinship: A Cultural Account*. Englewood Cliffs, NJ: Prentice-Hall.

Schneider, David (1972) "What Is Kinship All About?" In *Kinship Studies in the Morgan Centennial Year*, ed. P. Reining. Washington, DC: Anthropological Society, pp. 32–63.

Sidel, Ruth ([1986] 1992) *Women and Children Last: The Plight of Poor Women in Affluent America*. New York and London: Penguin.

Sidel, Ruth (1996) *Keeping Women and Children Last: America's War on the Poor*. New York and London: Penguin.

Stacey, Judith (1996) *In the Name of the Family: Rethinking Family Values in the Postmodern Age*. Boston: Beacon Press.

Strathern, Marilyn (1980) "No Nature, No Culture: The Hagen Case." In *Nature, Culture and Gender*, ed. Carol MacCormack and Marilyn Strathern. Cambridge: Cambridge University Press.

Strong, Pauline Turner (2001) "To Forget Their Tongue, Their Name, and Their Whole Relation: Captivity, Extra-Tribal Adoption, and the Indian Child Welfare Act." In *Relative Values: Reconfiguring Kinship Studies*, ed. Sarah Franklin and Susan McKinnon. Raleigh, NC: Duke University Press.

Tylor, E. B. (1889) "On a Method of Investigating the Development of Institutions: Applied to Laws of Marriage and Descent." *Journal of the Anthropological Institute*, 18: 245–72.

Waring, Marilyn (1990) *If Women Counted*. San Francisco: Harper.

Weston, Kath (1990) *Families We Choose: Lesbians, Gays, Kinship*. New York: Columbia University Press.

Young, Iris (1995) "Mothers, Citizenship, and Independence: A Critique of Pure Family Values." *Ethics*, 105: 535–56.

Symbols of Category Membership
Penelope Eckert

WHAT MAKES SOMEBODY A BURNOUT?

You know, maybe somebody who smokes all the time, you know, smokes marijuana and stuff, but you know, everybody does that. You could call me a Burnout. You know, I've did that . . . maybe, maybe it's the way they dress. It's a lot of things, I think. Your look, you can wear these leather – and these wallets with chains and look really bad, you know – lot of people say, "Oh, that guy's got to be a Burnout."

The Jock and Burnout categories emerge upon entrance to junior high school, where they develop in mutual opposition through a rapid foregrounding and differentiation of selected values, behavior, and symbols. Unstructured differences that have developed through elementary school are imbued with significance as they are thrown into opposition, and the opposition itself gains hegemony as it absorbs more and more aspects of everyday life. In an effort to differentiate themselves, the two categories progressively separate their worlds, developing opposing territories, appearances, demeanors, and activities. The underlying ideologies that separate Jocks and Burnouts are in turn strengthened by the increasing range of external manifestations associated with them.

The differences between Jock and Burnout social structure and norms are not very apparent in the daily business of life. In fact, by the time the cohort reaches graduation, Jocks and Burnouts know precious little about each other. What everyone knows of their differences is what shows – the symbolic manifestations of category affiliation. Ask high school students or recent graduates about the social categories in their school, and they will begin with how they dress, where they hang out, or what substances they use. Clothing and other forms of adornment, ways of speaking, territory, and even substance use and school performance all have symbolic value in the adolescent context. However sub-

consciously, they all stand for deeper cultural differences that may themselves not be accessible to all who participate in the symbolic system. Differences in symbolic behavior are commonly taken as the only differences between the categories – and such things as clothing differences are regarded as if they had social value in themselves rather than simply in association with an evaluation of the people who wear them. Category symbols attain their value from association with clear differences in both form and content, developing around salient social differences between the categories and maximizing distinctness in visible form.

Clothing and adornment is perhaps the most powerful symbolic subsystem in the Jock–Burnout opposition. An individual's bodily adornment is seen simultaneously with the individual and thus provides the guarantee that the individual will not be separated from his or her social identity. To the extent that they are inseparable from the person, other portable symbols, such as books, radios, cigarettes, and sports paraphernalia, are also effective indicators of social identity, as are cars. Musical taste can be unambiguously displayed through the use of radios. Styles of demeanor and movement rely to a great extent on action and interaction, as does language. Finally, territorial and activity displays are limited to specific settings. All of these areas of behavior are fully exploited to express social category affiliation, and because adornment is the only ever-present symbolic subsystem, it is manipulated to incorporate as many of the elements of other subsystems as possible. Musical tastes can be displayed on T-shirts; activities, on activity-specific clothing (such as motorcycle boots or football jerseys); language style and demeanor, in action and in messages on buttons and T-shirts; territory, on jackets (such as the DETROIT jackets worn by some Burnouts).

Just as the Jock and Burnout categories develop in mutual opposition, so do their symbols. Elements of behavior that come to represent one category will be rejected by the other, and they may be exploited by the other category through the development of a clearly opposed element. Thus the Burnouts not only avoid the pastel colors that characterize Jock clothing, but they consistently wear dark colors. (This opposition could, of course, be expressed in reverse – the Jocks avoid dark colors and consistently wear pastels.) At the same time, these colors have positive significance: Pastel colors are associated in our society with youth, innocence, and gaiety, while dark colors are associated with sombreness, age, and sophistication – all qualities that are associated with the categories that wear them.

Many Jock and Burnout symbols stand above all for differences in economic means, perception of life stage and adult domination, and school and local orientation. Jocks are locally oriented both to the school and to the local community, while Burnouts are oriented away from the school, toward the neighborhood, and toward Detroit. Jocks embrace adult norms for the adolescent life stage, while Burnouts constantly lay claim to adult status. Finally, Jocks associate themselves with the middle class and its relative affluence, while Burnouts associate themselves with the working class and its relatively limited material means.

School Territories

Jock and Burnout use of school facilities is symbolic of differences in attitudes toward the school and in orientation to the adolescent life stage. The Jocks accept the facilities provided by the school and use them in rough conformity to school expectations – they store their coats and books in lockers, use the bathrooms for their intended purpose, and eat in the cafeteria. Burnouts, on the other hand, express their counter-cultural position in the school by transforming the school facilities to suit their needs and identities (see Willis, 1977, for a discussion of such transformation). To a certain extent, their use of the school is built around cigarette smoking, which, as will be discussed later, is a key symbol in the Jock–Burnout split. In schools across the country,

Burnouts' smoking leads them to hang out in doorways and stairwells, parking lots, bathrooms, breezeways, and loading docks. This use of marginal areas has added significance in its representation of Burnouts' more generally marginal place in the school. This marginalization not only is imposed through the school's rejection of Burnout values, but is embraced by Burnouts in their rejection of the school as a comprehensive social institution. While the Jocks center their social lives in the school and accept the school as a "home away from home," the Burnouts energetically deny any such function of the school. The Jocks embrace whatever facilities the school offers them. In contrast, the Burnouts pick and choose. They use facilities that reflect recognition of their adult status and needs – the courtyard, vocational classrooms, parking lot. They shun those that reflect the school's parental role of providing food and living space, namely, lockers and the cafeteria. Those they cannot shun – the bathrooms – they transform into alternative smoking areas.

Lunchtime Territories

In addition to seeking marginal spaces, Burnouts reject school facilities that represent the school's in loco parentis role. One such facility is the cafeteria. Although the food in the Belten cafeteria is quite good, the Burnouts are overwhelmingly critical of it. The common Burnout claim that cafeteria food has made people sick implies a rejection of not only the school's right but its ability to assume a parental role. The few Burnouts who do eat in the cafeteria occupy the most marginal table in the room – a table off to the side and next to the rear exit, where they can be "half in and half out" of the cafeteria and separate from the main cafeteria activity.

DO YOU EAT IN THE CAFETERIA?
Sometimes. . . . When it looks edible. When it doesn't look like it's moving around at you.

OH GOD. WHO DO YOU EAT WITH USUALLY?
All the Burnouts, you know, just anybody who comes along and sits at the table . . . right next to the first line. We just sit there and chow down, and talk.

Many Burnouts do not eat lunch at all, and of those who do the overwhelming majority limit themselves to packaged food, which they can carry out to the courtyard. The Belten cafeteria provides two hot food lines leading from the main entrance and a fast-food line leading from a side hall (and emptying near the Burnout table referred to above), where Burnouts buy their cookies or potato chips. One Burnout demonstrated the norm against eating in the cafeteria, in her reaction to a friend's insistence that she did eat there, and her proud denial of engaging in legitimate transactions with the school.

DO YOU EVER EAT IN THE CAFETERIA?
In there? Huh-uh.
[friend speaking] Yeah, you do.
Bullshit. I never eat in there.
[friend] Come on.

NOT EVEN WHEN THE WEATHER IS REAL BAD?
No, I used to chow in the hall. Or I don't eat at all.

BUT DO YOU EVER, LIKE, BUY FOOD THERE AND THEN GO OUT INTO THE COURTYARD?
Yeah. Well, I don't buy food. . . . Everybody rips off from them. I remember one time I went up to the chip rack, you know. I had Linda and them stand behind me, and when they weren't looking I'd whip chip bags back there. And they're cramming them in their purse. We'd walk out, we were munching down.

High school cafeterias everywhere show strict territorial specialization. A high school in a neighboring town shows a stratified use of the cafeteria, with the Burnouts (called "Freaks" in this school) eating near the outside doors at the bottom of the cafeteria so they can slip out for a smoke, and the Jocks at the top of the cafeteria – an area actually elevated above the rest. The "In-betweens" occupy the middle area. The Belten cafeteria is set up with long tables along three walls and round tables in the middle. The human geography of the cafeteria varies between lunch periods and semesters, but by and large the Jocks occupy the tables on the west wall and an occasional round table, while the fast-food line and the Burnout table are on the east wall. Some people refer to the tables along the west wall as the "Jock tables."

Burnouts are not the only ones who eat elsewhere than in the cafeteria. Members of the choir, which rehearses before and after lunch, frequently eat in the choir room; those who work in the student store sometimes eat in the room behind the store;

many on the yearbook staff eat in the yearbook room; ROTC members sometimes eat in the ROTC room; and a few people eat in various classrooms and faculty spaces. Lunch periods are so routinized that I knew exactly where to find most people during that time. People always eat in the same place with the same people, and if they don't stay there for the whole period, they retire to a specific place to wait for the bell to ring. In-between people who smoke may go to the courtyard, a few go to the library or to the room where their next class meets (if they can get past the hall monitors), and many stand, always in the same place, in the cafeteria lobby and the gym hall. The Jocks who are not in any of the specialized areas stand directly in front of the main entrance to the cafeteria and in front of the student store opposite, the Burnouts who are not in the courtyard stand in the hall by the radiator at the courtyard's main entrance, and the In-betweens congregate between the two areas. Students clearly see this after-lunch standing around as a significant activity, and some remain in the cafeteria expressly to avoid it.

AFTER LUNCH, DO YOU STAY IN THE LUNCHROOM?
Mm hmm. I hate standing out in the hall. I feel like I'm on exhibit. Bothers me. You just stand there, and everybody else looks around, it's all crowded. Don't like it. I'd rather just sit.

The Courtyard

The locus of Jock–Burnout territorial separation is the courtyard. Whereas the cafeteria is in the public domain, the courtyard is Burnout territory by virtue of its designation as the authorized smoking area. The close association between Burnouts and the courtyard comes out repeatedly in conversation, as Burnouts are commonly described as "the people who smoke" and "the people in the courtyard." One Jock accounted for his split-up with several junior high friends in the following way:

Like there's a few others . . . who also go here who I don't hang around with at all any more, I mean, not that I, you know, wouldn't want to, it's just, we just went different ways in tenth grade and ever since.

HOW DID YOU GO DIFFERENT WAYS?
They went into the courtyard and I went into the student government.

Burnouts who do not smoke go regularly to the courtyard, but few other nonsmokers do, since smoking is the only legitimate excuse for a non-Burnout to be in Burnout territory. Those non-Burnouts who do go into the courtyard are apt to be labelled as Burnouts by many of the people in the school, both because of their use of the courtyard and because they smoke. These people stick to the southwest corner of the courtyard, which is recognized among those in the courtyard as neutral – a distinction not recognized by those who do not frequent the courtyard. The courtyard is the one place in the school that the Burnouts consider their own, and their care for the courtyard contrasts with the graffiti found on the walls that lead to it. This care was described by one In-between smoker who frequents the southwest corner of the courtyard.

I've always, I've always liked it out here. It's just, just, besides the litter. But there's not really that much, because, um, like people, you know, a lot of, most of the Burns come out here, you know, the Burnouts that think they're real cool and stuff. They come out here and, um, and, you know, if they see litter, believe it or not, they'll pick it up. Because, you know, like they, they, this is the one part they can say is theirs, you know, because all the really popular people really don't come out here. . . . It, it really is nice, you know, it's big, and, I don't know, it's nice. They have, they have flowers, and people really don't pick the flowers and stuff, you know, like, and they don't step on the little, like we plant trees in here sometimes, and they don't pick them and everything, you know, and throw them away, and just. . . . I think a lot of people take care of it because they look, they look at other high schools, and, you know, like they have nothing at all.

Smoking and the courtyard (probably because of its association with smoking) are the most widely recognized Burnout symbols and are therefore the most carefully maintained areas of differentiation. Presence in the courtyard is recognized as an unambiguous social statement. One In-between gave the following explanation for why she and her best friend do not go into the courtyard:

DO YOU EVER GO IN THE COURTYARD?
No.

ANY PARTICULAR REASON?

I've well, let's see. Julie and I are, you might say we party. I mean, there's Jocks and Jells like that. But we don't smoke cigarettes. And I think – I don't know – I get the impression that if people who don't smoke cigarettes go out there, everybody automatically thinks, "Oh, they want to be a Jell." So I wouldn't want everybody saying, "Oh, what are you, um, trying to be a Jell now?" or something.

Avoidance of the courtyard incurs considerable inconvenience, because the courtyard provides a shortcut between classes and from classes to the cafeteria. Some In-betweens will use this shortcut between classes but will not go there during lunch:

I don't go out in the courtyard because [of] all the smokers and stuff. . . . I'll go outside and walk through it, probably, but I won't stay out there.

Most Jocks go through their high school years without ever setting foot in the courtyard. Some say this is because of the smoke, although in a large outdoor area like the courtyard, it is easy to avoid other people's smoke.

AND WHEN YOU'RE CHANGING CLASSES, DO YOU EVER WALK THROUGH THE COURTYARD TO TAKE A SHORTCUT?
No. No, I don't . . . even if it were longer inside, I'd stay inside. Because there's a lot of that smoke, you know, and stuff, especially near the areas where people are allowed to smoke. And it gets in my hair and I have to wash it. That's the only reason. It smells bad, it really reeks.

Others cite the Burnouts themselves as a reason not to go into the courtyard.

DO YOU EVER GO INTO THE COURTYARD?
Hm mm. Something might bite us. . . . They're dangerous animals. They're so funny. It's like watching prehistoric man out there. It's so funny, because one time we saw, these two guys were acting like "Kung Foo Joe" you know, and me and Sally were, "I don't believe it."

Many cite fear of ridicule as the main reason for avoiding the courtyard. A few say that because presence in the courtyard implies smoking, they would run the risk of expulsion from a team if they were seen there. The following Jock, who prides himself on his ability to get along with Burnouts, evoked the more general significance of territory in his account of why he never goes into the courtyard. The confusion of his account reflects the fact that his behavior toward the courtyard has been so strongly dictated by social norms that he has not incorporated it into his personal ideology.

I think I've walked through the courtyard twice, and both the times, it was like after school and nobody was around. I never walk through the courtyard.

EVEN TO CHANGE CLASSES AND STUFF, YOU DON'T DO THAT? Nope.

HOW COME?

Well, for one thing, there's other ways to get around, you know, if you want to walk through. And when it's cold, I can't see people standing out in the courtyard, that doesn't make sense. But just being out in the courtyard has a lot of significance. When people see you out there, even if you're out there just to walk by and everything, if somebody walks by, you catch their attention, if you've never been out there before, and, you know, somebody sees you, they might think something. I think, you know. But it – that's not why. Because I really, I really don't care what people think about me, as long as, you know, I do what I think is right. But it's just the idea of having – having to walk through there. It doesn't, you know, it doesn't make sense. If you want to get somewhere, you don't have to walk through the courtyard. It's – I don't know, I don't know how to explain it. It's like, it's territory which you don't have to go through. If it's going to cause problems, why – you know, avoid it. . . . I think it – I think when you walk through the courtyard, you're easily – it's easy to get a label . . . and if you talk to the people out there that have the reputation of, you know, always around drugs, or, you know, having any kind of influence with drugs, then you're going to get labelled that way. I mean, if you're inside the building, that's a different story, you know, if somebody walks by and sees you talking to somebody that, you know, is around drugs, they're not going to think too much about it because they'll say, "Well, maybe they're just talking about a class or something." They don't know what you're talking about. But once you're outside, it's like, you're in his shop. He can tell – you know, it's like you're working with him on his type of you know, his thing, so, I don't know.

Because cigarette smoking is a universal Burnout symbol, Burnouts across the country occupy high school smoking areas: In one California high school, the Burnouts are called "Sectioners" by virtue of the fact that they hang out in the smoking "section." Most schools that permit smoking designate unattractive outdoor areas in the back for this purpose, and one school in the Detroit area co-opted the Burnouts' choice of territory by tearing out the fixtures and stalls from one boys' and one girls' bathroom and designating them as sex-segregated smoking areas. The central location and attractiveness of the courtyard in Belten provides an unusually habitable and nonmarginal Burnout territory. I have been told by students from the wealthier Neartown high school that the proof that Belten has a "Burnout problem" is that it allows this category its own territory. However, while the courtyard is Burnout territory, almost the entire rest of the school is Jock territory. As a number of Burnouts have pointed out, "the Jocks own the school." The Jocks can afford to have their territory defined residually in relation to the Burnouts', because they dominate so much of the functional area of the school. They can regularly be found during their free time in the student activities office, in the various areas of the athletic department (gym, multi-purpose room, faculty offices), in the music rooms, and in classrooms and teachers' offices. Territorial disputes do not arise in Belten, probably because there is adequate territory for both categories. In a nearby town, where Burnouts hang out in stairwells and vestibules, the "Freaks" occasionally invade the opulent central lounge that is known as Jock territory. The invasions have taken place on boys' varsity game days, when symbolism is at its height and Jocks are wearing their game day "uniforms": uniforms for cheerleaders and pompom girls, jackets and ties for players.

Lockers

Just as the courtyard is home base for the Burnouts, the Jocks' home base is their lockers. Each class is assigned lockers in a specific area of the school, and with seniority each class graduates from the least to the most prominent location in the school – freshman and sophomore lockers in the back halls, junior lockers in the upstairs front hall, and senior lockers in the front hall on the main floor. Lockers serve as age-segregated gathering places, each area named for the class it houses: "Senior Hall," "Junior Hall," "Sophomore Hall." It is significant that Burnouts do not acknowledge these names. Two people are assigned to a locker at the beginning of the school year. Jocks generally visit their lockers between classes and spend a lot of time "fooling around" at their lockers before and after school. One peripheral junior Jock described her feelings about Junior Hall in much the same way that Burnouts describe the courtyard:

I like that hall too, because I know everybody. Junior Hall. I can say "Hi" to everybody. I don't feel left out.

In one school in the Detroit area, the senior Jocks are particularly territorial about Senior Hall, and most underclasspeople take detours rather than risk harassment by walking down it. The lockers in this hall are elaborately decorated – some Jock boys have carpeted the insides of their lockers, and joke about installing stereos. They spend long periods of time sitting against the wall opposite their opened and impressively adorned lockers. At Belten, Jocks decorate the outsides of locker doors for important events: birthdays, performances, and games. For Valentine's day, girls anonymously decorate the lockers of the boys' starting varsity basketball team. The location of prominent people's lockers is important information and is frequently essential to the interpretation of the signs that appear on them, such as "Nice going, Joe!"

Locker sharing, virtually always among members of the same sex, is as close as Jocks can come to living together and as such is an important sign of friendship. People frequently affirm the importance of a friendship by pointing out that the friend is their "locker partner." In keeping with the Jock norm against limiting themselves to a "best friend," [. . .], many share a locker with as many as five people.

And now it's like all three of us, and Laurie Smith is good friends with us too. We all share a locker. All four of us. It doesn't have a lock on it either.

DO THEY USUALLY ASSIGN LOCKERS TO FOUR PEOPLE OR DO YOU JUST – THEY ASSIGN IT TO A COUPLE OF PEOPLE AND EVERYBODY ELSE MOVES IN?

Two. Two people for each locker, and like we, "this isn't even anybody's locker, I don't think." We just kind of, "Oop, no one's in this locker."
IS THAT REALLY IMPORTANT, WHO YOUR LOCKER PARTNER IS?
It is, because I wouldn't see Alice during the day if we weren't locker partners. I wouldn't – I'd see Laurie a couple of times, but not, you know, I wouldn't see Alice at all. Because we don't have any classes or even lunch or anything.

This girl's pride at not having a lock on the locker is reminiscent of pride at living in a "good neighborhood," and contrasts with the Burnouts' claim that stuff gets stolen from lockers.

The first week of school brings almost a total reshuffling of lockers, as people move into lockers with their friends and as rows of lockers are taken over by networks. By virtue of this reshuffling, the Jocks in each grade occupy a specific area of lockers in their hall. The locker houses not only school paraphernalia, but personal effects. The insides of lockers are frequently decorated with signs and pictures.

Burnouts do not keep much in their lockers, rarely visit them, and never "fool around" at them. Because they go into the courtyard between classes, Burnouts do not have time to go to their lockers, and scorn those who do. But they also claim that lockers are unsafe, that the locks never work, and that things get stolen from them. This claim, along with their claim that cafeteria food is bad for you, amounts to a denial of the adequacy of the school's parental ability, further justifying their rejection of the school's claim to a parental role. Adding to the Burnouts' hostility toward lockers is the school's reservation of the right to examine lockers for drugs – a right that Burnouts argue against strongly, claiming that lockers should be private space and inviolable. Since the lockers are not to be treated as adult living space but as the living space of a child subject to parental supervision, the Burnouts will not use them.

Looking and Acting Different

Smoking

Drugs and alcohol have come and gone as symbols of rebellion for adolescents, but the one classic and enduring magical substance is tobacco. While the Burnouts may be named for drug use, their key symbol is – as it was for the hoods of the 1950s and the greasers of the 1960s – the cigarette. Cigarette smoking is the pivotal issue in the beginning of seventh grade and remains the key symbol (Ortner, 1973) of the Burnout category throughout high school, even after more potent symbols of rebellion, such as drugs, became part of the opposition. The Burnouts are most frequently described as "the people who smoke," and Jocks continue to shun cigarettes, even after a number of them begin to smoke pot covertly. The cigarette's symbolic value within the adolescent culture undoubtedly arises from its condensation of referents and its portable, displayable, consumable, and quasi-illicit properties. The cigarette is most commonly interpreted as a symbol of adulthood, but is also associated with rebellion, machismo, sophistication or "coolness," independence, and vice. Burnouts display cigarette packages rolled in T-shirt sleeves or protruding from shirt pockets or purses, and requests for cigarettes or elaborate craving gestures are common forms of greeting. In keeping with the Burnouts' norms of sharing, [. . .] cigarette sharing with an extended network serves to solidify social relations. Cigarettes are the ideal commodity for such a system of exchange, since they are relatively inexpensive and carry additional value in themselves as a symbol of Burnout identity. Several Burnouts report having used cigarette exchange as a way of making friends when they first arrived at Belten.

HOW DID YOU MEET?
She comes up to me, "Got a smoke?" I go, "Yeah." And then, then the other day, "You got a smoke?" And then, and one day, a couple days later, I go, "Hey, you," because I didn't have no smokes, I go, "You, you owe me a couple smokes." She goes, she goes, "Oh, really?" Then I don't know, I don't know how I got to know her.

I usually, when I come into a new school, I've learned to make friends real quick because I've moved so many times, so I just walk up to someone, you know, "You want a cigarette?" "Yeah," and start talking, and "yeah, check out that girl over there," or something, you know, just get something going.

The symbolic status of smoking for the Burnouts is reflected in and matched by the Jocks' vocal and passionate opposition to smoking. Jocks overwhelmingly do not smoke: Of 49 Jocks asked, only 2 reported being smokers, and neither smokes at or near the school or at school functions; of 38 Burnouts, 35 reported being smokers. Of 20 In-betweens, 9 reported being smokers. Opposition to smoking is an important Jock norm, and Jocks join the school in its campaign against smoking. One of the prestigious extracurricular activities at Belten is the "Smoking Committee," a group that gives anti-smoking presentations in elementary schools around the area. The status of this committee and other anti-smoking activities as part of the institutional structure of the school brings the Jock alliance with the school squarely into the Jock–Burnout opposition (Eckert, 1983). The Jocks and the school, together, condemn and oppose the Burnouts in this "unhealthy," "smelly," and "self-destructive" behavior. One girl's account of how one of her teachers helped shepherd her back into the fold illustrates the symbolic value of smoking.

In junior high I was really bored with like, you probably experienced this too, it just, you just get really bored with the whole situation . . . and, um, and like the Burnouts always seemed like they were, they had so much fun, you know, they were always the neat people to be with, so I started getting mixed up with them a little bit. And so, um, I got my first D that I ever got in math. And my math teacher always like teased me in front of the class, you know. And like we'd draw like, um, geometric figures, and one time there was one like this, I'll never forget, like a, a cigarette box with a, a cigarette sticking out, and he said, "Denise, what does that look like to you?", you know. And then this one guy said, "A pack of cigarettes," and like they'd always, like, because they were all like really straight kids in AP math. And so I think that helped me a lot, though, to have all of that, because it, it made me, I don't know, it just kind of made me realize what was going on.

Clothing

The stranger to the high school notices a variety of clothing, but just as the geography of the school becomes meaningful only when one begins to see how various people use the building, the clothing styles take on meaning as one begins to notice that certain patterns of clothing appear in certain parts of the school, and eventually as one comes to know the social significance of these patterns. Clothing is a particularly powerful social maker because it is regularly renewed and never separated from the individual in public situations. Just about every component of external clothing has indexical or symbolic value in the category system.

Throughout society, clothing style signals economic means, access to information, and specific group identity. Economic means are reflected both in a rapid turnover of clothing – exhibited through wardrobe size and swift style changes – and in the quality and expense of individual items. Within any social group, the specific items and combinations of items one chooses reflect group consensus. These subtler differences, which can be achieved only through private information, are the ultimate indication of group membership. The relative paucity of an outsider's or a marginal individual's information may prevent that individual from even knowing that he or she is not completely "in style" with the target group. Each group's style is thus a function of specific identity, information (including both verbal information and exposure), economic means, practical needs, and an ideology based on all of these. As a social marker of group membership, clothing style is closely associated with the social and cultural characteristics of groups and can elicit powerful emotional reactions. Style is not interpreted simply as an indication of social affiliation but as a direct and intentional expression of group values, a marker of group boundaries, and thus a rejection of alternative values. Failure to conform to group style, therefore, is taken to signal lack of solidarity.

The significance of clothing is not equal for men and women. In American society, women are expected to pay more attention than men to clothing style. Women's style encompasses a wider range than men's, and even includes much of men's style. In general, women wear more accessories than men, and their clothes include a wider range of colors and of cuts. The difference between women's informal and formal wear is greater, and women's adornment extends beyond clothing and accessories to cosmetics and labor-intensive hair styles. Differences in adornment serve as simple gender markers, but women's greater stylistic elaboration is also an in-

dication of their greater reliance on symbolic means of signalling social status in a society that denies them equal access to social mobility through action. Adolescent girls have to work harder to achieve social status and are far more constrained by physical attractiveness than boys. In addition, girls are more constrained by social distinctions than are boys and must take greater care to signal the appropriate identity through the full range of symbolic means. Just as boys are freer than girls to cross category boundaries, they are less bound by category-specific clothing styles.

Jock and Burnout clothing is clearly differentiated on the basis of cost. Jocks, particularly girls, strive for a good number of outfits and consciously avoid wearing the same thing too closely in succession. Expense of clothing is apparent in the quality of cut, fit, and fabric, and in the more obvious designer labels. Most Belten Jock girls shop, frequently in pairs or groups, in the mid- to somewhat higher-priced stores in major shopping malls in the Detroit suburban area. Burnouts, much of whose solidarity is based on relative lack of economic means, pride themselves on not being concerned with clothing as a status symbol and maintain somewhat more limited and inexpensive wardrobes. Even those Burnouts who can afford to dress on a Jock scale tend not to, as an expression of solidarity with those who cannot. Lack of means is in itself a positive value, and Burnouts criticize Jocks for what they see as unnecessarily expensive and competitive dressing. The Burnout taboo on competitive dressing reflects not only solidarity in lack of means, but the more general disapproval of social competition. [. . .]

Many Jocks' enhanced economic status is indeed reflected in their ability to follow the fashions and in their emphasis on "designer" clothing, particularly Calvin Klein jeans and Izod shirts. The economic aspects of Jock clothing, like the social value of economics in general, are not absolute but geared to the dominant means of the main Jock group. While in some wealthier schools around the Detroit area, Jocks wear entire Izod outfits, it is frowned upon in Belten to wear more than one Izod item at a time or even to own more than one or two. The preppy look, therefore, is not adopted with abandon at Belten. The stigmatization of "preppy Jocks" as conspicuously wealthy extends to the entire preppy look, as reflected in one Jock boy's strong reaction to one group of girls' habit of wearing their collars up.

> Like some of the people are wealthy, you know, and I hate Preppies, I mean, I hate people who wear their collar up and stuff, like, you know, that's totally stupid, I mean, if so many people do it, I guess it's not stupid, but it looks dumb, I don't know why they do it. And there's one girl . . . she'll ah, wear her collar up, and whenever you say anything, or happen to mention "Preppy," she'll make sure it's up – you know, make sure it's really good and up there.

Burnout fashion includes some elements that spread from working class urban areas and some outmoded elements of Jock style. In the early 1980s, Burnouts were wearing the bell-bottomed jeans popular among Jocks five years before, and Burnouts boys' long hair styles are another throwback to that era. In 1986, Burnout girls were wearing the straight-legged jeans and feathered hair style fashionable among Jocks in the early 1980s, while Jocks had moved on to short, pegged jeans and permed hair styles. The chronological relation between certain Jock and Burnout styles is not an indication that fashions simply pass from Jocks to Burnouts, for Burnouts' current jeans and hair styles correspond also to current young adult working class fashion and to the fashions currently worn by certain hard rock and country music stars. Just as Jocks follow mainstream adult influence in clothing, Burnouts follow the fashions of working class adults and the entertainers that appeal to them. Certain elements of style never adopted by Jocks reflect "country" influence, such as the buckskin "squaw boots" popular among Burnouts in the early 1980s and still popular today.

Bell-bottoms were a particularly strong Burnout index in the early 1980s and, of all the Burnout indices, the greatest object of disparagement among Jocks. Bell-bottoms are the most salient, and the first mentioned, item of Burnout fashion at Belten. This is reflected in one In-between's characterization of the lower socioeconomic school in Neartown as a place where "they wear bell-bottoms 10 feet wide." This reference to the specific width of the bell-bottoms reflects the significance of the width con-

tinuum. Jeans in the early 1980s ranged all the way from the wide bells of the early 1970s through the slightly more conservative flares, to the mainstream straight legs, and finally to the new and very fashionable pegged baggies. Among the latter two cuts, the prestige hierarchy of designer names had become an additional element of style. Even ignoring brand name, the casual observer could notice before long that jean leg width and school territory were closely related, particularly in the distribution of jeans in after-lunch territories in Belten (see Eckert, 1982). The geographic continuum from the lobby directly in front of the cafeteria (Jock territory), down the gym hall, and into the courtyard (Burnout territory) corresponds to a striking continuum in jean leg width. As one moved from the Jock to the Burnout territory, the average jean width gradually increased.

This distribution reflects not simply an opposition between bells and straight legs, but a width continuum corresponding to the social continuum. Just as the school population boasts a mass of In-betweens in addition to Jocks and Burnouts, the cut of jeans presents in-between alternatives. Not only are there more bells in the courtyard and more straight legs in the cafeteria lobby, but there are more flares in the transitional area. This continuum is repeated in the styles worn by students who spend time together. Quantitative observations of casual groups of students showed that people walking together commonly wear the same cut of jeans. However, pairs and groups also show combinations within a limited range of the jeans continuum: bells with flares, flares with straight legs, straight legs with baggies. Virtually no groups or pairs reflect jumps in the continuum.

While Jocks wear polo shirts, button-down shirts, and crew-neck sweaters, Burnouts overwhelmingly wear rock concert T-shirts. These T-shirts have the double symbolic value of displaying lack of means and of advertising the Burnout taste for hard rock. Burnouts girls wearing sweaters do not sport the "preppy" look of woolen crew necks, but opt for patterned sweaters frequently made of synthetic materials.

The most richly symbolic element of Burnout upper body wear is the jacket. The Burnouts signal their peripheral relation to the school – the fact that they are "just passing through" – by wearing their jackets all day in school. They say that they wear their jackets because they go into the courtyard between classes, because their lockers are not safe to keep anything in, and because it facilitates skipping out on the spur of the moment. The jacket worn in school very closely signals all of these elements of Burnout culture.

Certain elements of Burnout clothing also symbolize urban identification. Some Burnout boys signal their affiliation with Detroit by wearing black jackets with DETROIT written in white on the back. This urban style stands in clear opposition to the frequent Jock letter jacket, which indicates local and school orientation and participation in sports. In the early 1980s, most Burnout boys wore lined jeans jackets, which gradually gave way to the current urban fashion of hooded sweatshirts under unlined jeans jackets. Familiarity with and competence in the tougher and more crime-ridden urban environment is also symbolized by two elements of male style – metal studs, particularly on leather jackets and wrist bands, and chains attaching the wearer's wallet to his belt loop.

Sports

Sports present a complex picture in the Jock–Burnout opposition. Many Burnouts are good athletes and pride themselves on their physical abilities. Their resentment that the Jocks' involvement in school sports implies athletic superiority, and the fact that some good Burnout players defected from school teams, gives rise to considerable competition wherever Jocks and Burnouts come into contact in an athletic context. As one Burnout said:

> God, in gym, man, it's Jocks against the Burnouts whatever you're doing, man. That's where, you know, it gets let out a little bit.

During junior high, there was at least one Jock–Burnout game, but, as one Jock describes below, the school tried to discourage such competition:

> Like when we were in Rover we used to have a Jock–Burn football game, Jock–Burn baseball game

and stuff, you know. . . . Like they'd come up and ask one of our – you know, one of the guys from the football team, "Hey, you want to have a game?" You know, "You guys think you're so great." They're just, not really mean, they're just, you know, goofing around. Just, you know, for something to do. So, I don't know, it's just anybody, just some – they get an idea or we get an idea and we. . . . Except our coach found out and he goes, "Yeah, I'm gonna be driving down, driving by [the park] today, and if I see any of you guys out there, uh, don't be – don't be coming back to practice" or something.

WHY?

I don't know, it's just, he didn't want no one getting hurt and stuff, you know how that goes, and he just thought it was a dumb thing to do to have a – he just thought it was dumb having a distinction too, you know. But if some of the Burnouts, or whatever, would have just played football, we could have been a lot better, so he was kind of mad because they'd – they'd stay away just because, you know, kind of peer pressure.

While Burnouts were on school teams, particularly football, in junior high, their numbers fell off as they reached high school. Several factors contributed to this disaffection. Since the Jocks' corporate mentality leads them to form social networks around school activities, school sports enhance their social lives. The Burnouts, on the other hand, for whom social networks are primary, found that the time taken up by afternoon practices threatened the solidarity of their peer groups and excluded them from group activities. Coaches' disciplinary actions were another factor: Burnouts who missed practices or were caught using forbidden substances were suspended and dropped from teams. In keeping with their hostility toward the school's parental presumptions, Burnouts came to consider school athletics as a threat to their personal autonomy. One Burnout explained that the coaches' attention to substance use contradicted meritocratic selection – that a coach should be concerned simply with the individual's athletic performance regardless of his or her life-style. Eventually, Burnouts began to feel that they were being discriminated against, in team selections and in interactions with their teammates, on the basis of their category affiliation. As a result of all these factors, most Burnouts confine their athletic activities to city and commercial teams and to informal games.

Co-ed pickup games in neighborhood parks are a common Burnout activity in good weather. These games are as much social activities as athletic events, and all levels of skill are accepted. Particularly significant in these games are the cigarette breaks. On several occasions in games in which I participated, play was interrupted while a "runner" ran onto the field to pass a cigarette around to players stranded on base – a clear affirmation of Burnout solidarity in an activity that might otherwise be identified as "Jock."

Language

Perhaps the strongest evidence of the depth of the difference between Jocks and Burnouts lies in their use of language. There are the obvious, conscious differences – the Burnouts' more frequent and public use of obscenities and of specialized vocabulary such as drug-related slang. On a somewhat less conscious level, there are differences in routine expressions such as greetings. While Jocks tend to use the common short greeting "hi" when they come across a casual acquaintance, Burnouts overwhelmingly use the longer "how 'ya doin'." These particular greeting differences are repeated in the larger society between middle class and working class speakers. While such differences are not consciously maintained, they are recognized when pointed out to speakers.

Grammar is a conscious marker of Jock and Burnout affiliation – both in recognition and in use. The Burnouts are overwhelmingly seen as speaking "ungrammatically," that is, as using nonstandard grammar. Standard grammar is the grammar used by the powerful society's mainstream and embraced by its institutions, including the school. Its forms are not necessarily more conservative historically, nor is it any more systematic, logical, or beautiful. The use of standard grammar simply signals one's membership in and identification with the national mainstream. At times the use of nonstandard grammar may reflect sufficient isolation from the mainstream to prevent significant exposure to standard language, but its more important mechanism is its social symbolic value in the local non-mainstream community. And as with any symbolic material, the use of nonstandard grammar can reflect rejection of mainstream society and identification with the local non-mainstream community.

The multiple negative (such as *I don't know nothing*) is among the most commonly cited features of nonstandard grammar. (Multiple negation has been absurdly associated with a variety of cognitive shortcomings, with which it was never connected in the sixteenth century, when it was standard in English.) All the students in Belten High have access to standard negation; all of them use it at least some of the time, but many of them also use multiple negation. The Burnouts use far more multiple negatives than Jocks. The Burnouts used multiple negation in their tape-recorded speech with a probability of .720, while the Jocks used it with a probability of .280 (sig. = .006). None of the speakers in either category used multiple negatives all the time. The variable use of multiple negation may mean that the speaker uses standard negatives when he or she is speaking carefully but multiple negation is more natural. It may also mean the opposite: that standard negation is more natural but the speaker intentionally uses multiple negation on occasion. Finally, it may mean that the speaker's usage depends on the situation and the kind of impression he or she is trying to make or the connotations he or she wants to give to the utterance. No doubt all of these apply within the community of speakers at Belten. There is certainly no question that much of the Burnouts' use of multiple negation, and the Jocks' use of standard negation, is symbolic of category affiliation and of the relation to schooling associated with that affiliation.

While vocabulary, greetings, and grammatical patterns function on a relatively conscious level, there are also patterns of pronunciation that differ between Jocks and Burnouts. Some of these are used almost entirely unconsciously. One such pattern is in the pronunciation of several vowels that are in the progress of undergoing historical change in the Detroit area, almost entirely without the awareness of the speakers who are actually implementing the change. For example, there is a tendency in the Detroit area for speakers to back the vowel that occurs in *lunch* so that is sounds more like the vowel in *launch* (there are many such pairs – punch/paunch, but/bought, cut/caught). This change is spreading outward from the urban area, and in Neartown as in other suburbs around the Detroit area the Burnouts lead significantly in this change. In a sample that includes only people who grew up in Neartown, not recent arrivals from Detroit, the Burnouts back this vowel with significantly greater frequency than the Jocks. (This change is discussed in detail in Eckert, 1988.)

Together, these kinds of linguistic features differentiate the Jocks and the Burnouts and serve as powerful symbols of category membership. They are not simply class markers picked up in the neighborhood or the home. It is well known that children acquire their dialects from their peers rather than their parents, and that dialects tend to settle in the preadolescent years – in fact, at the very time that the Jock and Burnout categories are forming. The clearest indication that these linguistic features are acquired as a function of category affiliation, though, is the fact that while they correlate statistically with category affiliation, they do not correlate with parents' socioeconomic class. That is, there is sufficient class crossover in the categories [. . .] so that the effects of home can be separated from the effects of peer affiliation.

The Growth of Symbolic Oppositions

In seventh grade, the Burnouts aggressively display their counter-school values through the adoption of distinct public behavior with clear symbolic value related to claims on adult status and to orientation to the school. Smoking, drinking, occupation of the illicit smoking area adjacent to the school, and gathering outside of dances and roller skating rinks to smoke and drink are unambiguous in their meaning. The Jocks' development of strong and vocal norms against all of these activities, and their central participation in school social activities (as opposed to hanging out at the periphery), comes to signal opposition to the Burnouts' behavior. This symbolic behavior is supplemented as increasing domains of everyday life are incorporated into the set of oppositions. The clear association of any piece of behavior with one category will lead to the adoption of opposing behavior by the other. As more domains and details of behavior are incorporated as category symbols, the oppositions become mutually reinfor-

cing, developing a structured symbolic system with its own impetus. Clothing, territory, substance use, language, demeanor, academic behavior, and activities all ultimately serve as conscious markers of category affiliation. In each of these areas, the behavior of one category is carefully opposed to that of the other, and one can see clearly that the two sets of behavior have grown in relation to each other. This ever-enlarging set of oppositions strengthens the hegemony of the category system in adolescent life and increasingly restricts individual perceptions and choice.

The elaboration of the system of oppositions exerts increasing constraints on individual behavior, narrowing individuals' personal options and view of the world. Since the two categories develop in mutual opposition, behavioral choices are typically binary, offering alternatives that are seen as opposites and excluding other choices altogether from the range of accepted behavior. As rock concert T-shirts and polo shirts become associated with Burnouts and Jocks, respectively, the choice of a third alternative, such as a frilly blouse, becomes anomalous and is taken to indicate that the individual wearing it does not know the adolescent clothing system. The limitation to the binary choices associated with the category system is reinforced by the adolescent need to deny parental domination of personal behavior, particularly behavior, such as clothing choice, that does not have a clear "good" or "bad" association in the real world. This denial must take the form of participation in the system of socially meaningful choices offered within the adolescent community.

The oppositional system also focuses attention on those areas of behavior that it has made salient, making attention to other areas anomalous. Lunch, for instance, is either bought in the cafeteria or brought in an inconspicuous paper bag. An individual who chose to bring lunch to school in a conspicuous and carefully chosen container would be viewed as paying attention to the wrong things and thus as not knowing what is important in adolescent society. It would also suggest that the individual is participating in some system outside the local adolescent community. In the case of the lunch container there might also be a childish connotation carried over from elementary school lunch boxes, while an individual who carried a newspaper in school would be viewed as trying to look excessively adult. The system of oppositions is further strengthened by the links established among the binary choices, encouraging an association among otherwise independent areas of behavior. The value of smoking and rock concert T-shirts as Burnout symbols links them in an implicational relationship, so that the individual who wears rock concert T-shirts will be assumed also to smoke. This is also apt to be true, because those in need of a clear social identity are likely to make the entire range of choices consonant with one or the other category. Thus, in the development of the system of oppositions, individual traits lose their independence and form a network of associations, resulting in an increasingly powerful system. As the system of oppositions develops, each pole becomes increasingly specified and constrained. The consequences can be far-reaching, because the oppositions dominate not only temporary behavior, such as clothing, but choices with lasting implications, such as curriculum choice, academic effort, and substance use.

The Jock and Burnout categories represent the two extremes in relation to adults, and the oppositions associated with each term of the Jock–Burnout split represent choices that adolescents and preadolescents see themselves confronted with in the process of disengagement from the family. Ambivalence over disengagement leads to confusion over a variety of decisions, particularly those that involve the assumption of adult roles and rebellion against parents. These decisions are played out in the continual exercising of oppositions, which set up the social world in terms of binary choices and simplify the appearance of the choices to be made. At the same time, the category system provides group support for these choices: The decision to smoke is no longer an individual transgression, but is condoned and supported not only by individuals in one's group but by the existence of a social category characterized by these choices. The institutionalization of the opposition provides social sanction for either choice. Thus the decision not to smoke, if it appears to be simply obedience to one's parents, is at least as threatening to one's image as the decision to smoke. Status within a category characterized by non-smoking allows the individual to feel independent from the family while choosing parentally approved behavior.

The simplification of choice within the category system leads to oversimplification of values, and the overwhelming judgments of "good" and "bad" associated with the categories prevent individuals from recognizing the independence of many of the decisions they are faced with. The close association of traits within either category is powerful enough to force individual decisions, not on the merits of the issues at hand, but as a simple requirement and expression of category affiliation and participation in adolescent society. Thus a Burnout will find it difficult to avoid smoking or to participate in a school activity, while a Jock will feel pressured to invest in a wardrobe and to participate in activities that he or she may find uninteresting.

Obviously not everyone in Belten High School describes himself or herself as a Jock or a Burnout. In fact, only about 30 percent or 40 percent of them do. But this does not make these categories any less powerful in the social structure of the school. The fundamental status of these categories is underscored by the fact that almost all those who are not professed Jocks or Burnouts describe themselves and are described as "In-betweens."

> When people go into classifying, you know, you got the Jocks and the Jells, and then there's the In-betweeners, or whoever you want to say, you know.

The status of In-between is a by-product of the oppositional system, dominated by the same binary choices that constitute the opposition between Jocks and Burnouts. Most of the In-betweens do not choose alternative behavior, but simply mix Jock and Burnout choices. People who choose alternatives are generally referred to as "weirdos" or "nerds." The In-betweens describe themselves in terms of which choices they share with either category, and sometimes as occupying a place in a continuum between the poles, defined by the number of traits chosen from either pole. As the cohort matures, the population of the school increasingly constitutes such a continuum, but retains a significant cluster of people near each pole. There is continuous feedback of the separation and hostility between the categories and the symbolic oppositions that develop in association with them. This feedback increasingly isolates the members of each category, so that by the time the cohort reaches eleventh grade, they know relatively little about each other. As one Burnout said in his junior year:

> I don't know the Jocks any more. I don't have anything to do with them. It's hard to remember their names.

References

Eckert, P. (1982). "Clothing and Geography in a Suburban High School." In C. P. Kottak (ed.), *Researching American Culture* (pp. 139–44). Ann Arbor: University of Michigan Press.

Eckert, P. (1983). "Beyond the Statistics of Adolescent Smoking." *American Journal of Public Health*, 73, 439–41.

Eckert, P. (1988). "Sound Change and Adolescent Social Structure." *Language in Society*, 17, 183–207.

Ortner, S. B. (1973). "On Key Symbols." *American Anthropologist*, 75, 1338–46.

Willis, P. (1977). *Learning to Labour*. Westmead, Farnborough, Hants., England: Saxon House.

Kinship Systems

A. M. Hocart

When we explore a new language, we infer the meaning of words from the objects to which they are applied. The first object gives us a preliminary definition. That may chance to be right, but further experience may compel us to revise it. Thus I may first hear the word "table" used of a list of facts in a book, and so translate it "page." By degrees I shall learn better.

This caution is generally borne in mind by students of literary languages, but it is too often lost sight of in the study of non-literary languages. A great many investigators never get beyond the first use of the word that happens to come their way. Miss Lucy Mair has produced a striking example in the *Bulletin of the School of Oriental Studies*, vii, 918. An investigator heard the Uganda word *obuko* applied to palsy. He entered it in his dictionary as "palsy." It really refers to marriage rules, to a breach of which palsy is the consequence.

One of the most flagrant cases is the translation of the so-called classificatory kinship terms. The person most commonly called *tama* in Melanesia, the one most in evidence, is a man's father. He is the man who will be named if you asked, "Who is your *tama*?" So *tama* has been duly set down as "father." The same has been done with other kinship terms in Melanesia and elsewhere. It was soon noticed, however, that other men besides the father are called *tama*. By all rules the first translation should have been dropped, and a new one found to cover all the different *tamas*, and thus express the essence of *tama*-ship. Unfortunately, no single word can do so, and it has remained in the literature of the South Seas as "father," with the proviso that it is "extended" to cover father's brother, father's father's brothers' sons, and so on. Ever since we have been racking our brains to explain how Melanesians can call their uncles, and even remote cousins, "fathers."

The effect on theory has been disastrous. The order in which we have learned the uses of *tama* and similar words has been confused with the order of development in actual history. Because we first took it to mean father we slip unwittingly into the assumption that it meant father originally.

This fallacy has now received official expression in the term "kinship extensions." That expression implies that the meaning father is primary and that all other uses result from extending the term to an ever-widening circle of kinsmen.

It is curious that this doctrine, which is historical since it describes a process of development in the past, is championed most stoutly by those who are forever gibing at origins, evolution, historical reconstruction. This is a historical reconstruction, or what is?

The only way of proving that a process has taken

place in the past is by recognized historical methods: either produce documents or resort to the comparative method. It is perhaps fortunate in this case that we have little documentary evidence and so must rely on the much more reliable comparative method.

Before we can apply it we must get our facts right. To that end let us forget all we have ever been told about the meaning of classificatory terms and rediscover the language, taking Fijian as an example. Evidently *tama* cannot mean father since it includes cousins to the *n*th degree, even cousins too young to have children; in fact, a man is born a *tama*. We notice, however, that all those cousins have one thing in common: they are once removed; in other words, they are of the generation next to Ego, and, to be more precise, to the one immediately before. Not all the members of this generation, however, are *tama*. There are two sides to that generation, the father's and the mother's; only those on the father's side are *tama*. That is evidently the meaning of *tama*, so our final definition will run:

tama = all males of the previous generation on the father's side.

Repeating the process we go on.

vungo = all males of the generation immediately above and below Ego on the mother's side;
tavale = all males of the same generation on the mother's side.

And so on. When our list is complete we find that all the terms fall into two sets, one set belonging to the father's side, the other to the mother's. Each term refers to a particular generation within one side. In short, these terms do not express consanguinity, as we have unfortunately been accustomed by Morgan to believe, but they fix the place of any relative according to generation and side. If I call a man *tuaka* it is clear that he is of my generation on my father's side, and senior to me; a *wati* is a woman of my generation on the side from which my mother comes.

This last term affords an excellent illustration how a particular use is mistaken for the true one, and the true one comes to be looked upon as an improper one. A Fijian introduces his wife as *wati*, so the word is noted as "wife." When it is found there are hundreds of *watis* who are not his wives, the first translation is not abandoned, but all other uses are explained as extensions: these women, it is explained, are called wives because he might marry any of them if the family so decided; they are wives by anticipation, "potential wives." Upon this muddled lexicography has been built up a whole edifice of primitive promiscuity.

Exactly the same usage exists in Arabic. Arabic-speaking husbands can often be heard addressing their wives as *bint 'amm*; but they also call their paternal uncles' daughters *bint 'amm*. We do not translate "wife," "potential wife," because we know that *bint* is daughter, and *'amm* is paternal uncle; therefore *bint 'amm* means "cousin on the father's side." When a man marries his cousin, as it is best to do, he goes on calling her "cousin" as he has been accustomed to since childhood. The Fijian and the Ashanti do exactly the same.

We can remember the time when an English youth would refer jocosely to his father as "The Governor." No one has ever suggested that this was primary and that the word has been extended to colonial administrators.

All our difficulties spring from a preconceived idea that kinship terms everywhere try to express the same thing as they do in Aryan and Semitic languages, and that in those languages they show the place on the family tree. The result is that in a certain African language the term *nana* is rendered father's father, father's father's brother, and so on through thirty-four European relationships, and then it does not exhaust all the possibilities. And what is the outcome of all this painstaking? We have a list of cases, but we have not got the meaning. It is as if a dictionary under "hot" told us "the sun is hot, pepper is hot, A's temper is hot, the discussion is hot," and left it at that. If we go to the trouble of extracting the meaning of *nana* from the cases we find it simply means "any relative two generations above or below."

At this point we may be asked what evidence

have we that the people themselves understand kinship terms in this sense. The same evidence as we have for the meaning of any word, what is common to the cases in which it is used.

As regards the Chinese system we have more, we have the definite statement of a Chinaman. Mr H. Y. Feng produces documentary evidence that the Chinese system was once a cross-cousin system, and so it is akin to the Fijian. As in cross-cousin systems the kinsfolk are still divided into two: those of the same patronymic, and those of another. These sides he chooses to call "sibs." Besides this vertical division, there is a horizontal one into generations. "These two factors, sib and generation," he sums up, "not only pervade the whole system but regulate marriage." A man marries a woman of another patronym of the first generation.[1]

The hill tribes of Viti Levu, Fiji, indicate very clearly what their kinship terms mean to them. Every hillsman assumes all other hillsmen to be his kinsmen. He is not concerned how near or how far related a stranger may be; he does not search the pedigrees to find out how they are related. All he wants to know is their respective generations. That is easy, because the whole population is divided into two alternate generations called *tako* and *lavo*. If both are *tako* or both *lavo* they are of the same generation, and then the senior is *tuka*, the junior *tadhi*, terms which have unfortunately been translated (by myself among others), as elder and younger brother. Evidently they mean nothing of the kind, since a man's grandfather is his *tuka* as well as his elder brother. The words simply mean "of the same one of the two generations, on the same side, senior," or "junior," as the case may be. If one man is *tako*, the other *lavo*, then they are related as *tama* and *luve* – that is as one generation to the other. In the case of relatives who are known, and whose side is therefore known, two sets of terms exist, just as in all cross-cousin systems. The line and the generation is what the Fijian looks for in his kinship system, not propinquity.

Why should he be so interested in the generation and so little in the nearness of kin? Because nearness is of little importance in public affairs; generation and line are all important. If a chief, chieftain, or priest dies it is not the next of kin that succeeds, as with us, but the next senior of his generation, no

matter how distant; if the deceased was the last of his generation, then it goes to the most senior of the next. A Lauan expresses the rule thus: "X was not made chief, because his *tama* was living." We are not rendering the meaning at all by translating *tama* "father," because X's father was dead. What is meant is that X could not succeed because there was still a member of the previous generation on his father's side to come before him.[2]

We now understand why members of the same generation and side are so carefully distinguished as senior and junior (commonly rendered "elder brother and younger brother, classificatory"). The order of seniority is all important. With us only one of a group of brothers has to have his status made clear in royal and titled families; so among such families he bears a special title "heir" which singles him out; the rest are lumped together as brothers, for their seniority is normally of little importance, since they drop out of the succession. It is only when the holder has no issue that the seniority of his younger brothers need be remembered.

It is not the whole of a generation that succeeds, but only those in the male line. Therefore the female line has to be distinguished from the male by special terms. Since the female line is completely excluded, seniority does not come into consideration at all in their case, so no distinction is made between senior and junior.

Generation, line, and seniority decide not only succession, but everyday behavior. The duties in the ritual are fixed in the same way.[3]

In short, what we seek most is the next of kin, and so we run up and down the family tree. The Fijians (and the Australian aborigines, and the rest) do not, because there is no point in doing so. All they want is such information as will enable them to place each man on the correct side in the right generation. An inquiry proceeds thus: "How are you related?" "Of the same side and generation." "Why?" "Because our fathers were of the same side and generation." Or else: "We belong to successive generations on opposite sides, because he is of my mother's side and generation."

If the users of classificatory systems can get on without pedigrees, surely the field-worker can. He would be all the better for it in working out the system. He would cease to see the system thus:

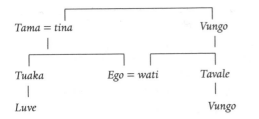

and learn to see them thus:

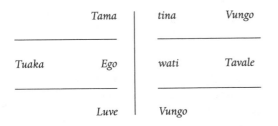

I do not mean that pedigrees are useless. There are many investigations that are impossible without them, but they have exercised a pernicious influence on the theory of classificatory systems.

Some systems are more complicated, some less, than the typical cross-cousin system from which our illustrations have been drawn, but the principle remains the same. It is all a matter of how many lines and how many generations are distinguished.

Since classificatory terms have no real equivalents in our language we must either use cumbrous circumlocutions or condensed symbols. We must choose between saying: "A boy is circumcised by a man one generation up on the opposite side"; or else represent that man by something like this:

$\frac{1 \text{Op}}{\text{Ego}}$ I leave it to others to work out something on these other lines. It would be easy enough but for the Australian systems. Anyhow we cannot go on identifying these classificatory terms with our kinship terms which mean something quite different.

We are now in a position to examine more fruitfully the theory of kinship extension. In a paper of this dimension it is only possible to outline the evidence, and the more so as nothing has been done to deal systematically and comparatively with the problem, except in the case of Aryan languages. I can only sum up here the results of bringing up to date Delbruck's survey of Aryan kinship terms. The reader will find a detailed discussion in the *Ceylon Journal of Science*, sec. G, i, 179; ii, 33.[4]

The conclusion is that our own kinship terms appear to have once been used in a classificatory sense. The word father, for instance, meant originally not the procreator, but any man who conferred life on another, whether by sacramental intercourse with the mother or by some other ritual act, but not by the mere unconsecrated infusion of semen. It also applied to all the kinsmen of the father's side and generation, because they are ritually interchangeable with the father. At a very early date, before the splitting up of the parent Aryan tongue, this and other terms were narrowed down to their present use; but the original use still persists in connection with ritual, e.g. godfather, lay brother, etc. The present usage is thus a result of contraction, not of extension, and is based on modern physiology, not on a theory of sacraments.[5]

The Semitic evidence wants working out in detail, but a superficial examination provisionally points the same way.

Are we to believe that speakers of Aryan and Semitic started with a classificatory system and ended with a genealogical one, while the rest of the world reversed the process, extended terms which meant properly begetter, bearer, begetter's begetter, and so on, to cousins so distant that kinship is only presumed? It is hardly probable, but if anyone believes it happened so, let him produce some evidence.

He might point out that classificatory terms are constantly used like ours, that in Melanesia *tama* is often understood to mean the father and no one else. Is this the original use, as is constantly assumed by the "extensionists," or is it the beginning of contraction? Only definite cases can decide this question.

If a Fijian asks, "Have you a *wati*?" it is obvious he cannot mean, "Have you kinswomen of your generation on your mother's side?" because, where kinship is unbounded, no man is without such kinswomen. What is meant is "Do you own such woman?" – in short, "Are you married?" There is not a boy who has not got kinswomen two generations before him, so the statement "he has a kinswoman two generations up" can only refer to one of them, the nearest. The meaning is: "He is a boy who has been much under the care of his grandmother, and so known a good deal of old women's lore." This is an excellent example how the meaning of words is filled in by the rest of the sentence and by custom. Here custom narrows down the dictionary meaning not only to one person, but to one characteristic of that person. If a Frenchman talks of "ma femme" he refers to one woman only, not any woman connected with him, not his servant, or even his mistress, but the one with whom he has contracted a permanent alliance recognized by the state, and possibly by the Church. No one has ever suggested this is the original meaning of the word, and that it has been extended to all women. It is not always necessary to have a possessive. If an Englishman says "The King," everyone understands he means the King of England. It does not follow that originally the title meant that king only, and has been extended to other kings.

In all these cases words designating whole classes of men are restricted by the singular, the definite article, or some other sign of definiteness to one person, the context and custom further define who that one person is. "My *tama*" is the *tama* of the family circle; "the Captain" is the commander of the speaker's company; "herself" is the speaker's wife. It is easy to see how, as the household emancipates itself from the clan or kindred, kinsmen outside the household drop more and more into the background, the direct line father-grandfather monopolizes the attention, and so the kinship terms. The father always stands out among the men of his generation; but he stands out more than ever when the household forms a closed body with its own household cult. That cult now no longer descends from brother to brother, but from father to son, so that the other members of the father's generation can no longer be regarded as being on the same footing as the father.

In the use of *tama* to mean "father," *wati* to mean "wife," we have the germ, not the survival of a genealogical system.

A short review of the facts thus raises a presumption that the classificatory terms are not due to extension, but that our habit of denoting nearness of kin is the result of contraction.[6] Finally, to establish this presumption it would be necessary to show that it fits all the facts, not only of kinship, but of social organization generally. Among the most important facts are the ritual functions of kinsmen. The first task is to collect them all and to try and find the underlying principle why it is, for instance, that the men of the father's side and generation provide the regalia for initiation, while the men of the mother's generation and side carry out the operation. Until that has been done all discussions as to the ultimate meaning of classificatory systems, or indeed of kinship systems in general, must remain idle guesswork.

Note. – Miss Margaret Mead has made a very intensive study of these functions in the Admiralty Islands.[7] Only a comparative study, however, can explain.

I only know of one serious attempt to prove the extension theory, that is, if I have understood Prof. E. E. Evans-Pritchard aright. In his paper on "The Nature of Kinship Extensions"[8] he shows with admirable objectivity how the Azande child learns to extend the terms and the behavior from the immediate family circle to wider circles. Presumably these children are repeating the phylogenetic evolution. But our children begin by calling all adult men *dada*, and are taught to limit it to one man. There is obviously a flaw in an argument that leads to contradictory results. The flaw is that the conditions under which a child learns a language, or behavior, generally do not reproduce those under which evolution has taken place. As Vendryes says: "Children only teach us how an organized language is acquired; they do not give us an idea what language can have been at the beginning of its evolution." Substitute "behavior" for "language," and the statement remains equally true. Biologists have for some time recognized the fact that the growth of the human body does not exactly reproduce the evolution of the race. The chief merit of Prof. Evans-Pritchard's paper is that it gives us the Azande point of view in their own words and actions, and does not romance about what is going on inside their minds.

Notes

1 "Teknonymy and the Chinese Kinship System," *Amer. Anthr.*, 1936, p. 60.

2 These remarks apply equally to the Aranda who have the same system of succession, according to Strehlow. It is also found in Ceylon where the classificatory system prevails (*Ceylon Journal of Science*, sec. G, i, 75; Geigler, *Culavansa*, i, 20ff.).

3 See my *Lau Islands*, pp. 35ff., and *The Progress of Man*, pp. 259ff.

4 R. S. Rattray made a move in the right direction by dividing up his kinship terms into generations; but he stopped half-way. *Ashanti*, pp. 24ff.

5 Supplemented by my *Progress of Man*, pp. 261ff.

6 From a manifesto by Infante Don Alfonso Carlos and King Alfonso's reply it appears that the Royal House of Spain can use "Uncle" and "Nephew" of second cousins once removed, as in classificatory systems.

7 "Kinship in the Admiralty Islands," *Anthr. Papers of the American Museum of Natural History*, vol. xxxiv, Pt. ii, 20ff.

8 *Man*, 1932, p. 7.

---

1 Cut out a letter to Ann Landers, Ms. Manners, Ask Beth, or local equivalent and attach it to the answer. What notions of the person, of proper social relations, are implied in both the letter and the answer? What cultural values are being drawn upon? Would you have answered the letter differently? Why?

2 Pretend you do not understand the local language. (For most of you using this book, this will probably be English; some of you may be studying in English in a non-English-speaking setting.) Observe and/or listen to interactions in one place for a period of time (e.g., a half-hour in a busy place, perhaps longer elsewhere). Note the ways in which people greet each other, and leave each other. Apart from the specific words used, what is done to indicate this is a "greeting" or a "leave taking"? Do you detect any patterns? Are there any significant differences when the interaction is between/among men, between/among women, or between/among individuals of different genders? Different ages?

EXERCISES

6

Our Bodies, Our Selves

*Are we our bodies or do we **have** bodies? Different concepts of the body, the gendered body, the physical body, the social body. Techniques and modifications of the body. Tattoos. Body parts and organ transplants. Traffic in body parts. Body image, advertisements, and eating disorders. Bodies before and after death.*

Our Bodies, Our Selves

The title of this chapter is also the title of a book by the Boston Women's Health Collective. Appalled by the lack of information about their bodies available to women in the 1960s, this "consciousness-raising" group gathered the information, pooled their knowledge, and published it in 1973. That first edition was a thin booklet on newsprint; the 1992 edition has a commercial publisher and is heavy with 752 pages. It remains a highly acclaimed resource for women. Our bodies *are* ourselves.

Our bodies are what allow us to occupy space, experience the sensual world, and interact with others. We take them for granted as coextensive, coexistent with ourselves; indeed, they are so much a part of us that they seem inseparable. Yet the way we often think and speak of them implies something different. Each of us *has* or *is* a body – but there is a world of difference between the choice of verb. Do I *possess* my body? Or, *am* I my body? Who is the *I* who *has* a body? How am *I* distinguished from *my* body? If I *have* a body, does that imply *I* am somehow separate from it? Alternatively, if I *am* my body, what does that imply about my mind, about my soul? Is my mind subsumed by my brain? Is the *mind–body problem*, as it is known, a problem confronted by people everywhere, or is it the result of a particular philosophical tradition? Is it the secularized form of Christian *body–soul* dualism? These are important issues dealt with primarily by philosophers and theologians. I forefront them here to alert you to the way notions of the body, and treatments of it, are embedded in wider cultural frames of meaning.

Anthropologists have always been interested in the ways that peoples around the world think about and treat their bodies – about the different features acknowledged, emphasized, or muted, about techniques and rituals of the body, about bodily adornment (see chapter 8), about sex and gendered bodies, about diseased and dead bodies, about the ways societies discipline and subject bodies, as well as the symbolic uses of the word "body" in terms such as "the social body," or the "body politic." Books have been written about each of these aspects of the body; in this chapter I wish only to point out some of the terrain for your exploration. But before we begin, there is a major point, rarely made, that appears to undermine the entire enterprise – *there is no such thing as "the body."*

It is undeniable that each of us has or is a body, and share certain aspects of bodiliness such as flesh, blood, and bones as well as a susceptibility to illness, aging, and death. Although bodiliness is part of what it means to be human, to speak of it in general terms, even within a specific culture, is to miss a crucial point – that there is no such thing as "the body," because all societies make a distinction between bodies that are female and those that are male. "The body" is an abstraction – one made possible by a particular kind of language (see Whorf 1956 and this volume, chapter 4). This kind of abstraction and nominalization is something that is not possible in all languages. This shorthand allows those of us who speak Indo-European languages to construct whole theories about abstractions like "the body," "truth," and "beauty."

Because there is no such thing as "the body," male and female bodies have different meanings. One or the other may be more associated with the very notion of bodiliness. For example, in Western cultures it is the female body that has represented or symbolized bodiliness, despite the fact that all of us, male and female alike, are equally susceptible to the ravages of corporal existence. Why that association? In the West we tend to think of bodies as natural entities, as part of animal nature, but it is women's bodies, in particular, that become associated with nature. This is so because reproduction is considered a natural phenomenon, and women are the ones primarily associated with reproduction (see Ortner 1974). But, as we saw in chapter 5, this was not always the case. Clearly, these associations are cultural, not natural.

Bodies surely have physical limits as well as potentialities that cannot be ignored, but they exist in complex matrices of meaning, desire, and power. Bodies are not, and cannot be, solely natural, self-evident entities, for there is no such thing as a "natural" body outside the grip of culture. Rather, as Susan Bordo reminds us, "We are creatures swaddled in culture from the moment we are designated one sex or the other, one race or another" (Bordo 1993: 36). Bodies are molded and shaped by culture – not only by what we eat, how we sleep or walk, but also how we experience our bodies (with pride, disgust, confidence, or pain, and by images and cultural icons) – which includes the social control and discipline exerted on them.

Body Experience

Our sense of our body begins so early that we have no conscious memory of it; but whether we were welcomed into the world or unwanted and emotionally rejected;

whether we were held often with love or left alone for long periods; whether we were fed when we cried or cried because we were starving, are the bedrock upon which both our bodies and our self-image are built. Then we are taught how to walk, how to eat, how to comport ourselves – instructions infused with cultural images of appropriate behavior. We are praised, criticized, shamed, or blamed for our ability or inability to live up to the cultural prescriptions. So much of our early training has to do with control of our bodies and their functions. Why do people in some cultures insist on early toilet training while others assume it will happen when the child is ready? Why do people in some cultures swaddle their babies, while others barely cover them? Why is it acceptable in one culture that the whole family sleep together and experience bodily warmth and skin contact whereas in another culture, among the dominant group in the United States for example, such practice is thought to impede the development of independence and have deleterious effects on psychological and sexual health? Almost any bodily practice you can think of will have contrasting evidence from another culture – a clear indication that different societies have very different notions about bodies and bodiliness.

A childcare guide, like the popular manual of Dr. Spock, is an excellent guide to beliefs about appropriate bodily practice and discipline held by a majority of people in the United States, even though it is couched in universalistic language. But what if Dr. Spock had been born in Bali? What advice would he have given then? These questions sparked Judy DeLoache and Alma Gottlieb to conceive a book that would make alternative forms and norms of childrearing explicit in order to point out that there is no *natural* way to accomplish this task. By providing other examples of successful childrearing, they also highlighted the ways in which our own practices are deeply embedded in a particular cultural milieu. Since not all cultures have a tradition of childcare manuals written by experts, they asked anthropologists, historians, and psychologists to write a guide from the point of view of the cultures they had studied – *as if* they were the local expert(s). The resulting book, *A World of Babies* (DeLoache and Gottlieb 2000), is a collection of such imagined but culturally accurate childcare guides. In my own contribution I took on the persona of the granddaughter of the village midwife recording her views about childcare for posterity – a role not so different from my anthropological one. Here are a couple of examples from my fieldwork. In the Turkish village where I worked (and in many others I visited), babies are tightly swaddled, even in summer. People told me they do this to make a baby feel more secure and to protect him or her from drafts, which are thought to bring illness. They were aghast when I told them that in hot weather Americans often dress their babies only in a shirt and diaper and that their little legs and arms are left free. Americans (and their doctors) believe that babies must crawl in order to lay down pathways in the brain that affect eye–hand coordination. I never saw a baby crawl in the Turkish village but they seemed to have no difficulty with such coordination.

In Europe and the United States, childcare guidebooks are common, yet many cultural values of bodies and norms of bodily behavior are conveyed implicitly by non-verbal means. We are instructed by words as well as actions how to experience our bodies; our bodily experience is also conditioned by images of bodies that are held up as ideal in a society.

Body Image

Images of bodies come from many sources – parents and other caretakers, siblings, relatives and friends, and later from peer group, the media, cultural icons and heroes. In the past, images of culturally valued bodies might simply have been pointed out among the group of people, or in sculptures or paintings, but the invention of photography and other visual media has released a flood of images. Today, in modern industrialized nations, it is primarily from these media that people derive their images of ideal bodies and attempt to conform to them. While these images affect both men and women, they affect them differentially. I will discuss women first because women, much more than men, have been valued *for* their bodies – for how they look more than for what they do. Female attractiveness, we are told, is what will "get the man." We live in a culture where "a woman with an IQ of 180 who is not lovely is likely to marry ugly, be paid modestly well and secretly despise herself until the day she dies. A woman with an IQ of 100 and beauty in the 99th percentile is likely to marry a physician or an investment banker, have a maid and be admired by all her neighbors" (psychologist Rex Beaber, quoted in *People*, October 30, 2000, p. 108). No doubt this comment is an exaggeration, but nevertheless stereotypes encode important cultural notions. Even if partially true, it is a sad commentary on both our culture, which does not know how to value women's intelligence, and on those men who prefer beauty to brains and seem content to be with women who are their intellectual inferiors.

Women display male wealth and prestige on and by their bodies. In the West it is the thin, elegant woman who displays the wealth and prestige of her husband. The same is true among the urban educated elite in Turkey. But in the rural areas, it is round, plump women who demonstrate for all to see that they are provided for, that they have enough to eat. This reflects honor and prestige on their husbands. Fat is also beautiful among numerous groups in Africa. At a festival in Niger, women "compete to become the heaviest. They train for the beauty contest by gorging on food, especially millet, and drinking lots of water on the morning before the contest" (Onishi, *New York Times*, February 12, 2001). And some of them have resorted to using steroids to build bulk. "The world is a funny place," commented a doctor in Niger. "In America, you are rich, you have everything, and the women there want to become so thin as if they had nothing. Here in Africa, we have nothing, the women who buy these products [steroids and other weight-inducing drugs] have nothing, but they want to become fat as if they had everything." Despite the differences in the ideal of beauty, the "motivations appear the same: seeking men's approval."

Women will struggle with body image until the hold of that motivation is broken, and men, not just women, must help in this endeavor. "Fathers can help daughters in the body-image battle," proclaimed another article in the *New York Times* (September 18, 2000), perhaps more than mothers for the very reason that mothers are, themselves, also struggling with the same issues. One father, concerned about what his teenage daughters confronted every day in the media, the movies, and from peers, started an organization "dedicated to enhancing fathers' relationships with their daughters, but also, more specifically, to girls' relationships with their bodies." Girls need to be educated and supported in this area; boys need to learn how to appreciate girls and women for who they are and not just for their bodies.

Images of female attractiveness vary over time, even in the same culture. To understand that, we do not need to go back to the rounded, fleshy bodies painted by Rubens or even Renoir; all we need to do is to take a look at movies from the 1950s. At that time in the United States, the idols of feminine beauty were Marilyn Monroe, Ava Gardner, and Elizabeth Taylor; these women were buxom and curvaceous. Since then the ideal has changed dramatically – from US size 10 or 12 (UK size 12 or 14) to US size 2 or 4 (UK size 6 or 8). What has happened in just 40 years? More importantly, *why* has this change occurred?

Growing up in the 1950s, my friends and I were certainly concerned about our looks, and it was clear we would never measure up to the film idols mentioned above. However, we focused more on skin and hair, and how to develop larger breasts. No one I knew ever went on a diet or purposefully "worked out." We had gym class, of course, and played field hockey or basketball, volleyball, or softball because we had to. Some played on the high school teams. Others of us simply swam, or hiked, or skied because we liked to do those things. Even in college, I knew only one or two women who dieted and they were thought by the rest of us to be a little strange. We never heard of anorexia or bulimia; if they existed then, they must have been extremely rare.

Today, at the beginning of the twenty-first century, they appear to be epidemic. "According to the National Association of Anorexia Nervosa and Associated Disorders, roughly 7 million American girls and 1 million boys struggle with eating disorders. The mortality rate from anorexia – estimated between 10 and 20 percent – is the highest of any mental disorder" (*People*, October 30, 2000, p. 109). A poll conducted in 1996 showed that "young girls are more afraid of becoming fat than they are of nuclear war, cancer, or losing their parents" ("Facts and Figures" from the Council on Size and Weight Discrimination). Such a perspective on life bodes ill for the future of our society, especially since this myopic fixation on the body is particularly strong among middle- and upper-class white, educated girls and young women – those who "have everything." No wonder it seems like self-indulgence to those less fortunate.

This focus on the body prevents these girls from becoming involved in larger social and political issues, and sometimes also detracts from their studies. Their energy is channeled to their bodies rather than into projects to protect the environment or to eliminate nuclear weapons; that is, they "make the body into an all-consuming project in ways young women of the past did not" (Brumberg 1997). According to Brumberg, no one

could foresee that as American women shed their corsets, they would adjust their waistlines to a different set of expectations and constraints that would be even harder and tougher than cotton laces and whalebone stays. Over the course of the twentieth century, girls' bodies have been a critical index of our social and economic life, in ways that we are just beginning to understand. (p. 213)

For many young women, the "body project" continues in college. College is seen by many women as the means to get a man, rather than to get a life, and the way to get a man is through the body. In my "Investigating Culture" classes I ask students, anonymously, to write a page describing how they feel about their bodies, whether they ever dieted, whether they ever tried to make their body conform to some ideal. In general, the men say they are satisfied, a few admit they work out to "tone up." But the papers of the women make me want to cry. "I am very dissatisfied with my body and have been ever since I was a little girl." "I hate myself, I hate my stomach and my arms. . . . I wish I was shorter. I wish my tummy was firmer and I wish my hips were smaller." A more serious case: "I used to play five to ten hours of tennis a day and not eat . . . well I'd eat once or twice a week (an apple and some carrot sticks, maybe some pretzels) . . . I'd play all summer and I'd pass out on the courts and my friends would have to carry me home." A few confessed that they were becoming somewhat more accepting of their bodies. The black women, generally, seemed to have fewer problems with eating and were much more accepting of their bodies. While I know many female students who are not so self-absorbed, nevertheless, even the brightest and most ambitious tell me that practically everyone they know is on a diet, that some of them have been dieting since grammar school. When they go through the cafeteria line in the dorm, they feel everyone else is watching what kind of food and how much of it they are putting on their plates. In this era of unprecedented freedom for women, they are being policed by themselves and their peers.

"Barbie," a doll invented by Ruth Handler and introduced in 1959, was more busty than Twiggy, but was still an impossible model for a woman to emulate. Her shape if transferred to a human female would be 39–21–33 and her legs were out of proportion to the rest of her body.

The origin of the ideal of the very thin body is often attributed to the British model Twiggy (*née* Leslie Hornby) who, in 1966, became an overnight sensation and changed the image of female attractiveness. At 16, Twiggy was 5 ft 7 in, rail thin, flat-chested, and weighed only 87 lbs – an impossible weight for most women, since the average American woman is 5 ft 4 in, weighs 140 lbs, and wears a size 14 dress (Council on Size and Weight Discrimination, 1996). However, over the past few decades, the ultra-thin body has become the ideal, and in order to reach it, young women have been starving themselves, literally. Many of the diets they follow have fewer calories than were allotted to women in concentration camps (see Wolf 1991: 195); indeed, the women with the most severe cases of anorexia look as if they *were* in a concentration camp.

Naomi Wolf also notes that "in India, one of the poorest countries in the world, the very poorest women eat 1,400 calories a day, or 600 more than a Western woman on the Hilton Head Diet" (p. 193).

Anorexia nervosa, the medical term for this disease of self-starvation, is often not recognized as a disease and that, as well as issues of etiology or cause, makes it one that is very difficult to treat. No doubt many of you are aware of this health concern and may know someone who is anorexic. A number of theories have developed to account for this illness. Early on, theorists assumed the young women were simply retreating from womanhood – that they resented the changes in their bodies and wanted to remain pre-pubescent. By starving themselves, some of them ceased to menstruate. A corollary of this view is the idea that these young women had a fear of womanhood and its implications, particularly sex and reproduction. Becoming emaciated was a way, possibly, to prevent sexual advances they were not ready for. Might this illness be interpreted as a sign that women are being forced into sexuality too early?

Darwin believed that female beauty and sex appeal were important evolutionary strategies for procuring male partners for reproduction. If true, and there is considerable debate about it, what does the current image of the ultra-thin, almost boyish female body, in which quite commonly menstruation does not occur, convey about femininity, masculinity, the culture, and the future which is tied to reproduction?

Other theories situate the problem in the mother–daughter relationship or in a "dysfunctional family." But as one theorist said, it is just not possible that 60–80 percent of families are dysfunctional. More socially oriented theorists have suggested, instead, that anorexia must be analyzed in its full cultural and social context. The disease has to be a combination of individual and social factors, if for no other reason than that the individual must carry out the regime prescribed by the culture. That involves her volition, her will.

Dieting and becoming extremely thin obviously take an enormous amount of willpower. This can bring a great deal of satisfaction to the person who can do it. It shows that you have discipline and control, that you can overcome the temptations of ice cream, chocolate, and other delicious foods depicted in the advertisements and displayed in the stores. I have actually witnessed anorexic women in upscale gourmet markets feasting their eyes on the food displays, and then walking away without buying anything. However, this *experience* of power and control needs to be placed in a wider framework of the cultural demands put on women to be thin; while *felt* as powerful, the practices are really training them in docility to cultural ideals (see Bordo 1993: 27). Instead, we need to ask what is this denial all about? Why is there such a vilification of plumpness, of flab or fat? Where does it come from? Who is creating these images and for what purposes? Who is hurt by them and who profits?

The hatred of the flesh has, admittedly, a long history in Christianity, where flesh is/was imagined as a snare that imprisoned the soul. Those who aspired to be saintly often mortified the flesh, but the ways were different for men and women. In the fifth to seventh centuries some of these men, known as stylites (see chapter 1), went into the desert and sat atop pillars; others made pilgrimages on their knees while flagellating themselves. Women, in contrast, tended to deny themselves food, as a way to deny the appetites of the body and achieve spiritual illumination.[1] "Fasting, aimed at spiritual purification and domination of the flesh, was an important part of the repertoire of Christian practice in the Middle Ages" (Bordo 1993: 185). The aim was the development of the soul, not the elimination of fat. Indeed, it is interesting that so many spiritual exercises actually focused on the body. While some encourage acts of excess and license, most focus on quelling the body's movements, appetites, and/or desires, and this is true whether the religious practice is Christian, Buddhist, or Hindu. The body, however, is not the object. Instead, the goal is to forget or ignore body.

Anorexia has occasionally been compared to these medieval practices, but there is a huge difference. The modern incarnation of these religious practices is not tied to any religious or spiritual beliefs; instead, the practices of denial have become the religion. We "have elevated the pursuit of the fat-free, lean body into a new religion. It has a creed: 'I eat right, watch my weight and exercise' . . . [and] in following the creed, one is guaranteed beauty, energy, health, and a long successful life" (Seid 1994: 4). Perhaps it *is* the religion of late capitalism.

> On the one hand, as producers of goods and services we must sublimate, delay, repress desires for immediate gratification; we must cultivate the work ethic. On the other hand, as consumers we must display a boundless capacity to capitulate to desire and indulge in impulse; we must hunger for constant and immediate satisfaction. The regulation of desire thus becomes an ongoing problem, as we find ourselves continually besieged by temptation, while socially condemned for overindulgence. (Bordo 1993: 199)

As women have been turned more into consumers than producers, they are being asked to consume more and more of all the products, including a rich variety of foods not available in the 1950s. At the same time, they are being given a contradictory message that to be beautiful and attractive they must be thin, and this demands denial. One way of promoting these contradictory claims is very seductive: you can have both at once – *fat-free* chocolate decadence! Of course, fat-free does not necessarily mean low-calorie; however, you can always burn off the calories by using a new exercise machine.

No one will deny that having a healthy and fit body is an important goal. The concern has to do with the *obsession* to be thin and the narrowing of *focus* on the self, the body, and food. The authors who write most eloquently about the contemporary obsession with food and with slenderness have often had personal experience of it (see especially Kim Chernin, Naomi Wolf, and Susan Bordo).

But none of us is immune from the dictates of culture. Not all of us will become anorexic but many, maybe most, women struggle with their body image. Even the most staunch feminist knows that a slim, toned body has more respect, will be listened to, and gets more attention than a fat, soft, flabby body. During the summer of 2000 when I began to write this book, I decided that I did not want to be a plump "old lady." If I didn't lose the weight then, I might not be able to do so later. I had six months before I would turn 60. I wanted to give a big dance party and had always wanted to wear a black sequin dress. I joined Weight Watchers, lost 25 lbs, gave the party, and wore the dress. I can't deny that I feel, let alone look, much better and that *does* affect one's attitude, which carries into all areas of one's life. Because of my success, I was asked to work for Weight Watchers! I imagined myself the next Duchess of York. So, ironically and quite coincidentally (or is it?), as I am writing this chapter on the body, I am also working part-time for the local branch of Weight Watchers. (Of course, I can legitimate it as part of my research.) Surely, it has given me more insight into the terrible anxieties that women of all ages and sizes have about their weight. People are impatient and want change fast; rather than changing their relation to food and watching what and how much they eat, many try one or another fad diet in the attempt to shed the pounds quickly. The evidence of numerous studies shows that people who do that tend to gain it all back, and often more. Regardless, *all* weight-reduction programs – with their meetings and dues, their books and their foods – make billions off of women's dissatisfaction (over $40 billion a year, according to the 1996 Council on Size and Weight Discrimination). The diet industry feeds women's dissatisfaction in order to continue to reap the profits. They are collusive, and this should give women pause.

"A Body to Die For" was the title of a Special Report in the October 30, 2000 issue of *People* magazine. The cover screamed, in large letters, DYING TO BE THIN. The report told the poignant "stories of six people who, like so many, were consumed by the battle to lose weight. Three sought help from liposuction, two took pills, one starved herself – and all paid with their lives" (p. 109). The one who starved herself was a bright and very attractive college student who had everything to live for, but became anorexic; her 5 ft 7 in frame wasted to 88 lbs. As she was slipping in and out of consciousness, she told her heartsick parents, "I don't want to be fat. I want to die" (p. 111). Fatness had become a sin worse than death.

Male Bodies

When we think about bodies and struggles over body image, we generally think of women. But increasingly in contemporary American society, and perhaps somewhat less so in Europe, men are becoming more and more concerned not just with weight, but also with their bodies. "Why are men so much more concerned about their bodies today than they were 50 years ago?" This question was the first line in a *New York Times* article, October 7, 2000. It was also the question that provoked a research project at Harvard Medical School published as *The Adonis Complex: The Secret Crisis of Male Body Obsession* (Pope, Phillips, and Olivardia 2000). The authors noted that

> men of the 1950s or 1960s didn't worry about their muscularity; they didn't pour money into gym dues or protein supplements or weight machines for the basement. Similarly, male eating disorders, such as binge eating and vomiting, were almost unknown. Most men hadn't even heard of a body fat measurement, nor did they worry greatly about how much body fat they had. And for all practical purposes, there was no such thing as a "personal trainer." (p. 27)

But since that time, men's dissatisfaction with their body image has grown dramatically; according to a 1997 study, "*43 percent – nearly half* – of the men in this survey reported that they were dissatisfied with their overall appearance" (p. 27; emphasis in the original). These researchers attribute this growing concern to a number of factors, notably to the use and display of male bodies in advertisements, the use of steroids, and boys' action toys.

The changes in G. I. Joe since his first appearance in 1964 are illustrative (see figure 6.1). The original doll, if he were a man, would be "5 feet 10 inches tall, he would have a 32-inch waist, a 44-inch chest, and a 12-inch bicep – a perfectly

Figure 6.1 The evolution of GI Joe, from *The Adonis Complex* by Harrison G. Pope, Katharine Phillips, and R. Olivardia (New York: Free Press, 2000), p. 41. Courtesy Simon & Schuster/Zachary Shuster Harmsworth.

respectable physique" (p. 41). Since then, he has gone through a number of trans-formations, each one becoming more and more muscular until the arrival of G. I. Joe Extreme in the mid-1990s. If he "were full-sized, he would have a 55-inch chest and a 27-inch bicep . . . bigger than that of most competition bodybuilders" (p. 42). The same kinds of changes have occurred in other action toys for boys – characters from *Star Wars*, and those with names like Gold Ranger, Iron Man, Batman, and Wolverine. "All have physiques suggestive of steroid-using bodybuilders" (p. 43). If these are the models toy makers present to our young boys, we should not be sur-prised that so many of them feel physically inadequate. More and more men are reported to be afraid to go to the beach or appear in public without a shirt because they do not measure up (see Hall 1999). They fear being judged on the basis of their bodies.

Curiously, there are societies that stress male beauty and attractiveness, a situ-ation that Darwin's theory of sexual dimorphism and evolution, mentioned above, does not account for. David Gilmore, in "The Beauty of the Beast: Male Body Imagery in Anthropological Perspective," discusses societies in which men are the objects of desire, their bodies put on show, literally. The Fulani of Africa, for example, "stage male beauty contests with women judges" (Gilmore 1994: 197)! Among this group, it is the men who adorn the body, use make-up, preen, strut, and display themselves while women judge them.

In the West, too, there have been times when males exhibited the cultural ideals of beauty and attractiveness. Ancient Greece is a notable example, as the numerous sculptures of nude males amply display. The male form epitomized the ideal. "The Platonic association of the 'beautiful' with the 'good,' the belief that physical beauty is a sign of interior or spiritual beauty, originates with the Greeks and runs as a thread throughout Western Christian civilization" (Gilmore 1994: 212). In eighteenth-century Europe, men of the elite classes adorned themselves with velvet coats, wigs, make-up, perfume, gold jewelry and elegant shoes, hose, boots, and hats. This is not to imply that women during that time were drab creatures. They, too, wore elaborate costumes and powdered wigs, but what is unusual is that men were similarly objects of beauty. Male bodies were also idealized in Nazi Germany, as we shall see below.

However, today's increasing focus on male bodies represents not a shift of the cultural ideal of beauty from women *to* men, but rather that both are being objectified, made into *objects* of desire. Formerly, it was primarily women's bodies that were used in advertisements to sell anything from cars to vodka (see figure 6.2). When men appeared in ads, for example the Marlboro man, their sexiness was due not to their naked bodies but to an extension of their activities. Since the 1950s "the percentage of ads depicting women in some state of undress remained relatively stable. . . . By contrast, the percentage of ads depicting undressed men rose sharply, from less than 5% in 1950 to as much as 35% in the 90s" (Pope, quoted in Eakin 2000: 19). The ads for the perfume Obsession are emblematic: not only does the female model resemble an emaciated waif, but the naked male torso is on display.

From one perspective, men are finally getting to feel what women have endured for a very long time. However, it doesn't seem to make them more sympathetic, nor have they launched a crusade, comparable to the women's movement, to *oppose* the cultural models and the exploitation. Instead, more and more of them desire to reach the ideal. To add bulk and develop muscles, and especially to gain the "six-pack" abs depicted on so many of the ads, they must work out. And all this regardless of whether women actually find these attributes attractive.

Like the women who are so focused on their bodies, on dieting, and working out, leaving little time or energy for more important projects, so too are men. Referring to one of the men they interviewed, Pope said: "He puts all his hopes and dreams into his workouts and not into his daily life" (Pope et al., 2000: 7). Pope and his associates discuss the very poignant case of a young man who gave up a promising career because he needed more time to work out. Instead, he became a personal trainer in a gym because "it was the only job I could think of that gave me enough time to do my own training" (p. 8). He admitted to the researchers that during the day 90 percent of the time his thinking

> would have something to do with either my weightlifting, my diet, or the way I look. I can't go past a mirror without posing just for a minute to check out my body – as long as I'm sure nobody's watching. I even check myself out when I see my reflection in a store window or car window. . . . Sometimes when I'm in a restaurant, I even study my reflection in the back of a spoon. (p. 9)

It is often said that men spent 99 percent of their time thinking about sex; now, instead, many are thinking more about their bodies. What has happened? This man's obsession with his body wrecked a very satisfactory relationship with a woman because he had no time left to spend with her after his hours at work and workouts.

> If that is true or nearly so, no wonder the world is in such a mess; the political leaders have only 1 percent of their brain power and concentration available for attending to world problems.

Figure 6.2   An advertisement for vodka that uses a woman's body to sell the product. Reproduced by permission of Swardlick Marketing Group.

The researchers conclude that the "Adonis Complex" has arisen primarily because of "two sociocultural factors that distinguish the present generation from every generation before it: the availability of anabolic steroids and the increasing parity of women" (p. 60). "As women have entered the work force and become heads of families, men have had to relinquish their traditional roles as fathers, soldiers and breadwinners . . . which leaves their bodies as the only way to demonstrate their masculinity" (*New York Times*, October 7, 2000). Surely there are other ways to conceive of masculinity. Conclusions that blame the women's movement and women's entrance into traditional male occupations could be used to push women back into the home and sabotage the gains women have earned in the past 30 years. These researchers fail to consider how "feminist thought and conversation has created room for alternatives to traditional masculinity" (Hall 1999), and it is clear they have not listened to those conversations.

Although they decry the ads and the toys, Pope et al. do not consider the role of capitalism in the deformation of roles as well as bodies. Their research lacks a critique of an economy that has made it imperative that both men and women work in order to consume the products (and the lifestyle) that fuel the economy. Nor do they imagine a more egalitarian model in which both genders can be sexy and be parents, can work outside the home and do the "dependency work" (Kittay 1996: 219) of caring for children, the sick, the disabled, and the elderly, and in which both can be breadmakers as well as "breadwinners." This is obviously much more difficult; not only would it demand a change in the definition of male roles, but it would also require a total restructuring of the economy and of the ways in which we live and work; it would demand a change in institutions and in values.

Body Modifications

Dieting and "working out" are two common ways in which men and women attempt to modify and transform their bodies. They are not the only ways: corsets or girdles are another, so too are breast implants, liposuction, botox injections, and straightening teeth. Because some of these practices are (or have been) widespread, they seem almost "normal," while those of others are exoticized and deplored, for example the use of neck rings to elongate the necks of Padung women of Burma (Myanmar), or the Chinese practice of binding women's feet (to be discussed in chapter 8). These are only a few examples by which women's bodies are molded to cultural norms of feminine beauty. These forms are externally accomplished, but there are other ways in which the bodies of women and men are transformed – ways that involve the skin (scarification, piercing, tattooing), and still others that change or remove parts of the body to accomplish the cultural ideal (filing or removal of teeth, removal of a finger joint, subincision, circumcision, infibulation, castration). I cannot possibly discuss all of the forms here but mention a few that you or your friends may practice and some that have received international attention.

Tattooing and scarification

These might more logically be considered under the category of bodily adornment dealt with in chapter 8, but will be briefly noted here since they do involve penetration of the skin. Scarification is practiced among a number of peoples, e.g. the Nuer and Dinka in Africa, whereby designs are created *on* the body by scars that are ritually applied at specific times such as at initiation. Tattooing is an ancient practice among a number of peoples: the faces and hands of Muslim women in the southeastern part of Turkey and among some Bedouin groups are tattooed. These designs are generally geometric and abstract and in deep blue and red. A very different kind of tattooing occurs among a dwindling number of Japanese men: a full body tattoo. Called *horimono* from the word *hori* meaning "to carve," this practice is quite ancient but today is frowned upon. This art that seems to cry out for display is, ironically, concealed. The men who get such tattoos cover them up, do not venture to beaches or steam baths, and a few have even been able to keep the knowledge from their colleagues, their wives (by changing and bathing in the dark), and their children (*San Francisco Chronicle*, September 1, 2002). Nevertheless, it forms a bond between these men who expose them to each other on their annual pilgrimage to a shrine outside of Tokyo.

These forms of tattoo are not at all like the hearts and flowers, ships, pin-ups, crosses or "Mother" that were / are common among some Americans; they are an ancient cultural form traditionally prescribed by the culture, even though today, the Japanese men are *choosing* to continue it. In the United States, tattoos are no longer associated with sailors or motorcyclists, but since the 1990s tattooing has been a growing fad among many young high school and college-age men and women. Tattoos are no doubt desired for purposes of identity and possibly for sexual titillation; they may also, like piercing, be interpreted as symbols of rebellion against parents or what they stand for, namely, bourgeois society. More recently, a number of people including firefighters have gotten tattoos to remember someone they lost during the attack on the World Trade Towers on September 11, 2001. A photograph exhibit, "Indelible Memories: Sept. 11 Memorial Tattoos Photographed by Vinnie Amessé," was held at the Staten Island Historical Society during Spring 2003.

While some of the young people have small tattoos – a flower on the breast or a snake at the base of the spine or a "bracelet" around the ankle – others are going in for much more extreme forms of tattooing, scarification, and piercing. For example, law enforcement officials in Utah and California have noticed a marked increase in tattoos among prisoners who join white supremacist groups while they are in prison. Such tattoos either proclaim "white power" or depict hate slogans against targeted groups (Madigan, *New York Times*, April 5, 2003).

Some extreme practices of marking the body could also be interpreted as a means of rebellion; however, according to one advocate, "the most important thing you learn is that you are not your body, you just live in it" (Vale and Juno 1989: 29).[2] These "modern primitives," as they are called, are of the opinion that you *have* rather than you *are* your body. Overcoming pain and daring to step outside of conventional society is expressed in terms of *control* in the last place where they feel they can exercise this – the body (not unlike explanations given by anorexics). Some of them also feel that their practices are part of a spiritual process that puts them in touch with authentic primitives and the types of rituals they have had to endure. However, as British cultural analyst Christian Klesse (2000) notes, the modern primitives have idealized and romanticized "primitive society," which is decontextualized, dehistoricized, universalized, and essentialized. They take only one aspect of it (bodily modification) to represent that society. Furthermore, they perpetuate the dichotomy not only of primitive vs. modern but also of nature (in this case, the body) vs. culture which has characterized a major but no longer sustainable tradition in the West.[3]

Body piercing

Body piercing has also been widely practiced cross-culturally but, again, the meaning must be explored in each culture. In her book *The Body Project*, Brumberg notes: "unlike aboriginal societies, where the part to be pierced is determined by

Figure 6.3   Example of *horimono* at Matsuri festival, Tokyo, 1998. Photo © Bruce Gilden/Magnum Photos.

long-standing ritual and tradition, contemporary teens face an array of piercing options" (1997: 131). Yet we should not forget that the notion of *choice* is a very long-standing and important tradition in America even as our choices are quite narrowly confined; for example, we can choose between Lancôme, Estée Lauder, or Max Factor yet they are all cosmetics, made of the same ingredients, and do a very similar job. Marketed as choices, they really reflect status, identity, and lifestyle.

In the United States, piercing used to be limited to ear piercing and was desired so women could wear earrings without the fear of losing them as was so common with screw-ons or clip-ons. In the mid-1960s I remember I wanted to have pierced ears but was afraid both of the pain and of the possibility I would make a mess of it. People I knew were piercing their ears themselves – with an ice cube and a needle. I tried one but it got infected and so I dropped the whole idea. Not until years later when my daughter was in eighth grade and all her friends were getting their ears pierced did I reconsider. And by that time professionals performed the brief operation with a stapler-like machine that inserted a gold stud as the hole was being pierced. I went with my daughter – she was braver and went first; I grit my teeth, held her hand, and then had mine done.

Figure 6.4   George Henrique showing the tattoo of his daughter Michelle, who died in the 9/11 disaster. Photo by Vinnie Amessé.

In contrast, today many young women (and a few men) have their ears pierced, some have multiple ear piercings; in addition men as well as women have nose, eyebrow, lip, tongue, and navel piercings. Some indicate sexual orientation, others are said to increase sexual pleasure, and some border on S/M practices. Those referred to as "modern primitives" engage in even more intimate body piercings – of the nipples, the penis, the labia and clitoris – that seem to play along the boundaries of more institutionalized torture and mutilation,[4] and thus could be seen as trivializing those practices.

Circumcision

Another widespread, and seemingly quite normal, form of body modification is, of course, circumcision. Although circumcision is practiced among a number of peoples, I will discuss, briefly, only that prescribed for Jews and Muslims. Both attribute the practice to Abraham, who instituted it after his sojourn in Egypt. Jews circumcise boys when they are babies (traditionally, on the eighth day) since Isaac was a baby when he was circumcised, while Muslims, who trace their descent from Abraham's son Ishmael, tend to perform it sometime between the ages of 7 and 13, because Ishmael was already a grown boy when he was circumcised, and thus among some Muslims, circumcision is viewed as a test of manhood.

Some biblical scholars claim that circumcision of Jewish boys is related to sacrifice, especially the sacrifice of the first born: "Sanctify unto me all the first-born, whatsoever openeth the womb among the children of Israel, both of man and of beast. It is mine" (Exodus 13: 2; see also Exodus 22: 29). Jewish scholar Jon Levenson goes even further when he sees circumcision "as a sublimation for child sacrifice in ancient Israelite religious practice" (1993: 51), that is, as a *pars pro toto* (a part for the whole – the foreskin for the child). I disagree with this interpretation, first because there is no proof that child sacrifice was practiced by either the ancient Israelites or any of their neighbors (see Delaney 1998). More important is that circumcision was a sign of the covenant God made with Abraham and the context is fruitfulness and procreation, not sacrifice:

> And I will make thee exceedingly fruitful, and I will make nations of thee, and kings shall come out of thee. And I will establish my covenant between me and thee and thy seed after thee in their generations for an everlasting covenant. (Genesis 17: 5–8)

Howard Eilberg-Schwartz, a scholar of ancient Judaism, agrees, and thinks that language such as "uncircumcised trees" offers a clue – that "cutting away the foreskin is like pruning a fruit tree . . . both increase the desired yield. One might say that when Israelites circumcise their male children, they are pruning the fruit trees of God" (1990: 152). What neither he nor most other scholars have asked, however, is why is the covenant between God and humans signed on *male* flesh? Why is the male sexual organ seen as *the* organ for the transmission of life? For me, the answer is in the word *seed* – the ancient, though still prevalent, notion that the male "seed" contains the child and that the female was/is seen as merely the nurturing medium (soil) in which it is planted (see Delaney 1991, 1998). In any case, circumcision was clearly a distinguishing mark that separated one people – the people of Abraham – from all others.

The medical, as opposed to ritual, circumcision of male babies has been routinely practiced in the United States for decades for supposed hygienic reasons, although today there is a movement to stop the practice for lack of convincing evidence that an uncircumcised penis is more likely to develop infections or cancer if proper habits of cleanliness are not instilled. In addition, many people, doctors included, feel that it *is* painful and accidents have happened.

Female genital cutting

Female "circumcision" or genital cutting (FGC), also referred to as female genital mutilation (FGM),[5] is not at all similar to circumcision of males, even though it is sometimes referred to as female circumcision. Male circumcision is often thought to increase sexual pleasure, while FGC – primarily, the excision of the clitoris – is designed to do just the opposite, to cut out sexual pleasure. In the most severe form of FGC – infibulation – not only is the clitoris cut off but also the labia minora; then the labia majora are sewn together leaving only a small opening to allow for urination and menstrual flow. Sex initiated at marriage is usually extremely painful and often leads to infections and other serious health problems that can make birth very difficult. Estimates suggest that 100 million women are now living with FGC and another 2 million girls (between the ages of 5 and 6) every year are at risk. Although the majority of FGCs are done in 28 countries across the mid-belt of Africa, it also occurs among immigrants from those countries in Europe and North America. Although primarily associated with African Muslims, the practice itself is pre-Islamic and has been practiced by African Jews and Christians as well as those who follow more traditional religious teachings. Westerners have been appalled by the practice and have lobbied to get it included, under the concept of the right to bodily integrity, in the International Bill of Human Rights. Only recently in the United States has escape to avoid the practice been allowed as reason for asylum.

> The most severe form, pharaonic circumcision or infibulation, is practiced primarily in Sudan, Somalia, Eritrea, and Djibouti.

In many cultures, including our own (at certain times), female sexuality is culturally construed as rampant and uncontrollable and therefore measures need to be taken to control it. While not explicitly focused on the sexual organs, some practices such as "covering" (i.e., veiling), enclosure in the house, bound feet, and so forth are measures taken to contain female sexuality and ensure paternity of the children – "circumcision" is only the most extreme.

Yet it would be wrong to assume such an operation has been practiced only in other, particularly African, cultures. While many Western women protest these "surgical" procedures, they are often unaware of the history of this practice in Europe and the United States. During the nineteenth century and well into the twentieth, clitoridectomy was performed on thousands of women, because of masturbation and/or because of mental imbalance or retardation. Again, these surgical procedures were performed because of beliefs about female sexuality and the idea of the hysteria (literally, "wandering womb") (see Ehrenreich and English 1973, 1979).

While Western feminists have been appalled by female genital cutting, they too often act like cultural imperialists without any sensitivity to the local meanings and understanding. To barge in and say "this is wrong" will only create defensiveness and resistance; in order to change practices, you must work from the meanings and values that the people themselves find in them.[6] Anthropologists often go to the other extreme: while they generally believe in the "rights of people to pursue their traditional practices and values" (Gruenbaum 2001: 29), they also need to ask just whose interests do these practices serve. It is all too easy to blame men for FGCs; however, the practices are more often enforced by elder women who claim that "uncircumcised" girls will not be desirable as marriage partners, and they want their daughters to be marriageable. At the same time, it is important to recognize that it is still patriarchal ideas about beauty and desirability that prevail; it is these ideas that need to be changed if the practice is to be stopped. Perhaps there is a lesson to be learned from the way in which the Chinese ended footbinding. They formed "pledge societies" whereby the parents of girls pledged they would not bind the feet of their daughters while parents of boys pledged they would not let their sons marry girls with bound feet. First, of course, they had to be convinced that the practice was harmful.

Another way is through the medium of humor. Sia Amma, a Liberian native, staged a humorous performance inaugurating the First Annual International Clitoris Celebration in Oakland, California, in March 2003 as part of her effort to end the practice of female genital cutting. She also founded "Global Women Intact," a non-profit organization devoted to educating African people about the practice, and every year she returns to Liberia and Senegal and gives a class, "Clitoris 101," to girls and women there.

Castration

One of the most extreme measures ever taken to control sexuality concerns men – castration – a procedure whereby the testicles are removed. Like women who have undergone FGC, castrated men are more docile and thus useful as guards of female quarters such as the *harem* (which refers not to the women themselves but to their living quarters). The institution of *eunuch* (from the Greek "keeper of the couch") guards reached its epitome in the Byzantine court in Constantinople[7] from which it was adopted by the Ottomans with whom it is usually associated, and it was an element in the slave trade. During the sixteenth century the practice entered Europe in the form of *castrati* – men who underwent the operation before puberty – whose voices remained soprano or rich contralto needed for choirs and operas, since women were banned from performing on stage. This practice should be distinguished from that of chemical "castration" proposed, in the mid-1990s, for sex offenders in the United States. In no way does it resemble physical castration, especially since the process can easily be reversed once the medication is halted. Moving from transformations or modifications of the body, let us turn now to bodily techniques.

Techniques of the Body

I first began to think about techniques of the body when I found I could not squat with my feet *flat* on the floor or the ground as could the Turkish villagers among whom I lived. Even the elderly could squat comfortably for long periods of time. They squatted while they prepared food for cooking, or did the dishes, or waited for someone, or simply while watching the world go by. I practiced and eventually was able to do it, but it quickly became painful and was definitely *not* comfortable. It occurred to me that one had to develop this technique from childhood, training the tendons and muscles to keep them from tightening. I do not know why this practice developed among Turks – perhaps it relates to their nomadic past when chairs were not used. Even today, village Turks do not often use chairs although they are becoming *de rigueur* as part of the trousseaux of the young. Instead, they sit on cushions on the floor or on a *divan* (a kind of day bed set against the walls with firm cushions lined along the back edge) where they can draw their legs up and under them.

Marcel Mauss, French anthropologist and nephew of Emile Durkheim, published a ground-breaking article in 1934, titled "Techniques of the Body." In it, he commented that one "can distinguish squatting mankind and sitting mankind . . . people with chairs and people without chairs" (1973: 81). He was the first anthropologist to draw attention to the variety of bodily techniques and propose they be studied systematically. He noticed how swimming techniques had changed even in his lifetime and were quite different elsewhere. Although he was quite aware of the biophysical limits on body movement and posture as well as individual idiosyncrasies, he claimed that there were significant cultural patterns that were transmitted by example and by oral explanation. Bodily techniques "are assembled by and for social authority," and they become habitual. Mauss used the word *habitus* – a kind of acquired ability but more than habits. The word was later made a key concept by Pierre Bourdieu, for whom it meant a system of "durable dispositions" that are taught not only by word but by example and by imitating. He states this quite eloquently when he says: "The book from which children learn their vision of the world is read with the body" (Bourdieu [1972] 1977: 90). This concept was quite useful to me in the village as I watched the ways Turkish children moved or were allowed to move, how they learned to become not just Turkish, but a Turkish girl or boy. As young children both girls and boys could roam around their neighborhoods quite freely; however, since boys were more socially valued they were supposed to conduct themselves with decorum while girls could run about, shriek, and act silly. This behavior changed drastically as they approached adolescence; then boys were expected to be *delikanlı* (crazybloods) while girls had to become *kapalı* (covered), which meant not just covering their hair with headscarves, but covering their bodies with voluminous clothing that also restricted their movements, and enclosing them in the house.

There is usually no question that *training* in bodily techniques is involved when the issue is yoga, tai chi, or sports, but people are generally more skeptical when the focus is normal, everyday activities such as walking. Nevertheless, there are very different ways of walking, not only among the Maori where mothers supposedly train their daughters to walk with a "loose-jointed swinging of the hips" – a walk that has a special name – but also between the French and the British (Mauss 1973: 72). Europeans claim they can spot Americans by the way they walk.

Mauss's classification of bodily techniques included:

1 those of birth and obstetrics: why, for example, is it considered normal in the United States to give birth lying down where in many other societies it is done squatting or even standing?
2 of infancy: here he discussed methods of carrying babies, and also distinguished societies with and without cradles. What, I wonder, are the implications of a crib?
3 of adolescence: issues relating to puberty such as techniques for removing facial and body hair, of ejaculation and menstruation. This is also a time when youths

in some societies are initiated into techniques of sexual behavior including kissing, intercourse, etc. Although "[n]othing is more technical than sexual positions, very few writers have had the courage to discuss" them, yet because they vary considerably cross-culturally, they might provide interesting insight into the culture.

Under techniques of "adult life" Mauss included bodily techniques such as sleeping that actually span age groups. He distinguishes "between societies that have nothing to sleep on except the 'floor,' and those that have instrumental assistance . . . people with mats and people without . . . people with pillows and those without" (p. 80), and those, like Japanese and some African groups, that make a kind of "bench" to support the neck. "The Masai can sleep on their feet," others can sleep on horseback, and Mauss acknowledges that he learned to sleep standing up, or on rocks, during World War I. There are techniques of dancing, of jumping, of climbing, of pulling and lifting and throwing, of coughing and spitting (a great example was in the film *Titanic*), and of bodily hygiene, for example bathing, care of the teeth, hair, etc. (see Miner 1956), and all of these techniques are inflected by gender, age, and efficiency.

Body Orientation

How techniques of the body actually illuminate cultural values and beliefs is a question that is still very much understudied. More utilized has been bodily orientation, particularly right–left polarization and its meanings. Here, Robert Hertz was prescient. His ground-breaking article "The Pre-Eminence of the Right Hand: A Study in Religious Polarity," originally published in 1909 (and included in Needham's 1973 volume *Right and Left: Essays on Dual Symbolic Classification*), has become an anthropological classic. It begins:

> What resemblance more perfect than that between our two hands! And yet what a striking inequality there is! . . . Every social hierarchy claims to be founded on the nature of things. . . . Aristotle justified slavery by the ethnic superiority of the Greeks over barbarians; and today [keep in mind this was 1909] the man who is annoyed by feminist claims alleges that woman is *naturally* inferior. Similarly, according to common opinion, the pre-eminence of the right hand results directly from the organism and owes nothing to convention or to men's changing beliefs. But in spite of appearances the testimony of nature is no more clear or decisive, when it is a question of ascribing attributes to the two hands, than in the conflict of the races or the sexes. (1973: 3)

The idea that inequality is bound up with systems of classification which are, at root, symbolic, cultural, conventional, and thus humanly constructed, is an idea of utmost importance, yet it is one that few people seem to have learned since Hertz first articulated it nearly a century ago. His response to studies that claimed we are right-handed *because* we are left-brained could still be used today. Even if there is a strong correlation between right-handedness and the development of the left hemisphere of the brain, there is nothing to prevent us from turning the claim around and saying: "we are left-brained because we are right-handed" (1973: 4). It is a good example of a chicken–egg problem.

So, even if there is a slight inborn preference for the right hand, that is "not enough to bring about the absolute preponderance of the right hand if this were not reinforced and fixed by influences extraneous to the organism" (p. 5). If the left were, indeed, naturally weaker, wouldn't that be reason to develop and strengthen it? That does not happen; instead, children have been trained to use the right hand, have sometimes had restraining devices attached so they could *not* use the left hand, and have sometimes been punished for using the left hand. My sister, who is left-handed, recalls that during the year we spent in Catholic school, the nuns repeatedly hit her left hand. She was only a first-grader. Rather than let children develop either hand or use both, many, if not most, cultures prescribe that the right be developed while the use of the left is thwarted, repressed, or given only the most odious tasks. In Turkey, as in India, the left hand is used to wash the genital area after defecation; because of this it is not supposed to touch food.

In the United States, there has been a gradual loosening of prescriptions to use the right hand at school, but it has not disappeared. My daughter was quite ambidextrous as a child but this so disconcerted her teachers and her doctor, who, like them, believed that ambidexterity might confuse or scramble the proper brain development, that they required she decide which hand she was going to use. Although she learned to use the right hand for writing and some other tasks, she "freaks people out" when she plays tennis or ping pong because she can switch hands with dexterity. I do not know if this would be allowed in professional sport matches.

Some research suggests that left-handed people die younger than right-handed people, primarily because of accidents in a world built to accommodate right-handed people: "Everyday implements, such as scissors, gearshifts and can openers, even the direction in which the threading of screws is angled, is biased toward right-handed use" (*New York Times*, August 29, 1989). I recall the difficulties in trying to teach my left-handed sister to knit. The researchers also claimed that less obvious examples such as "traffic patterns are designed to utilize the clockwise turning bias of the right-hander." Whether the same is true for the British, who drive on the left and whose cars have the gearbox on the left side of the driver, is something they will have to answer.

The very words for *left* and *right* carry loaded meanings: dexterity comes from the Latin *dextra* (right hand); the left hand is *sinistra*, from which, obviously, comes the word sinister. French for left, *gauche*, has become in English *gawky*; while right, *droit*, means the law. In Turkish right is *sağ* and left is *sol*; *sağ* is used in all kinds of expressions such as *sağ olsun* – may you be well. One need hardly mention how right and left are used for political leanings and parties or that Jesus sat on the *right* hand of God. Although today, *left* and *right* signify secular values and political orientations, Hertz argues that the polarity itself, like so many other things we have discussed, has theological/religious underpinnings; that is, the meaning of polarity – the opposition of right and left – derives from and is justified by recourse to something beyond the *nature* of the two hands.

The Social Body

Anthropologists, among others, are quite familiar with the notion of society as a "body." Herbert Spencer, an influential nineteenth-century social thinker, noted: "A dim perception that there exists some analogy between the body politic and a living individual body, was early reached, and from time to time re-appeared in literature" (cited in McGee and Warms 2000: 13 [1860]) but had not been scientifically explored. He argued that the social organism was like individual organisms in at least three ways: (1) they augment in mass (grow bigger); (2) there is increasing complexity of structure; and (3) the various parts gradually acquire mutual dependence. This idea was picked up by Emile Durkheim, who wanted to know what held modern society together. Durkheim theorized that there are two basic types of social solidarity that relate to the division of labor: "organic" and "mechanical." Modern, industrialized societies, he believed, functioned "organically"; each sector was devoted to only one kind of labor, only a part of the functioning whole. In primitive societies he believed that the division of labor was far less differentiated; each person could reproduce all of the needed functions. While I think the nomenclature is deceptive since modern societies are more dominated by machines and primitive ones are much closer to the organic world, and in the latter there is considerable division of labor, nevertheless there is a valid point, namely, that in order to be a *society*, the population itself has to be regulated and the tasks have to be both distributed and integrated for the society to function. Bodies are shaped by cultural values and ideals, by families and peers, but also in a more forceful way by governments – whether chiefs, tribal councils, kings, or the modern state – all of which attempt to regulate and subject individual bodies to the social order.

Mary Douglas, a famous British anthropologist working in the Durkheimian tradition, suggests that the "body is a model which can stand for any bounded system. Its boundaries can represent any boundaries which are threatened or precarious" ([1966] 1999: 116). She goes on to say that we "cannot possibly interpret rituals concerning excreta, breast milk, saliva, and the rest unless we are prepared to see in the body a symbol of society, and to see the powers and dangers credited to social structure reproduced in small on the human body" (p. 116). This was and continues to be a highly creative and useful suggestion. However, it is also a useful place to point out the differences between British social anthropology and American cultural anthropology. While I agree with Douglas that the body is a rich source of symbols, we cannot assume that their meaning is naturally determined or universal. That is, I do not assume that the human body and its various parts are perceived the same way in all societies, or even that there is consensus about what is "natural." Thus, the body's use as a model for society cannot be assumed *a priori* but must be investigated in each case.

Furthermore, Douglas does not specify which kind of body – male or female – shall stand as the model for the society. In Turkey, only the male body is thought to be "bounded" and self-contained; the female body is relatively unbounded. It sprouts breasts, its belly distends in pregnancy, it also leaks in menstruation and lactation. It is imagined as naturally "open," especially to sexual advances from men, and, thus, social measures must be taken to bind and contain it. As noted above, this is symbolized by various forms of "covering."

Although the male body is the symbolically bounded body, it is the female body that forms the symbolic model for the society, due, perhaps, to the symbolic equation between the female body and the physical land as in *Anavatan* (Motherland). Because of the cultural understandings of the openness and vulnerability of the female body, "[b]oundaries thus become a focus of anxiety, and exits and entrances are controlled and under surveillance" (Delaney 1991: 278). This is true whether the boundary is the female body, the house, the village, or the nation. Outside influences, whether the presence of foreigners at the center of Ottoman economy, or the seductive attractions of the West, have been imagined as corrupting the country as an illicit relationship would pollute and corrupt a woman. The economic "capitulations" demanded by the foreign powers prior to World War I were felt by Turks as if Turkey was prostituting itself. When the country was going to be dismembered and the parts given to the Allies, Mustafa Kemal rallied the people to fight to save the "Motherland." In the nation he created, he was given the name Atatürk, which means Father Turk or Father of the Turks. The gendered symbolism intensifies the meaning of the patrol and control of Turkey's borders and points of entry, especially over the Dardanelles and the Bosphorus – the narrow waterways leading straight to the heart of the country, Istanbul. They patrol the "Motherland" as they patrol and surveil (protect) *their* women – mothers, sisters, daughters.

Body and Nation[8]

The Turkish example shows how easily the "social" body can blend into the "national" body. But again, we must ask which bodies. Generally, women *symbolize* the nation – its physical land mass and boundaries – but it is usually men (or symbolic men, as in the case of the "Iron Maiden" Margaret Thatcher) who *represent* it – both as heads of state and as its defenders. When nations were being formed in Europe, it was the generalized female body that was used to symbolize it – whether as Britannia, Germania, or Marianne (for the French Republic). In the United States, although Columbia was proposed at the Columbian Exposition in Chicago in 1898, it is really "Lady Liberty" (the Statue of Liberty) that has assumed this place. (We will return to this in chapter 9.) But beyond symbolics, bodies and nation are intertwined in other ways.

In Nazi Germany, for instance, there developed a cult of the body, especially the nude male body, which was imagined as "the temple of manliness" (Mosse 1985: 46). Germany was to become a *manly* nation, the ideal was to be achieved by promoting fresh air, exercise, and a natural diet.

> The stereotyped embodiment of manliness was modeled on an ideal of male beauty born in the eighteenth-century Greek revival, while the image of the woman in German or English national iconography was frequently fashioned after traditional portrayals of the Virgin Mary. (Mosse 1985: 23).

The ideal woman was wholesome and chaste until marriage, and only those deemed suitably Aryan were encouraged to reproduce the nation. At the heart of Nazi ideology, though relatively unknown, was the Lebensborn movement. "Lebensborn" means "source," and it was to be the fountain that would supply the revitalized nation with its vital new citizens. Young women with the "proper" Aryan background and features were encouraged to mate with similarly approved SS officers. They did not need to get married; the Führer was the putative father and the children would be raised in state-run homes. The film *Of Pure Blood* discusses some of the features of the movement and tells the stories of some of the children raised there. They are heart-rending – many died, deprived of the close nurturing care more typical of families, while others became listless and retarded. At the end of the war, those still alive suffered from not knowing who their parents were. The idea of a "pure" blood that constitutes the nation clearly has racist implications. "Aryan" Germans were encouraged to marry only other "Aryans," for otherwise they would be polluting the pure blood of the nation (see Linke 1999: 198 ff.).

Reproduction, while seemingly a private issue, is intimately tied to building the nation and to nationalism. Women are recruited to reproduce the nation, that is, to produce its citizens. However, only certain kinds of women are sought for this project. France, for example, encourages "French" women to get pregnant and give birth to children and pays them stipends if they do; it is not happy when North Africans proliferate because most of them are not citizens. In 1983, Israel, fearful that its Jewish population was declining, passed "the Law on Families Blessed with Children . . . giving a whole range of subsidies to families with more than 3 children" (Yuval-Davis 1987: 83). Of course, only Jewish women married to Jewish men were eligible. In addition, in many countries, only male citizens are able to pass on citizenship to their children. For example, if a Turkish woman living in Turkey is married to a French man, their children will not automatically be Turkish. Children born *in* the United States are citizens, but many women will be shocked to learn that a child born abroad, prior to 1934, to an American citizen mother married to a non-citizen, were not, although fathers married to foreign women had had that right since 1855. As stated in *Montana v. Kennedy* (366 US [1961]):

> The court ruled that a child born abroad prior to May 24, 1934, to an American citizen mother did not acquire American citizenship at birth, since at that time citizenship at birth was transmitted only by a citizen father. Although subsequent legislation conferred upon American women the power to transmit citizenship to their children born abroad, such legislation was not retroactive and did not bestow citizenship on persons born before the enactment of such legislation.

And even then, citizenship would not descend until the child returned and resided in the United States for a five-year continuous period prior to his or her eighteenth birthday.

There are other ways in which bodies are deeply entwined with the nation. In times of war, for example, governments have been able to commandeer (male) bodies to fight and be killed. The modern nation-state has literally been built on the bodies of men. Benedict Anderson argued in his influential book, *Imagined Communities* (1983), that the idea of the nation is one that people have been willing to sacrifice their lives for. Although many civilians lost their lives in the creation of nation-states, it has usually been male bodies that are conscripted to fight, and die, for the nation. The use of their bodies has been legitimated through rhetorics of honor and glory so they will not seem to have died in vain. Today, with the threat of nuclear weapons and other varieties of modern warfare, the *collateral* damage to human bodies is tremendous. It is clear that the nation controls our bodies in myriad ways, some of which we are not aware of or only become so when that control impinges on us personally.

Rights in our bodies/rights to our bodies

Citizens of the United States assume that we possess our bodies, but this is true only to a limited extent. The state, by deciding who shall receive health care and who shall have access to good food and housing, literally shapes the bodies of its inhabitants. It can decide who can do what kinds of work and how many people are allowed to occupy an apartment, house, or bedroom, disciplining the spaces bodies can occupy. It can scrutinize and even block certain kinds of bodies from entering the country: bodies with disabilities, AIDS, mental deficiencies, and particular kinds of sexual orientation. Finally, it has the power to discipline the bodies of those who transgress its rules and regulations.

The United States, thought to be a multicultural society, nevertheless attempts to discourage some groups from reproducing, and has in the past even sterilized members of stigmatized racial groups or the genetically impaired. Today, poor women are the target for state population control policies. Believing that poor women reproduce only to gain added, but extremely minimal, welfare benefits, the United States is one of the most punitive of all industrialized nations with regard to "welfare" for single or poor mothers.

> Poor children in the United States are poorer than the children in most other Western industrialized nations . . . only in Israel and Ireland are poor children worse off than poor American youths. (Keith Bradsher, reporting on the Luxembourg Income Study, *New York Times*, August 14, 1995; see also an op ed piece by Richard Russo, same day)

This was confirmed independently by a three-year study financed by the Carnegie Foundation entitled "Starting Points: Meeting the Needs of Our Youngest Children" (1994).

Although it takes two to make a child (with conventional methods), women, not men, are the targets of birth control devices and programs, despite the fact that the majority of out-of-wedlock teenage pregnancies are the result of intercourse with men over the age of 21 – men who, thus, have much easier access to such devices. In addition, "virtually all sterilization abuse (as well as proposals for less drastic bodily invasions, such as the use of Norplant) is directed against women on welfare" (Bordo 1993: 76). There was a huge outcry when chemical sterilization (which was called *castration*) of convicted male sex offenders was proposed; it was held that their reproductive rights could not or should not be infringed. But there was hardly any defense for the welfare mothers who would be subjected to Norplant or other forms of sterilization.

In the United States, where individual freedom is assumed and where state intervention into personal lives is generally abhorred, women's control over their bodies is quite limited. Philosopher Susan Bordo argues that two different traditions have influenced both law and medicine concerning individual rights: "one for embodied subjects, and the other for those who come to be treated as mere bodies despite official rhetoric that vehemently forswears such treatment of human beings" (1993: 72). Bodily integrity is held in such high regard that "judges have consistently refused to force individuals to submit without consent to medical treatment even though the life of another hangs in the balance" (p. 73). You cannot be forced to donate bone marrow to save the life of your already born and living child, but there are people who believe you should be forced to continue a pregnancy and give birth against your wishes, without your consent. Very often, these same people do not support welfare. Bordo decries the way women's bodies are being imagined as "fetal incubators"; in some of the rhetoric, the fetus's *personhood* takes precedence over that of the woman involved. We must ask, as the title of Bordo's article does, "Are Women Persons?"

Traffic in Body Parts

When we think about "the body" we generally think of the whole body. Although our language distinguishes different body parts – arms, toes, heart, liver, etc. – they are integral parts *of* the body; they are continuous with and connected to it. We do not normally think of them as separate and partible. Yet, due to recent technical advances in medical practice, we also know that some of these body parts are partible. For example, a living person is able to give half a lung or kidney to another person, and not necessarily die in the process. However, science has also developed techniques for "harvesting" organs such as hearts, livers, and eyes from cadavers, and preserving them until they are able to transplant them into living people who need them. People are being encouraged to donate their organs when they die. In the United States, people are given forms to sign when they go to get or renew their driver's license so that if they are involved in a fatal accident, their organs can be taken.

This technology is, obviously, life-saving for many people, but there is a dark specter looming behind it – the traffic in body parts. While there is a long tradition in the West that the body should remain outside market transactions, selling the body – whether into slavery or prostitution – is against the law. Selling *parts* of the body is also against the law

in virtually every country (Iran is perhaps the only exception) and has been condemned by all of the worlds' medical associations. In the United States, the National Organ

Transplant Act, passed in 1984, calls for as much as a $50,000 fine and five years in prison if a person is convicted of buying or selling human organs. . . . Yet in Israel and a handful of other nations, including India, Turkey, China, Russia, and Iraq, organ sales are conducted with only a scant nod toward secrecy. (Finkel 2001: 28)

However, since it is normally poor people who sell their organs, some people, including doctors like Michael Friedlaender who performs transplant operations at Hadassah University Hospital in Jerusalem, think they ought to be paid. "After all, Friedlaender points out, everyone else in the transaction profits – the doctors, the hospital, the nurses and of course the recipient. 'Why,' he wonders, 'does the person losing the most have to do it for free?'" (Finkel 2001: 32). There is a certain logic to his point.

However, others such as Lawrence Cohen and Nancy Scheper-Hughes, medical anthropologists at the University of California, Berkeley, and co-founders of Organ Watch, strongly disagree precisely because the donors tend to be the poorest and most vulnerable people (Cohen 1999; Scheper-Hughes 2000). According to Scheper-Hughes, "the flow of organs follows the modern routes of capital: from the South to the North, from Third to First World, from poor to rich, from black and brown to white, and from female to male" (2000: 193). The traffic in organs replicates global inequalities and works to further enforce them. It is very difficult to maintain the line (or fiction) between voluntary donation and coercion in such cases since poor people are vulnerable to coercive tactics and rhetoric, whether within the family or from outside. For example, in India, where Cohen has conducted extensive field-work, it is mostly women who "donate" a kidney. Husbands "made it clear that if the men had to do heavy labor, it was only fair that the women contribute to the family income by selling a kidney." But, he went on, "in none of the cases did selling an organ significantly improve the family's fortune in the long run" (Cohen, cited in Finkel 2001: 33). There is even a slum outside the city of Chennai that is "nick-named 'Kidneyvakkam' because so many of the residents had undergone the oper-ation" (Cohen 1999: 137).

Are the bodies of poor people going to be viewed as commodities, as resources for spare parts? It seems this is already happening, according to Japanese social the-orist Tsuyoshi Awaya, who has coined the term "neo-cannibalism" to describe the phenomenon. "We are now eyeing each other's bodies greedily as a source of detachable spare parts with which to extend our lives" (Awaya, cited in Scheper-Hughes 2000: 198). Condemned and executed prisoners in China have already been used in this way; and there are fears that certain groups such as "street children" are also being used for this purpose (e.g. the film Central Station). Whether these fears are grounded in fact I do not know. But even as rumors, as "weapons of the weak" – that is, as a form of protest by those most vulnerable – they have had a powerful effect. Apparently, several countries will no longer allow international adoption due to fears that the children are being used for their organs. Clearly, international guide-lines for obtaining and transplanting organs need to be developed and enforced to stop the trafficking in body parts. More important, there has to be a better way to solve the problem of poverty than by dismembering the poor.

If you believe that you *are* your body, who are you if you have parts from someone else? If you believe the body should be buried (or burned) intact, what is the status of a body from which an organ (or organs) has been removed? What are the implications for death (Lock 2002)? Different religions and religious people have different feelings about this; Judaism and Islam, for example, believe the body should be buried intact, and religious officials seem more ambivalent about donation than they are about accepting organs. Surprisingly, Christianity does not seem to have such qualms (Finkel 2001: 28).

Or maybe it is not so surprising since there was a "trafficking in holy body parts" (Bynum 1995: 327) among Christians during the Middle Ages. "By the twelfth century," according to medievalist Caroline Walker Bynum, "the faithful were enthusiastically fragmenting bodies . . . so that parts could be given to religious communities that wished to share in the saint's power and presence" (p. 201). In addition, there seemed to be a hierarchy of parts – hearts went to abbeys, entrails to lesser churches. Sometimes the parts were buried, and thus the same saint could be buried in two (or more) places. But more often they were "divided up to provide relics" (p. 201). At first reliquaries were elaborate constructions in the shape of churches and made of gold encrusted with gems; later they came to resemble the part that they housed, like the hand of John the Baptist that I have seen in the collection at Topkapı Palace, Istanbul. Because of the enthusiasm for fragments of saints' bodies, it sometimes happened that a particular saint might end up with more parts than he or she started with! In a sense, the "enthusiasm for bodily partition was made possible by the confidence in ultimate victory over it" (p. 213), for God would reunite all the parts at resurrection. Despite the view that the earthly body was a house of rot and corruption, it would be wrong to conclude that the practices of fragmentation and partition suggest "either dualistic rejection of the body or the equation of self with soul" (p. 328); instead, the whole person, the true person, *is* the resurrected body.

Dead (and Dying) Bodies

The way we think about and treat dead bodies very much depends on what we think about bodies more generally. This relates to the issue of whether we believe, as poet Erica Jong poignantly put it, "Flesh is merely a lesson. We learn it and pass on" (1979: 24). The way we treat dead bodies depends on whether we believe we are merely our bodies, whether our bodies are the casing for the soul or spirit, or whether these aspects of the person are inseparable. Americans are particularly squeamish about the whole topic of death; for a society so focused on youth and fitness, the deterioration of the body is a terror to be avoided at all costs, the idea of death is anathema. As noted in chapter 2, elderly dying people are often shunted away out of sight – to nursing homes or hospitals. Except for those present at a death, most people rarely see a dead body. In the United States, the body is treated as so much dead matter, whisked away as quickly as possible and delivered to a funeral home to be prepared either for burial or for cremation. Personally, I find something quite barbaric in this treatment, and at the death of one of my parents I postponed informing the attending staff so that I could sit with the body for a time.

Is Life the Incurable Disease?

> Is life the incurable disease:
> The infant is born howling
> & we laugh,
> the dead man smiles
> & we cry,
> resisting the passage,
> always resisting the passage,
> that turns life
> into eternity.
>
> Blake sang alleluias
> on his deathbed.
> My own grandmother,
> hardly a poet at all,
> smiled
> as we'd never seen her smile
> before.
> Perhaps the dress of flesh
> is no more than a familiar garment
> that grows looser as one diets
> on death, & perhaps discards it
> or gives it to the poor in spirit
> who have not learned yet
> what blessing it is
> to go naked?

Erica Jong, *At the Edge of the Body* (1979)

There are some societies where the family and close friends sit with the body for quite a while after death to let the spirit adjust to its new condition, fearing that haste will bring misfortune on the living. The *Tibetan Book of the Dead*, for example, suggests a period of 33 days to allow the spirit to negotiate the different levels of *bardo* existence. Then the body is exposed to let birds of prey pick the flesh clean, and the bones are collected, cleaned, and placed in jars.

During my fieldwork I became quite preoccupied with death because the villagers were gravely concerned about what they should do if I died there. I had never really given it much thought, but confronted with it daily I was forced to try to clarify my beliefs. But, in fact, I dealt with it by giving the headman the telephone number of the American Embassy. People have different views in different contexts, and I was no exception. Still, this preoccupation helped me to learn about their views.

When a person dies in that Muslim village, everyone is immediately aware of it. Floating over the village is the sound of the *ezan* (call to prayer) broadcast from the minaret but outside of its regular schedule. Everything happens very quickly because bodies must be buried within 24 hours. The dead body is washed, usually by the oldest female relative, and the orifices of the body plugged with cotton wool. Then it is immediately wrapped in a length of white cloth called a *kefen*. If the person who died is male, his body is first taken to the mosque where all the men of the village have gathered to pray for him. Bodies of women are taken directly to the cemetery. Women do not go to the mosque but gather, instead, at the home of the deceased's family where they mourn by singing tales about the dead person, cry and wail, and comfort the survivors.

Bodies must be *buried* intact because villagers believe the dead will be interrogated by an angel before they may enter Paradise. The questions are simple and all villagers have memorized the answers in Arabic, the language of the Prophet and the Qur'an. What is your religion? Who is your prophet? Did you keep *oruç* (the fast of Ramazan)? Did you perform *namaz* (daily prayers)? And, for women, Did you keep your hair covered? It is said that for every strand of hair exposed, a woman will burn 90 days in hell. Not surprisingly, hell is imagined as being occupied primarily by women.

Thus, Turks will not countenance cremation, and many of the village Turks would not fly in an airplane because of the possibility of a crash and consequent burning. They took buses not planes to Mecca when they went on the *hajj*. Of course, many urban and even some village Turks have flown, and Turkey, like all Muslim countries, has a national airline (and several private ones) and a number of modern airports. When a Turk who has been working in Europe dies, quite often the body will be flown home to be buried in the soil of that person's natal village.

In the contemporary United States, there are a number of options for dead bodies and whichever is chosen is often related to the person's religious beliefs. Jews and Christians, generally, believe the body should be buried. Though the phrase "ashes to ashes, dust to dust" might conceivably include cremation, that has not been the general practice. When cremation is chosen, it is not uncommon that the ashes are then buried; others keep them in special urns, still others scatter them in places that the deceased was attached to. Some people, like my mother, donate their dead bodies to hospitals so that students may learn from them; others donate parts so that others might live.

Immortality and Cryonics

For the devout believer, Christianity takes the sting of death away (1 Corinthians 15: 55). Death is transcended by the resurrection of the body (and soul). There is a belief in some kind of continued existence in Heaven. But in a secular society influenced by Christianity, there are some who seek an earthly immortality – some are attracted to the idea of cloning, others to cryonics.[9] Cryonics, a word coined in 1965, "is a specific term referring to the freezing of people for future revival" (Alcor Life Extension Foundation [1989] 1993: 6). Although the idea is not particularly new, the ability to put it into practice is. Today there are several facilities where this technology is available *and* there are already about 100 people who are frozen and stored at one of these facilities. This practice received considerable attention in July 2002 when the body of baseball hero Ted Williams was delivered to Alcor. Some clients have elected to have only their head/brain frozen, believing that their unique personality is stored in the brain rather like information in a computer.

In part the beliefs and practices of the cryonicists came about with the realization that there are currently several clinical definitions of death – when the heart stops beating, when a person stops breathing, or when brain activity stops – and all of these can sometimes be reversed due to modern technology. According to Robert Ettinger, one of the founders of the movement, a person "dies little by little usually, in imperceptible gradations, and the question of reversibility at any stage depends on the state of medical art" (1964: 3). He proposed that if the supposedly dead body could be frozen quickly enough, it might be able to remain in a state of "suspended death" indefinitely – at least until technology is developed whereby it can be re-animated and cured of whatever had killed it in the first place, either with new medicines, cloning techniques, or cell revitalization. Death, in their new jargon, becomes merely "deanimation"; in this state they await "reanimation." Cryonicists also discuss the possibility of "suspended animation" or "suspended life," where people who are old or feeble might wish not to wait until natural death but be frozen before that event. Unanswered is whether this would be called "euthanasia," and if so, then laws would have to be passed to allow this procedure. A question that needs much more investigation is why most of the participants involved in the cryonics enterprise are white, middle class, and male. Why is it primarily men who desire personal earthly immortality? How would notions of time change if the possibility for immortality existed? Why is life not enough?

Notes

1 See especially Bynum (1987) and Bell (1985).
2 Vale and Juno's book *Modern Primitives* (1989) is a documentary of a variety of these contemporary practices.
3 See Kuper's *The Invention of Primitive Society* (1988) for a discussion of the way the notion of "primitive society" was invented in the mid-nineteenth century in an evolutionary framework as a mirror to Western society. We have already talked of the way the body (nature) is constructed within culture and does not exist outside it.
4 See, for example, Elaine Scarry's book *The Body in Pain* (1987).
5 The term female genital *mutilation* is offensive to Sudanese women (and others) because it is not seen as mutilation. The English speakers among them use "circumcision," while others prefer the term female genital "cutting" (Gruenbaum 2001, and talk at Stanford January 16, 2003).

6 For culturally sensitive accounts that at the same time do not condone the practice, see especially the work of anthropologists Janice Boddy (1982, 1989) and Ellen Gruenbaum (2001). For an Egyptian doctor's perspective, see Nawal El Sadaawi's *The Hidden Face of Eve* (1980).

7 See Kathryn M. Ringrose's "Living in the Shadows: Eunuchs and Gender in Byzantium," in *Third Sex, Third Gender: Beyond Sexual Dimorphism in Culture and History*, ed. Gilbert Herdt (New York: Zone Books, 1994).

8 Recently, an enormous literature has developed on this topic. See, for example, Anthias and Yuval-Davis (1992); Linke (1999); Mosse (1985); and Parker, Russo, Sommer, and Yeager (1992).

9 My information about cryonics was supplied by Tiffany Romain, a graduate student in my department, who is making this study the basis of her doctoral dissertation.

Bibliography

Alcor Life Extension Foundation ([1989] 1993) *Cryonics: Reaching for Tomorrow*.

Anderson, Benedict (1983) *Imagined Communities*. London: Verso.

Anthias, Floya and Yuval-Davis, Nira, in association with Harried Cain (1992) *Racialized Boundaries: Race, Nation, Gender, Colour and Class and the Anti-Racist Struggle*. London: Routledge.

Bell, Rudolph (1985) *Holy Anorexia*. Chicago: University of Chicago Press.

Bettleheim, Bruno (1954) *Symbolic Wounds: Puberty Rites and the Envious Male*. New York: Free Press.

Blacking, John, ed. (1977) *The Anthropology of the Body*. London: Academic Press.

Boddy, Janice (1982) "Womb as Oasis: The Symbolic Context of Pharaonic Circumcision in Rural Northern Sudan." *American Ethnologist*, 15 (1): 4–27.

Boddy, Janice (1989) *Wombs and Alien Spirits: Women, Men, and the Zar Cults in Northern Sudan*. Madison, WI: University of Wisconsin Press.

Bordo, Susan (1993) *Unbearable Weight: Feminism, Western Culture, and the Body*. Berkeley: University of California Press.

Boston Women's Health Book Collective (1992) *The New Our Bodies, Ourselves*. New York: Simon & Schuster.

Bourdieu, Pierre ([1972] 1977) *Outline of a Theory of Practice*. Trans. Richard Nice. Cambridge: Cambridge University Press.

Brownmiller, Susan (1984) *Femininity*. New York: Fawcett Columbine.

Brumberg, Joan Jacobs (1997) *The Body Project: An Intimate History of American Girls*. New York: Random House.

Bynum, Caroline Walker (1987) *Holy Feast and Holy Fast: The Religious Significance of Food to Medieval Women*. Berkeley: University of California Press.

Bynum, Caroline Walker (1995) *The Resurrection of the Body in Western Christianity, 200–1336*. New York: Columbia University Press.

Chernin, Kim (1981) *The Obsession: Reflections on the Tyranny of Slenderness*. New York: Harper & Row.

Cohen, Lawrence (1999) "Where It Hurts: Indian Material for an Ethics of Organ Transplantation." *Daedalus*, 128 (4): 135–65.

Delaney, Carol (1991) *The Seed and the Soil: Gender and Cosmology in Turkish Village Society*. Berkeley: University of California Press.

Delaney, Carol (1998) *Abraham on Trial: The Social Legacy of Biblical Myth*. Princeton: Princeton University Press.

DeLoache, Judy and Gottlieb, Alma, eds. (2000) *A World of Babies: Imagined Childcare Guides for Seven Societies.* New York: Cambridge University Press.

Disch, Estelle (1997) *Reconstructing Gender: A Multicultural Anthology.* Mountain View, CA: Mayfield.

Douglas, Mary ([1966] 1999) *Purity and Danger: An Analysis of the Concepts of Pollution and Taboo.* London: Routledge & Kegan Paul.

Eakin, Emily (2000) "In This Woman's World, What's a Guy to Do? Sweat." *New York Times,* October 7.

Ehrenreich, Barbara and English, Deidre (1973) *Complaints and Disorders: The Sexual Politics of Sickness.* Old Westbury, NY: Feminist Press.

Ehrenreich, Barbara and English, Deidre (1979) *For Her Own Good: 150 Years of the Experts' Advice to Women.* New York: Anchor Books.

Eilberg-Schwartz, Howard (1990) *The Savage in Judaism: An Anthropology of Israelite Religion and Ancient Judaism.* Bloomington: Indiana University Press.

El Sadaawi, Nawal (1980) *The Hidden Face of Eve: Women in the Arab World.* Trans. and ed. Sherif Hetata. London: Zed Press.

Ettinger, Robert C. W. (1964) *The Prospect of Immortality.* New York: Doubleday.

Featherstone, Mike, ed. (2000) *Body Modification.* London: Sage.

Finkel, Michael (2001) "This Little Kidney Went to Market: Complications." *New York Times Magazine,* May 27, pp. 26–59.

Gilmore, David (1994) "The Beauty of the Beast: Male Body Imagery in Anthropological Perspective." In *The Good Body: Asceticism in Contemporary Culture,* ed. Mary G. Winkler and Letha B. Cole. New Haven: Yale University Press, pp. 191–214.

Gruenbaum, Ellen (2001) *The Female Circumcision Controversy.* Philadelphia: University of Pennsylvania Press.

Hall, Steven (1999) "The Troubled Life of Boys: The Bully in the Mirror." *New York Times,* August 22.

Hertz, Robert ([1909] 1973) "Pre-Eminence of the Right Hand: A Study in Religious Polarity." In *Right and Left: Essays on Dual Symbolic Classification,* ed. Rodney Needham. Chicago: University of Chicago Press.

Jong, Erica (1979) *At the Edge of the Body.* New York: Holt, Rinehart, & Winston.

Kittay, Eva (1996) "Human Dependency and Rawlsian Equality." In *Feminists Rethink the Self,* ed. Diana Tiejtens Meyers. Colorado: Westview Press.

Klesse, Christian (2000) "'Modern Primitivism': Non-Mainstream Body Modification and Racialized Representations." In *Body Modification,* ed. Mike Featherstone. Thousand Oaks, CA: Sage Publications.

Kuper, Adam (1988) *The Invention of Primitive Society: Transformations of an Illusion.* New York: Routledge.

Levenson, Jon (1993) *The Death and Resurrection of the Beloved Son: The Transformation of Child Sacrifice in Judaism and Christianity.* New Haven: Yale University Press.

Linke, Uli (1999) *Blood and Nation.* Philadelphia: University of Pennsylvania Press.

Lock, Margaret (2002) *Twice Dead: Organ Transplants and the Reinvention of Death.* Berkeley: University of California Press.

McGee, Jon and Warms, Richard (2000) *Anthropological Theory: An Introductory History.* Mountain View: Mayfield Publishing.

Mascia-Lees, Frances E. and Sharpe, Patricia (1992) *Tattoo, Torture, Mutilation, and Adornment: The Denaturalization of the Body in Culture and Text.* Albany: State University of New York Press.

Mauss, Marcel ([1934] 1973) "Techniques of the Body." *Economy and Society,* 2 (1): 70–88.

Miner, Horace (1956) "Body Ritual Among the Nacirema." *American Anthropologist*, 58: 503–7.

Mosse, George L. (1985) *Nationalism and Sexuality: Middle-Class Morality and Sexual Norms in Modern Europe*. Madison, WI: University of Wisconsin Press.

Ortner, Sherry (1974) "Is Female to Male as Nature is to Culture?" In *Women, Culture, and Society*, ed. Michelle Rosaldo and Louise Lamphere. Stanford: Stanford University Press.

Ottenheimer, Martin (1996) *Forbidden Relatives: The American Myth of Cousin Marriage*. Urbana and Chicago: University of Illinois Press.

Parker, Andrew, Russo, Mary, Sommer, Doris, and Yeager, Patricia, eds. (1992) *Nationalisms and Sexualities*. New York: Routledge.

Pope, Harrison G., Jr., Phillips, Katharine A., and Olivardia, Roberto (2000) *The Adonis Complex: The Secret Crisis of Male Body Obsession*. New York: Free Press.

Scarry, Elaine (1987) *The Body in Pain: The Making and Unmaking of the World*. New York: Oxford University Press.

Scheper-Hughes, Nancy (2000) "The Global Traffic in Human Organs." *Current Anthropology*, 41/2 (April): 191–224.

Seid, Roberta P. (1994) "Too Close to the Bone: The Historical Context for Women's Obsession with Slenderness." In *Feminist Perspectives on Eating Disorders*, ed. Patricia Fallon, Melanie A. Katzman, and Susan C. Wooley. New York: Guilford.

Suleiman, Susan Rubin, ed. (1986) *The Female Body in Western Culture: Contemporary Perspectives*. Cambridge, MA: Harvard University Press.

Turner, Bryan (1984) *Body and Society: Explorations in Social Theory*. Oxford: Blackwell.

Yuval-Davis, Nira (1987) "The Jewish Collectivity and National Reproduction in Israel." In *Women in the Middle East*. London: Khamsin.

Vale, V. and Juno, Andrea (1989) *Modern Primitives: Tattoo, Piercing, Scarification: An Investigation of Contemporary Adornment and Ritual*. London: Re/Search Publications.

Whorf, Benjamin (1956) *Language, Thought and Reality*. Cambridge, MA: MIT Press.

Wolf, Naomi (1991) "Hunger." In *The Beauty Myth: How Images of Beauty Are Used Against Women*. New York: Anchor Books, Doubleday.

Body Ritual Among the Nacirema
Horace Miner

The anthropologist has become so familiar with the diversity of ways in which different peoples behave in similar situations that he is not apt to be surprised by even the most exotic customs. In fact, if all of the logically possible combinations of behavior have not been found somewhere in the world, he is apt to suspect that they must be present in some yet undescribed tribe. This point has, in fact, been expressed with respect to clan organization by Murdock (1949: 71). In this light, the magical beliefs and practices of the Nacirema present such unusual aspects that it seems desirable to describe them as an example of the extremes to which human behavior can go.

Professor Linton first brought the ritual of the Nacirema to the attention of anthropologists twenty

R
E
A
D
I
N
G
S

years ago (1936: 326), but the culture of this people is still very poorly understood. They are a North American group living in the territory between the Canadian Cree, the Yaqui and Tarahumare of Mexico, and the Carib and Arawak of the Antilles. Little is known of their origin, although tradition states that they came from the east. According to Nacirema mythology, their nation was originated by a culture hero, Notgnihsaw, who is otherwise known for two great feats of strength – the throwing of a piece of wampum across the river Pa-To-Mac and the chopping down of a cherry tree in which the Spirit of Truth resided.

Nacirema culture is characterized by a highly developed market economy which has evolved in a rich natural habitat. While much of the people's time is devoted to economic pursuits, a large part of the fruits of these labors and a considerable portion of the day are spent in ritual activity. The focus of this activity is the human body, the appearance and health of which loom as a dominant concern in the ethos of the people. While such a concern is certainly not unusual, its ceremonial aspects and associated philosophy are unique.

The fundamental belief underlying the whole system appears to be that the human body is ugly and that its natural tendency is to debility and disease. Incarcerated in such a body, man's only hope is to avert these characteristics through the use of the powerful influences of ritual and ceremony. Every household has one or more shrines devoted to this purpose. The more powerful individuals in the society have several shrines in their houses and, in fact, the opulence of a house is often referred to in terms of the number of such ritual centers it possesses. Most houses are of wattle and daub construction, but the shrine rooms of the more wealthy are walled with stone. Poorer families imitate the rich by applying pottery plaques to their shrine walls.

While each family has at least one such shrine, the rituals associated with it are not family ceremonies but are private and secret. The rites are normally only discussed with children, and then only during the period when they are being initiated into these mysteries. I was able, however, to establish sufficient rapport with the natives to examine these shrines and to have the rituals described to me.

The focal point of the shrine is a box or chest which is built into the wall. In this chest are kept the many charms and magical potions without which no native believes he could live. These preparations are secured from a variety of specialized practitioners. The most powerful of these are the medicine men, whose assistance must be rewarded with substantial gifts. However, the medicine men do not provide the curative potions for their clients, but decide what the ingredients should be and then write them down in an ancient and secret language. This writing is understood only by the medicine men and by the herbalists who, for another gift, provide the required charm.

The charm is not disposed of after it has served its purpose, but is placed in the charm-box of the household shrine. As these magical materials are specific for certain ills, and the real or imagined maladies of the people are many, the charm-box is usually full to overflowing. The magical packets are so numerous that people forget what their purposes were and fear to use them again. While the natives are very vague on this point, we can only assume that the idea in retaining all the old magical materials is that their presence in the charm-box, before which the body rituals are conducted, will in some way protect the worshipper.

Beneath the charm-box is a small font. Each day every member of the family, in succession, enters the shrine room, bows his head before the charm-box, mingles different sorts of holy water in the font, and proceeds with a brief rite of ablution. The holy waters are secured from the Water Temple of the community, where the priests conduct elaborate ceremonies to make the liquid ritually pure.

In the hierarchy of magical practitioners, and below the medicine men in prestige, are specialists whose designation is best translated "holy-mouth-men." The Nacirema have an almost pathological horror of and fascination with the mouth, the condition of which is believed to have a supernatural influence on all social relationships. Were it not for the rituals of the mouth, they believe that their teeth would fall out, their gums bleed, their jaws shrink, their friends desert them, and their lovers reject them. They also believe that a strong relationship exists between oral and moral characteristics. For example, there is a ritual ablution of the mouth for children which is supposed to improve their moral fiber.

The daily body ritual performed by everyone includes a mouth-rite. Despite the fact that these people are so punctilious about care of the mouth, this rite involves a practice which strikes the uninitiated stranger as revolting. It was reported to me that the ritual consists of inserting a small bundle of hog hairs into the mouth, along with certain magical powders, and then moving the bundle in a highly formalized series of gestures.

In addition to the private mouth-rite, the people seek out a holy-mouth-man once or twice a year. These practitioners have an impressive set of paraphernalia, consisting of a variety of augers, awls, probes, and prods. The use of these objects in the exorcism of the evils of the mouth involves almost unbelievable ritual torture of the client. The holy-mouth-man opens the client's mouth and, using the above mentioned tools, enlarges any holes which decay may have created in the teeth. Magical materials are put into these holes. If there are no naturally occurring holes in the teeth, large sections of one or more teeth are gouged out so that the supernatural substance can be applied. In the client's view, the purpose of these ministrations is to arrest decay and to draw friends. The extremely sacred and traditional character of the rite is evident in the fact that the natives return to the holy-mouth-men year after year, despite the fact that their teeth continue to decay.

It is to be hoped that, when a thorough study of the Nacirema is made, there will be careful inquiry into the personality structure of these people. One has but to watch the gleam in the eye of a holy-mouth-man, as he jabs an awl into an exposed nerve, to suspect that a certain amount of sadism is involved. If this can be established, a very interesting pattern emerges, for most of the population shows definite masochistic tendencies. It was to these that Professor Linton referred in discussing a distinctive part of the daily body ritual which is performed only by men. This part of the rite involves scraping and lacerating the surface of the face with a sharp instrument. Special women's rites are performed only four times during each lunar month, but what they lack in frequency is made up in barbarity. As part of this ceremony, women bake their heads in small ovens for about an hour. The theoretically interesting point is that what seems to be a preponderantly masochistic people have developed sadistic specialists.

The medicine men have an imposing temple, or *latipso*, in every community of any size. The more elaborate ceremonies required to treat very sick patients can only be performed at this temple. These ceremonies involve not only the thaumaturge but a permanent group of vestal maidens who move sedately about the temple chambers in distinctive costume and headdress.

The *latipso* ceremonies are so harsh that it is phenomenal that a fair proportion of the really sick natives who enter the temple ever recover. Small children whose indoctrination is still incomplete have been known to resist attempts to take them to the temple because "that is where you go to die." Despite this fact, sick adults are not only willing but eager to undergo the protracted ritual purification, if they can afford to do so. No matter how ill the supplicant or how grave the emergency, the guardians of many temples will not admit a client if he cannot give a rich gift to the custodian. Even after one has gained admission and survived the ceremonies, the guardians will not permit the neophyte to leave until he makes still another gift.

The supplicant entering the temple is first stripped of all his or her clothes. In every-day life the Nacirema avoids exposure of his body and its natural functions. Bathing and excretory acts are performed only in the secrecy of the household shrine, where they are ritualized as part of the body-rites. Psychological shock results from the fact that body secrecy is suddenly lost upon entry into the *latipso*. A man, whose own wife has never seen him in an excretory act, suddenly finds himself naked and assisted by a vestal maiden while he performs his natural functions into a sacred vessel. This sort of ceremonial treatment is necessitated by the fact that the excreta are used by a diviner to ascertain the course and nature of the client's sickness. Female clients, on the other hand, find their naked bodies are subjected to the scrutiny, manipulation and prodding of the medicine men.

Few supplicants in the temple are well enough to do anything but lie on their hard beds. The daily ceremonies, like the rites of the holy-mouth-men, involve discomfort and torture. With ritual precision, the vestals awaken their miserable charges each dawn and roll them about on their beds of pain while performing ablutions, in the formal movements of which the maidens are highly trained. At other times they insert magic wands in the supplicant's mouth or force him to eat substances which are supposed to be healing. From time to time the medicine men come to their clients and jab magically treated needles into their flesh. The fact that these temple ceremonies may not cure, and may even kill the neophyte, in no way decreases the people's faith in the medicine men.

There remains one other kind of practitioner, known as a "listener." This witch-doctor has the power to exorcise the devils that lodge in the heads of people who have been bewitched. The Nacirema believe that parents bewitch their own children. Mothers are particularly suspected of putting a curse on children while teaching them the secret body rituals. The counter-magic of the witch-doctor is unusual in its lack of ritual. The patient simply tells the "listener" all his troubles and fears, beginning with the earliest difficulties he can remember. The memory displayed by the Nacirema in these exorcism sessions is truly remarkable. It is not uncommon for the patient to bemoan the rejection he felt upon being weaned as a babe, and a few individuals even see their troubles going back to the traumatic effects of their own birth.

In conclusion, mention must be made of certain practices which have their base in native esthetics but which depend upon the pervasive aversion to the natural body and its functions. There are ritual fasts to make fat people thin and ceremonial feasts to make thin people fat. Still other rites are used to make women's breasts larger if they are small, and smaller if they are large. General dissatisfaction with breast shape is symbolized in the fact that the ideal form is virtually outside the range of human variation. A few women afflicted with almost inhuman hypermammary development are so idolized that they make a handsome living by simply going from village to village and permitting the natives to stare at them for a fee.

Reference has already been made to the fact that excretory functions are ritualized, routinized, and relegated to secrecy. Natural reproductive functions are similarly distorted. Intercourse is taboo as a topic and scheduled as an act. Efforts are made to avoid pregnancy by the use of magical materials or by limiting intercourse to certain phases of the moon. Conception is actually very infrequent. When pregnant, women dress so as to hide their condition. Parturition takes place in secret, without friends or relatives to assist, and the majority of women do not nurse their infants.

Our review of the ritual life of the Nacirema has certainly shown them to be a magic-ridden people. It is hard to understand how they have managed to exist so long under the burdens which they have imposed upon themselves. But even such exotic customs as these take on real meaning when they are viewed with the insight provided by Malinowski when he wrote (1948: 70):

> Looking from far and above, from our high places of safety in the developed civilization, it is easy to see all the crudity and irrelevance of magic. But without its power and guidance early man could not have mastered his practical difficulties as he has done, nor could man have advanced to the higher stages of civilization.

References Cited

Linton, Ralph (1936) *The Study of Man.* New York: D. Appleton-Century.

Malinowski, Bronislaw (1948) *Magic, Science, and Religion.* Glencoe: Free Press.

Murdock, George P. (1949) *Social Structure.* New York: Macmillan.

1   Cut out two advertisements from any popular magazine, one that features a man and one that features a woman. For each ad do three things. First, describe the person in the ad: body image, stance, expression, and so on. Second, discuss why you think this particular image helps to sell whatever product is being advertised. Third, discuss how this particular image communicates something about the culture's notions of males and females. You might ask a couple of friends to comment on the photos as well and include their comments in your analysis.

2   Can you think of an example in your own life when you were aware of trying to make your body, or part of it, conform to the cultural norm or standard? How did you do it? If you cannot readily think of such an example – or would prefer not to share it – ask someone else if they'd be willing to tell you about such an experience in their life.

7

Food For Thought

What constitutes food? What makes a meal? What does it mean to say that "food is love"? Relation of food to the environment. Fast food, slow food, genetically modified food ("Frankenfood"). Food and sex. Food and civility. Food and religion. Cooking.

Food For Thought

A hundred years from now anthropologists and other descendants, upon looking back on our best-selling reading lists, will be curious to know just when it was that food and chefs and things culinary, and books about them, replaced sex as our main sensuous nourishment. (Arnold 2001: B3)

Introduction

You may not agree that food has usurped the place of sex in y/our culture, but the ascendance of interest in food, cooking, chefs, and restaurants cannot be denied. The journalist quoted above was struck by the number of books about food on the best-seller list – three as he wrote, one just off the list after 15 weeks, and others soon to appear on it. Tastes in reading, like tastes in food, change with the times and provide an interesting avenue for investigating a culture. In addition to books about food, more than 2,000 cookbooks were published in the year 2000 alone. Surely, this is food for thought. Ruth Reichel, one of the best-selling authors and editor of *Gourmet* magazine, suggested that the explosion of interest in food is a sign that we are finally "getting away from our Puritan roots and no longer are embarrassed about thinking about food" (cited in Arnold 2001), that is, we are able to view food sensually and aesthetically rather than merely as a source of energy and survival.

In this chapter I lay out a smorgasbord of ideas about the ways food shapes culture and culture shapes food. It is not a chapter about the nutritional value of food – about vitamins, minerals, and food as an energy source – but about the culturally constituted nature of food and meals. These are interlarded with issues of classification, religion, identity, civility, pleasure, economics, and the environment. Throughout, be attentive also to the way the topic draws with it the topics from the previous chapters – space, time, language, social relations, and body.

(1) Regarding space, for example, think of all the places where you can obtain food and the spaces needed to grow food, which includes the pasturing of animals. *Consuming Geographies: We Are Where We Eat* (Bell and Valentine 1997) is organized around social spaces of food consumption – body, home, community, city, region, nation, and finally, the globe.

(2) The temporal dimension not only is indicated by the specific seasons when certain food becomes available, but also is present in the times of our daily meals. Each meal has a different meaning, as do the meals of different days of the week, let alone holiday meals associated with the ritual calendar.

(3) Linguistically, there is an enormous lexicon of terms for food, beginning, one might say, with the raw and cooked – also the title of a book by French anthropologist Claude Lévi-Strauss[1] – and roasted, boiled, broiled, baked, grilled, sautéed, and steamed, to mention only a few.

Roland Barthes, a French structuralist, sees all foods as "signs in a system of communication" ([1957] 1972: 63). The messages expressed by means of food can involve love or disdain, profligacy or stinginess, tradition or *avant garde*, ideas about gender, and the condition of, or concern for, health. As with language, there are rules of combination and substitution – that is, what goes with what, the order of the components, and what are suitable substitutes. Moreover, food terms are used metaphorically to speak of other things, for example a person who asks "Have you got any bread on you?" is not asking for food but to find out how much money you have in your pocket. "What's your beef?" does not mean what cut of meat you want but what is your gripe.

(4) "Eating together lies at the heart of social relations" (Counihan 1999: 6); it is a kind of training ground in civility (Flammang, forthcoming). The etymology of the word *companion* has to do with breaking bread with someone.

(5) Finally, and obviously, food is essential for our bodies and, as we have just seen, it is also intimately related to our body image. Food is a consuming passion.[2]

We Are What We Eat

Food is also a very strong cultural marker, and thus an integral part of a person's identity. In 1825, Jean Anthelme Brillat-Savarin, a French politician-gourmet, said: "Tell me what you eat, and I will tell you who you are."[3] The statement was meant not primarily in terms of ethnic identity but of the stage a nation had reached in the scale of civilization, a scale which, at that time, was assumed to be unilinear and progressive. Naturally, France, with its subtle, refined, and sophisticated cuisine, was assumed to be the epitome. Today, anthropologists are far more likely to approach food as an index to culture, not in the sense of "high" vs. "low" culture, but of particular cultures and ethnicities. Nevertheless, elements of cultural ascendancy, even snobbishness, persist in statements like the following: "French subtlety of thought and manners is said to be related to the subtlety of their cuisine, the reserve of the British to their unimaginative diet, German stolidness to the quantities of heavy food they consume, and the unreliability of the Italians to the large amounts of wine they drink" (Farb and Armelagos 1980: 40). Despite those stereotypes, food is a quintessential symbol of *identity* – we are what we eat – both individually and culturally. "A people's cuisine, or a particular food, often marks the boundary between the collective self and the other, for example, as a basis of discrimination against other peoples" (Ohnuki-Tierney 1993: 3), or merely just a distinguishing trait, as in the case of Marmite.

Marmite is a brownish vegetable extract with a toxic odor, saline taste and an axle grease consistency that has somehow captivated the British. . . . They buy it at a 24 million-jar-per-year clip that has enshrined it as a national symbol right up there with the royal family and the Sunday roast. (Hoge, *New York Times*, January 24, 2002)

> When I was working on an archaeology project sponsored by the British Institute of Archaeology in Turkey, Marmite was the spread of choice among all the British members. Americans, on the other hand, brought peanut butter.

Indeed, so much is it a symbol of being British that several "members of Parliament asked the Commons to affirm the Britishness of Marmite," especially because of "its lack of appeal for the majority of the world's population" (*New York Times*, February 27, 2002)!

Clearly, one of the most important ways that people reproduce themselves as British, or Turkish, or Chinese, or American is by the food they eat. This is something often ignored by biologists, developers, and aid planners, and the absence of such awareness has had a number of embarrassing, and in some cases tragic, consequences. During a particularly bad famine in part of Africa some years ago, the United States sent an enormous supply of wheat to ease the hunger. However, it turned out that the people did not eat wheat and didn't know what to do with it, so the starving continued. Americans, I think, would balk if they were suddenly told they had to eat grubs – unless they were a contestant on the television show *Survivor*. There are many species of plants and animals that are edible but only some of them become food. Those that become food vary cross-culturally. Why is it that Germans eat pork while for Jews and Muslims it is forbidden? Why is beef the heart of a meal for many British and Americans, but it is sacred and not eaten in India? Why is the dog elevated to sacred status in Britain and the United States, but is eaten in Vietnam and elsewhere? All of these meats are edible; it is culture that deems them inedible. Eating is not just about surviving, about getting a certain amount and kind of nutriments; what we eat is who we are as a people. People "survive in a definite way. They reproduce themselves as certain kinds of men and women, social classes, and groups, not as biological organisms or aggregates of organisms ('populations')" (Sahlins 1976: 168).

Because of the strong association between food and identity, some people find it difficult, for instance, to sample food from a culture very different from their own because the food will be unfamiliar and they do not like to try new things. That was certainly true among many Turks I met. Turkish cuisine is considered to be one of the great cuisines in the world and Turks have strong feelings about it. They do not, or did not, see the point of trying foods of different cultures/ethnicities; perhaps they thought it would dilute their Turkishness. Until very recently, there were few restaurants featuring foods of other nations; indeed, Turkey was not really a restaurant culture. Today, this is changing rapidly, partly in response to tourism, and now, at least in the major cities, one can find all kinds of ethnic restaurants as well as French cafés, pizza parlors, Chinese take-out, and even sushi bars, as well as the ubiquitous McDonald's. Food may be becoming globalized and creolized, but attachments of people to their own local, regional, and national dishes remain remarkably strong.

The French notion of *terroir* is related to these sentiments. Although there is no exact English equivalent, it means that an agricultural product carries with it something of the "flavor" of the place where it was grown. "For terroir's most ardent promoters, it is axiomatic that the finest fruits and vegetables are those truest to their roots; those whose taste reflects the interplay of soil, climate, topography, and ritual" (Steinberger, *New York Times*, April 14, 2001). Although normally the term is applied to wine making, where the specific region, light, soil, and type of vine are all thought to contribute to the distinctive style of the wine produced in that place, it can, nevertheless, be applied to any agricultural product. Not surprisingly, the French have a very ambivalent attitude to the commercialization and globalization of foodstuffs.

Because food is an important symbol of identity, "a nation's diet can be more revealing than its art or literature" (Schlosser 2001: 3). Italians, according to Alessandra Farkas, a correspondent for Italy's leading newspaper, are identified not just with pasta but especially with the meat and tomato sauce called *ragù*. "The sauce is the center of everything, it's like a cultural force. . . . [I]t's like chicken soup for American Jews – it holds generations together" (Asimov, *New York Times*, November 3, 1999). Meanwhile, people in Argentina eat steak "as if it were a national obligation" (Christian, *New York Times*, May 28, 1988) and eat more of it than any other people in the world. For Japanese, it is rice.

A similar issue regarding basmati rice erupted in India when the United States tried to patent a type of it. Protesters accused the US firm of "bio-piracy and theft of indigenous plant wealth" (*New York Times*, May 25, 2001) and feel that the term should only be applied to rice grown on "Indian soil [and] irrigated by waters from the Himalayan rivers," much as the appellation "champagne" can only be used for sparkling wines made from grapes grown in the Champagne district of France.

This is the thesis of Ohnuki-Tierney's well-researched discussion of *Rice As Self: Japanese Identities Through Time* (1993). "The symbolic importance of rice has been deeply embedded in the Japanese cosmology both of the elite and the common folk: rice as soul, rice as deity, and ultimately rice as self" (p. 8). Rice is the symbol of commensality – of eating together – whether a feast for the gods or in daily meals among humans. It is also a kind of sacred medium of exchange. It is relatively easy for Japanese to distinguish themselves from Westerners (meat eaters and bread eaters), but so too do they distinguish themselves from other rice-eating peoples. At issue is not the *kind* of rice (short-grained vs. long-grained), since the Japanese are vehemently opposed to the importation of rice from California even though its short-grain variety is very similar to their own and is much cheaper than the home-grown variety. Japanese will pay the additional cost to have *Japanese* rice grown in Japanese rice paddies. For rice is not only a symbol of the self, it is also a symbol of the land – its spatial and temporal dimensions – that is, both its territorial and historical meanings. "As a metaphor of self, rice paddies are *our* ancestral land, *our* village, *our* region, and ultimately, *our* land, Japan" (p. 10). By ingesting Japanese rice, one incorporates the spirit of Japan, creating an identity between self and nation. Similar studies could be done for other cultures.

While rice may be a "key symbol" (Ortner 1973) that opens up the investigation of Japanese identity, anthropologist Anne Allison argues that such identity is an example of the working of an "ideological state apparatus," by which she means the institutions that "exert power not primarily through repression but through ideology" (1991: 196). While the primary purpose of schools is assumed to be education, educational practices are also ways "of indoctrinating people into seeing the world a certain way and of accepting certain identities as their own within that world" (Allison 1991, quoting Althusser). It is similar to what Sylvia Yanagisako and I have called "naturalizing power," "the ways in which differentials of power come already embedded in culture . . . for power appears natural, inevitable, even god-given" (1995: 1) – that is the way the world simply is.

> [O]ne look at a typical child's *obento* – a small box packaged with a five- or six-course miniaturized meal whose pieces and parts are artistically arranged – would immediately reveal [that] no food is "just" food in Japan. What is not so immediately apparent, however, is why a small child with limited appetite and perhaps scant interest in food is the recipient of a meal as elaborate and as elaborately prepared as any made for an entire family or invited guests. (Allison 1991: 196)

The state apparatus has made it seem normal that Japanese mothers would spend enormous amounts of time, skill, and money in a daily routine of making a variety of tiny, beautiful, bite-sized morsels for the lunch boxes of their nursery school children, and the children, even if they do not appreciate the artistry, are learning that they deserve such attention. In this way, the state forms particular kinds of people by means of the food they eat.

Some people revel in trying different kinds of food; they consume the culture, literally. Sometimes this is taken to extremes. "The idea that you are what you eat has been enthusiastically promoted for years by Den Fujita, the eccentric billionaire who brought McDonald's to Japan three decades ago. 'If we eat McDonald's hamburgers and potatoes for a thousand years,' Fujita once promised his countrymen, 'we will become taller, our skin will become white, and our hair will be blonde'" (Schlosser 2001: 231). Americans, apparently, take a different approach. Playing with Brillat-Savarin's dictum, Donna Gabaccia, in her book *We Are What We Eat: Ethnic Food and the Making of Americans* (1998), thinks that

> our food reveals that we are cosmopolitan and iconoclasts; we are tolerant adventurers who do not feel constrained by tradition. . . . What unites American eaters culturally is how we eat, not what we eat. As eaters, all Americans mingle the culinary traditions of many regions and cultures within ourselves. We are multi-ethnic eaters. (1998: 225–6)

My Turkish friends did not put such a positive spin on this mingling; by eating anything and everything, we reveal we have no culture. The multi-ethnic mixtures in our stomachs make us into mongrels.

What is Food?

Take, for example, the artichoke. Who, coming upon this thorny thing for the first time, could ever have imagined eating it? Indeed. I was 20 before I first saw as well as ate an artichoke; my first meeting with an artichoke coincided with the first meeting of my Bostonian (soon-to-be) in-laws. I do not know which was more intimidating.

We need food to survive, that is a given, but what counts as food? Food, in the United States, has until recently been classified into four food groups: (1) meat, fish, and poultry; (2) grains; (3) dairy products; and (4) fruits and vegetables. In 1991 a physicians' group recommended that this be completely changed and that four new groups be substituted: (1) fruits, (2) legumes (including beans, peanut butter, and soybeans), (3) grains, and (4) vegetables, with meat and dairy products being options. This is also known as a *vegan* diet. While this was not officially adopted, the United States Department of Agriculture (USDA) was in the process of changing its recommendations for a healthy diet, recommendations that greatly reduced the role of meat and dairy products. On April 24, 1991, the USDA sent its proposal, the Eating Right Pyramid, to the printer to replace the food wheel used since the 1950s; the next day, the Agriculture Secretary, Edward R. Madigan, cancelled it. Although he denied it, it is widely suspected that the reason was "because meat and dairy producers objected to what they felt was the pyramid's negative depiction of their products" (Burros, *New York Times*, May 8, 1991). The Department of Agriculture is clearly in a double-bind – needing to promote the nation's health and, at the same time, promoting the health (or is it the wealth?) of the meat and dairy industries. Meat and dairy products are now included in the revised Food Pyramid just below fats, oils, and sugars, implying they should be eaten sparingly (see figure 7.1).

Regardless, the old "meat and potatoes" definition of a main meal is surely changing. Since the débâcle over the Food Pyramid, nutritionists have chosen to talk of the healthy diet as the "Mediterranean diet," which is essentially the same thing as originally proposed by the USDA. "The characteristics of the Mediterranean diet [are] simple 'peasant' food, with emphasis on pastas and breads, grilled fish, fresh fruit and vegetables, red wine, and especially olive oil" (Bell and Valentine 1997: 156). This diet, celebrated in Britain as well as in the United States in restaurants, advertisements, and on supermarket shelves, is thought to be far healthier than what the British and Americans have been eating, and it is also thought to be responsible for the longevity of the Mediterranean peasantry. The popularity of this diet began as more and more British and Americans toured the Mediterranean area, but it is also credited to the well-known British food and cookbook writer Elizabeth David, who was the first to bring a bit of culinary sunshine to the colder northern climes. Nevertheless, it is worthwhile to point out, as did Bell and Valentine, that the whole notion of a "Mediterranean" diet is a *construction* – one that glosses over significant national, ethnic, and local variations. The only things that North African, Syrian, and Greek cuisines have in common are the ingredients, not the culturally distinctive ways they are used to make particular dishes that combine to make a meal.

THE FOOD GUIDE PYRAMID
Number of servings per day

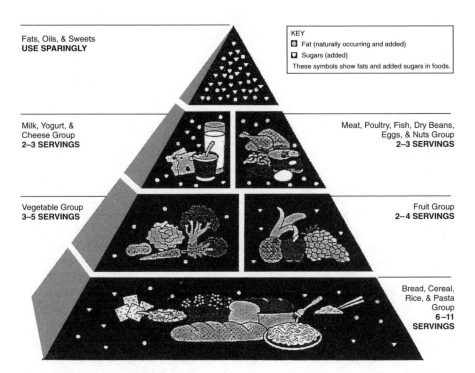

Fats, Oils, & Sweets
USE SPARINGLY

KEY
▢ Fat (naturally occurring and added)
▢ Sugars (added)
These symbols show fats and added sugars in foods.

Milk, Yogurt, &
Cheese Group
2–3 SERVINGS

Meat, Poultry, Fish, Dry Beans,
Eggs, & Nuts Group
2–3 SERVINGS

Vegetable Group
3–5 SERVINGS

Fruit Group
2–4 SERVINGS

Bread, Cereal,
Rice, & Pasta
Group
**6–11
SERVINGS**

Figure 7.1 The USDA Food Pyramid.

Clearly, food is more than a matter of calories, vitamins, and minerals. It is a matter of culture and, within that, of individual preference. What is considered food by one person or one culture is considered inedible to another. "One man's meat is another man's poison," as the old adage succinctly states.

Classification systems

What counts as food in any particular culture, and what foods are preferred or forbidden, is intimately related to a system of classification that, in many cases, has roots in religious prescriptions. According to Genesis, for example, humans as well as animals were originally to be vegetarian.

> Behold, I have given you every herb bearing seed, which is upon the face of all the earth, and every tree, in which is the fruit of a tree yielding seed; to you shall it be for meat.

And to every beast of the earth, and to every fowl of the air, and to every thing that creepeth upon the earth, wherein there is life, I have given every green herb for meat: and it was so. (Genesis 1: 29–30)

But not every fruit was given as food; eating the apple changed the human condition forever (Genesis 3). Only after the Flood and Noah's saving of the animals did God grant them as food.

Leviticus 11: 1–32, 39–47 – Clean and Unclean Animals

11   And the LORD said to Moses and Aaron,[2] "Say to the people of Israel, These are the living things which you may eat among all the beasts that are on the earth.[3] Whatever parts the hoof and is cloven-footed and chews the cud, among the animals, you may eat.[4] Nevertheless among those that chew the cud or part the hoof, you shall not eat these: The camel, because it chews the cud but does not part the hoof, is unclean to you.[5] And the rock badger, because it chews the cud but does not part the hoof, is unclean to you.[6] And the hare, because it chews the cud but does not part the hoof, is unclean to you.[7] And the swine, because it parts the hoof and is cloven-footed but does not chew the cud, is unclean to you.[8] Of their flesh you shall not eat, and their carcasses you shall not touch; they are unclean to you.

9   "These you may eat, of all that are in the waters. Everything in the waters that has fins and scales, whether in the seas or in the rivers, you may eat. [10]But anything in the seas or the rivers that has not fins and scales, of the swarming creatures in the waters and of the living creatures that are in the waters, is an abomination to you.[11] They shall remain an abomination to you; of their flesh you shall not eat, and their carcasses you shall have in abomination.[12] Everything in the waters that has not fins and scales is an abomination to you.

13   "And these you shall have in abomination among the birds, they shall not be eaten, they are an abomination: the eagle, the vulture, the osprey,[14] the kite, the falcon according to its kind,[15] every raven according to its kind,[16] the ostrich, the nighthawk, the sea gull, the hawk according to its kind,[17] the owl, the cormorant, the ibis,[18] the water hen, the pelican, the carrion vulture,[19] the stork, the heron according to its kind, the hoopoe, and the bat.

20   "All winged insects that go upon all fours are an abomination to you. [21]Yet among the winged insects that go on all fours you may eat those which have legs above their feet, with which to leap on the earth.[22] Of them you may eat: the locust according to its kind, the bald locust according to its kind, the cricket according to its kind, and the grasshopper according to its kind.[23] But all other winged insects which have four feet are an abomination to you.

24   "And by these you shall become unclean; whoever touches their carcass shall be unclean until the evening,[25] and whoever carries any part of their carcass

Every moving thing that liveth shall be meat for you; even as the green herb have I given you all things. But flesh with the life thereof, which is the blood thereof, shall ye not eat. (Genesis 9: 3–4)

The last sentence could still be seen as an injunction against eating warm-blooded animals but is, instead, interpreted as only eating meat from which the blood has been drained (as is true in kosher or halal meat). In any case, some contemporary vegetarians believe that we might return to Eden if we would only return to the original vegetarian dispensation.

shall wash his clothes and be unclean until the evening.[26] Every animal which parts the hoof but is not cloven-footed or does not chew the cud is unclean to you; every one who touches them shall be unclean.[27] And all that go on their paws, among the animals that go on all fours, are unclean to you; whoever touches their carcass shall be unclean until the evening,[28] and he who carries their carcass shall wash his clothes and be unclean until the evening; they are unclean to you.

29   "And these are unclean to you among the swarming things that swarm upon the earth: the weasel, the mouse, the great lizard according to its kind, [30]the gecko, the land crocodile, the lizard, the sand lizard, and the chameleon. [31]These are unclean to you among all that swarm; whoever touches them when they are dead shall be unclean until the evening.[32] And anything upon which any of them falls when they are dead shall be unclean, whether it is an article of wood or a garment or a skin or a sack, any vessel that is used for any purpose; it must be put into water, and it shall be unclean until the evening; then it shall be clean. . . .

39   "And if any animal of which you may eat dies, he who touches its carcass shall be unclean until the evening,[40] and he who eats of its carcass shall wash his clothes and be unclean until the evening; he also who carries the carcass shall wash his clothes and be unclean until the evening.

41   "Every swarming thing that swarms upon the earth is an abomination; it shall not be eaten.[42] Whatever goes on its belly, and whatever goes on all fours, or whatever has many feet, all the swarming things that swarm upon the earth, you shall not eat; for they are an abomination.[43] You shall not make yourselves abominable with any swarming thing that swarms; and you shall not defile yourselves with them, lest you become unclean.[44] For I am the LORD your God; consecrate yourselves therefore, and be holy, for I am holy. You shall not defile yourselves with any swarming thing that crawls upon the earth.[45] For I am the LORD who brought you up out of the land of Egypt, to be your God; you shall therefore be holy, for I am holy."

46   This is the law pertaining to beast and bird and every living creature that moves through the waters and every creature that swarms upon the earth,[47] to make a distinction between the unclean and the clean and between the living creature that may be eaten and the living creature that may not be eaten.

I will return to the issue of vegetarianism below; here I wish to direct you to the biblical classification of permitted and tabooed foods first outlined in Leviticus 11 and Deuteronomy 14. The meaning of the lists has perplexed numerous commentators for centuries. A major question has been why did Jews forbid pork? Was it a matter of hygiene, a recognition that occasionally people became ill from eating the meat, or because of the scavenging eating habits of pigs? Anthropologist Mary Douglas, in her famous 1966 essay "The Abominations of Leviticus," took issue with people who explained the prohibitions in terms of hygiene – that is, that there is an underlying medical reason for the prohibition. Douglas calls such people "medical materialists" (1966: 33).

> For Maimonides himself, the great twelfth-century prototype of medical materialism, although he could find hygienic reasons for all the other dietary restrictions of Mosaic law, confessed himself baffled by the prohibition on pork, and was driven back to aesthetic explanations, based on the revolting diet of the domestic pig. (p. 32)

But that is *not* the reason given in the Bible. Indeed, "nothing whatever is said about its dirty scavenging habits" (p. 56). Pig is forbidden because it does not fit into the categories of the classification system – namely, those of cloven-hoofed, cud-chewing animals. Douglas's argument places the food prohibitions in a context of a system of classifications; certain animals are ambiguous or anomalous – they do not fit the system of classifications and thus become tabooed. While "cloven-hoofed, cud-chewing ungulates are the model of the proper kind of food for a pastoralist," a pig is cloven-hoofed but not ruminant. That "is the only reason given in the Old Testament for avoiding the pig" (Douglas 1966: 56). Since it does not fit the classification, it is outlawed. The primary issue about kosher rules is holiness and how to maintain a state of purity. "Holiness requires that individuals shall conform to the class to which they belong. . . . Holiness means keeping distinct the categories of Creation" (p. 54). Clearly, the pig transgressed those lines.

Hers is a very compelling and important argument and points out why people become morally exercised when others purposefully transgress the boundaries; it amounts to sacrilege. However, Douglas's argument does not address the question of what motivates this particular classification; after all, classifications do not exist in nature but are humanly constructed, and there is no objective reason for the classification.[4]

In a very different vein, novelist Jorge Luis Borges poked fun at the seeming naturalness of Western classifications when he suggested that any "creature, instead of belonging to groups like 'insects' or 'amphibians,' could be classified in one of these categories: 1) belonging to the Emperor, 2) embalmed, 3) tame," etc. (Rothstein, *New York Times*, May 12, 2001, A19). While fantastic to our modern scientific sensibilities, this classification does force us to think about how Europeans/Americans categorize the natural world, and why. "Do we create a narrative account, giving each animal a proper place, as in the biblical story of creation? Is there a hierarchy in our orderings, in which we judge animals by their usefulness to us or by their place in an evolutionary ladder?" (ibid.). Why should humans be at the top of the ladder? Do other people organize the world this way? If not, why not, and what are the implications?

British animals

Edmund Leach, another British anthropologist, made an attempt to decipher the classification of animals, not of Genesis, but of the British. Although the focus of his article "Anthropological Aspects of Language: Animal Categories and Verbal Abuse" (1964), discussed in chapter 4, is on the issue of taboo, his analysis depended on the classification system of food. He noted that while there is "a vast range of materials which are both edible and nourishing, . . . only a small part of this edible environment will actually be classified as potential food. Such classification is a matter of language and culture, not of nature" (1964: 30–1). He went on to distinguish three major categories:

1   Edible substances that are recognized as food and consumed as part of the normal diet.
2   Edible substances that are recognized as possible food, but that are prohibited or else allowed to be eaten only under special (ritual) conditions. These are substances which are *consciously tabooed*.
3   Edible substances that by culture and language are not recognized as food at all. These substances are *unconsciously tabooed* (Leach 1964: 31).

The difference between 2 and 3 is illustrated by the contrast between the Jewish prohibition on eating pork with the English objection to eating dog. In the first case, it is admitted that pork is food but Jews will not eat it, while the second case depends on a categorical assumption that dogs are *not* food (p. 32), even though they are perfectly edible and, in some places, are bred for food. Marshall Sahlins, an American anthropologist, does a *cultural* analysis of animals and food.

American logic

Animals who share our beds and table are like "one of the family" and it would be unthinkable to eat them. According to Sahlins:

> America is the land of the sacred dog. . . . They roam the streets of major American cities at will, taking their masters about on leashes and depositing their excrements at pleasure on curbs and sidewalks. A whole system of sanitation procedures had to be employed to get rid of the mess. . . . Within houses and apartments, dogs climb upon chairs designed for humans, sleep in people's beds, and sit at table after their own fashion awaiting their share of the family meal. All this in the calm assurance that they themselves will never be sacrificed to necessity or deity, nor eaten even in the case of accidental death. (1976: 171–2)

His analysis of the American food system goes beyond the classificatory systems constructed by Douglas and Leach by considering the *meanings* of the categories and associations. His book *Culture and Practical Reason* (1976) is a major critique of economic explanations for cultural phenomena. One of the most telling examples he presents concerns food, specifically beef.

Why is it that beef, especially in the form of steak, is the most prized and the most expensive cut of meat even though "its absolute supply is much greater than that of tongue" (p. 176)? Doesn't this contradict one of the fundamental premises of economic rationality based on notions of supply and demand whereby scarcity is related to price? Steak is not the scarce item. Nor is there a natural desire for steak since many people(s) do not eat it and find it repulsive. "Taste," says Nick Fiddes in his book *Meat: A Natural Symbol*, "reflects rather than explains preferences" (1991: 6), and is related to an entire cosmology – distinctive views of how and what the world is.

It is "symbolic logic which organizes demand" (p. 175) according to Marshall Sahlins, not economic rationality, or, rather, economic rationality follows symbolic logic. For example, he points out that "innards" – liver, kidney, heart, and intestine – like tongue, are scarce in relation to steak, but they are cheap. He also notices how we disguise the provenance of muscle meat with terms like steak, chuck, roast, and chops but refer to internal organs by the same terms we use for human organs. "Edibility is inversely related to humanity" (p. 175), Sahlins claims, thus people who eat innards – who are most often poor and most often black – can be seen as less than human, and the entire meat system can be seen as a sustained metaphor on race, class, and cannibalism. "Black is in American society as the savage among us" (p. 176) – "us" here referring to white middle-class Americans. Blacks, however, subvert and recoup this ascription when they rename innards "Soul Food."

While there is always some play in the system, we must not be lulled into thinking such classification systems are merely play, for "the symbolic scheme of edibility joins with that organizing the relations of production to precipitate, through income distribution and demand, an entire totemic order, uniting in a parallel series of differences the status of persons and what they eat" (Sahlins 1976: 176). That is, the scheme of edibility is a way of naturalizing and reinforcing class and ethnic differences.

Artichokes were a west coast vegetable having been introduced by Italians who emigrated to the area around Half Moon Bay, California, now known as the artichoke capital of the world.

The artichoke with which I began this section is a useful example of the way food can index status or class. In the 1960s when I first encountered one, artichokes were exotic and relatively rare on the east coast; I do not recall seeing them on the shelves of standard supermarkets. Being able to appreciate them, knowing where to find them, how to cook and how to eat them was a sign of elite status – of having what Pierre Bourdieu calls "cultural capital." At that memorable luncheon, I was made aware, without any word being spoken, that I was clearly and obviously outclassed.

What Makes a Meal?

Just as what counts as food is related to a classification system, so too are meals and menus. Is a hotdog bought from a street vendor and eaten on the street considered a meal? What if you add french fries and a coke? What about pizza ordered in? In order to understand what a meal is, one first needs to think about it in contrast with all the other ways food may be obtained and eaten, and second, to consider the kinds of food that make a meal, the places a meal may be eaten and with whom. In "Deciphering a Meal" (1975), Mary Douglas began at home – in Britain and with her own family.

> Between breakfast and the last nightcap, the food of the day comes in an ordered pattern. Between Monday and Sunday, the food of the week is patterned again. Then there is the sequence of holidays and fast days through the year, to say nothing of life cycle feasts, birthdays, and weddings. (Douglas 1975: 251)

The classification of meals consists not just in their order – in the day, the week, and the year – but also in the kinds of foods appropriate for each meal and the kinds of people with whom one "breaks bread."

In Britain there are, according to Douglas, "two major contrasted food categories . . . meals versus drinks. . . . Meals are a mixture of solid foods accompanied by liquids. With drinks the reverse holds" (pp. 254–5). Both the meal category and "drinks" category have names: breakfast, lunch, supper, cocktails, or tea. The drinks category is, appropriately, more fluid and is not nearly as structured as a meal. It also often involves standing rather than sitting at a table.

The food categories also correlate with social categories. "Drinks are for strangers, acquaintances, workmen, and family. Meals are for family, close friends, honored guests. The grand operator of the system is the line between intimacy and distance" (p. 256). As we noted in chapter 5, French people find the American custom of inviting newly met acquaintances home to dinner very odd; conversely, Americans think the French are very cold and unfriendly because they rarely invite their new (American) friends to dinner in their homes. Being invited to a French home for dinner marks a significant shift in the quality of the relationship that might not be appreciated by an American guest for whom such behavior seems normal.

In India, caste membership will determine those with whom one may eat. Among the upper classes in Britain and France (and no doubt elsewhere), children do not regularly eat with their parents, and in quite a number of societies men and women do not eat together. In addition,

> Meals properly require the use of at least one mouth-entering *utensil* per head, whereas drinks are limited to mouth-touching ones. . . . Meals require a *table*, a *seating* order, *restriction* on movement and on alternative occupations. There is no question of knitting during a meal. . . . (Furthermore), a meal is not a meal if it is all in the bland-sweet-sour dimensions. A meal incorporates a number of contrasts, hot and cold, bland and spiced, liquid and semi-liquid, and various textures. It also incorporates cereals, vegetables, and animal proteins. (Douglas 1975: 255–6; emphasis mine)

Before turning to the food and menus, let us briefly explore some of the conditions that make a meal a meal.

Setting the table

Douglas began with "mouth-entering utensil," of which chopsticks would qualify, but there are some peoples who use their fingers or bread to scoop food. The

Breakfast Around the World

What follows are traditional, or culturally dominant, menus in each culture. It by no means assumes that all people in each culture eat these meals, nor does it deny that many people go hungry and have no breakfast, let alone other meals.

United States

A common breakfast is orange juice, cold cereal with milk and sometimes fruit, and coffee. Alternatives: (a) toast or English muffin with butter and jam; (b) bacon and eggs and toast. (Some people get all of these combined in an Egg McMuffin.) On weekends Americans sometimes merge breakfast and lunch and call it *brunch*. This meal includes more elaborately prepared and presented foods: an omelet instead of just eggs, various cold meats or smoked salmon, bagels and cream cheese. Some people serve champagne at this meal, sometimes mixed with orange juice and called a "mimosa." Restaurants have capitalized on the craze for brunch and offer a veritable cornucopia of foods, lavishly presented.

Turkey

A *sine qua non* of a proper Turkish breakfast is bread, as it is of every meal. Indeed, food is equated with bread. Turks do not say: "have you eaten (food)?" they say "*ekmek edin mi?*"—have you eaten bread? In the city the *kapacı* (resident doorman) goes out for bread (crusty sour-dough type bread) every morning and delivers to each apartment in the building; in the village, round flat breads (like a large English muffin) are warmed up and eaten with white feta-like cheese, olives, tomatoes, and cucumbers in season. Sometimes in the village we would also have peppers, potatoes, and onions fried in olive oil—one of my favorites.

manner of eating will also indicate quite a lot about the cultural notions of proper food. However, for the purposes of this discussion, the example of a meal in my mind will be one familiar to Europeans and Americans and includes forks, knives, and spoons. That leads one to think of the industries behind every meal. *First* are the manufacturers who produce the utensils, whether of stainless steel or sterling silver. Among the elite sterling silver is essential, a place setting includes far more than the three items above, and there is an intricate etiquette involved in the appropriate placing of each item. Among each type of flatware there are hundreds, if not thousands, of patterns, and a huge amount of money is spent on advertising them. Women, in particular, are advised to choose a pattern so that when they get married they can register it at various gift stores.

Second are the manufacturers of dinnerware, for in addition to utensils you need dishes to put the food on. Again, the distinctions and patterns are numerous and a

Japan

I was surprised to see a Japanese breakfast available at a hotel in Istanbul, Turkey. It consisted of miso soup, steamed spinach leaves, rice, grilled fillet of salmon, and green tea. I asked a Japanese anthropologist if this is a traditional Japanese breakfast. She said she would add eggs and pickles.

The Netherlands

Dark (wheat) bread, cold ham and a variety of cheeses, butter and jam. One of my favorites is a honey-spice loaf cake but now I hear it is intended primarily for children. Today my informants tell me that many people have shifted to corn-flakes and other cereals.

Bhutan

A Bhutanese friend informs me that traditional breakfast among more well-to-do Bhutanese who live in the western part of the country is rice, dried yak meat, and butter tea (a mixture of tea, salt, butter, and baking soda). Farmers in the eastern part tend to be poorer and eat rice with pepper curry mixed with cheese. They only drink butter tea on special occasions because it is expensive and instead drink sugared tea without milk.

Ivory Coast

Among the Beng breakfast could consist of leftover *foufou* (cooked yams pounded into a ball) with sauce or corn porridge sweetened with ripe bananas. If people have money they might buy a loaf of French bread from a local trader and serve it with freshly made peanut butter.

lot is communicated wordlessly about class, income, taste, and lifestyle depending on the china used at a particular meal. For example, many middle- and upper-class families have several sets of china – fine china for fancy dinner parties and pottery dishes for everyday fare. Some people are fortunate to be given or to inherit as a family heirloom, passed down from one generation to another, a set of china or sil-verware, or both.

The *third* industry that provisions a dinner table is the makers of glassware – lead crystal versus ordinary glass, stemware versus tumblers. *Fourth* are the makers of table linens, of which only some are actually made of linen, many more are made of cotton and synthetic fabrics and, today, even plastic. In this category, there are tablecloths as well as placemats, and each, generally, denotes the level of formality.

Figure 7.2   A place setting from a homeware catalogue.

The *fifth* industry involved in making a meal is furniture. Picnics notwithstanding, a proper meal generally demands a table: indeed, witness the oxymoron "picnic table." Some people eat at a table in the kitchen while others eat in a dining room; usually the type of table is different. In the 1950s for instance, the big new thing was a Formica-topped kitchen table. Its selling point was that it wouldn't stain as does wood, it didn't need polishing, and it was easy to clean. At my house and among those of my acquaintances, dining rooms and dining tables were reserved for special holiday dinners or when other people were invited. Dining tables more typically are of wood, though sometimes of glass.

Turkish villagers, at least where I worked, did not eat at tables. Instead, they sat on the floor around a large copper tray raised off the floor by a small round wooden support. A cloth was placed beneath the tray and each person picked up an edge to cover his or her legs and clothes; that is, it functioned as a napkin. Often we did not use plates, but each person had his or her own spoon or fork and simply took food from the communal dish. All family members sat around the tray; but in some villages men ate first and then the women and children.

Seating arrangements in American families (when they eat together) generally include every family member unless small children eat first and are put to bed before the "grown-ups" eat. A traditional seating plan has the head of the household, usually the father, sitting at the head of the table; most other family members have their regular seats. At a dinner party, the host or hostess often pays considerable attention to the seating plan and tries to put people with similar interests together, and also to alternate by sex.

All this before we even get to the food served. And I have not yet even mentioned the work in the background, the preparation and cooking. There is a vast industry that supplies cooking utensils – the pots and pans and mixers and processors and stoves and microwaves. Not surprisingly these items, too, have myriad producers, prices, and designs, and, again, these differences often relate to class and income, lifestyle and taste. There is no room to go into detail in this fascinating area; I state this merely to draw attention to the vast areas for research in relation to food besides the food itself. It is clear that what makes a meal a meal involves much more than merely food.

In addition to a table, the setting and the seating, Douglas claimed there is a "restriction on movement and on alternative occupations." People are meant to keep seated while at table, though children often get restive and are sometimes "excused" early. Douglas's definition would seem to exclude those who listen to music or the radio or watch television, as is the case among Turks both rural and urban, while they eat. Would she consider it a meal if you eat alone? Would you?

The inclusion of a seating order in Mary Douglas's definition of a meal seems to imply that a real meal involves more than one person. Sociologist Janet Flammang is more explicit: "Table conversation is an art of give and take, where we think before we speak so we do not disrupt the pleasures and sharing of the group" (forthcoming). She believes that the "table is where we learn the art of conversation, especially across generations, learn to feel connected, and learn to trust ourselves and others." For her,

> [C]ivility at the table is a cornerstone of civil society and democratic process. . . . A democratic process is deliberative: people think and give reasons for what they think in trying to persuade others to agree with them. People will be more persuasive to the degree that they understand both what they think and what others think. This mutual self- and other-understanding comes primarily from conversations,

and people begin to learn this as children sitting with the family at mealtimes. This is clearly an idealistic view of the family dinner table, for there are numerous families where dinner times are tension ridden and conversation is minimal.

Nevertheless, the model she presents conveys an important message at a time when American families, of whatever type, are spending less time together and hardly ever eat together anymore. Flammang believes there is a relationship between the breakdown in family dining and the breakdown in civility. Her forthcoming book *Women and the Politics of Food* explores the social costs and the possible alternatives that do not depend on putting women back in the kitchen nor assume that women's lives have been improved by staying out of it. Instead, she advocates that we all need to become more involved with food and its preparation. Now that the table is set and the people are gathered around it, let us move on to the food, to the actual components of a meal.

Menu

Any discussion of meals entails a discussion of the menu. Not only do menus vary considerably cross-culturally, but "there is an implicit order governing the idea of what constitutes a meal both in terms of appropriate foodstuffs and the order of eating them" (James 1990: 676). We do not begin with dessert, as every child who wants ice cream first quickly learns. The order will depend on what type of meal it is: a quick breakfast on a weekday or the "soup to nuts" menu (soup, fish course, meat course, salad, cheese, dessert, coffee, nuts, cordials) considered appropriate for elite dinner parties. As a Fulbright fellow in Belgium, I was treated to several very elegant meals where the courses were separated by sorbets to cleanse the palate.

For each item in the order there are acceptable substitutions: for the soup course one might substitute a cream soup for consommé, and for the fish course one could have halibut, tuna, or salmon. All are equally fish, and each can be prepared in any number of ways. The same rule applies to all courses. Among some people color is important – one would not want every food in the meal to be the same color. I recall one home meal in Belgium where everything was kind of whitish – the soup, endive, rice, white fish! Although it did not taste bland, it looked that way; I felt it was unappealing.

There are some meals where substitutions can only be made in very narrow compass. Holidays have special foods though these may vary by region, ethnicity, and family. For example, my family always had roast beef and Yorkshire pudding for Christmas, but many others had duck or turkey. Some people have spring lamb at Easter, perhaps symbolic of the "paschal lamb," but others have ham, something that seems to me a direct affront to Jews especially when Passover occurs around the same time. Gillian Feeley-Harnik, anthropologist at the University of Michigan, explores the way food became a means for the emerging theological differences between Jews and early Christians in her 1981 book *The Lord's Table: Eucharist and Passover in Early Christianity*.

Thanksgiving is a major holiday in the United States. The story we are told is that the Pilgrims instituted this to thank the Native Americans for helping them through a terrible winter. While they did have a harvest celebration in October 1621, there were hardly any Native Americans left around Plymouth because the Pawtuxet who lived there had been wiped out by an epidemic. While the Pilgrims did continue to hold harvest feasts, it did not become a national holiday until it was proclaimed by Abraham Lincoln in 1863. "It can be read as a first salvo in his re-election campaign . . . and of our bloody crucible as a people, [during] the Civil War" (Quinn, *New York Times*, November 24, 1994).[5]

The Thanksgiving meal has been represented by whole roasted and stuffed turkey along with gravy, cranberry sauce, pearl onions, yellow squash, a green vegetable, salad, and pumpkin pie. An article in the *New York Times* just before Thanksgiving in the year 2000 featured innovations being made by different people around the country. For example, a family in Georgia served *fried* turkey and turnip greens, while a Vietnamese family in California stuffed their *brined* turkey with shitake mushrooms and lotus seeds, and a gay couple in Massachusetts *replaced* turkey with a crown roast of pork stuffed with brandied dried fruit and sausage. The article concluded: "That's what makes the holiday so great. After all, this is America. You're free to create your own traditions" (Hesser, *New York Times*, November 15, B1). I am not so sure. Is it still Thanksgiving without a turkey?[6] Meanwhile, Chinese immigrants from Fujian Province now living in New York City use the day "for the new tradition of a Thanksgiving Day matrimonial marathon" (Sachs, *New York Times*, November 29, 2002) accompanied by traditional Chinese wedding banquets.

Main meal

Douglas's family rejected soup and pudding as a meal because it has only "a begin-ning and an end and no middle" (1975: 250), the implication being that the main meal must consist of, at least, three courses. Meat is at the center of the main meal in both Britain and the United States. In Britain, according to Douglas (1975) and James (1990), meat could be fish and either should be accompanied by two veget-ables. In the United States, until recently, the main meal had to have "meat and pota-toes" with vegetables or salad on the side. For many people in both Britain and the United States, a meal of only vegetables is not a meal at all. But why? The answer appears obvious – meat is "high in strength-giving protein, and simply because when cooked it tastes good and is satisfying" (Fiddes, 1991: 1), but, as noted, plenty of people flourish with little or no meat and taste is surely a matter of culture and upbringing. Growing up in the 1940s and 1950s, I simply assumed that a proper evening meal con-sisted of meat (including occasionally fish or poultry), potatoes or other starch, and a vegetable. Once learned as a "proper meal," the habit is dif-ficult to break, and to this day, I tend to follow that pattern except for occa-sional pasta dishes or a stew that would combine all in one dish. Dessert, in those days, at least at my house, was relatively simple – fruit, often canned, or jello, and when we got a freezer, ice cream.

> In the 1950s home freezers changed the foodways of American households. I recall my mother ordering a "side of beef" to be cut into chops, steaks, and roasts in suitable portions for our family of six and put in the freezer until needed; vegetables were no longer canned but frozen and soon could be bought in packages already frozen.

But why meat?

Many of us, and the society in general, consider meat eating normal; it is part of our *habitus*, of what we take for granted. Yet recall the biblical injunction against meat eating (see p. 279). We tend to think that only vegetarianism is ideological; it is much more difficult for us to realize that meat eating is also ideological for it embodies ideas, categories, and values that *go without saying*. Fiddes shows that vegetarianism is not substantively defined but is defined only in relation to meat eating; it is the avoidance of meat eating.

Building on the work of Douglas, Leach, Sahlins, and others, Nick Fiddes argues that "our use of meat as food reflects our categorization of, and our relations towards, animal competitors, companions, and resources . . . that it tangibly represents human control of the natural world" (1991: 2). This idea has been with cultures influenced by the Bible for a very long time. Recall the biblical license: "Let them have dominion over the fish of the sea, and over the birds of the air, and over the cattle, and over all the earth, and over every creeping thing that creeps upon the earth" (Genesis 1: 24). Fiddes continues: "Consuming the muscle flesh of other highly evolved animals is a potent statement of our supreme power" (1991: 2). Incorporating their flesh, we consume their power.

Of Meat and Men

"People with power have always eaten meat" (Adams 1991: 26), and that implies not just class distinctions but also gender distinctions. While Sahlins barely mentions the association of men and meat in his discussion, this is the main theme in the work of both Nick Fiddes and Carol Adams. There are two major dimensions I wish to discuss *vis-à-vis* gender and meat; first, the idea that women *are* meat, and second, that men, in many cultures, have traditionally had rights to meat.

Some of the gender symbolism of meat eating may have begun with "Man the Hunter," or at least the cultural myth and ideology of man the hunter. We do not eat lion meat, according to Fiddes, because it would blur the categories of Man the Hunter and Lion the Hunter. This seems a better reason than the one given by Leach, who said we don't eat lions because they are wild, beyond our pale. In any case, Man the Hunter is portrayed dragging home the meat. When this is combined with the idea that women are meat, we get the numerous cartoons of primitive man dragging home a woman by the hair. "Man is the hunter; woman is his game" (Tennyson, cited in Fiddes 1991: 144), a statement that casts all men as sexual predators.

There are numerous words that can be applied indiscriminately to either food or women, e.g. appetizing, delicious, succulent. Fiddes notes how Alex Comfort named his *Joy of Sex* after the classic American cookbook bible *The Joy of Cooking* (Rombauer and Rombauer Becker, 1931), including chapter titles that continue the culinary metaphor: Starters, Main Courses, Sauces and Pickles (Fiddes 1991: 144). The symbolic equation of women with food, and specifically, meat, can have violent implications. Adams tells how she came across what seemed at first sight to be a typical meat diagram in a Boston meat market – the kind that outlines where the rib, chuck, loin, rump part of meat come from – except on closer inspection, the diagram was a woman's body. Might there be a connection, she asks, between the butchering and dismembering of animals and the killing and dismemberment of women's bodies by men? I recall that a cover of *Hustler* magazine depicted a woman's body going head first through a meat grinder.

Meat is associated with strength and virility, but if women *are* meat, then just whose strength are men incorporating when they eat it? Oddly, this contradiction has not been noticed or commented on by the authors cited. But the associations between meat and masculinity may also be why some people think that vegetarian men are gay; after all, *Real Men Don't Eat Quiche* (Feirstein, 1982). The association between men and meat is no doubt behind the prominence of meat on the training tables of athletes and soldiers. During World War II, for example, the consumption of meat by what Russell Baker called the "American warrior" was "about two-and-a-half times that of the average citizen" (Adams 1991: 32).

In patriarchal societies, men often eat their meals first and, thus, get "the lion's share" of the choicest cuts of meat while women get the leftovers. Turkey is a patriarchal society, and in the village where I worked people ate little meat at regular daily meals – sometimes a bit of minced meat in a stew. Although it was a fairly prosperous village, most people could not afford to each much meat. Since meat was intended for the market, whatever they ate meant that much less to sell and thus less income. But at special feasts such as weddings, or before a few villagers were to leave on the *hajj* (pilgrimage) to Mecca, a number of sheep were slaughtered and roasted, and the whole village gathered for the meal. However, on these occasions, men ate together and ate *before* the women who served them. The delicious smell wafted over the village making everyone hungry for their share. Often there was little left by the time the women and children were ready to eat. Having not had much meat for several months, I can still recall my lust as well as my guilt as I fell upon my portion of the roasted lamb which I, as an "honored guest," was served in their midst.

Not all patriarchal societies are meat eating, however. India is a patriarchal society but, among Hindus, cows are sacred and are not eaten. A Hindu student made the interesting suggestion that the "Mad Cow disease" scare in Britain is a kind of revenge for the way they colonized and incorporated India in their commonwealth.

When meat is scarce, it is usually women who go without even when they are pregnant or nursing – a time when they need it more than men. Most of the women in "my" village were anemic. "Meat is a constant for men, intermittent for women, a pattern painfully observed in famine situations today. Women are starving at a rate disproportionate to men" (Adams 1991: 26; see also Fiddes 1991: 158ff.). In many countries, women do without meat, and in Britain and the United States, one occasionally hears news reports of "domestic abuse," i.e. wife beating, if the man of the house did not get meat for his dinner.

In addition to the supposed need of meat for strength, men are also thought to need it for "brain food." This idea and the statement below depend on the prior categorization that men do *head* work while women do *hand* work. George Beard, a nineteenth-century medical doctor influenced by Darwin, advocated that:

In proportion as man grows sensitive through civilization or through disease, he should diminish the quantity of cereals and fruits, which are far below him on the scale of evolution, and increase the quantity of animal food, which is nearly related to him in the scale of evolution, and therefore more easily assimilated. (Cited in Adams 1991: 30)

This ideological statement has little to do with nutrition, and the assimilation of animal flesh is not easier for humans than the assimilation of plants. Instead, his evolutionary schema seems to follow more closely biblical valuations: recall that when Cain "brought of the fruit of the ground an offering unto the Lord" (Genesis 4: 3), God had no respect but instead preferred Abel's offering of a "firstling of the flock." Cain became angry and, as the story goes, rose up and killed his brother. However, no reason is ever given for God's preference. Personally, I think that the story symbolizes the tension between the practices and beliefs of the agricultural-ists of Mesopotamia and the nomadic pastoralists who were, through Abraham, to become the "chosen people" of God. The chosen food symbolized the people chosen.

Food and Worldview

Food is intimately related to religion/worldview whether it is biblical, Hindu, Buddhist, Hopi, or even that promoted by the "health food" movement. Anthro-pologist Jill Dubisch investigated the health food movement in the United States and claimed that the analysis of its "underlying world view reveals that, as a system of beliefs and practices, the health food movement has some of the characteristics of a religion" ([1981] 1997: 62). Its roots go back to mid-nineteenth-century "hygien-ists" such as Sylvester Graham, of graham cracker fame, who "preached that good health was to be found in temperate living. This included abstinence from alcohol, a vegetarian diet, consumption of whole wheat products, and regular exercise" (p. 63) – quite a contrast to Beard, who wrote somewhat later, after Darwin's work was published.

The health food movement resurfaced in the counter-cultural 1960s. According to Dubisch, becoming part of the movement often involves a kind of "conversion experience," perhaps one that includes healing from an ailment. Such an experience demands a reorganization of one's kitchen and also one's life; it demands a psy-chological reorientation – a different way of perceiving the world and one's own place in it. It

> means learning and accepting the general features of the health food world view. To begin with, there is great concern, as there is in many religions, with purity, in this case, the purity of food, of water, of air. In fact, there are some striking similarities between keeping a "health food kitchen" and the Jewish practice of keeping kosher. Both make distinctions between proper and improper foods, and both involve exclud-ing certain impure foods (whether unhealthful or non-kosher) from the kitchen and table. In addition, a person concerned with maintaining a high degree of purity in food may engage in similar behavior in either case – reading labels carefully to check for impermissible ingredients and even purchasing food from special establishments to guarantee ritual purity. (p. 64)

Devotees of health food categorize food either as "health food" or "junk food"; the former is believed to promote well-being and bestow *mana* (a kind of beneficial

Figure 7.3   An apple as "health food".

power), while the latter is *taboo* and, if eaten, conveys malignant power. Foods that are felt to be health promoting are dark bread instead of white, honey instead of sugar, yogurt instead of ice cream, and tofu or soybeans in place of beef. Especially singled out for opprobrium are McDonald's hamburgers, french fries, and coke – the "all-American" favorites.

Health food is not just about achieving a healthy body – it is a way of establishing a healthy relationship with society and getting in tune with the universe. Growing your own food, baking your own bread, perhaps raising a cow and making cheese are thought to foster independence and self-reliance – a pioneer ethos. Emotional, spiritual, and social problems are linked to nutrition, and at the cosmic level, health food is allied with nature and is life affirming while junk food is a symbol and symptom of a death-oriented destructive culture (p. 67). In many ways the movement is nostalgic – harking "back to a 'golden age' which it seeks to recreate and assumes that many of the ills of the contemporary world are caused by society's departure from this ideal state" (p. 69) – Eden, once again.

Fast food

At the opposite end of the food spectrum from "health food" is "fast food." Fast food, itself, is not new if one considers street kebabs in Turkey, fish and chips in Britain, noodles in China, and station box lunches in Japan. What is new is the standardization and automation. "During a relatively brief period of time, the fast food industry has helped to transform not only the American diet, but also our landscape, economy, workforce, and popular culture" (Schlosser 2001: 3). In his extraordinary book, *Fast Food Nation: The Dark Side of the All-American Meal* (2001), Eric Schlosser has meticulously documented the ways that the quintessential American meal, namely a hamburger and fries, has changed our relation to food, the environment, and each other. While most of us take "fast food" for granted and find it convenient, few of us know anything about the history and the darker side of the industry and the consequences for our society as a whole.

Horn and Hardart's "automat" might also be classified as fast food. The restaurant had tables and chairs but its walls were lined with what were really vending machines: the food was already prepared and put in little window boxes. You selected your choice, put in the money, and got your food. There was a lot more choice in a typical automat than at a fast food restaurant today. The first automat opened in 1902; they were popular during the Depression and were still in operation when I was a child (in the 1940s) and visited them in New York with my grandmother.

The origins of the fast food industry are set in late 1940s and early 1950s in California and are bound up with the increasing use of automobiles and, thus, the need for restaurants to be located on the road and outside the city centers. Carl Karcker, the founder of Carl's Jr., first began with a hot dog stand; later he opened a drive-in restaurant as did the McDonald brothers. But sometime in 1948 the McDonald brothers transformed their operation. Not only did they reduce the number of items on their menu, basically to hamburgers, french fries, and milkshakes; they also replaced dishes and glassware with paper cups and plates. In addition, they

> divided the food preparation into separate tasks performed by different workers. To fill a typical order, one person grilled the hamburger; another "dressed" and wrapped it; another prepared the milk shake; made the fries; and another worked the counter. For the first time, the guiding principles of a factory assembly line were applied to a commercial kitchen. The new division of labor meant that a worker only had to be taught how to perform one task. (Schlosser 2001: 20)

> The McDonald brothers' system caught the attention of Ray Kroc, who convinced them to sell him the franchise rights to spread McDonald's across the nation and eventually the world.

This deskilling of workers was touted as a benefit for anyone wishing to set up a franchise since it was more difficult to find skilled cooks. Their Speedee Service system transformed the restaurant business and was quickly imitated by others such as Carl's Jr., Burger King, and Kentucky Fried Chicken, but it is McDonald's that symbolizes the phenomenon, as

Figure 7.4   Food automat, 977 Eighth Avenue, Manhattan, 1936. Photo by Berenice Abbott/ Museum of the City of New York.

Figure 7.5   Cartoon by Pete Mueller, 'I'm optional, you're optional, fries are not'. © Pete Mueller.

its use in new words such as McDonaldization, McWorld, McThink, McDollars, or, in negative mode, McGarbage, McGreedy, and McProfits, indicates.

A new McDonald's opens every 3 hours and there are now more than 28,000 worldwide.[7] "The company annually hires about a million people, more than any other American organization, public or private" (Schlosser 2001: 4). If true, that is a depressing statistic that does not bode well for the future workforce. While some people deplore McDonald's food and work tactics, the behavior of numerous others, according to Conrad Kottak (1982), reveals that it functions not only as a place to get a fast meal, but also as almost a sacred site (with golden arches and, in some places, stained-glass windows), a pilgrimage destination, and a refuge, especially when one is in unfamiliar territory. And I confess that once in Paris, the mecca of wonderful food, I slipped into a McDonald's just to feel "at home" – to hear English and to have a familiar "quarter-pounder with special sauce," a coke, and french fries! And discovered that it had become, at least among young people, a trendy place to gather.

Despite its enormous success and increasing popularity, some people fear the "Americanization" of the world and worry that it "threatens a fundamental aspect of national identity: how, where, and what people choose to eat" (Schlosser 2001: 44). It counters this by being extremely pliable and by adapting local tastes, for example: McDöner (Turkish döner kebab in Germany), McChao (fried rice in China), and McLaks (grilled salmon in Norway), and in Israel Big Macs have no cheese in respect for kosher diet that separates meat and milk products (Watson 1997).

Margaret Visser, a Canadian classicist who turned her attention to food in her 1986 book *Much Depends on Dinner*, thinks the popularity of these "standardized mass-produced processed dishes" might be an expression of democracy, "for nothing more directly expresses our loathing for hierarchy than the pre-cut, pre-coated, ground and reconstituted portions – often computer calculated to be *equal* – which we get as fast-food" (Visser, quoted in interview with Trish Hall, *New York Times*, June 15, 1988). She may have a point, but this is a cookie-cutter image of democracy; equal doesn't always mean, or need to mean, the same. Equal *access* to good food might be a better expression of democracy.

In the year 2000 Americans spent more than $110 billion on fast food; it is more than they spend "on higher education, personal computers, computer software, or new cars. They spend more on fast food than on movies, books, magazines, newspapers, videos, and recorded music – combined" (Schlosser 2001: 3). Americans are hungry. Schlosser continues: "On any given day in the United States about one-quarter of the adult population visits a fast food restaurant," and so do millions of children who are, increasingly, the targets of advertising. Virtually all children in the United States know about McDonald's, and most have probably visited one not once but many times, some several times a week. However, children who early on become accustomed to, if not addicted to, fast food do not easily abandon it. Obesity in children and in the general population has paralleled the growth of the fast food industry, and the same is true in other nations after they have introduced fast food. Schlosser does not claim fast food is the only cause, but it is certainly a contributing one; nevertheless, obesity contributes to and exacerbates numerous health problems which, in turn, contribute to the rising health care costs.

The enormous demand for meat and potatoes, even in these new forms, has a concomitantly enormous impact on our environment. According to Sahlins: "The exploitation of the American environment, the mode of relation to the landscape, *depends on the model of a meal* that includes a central meat element" (1976: 171). What he means by this is that an enormous amount of land (80 percent of the arable land in comparison with a mere 3 percent taken up by cities) is devoted to feed grains for cattle and their pasturage, "[a]ll of which would change overnight if we ate dogs" (Sahlins 1976: 171), became vegetarian, or adopted the diet recently proposed by the USDA.[8] What Sahlins is trying to get across is that there is nothing of economic rationality in the use of our lands. Rather, the use is determined by the cultural logic of foods and meals and the meaningful distinctions and identities we create.

Another issue related to the land concerns how the fast food industry has changed the *way* the food is grown. In a very short period of time, a few companies have managed to buy out, take over, and dominate the production of both beef and potatoes, a process that has forced thousands of small farmers into virtual *serfdom* for the large agribusinesses or out of business and a life. Quite a number of these people have committed suicide because of the end of their way of life and the farm which had been in their family for generations. "The suicide rate among ranchers and farmers in the United States is now about three times higher than the national average" (Sahlins 1976: 146). This tragedy was borne out by anthropologist Eric Ramirez, whose dissertation research was devoted to this problem in Oklahoma (2001).

Another human tragedy unfolds with the workers in the "modern" slaughterhouses. No longer butchers, a highly skilled occupation, these workers have been demoted to manning one particular station at one particular instant in the assembly line. It is now perhaps one of the most dangerous jobs in the United States; most of the workers are immigrants, have no benefits, but risk life and limb every day. Because of the speed-up in the production process, there is also much more room for accidents such as the spillage from intestines that can contaminate an entire line of meat. Such meat will not necessarily be disposed of but may easily end up in restaurants and even schools, as we learn only after the fact, after incidents of food poisoning get reported in the news.

The human tragedy is paralleled by what happens to the cattle. Traditionally, cattle were raised in pastures calculated as 30 acres for each head of cattle; today, in part because of the rising costs of land for real estate but also because of the value of *efficiency*, most of the cattle are housed in pens where they can barely move and where they are stuffed full of chemicals, hormones, and feed other than the grasses of their normal diet. Cows are vegetarian, yet feed companies have been using the waste parts of animals, including the nerves and brains, in their feed, a procedure that has been definitely linked to bovine spongiform encephalopathy (BSE), otherwise known as Mad Cow disease. When the cattle are fattened up, they are put on conveyor belts into the slaughterhouse where one is killed and processed every minute. No wonder there are accidents and spillage.

Where does all this automation and speed-up lead? Because of the way cattle are raised and processed, the food has little taste. Whatever taste there is is derived from chemical additives, often made at perfume factories. The same is true for the fries. McDonald's used to fry their potatoes in 93 percent beef tallow which gave them their distinctive taste. However, they did not disclose this fact, and after being sued by a group of vegetarians they switched to vegetable oil, but continue to use chemical additives to simulate the smell of the former fries.

This overview is far too brief, but I hope it is enough to whet your appetite for more information. Fast food has changed our lives; not only *what* we eat, *how* we eat, and *where* we eat, but it has also contributed to a deterioration of land and farming, compassion for workers and animals, and in the patterns of civility that accompany dining. In the long run that may be its most deleterious effect, for it can incorporate the other concerns. Although it is true that families eat at McDonald's and other fast food chains, the experience is very different from that of families eating a home-cooked meal around the table and talking about the day's activities, or even from that of eating in a restaurant where thought is put into the selection and presentation of food, and where preparation is both a skill and an art. People who eat at fast food restaurants are generally people "on the run," people too busy to have a "normal" meal. Perhaps fast food is quintessentially American because it both symbolizes and embodies the value we place on speed and efficiency.

Anomalous Foods: Betwixt and Between

There are some edible things that are, nevertheless, classified as non-food. In a health-conscious world, British anthropologist Allison James wonders why it is that despite the warnings and the knowledge that confectionery, or candy as Americans refer to it, is full of sugar and often high in fat, the consumption of it is actually increasing in Britain. In a report in 1988, Britons spent £3,285 million on confectionery but only £2,375 million on staples like bread, and only £650 million on cereals. It is not enough simply to say that Britons have a sweet tooth; one needs to ask why. James resorts to classification systems whereby confectionery is both food and non-food, yet it is not the same as "junk food," which still qualifies as food. Because of the "place which confectionery occupies in the system of food classification is between 'real' and 'junk' food, and as a 'liminal' foodstuff, confectionery has the symbolic power both to mediate social relationships and to confer particular sets of social meanings" (James 1990: 666). Never part of a meal, yet still something to be eaten, it stands outside the major classifications and thus can act as go-between, sweetening the path of social relations. It makes an appropriate gift in place of flowers or wine when one is invited to dinner. Confectionery has become a symbol of love, not only between parents and children but between men and women. For example, confectionery, especially chocolate, is an appropriate gift from men to women on Valentine's Day. The ability of candy to sweeten social relations depends first of all on the classification of sweet as good and pleasurable.[9]

Frankenfood[10]

Just as we begin to think we know what food is and is not, and what its meanings are, a whole new category emerges that confounds all the traditional classifications, and that is the newly *made* genetically modified foods, GMFs, or in a more ghoulish mode, *frankenfood*, as the British refer to them. These *transgenic* foods – the new chimera – fuse genetic material not only from two different kinds of plants – as occurs in hybrids – but from two different species altogether. Thus we have tomatoes with fish genes, potatoes with chicken genes, tobacco with hamster genes, and corn plants with firefly genes (Rifkin 1998: 81). No wonder people are wary. Are these things safe to eat? Are they really foods? What will be the long-term effect on the environment? At a deeper level the anxiety may be related to the belief that we are what we eat; if we eat transgenic food, the question looms: what will we become?

The scientists who are developing these foods or, more accurately, the seeds, glorify their usefulness: they make plants resistant to bugs, they lace rice with vitamin-enriched bacteria, and they can insert genes that will prevent frost damage and thus, theoretically, prevent financial loss for farmers. All of these alterations will, they claim, help the starving peoples of the Third World. However, a *Nova Frontline* special (April 24, 2001) said that genetically modified food will not relieve world hunger but will, instead, make the Third World more dependent on the companies that hold the patents on the seeds.[11] The developers seem not to have learned the lesson from the aid workers who, as we noted, became aware that even hungry people will reject edible food if it does not fit their classification system. Turkish villagers also told me that they rejected a new, "improved" strain of wheat because the flour made from it produced inferior bread.

If the main problem is not scarcity of food but distribution as many economists believe, then there is no guarantee that genetically modified food is going to solve the problem of hunger. Most of the world's food is consumed by people living in

Figure 7.6 "Frankenfoods." Genetically Modified Specials, by Jesse Gordon and Knicker-bocker Design. From *New York Times* (July 15, 2000).

the rich nations of the First World. We sample the world's smorgasbord while the rest of the world gets the crumbs or gleanings. It is unlikely that a technological fix will solve what is essentially a social problem.

Consumers worry about what we are doing to our bodies and to the world's ecosystem. Monarch butterflies apparently died eating genetically modified corn pollen (*Nova Frontline* special, April 24, 2001). Europeans demanded that all transgenic foods be labeled but the United States, which is at the forefront of the development of these foods, determined it was unnecessary. The scare during 2000–1 about the possibility of inducing allergies from the genetically modified corn in Taco Bell tortilla shells helped to generate more public interest. Still, the percentage of consumers involved in these issues is small and many of them are not fully aware of the potential consequences of GMFs, especially that, once planted, the process is irreversible. These species cannot be contained within the boundaries of a field; they cross-fertilize and tend to take over existing species, which will result in massive extinctions of traditional plants. Some people are concerned about the consequent narrowing of the gene pool and feel it is presumptuous of scientists to "play God" by deciding which species will be preserved and which will perish. Are GMFs Lucifer in disguise?[12]

Farmers' markets

The ingredients for the food were produced by local organic farms and ranches. The celebration on the University of California's Berkeley campus began with a reception at the Campanile that featured pork specialties from Panzano and panisses, radishes, and almonds. Lunch was served on the Esplanade: summer vegetable salads, Provençal fish soup cooked in the fireplace, spit-roasted barons of Canfield Farm lamb with chanterelles, spicy lamb and mint sausages, fresh shell beans, herb salad, cheese from Jean d'Alos, apple and plum jellies, mulberry ice cream cones, friandises and tisane. Surprisingly, the wines were not local California wines.

In response to the manufacturing of our food, whether as fast food or as GMFs, some people clamor for farmers' markets in the hopes of finding a hint of the "authentic" tastes of their childhoods, when "a tomato tasted like a tomato." For some this means primarily "organic," foods grown without chemical additives and pesticides; for others it means produce locally grown by small, traditional farmers. While farmers' markets and food stands with fresh local produce have been around for a long time, there has been increasing interest in them.

Alice Waters, the founder and owner of Chez Panisse, an upscale restaurant in Berkeley, California, has been an important force in this development. She could rightly be called the new Julia Child because the transformation she has brought about in people's notions about food and dining has been just as powerful and far-reaching. But it is a different kind of transformation. Unlike Child, who was trained in the classic French tradition and emphasized recipes and method, Waters is more concerned not just with what we eat but where and how it is grown. Her "delicious revolution" has five component parts – land, food, meals, conversation, and community (Flammang, forthcoming). Rather than sampling the global smorgasbord, she emphasizes seasonal organic produce from *local* growers. At the celebration party for the 30th anniversary of Chez Panisse (August 2001), there "was no caviar, no *foie gras*, no truffles, no shellfish, none of the luxury ingredients other lovers of fine food might have chosen" (Apple, Jr., *San Francisco Chronicle*, August 29, 2001). Good food need not mean exotic.

An International School Lunch Tour

Congress has vowed to take up the highly polarized issue of school lunches this spring with the reauthorization of the law that helps states pay for school lunches. The attention comes not a moment too soon. While school lunches have never approached haute cuisine, some of us can recall a time when trays of mystery meat and creamed corn offered a sort of bonding experience, something we suffered through together, like showers after phys. ed.

Today few children work up enough sweat in school to require a shower, and many are swapping the government-sanctioned "meat and two veggies" lunch for candy bars, ice cream and soda from the cafeteria vending machines. And who can blame them? Choosing soggy broccoli, gray pot roast and an apple over pizza, chips and chocolate cupcakes seems, well, almost un-American.

The problem, of course, is that American children are among the fattest in the world, and the readily available junk food has plenty to do with setting up unhealthy eating habits. Meanwhile, other nations focus on the basics: appetizing yet healthful, these lunches offer children all the choice they need.

Ellen Ruppel Shell, codirector of the Knight Center for Science and Medical Journalism at Boston University and author of "The Hungry Gene: The Science of Fat and the Future of Thin."

Russia
SCHOOL 1529, MOSCOW

On the Menu:

Beef
Potato and wheat soup
Boiled rice
Mandarin orange compote
Wheat bread
Rye bread
Fresh tomato

Whole grains and fresh fruit enliven this hearty selection.

France
ÉCOLE ÉLÉMENTAIRE
RUE ST. BERNARD, PARIS

On the Menu:

Ham with lentils
Salad with tomatoes, corn, soy and Gruyère
Yogurt with sugar
Baguette slices

Banana
Water

*Four fresh vegetables and banana: French
children get their "five a day" on a single tray.*

Mexico
LÁZARO CÁRDENAS GRAMMAR
SCHOOL, MEXICO CITY

On the Menu:

Meat
Rice, corn and squash
Horchata (water mixed with
oatmeal and sugar)
Apple

A big dose of starch, but very little sugar or fat.

South Korea
ELEMENTARY SCHOOL, TAEGU

On the Menu:

Rice
Chicken soup
Squid with hot sauce
Fried sweet potatoes
Radish kimchi

*High in flavor, low in fat, and varied enough to
keep even finicky eaters interested.*

USA
SOUTH AVENUE SCHOOL,
BEACON, NY

On the Menu:

Pot roast
Mashed potatoes
Broccoli
Apple
Milk

*The gravy and chocolate milk may go down
easy, but they don't do much to enhance the
nutritional value of this fat-heavy meal.*

In her search for fresh, local ingredients, Waters "discovered" and came to depend on a number of local, small-scale farmers and foragers with whom she established intimate relations unmediated by the middlemen of commercial food provisioning. She realized how much she and her restaurant were part of a wider interconnected community. As "a restaurant," she said, "we are utterly dependent on the health of the land, the sea, and the planet as a whole, and that this search for good ingredients is pointless without a healthy agriculture and a healthy environment" (Waters, in Clark 1990: 113). She has tried to show that "sustainable agriculture – a careful way of farming that maintains the quality of the soil for future generations – was possible and profitable" (Severson, *San Francisco Chronicle*, August 19, 2001).

As her philosophy developed, so did her political action: she worked with Catherine Sneed on the Garden Project whereby inmates from the San Francisco County Jail learned to work as organic farmers, a process that had a profound effect on their lives. It gave them "the kind of skills to nourish themselves physically and spiritually. And it shows that even the most difficult segments of society can find hope and self-worth if they're given just a small opportunity" (Waters, quoted by Garcia 1999). At first they donated their produce to homeless shelters but have since been allowed to sell directly to customers, which include many of the fancy Bay area restaurants.

This project gave Waters the idea for the Edible Schoolyard. After driving by a school with a large but unkempt yard and learning that it also had an abandoned kitchen and cafeteria (replaced by fast food concession stands on the playground), she conceived the idea to start a program similar to that for the prisoners. Not only did the children learn how to grow vegetables and about the care necessary to make them flourish, but they also became much more interested in the food they were eating. As Waters commented, "in about six weeks these kids go from saying 'I don't like salad' to saying 'You've gotta try the arugula!'" (see Flammang, forthcoming). The excitement they have in eating what they have grown is contagious and is passed along to family and friends; this may truly be the beginning of training in the civility that is perhaps the goal of the "delicious revolution."

The Edible School and other projects like it are now funded in part by the Chez Panisse Foundation set up in 1996, whose statement of purpose is "to support educational and cultural projects that promote sustainable agriculture, strengthen community, and reinforce self-esteem by creating opportunities for people to grow, prepare, and share their food" (quoted in Flammang, forthcoming).

In addition to the health food movement, organically grown food, and farmers' markets is a relatively new international movement called (appropriately) "Slow Food" that began in Italy in 1986. It now boasts more than 65,000 members in 45 countries, an indication that a reaction is setting in against fast food and the "fast life, which manifests itself through the industrialization and standardization of our food supply and the degradation of our farmland" (www.SlowFoodUSA.com, September 4, 2001). Not unlike Alice Waters (who is a member of a California branch), this movement "believes that pleasure and quality in everyday life can be achieved by slowing down, respecting the convivial traditions of the table and celebrating the diversity of the earth's bounty." Instead of creating fast, convenient foods for our fast-paced lives, they draw attention to the relation between food, social relations, the environment, and time. As we saw in chapter 3, time is the one thing

Figure 7.7   "Food porn." Photo © Food Features.

Americans seem to have less and less of because we are working more than ever before. Are we really "getting away from our Puritan roots," as Ruth Reichel believes? Or are they becoming more exposed? What is the relation between them and the increasing interest in food, cooking, and cookbooks?

Cookbooks and cooking

In many parts of the world, traditional recipes are handed down from generation to generation. Where one learns by example, by helping to prepare meals, there is no need for a cookbook. In the Turkish village, for example, I was told there were only three ways to prepare green beans! In modern urban society where people do not live close to their parents or other relatives, and have often reached the age of maturity without knowing how to cook, cookbooks became a necessity. Obviously, they require a literate readership, for in order to use a cookbook, you have to know how to read. Beyond teaching the basics – how to boil, broil, roast, or fry – cookbooks serve myriad purposes. For the neophyte cook, they help create menus that serve both to dissipate boredom and to ease the anxiety of entertaining. For immigrants displaced from the homeland, they can help keep alive the flavors and aromas of home while simultaneously helping them adapt to their new home.

According to anthropology student Malindo Lo, Chinese cookbooks written by Chinese Americans are often quite nostalgic and attempt to evoke an authentic past which the immigrants may never have experienced (Lo 2001). For the more advanced cook, preparing meals from certain cookbooks is a means to impress friends. In the 1960s and 1970s, when I lived in Cambridge, Massachusetts, I remember the subtle competition among friends to reproduce the recipes from Julia Child's cookbooks.[13] Not only was Cambridge her home at the time, but she had just launched the extremely popular television series *The French Chef*. (I used to walk by her house and liberate food magazines from her trash can!) She is certainly responsible for raising the level of appreciation of food and its preparation in the United States. Today, a number of other chefs have followed her lead – witness the proliferation of cooking programs on television. However, an interesting research question would be to discover how many viewers actually cook the recipes demonstrated on the programs versus those who watch them purely for entertainment? And why this form of entertainment? Similarly, how many people cook the recipes from the beautifully illustrated cookbooks they buy?

Reading cookbooks can whet appetites and spur people to cook; but for many others they provide vicarious pleasure – a culinary voyeurism or "food porn"[14] – for those who know full well they will never have the time to do so. This returns us to where we began this chapter. Does the increased interest in cooking, food, and cookbooks indicate a revolution in our approach to food, or might it also indicate a nostalgia for the delicious, nutritious sensuousness of food that we have lost? Working so hard and so long has made people too tired for sex, so perhaps they have turned to food as the last resort, the last pleasurable refuge. Even though they do not have time to prepare the luscious meals they see in cookbooks or on television, they can still savor the simulacra of them.

Cooking, for Lévi-Strauss, represented the transition *from* nature *to* culture. It represented for him a major event in human evolution; it is what distinguishes us from the animals. But it also symbolizes the transformation *of* nature, a magic trick we perform everyday. Even more important, cooking helps us to realize that there are other ways of transforming nature into culture besides domination and exploitation. Perhaps, as the only animal species that cooks its food, the lessons learned from cooking and the civility of the table are what make us fully human.

Bon appétit!

Notes

1   In it, he "argues that a universal feature of human thought involves linking the distinction between raw ingredients and cooked food with the fundamental distinction between nature and culture" (Beardsworth and Keil 1997: 61). Central to this distinction is his "culinary triangle," whereby raw food "becomes cooked food through a *cultural* transformation . . . [and] cooked food may be reclaimed by nature through the *natural* transformation of rotting" (p. 61; emphasis mine).
2   See the book of the same title by Peter Farb and George Armelagos (1980).

3   There are similar sayings among Hindus (see Parry 1985: 613), Germans, and others from the ancient past to the present (Ohnuki-Tierney 1993: 3).

4   In response to criticism from Bulmer (1967) and Tambiah (1969), Douglas revised her opinion (1975) and began an investigation of the relationship between metaphysical systems (or religions) and the classifications of everyday life.

5   See also Janet Siskand's "The Invention of Thanksgiving," *Critique of Anthropology*, 12/2 (1992): 167–91.

6   Turkey, the bird, also known as *meleagris gullopavo* or *americana sybestris auis*, is native to North America. Apparently the 1494 Tordesillas Treaty forged by the pope in Rome granted commercial enterprises to the Portuguese who then brought the fowl to their colony in Goa, India, from whence it was taken to Egypt, then part of the Ottoman Empire. In Turkish, the bird is known as *hindi* (from India). When Ottoman traders took some of these birds to the British Isles, it was designated *turkey*. Thus, according to H. B. Paksoy, a Turkish historian who wrote about this, the Pilgrims were already familiar with *turkey*. Benjamin Franklin suggested that it be designated as the symbol of the new republic but instead the bald eagle was given the honor (Paksoy, "Türk Tarihi, Toplumların Mayası, Uygarlık," *Annals of Japan Association for Middle East Studies*, 7 (1992): 173–220, translated and sent to me by Levent Soysal).

7   In 2003 there were reports that the number of franchises of McDonald's was decreasing and that some had also closed.

8   Frances Moore Lappé, author of *Diet for a Small Planet*, notes that "We feed almost half of the world's grain to livestock, returning only a fraction in meat – while millions starve. It confounds all logic" ([1971] 1991: xvii). Indeed, *"it takes 16 pounds of grain and soybeans to produce just 1 pound of beef in the United States today"* (p. 9).

9   See Mintz (1985), who discusses the dark side of the sugar industry. We will address this in chapter 9.

10   An excellent *Nova Frontline* special with this title was aired April 24, 2001 and can be ordered from PBS.

11   The Bush administration is attempting to force Europe to accept GMFs, claiming the European position is immoral because it leads to starvation in the developing world (Becker, *New York Times*, January 10, 2003). I think it is more a matter of having another market for US food products.

12   See also Kimbrell (2002).

13   During that time I, and many of my friends, saw no contradiction between cooking good food and preparing elegant dinners for our friends and marching for civil rights or against the war in Vietnam. Merry White, a close friend, and for a time my next-door neighbor, was and is an excellent cook, has written several very good cookbooks, and is now a sociologist-anthropologist at Boston University where she teaches courses about food and about Japan. I credit her with developing my interest in food.

14   I came across this term in an article by Anthony Bourdain in the *San Francisco Chronicle*, September 4, 2001; I do not know whether he is the originator of it.

Bibliography

Adams, Carol J. (1991) *The Sexual Politics of Meat: A Feminist-Vegetarian Critical Theory*. New York: Continuum.

Allison, Anne (1991) "Japanese Mothers and *Obentos*: The Lunch-Box as Ideological State." *Anthropological Quarterly*, 64 (4): 195–208.

Arnold, Martin (2001) "Food Beats Sex in Best Sellers." *New York Times*, May 24.

Barthes, Roland ([1957] 1972) *Mythologies*. New York: Hill and Wang.

Beardsworth, Alan and Keil, Teresa (1997) *Sociology on the Menu: An Invitation to the Study of Food and Society*. London: Routledge.

Bell, David and Valentine, Gill (1997) *Consuming Geographies: We Are Where We Eat*. London: Routledge.

Bulmer, R. (1967) "Why is the Cassowary not a Bird? A Problem of Zoological Taxonomy Among the Karam of the New Guinea Highlands." *Man*, n.s., 2: 5–20.

Clark, Robert, ed. (1990) *Our Sustainable Table*. San Francisco: North Point Press.

Counihan, Carole M. (1999) *The Anthropology of Food and the Body: Gender, Meaning and Power*. New York: Routledge.

Counihan, Carole M. and Kaplan, Steven L. (1998) *Food and Gender: Identity and Power*. Amsterdam: Harwood.

Douglas, Mary (1966) "The Abominations of Leviticus." In *Purity and Danger: An Analysis of the Concepts of Pollution and Taboo*. London: Routledge & Kegan Paul, pp. 42–58.

Douglas, Mary (1975) "Deciphering a Meal." In *Implicit Meanings: Essays in Anthropology*. London and Boston: Routledge & Kegan Paul, pp. 249–75.

Douglas, Mary (1984) *Food in the Social Order: Studies of Food and Festivities in Three American Communities*. New York: Russell Sage.

Dubisch, Jill ([1981] 1997) "You Are What You Eat: Religious Aspects of the Health Food Movement." In *Magic, Witchcraft, and Religion: An Anthropological Study of the Supernatural*, 4th ed., ed. Arthur C. Lehmann and James E. Myers. Mountain View, CA: Mayfield, pp. 62–70.

Farb, Peter and Armelagos, George (1980) *Consuming Passions: The Anthropology of Eating*. Boston: Houghton Mifflin.

Feeley-Harnik, Gillian (1981) *The Lord's Table: Eucharist and Passover in Early Christianity*. Philadelphia: University of Pennsylvania Press.

Feirstein, B. (1982) *Real Men Don't Eat Quiche*. London: New English Library.

Fiddes, Nick (1991) *Meat: A Natural Symbol*. London: Routledge.

Flammang, Janet (forthcoming) *Women and the Politics of Food*.

Gabaccia, Donna R. (1998) *We Are What We Eat: Ethnic Food and the Making of Americans*. Cambridge, MA: Harvard University Press.

Garcia, Ken (1999) "Jail Sentences Reduced to Thyme Served: Unique Garden Program for Inmates," *San Francisco Chronicle*, April 17.

Goody, Jack (1982) *Cooking, Cuisine and Class: A Study in Comparative Sociology*. Cambridge: Cambridge University Press.

James, Allison (1990) "The Good, the Bad and the Delicious: The Role of Confectionery in British Society." *Sociological Review*, 38 (4): 666–88.

Kass, Leon R. (1994) *The Hungry Soul: Eating and the Perfecting of Our Nature*. Chicago: University of Chicago Press.

Kimbrell, Andrew, ed. (2002) *Fatal Harvest: The Tragedy of Industrial Agriculture*. Washington, DC: Island.

Kottak, Conrad, ed. (1982) *Researching American Culture*. Ann Arbor: University of Michigan Press.

Lappé, Frances Moore ([1971] 1991) *Diet for a Small Planet*. New York: Ballantine Books.

Leach, Edmund (1964) "Anthropological Aspects of Language: Animal Categories and Verbal Abuse." In *New Directions in the Study of Language*, ed. Eric Lenneberg. Cambridge, MA: MIT Press, pp. 23–63.

Lévi-Strauss, Claude (1966) "The Culinary Triangle." *Partisan Review*, 33: 586–95.

Lévi-Strauss, Claude ([1968] 1978) *Mythologiques*, vol. 3: *The Origin of Table Manners*. Trans. J. and D. Weightman. New York: Harper & Row.

Lo, Malinda (2001) "'Authentic' Chinese Food: Chinese American Cookbooks and the Regulation of Ethnic Identity." Unpublished paper, Department of Cultural and Social Anthropology, Stanford University.

Macbeth, Helen (1997) *Food Preferences and Taste: Continuity and Change*. Providence, RI: Berghahn Books.

Mintz, Sidney (1985) *Sweetness and Power: The Place of Sugar in Modern History*. New York: Viking Press.

Ohnuki-Tierney, Emiko (1993) *Rice As Self: Japanese Identities Through Time*. Princeton: Princeton University Press.

Ortner, Sherry (1973) "On Key Symbols." *American Anthropologist*, 75: 1338–46.

Parry, Jonathan (1985) "Death and Digestion: The Symbolism of Food and Eating in North Indian Mortuary Rites." *Man*, 20: 612–30.

Ramirez, Eric (2001) "Troubled Fields: Men, Emotions and the Oklahoma Farm Crisis, 1992–94." Ph.D. dissertation, Stanford University, Department of Cultural and Social Anthropology.

Rifkin, Jeremy (1998) *The Biotech Century: Harnessing the Gene and Remaking the World*. New York: Jeremy P. Tarcher/Putnam.

Sahlins, Marshall (1976) *Culture and Practical Reason*. Chicago: University of Chicago Press.

Schlosser, Eric (2001) *Fast Food Nation: The Dark Side of the All-American Meal*. Boston: Houghton Mifflin.

Tambiah, S. J. (1969) "Animals are Good to Think and Good to Prohibit." *Ethnology*, 8 (4): 423–59.

Visser, Margaret (1986) *Much Depends on Dinner*. Toronto: McClelland & Stewart.

Visser, Margaret (1991) *The Rituals of Dinner: The Origins, Evolution, Eccentricities, and Meaning of Table Manners*. New York: Grove Weidenfeld.

Waters, Alice (1990) "The Farm–Restaurant Connection." In *Our Sustainable Table*, ed. Robert Clark. San Francisco: North Point Press, pp. 113–22.

Watson, James L., ed. (1997) *Golden Arches East*. Stanford: Stanford University Press.

Westwood, Sallie and Bhachu, Parminder, eds. (1988) *Enterprising Women*. London: Routledge.

Yanagisako, Sylvia and Delaney, Carol (1995) *Naturalizing Power: Essays in Feminist Cultural Analysis*. New York and London: Routledge.

Videos

American Eats: History on a Bun. A & E Home Video, August 21, 2001.

Dim Sum, dir. Wayne Wang, 1985.

Eating: A Very Serious Comedy About Women and Food, dir. Nelly Alard, 1990.

Frankenfood, PBS *Frontline* special. April 24, 2001.

You Are What You Eat: Religious Aspects of the Health Food Movement

Jill Dubisch

Dr. Robbins was thinking how it might be interesting to make a film from Adelle Davis' perennial best seller, *Let's Eat Right to Keep Fit*.

Representing a classic confrontation between good and evil – in this case nutrition versus unhealthy diet – the story had definite box office appeal. The role of the hero, Protein, probably should be filled by Jim Brown, although Burt Reynolds undoubtedly would pull strings to get the part. Sunny Doris Day would be a clear choice to play the heroine, Vitamin C, and Orson Welles, oozing saturated fatty acids from the pits of his flesh, could win an Oscar for his interpretation of the villainous Cholesterol. The film might begin on a stormy night in the central nervous system. . . .

Tom Robbins, *Even Cowgirls Get the Blues*

I intend to examine a certain way of eating, that which is characteristic of the health food movement, and try to determine what people are communicating when they choose to eat in ways which run counter to the dominant patterns of food consumption in our society. This requires looking at health foods as a system of symbols and the adherence to a health food way of life as being, in part, the expression of belief in a particular world view. Analysis of these symbols and the underlying world view reveals that, as a system of beliefs and practices, the health food movement has some of the characteristics of a religion.

Such an interpretation might at first seem strange since we usually think of religion in terms of a belief in a deity or other supernatural beings. These notions, for the most part, are lacking in the health food movement. However, anthropologists do not always consider such beliefs to be a necessary part of a religion. Clifford Geertz, for example, suggests the following broad definition:

a *religion* is: 1) a system of symbols which acts to 2) establish powerful, pervasive, and long-lasting moods and motivations in men by 3) formulating conceptions of a general order of existence and 4) clothing these conceptions with such an aura of factuality that 5) the moods and motivations seem uniquely realistic. (Geertz, 1965: 4)

Let us examine the health food movement in the light of Geertz's definition.

History of the Health Food Movement

The concept of "health foods" can be traced back to the 1830s and the Popular Health movement, which combined a reaction against professional medicine and an emphasis on lay knowledge and health care with broader social concerns such as feminism and the class struggle (see Ehrenreich and English, 1979). The Popular Health movement emphasized self-healing and the dissemination of knowledge about the body and health to laymen. One of the early founders of the movement, Sylvester Graham (who gave us the graham cracker), preached that good health was to be found in temperate living. This included abstinence from alcohol, a vegetarian diet, consumption of whole wheat products, and regular exercise. The writings and preachings of these early "hygienists" (as they called themselves) often had moral overtones, depicting physiological and spiritual reform as going hand in hand (Shryock, 1966).

The idea that proper diet can contribute to good health has continued into the twentieth century. The discovery of vitamins provided for many health food people a further "natural" means of healing which could be utilized instead of drugs. Vitamins were promoted as health-giving substances by various writers, including nutritionist Adelle Davis who has been perhaps the most important "guru" of health foods in this century. Davis preached good diet as well as the use of vitamins to restore and maintain health, and her books have become the best sellers of the movement. (The titles of her books, *Let's Cook It Right*, *Let's Get Well*, *Let's Have Healthy Children*, give some sense of her approach.) The health food movement took on its present form, however, during the late 1960s when it became part of the "counterculture."

Health foods were "in," and their consumption became part of the general protest against the "establishment" and the "straight" lifestyle. They were associated with other movements centering around social concerns, such as ecology and consumerism (Kandel and Pelto, 1980: 328). In contrast to the Popular Health movement, health food advocates of the sixties saw the establishment as not only the medical profession but also the food industry and the society it represented. Food had become highly processed and laden with colorings, preservatives, and other additives so that purity of food became a new issue. Chemicals had also become part of the food growing process, and in reaction terms such as "organic" and "natural" became watchwords of the movement. Health food consumption received a further impetus from revelations about the high sugar content of many popular breakfast cereals which Americans had been taught since childhood to think of as a nutritious way to start the day. (Kellogg, an early advocate of the Popular Health movement, would have been mortified, since his cereals were originally designed to be part of a hygienic regimen.)

Although some health food users are member of formal groups (such as the Natural Hygiene Society, which claims direct descent from Sylvester Graham), the movement exists primarily as a set of principles and practices rather than as an organization. For those not part of organized groups, these principles and practices are disseminated, and contact is made with other members of the movement, through several means. The most important of these are health food stores, restaurants, and publications. The two most prominent journals in the movement are *Prevention* and *Let's Live*, begun in 1920 and 1932 respectively (Hongladarom, 1976).

These journals tell people what foods to eat and how to prepare them. They offer advice about the use of vitamins, the importance of exercise, and the danger of pollutants. They also present testimonials from faithful practitioners. Such testimonials take

the form of articles that recount how the author overcame a physical problem through a health food approach, or letters from readers who tell how they have cured their ailments by following methods advocated by the journal or suggested by friends in the movement. In this manner, such magazines not only educate, they also articulate a world view and provide evidence and support for it. They have become the "sacred writings" of the movement. They are a way of "reciting the code" – the cosmology and moral injunctions – which anthropologist Anthony F. C. Wallace describes as one of the important categories of religious behavior (1966: 57).

Ideological Content of the Health Food Movement

What exactly is the health food system? First, and most obviously, it centers around certain beliefs regarding the relationship of diet to health. Health foods are seen as an "alternative" healing system, one which people turn to out of their dissatisfaction with conventional medicine (see, for example, Hongladarom, 1976). The emphasis is on "wellness" and prevention rather than on illness and curing. Judging from letters and articles found in health food publications, many individuals' initial adherence to the movement is a type of conversion. A specific medical problem, or a general dissatisfaction with the state of their health, leads these converts to an eventual realization of the "truth" as represented by the health food approach, and to a subsequent change in lifestyle to reflect the principles of that approach. "Why This Psychiatrist 'Switched'," published in *Prevention* (September, 1976), carries the following heading: "Dr. H. L. Newbold is a great advocate of better nutrition and a livelier life style. But it took a personal illness to make him see the light." For those who have experienced such conversion, and for others who become convinced by reading about such experiences, health food publications serve an important function by reinforcing the conversion and encouraging a change of lifestyle. For example, an article entitled "How to Convert Your Kitchen for the New Age of Nutrition" (*Prevention*, February, 1975) tells the housewife how to make her kitchen a source of health for her family. The article suggests ways of reorganizing kitchen supplies and reforming cooking by substituting health foods for substances detrimental to health, and also offers ideas on the preparation of nutritious and delicious meals which will convert the family to this new way of eating without "alienating" them. The pamphlet, *The Junk Food Withdrawal Manual* (Kline, 1978), details how an individual can, step by step, quit eating junk foods and adopt more healthful eating habits. Publications also urge the readers to convert others by letting them know how much better health foods are than junk foods. Proselytizing may take the form of giving a "natural" birthday party for one's children and their friends, encouraging schools to substitute fruit and nuts for junk food snacks, and even selling one's own baking.

Undergoing the conversion process means learning and accepting the general features of the health food world view. To begin with, there is great concern, as there is in many religions, with purity, in this case, the purity of food, of water, of air. In fact, there are some striking similarities between keeping a "health food kitchen" and the Jewish practice of keeping kosher. Both make distinctions between proper and improper foods, and both involve excluding certain impure foods (whether unhealthful or non-kosher) from the kitchen and table. In addition, a person concerned with maintaining a high degree of purity in food may engage in similar behavior in either case – reading labels carefully to check for impermissible ingredients and even purchasing food from special establishments to guarantee ritual purity.

In the health food movement, the basis of purity is healthfulness and "naturalness." Some foods are considered to be natural and therefore healthier; this concept applies not only to foods but to other aspects of life as well. It is part of the large idea that people should work in harmony with nature and not against it. In this respect, the health food cosmology sets up an opposition of nature (beneficial) versus culture (destructive), or, in particular, the health food movement against our highly technological society. As products of our industrialized way of life, certain foods are unnatural; they produce illness by working against the body. Consistent with this view is the idea that healing, like eating, should proceed in harmony with nature. The assumption is that the body, if allowed to function naturally, will tend to heal itself. Orthodox medicine, on the other hand, with its drugs and surgery and its nonholistic approach to health, works against the body. Physicians are frequently criticized in the literature of the movement for their narrow approach to medical problems, reliance on drugs and surgery, lack of knowledge of nutrition, and unwillingness to accept the validity of the patient's own experience in healing himself. It is believed that doctors may actually cause further health problems rather than effecting a cure. A short item in *Prevention*, "The Delivery is Normal – But the Baby Isn't," recounts an incident in which drug-induced labor in childbirth resulted in a mentally retarded baby. The conclusion is "nature does a good job – and we should not, without compelling reasons, try to take over" (*Prevention*, May, 1979: 38).

The healing process is hastened by natural substances, such as healthful food, and by other "natural" therapeutic measures such as exercise. Vitamins are also very important to many health food people, both for maintaining health and for healing. They are seen as components of food which work with the body and are believed to offer a more natural mode of healing than drugs. Vitamins, often one of the most prominent products offered in many health food stores, provide the greatest source of profit (Hongladarom, 1976).

A basic assumption of the movement is that certain foods are good for you while others are not. The practitioner of a health food way of life must learn to distinguish between two kinds of food: those which promote well-being ("health foods") and those which are believed to be detrimental to health ("junk foods"). The former are the only kind of food a person should consume, while the latter are the antithesis of all that food should be and must be avoided. The qualities of these foods may be described by two anthropological concepts, *mana* and *taboo*. *Mana* is a type of beneficial or valuable power which can pass to individuals from sacred objects through touch (or, in the case of health foods, by ingestion). *Taboo*, on the other hand, refers to power that is dangerous; objects which are taboo can injure those who touch them (Wallace, 1966: 60–1). Not all foods fall clearly into one category or the other. However, those foods which are seen as having health-giving qualities, which contain *mana*, symbolize life, while *taboo* foods symbolize death. ("Junk food is . . . dead. . . . Dead food produces death," proclaims one health food manual [Kline, 1978: 2–4].) Much of the space in health food publications is devoted to telling the reader why to consume certain foods and avoid others. ("Frozen, Creamed Spinach: Nutritional Disaster," *Prevention*, May, 1979. "Let's Sprout Some Seeds," *Better Nutrition*, September, 1979.)

Those foods in the health food category which are deemed to possess an especially high level of *mana* have come to symbolize the movement as a whole. Foods such as honey, wheat germ, yogurt, and sprouts are seen as representative of the general way of life which health food adherents advocate, and Kandel and Pelto found that certain health food followers attribute mystical powers to the foods they consume. Raw food eaters speak of the "life energy" in uncooked foods. Sprout eaters speak of their food's "growth force" (1980: 336).

Qualities such as color and texture are also important in determining health foods and may acquire symbolic value. "Wholeness" and "whole grain" have come to stand for healthfulness and have entered the jargon of the advertising industry. Raw, coarse, dark, crunchy, and cloudy foods are preferred over those which are cooked, refined, white, soft, and clear (see table 7.1).

Thus dark bread is preferred over white, raw milk over pasteurized, brown rice over white. The convert must learn to eat foods which at first seem strange and even exotic and to reject many foods which are components of the Standard American diet. A McDonald's hamburger, for example, which is an important symbol of America itself (Kottak, 1978), falls into the category of "junk food" and must be rejected.

Just as the magazines and books which articulate the principles of the health food movement and serve as a guide to the convert can be said to comprise the sacred writings of the movement, so the health food store or health food restaurant is the temple where the purity of the movement is guarded and maintained. There individuals find for sale the types of food and other substances advocated by the movement. One does not expect to find items of questionable purity, that is, substances which are not natural or which may be detrimental to health. Within the precincts of the temple adherents can feel safe from the contaminating forces of the larger society, can meet fellow devotees, and can be instructed by the guardians of the sacred area (see, for example, Hongladarom, 1976). Health food stores may vary in their degree of purity. Some sell items such as coffee, raw sugar, or "natural" ice cream which are considered questionable by others of the faith. (One health food store I visited had a sign explaining that it did not sell vitamin supplements, which it considered to be "unnatural," i.e. impure.)

People in other places are often viewed as living more "naturally" and healthfully than contemporary Americans. Observation of such peoples may be used to confirm practices of the movement and to acquire ideas about food. Healthy and long-lived people like the Hunza of the Himalayas are studied to determine the secrets of their strength and longevity. Cultures as yet untainted by the food systems of industrialized nations are seen as examples of what better diet can do. In addition, certain foods from other cultures—foods such as humus, falafel, and tofu—have been adopted into the health food repertoire because of their presumed healthful qualities.

Peoples of other times can also serve as models for a more healthful way of life. There is in the health food movement a concept of a "golden age," a past which provides an authority for a better way of living. This past may be scrutinized for clues about how to improve contemporary American society. An archaeologist, writing for *Prevention* magazine, recounts how "I Put Myself on a Caveman Diet – Permanently" (*Prevention*, September 1979). His article explains how he improved his health by utilizing the regular exercise and simpler foods which he had concluded from his research were probably characteristic of our prehistoric ancestors. A general nostalgia about the past seems to exist in the health food movement, along with the feeling that we have departed from a more natural pattern of eating practiced by earlier generations of Americans (see, for example, Hongladarom, 1976). (Sylvester Graham, however, presumably did not find the eating habits of his contemporaries to be very admirable.)

Table 7.1   Health food world view

	Health Foods	Junk Foods	
cosmic	LIFE	DEATH	
oppositions	NATURE	CULTURE	
	holistic, organic	fragmented, mechanistic	
basic	harmony with body and	working against body and	undesirable
values	nature	nature	attributes
and	natural and real	manufactured and artificial	
desirable	harmony, self-sufficiency,	disharmony, dependence	
attributes	independence		
	homemade, small scale	mass-produced	
	layman competence and	professional esoteric	
	understanding	knowledge and jargon	
	whole	processed	
beneficial	coarse	refined	harmful
qualifies	dark	white	qualities
of food	crunchy	soft	
	raw	cooked	
	cloudy	clear	
	yogurt*	ice cream, candy	
specific	honey*	sugar*	specific
foods with	carob	chocolate	taboo
mana	soybeans*	beef	foods
	sprouts*	overcooked vegetables	
	fruit juices	soft drinks*	
	herb teas	coffee,* tea	
	foods from other cultures:	"all-American" foods: hot	
	humus, falafel, kefir, tofu,	dogs, McDonald's hamburgers,*	
	stir-fried vegetables, pita	potato chips, Coke	
	bread		
	return to early American	corruption of this original	
	value, "real" American	and better way of life and	
	way of life	values	

* denotes foods with especially potent *mana* or *taboo*.

The health food movement is concerned with more than the achievement of bodily health. Nutritional problems are often seen as being at the root of emotional, spiritual, and even social problems. An article entitled "Sugar Neurosis" states "Hypoglycemia (low blood sugar) is a medical reality that can trigger wife-beating, divorce, even suicide" (*Prevention*, April 1979: 110). Articles and books claim to show the reader how to overcome depression through vitamins and nutrition and the movement promises happiness and psychological well-being as well as physical health. Social problems, too, may respond to the health food approach. For example, a probation officer recounts how she tried changing offenders' diets in order to change their behavior. Testimonials from two of the individuals helped tell "what it was like to find that good nutrition was their bridge from the wrong side of the law and a frustrated, unhappy life to a vibrant and useful one" (*Prevention*, May 1978: 56). Thus, through more healthful eating and a more natural lifestyle, the health food movement offers its followers what many religions offer: salvation—in this case salvation for the body, for the psyche, and for society.

Individual effort is the keystone of the health food movement. An individual can take responsibility for his or her own health and does not need to rely on professional medical practitioners. The corollary of this is that it is a person's own behavior which may be the cause of ill health. By sinning, by not listening to our bodies, and by not following a natural way of life, we bring our ailments upon ourselves.

The health food movement also affirms the validity of each individual's experience. No two individuals are alike: needs for different vitamins vary widely; some people are more sensitive to food additives than others; each person has his or her best method of achieving happiness. Therefore, the generalized expertise of professionals and the scientifically verifiable findings of the experts may not be adequate guides for you, the individual, in the search of health. Each person's experience has meaning; if something works for you, then it works. If it works for others also, so much the better, but if it does not, that does not invalidate your own experience. While the movement does not by any means disdain all scientific findings (and indeed they are used extensively when they bolster health food positions), such findings are not seen as the only source of confirmation for the way of life which the health food movement advocates, and the scientific establishment itself tends to be suspect.

In line with its emphasis on individual responsibility for health, the movement seeks to deprofessionalize knowledge and place in every individual's hands the information and means to heal. Drugs used by doctors are usually available only through prescription, but foods and vitamins can be obtained by anyone. Books, magazines, and health food store personnel seek to educate their clientele in ways of healing themselves and maintaining their own health. Articles explain bodily processes, the effects of various substances on health, and the properties of foods and vitamins.

The focus on individual responsibility is frequently tied to a wider concern for self-sufficiency and self-reliance. Growing your own organic garden,

grinding your own flour, or even, as one pamphlet suggests, raising your own cow are not simply ways that one can be assured of obtaining healthful food; they are also expressions of independence and self-reliance. Furthermore, such practices are seen as characteristic of an earlier "golden age" when people lived natural lives. For example, an advertisement for vitamins appearing in a digest distributed in health food stores shows a mother and daughter kneading bread together. The heading reads "America's discovering basics." The copy goes on, "Baking bread at home has been a basic family practice throughout history. The past several decades, however, have seen a shift in the American diet to factory-produced breads . . . Fortunately, today there are signs that more and more Americans are discovering the advantage of baking bread themselves." Homemade bread, home-canned produce, sprouts growing on the window sill symbolize what are felt to be basic American values, values supposedly predominant in earlier times when people not only lived on self-sufficient farms and produced their own fresh and more natural food, but also stood firmly on their own two feet and took charge of their own lives. A reader writing to *Prevention* praises an article about a man who found "new life at ninety without lawyers or doctors," saying "If that isn't the optimum in the American way of living, I can't imagine what is!" (*Prevention*, May 1978: 16). Thus although it criticizes the contemporary American way of life (and although some vegetarians turn to Eastern religions for guidance—see Kandel and Pelto, 1980), the health food movement in general claims to be the true faith, the proponent of basic American-ness, a faith from which the society as a whole has strayed.

Social Significance of the Health Food Movement for American Actors

Being a "health food person" involves more than simply changing one's diet or utilizing an alternative medical system. Kandel and Pelto suggest that the health food movement derives much of its popularity from the fact that "Food may be used simultaneously to cure or prevent illness, as a religious symbol and to forge social bonds. Frequently health food users are trying to improve their health, their lives, and, sometimes the world as well" (1980: 332). Use of health foods becomes an affirmation of certain values and a commitment to a certain world view. A person who becomes involved in the health food movement might be said to experience what anthropologist Anthony F. C. Wallace has called "mazeway resynthesis." The "mazeway" is the mental "map" or image of the world which each individual holds. It includes values, the environment and the objects in it, the image of the self and of others, and the techniques one uses to manipulate the environment to achieve desired end states (Wallace, 1970: 237). Resynthesis of this mazeway—that is, the creation of new "maps," values and techniques—commonly occurs in times of religious revitalization, when new religious movements are begun and converts to them are made. As individuals, these converts learn to view the world in a new manner and to act accordingly. In the case of the health food movement, those involved learn to see their health problems and other dissatisfactions with their lives as stemming from improper diet and living in disharmony with nature. They are provided with new values, new ways of viewing their environment, and new techniques for achieving their goals. For such individuals, health food use can come to imply "a major redefinition of self-image, role, and one's relationship to others" (Kandel and Pelto, 1980: 359). The world comes to "make sense" in the light of this new world view. Achievement of the desired end states of better health and an improved outlook on life through following the precepts of the movement gives further validation.

It is this process which gives the health food movement some of the overtones of a religion. As does any new faith, the movement criticizes the prevailing social values and institutions, in this case the health-threatening features of modern industrial society. While an individual's initial dissatisfaction with prevailing beliefs and practices may stem from experiences with the conventional medical system (for example, failure to find a solution to a health problem through visits to a physician), this dissatisfaction often comes to encompass other facets of the American way of life. This further differentiates the "health food person" from mainstream American society (even when the difference is justified as a return to "real" American values).

In everyday life the consumption of such substances as honey, yogurt, and wheat germ, which have come to symbolize the health food movement, does more than contribute to health. It also serves to represent commitment to the health food world view. Likewise, avoiding those substances, such as sugar and white bread, which are considered "evil" is also a mark of a health food person. Ridding the kitchen of such items—a move often advocated by articles advising readers on how to "convert" successfully to health foods—is an act of ritual as well as practical significance. The symbolic nature of such foods is confirmed by the reactions of outsiders to those who are perceived as being inside the movement. An individual who is perceived as being a health food person is often automatically assumed to use honey instead of sugar, for example. Conversely, if one is noticed using or not using certain foods (e.g., adding wheat germ to food, not eating white sugar), this can lead to questions from the observer as to whether or not that individual is a health food person (or a health food "nut," depending upon the questioner's own orientation).

The symbolic nature of such foods is especially important for the health food neophyte. The adoption of a certain way of eating and the renunciation of mainstream cultural food habits can constitute "bridge-burning acts of commitment" (Kandel and Pelto, 1980: 395), which function to cut the individual off from previous patterns of behavior. However, the symbolic activity which indicates this cutting off need not be as radical as a total change of eating habits. In an interview in *Prevention*, a man who runs a health oriented television program recounted an incident in which a viewer called up after a show and announced excitedly that he had changed his whole lifestyle—he had started using honey in his coffee! (*Prevention*, February 1979: 89). While recognizing the absurdity of the action on a practical level, the program's host acknowledged the symbolic importance of this action to the person involved. He also saw it as a step in the right direction since one change can lead to another. Those who sprinkle wheat germ on cereal, toss alfalfa sprouts with a salad, or pass up an ice cream cone for yogurt are not only demonstrating a concern for health but also affirming their commitment to a particular lifestyle and symbolizing adherence to a set of values and a world view.

Conclusion

As this analysis has shown, health foods are more than simply a way of eating and more than an alternative healing system. If we return to Clifford Geertz's definition of religion as a "system of symbols" which produces "powerful, pervasive, and long-lasting moods and motivations" by "formulating conceptions of a general order of existence" and making them appear "uniquely realistic," we see that the health food movement definitely has a religious dimension. There is, first, a system of symbols, in this case based on certain kinds and qualities of food. While the foods are believed to have health-giving properties in themselves, they also symbolize a world view which is concerned with the right way to live one's life and the right way to construct a society. This "right way" is based on an approach to life which stresses harmony with nature and the holistic nature of the body. Consumption of those substances designated as "health foods," as well as participation in other activities associated with the movement which also symbolize its world view (such as exercising or growing an organic garden) can serve to establish the "moods and motivations" of which Geertz speaks. The committed health food follower may come to experience a sense of spiritual as well as physical well-being when he or she adheres to the health food way of life. Followers are thus motivated to persist in this way of life, and they come to see the world view of this movement as correct and "realistic."

In addition to its possession of sacred symbols and its "convincing" world view, the health food movement also has other elements which we usually associate with a religion. Concepts of *mana* and *taboo* guide the choice of foods. There is a distinction between the pure and impure and a concern for the maintenance of purity. There are "temples" (health food stores and other such establishments) which are expected to maintain purity within their confines. There are "rabbis," or experts in the "theology" of the movement and its application to every-

day life. There are sacred and instructional writings which set out the principles of the movement and teach followers how to utilize them. In addition, like many religious movements, the health food movement harkens back to a "golden age" which it seeks to recreate and assumes that many of the ills of the contemporary world are caused by society's departure from this ideal state.

Individuals entering the movement, like individuals entering any religious movement, may undergo a process of conversion. This can be dramatic, resulting from the cure of an illness or the reversal of a previous state of poor health, or it can be gradual, a step by step changing of eating and other habits through exposure to health food doctrine. Individuals who have undergone conversion and mazeway resynthesis, as well as those who have tested and confirmed various aspects of the movement's prescriptions for better health and a better life, may give testimonials to the faith. For those who have adopted, in full or in part, the health food world view, it provides, as do all religions, explanations for existing conditions, answers to specific problems, and a means of gaining control over one's existence. Followers of the movement are also promised "salvation," not in the form of after-life, but in terms of enhanced physical well-being, greater energy, longer life-span, freedom from illness, and increased peace of mind. However, although the focus is this-worldly, there is a spiritual dimension to the health food movement. And although it does not center its world view around belief in supernatural beings, it does posit a higher authority—the wisdom of nature—as the source of ultimate legitimacy for its views.

Health food people are often dismissed as "nuts" or "food faddists" by those outside the movement. Such a designation fails to recognize the systematic nature of the health food world view, the symbolic significance of health foods, and the important functions which the movement performs for its followers. Health foods offer an alternative or supplement to conventional medical treatment, and a meaningful and effective way for individuals to bring about changes in lives which are perceived as unsatisfactory because of poor physical and emotional health. It can also provide for its followers a framework of meaning which transcends individual problems.

In opposing itself to the predominant American lifestyle, the health food movement sets up a symbolic system which opposes harmony to disharmony, purity to pollution, nature to culture, and ultimately, as in many religions, life to death. Thus while foods are the beginning point and the most important symbols of the health food movement, food is not the ultimate focus but rather a means to an end: the organization of a meaningful world view and the construction of a satisfying life.

References

Ehrenreich, Barbara and English, Deidre (1979) *For Her Own Good: 150 Years of the Experts' Advice to Women.* Garden City, NY: Anchor Press/Doubleday.

Geertz, Clifford (1965) "Religion as a Cultural System." In Michael Banton, ed., *Anthropological Approaches to the Study of Religion.* ASA Monograph 3. New York: Frederick A. Praeger.

Hongladarom, Gail Chapman (1976) *Health Seeking Within the Health Food Movement.* PhD dissertation, University of Washington. (Xerox University Microfilms, Ann Arbor.)

Kandel, Randy F. and Pelto, Gretel H. (1980) "The Health Food Movement: Social Revitalization or Alternative Health Maintenance System." In Norge W. Jerome, Randy F. Kandel, and Gretel H. Pelto, eds., *Nutritional Anthropology.* Pleasantville, NY: Redgrave Publishing Company.

Kline, Monte (1978) *The Junk Food Withdrawal Manual.* Total Life, Inc.

Kottak, Conrad (1978) "McDonald's as Myth, Symbol and Ritual." In *Anthropology: The Study of Human Diversity.* New York: Random House.

Shryock, Richard Harrison (1966) *Medicine in America: Historical Essays.* Baltimore: Johns Hopkins.

Wallace, Anthony F. C. (1966) *Religion: An Anthropological View.* New York: Random House.

Choose some place that food may be obtained (restaurant, shop, stand, grocery store, etc.). I prefer that you go off campus/outside the university. You may do this exercise with a partner.

1   What is the name of the place and its location? Describe the place. What is the arrangement of space, what kind of atmosphere is conveyed? How formal or informal is it?

2   What kind of food is available? What kinds of people (specify by age, gender, ethnic identity, class, etc.) frequent this place? What kinds of workers are employed? What are the most popular times for visiting this place? Talk to the owner, manager, workers, and patrons for their views about these questions. Do you agree with their assessments?

3   If you can talk to the owner or manager, try to find out the history of the place and also why he or she thought they could make a success of it (i.e., what need or niche are they filling)?

8
Clothing Matters

Clothing does more than cover the body; it is also a cultural index of age, gender, occupation, and class. Is it then true that "clothing makes the man"? Haute couture, sweat shops, clothing and the economy.

Clothing Matters[1]

"Man is born naked, but is everywhere in clothes."

This play upon Rousseau's "man is born free but is everywhere in chains" surely
provokes a question of whether we are imprisoned by clothes or "slaves to fashion."
It was also anthropologist Terence Turner's way of beginning an article describing
the body adornments of the relatively naked Kayapo of South America (1980). The
body, he argued, even among peoples regarded as "primitive," is never completely
naked; everywhere humans have done something to modify the naked state whether
it be the body paint of the Kayapo, the tattoos and body piercing of the new, urban
tribalists, the boots and hats of American cowboys, or the full black veils worn by
many Muslim women. The fact that everyone everywhere (most of the
time) wears clothes or their equivalent is obvious, but why the variety and
what does it mean?

Nudity is, therefore, no more
natural than wearing clothes.

Clothes do not merely protect us from the elements, they also express
cultural meanings and identities and serve as markers of status, age, and
gender as well as occupation, activity, degree of formality, and a host of other things.
Like other non-verbal signs, these markers not only distinguish individuals and
groups from each other, they are also a means whereby we tend to "place" people
in their social context. Walk down a busy street and observe the clothes people are
wearing. Based only on their clothes, what can you surmise about them?

Not only do clothes encode cultural values and social distinctions, they also form
a system – there is sense and reason behind what composes an "outfit." Like com-
posing a sentence (or a meal, see chapter 7), clothing has a certain syntax, a lexicon
of items and rules of combination that compose an outfit appropriate for the

occasion. This was the conclusion reached by French semiotician Roland Barthes. Drawing on the work of linguist Ferdinand de Saussure, Barthes examines *The Fashion System* ([1967] 1983). Rather than conducting an ethnographic study, however, he chose to investigate only the *discourse* about clothing, that is, the way clothing is discussed and written about in fashion magazines. That is surely an interesting aspect of the clothing system, but it leaves out the very aspects that anthropologists are interested in, namely, the non-verbal way it encodes the wider cultural system and reflects back to it.

Anthropologist Marshall Sahlins picks up where Barthes leaves off. Beyond the features emphasized in discourse, Sahlins makes the point that the perceptual differences alone do not determine their meaning, but only as they are drawn into the symbolic or cultural system. We must attend to style as well as texture, fabric, color, and line, all of which constitute a total ensemble and its meanings. For example, certain fabrics can index class and also gender: cashmere is a luxury wool associated with the upper class; more generally, wool is usually associated with men and silk with women. Women wear wool, of course, but its masculine connotations make it more business-like. Similarly, most of us must have wondered at some point why it is that "[t]he overlap of a blouse, a jacket or a coat determines the sex of the article. By buttoning a garment on the right side, it becomes suitable for men only and definitely unsuitable for women. Whatever the quaint explanations of folkore are, the right side of the body has always been male, the left side female; this orientation survived despite its irrationality" (Sahlins 1976: 190, quoting Rudolfsky 1947). The meanings of these orientations are relative to Western societies, whether they extend beyond them is open to investigation.

Turning to color, we know that red is the most saturated and most advancing color, it catches the eye. Wearing red draws attention to the self; it has been the color associated with prostitutes. As a teenager in the 1950s, I was not allowed to wear red because of that association. But red does not *mean* the same thing everywhere. In many countries, but not all, one of the meanings of red is danger. This may be why it is used in traffic signals. Red can also symbolize blood; but again, there are a number of meanings of blood. For example, it may not symbolize the blood of killing and death, but rather may symbolize the life-blood of kinship relations. In Turkey, red is the traditional color of the wedding dress; today, more often, a bride might wear a red sash or red veil. In that context, red symbolizes the blood relation through males – the patriline – which, when she gives birth to a son, will continue.

Because clothes can represent so many things – about people, about culture, about the economy – they are spectacular clues we can use for our sociocultural investigation.[2] In this chapter, we will briefly discuss why notions of modesty or protection are inadequate to explain the phenomenon of clothing, and then move on to what clothes accomplish besides a modest protection from the elements.

Modesty

Perhaps the earliest theory, at least in the West, to explain the adoption of clothes was rooted in the Bible. In Genesis, Adam and Eve "were both naked, the man and his wife, and were not ashamed" (Genesis 2: 25). After eating the fruit from the "Tree of Knowledge of Good and Evil," which God had forbidden them, their eyes "were opened, and they knew that they *were* naked; and they sewed fig leaves together, and made themselves aprons" (Genesis 3: 7). This theory explains the origin and continuing necessity of clothes in terms of modesty. And, like those who think that if we returned to a vegetarian diet we would recreate Eden, so too do some of those who espouse nudity think that will bring about the Primeval Garden before the Fall.

But people in different societies feel quite differently about their bodies and its exposure; modesty, as cultural anthropologists claim, is a learned behavior, not instinctual. "Australian aborigines, for example, are indifferent to their nakedness but are deeply embarrassed if seen eating" (Laver 1969, cited in Rubenstein 1995: 17). In addition, modesty is inflected very differently according to gender. Women in a number of societies are required to dress modestly, but what that means in practice varies considerably – in some places it means a long black veil that covers the entire body, elsewhere it might mean a ban on sleeveless dresses, no skirts above the knee, or no bare midriffs in school. The concept of modesty has particular salience in cultures influenced by the monotheistic, Abrahamic religions – Judaism, Christianity, and Islam – because of the definitions and meanings of gender, but it cannot be a universal criterion of a theory of clothing.

Another commonsense view is that clothing must have originated to protect us from the elements – from the extremes of temperature and from moisture. Without fur to keep us warm, we "borrow" it from those animals who do. This, then, would be the underlying rationale for the vogue of fur coats. While most of us want some protection from the elements and have devised all kinds of clothing to keep us dry in the rain, warm in the snow, and cool at the beach, it has long been noted that some peoples can withstand extreme changes in temperature even while relatively naked. Darwin reported that while he and his crew huddled next to the fire and wrapped themselves in blankets yet remained cold, the people in Tierra del Fuego, "all naked, were some distance from the fire and yet perspiration streamed down their bodies" (Wulsin 1968, cited in Rubenstein 1995: 19). B. Spencer and F. J. Gillen, one a missionary and the other a government employee who spent many months among the Australian aborigines in the late nineteenth century and wrote a number of books that can rightfully be called anthropological, noted that the aborigines, too, were able to withstand inclement weather and tolerate significant changes in the temperature without being greatly discomfited. Some theories and practitioners of meditation and yoga claim they, too, are able to ignore changes in temperature. Whether they actually *ignore* these changes or whether they are able to make their bodies feel warm if they are cold or feel cool when they are hot, I am not sure, but in either case, it is an issue of mind over matter.

Even if modesty and protection are part of the rationale for clothing, they do not explain the variety of clothing around the world. Adaptationists would, no doubt, try to argue that people dress in accord with their environment – wearing few clothes where it is hot and more clothes where it is cold. However, I was disabused of this theory when I was travelling in a desert area near Haran, Turkey (allegedly Abraham's home) and the temperature was 120 degrees Fahrenheit. The people were dressed in heavy woolen and thick velvet clothing in dark colors.

Clearly, it was cultural factors – ideals of beauty, beliefs about gender, and, to be sure, notions of modesty in that culture – that determined what the people wore.

Still, another explanation is that people have a desire to adorn themselves – whether for self-expression or to ward off the evil spirits or to create group identity or, as some feminists claim, for the pure pleasure we derive from doing so. Adornment is an aspect – even a major aspect – of clothing; however, as a theory, it reduces the extraordinary variety of clothing and cannot account for what is culturally significant and meaningful. Rather than attempting to formulate one universal theory that would account for all clothing – something I am not sure is even possible – perhaps it is more productive to entertain and explore all of them as they may illuminate particular cultural practices. We must not become satisfied with the latest fashion in theory, but begin, perhaps, with fashion itself.

Distinctions

One of the first things you can deduce about clothing is that it creates distinctions – of status, age, gender, and activity. Some distinctions are, or seem, more obvious than others. Some are life-cycle statuses. For example, there is a difference between the clothing worn by children and that worn by adults. Yet, this may be a fairly recent phenomenon in the West, for if paintings from medieval times to mid-twentieth century can be taken as evidence, children had been wearing merely diminutive versions of adult clothing. In many cultures one can tell by the clothing a woman wears whether she is marriageable, already married, or widowed. The only signifier in the West is the wedding ring and not all married people even wear that. In some societies people who have children or grandchildren have a special status that is indicated by special clothing or article of clothing. (When I became a grandparent, I longed for some sign that would display my new status – and my delight – to the world.) Mourning, too, is very often exhibited by special clothing. In the West, people in mourning tend to wear black, at least to a funeral, but elsewhere a widow (more rarely a widower) will wear black for the rest of her life and it can indicate she is no longer marriageable.

Clothing matters especially at the highest social level. In Britain, at certain ceremonial occasions there is no mistake about who is queen; she is the one who wears a crown, a blue ribbon across her chest, and an ermine trimmed cape. The specially designed clothes and the elaborate hats that British royalty wear are also distinguishing marks. People want royalty to *look* like royalty and thus are willing to provide huge amounts of money from the public purse so they can keep up their appearance. The president of the United States is not royalty but *primus inter pares* (first among equals), and there are no sartorial signs to represent his status; still, he needs to look worthy of the job, he needs to *look* presidential. During the United States presidential election of 2000, the candidates' clothes were commented on in the newspapers and television almost every day. In an article titled "Read My Clothes,"[3] Bellafante and Trebay discussed the various "statements" that were made by the clothing choices of Mr. Bush and Mr. Gore. "With no conclusive vote count, the candidates have been forced to perform their roles symbolically . . . both have made numerous costume changes appropriate to their roles" (Bellafante and Trebay, *New York Times*, September 21, 2000); the authors note, however, that Mr. Gore's attempts at casual attire tended to backfire because it seemed forced, whereas George W. appeared comfortable in his ranch wear and cowboy hat. Perhaps it was Gore's clothes, not the *chads*, that cost him the vote.

Certain professional statuses are denoted by clothing, especially those in religious orders, the judiciary, and the military. Among the religious, however, there are distinct differences in the attire worn by those in monastic orders versus the priestly groups. Traditionally, monks are clothed in simple homespun shifts tied with a piece of rope and differences in rank were minimized; within priestly groups, the hierarchical differences are pronounced: the miter and white clothing of the pope, the red robes of the cardinals, the purple of bishops, green of abbots, and plain black of parish priests. Judges also don distinctive robes when they are in court, and in Britain they still wear white wigs. Academic robes, seen today only at graduation exercises, are emblazoned with school colors, emblems of highest degree, and branch of study.

Figure 8.1 Bizarro cartoon by Piraro, 1999, courtesy of Allsorts Media/King Features Syndicate.

Not surprisingly, the military distinguishes its different ranks by means of clothing (and the badges and stripes attached); because it is an extremely hierarchical institution, one needs to know who is in command. Clothing also distinguishes the different branches, e.g. army, navy, airforce, marines, each having distinctive uniforms and aura. Military clothing can become a focus of intense controversy. For instance, in March 2001, when the United States Army issued a new type of hat (a black beret) to every officer and soldier, the special branch called the Rangers who, until then, had been the only ones permitted to wear the beret, organized a march from Georgia to Washington, DC, in protest. If every soldier could wear the beret, they lost their badge of distinction (*New York Times*, March 12, 2001).

The US Navy had two decades of debate over whether "its men may carry umbrellas while in uniform" and finally decided they may. However, for many of the top brass "a military man protecting himself from the rain with an umbrella looks too effete" (*New York Times*, November 11, 1987) and undermines the masculine image they wish to project. In an attempt to salvage some of the image, they issued strict rules about how and when an umbrella may be carried: "the Navy is requiring that umbrellas be plain black, that they cannot be carried in formations, that they must not be used as walking sticks and that they must be carried in the left hand to leave the right hand free for saluting" (ibid.).

The business suit, often imagined as the uniform of the corporate world, creates a distinction between "white-collar" and "blue-collar" workers even though not all workers in either category wear only white or blue shirts. While the rules may be unstated, anyone applying for a "white-collar" job at a big company, whether in business or a law firm, better know them. You might think the only thing that matters is brains, ability, training, and the résumé, but clothing also matters. Do you think a person who showed up in a sports coat, open shirt, and khaki pants would be hired? What would such behavior indicate to those hiring? College students, accustomed to casual attire, often need special classes to help them choose appropriate clothing for job interviews. First impressions count, there is no second chance. If you ignore the importance of appearance, you give the impression of not being very serious about the job. One guide (on the web) for young men even specifies *what* you should wear: a suit that is either gray or navy, and single-breasted. It also specifies *how* you should wear it: the jacket should be buttoned (except for the bottom button) when you enter the interview office. Then you may unbutton it when you sit down. Another website had several pages on pants – proper length, pleats and creases, where the waistband should fall, and whether or not to have cuffs. A white, long-sleeved shirt with a straight point collar is advised and on the matter of ties, stripes or small patterns are recommended; "small patterns in a tie are associated with the upper middle class and that is usually the group to which your interviewer belongs" (www.manslife.com, July 26, 2001). Burgundy is a good color, and in any case a tie should have no more than three colors. "The tie should be long enough to reach your belt buckle, and don't

---

In 2002, the army updated its rules about appropriate attire: braids and cornrows (but not dreadlocks) are permitted, dyed hair must look "natural," and "baldness, natural or otherwise, is authorized." Pale nail polish is permitted for women, but not "fire-engine red, purple, blue, black" or camouflage. "Men are not allowed to show body piercing on military installations." Does that mean they can do so elsewhere? What about women with tongue piercing or nose rings? The above information was reported in *New York Times*, January 9, 2002. In addition, women stationed in Saudi Arabia are no longer required to wear the chador when they go out.

I am reminded of a poem by T. S. Eliot, "The Love Song of J. Alfred Prufrock," in which there are numerous references to clothes and the decisions and indecisions regarding them as well as a line about wearing "the bottoms of my trousers rolled."

forget the all important dimple – the indentation under the knot." The guide goes on to discuss shoes, socks, and belts as well as grooming tips. These rules should dispel women's beliefs that men's clothing seems simple compared with their own. Although the range is quite narrow, putting together a "dress for success" look takes time, attention to detail, and money. Furthermore, it is not only at the time of the interview that clothing matters; you need to keep up the image if you wish to climb the corporate ladder. "If you want a promotion you must look like you deserve it and can fit into the post."

In the 1950s, the corporate ideal was epitomized by *The Man in the Gray Flannel Suit*, a book about the compromises made by men in corporate America and played with style by Gregory Peck in the film of the same title. The suit and what it implied may have been one reason so many of us in the 1960s rebelled against that image and the lifestyle that went with it. After that brief respite (1960s and early 1970s), the rules and corporate lifestyle returned with a vengeance.

All of the distinctions made by clothes discussed so far have to do with authority; they don't just symbolize authority, they embody it, and this is true even when the clothes are very casual, as in the case of the physicists that anthropologist Sharon Traweek studied at SLAC (Stanford Linear Accelerator). She noted how easy it was "to distinguish between groups at the cafeteria. The physicists are dressed most casually, in shirts with rolled sleeves and jeans or nondescript slacks" (1988: 25), followed with increasing formality by engineers, technicians, administrators (in business suits), and secretaries. The people with the most authority and high status were able to wear the most casual clothing. Whether the business suit of the corporate world or the casual dress of the physicists, the specific garments permit the wearer to display his authority. I use the word *his* purposely because authority has traditionally been (and is still symbolically) male.

When women began to enter professions that were predominantly male, they adopted a form of business suit and tie so as to minimize their femininity and project an aura of authority. There continue to be all kinds of guides to help women "dress for success" with tips of what to wear and not to wear to the office. In the film *Erin Brockovich*, based on the true story of a woman by that name, the lead character was criticized, especially by her female co-workers, for her sexy clothes – the low-cut blouses exposing her cleavage, the high heels and mini-skirts were deemed unacceptable attire in the law firm where she was hired and then fired. Only after her boss realized she was onto a big case did he rehire her. While Brockovich was able to get away with wearing such clothes at a business firm, other women should not count on being able to follow her example.

Gender and Clothes

A major distinction created by means of clothes is, of course, gender. Everywhere men and women wear different kinds of clothes. In the contemporary United States, this begins at birth: girls are dressed in pink, boys in blue – a custom many will be surprised to learn developed after World War II (Garber 1992: 1). The color coding is not always carried out in practice, and one can find somewhat neutral colors for babies – white, yellow, pale green – but in general girls are associated with pink and boys with blue. Studies today show that people respond differently to baby girls and boys when the only clue they have to go on is the color, and maybe the style, of their clothing. Gregory P. Stone "observed that dressing a newborn in blue begins a sequence of interaction that is different from the one experienced by a baby dressed in pink. . . . The color acts as a cue or stimulus that influences how people behave toward the child and how that child is expected to conduct himself or herself. It is the response of others to gender-specific attire that encourages gender-appropriate behavior," concluded Stone (Rubenstein 1995: 83–4). People use a different tone of voice, different words, and different ways of holding and handling a baby depending on whether they think it is a boy or a girl – generally a softer, gentler tone and touch with girls than with boys. From these responses, repeated thousands of times over the next few years, a child develops a sense of the meaning of his or her gender which has very little to do with his or her genitalia.

Visit any department store and notice the differences in clothes for little girls and boys. Outfits for little girls often have frills or lace; there are flowered dresses in baby and toddler sizes; boys' clothing tends to use more somber or fully saturated colors, plaids and stripes, and tends to be small versions of adult clothes. In the United States, working-class families and those from certain ethnic groups will often dress their children in fancy and quite pronouncedly gender-specific clothes, while many middle-class parents have begun to dress their small children in gender-neutral clothing – pants and tops – made of material that is machine washable and does not need ironing. At adolescence clothing is a marker that dramatically differentiates the genders.

In Turkey, in the village at least, little girls and boys were dressed quite similarly in simple pants and tops. In the United States where we assume there is more gender equality than in Turkey, ironically we mark the gender of children more strongly. Nevertheless, once in the village when a little boy was playing with a headscarf, his mother kept shouting: "No, take that off. You are male, you are male."

A more basic question is why clothes are gendered in the first place. The differences cannot really be seen as functional because the differences are neither constant nor universal; for example, in different times and places men have worn skirts (Scottish kilts, priestly vestments, Arab jellaba, Greek/Albanian *fustanellas*) and women have worn pants (Turkish *şalvar*, bloomers). But in any particular culture, there are clothes meant for women, and clothes meant for men, and if one does not conform, one is seen as unusual or deviant. Today, it is easier and more acceptable for women to wear men's clothes than vice versa, but that has not always been the case.

In Shakespeare's England, only men could be actors and perform on stage, thus men played women's parts and dressed accordingly. (The film *Shakespeare in Love* plays upon this convention cleverly.) Although not

---

Not only are children often dressed in gender-specific colors but these differences are elaborated in their games and toys. When my first grandson was around a year and a half old, he was very interested in babies (as many children are). I decided to get him a baby doll so he could learn how to hold and play with one. I looked everywhere but I could not find a doll dressed in blue. Although I had capitulated to the gender stereotyping of color, I wanted a doll he could identify with. All dolls, because they were dressed in pink, were gendered female! Not only were dolls gendered female, but the color coding implied that only girls play with dolls, or should. What kind of message is subtly (or insidiously) conveyed about babies, about boys? When they saw my grandson with a doll, some of the parents in his neighborhood were aghast and would not let their sons play with him. They were already dressing their little boys in copies of army camouflage and handing them copies of automatic weapons to play with.

exactly cross-dressing, eighteenth-century noblemen wore clothing made in colors and of luxurious fabrics such as velvet and silk, adorned with lace, that today are symbolically feminine. In the mid-nineteenth century, two years after the first Women's Rights Convention in Seneca Falls (1848), Amelia Bloomer introduced a kind of trousers to be worn beneath dresses. The leaders of that first feminist movement – Elizabeth Cady Stanton, Susan B. Anthony, Lucy Stone, and Sarah and Angelina Grimké – wore them on their speaking circuits and advocated them as an alternative to conventional dress. Others felt "that trousers represented a usurpation of men's rights and prerogatives" and were vehemently opposed to them. Bloomer was not the first to suggest pants for women since women in utopian, often socialist, communities like New Harmony or the Oneida had preceded her. However, in those communities, trousers were associated with free love and sexual license. Those meanings were projected onto the feminists' use of pants and since that was not the image they wanted to convey, they soon abandoned them.

In contemporary Western society, many women wear pants much of the time and not just for leisure wear; Hillary Clinton as the president's wife was often seen in pants. (Of course, some people feel she wears the pants in the family.) Women's business suits now sometimes come with either skirt or pants (sometimes both), and there are even tuxedos designed for women, and not only lesbian women wear them. One need think only of Katharine Hepburn, Marlene Dietrich, and Greta Garbo to realize the erotic undercurrent of women in men's wear.

Cross-dressing

For women, there is clearly a continuum more than a strict dichotomy; many women wear clothes that are fashioned to resemble men's clothes, others wear clothes that have actually been made *for* men, and still others are much more self-consciously cross-dressing, but it does not raise concerns the way it does when men wear items of women's clothing. For men, the line is more strictly drawn. While women can wear men's clothes and even seem sexy and erotic in them, hardly anyone would assume they have some kind of psychological problem; whereas if men dress in clothes deemed female, people assume they have deep-seated problems and/or are gay. From observations in my grandsons' nursery schools, it was clear that little boys, like little girls, love to dress up in all kinds of clothes. When, how, and why is this beat out of them? When men "cross-dress" and wear women's clothes, they, like the clothes, become a marked category with quite specific meanings and consequences.[4] Not only are they stigmatized and ridiculed but are also punished. Writing in the *San Francisco Chronicle* (July 22, 2001), Bruce Mirken said that "To hear people tell it, the greatest threat we face – working to undermine the very fabric of our civilization even as I write this – is men wearing dresses" – not terrorism, not nuclear war, not global warming.[5] Clearly, we have *Vested Interests* in our clothing categories, as Marjorie Garber eloquently discusses in her book of that title.

Cross-dressing is, according to Garber (1992), a worldwide phenomenon with a long history. Sometimes one can cross-dress on specific occasions, such as Halloween

CASEY SHAW AND JASON WHITON FOR USAWEEKEND

"At first it was just a disguise, but then I started to like it."

Figure 8.2   Wolf cartoon by Casey Shaw and Jason Whitfield for *USA Weekend San Francisco Chronicle*, July 14, 2002.

or at a masked ball, and it does not necessarily have any deep or long-term bearing on one's gender role; in other places cross-dressing is a lifelong habit and coincides with a cross-gender role regardless of whether the sexual role, too, is adopted. Then, there are some people in some societies who dress in the clothing of neither one nor the other but adopt elements of both male and female clothing. I will briefly mention a few of these. Because it is so unusual or less well known, I give somewhat more space to the Albanian case.

1 "Sworn Virgins of Albania"

In Albania, according to a fascinating study by anthropologist Antonia Young, there are women who dress like men and take on all the rights, duties, and role of men except for sex. Once they take a vow to remain celibate and abstain from marriage, they are called "sworn virgins"; thenceforth they live like men.[6] Those who take this vow and adopt this role sometimes do it to avoid an unwanted arranged marriage;

more often it is done to retain the patrimony in the family when there is no son to inherit it. Once they take these vows, they wear traditional men's trousers, shirts, and hats though some of the younger, more urban ones have leather jackets and sunglasses. They become the heads of extended households over whom they have authority to make all major decisions concerning education, marriage, employment, even clothing and the purchase of a rifle for the young men as they come of age. They also represent the family at village meetings. The division of labor is strict and they, like all the other men, do all "heavy manual work: ploughing, hoeing, harrowing, manure spreading, chopping wood, scything, mowing, harvesting, watering and maintaining irrigation systems, protecting animals and property; it also includes being a host: talking to visitors, drinking and smoking with them, and avenging family honour" (Young 2000: 32). According to Young, this task takes precedence above all the others. Finally, they are buried as men.

Young makes clear that theirs is a social not a sexual role. As far as Young and others have been able to ascertain, the "sworn virgins" are not lesbians; indeed, she believes the concept is alien to them. Nor do the concepts of "third gender," transsexual, transgender, or even cross-dresser help to illuminate what is going on here (p. 124). They differ in a number of ways from other "cross-dressers" not only because they take it on for life, but also "this change is in no way seen as deviant within their society; it is not the result of some psychological or physiological difference, but as a status within an orderly pattern of statuses. . . . The accepted status is marked in a logical and regular fashion by the *adoption of appropriate dress*" (p. 113; emphasis mine). Nor is there any question of "sexual deviance." Young goes on to note that the role of the sworn virgin "is a dramatic illustration of the sociological concept of 'putting on a role,' rather than an occasion on which some inner self is permitted to 'come out'" (p. 113; thus, siding with the first opinion and challenging the second stated by Woolf, see below).

2 Billy Tipton

Another case of one who cross-dressed for life is Billy Tipton, a jazz musician who was found at his death in 1989 to have been a woman. He was married and had two (adopted) sons, and both his wife and sons never knew that he was a she underneath so well did s/he accomplish the role. His adoption of men's clothing is often interpreted, as is the Albanian case, in terms of socioeconomic necessity. Garber challenges this and wonders why it is that we have to normalize the transvestism by "interpreting it in the register of socio-economic necessity. A patriarchal culture had ordained that jazz musicians were, or ought to be male; therefore, it is claimed, Billy Tipton cross-dressed" (Garber 1992: 69). Instead, she suggests that it is the transvestite who has the possibility of disrupting the rigid patriarchal binary (p. 70), the potential to loosen its hold and the damage that it creates. Why, asks Garber, couldn't Billy Tipton's transvestism be merely professional and public, one that could be left at the door of his house? What made him think it was necessary to continue the charade?[7] At the same time, Garber gives short shrift to the differing reasons women and men have for cross-dressing. It is quite reasonable that women might choose to wear men's clothing to obtain privileges only men have – whether that might be to travel unmolested, as did numerous women in the eighteenth and nineteenth centuries such as Isabelle Eberhardt (see Blanch 1954); or to inherit property, as in the Albanian case; or to enter a profession closed to women, as did Billy Tipton. The reasons men choose to wear women's clothes are less obvious and, thus, in need of more explanation.

3 Bülent Ersoy

Bülent Ersoy, one of the most popular singers in Turkey during the 1970s and early 1980s, is the reverse of Billy Tipton. An attractive man with somewhat "feminine" features, he decided not just to wear women's clothes and adopt a female persona, but to undergo a sex-change operation to become the woman he felt he was "underneath." However, once that was accomplished, Parliament ruled that he could no longer perform in public because it categorized him/her as homosexual, and homosexuals were not allowed to perform in public. But was he really a homosexual? Almost daily there were articles in the newspapers describing how s/he was learning how to become a stereotypic woman – learning how to apply nail polish, do hair, wear heels and dresses and underwear. Transvestism was not well tolerated in Turkey; thus, whether Ersoy felt compelled to undergo the more drastic procedure to become a woman, or whether that was his/her own desire, is difficult to know.

4 "Third gender"

Some societies seem to tolerate a kind of intermediate status – neither male nor female. Rather than adopting the clothes and gender identity of one or the other, the person is able to don the clothes and personas of both and, in the process, create a kind of "third gender," at least for a certain period of time. This is what Norwegian anthropologist Unni Wikan claimed regarding the *xanith* in Oman, who are both male servants and homosexual prostitutes who perform the passive role (1977: 305). In this extremely sex-segregated society, the *xanith* were able to move freely in the women's quarters and participate in their activities. They do not wear the face mask (*burqa*) or other women's clothing:

> His clothes are intermediate between male and female: he wears the ankle-length tunic of the male, but with the tight waist of the female dress. Male clothing is white, females wear patterned cloth in bright colours, and transsexuals wear unpatterned coloured clothes. Men cut their hair short, women wear theirs long, the transsexuals medium long. (1977: 307)

Wikan goes on to describe how the *xanith*'s hairstyle, use of perfume and cosmetics, and gait follow neither the patterns used by men nor by women. While Wikan calls these men *transsexuals*, today we would reserve that term for those, like Bulent Ersoy, who actually change their anatomical sex. *Xaniths* are perhaps more appropriately called transgendered individuals or simply *xanith*. Unlike women, the *xanith* can move "about freely; but like women, he stays at home in the evenings, whereas men may spend their time in clubs and cafes" (p. 307). Despite being more like women and immersed in the women's area and activities, they retain their legal status as men and they can revert to male status if they marry and demonstrate that they can perform the male role in intercourse. According to Wikan, "[i]t is the sexual *act*, not the sexual organs, which is fundamentally constitutive of gender" (p. 309).

The berdache of certain Native American groups is another of these seemingly intermediate categories. Will Roscoe believes that "characterizations of berdaches as crossing genders or mixing genders, as men or women who 'assume the role of the "opposite" sex,' are reductionist and inaccurate" (1994) and argues for their place as third or even fourth gender (for the male and rarer female berdache). He also claims them as important resources for gay identity. In contrast, Ramón Gutierrez believes that the status/role of berdache arose as one consequence of conquest – as a form of humiliation.[8] I would be curious to learn whether there are significant differences – in both the role and numbers of persons who take on that role – depending on whether they occur in matrilineal or patrilineal societies.

From these examples, can we decide whether clothes merely recognize and express an innate gender difference or do they help create that image of difference? Virginia Woolf described these two perspectives in her novel *Orlando*, in which the title character goes through a series of changes from man to woman and back again. When Orlando puts on women's clothes, people respond to her in a certain way, treating her more delicately and paying her compliments among other things, and s/he, in turn, begins to act like a woman. Woolf constructs a debate between two camps of philosophers: one side concluded that clothes "change our view of the world and the world's view of us . . . that it is clothes that wear us and not we them" ([1928] 1960: 122–3). The other side inclined toward a different view. "Clothes," for them, "are but a symbol of something hid deep beneath. It was a change in Orlando herself that dictated her choice of a woman's dress and of a woman's sex" (p. 123). Contemporary versions of these positions are heard in the debates about sexual orientation. I am not sure the issue can ever be resolved in favor of one position or another, perhaps because the issue is too narrowly posed. In the West and in many Muslim societies, it is generally assumed that there are only two genders and each corresponds with genital sex. Thus, they should wear clothes appropriate to their gender and anything else is seen as weird or as deviant, and is socially punished. In recent years, these views have been changing dramatically in some places, yet the idea that there might be more than two genders has been difficult to accept. Perhaps it is we, in the West, who have such limited imaginations that we continually force both people and clothing into only two categories.

A "major flaw in Western discourse on transgenderism is that we find it very difficult to break away from the basic dichotomy of male–female in our analysis of gender. Even within the homosexual community we tend to see a breakdown according to traditional gender stereotypes, with one member of a partnership taking the 'active,' the other the 'passive' role" (Wood 1998, cited in Young 2000: 117). Thus, for example, we have "butch" clothes and "femme" clothes in the lesbian community. If this is the case, then Sahlins is right in claiming that, at the very least, we have six sartorial genders.[9] Geneticist Anne Fausto-Sterling claims that there are five naturally occurring sexes (1993). While some are more rare than others, she questions why we force them (surgically) to conform to either male or female. In any case, if her claim is true, then *cross*-dressing is a misnomer.

Clearly there are wide variations in definitions of gender and its expression in clothing. If gender is culturally constructed and not just an either/or category immutably rooted in nature, aren't we all "in drag"? We feel this more, perhaps, on formal occasions when it is obvious we are "dressing up." But I also recall a similar feeling when I had to dress in a certain way to go to work in an office. It felt as if I was putting on a costume. Even now, I continually try to figure out what is proper "professor" clothing. At the very least, we are "dressing up" to our culture's definition of what is appropriate attire for men and women.

Women's clothing is the *marked* category – meaning that it stands out. The concept of markedness is taken from linguistics, which uses it, for example, to talk about the way the female pronoun, *she*, is the marked one, for *he* can be used for either gender. Because women are symbolically the second sex, the inferior sex, the clothes they wear can absorb these meanings. That is the belief of those theorists who, following Simone de Beauvoir, viewed fashion as enslavement. In the same vein but more recently, the poet Adrienne Rich placed "dress codes" in the same category as purdah, foot binding, and the veil (Gaines and Herzog 1990: 3). In contrast to this rather puritanical view, some contemporary feminist theorists have admitted that they, and many women, get a great deal of pleasure – both aesthetic and erotic – from their clothes. Not only that, but performance theorists like Judith Butler argue that one can *try on* a variety of identities; clothes can be used to *épater la bourgeoisie*, to project an image of power, to disrupt gender categorization, and to impress and express many moods, identities, and whims. There is a lot of appeal in such a theoretical stance, but it seems, also, to ignore – to a great extent – the way in which identities and identifications are ascribed, not just performed. That is, they have a history and are interwoven with other domains and categories in a culture; they are not solely at the control of the person donning them. Does playing with the clothing of the other gender(s) really blur the boundaries of gender, or does it instantiate the genderedness of clothing even more forcefully?

Fashion

As the marked and supposedly inferior category, it is all the more surprising that women's clothes today are the focus of extraordinary elaboration. As noted above, this was not always the case in the West. In sixteenth through early nineteenth centuries, men's clothes, at least those of the elite, were elaborate, made of luxurious materials, and the focus of attention. Although some of this attention to male clothing has returned, in general, *haute couture* (high fashion) and the fashion industry are primarily concerned with fashioning women. The fashion industry makes a fortune from the designing and selling of women's clothes, in short, from making *fashion*.

Haute couture, almost synonymous with Paris, was actually founded/invented by a Londoner, Charles Frederic Worth, who moved to Paris in 1846 and set up his own dress-making business. He was also couturier to the court of Emperor Louis Napoleon who believed "that the production of fashion was essential to the well-being of the nation" (Rubenstein 1995: 146). Napoleon "wanted to encourage the well-to-do members of the aristocracy to support the economy by spending money on clothes" (p. 146). In order to show off his designs to potential clients, Worth hit upon the idea of what is known in the trade as the "fashion parade," when super-models strut down the "catwalk" showing off a designer's "models" – a term that applies not to the woman wearing it, but to the dress itself.

Worth also established the Syndical Chamber for Haute Couture, a group that decides which "houses" qualify for the label *haute couture*. Not every designer can qualify. In order to achieve this designation, a designer must meet the following criteria: "to employ a minimum of fifteen people at the workshops, to present to the press in Paris each season (spring/summer and autumn/winter) a collection of at least thirty-five runs consisting of models for daytime wear and evening wear" (Laurence Benaim, www.france.diplomatie.fr, July 19, 2001). As of this writing, there are 18 houses that warrant the accolade of *haute couture*, including Dior, Balmain, Cardin, Chanel, and Givenchy.

Internally, a *haute couture* establishment is extremely hierarchical. At "the bottom of the ladder are the '*arpettes*' or apprentices, who pin the fabrics and run from floor to floor. Next in line are qualified chief assistants, second assistants, fitters, chief and assistant sales staff. At the top of the pyramid is the designer. He is the great couturier and, in French, is always referred to by a masculine gender, regardless of whether the position is held by a man or a woman" (Jean-Louis Arnaud, www.france.diplomatie.fr, July 9, 2001). And there were a number of well-known female designers including Coco Chanel who designed the "Chanel suit" and the famous perfume, Chanel No. 5, and Elsa Schiaparelli known for her black and hot pink signature, among others.

High fashion really took off in the late 1940s and 1950s when Christian Dior proclaimed the "new look" in 1947 that emphasized fine shoulders and narrow waists and became the image of the ideal, not just of French women but of women around the world. The high fashion houses, providing extremely expensive, unique, luxurious clothes for a very small number of women, flourished until the 1970s; although they still put out designs, many have turned to *prêt-à-porter* (ready-to-wear) lines due, in part, to the social revolution of the 1960s with its ethic of equality and general disdain for extravagant displays by the ultra-rich.

What is curious, and calls out for further research, is why it was that high fashion arose and flourished in the very places that sparked the great social movements for liberty, equality, and fraternity. Social theorist G. Simmel, writing in 1904, felt that "fashion can only exist where social boundaries are permeable" – for if boundaries are rigid, the clothing of each class becomes more like a uniform. That may be part of an answer since it was during this time that there was more social mobility. Yet one could also argue that fashion emerged at this time because the aristocracy did not want to let go of their class privilege so easily. A more aesthetic reason might be that high fashion, like art, is something that inspires, gives dreams, added glamour, and sparkle to the more drab, domestic, complacent workaday world in which most people are enmeshed. High fashion does seem to have a "trickle-down"

Figure 8.3   A Dior evening dress, modeled by Barbara Goalen, 1947. © Hulton/Getty Images.

effect, as Emperor Napoleon recognized in the nineteenth century. He is said to have had Worth produce a new fashion "each season because everything the Empress wore created a demand first among upper-class women and then among the lower classes" (Saunders 1955, cited in Rubenstein 1995).

While high fashion continues to intrigue people, it is also more and more difficult to justify the extraordinary cost of such clothes – ranging from $20,000 for a women's suit to $60,000 and up for an evening gown – devoted to so few. At the 2001 Academy Awards, several movie stars admitted to borrowing dresses or buying high fashion second-hands. Prior to World War II, 35,000 people were employed in the *haute couture* industry; today there are only about 4,500 people, including seamstresses. There are fewer than 1,500 clients, down from more than 15,000, a change which is attributed by Benaim to a real change in lifestyles. The decline has also made it more difficult for these houses to stay afloat; a number of them have folded and others have been bought by conglomerates, for example, Dior belongs now to LVHM (the Louis Vuitton Moët Hennessy group).

Subcultural Style

If the decline of high fashion is attributed to the social upheavals of the 1960s, so too is its reinvention, as it incorporated some of the styles bubbling up from the counter-culture. Style was no longer dictated from the top, from *haute couture*, but arose from the psychedelic visions of grassroots. In response to seeing themselves marginalized, designers of *haute couture* appropriated some of the style of the counter-culture, for example, Yves St. Laurent's *Rive Gauche* ready-to-wear line.

Hippies, as some of the people of this era were known, reacted against the button-down, buttoned-up shirts of the business world, adopted gauzy or tie-dyed shirts they made themselves, drawstring pants, or long flowing dresses. To the consternation of the "straight" world (at the time "straight" meant the normal business world of the 1950s; it was the opposite of "hippie" not gay), men let their hair grow long, women went without bras, and both abandoned shoes or wore only sandals. At times everyone wore beads, feathers, and face paint, especially at the large "be-ins"[10] where people gathered to celebrate life and love.

Subcultural style did not actually begin with the hippie movement. Consider the beats of the 1950s. Regardless of whether one actually went "on the road," many of us longed to; the idea underlay our outlook on life. We could express our affiliation with the beats by adopting the costume. The color was black; *de rigueur* was a black sweater, paired with black pants or skirt. You had to smoke and drink black coffee and frequent dark smoky cafés where you had to be prepared to discuss existentialism or the latest *avant-garde* poet.

There were other precursors – the rock and roll styles of the late 1950s and early 1960s as well as the *zoot suiters* of the 1940s, and other theorists would, no doubt, project the history of subcultural style farther back. However, the 1960s seems to be a kind of watershed, perhaps because of the convergence of a number of social movements (civil rights, anti-war, communal, feminist, welfare rights, and drug-using and advocating groups) or, if not convergence, the fact that individuals participated in several of them at the same time. In addition, the movements were widespread, carried primarily by the youth who seemed to be much more mobile and interconnected than in earlier periods.

One of the first attempts, and perhaps the finest, to take subcultural style seriously and analyze it was made by Dick Hebdige, a British social theorist. In his book *Subculture: The Meaning of Style* (1979), he tracks the changes and the meanings of the clothing style of British youth from the 1950s to the late 1970s. Nevertheless, as backdrop perhaps, he begins with a discussion of the difference between the American beats and hipsters and showed that while both groups were "organized around a shared identity with blacks (symbolized by jazz), the nature of this identity, exposed in the styles adopted by the two groups, was qualitatively different" (1979: 48). He analyzed the stylistic differences in relation to the social differences – that is, the different social position and experience of the two groups. He said the hipster was typically

> a lower-class dandy, dressed up like a pimp, affecting a very cool, cerebral tone – to distinguish him from the gross, impulsive types that surrounded him in the ghetto – and aspiring to the finer things in life, like very good "tea," the finest sounds – jazz or Afro-Cuban . . . [whereas] . . . the Beat was originally some earnest middle-class college boy like Kerouac, who was stifled by the cities and the culture he had inherited and who wanted to cut out for distant and exotic places, where he could live like the "people," write, smoke and meditate. (Hebdige 1979: 48, citing Goldman 1974)

Hebdige continued this analysis in Britain where, again, it was blacks who served as the catalyst for the precipitation of a number of groups. He notes that the 1960s saw a rising immigrant, black (mainly West Indian) population becoming "established in Britain's working-class areas, and some kind of rapport between blacks and neighboring white groups had become possible" (p. 52). The various youth groups and styles that emerged were influenced by their relation and reaction not only to blacks but also to dominant cultural groups and institutions – parents, teachers, police, and to working-class or bourgeois culture.

Hebdige goes on to contrast the differences in style, in social position and class, and in music and philosophy between the Mods and Teddy Boys, between the skinheads and aficionados of Glam and Glitter rock, and finally punks, who combined "distorted reflections of all the major post-war subcultures" (p. 26), and whose primary target seems to be bourgeois society. It is not possible here to examine the minute details of their styles and the way they play off each other and the "parent" or mainstream culture, nor to trace their interconnections. For those interested, there is such a diagram or flowchart in the back of Ted Polhemus's wonderful book, *Street Style: From Sidewalk to Catwalk* (1994), which, along with spectacular photographs, also has brief descriptions of each group.

What was new in Hebdige's work was his attention not just to the myriad details of clothing that each group exhibited, and their taste in music, but also to their class position and occupational possibilities. Building on the work of British social theorist Stuart Hall and others, he "interpreted the succession of youth cultural styles as symbolic forms of resistance; as spectacular symptoms of a wider and more generally submerged dissent which characterized the whole post-war period" (p. 80). At the same time, it was not just some kind of *general* dissent, but one "produced in response to different conjunctures which positioned them differently in relation to existing cultural formations (immigrant cultures, the parent culture, other subcultures, the dominant culture)" (p. 81).

Still, these subcultures, he argues, were not merely *responding*, they were embodying or *dramatizing* their dissent. With punks, their tattered clothes held together with safety pins, the black leather, and the sartorial elements of bondage worked to exhibit, as a kind of living gallery, the decay and tatteredness of British society and their own bondage to it, but clearly, a life held together precariously. They *represented* the decline of British society and *presented* a challenge to it. Borrowing from a published interview with Sartre, Hebdige says he sought

> to acknowledge the right of the subordinate class (the young, the black, the working-class) to "make something of what is made of (them)" – to embellish, decorate, parody and wherever possible to recognize and rise above a subordinate position which was never of their choosing. (p. 139)

With their lack of options and narrow range of life choices in which many saw no future, it is hardly surprising their resistance and dissent were expressed so dramatically. What is surprising is that the violence of the clothes was not very often actualized. The Brixton race riots of 1980 in a section of London populated mainly by blacks were, according to social theorist Paul Gilroy, instigated in part because the police did not know how to interpret reggae sartorial and music styles and did not take seriously the deaths by fire of 13 young blacks who had attended a party (Gilroy 1987: 102–3). When blacks protested their handling of the case, the police instituted a "stop and search" operation, and it was this that seems to have triggered the riots. The mostly white punks seemed to have felt some sympathy and expressed "their hostility to both racist nationalism and nationalist racism in several records which recast reggae music in their own idiom" (p. 125), while their clothing symbolized their assault on the icons of Britishness – the Union Jack and the queen.

In this period of late capitalism, even punk clothes have been coopted and turned out as fashion. One can buy brand-name ripped and torn jeans for inflated prices, as well as safety pin earrings, and a range of bondage gear that formerly could only be found in kinky sex shops or catalogs. One gap in Hebdige's work, and one recognized by a number of theorists, is his lack of attention to gender, acknowledging nonetheless that these spectacular subcultural styles were primarily a male display.

Nothing ever stays the same. This is especially true of the fashion world. Some observers of the street scene in New York in the late 1990s noticed a strange shift in youth fashion. Kids were hanging out not in

> tattered jeans, worn leather coats, [or] combat boots [but in] puffy ski jackets, lots of polo shirts, lots of Gore-Tex and polar fleece. Designer logos (DKNY, Nautica, Ralph Lauren, North Face, Tommy Hilfiger) are de rigueur, as are bright Crayola colors. Industrial-strength sneakers and high-tech hiking boots are big; so are baseball caps and ski hats. The whole scene looks suspiciously like a tailgate party at an Ivy League football game. (Kakutani [1997], in Damhorst, Miller, and Michelman 1999: 398)

This was the *in* style worn, apparently, not just by the "preppy" white rich kids "speaking fluent ebonics and doing their best to be black teenagers," but also by black ghetto kids "as a talisman of the better life they wish they had" (p. 399). Not addressed in the article, however, was the way one's class position and income affect the ease or difficulty in obtaining the latest fashion. Certain teenagers have been known to kill in order to get a particular gold chain or pair of Adidas shoes, or get killed while trying to climb the social ladder by means of clothes.

One poignant story that captures both the longing and the tragedy of wanting to mold one's own identity into the fashionable image of the moment is "Alienation" by Julio Ramón Ribeyro; and it is included as the reading for this chapter. Of course, not all stories of longing end as tragically as his; nevertheless, the path of alienation – from one's body, friends, and culture – is rarely a happy one.

Politics of Clothes

While the vagaries of fashion, especially *haute couture*, tend to give the impression that clothing is frivolous, that would be a misinterpretation. Clothing, or particular articles of clothing, has enormous political implications. In this section I discuss only two examples – first, how Gandhi's clothing symbolized and incited a revolution in India, and second, the politics of headgear in Turkey.

Gandhi

Throughout his life Gandhi was very sensitive to the politics and implications of clothing. "No Indian leader took the problem of what to wear more seriously than Mohandas Karamchand Gandhi and probably no other leader changed his clothes so dramatically" (Tarlo 1996: 62). When he first went to England to study law, he tried to make sure he had obtained the appropriate clothes so as to blend more easily into his new surroundings. However, he had a number of embarrassing moments in this regard, beginning when he disembarked from the ship and discovered that he was the only man in white flannels. Tarlo believes that the "psychological impact of these incidents may be measured by the fact that he bothered to record them nearly forty years later" (p. 65).

After numerous sartorial changes that coincided with changes in his career, both in England and South Africa, he returned to India determined to throw off the yoke of British colonialism. At the same time he began to throw off all items of European clothing and experimented with a variety of native clothes until finally, on September 22, 1921, he published his intention to wear only a simple loincloth made of cloth spun and woven by hand. He "proposed to wear a loincloth for a period of just over five weeks, until the allotted deadline for *swaraj*," home rule (p. 72). It was not his intention to wear it for the rest of his life, it was a protest against the British, a symbol of his desire for home rule, and a sign, also, of sympathy with the poor.

> I wish to be in tune with the poorest of the poor among Indians. . . . How can these poor people afford a long shirt with a collar? Who will give them a cap? If we wear so many garments, we cannot clothe the poor, but it is our duty to dress them first and then ourselves, to feed them first and then ourselves. (*Complete Works*, 24: 456, quoted in Tarlo 1996: 75)

Once people took up spinning and weaving their own cloth and refused to import foreign cloth or wear clothes made from such cloth, Gandhi said he would revert back to his more "normal" clothes. When they did not do so, he continued to wear the loincloth as a sign of mourning, "that the people had rejected his version of progress and national development" (Tarlo 1996: 77). Nevertheless, it was an extraordinarily potent symbol of the power of one small man to change the world, for it was never the same after Gandhi.

Turkish headgear

In his delightful book *A Fez of the Heart* (1995), Jeremy Seal recounts the way in which headgear has paralleled political changes in the Ottoman Empire and the Turkish Republic. This was possible because Turkish "headgear has since time immemorial had a symbolic significance inconceivable in the West" (Seal 1995: 22). During the Ottoman period, the kind of clothes one could wear, the cloth and color of the clothes, and especially headgear were stipulated by law. "There was no other imperial power or state in the world like the Ottoman empire insofar as it had distinctive head-dress for every profession and for different classes and ranks of officials and military personnel" (Kumbaracilar n.d.: 3) not to mention religious personnel. One could tell at a glance to what group and rank a person belonged – an easy way to keep people under surveillance and, thus, under control.

In the early part of the nineteenth century, modernizing reforms were attempted including reform of headgear. In 1826 turbans were banned and the fez, adopted from North Africa, was instituted by state decree. The changes in headgear and regimes were also immortalized on tombstones – before 1826 tombstones were decorated with a variety of turbans carved on top of the thin stone slabs; after that date, the fez became routine. Thus, headgear also differentiates the dead and their era. Up until the revolution that created the Republic of Turkey the fez was the prescribed headgear for men. However, "[i]n 1925, the fez was outlawed and replaced by homburgs, panamas, bowlers, and flatcaps. And so a series of hats have provided the stepping-stones, the caravanserais, on the central theme of Turkish history, her great march westward toward the promised land represented by that ultimate measure of Westernization – the bare head" (Seal 1995: 21–2). Approaching that ideal, the most common headgear among men today is the flatcap – with a small brim in front. It is also highly functional. Because the cap can be turned around so that the brim is in back, it allows believers to touch their heads to the ground in prayer. Some devout Muslim men also wear embroidered skullcaps, similar to Jewish *yamakas*.

Women's headgear, not men's, is today the focus of heated controversy. The headscarf is an explosive issue not just in Turkey and other Muslim countries, but also in several European nations with large numbers of Muslim immigrants. Some women have been killed for not wearing the veil. It is scarcely a frivolous issue. When Atatürk banned the fez, he also encouraged women to go bareheaded, but he banned the wearing of the headscarf only for government employees such as teachers, nurses, lawyers, members of Parliament, etc. Women in the villages continued to wear their headscarves but many urban women abandoned them and adopted Western-style clothing.

Village headgear was never the long black covering mandated for women in Iran and Saudi Arabia. Instead, women's headcoverings in the village consisted of a number of different kinds of cloth depending on circumstance. The most common was a small thin gauze scarf in a variety of colors, often printed with flowers or other designs and edged with lace, beads, or tatting which displayed the woman's handwork. The scarf would be wound around the head so that some of it covered the shoulders; it was not tied under the chin like a kerchief. When visiting each other, some women would add a larger, longer white gauze scarf, and when going to town some of them, usually the older women, put on a large printed scarf that identified them as belonging to a specific area. In winter this was replaced by a large woolen scarf. For a visit to the city, younger women have adopted the kerchief and long loose coat of religious Muslims. The long black veils which totally cover the body are an urban phenomenon, and a very recent one. Indeed, when I first saw them in Istanbul, I assumed the women were visitors from Iran or Saudi Arabia. I was shocked to learn that some Turkish women had begun to take them up.

The polarization of Turkish society has intensified since the 1980s and that polarization is mirrored in women's clothing, each side provoking the other to extremes. Representing one extreme are young Western-oriented women who are wearing mini-skirts, tight tops with spaghetti straps, and high-heeled sandals; the other side is expressed by devout Islamist women who have adopted long coats and kerchiefs or the head-to-toe black veils. Although these women generally associate with others of like mind, occasionally one can see these two drastically different icons of Turkish womanhood walking and talking together. The universities have tended to stand staunchly behind Atatürk's ideas about headscarves, creating in the spring of 2000 a vociferous protest from women banned from taking their medical exams if they arrived with headscarf on.

When Merve Kavakçı, a member of Parliament, appeared for the first time in a headscarf, she fomented a huge debate that ended with the demand for her resignation. Ironically, people on the far right and on the left have joined forces over this issue, declaring that in a democracy people should be allowed to wear what they want. In principle that sounds like a good idea, but it is not so simple in Turkey, because the Islamists are using the rhetoric of democracy for undemocratic aims. The Islamists would not be so permissive towards the mini-skirted women if they were to achieve power. Far more important, in my mind, is that *none* of them has explored the meaning of hair in Turkish/Muslim society and why it is that women's hair must be covered.[11]

The covering of women's hair has a long history and did not begin with the Muslims. Orthodox Jewish women are also not allowed to show their hair; instead their own hair is shaved and they put on wigs. For centuries Christian women, too, covered their heads in keeping with biblical injunctions: "Every man praying or prophesying, having *his* head covered, dishonoureth his head. But every woman that prayeth or prophesieth with *her* head uncovered dishonoureth her head" (1 Corinthians 11: 4–5) because "the head of every man is Christ; and the head of the woman *is* the man" (1 Corinthians 11: 3). Thus began the custom of nuns both shaving their

Figure 8.4 (a and b) Turkish women's headwear.
Photos by author.

heads and wearing their distinctive habits. Lay Catholic women adopted veils, while Protestant women wore hats; both customs continue to this day even though they are in decline.

State rules

States have always had rules about attire, even if not as explicit as in the Ottoman Empire. In the 1950s in the United States, girls were not allowed to wear pants to school – not even in the freezing cold winters in upstate New York or Connecticut. And in 1962 I was nearly thrown out of college for wearing pants one day. Things changed dramatically in the mid-1960s and today, it seems, people do wear almost whatever they want to school. But this, too, causes problems. Girls have been accused of being too sexy and seductive when they wear short-shorts and halter tops, and boys wear baggy pants that seem always to be in imminent danger of falling down – both, to me, unseemly attire for school. Brand-name consciousness increases the competition that can spark violent antagonisms. It is no wonder that the subject of school uniforms has come up again in public discussion.

As I was writing this section I learned that New York state is requiring schools to adopt dress codes because of the increasing exposure of flesh and the sexualizing of young women. Teachers and administrators in schools have had enough of extremely short skirts, see-through blouses or low-cut tight tops with spaghetti straps, bare midriffs, etc. and are adopting dress codes. Most of the sanctions were for girls' clothing, but boys' low-slung and baggy pants were also banned (*New York Times*, "School Dress Codes vs. a Sea of Bare Flesh," September 11, 2001). Palo Alto in California has also banned similar clothing in school.

Uniforms

We generally take for granted the idea that our clothes express our personality, that our choice of clothes, insofar as is possible given our means, *says* something about us, expresses who we are. Thus, many Americans have a knee-jerk reaction against uniforms. Let me tell you about a profound experience that challenged and changed my view on this subject.

When I was a Fulbright fellow in Belgium I got the idea that I wanted to go down into a working coal mine. Do not ask me why. I think, in part, it was just because non-miners, especially women (who are thought to bring bad luck), are generally not permitted in the mine. But a friend arranged for me to go into the Beringen mine. It was one of the most extraordinary experiences in my life and one I would not want to repeat.

Before getting into the tiny cage that took us deep underground, I had to remove my own clothes, watch, jewelry – anything that could create static and cause a spark – and don the miners' uniform including the cap with lamp. At the bottom we got onto a small train that took us several lateral miles underground; these were mostly horizontal but they were continually going deeper. At the end of the train line we walked and then finally crawled between short stubby pillars supporting the weight of the world, literally, just above our heads. The noise was deafening – both from the mining equipment and from the huge fans circulating air. It was very scary and I became apprehensive, not only because of fear that I would be crushed, but also because I was the only woman among all these men. I could not leave until work ended that evening and I could never have found my way back through the labyrinthine paths.

Dressed in identical uniforms, everyone seemed to look the same. What became very apparent very quickly was that the individuality and personalities of the men stood out more precisely *because* they were wearing identical uniforms. I was thunderstruck. When we came up out of the mine and changed into our ordinary clothes, I became confused. I could hardly recognize the men I'd been in such close contact with all day and it was much more difficult to get a sense of their unique personalities even while we talked over drinks at their local pub. So impressive was this experience that it has stayed with me over the past 20 years and made me question the whole issue of uniforms and individual expression. Do we display our identity through clothes or are clothes a disguise?

Personally, I think uniforms would simplify our lives a great deal. We wouldn't have to think every morning, "What am I going to wear today?" Many people, of course, have to wear uniforms as symbols of their occupation, for example, the police, firefighters, the military, construction workers, doctors and lab technicians in hospitals, and often waiters/ waitresses and some maids. Even though uniforms symbolize authority of one kind or another so we know whom to address for a particular need, they do not necessarily coincide with class distinctions.

> Hating this daily agonizing ritual, my daughter and I came up with an idea of a clothing line suitable for all people – at school or at work, young or old, male or female. We were among those who really liked the style of the Mao suits worn in China: we would elaborate that basic plan and make jackets, pants, skirts, and jumpers in a variety of colors – magenta, aqua, yellow, green – not just dark blue. Our motto was to be "A billion people can't be wrong." I still think it is a great idea. Fashion designers beware!

Uniforms have been used in many private schools, both religious and secular, for a long time. Recently, public schools have begun to reconsider the issue of uniforms. The idea behind uniforms is that they are thought to foster a focus on learning rather than on clothing; students' minds are what matter, not their individual appearance. Uniforms also, of course, foster school identity and belongingness. Nevertheless, students will still make tiny adjustments to the uniforms both to express their individuality and/or resistance to its diminution. Some people, including some educators, think uniforms would cut down criminal behavior of some students, particularly those who cannot afford the latest fashion, and that they would also help to diminish the sexualized atmosphere in the classroom. Both of these are good reasons; others, however, say they curtail students' freedom to express their individuality and, therefore, are not appropriate in a democracy.

In Turkey, all children must wear school uniforms from first grade through high school. There, the purpose *was/is* democratic – poor children would be dressed exactly as rich children. The uniform expressed the idea that each child was equal before the law. That, at least, was the rationale. In practice, of course, it doesn't always work out that way. First, there is the distinction of gender – girls wear dresses while boys wear shirts and pants. At the end of grammar school or sixth grade, which is a kind of symbolic puberty, girls in the village don the headscarf, the primary symbol of sexual difference. When I was there, that also signaled the end of their schooling since the headscarf is not permitted in the secular public school system. I do not know how the village is complying with the new law that requires all children to complete the eighth grade.

In addition to gender are, of course, the differentials of income and class. Poor children, as in the village where I lived, wore hand-me-down uniforms, sometimes patched, faded, and rarely ironed. The white collars were often made of plastic so

Figure 8.5 Turkish schoolgirls in uniform. Photo by author.

Figure 8.6 Uniforms required of Turkish men going on *hajj*. Photo by author.

they could be kept clean. In the village it didn't really matter because most of them were in the same boat; but in the city where poor and richer kids attend the same schools, it could become more of a problem.

Cultural constraint

Uniforms, however, carry with them the idea of both cultural constraint (being "forced" to conform to the cultural norm or ideal) and social control (ease of surveillance) to which many people have strong objections. If fashion, in general, can be viewed as imposing constraints on the body, especially the female body, particular kinds of clothing enforce this even more. I am thinking of corsets and girdles, foot binding and high heels, Japanese kimono and Turkish *şalvar* – all of which also impede women's movement. No doubt you can think of many more examples. A major question is why do various societies wish to restrict the free movement of women? I will let you ponder this while I discuss some of the ways this has been done and what they imply about the society in question.

Linda Martin, a fashion historian, claims that "startling correlations appear between the design of female underwear and the exploration, expansion and acquisition of countries and continents by various civilizations" (Hatfield, *Boston Globe*, October 16, 1986). (If today's underwear is any indication, there is almost nothing left to explore and conquer.) The sixteenth century was also the time when early modern scientists were trying to bring the natural world under control. Since the natural world, or Nature, has been symbolically female, it is not so surprising that attempts were made to bring women's supposed unruly nature under control.

> In the sixteenth century, European women bound themselves into corsets of whalebone and hardened canvas. A piece of metal or wood ran down the front to flatten the breasts and abdomen. This garment made it impossible to bend at the waist and difficult to breathe. A farthingale, which was typically worn over the corset, held women's skirts out from their bodies . . . and made such simple activities as sitting nearly impossible. Queen Catherine of France introduced waist binding with a tortuous invention consisting of iron bands that minimized the size of the waist to the ideal measurement of thirteen inches. (Saltzberg and Chrisler, [1995] 1997: 136)

These extraordinary measures and measurements compressed the rib cage, leading to pulmonary problems and damage to internal organs. Rather than the bound feet of Chinese women, European women suffered from bound torsos. In the nineteenth century, *hysteria*, a psychological disease felt to be caused by a wandering womb, may instead have been caused by the very corsets made to hold it in check. But that was never considered in the theories, such as Freud's, used to explain the condition.

Steel stays, as well as whalebone, had also been used in corsets when the metal was no longer needed for armor, and they remained mainstays of women's fashion until 1914 when the steel was "needed for wartime production. By this time, [American] women were using 28,000 tons of steel per year for corset stays, enough to build two battleships" (Martin, in Hatfield 1986). Discarding the corset as part of the war effort made room for the freer, straighter, more boyish look of the "roaring twenties," a move that also coincided with the women's suffrage movement.

Bound feet

In China, the traditional idea of feminine beauty was tiny feet. In order to achieve this, the feet of small girls were "bound."

> Beginning at about age six to eight, the female child's four smaller toes were bent under the foot, the sole was forced to the heel, and then the foot was wrapped in a tight bandage day and night in order to mold a bowed and pointed four-inch-long appendage. Footbinding was extremely painful in the first 6 to 10 years of formative treatment. Complications included ulceration, paralysis, gangrene, and mortification of the lower limbs. (Mackie 1996: 1000)

Yet even this sounds too clinical for it does not indicate the broken bones, the blood- and pus-soaked bandages, and the odor. There was no way these women could escape an abusive husband or mother-in-law on such tiny "lotus" feet, which were apparently deeply erotic to men. Not only were the women hobbled for life, unable even to walk, they were taught early to endure tremendous pain for the purpose of beauty and the pleasure of men.

But it is too easy to dismiss this as a perversion of the Chinese or an ancient practice; we need only look at women today in modern post-industrial societies who are tottering around on stiletto-heeled, toe-crunching shoes and boots. One writer, in China for the celebration of the fiftieth anniversary of its revolution, captured an image that is unforgettable and worth quoting at length.

> In a single glance, I suddenly saw two women – separated by three generations, but standing less than 10 feet apart. A young man slowly wheeled a frail, elderly woman, curled up in a bicycle basket, through the treacherous traffic. Her five-inch long, bound feet dangled uselessly from under her skirt. Born before the revolution she could hardly walk.
>
> At the very same moment, a young woman, perhaps 20 years old, scantily dressed in a tight, short skirt and perched on four-inch high strapless platform shoes, tried to descend the steps that led to the subway station. She tottered precariously, her shoes slapping against her feet with every step. Born three decades after the revolution, she could hardly walk. (Rosen, *San Francisco Chronicle*, May 13, 2001)

Has anything changed, Rosen wondered. A friend with whom she discussed this issue said that women of today have a choice – they don't have to wear such shoes. Rosen retorted, "But isn't the young woman still a slave to fashion?" "Yes, but at least her feet won't be mutilated for life." "Oh really?" Wearing such shoes causes all kinds of foot problems in later years and we should not forget that it is far more likely a woman will fall and sprain or break her ankle and hurt other parts of her body as well. One man writing in response to the article made the suggestion that high-heeled shoes make a woman taller and therefore more imposing, giving her an image of power and an aura of authority as do a buttoned collar and a tightly knotted tie for a man. What he failed to realize is that these images of authority are, themselves, culturally produced.

Kimono

The Japanese kimono is a less obvious means to impede the movement of women, but it does so nonetheless. This garment, worn in various forms for more than a thousand years, is an extremely intricate ensemble. Originally worn by both men and women (with variations), the kimono was abandoned by men "a century ago in the name of modernity and efficiency" (Dalby 1993: 3) but became *the* symbol of Japanese womanhood.

Proper kimono attire consists of 18 different items, according to Yamanaka (1982), beginning with split-toe socks, *tabi*, through undershirts or half-slips, body pads, under-kimono, collars, undersash, obi, obi stays and cords and ending, finally, with *zori*, a special kind of sandal. Not only does it take quite some time to put on a kimono properly, but many women today must go to a special school to learn how, for the geisha are the only women who wear them as a matter of course every day.

Liza Dalby, an anthropologist who became a geisha for her research, describes how donning the kimono changed not only the way she moved but her very self. "A garment as demanding as the kimono, for example, requires a whole new personality, and, like learning a foreign language, it takes a while before we are no longer self-conscious. . . . Eventually the proper movements became natural, but in absorbing them I discovered that I had developed another self in kimono . . . [so that] after a while, I actually felt awkward speaking English when dressed as a geisha" (Dalby [1983] 1999: 105). Because the kimono constricts the body, one has to learn to walk with tiny mincing steps, "with turned-in feet, which makes a kimono rustle delicately." It affects one's movement in other ways too: "Driving a car or just sitting in a soft armchair are among the most awkward things a woman in kimono can do" (p. 327). When Dalby changed her mode of dress she also changed where and how she sat, how she walked, and innumerable other aspects of body gesture and language.

Şalvar

Wearing Turkish village *şalvar*, I, too, felt differently and apparently spoke differently. *Şalvar* are baggy trousers or bloomers cut from several yards of printed cloth, generally cotton or synthetic. Girls and women rarely had a choice of fabric, design, or color since the cloth was generally bought in town by the men in the family. No attempt was made to harmonize them with the blouses and knitted vests that completed the outfit, and the variations in color, pattern, and print often made me dizzy (see figure 8.5). Clearly a very different aesthetic was at work, one in which each item was valued on its own, not in relation to whether it went with anything else in the ensemble or not. Some people told me that the women's colorful outfits make them look like flowers, especially when they are out working in the fields.

Şalvar are cut into three pieces – two for the legs and one for the centerpanel that joins them. An elastic band is threaded at the waist. When my first pair were being made, I asked if I might have pockets so that I could carry my house key, my pad and pencil and dictionary around with

Although I dressed as village women did in *şalvar*, blouse, *yelek* (knitted vest), and headscarf, people began to comment on my color-coordinated outfits – something I could not relinquish easily since color and aesthetics are important to me.

Figure 8.7 Two Turkish women against tapestry. Photo by author.

me less noticeably. "No! Certainly not." Pockets are for men only. It became clear to me that women's hands were to be kept visible and busy knitting, sewing, working in the field, preparing food, or caring for babies and children. Thus, in order to carry my paraphernalia I had to make a small cloth pouch which could dangle from my wrist. The piece that joins the two leg sections together is attached near the ankle, making the *şalvar* almost like a long skirt seamed along the bottom with holes for feet. When I asked if that piece on my *şalvar* could be joined higher up so that I could walk at my usual pace, the answer was no. That would be unseemly, it would be more like men's pants.

Şalvar, I believe, symbolize other values. They make all women look both plump and pregnant. Turkish men, traditionally at least, gain prestige by a having plump wife – it shows he could afford to feed her well; a plump and pregnant wife was even better.

Functionally, *şalvar* are very satisfactory. Villagers do not normally sit on chairs; either they squat or sit on divans cross-legged or with their legs tucked under them. To squat in jeans or other tight pants cuts off the circulation, and sitting cross-legged is too revealing. *Şalvar* were roomy, modest, and comfortable. But, once again, women's free movement was very much restricted, not just socially but by the very clothes they wore.

No doubt practical, functional reasons can be found for any number of items of clothing, but whether those reasons are primary or whether they are secondary rationalizations is very difficult to tell. What is important is that one learns little about their cultural significance purely from pragmatic practice. If culture is really formed from practical interest, clothing could be interpreted from a functional point of view, but that hardly explains the variety of (often not very functional) designs;

such an approach also ignores that practical interests and desires are shaped within a system of values about what life is and how it should be lived.

Political Economy of Clothing

Anthropologist Marshall Sahlins asserts that the clothing system is a system of production, that what it produces is *social* distinctions not just the material items we call clothes. As he did with food (see chapter 7), he undermines our commonsense notions that we produce material goods *because* they directly reflect our needs and desires. Instead, he argues against this utilitarian view and suggests that our system of production is the realization of a symbolic scheme.

> For notice what is produced in the clothing system. By various objective features an item of apparel becomes appropriate for men or women, for night or for day, for "around the house" or "in public," for adult or adolescent. What is produced is, first, classes of time and place which index situations or activities; and second, classes of status to which all persons are ascribed. . . . Hence what is reproduced in clothing is this classificatory scheme. Yet not simply that. Not simply the boundaries, the divisions, and the subdivisions of, say, age-grades or social classes; by a specific symbolism of clothing differences, what is produced are the meaningful differences between these categories. In manufacturing apparel of distinct cut, outline, or color for women as opposed to men, we reproduce the distinction between femininity and masculinity as *known* to this society. That is what is going on in the pragmatic-material process of production. (1976: 181)

Because of the discriminations in the code, "the set of manufactured objects comprehends the entire cultural order of a society that it both *dresses* and *addresses*" (Sahlins 1976: 180). I like this phrase because it points out the double aspect of clothes – that they both conceal or cover the body and reveal or proclaim our identity – not the naked animal but the socialized, enculturated person.

In chapter 4 on language we noted how much we could tell about a person as soon as he or she opened his or her mouth; clothing provides non-verbal cues and is, perhaps, more unconscious. Let us think for a moment about some of the classifications encoded in clothes. First, time. There are clothes for nighttime and daytime wear, summer and winter and fall and spring, weekday and weekend, and holidays. There is also a "differentiation of the cultural space as between town and country, and within the town between downtown and neighborhood" (Sahlins 1976: 181), and the clothes we wear change according to *where* we wear them. In the modern (post-)industrialized world, a big distinction is made between work and leisure; this is not universal but emerged along with both industrialism and capitalism. Clothes encode categories of people – no longer just adults and children, but infants, toddlers, pre-schoolers, school age children, pre-teens, sub-teens, teens, juniors, adults, and the latest, over-60 group, and each of these categories is inflected by gender.

Occupations are encoded in attire – not just the obvious police, firefighters, surgeons and lab technicians, but also "white collar" and "blue collar." We grow up

Precious Cargo by Bob Morris

Gucci's got 'em for fall. Yohji and Helmut, too. Ralph is doing them in white cashmere, and of course, Old Navy has been pushing them since last winter. Yeah, the kids started it. But to get the back story on why a military-style staple of antifashion has become the chic signifier of the moment, you have to look beyond the trendy tribalism of extreme sports to the real deal: the cargo cults of Papua New Guinea.

After the Second World War, when the American military abandoned the South Pacific, the locals were thrown back into a stone-age existence. It was a downer, to put it mildly. Where were all those cigarettes, cans of fruit cocktail and other lovely supplies that had been dropping out of the sky? Tribal leaders assumed that all those airlifted goods were gifts from their dead ancestors. So to attract more cargo, they organized cults. With great ritualistic fervor, they built airstrips and radio transmitters out of bamboo. They carved shotguns, telephones and refrigerators from wood, then pretended to use them in elaborate ceremonies. Of course, all this carrying on never brought in any cargo. But maybe that wasn't as important as the optimism it created, as misguided people with hope in their eyes and wooden walkie-talkies in their hands looked to the sky for the things that would improve their lives.

In a similar way, fashion makes us all into cargo cultists. From the flattest flat to the longest skirt, from the biggest jeep to the tiniest cell phone, each new piece of cargo promises to renew our spirit, at least for an afternoon. When I first caught on to the cargo-pants thing, I went out and bought a pair right away. And I have to say, they have been working for me. Of course, I have nothing to carry in all those pockets, and I'd just as soon go skateboarding as join the Peace Corps. Still, every time I put mine on, they take me a step closer to feeling like a skinny, extreme athlete, alternative rocker, addict, model, stylist, raver, anthropologist, geologist, club kid, neohippie, hacker, slacker, hacky sacker, bushwhacker, anybody, in short, but who I am. I wear the pants; they help me do the dance.

Magic materialism: that's what fashion and cargo cults are all about.

thinking these categories are natural, but Sahlins is saying they are produced. Young people reading this book probably imagine that blue jeans have been around forever, that they are the natural choice for all kinds of leisure activities. They will be surprised to learn that they became that only in the 1960s during the Vietnam War and the conflict between youth and authority. In this conflict, which was also seen in terms of class conflict, the youth identified with unionized workers (who did wear blue jeans) and appropriated their clothing. According to Sahlins, "nothing could better prove the absence of practical utility in clothing, since work is one of the last things youth has in mind" (p. 184).

Figure 8.8 Cargo pants. © Alamy Images.

Globalization of the Clothing Industry

As we continue to make more and more subtle social and symbolic distinctions, we simultaneously open up new domains or niches for the production of objects. For example, it used to be that there was an article of clothing called a *sneaker*. This footwear was used for all kinds of sport activities – tennis, basketball, volleyball, bike riding, walking, and boating. Today, one needs different kinds of shoes for each sport, along with different kinds of outfits felt to be appropriate for each sport.

For every new distinction made in clothing, a new niche is opened for production. But how are these clothes made and where? In today's world, much of the clothing worn in the United States is made elsewhere. Look at the labels in your clothing and see what percentage of your wardrobe was made in your own country. "If the US is to remain competitive," said one executive quoted in the 1986 PBS film *The Global Assembly Line*, we must reduce costs, and this profit motive "compels companies to take labor offshore," meaning to Third World countries and "export processing zones" where they can pay workers shockingly low wages. For example, Sweatshop Watch, a California organization that monitors sweatshop abuses, published hourly wages for garment workers in 1995: China, 12 cents, Thailand, 38 cents, Philippines, 48 cents, compared with a wage of $9.95 for a worker in the United States. At least 50 countries now host "export processing zones" where the companies are not required to pay duty and thus the companies that establish businesses there do not contribute to that nation's income, which would help to alleviate some of the conditions of poverty. But that would, obviously, be counterproductive because it is that very poverty that enables them to hire workers so cheaply. While the work does bring income to individuals, they derive few benefits, work long hours, are often exposed to toxic chemicals, are not permitted to unionize, and are forced to meet quotas. If they do not, the company can threaten to take its work elsewhere. Is this not corporate blackmail?

In addition, an entire garment may not be made at one site but different parts of it may be farmed out to different places and then assembled in another. This fragmentation of work is one of the most blatant examples of Marx's idea of workers' alienation from the products of their labor. In these factories a worker, usually a woman "because they can do the delicate jobs better" (*The Global Assembly Line*), may only have responsibility for one seam, repeated over and over. Such fragmentation of work also contributes to the deskilling of the workforce, rendering them more as automatons than as talented seamstresses like those who work in *haute couture*.

But "sweatshops" are not just elsewhere, they are also found in the United States and other industrial countries. The term *sweatshop* was coined because the workers were "sweating" from pressure to produce high quotas and from working in places with little ventilation. Every now and then there is an exposé in the press describing the execrable conditions under which people, often immigrants (illegal or not), are working. One of the most shocking was exposed in 1995 in El Monte, California, not far from downtown Los Angeles.

> The workers were immigrants from Thailand. They were living and working in an apartment complex surrounded by barbed-wire fences. They worked over eighty hours a week for less than $2 an hour and were detained by the company owners until they had supposedly paid off the debt of their transportation. Some had labored in the factory for years, unsuccessfully pleading for their freedom. They were forced to shop at a store maintained on the premises by the factory owners, and often charging vastly inflated prices, which virtually assured that they would never get out of debt peonage and be able to buy their freedom. (Bonacich and Appelbaum, 2000: 165)[12]

The clothes they sewed were sold at some of the nation's largest retail stores but the retailers denied knowledge of the conditions under which these women worked. Their lawyer, Julie Su, claims they were making less than 60 cents an hour. Eventually, the 72 women won a law suit, were released from their virtual slavery, and awarded back pay. This aroused the ire of garment manufacturers who then vociferously opposed the Smithsonian exhibit, "Between a Rock and a Hard Place: A

History of American Sweatshops 1820–Present," which opened in the summer of 1998.

In addition to sweatshop production, there has been a proliferation of piecework done at home, mostly but not always by women and children. While this type of work has been going on for a long time, it has become more widespread, even necessary in the economic restructuring that occurred with the developing "niche" market. The "emergence of new systems of production has focused mainly on forms of *flexibility* that enable producers to adapt to volatile conditions in globalized markets. The use of subcontracting is one of the principal characteristics of these new systems" (Eraydin and Erendil 1999: 260; emphasis mine). Turkey has had an important textile industry for some time, but in the last part of the twentieth century textiles and clothing became its "most important export product" (p. 261). And Turkey has a large reservoir of cheap, flexible labor. In order for large companies to meet ever-changing demands, they subcontract work out either to small sweatshops or to a group of workers at home. This type of work can be integrated into the daily schedule when time is available and, thus, is often not seen as *work*. Such work is always temporary, at the whims of the market, has no benefits other than occasional income, and is not supervised (see White 1994). Children learn to do the work and it can seem to be merely apprenticeship. In this way, however, they are interpellated into the capitalist system.

> There was a massive demonstration in New York on August 17, 2001 by a new anti-sweatshop coalition organized by UNITE (Union of Needletrades, Industrial and Textile Employees) that included unions from many of the other countries (Mexico, Guatemala, Honduras, Hong Kong, Thailand, Nicaragua, Dominican Republic, Canada) where garment workers for firms such as Ann Taylor, Eddie Bauer, and Banana Republic are working in sweatshop-type operations.

It is no longer that the system of production comprehends a particular culture; increasingly, global capitalism (primarily from the United States and Western Europe) comprehends the rest of the world in its grip.

Notes

1   Taken from the title of a book by Emma Tarlo (1996).
2   Jenna Weissman Joselit, author of *A Perfect Fit: Clothes, Character, and the Promise of America* (Metropolitan Books, 2001), has also given a freshman seminar at Princeton titled "Getting Dressed," about the social and historical significance of clothes.
3   The title was a reference to the elder Bush's statement, "Read My Lips."
4   See, for example, the films *Priscilla, Queen of the Desert, Paris is Burning*, and *Ma Vie en Rose*.
5   This was written before 9/11.
6   See also René Gremaux's "Woman Becomes Man in the Balkans," in *Third Sex, Third Gender: Beyond Sexual Dimorphism in Culture and History*, ed. Gilbert Herdt (New York: Zone Books, 1994).
7   Middlebrook's psychological portrait may help to unravel this skein of tangled motives, both private and public (Middlebrook 1998).
8   For the issue of berdache and also "third gender" see: Roscoe (1991, 1994); Callender and Kochems, "The North American Berdache," *Current Anthropology*, 24/4 (1983); Trexler, *Sex and Conquest: Gendered Violence, Political Order, and the European Conquest of the Americas* (Cambridge: Polity Press, 1999); Gutierrez (1989); and also Serena Nanda on *hijras*, "Hijras: An Alternative Sex and Gender Role," in Herdt (1994), also *Neither Man nor Woman: The Hijras of India* (Belmont, CA: Wadsworth, 1990).

9   I think he meant "straight" men and women (2); "passive" homosexual men and women (2); and "active" homosexual men and women (2).

10   A "be-in" was an informal gathering, for no particular purpose except to be together, held in a public place like a park. Anyone could and did go to "hang out," although that phrase had not yet been coined.

11   See my article "Untangling the Meanings of Hair in Turkish Society" (1994).

12   I acknowledge Andrea Christensen, one of my student research assistants, for garnering this information.

Bibliography

Appadurai, Arjun, ed. (1986) *The Social Life of Things: Commodities in Cultural Perspective*. Cambridge: Cambridge University Press.

Ash, Juliet and Wilson, Elizabeth (1993) *Chic Thrills: A Fashion Reader*. Berkeley and Los Angeles: University of California Press.

Barthes, Roland ([1967] 1983) *The Fashion System*. New York: Hill & Wang.

Bastian, Misty L. (1996) "Female 'Alhajis' and Entrepreneurial Fashions: Flexible Identities in Southeastern Nigerian Clothing Practice." In *Clothing and Difference: Embodied Identities in Colonial and Postcolonial Africa*, ed. Hildi Hendrickson. Durham, NC: Duke University Press.

Blanch, Lesley (1954) *The Wilder Shores of Love*. New York: Simon and Schuster.

Bonacich, Edna and Appelbaum, Richard P. (2000) *Behind the Label: Inequality in the Los Angeles Apparel Industry*. Berkeley and Los Angeles: University of California Press.

Bourdieu, Pierre (1984) *Distinction: A Social Critique of the Judgement of Taste*. Cambridge, MA: Harvard University Press.

Craik, Jennifer (1994) *The Face of Fashion: Cultural Studies in Fashion*. London: Routledge.

Dalby, Liza Crihfield ([1983] 1999) "Kimono Schools." In *The Meanings of Dress*, ed. Mary Lynn Damhorst, Kimberly A. Miller, and Susan O. Michelman. New York: Fairchild.

Dalby, Liza Crihfield (1993) *Kimono: Fashioning Culture*. New Haven: Yale University Press.

Damhorst, Mary Lynn, Miller, Kimberly A., and Michelman, Susan O., eds. (1999) *The Meanings of Dress*. New York: Fairchild.

Davis, Fred (1992) *Fashion, Culture, and Identity*. Chicago: University of Chicago Press.

de la Haye, Amy and Wilson, Elizabeth (1999) *Defining Dress: Dress as Object, Meaning and Identity*. Manchester: Manchester University Press.

Delaney, Carol (1994) "Untangling the Meaning of Hair in Turkish Society." *Anthropological Quarterly*, 64 (4): 159–72.

Eraydin, Ayda and Erendil, Asuman (1999) "The Role of Female Labor in Industrial Restructuring: New Production Processes and Labor Market Relations in the Istanbul Clothing Industry." *Gender, Place and Culture*, 6: 259–72.

Fausto-Sterling, Anne (1993) "The Five Sexes: Why Male and Female Are Not Enough." *The Sciences* (March/April): 20–4.

Finkelstein, Joanne (1996) *Fashion: An Introduction*. New York: New York University Press.

Gaines, Jane and Herzog, Charlotte, eds. (1990) *Fabrications: Costume and the Female Body*. New York and London: Routledge.

Garber, Marjorie (1992) *Vested Interests: Cross-Dressing and Cultural Anxiety*. London and New York: Routledge.

Gilroy, Paul (1987) *There Ain't No Black in the Union Jack: The Cultural Politics of Race and Nation*. London: Hutchinson.

Goldman, Albert Harry (1974) *Ladies and Gentlemen – Lenny Bruce!!* New York: Random House.

Gremaux, René (1994) "Woman Becomes Man in the Balkans." In *Third Sex, Third Gender: Beyond Sexual Dimorphism in Culture and History*, ed. Gilbert Herdt. New York: Zone Books.

Gutierrez, Ramón (1989) "Must We Deracinate Indians to Find Gay Roots?" *Out/Look* (Winter): 61–7.

Hebdige, Dick (1979) *Subculture: The Meaning of Style*. London and New York: Methuen.

Herdt, Gilbert, ed. (1994) *Third Sex, Third Gender: Beyond Sexual Dimorphism in Culture and History*. New York: Zone Books.

Hollander, Anne ([1975] 1978) *Seeing Through Clothes*. New York: Viking Press.

Hotchkiss, Valerie R. (1996) *Clothes Make the Man: Female Cross-Dressing in Medieval Europe*. New York and London: Garland.

Jicai, Feng (1994) *The Three-Inch Golden Lotus: A Novel on Footbinding*. Trans. David Wakefield. Honolulu: University of Hawaii Press.

Mackie, Gerry (1996) "Ending Footbinding and Infibulation: A Convention Account." *American Sociological Review*, 61: 999–1017.

McVeigh, Brian J. (2000) *Wearing Ideology: State, Schooling and Self-Presentation in Japan*. Oxford: Berg.

Middlebrook, Diane Wood (1998) *Suits Me: The Double Life of Billy Tipton*. Boston: Houghton Mifflin.

Norton, John (1997) "Faith and Fashion in Turkey." In *Languages of Dress in the Middle East*, ed. Nancy Lindisfarne-Tapper and Bruce Ingham. Richmond, Surrey: Curzon Press with SOAS.

Polhemus, Ted (1994) *Streetstyle: From Sidewalk to Catwalk*. New York: Thames & Hudson (originally published to coincide with an exhibition at the Victoria and Albert Museum, London, Nov. 1994–Feb. 1995).

Ribeyro, Julio Ramón (1986) "Alienation." In *On Being Foreign: Culture Shock in Short Fiction*, ed. Tom J. Lewis and Robert E. Jungman. Yarmouth, ME: Intercultural Press.

Roscoe, Will (1991) *The Zuni Man-Woman*. Albuquerque: University of New Mexico Press.

Roscoe, Will (1994) "How to Become a Berdache: Toward a Unified Analysis of Gender Diversity." In *Third Sex, Third Gender: Beyond Sexual Dimorphism in Culture and History*, ed. Gilbert Herdt. New York: Zone Books.

Ross, Andrew, ed. (1997) *No Sweat: Fashion, Free Trade, and the Rights of Garment Workers*. New York and London: Verso.

Rubenstein, Ruth P. (1995) *Dress Codes: Meanings and Messages in American Culture*. Boulder, CO: Westview Press.

Sahlins, Marshall (1976) *Culture and Practical Reason*. Chicago: University of Chicago Press.

Saltzberg, Elayne A. and Chrisler, Joan C. ([1995] 1997) "Beauty is the Beast: Psychological Effects of the Pursuit of the Perfect Female Body." In *Reconstructing Gender: A Multicultural Anthology*, ed. Estelle Disch. Mountain View, CA: Mayfield.

Seal, Jeremy (1995) *A Fez of the Heart: Travels around Turkey in Search of a Hat*. New York: Harcourt Brace.

Tarlo, Emma (1996) *Clothing Matters: Dress and Identity in India*. Chicago: University of Chicago Press.

Traweek, Sharon (1988) *Beamtimes and Lifetimes: The World of High-Energy Physicists*. Cambridge, MA: Harvard University Press.

White, Jenny (1994) *Money Makes Us Relatives: Women's Labor in Urban Turkey*. Austin: University of Texas Press.

Wikan, Unni (1977) "Man Becomes Woman: Transsexualism in Oman." *Man*, 12: 304–19.

Woolf, Virginia ([1928] 1960) *Orlando: A Biography*. New York: New American Library.

Yamanaka, Norio (1982) *The Book of Kimono*. Tokyo: Kodansha International.

Young, Antonia (2000) *Women Who Become Men: Albanian Sworn Virgins*. New York: Berg.

Alienation (An Instructive Story with a Footnote)
Julio Ramón Ribeyro

Despite the fact that he was a mulatto named López, he longed to resemble less and less a defensive back on the Alianza Lima Soccer Team and increasingly to take on the look of a blond from Philadelphia. Life had taught him that if he wanted to prosper in a colonial city it was better to skip the intermediate stages and transform himself into a gringo from the United States rather than into just a fair-skinned nobody from Lima. During the years that I knew him, he devoted all of his attention to eliminating every tract of the López and *zambo*[1] within him and Americanizing himself before the bottom fell out and he would turn into, say, a bank guard or a taxi driver. He had to begin by killing the Peruvian in himself and extracting something from every gringo he met. From all this plundering a new person would emerge, a fragmented being who was neither mulatto nor gringo, but rather the result of an unnatural commingling, something that the force of destiny would eventually change, unfortunately for him, from a rosy dream into a hellish nightmare.

But let's not get ahead of ourselves. We should establish the fact that his name was Roberto, that years later he was known as Bobby, but that the most recent official documents refer to him as Bob. At each stage in his frantic ascent toward nothingness his name would lose one syllable.

Everything began the afternoon when a group of us fair-haired kids were playing ball on Bolognesi Plaza. We were out of school on vacation and some of us who lived in nearby chalets, both girls and boys, would meet at the plaza during those endless summer afternoons. Roberto used to go there too, even though he attended a public school and lived on one of the last backstreets left in the district rather than in a chalet. He would go there to watch the girls play and to be greeted by some fair-faced kid who had seen him growing up on those streets and knew he was the laundry woman's son.

In reality, he would go there like the rest of us, to see Queca. We were all infatuated with Queca, who, during the past couple of years, had the distinction of being chosen class queen, an honor bestowed upon her during festivities at the end of the school year. Queca didn't study with the German sisters of Saint Ursula, nor with the North Americans of Villa María, but rather with the Spanish nuns of Reparation. That was no big deal, nor the fact that her father was a blue-collar worker who drove a bus, nor that her house had only one story garnished with geraniums instead of roses. What was important then were her rosy skin, her green eyes, her long, brown hair, the way she ran, laughed, jumped, and her incomparable legs, always bare and golden and which, in time, would become legendary.

Roberto used to come only to watch her play; none of the boys who came from the other Miraflores neighborhoods, or even those who later came from San Isidro and Barranco, for that matter, could attract her attention. One time Peluca Rodríguez flung himself from the highest branch of a pine tree; Lucas de Tramontana drove up on a shiny motorcycle that had eight headlights; Fats Gómez broke the nose of the ice cream vendor who had the gall to whistle at us; and Armando Wolff donned several fine, new flannel suits with a bow tie. But not one of them caught Queca's eye. Queca favored no one; she preferred to talk with everybody, to run, skip, laugh, and play volleyball, leaving behind at nightfall a gang of teenage boys overwhelmed by intense sexual frustration that only a charitable hand underneath white sheets was able to console.

It was a fatal ball that someone tossed that afternoon, that Queca was unable to catch, and that rolled toward the bench where Roberto sat alone and observant. He had always waited for this moment. With a jump he landed on the grass, crawled between the flower beds, leaped over the hedge covered with passionflowers, stepped into a drainage ditch, and rescued the ball, which was just about to roll under the wheels of a car. But as he

[1] Ribeyro uses the term *zambo* to refer to a person who is a blend of Indian and Negro.

returned with it, Queca, who was now facing him with outstretched hands, seemed to be adjusting her focus, observing something that only now she was really seeing for the first time: a short, dark, thick-lipped being with kinky hair, something very ordinary that she probably saw daily, just as one sees park benches or pine trees. Abruptly, she turned away, terrified.

Roberto never forgot Queca's words as she fled: "I don't play with *zambos*." These five words decided his destiny.

Every human being who suffers becomes an observer, so Roberto continued going to the plaza for several years, but his look had lost all innocence. It was no longer a simple reflection of the world, but rather an organ of vigilance – penetrating, selecting, and examining.

Queca was growing up; her run was more moderate now, her skirts longer, her leaps weren't quite so bold, and her conduct around the gang had become more distant and selective. We were all aware of these changes, but Roberto observed something more: that Queca tended to turn away from her more swarthy admirers until, through successive comparisons, she focused her attention only on Chalo Sander, the one boy in the group with the fairest hair, the lightest skin, and the only one who studied in a school run by North American priests. By the time her legs were the most triumphant and well-turned, she was speaking exclusively to him. The first time she strolled to the levee holding hands with him we understood that she wasn't part of our turf anymore; there was nothing we could do but play the role of the chorus in a Greek tragedy, always present and visible, but irrecoverably separated from the gods.

Rejected and forlorn, we would gather on the street corner after one of our games, where we would smoke our first cigarettes, arrogantly fondle the newly discovered down of our mustaches, and comment on the hopeless state of things. Sometimes we would go into a bar owned by a Chinese named Manuel and have a beer. Roberto followed us around like a shadow, always scrutinizing us from the doorway, never missing a word of our conversation. Sometimes we would say, "Hi, *zambo*, have a drink with us," and he always said, "No thanks, another time," and although he smiled and kept his

distance, we knew that he shared in his own way our sense of loss.

And it was Chalo Sander, of course, who took Queca to the graduation party when we finished high school. We decided to meet in our favorite bar early that evening. We drank more than usual, plotted bizarre schemes, and spoke of kidnapping, of planning some kind of group attack. But it was all just talk. By eight o'clock we were in front of the modest little house with geraniums, resigned to being witnesses of our own privation. Chalo arrived in his father's car, sporting an elegant white tuxedo; a few minutes later he left the house accompanied by Queca, who, with her long evening grown and upswept hairdo, hardly resembled our once playful classmate. Queca, smiling and clutching a satin evening purse, didn't even see us. An elusive vision, the last, because never again would things be the same. All of our hopes died instantly, at that very moment that would never let us forget the indelible image that brought to a close a part of our youth.

Almost no one hung around the plaza anymore, some because they were getting ready to enroll at the university, others because they were moving to other neighborhoods in search of an impossible replica of Queca. Only Roberto, who was now a delivery boy for a bakery, returned to the plaza at nightfall, where other young boys and girls now became the new gang and played our games so naturally that it seemed as if they had invented them. Sitting on his solitary bench, Roberto appeared to pay little attention to the goings on around him, but in reality his eyes were always fixed upon Queca's house. That way he was able to confirm before anyone else that Chalo had been only one episode in Queca's life, a kind of rehearsal preparing her for the arrival of the original, of which Chalo had been a mere copy: Billy Mulligan, the son of a United States consulate official.

Billy was freckled, redheaded, wore flowered shirts, had enormous feet, a boisterous laugh, and the sun, instead of toasting him, made him peel; but he always came to see Queca in his own car and not in his father's car. Nobody knew where Queca first met him nor how he came to be there, but she began to see him often, until she saw only him – his tennis rackets, his sunglasses, his camera – while the outline of Chalo gradually grew more and more opaque, smaller, and more distant until it finally disappeared altogether. Moving from the group to the type, the type to the individual, Queca had shown her hand. Only Mulligan would take her to the altar and, when they were lawfully married, he would have every right to caress those things we had dreamed about in vain for so long.

Disillusionment generally is something that no one can tolerate; it's either soon forgotten, its causes evaded, or it becomes the object of ridicule and even a theme in literature. It turned out that Fats Gómez went off to study in London, Peluca Rodríguez wrote a really ballsy sonnet, Armando Wolff came to the conclusion that Queca was nothing but a social climber, and Lucas de Tramontana deceitfully boasted that he had laid her several times out on the levee. Roberto was the only one who learned a true, valuable lesson from all this; it had to be Mulligan or no one. What good was it to be blond if there were so many light-skinned braggarts who were desperate, lazy, and failures? There had to be a superior state, inhabited by those who could plan their lives with confidence in this gray city and who could effortlessly reap all the best fruits the land had to offer. The problem was how to become another Mulligan, since he was a *zambo*. But suffering, when it doesn't kill, sharpens ingenuity; so Roberto subjected himself to a long, thorough analysis and outlined a plan of action.

First of all he had to dezambofy himself. His hair wasn't a major problem; he dyed it with peroxide and had it straightened. As for his skin, he tried mixed starch, rice powder, and talcum from the drugstore until he found the ideal combination; but a dyed and powdered zambo is still a zambo. He needed to know how the North American gringos dressed, talked, moved, and thought; in short, exactly who they were.

Back then we saw Roberto marauding about during his free time in various locales that seemingly had nothing in common, except for one thing: they were usually frequented by gringos. Some saw him standing in front of the Country Club, others at the Santa Maria school gates; and Lucas de Tramontana swore that he caught a glimpse of him behind a fence at the golf course, and someone else spotted

him at the airport trying to carry some tourist's luggage; and then there were several who found him roaming about the halls of the US Embassy.

This phase of his plan was for him absolutely perfect. For the moment, he was able to see that the gringos were set apart from others by the special way they dressed, which he described as sporty, comfortable, and unconventional. Hence, Roberto was one of the first to discover the advantages of blue jeans, the virile cowboy look of the wide leather belt fastened by an enormous buckle, the soft comfort of white canvas shoes with rubber soles, the collegiate charm of a canvas cap with a visor, the coolness of a flowered or striped short-sleeved shirt, the variety of nylon jackets zipped up in front, or the sporty shirts displaying provocative, carefree slogans along with the logo of an American university.

None of these articles of clothing were sold in any department store but had to be brought from the United States, impossible for him to do. But, checking around, he discovered garage sales. Prior to returning to the United States, gringo families would announce in the newspaper their intention to sell everything they had. Roberto showed up on their doorstep before anyone else, acquiring in this way a wardrobe in which he invested himself and his life's savings.

With hair that was now straightened and bleached, a pair of blue jeans and a loud shirt, Roberto was on the brink of becoming Bobby.

All of this created problems. His mother said that no one would speak to him on the street, thinking he was pretentious. What was even worse, they would make jokes or whistle at him as if he were a queer. He never contributed a cent for food, he would stand for hours in front of the mirror, and he spent all his money on old clothing. His father, according to Roberto's black mother, may have been a worthless scoundrel who, like the magical Fu Man Chu, vanished only a year after they met, but at least he was never embarrassed to be seen with her, nor was he ashamed of being a pilot's mate on a boat.

In our group the first one to notice the change in Roberto was Peluca Rodríguez, who had ordered a pair of blue jeans through a Braniff purser. When the jeans came, he put them on and headed for the plaza to show them off, only to run into Roberto, who was wearing a pair identical to his. For days he did nothing but curse the *zambo*, saying he had ruined his act, that he had probably been spying on him to copy him. He even noticed that he bought Lucky Strike cigarettes and that he combed his hair with a lock falling over his forehead.

But the worst thing concerned his job. Cahuide Morales, the owner of the bakery, was a gruff, big-bellied, provincial mestizo who loved cracklings and native waltzes; and one who had broken his back for the last twenty years to make the business go. Nothing annoyed him more than for someone to pretend to be what he wasn't. Whether one was a mixed-breed or white didn't matter: what was important was *mosca, agua, molido*: He knew a thousand different words for money. When he saw that his employee had bleached his hair, he endured another wrinkle on his forehead; when he realized that Roberto had actually covered himself with powder, he swallowed a damn word that just about gave him indigestion; but when he came to work dressed like a gringo, the mixture of father, police, bully, and boss broke loose in him and he took Roberto by the scruff of the neck to the back of the store; Morales Brothers' Bakery was a serious business, and one would have to obey the rules; he had overlooked the makeup, but if he didn't come to work in uniform like the other delivery boys, he was going to boot him out the door with a swift kick in the ass.

Roberto was already on a roll and he couldn't go back now; he preferred the kick in the rear.

Those gloomy days were interminable as he looked for another job. His ambition was to go to work in a gringo's home as a butler, gardener, chauffeur, or whatever, but the doors were always shut in his face. His strategy lacked something, and that was a knowledge of English. Since he didn't have funds to enroll in a language academy; be bought himself a dictionary and began copying the words into a notebook. When he reached the letter C he threw in the towel; this purely visual knowledge of English wasn't getting him anywhere; but, then, there were always the movies, a school that would not only teach but also entertain.

In the balconies of the premier theaters he spent entire afternoons watching westerns and detective films in the target language. The plots were irrelevant; what mattered was the way the characters spoke. He wrote down all of the words he could understand and then repeated them until they were permanently recorded in his memory. By forcing himself to watch the films over and over again, he learned complete sentences and even entire speeches. In his room in front of the mirror he was suddenly the romantic cowboy making an irresistible declaration of love to the dance-hall girl, or the ruthless gangster uttering a death sentence while riddling his adversary with bullets. Besides, the movies nourished in him certain illusions that filled him with hope, leading him to believe he had discovered in himself a slight resemblance to Alan Ladd, who had appeared in one of the westerns dressed in blue jeans and a red and black plaid jacket. In reality, the only thing he had in common with him was his height and the yellow lock of hair he let dangle over his forehead. Dressed the same as the actor, he saw the film ten times in a row, always standing at the movie entrance after each showing, waiting for people to leave and hoping to overhear them say, but look, how strange, that guy looks like Alan Ladd. No one said it, of course; and the first time we saw him striking that pose, we laughed in his face.

His mother told us one day that finally Roberto had found a job, not in the home of a gringo as he had hoped, but possibly something better: the Miraflores Bowling Club. He waited tables in the bar from five o'clock in the afternoon until midnight. The few times that we went there we saw him excelling diligently. He waited on the natives in an unbiased, frankly impeccable manner, but with the gringos he was ingratiating and servile. As soon as one came in he was at his side, taking his order, and seconds later the customer had received his hot dog and Coca-Cola. He was encouraged to use words in English and, as he was answered in the same language, his vocabulary grew. Soon he possessed a good repertoire of expressions with which he won over the gringos who were delighted to see a native who understood them. Since Roberto was difficult to pronounce, the gringos were the ones who decided to call him Bobby.

And with the name Bobby López he was finally able to enroll in the Peruvian–North American

Institute. Those who saw him during that period say that he was the classic bookworm, the kind who never missed a class, or forgot his homework, or hesitated to question the teacher about some obscure grammatical concept. Apart from the white students who for professional reasons were taking courses there, he met others like himself who, although total strangers from different backgrounds and other neighborhoods, nourished the same dreams and led a life similar to his. He especially became a good friend of José María Cabanillas, a tailor's son from Surquillo. Cabanillas shared the same blind admiration for the gringos that he did, and years ago he too had begun to smother the *zambo* in himself with really enviable results. Besides having the advantage of being taller and lighter-skinned than Bobby, he resembled not Alan Ladd, who after all was a second-rate actor admired by a small group of snobbish girls, but rather the indestructible John Wayne. The two of them made an inseparable pair. They finished out the year with the best grades, and Mr. Brown held them up as examples to the rest of the students, speaking of "their sincere desire to excel."

As buddies they must have had long, pleasant conversations together. They were always going here and there, their rear ends stuffed into faded blue jeans, and always speaking in English to one another. But it's also true that no one could stomach them; they muddled things so badly that neither relatives nor friends could put up with them. That's why they rented a room in a building on Mogollón Avenue, where they lived together. It was there they created a sacred haven that allowed them to mix foreign culture with their own and to feel that in the middle of this dismal city they were living in a California neighborhood. Each one contributed what he could: Bobby, his posters, and José María, who was a music fan, his Frank Sinatra, Dean Martin, and Tommy Dorsey records. What a fine pair of gringos they made, stretched out on the sofa-bed, smoking their Lucky Strikes while listening to "Strangers in the Night" and staring at the bridge over the Hudson River stuck to the wall. With one big try, hop, they would be walking across that bridge.

Even for us it was difficult to travel to the United States. One had to have a scholarship, or relatives already there, or lots of money. For López and Cabanillas, none of these were possible. They saw no other way out but to cut loose like other near-whites, thanks to jobs as airline pursers. Every year when openings were announced, they both applied. They knew more English than anyone else, liked serving others, were self-sacrificing and enthusiastic; but nobody knew them, nobody recommended them, and it was obvious to the interviewers that they were dealing with powdered zambos. They were turned down.

They say that Bobby wept and pulled out his hair and that Cabanillas attempted suicide by jumping from a modest second-floor window. Within their refuge on Mogollón Avenue they spent the darkest days of their lives; the city, which had always sheltered them, had turned into a dirty rag they covered with insults and scorn. But eventually their spirits lifted and new plans surfaced. Since no one wanted anything to do with them here, they would have to get out any way they could. They had no choice but to immigrate disguised as tourists.

For an entire year they worked hard and deprived themselves of everything in order to save enough for their fare and set up a common fund that would allow them to survive abroad. As a result, the two of them were finally able to pack their bags and abandon forever that detested city in which they had suffered so much and to which they never wanted to return as long as they lived.

It's easy to predict the events that followed, and it doesn't take much imagination to complete this parable. In the neighborhood we had direct sources of information: letters from Bobby to his mother, news from travelers abroad, and finally the whole story from a witness.

Soon Bobby and José María spent in one month what they had thought would last them six months. They soon realized that all the Lópezes and Cabanillases in the entire world had congregated in New York – Asians, Arabs, Aztecs, Africans, Iberians, Mayans, Chibchas, Sicilians, Caribbeans, Mussulmans, Quecbuas, Polynesians, Eskimos, representatives of every origin, language, race, and pigmentation – all of whom had one common goal: the desire to live as a Yankee, for which they had surrendered their souls and altered their appearances.

The city tolerated them for several months, complacently, while it absorbed the dollars they had saved. Then, as if through a tube, it led them toward the mechanism of expulsion.

With great difficulty, they got an extension on their visas, while looking for steady jobs that would let them keep up with all the Quecas of the place; and there were many, although the girls just paraded in front of them, paying less attention to them than a cockroach would deserve. They wore out their clothes, Frank Sinatra's music became intolerable, and the mere thought of having to eat another hot dog, which was a luxury in Lima, turned their stomachs. From their cheap hotel they moved first to the Catholic shelter and then to a bench in a public park. Soon they discovered that white substance that fell from the sky, lightened their skin, and made them skate like idiots on the icy sidewalks, a substance which, by its very color, was nature's deceptive racist.

There was only one solution. Thousands of miles away, in a country called Korea, blond North Americans were fighting against some horrible Asians. According to the newspapers, the freedom of Western nations was in jeopardy and statesmen confirmed it on television. But it was so painful to send "the boys" to that place! They were dying like rats, leaving behind pale, grief-stricken mothers in tiny farmhouses with an attic full of old toys. Whoever went over there to fight for one year would be on easy street when he came home; naturalization, work, social security, integration, medals. Everywhere there were recruitment centers. To each volunteer the country opened its heart.

Bobby and José María enlisted so they wouldn't be deported. And after three months of training at an army base they left in an enormous airplane. Life was a marvelous adventure; the trip was unforgettable. Having been born in a poor, miserable, sad country, and having known the busiest city in the world, with thousands of deprivations, it's true; but all this was behind them because now they were wearing a green uniform, flying over plains, seas, and snow-capped mountains, clutching powerful weapons and were becoming young men still filled with promise, exploring the realm of the unknown.

The laundress María has plenty of postcards of temples, markets, and exotic streets, all written in a small fastidious hand. Where could Seoul be? There are lots of ads and cabarets. Then came letters from the front lines that described to us the first attack, which forced him to take a few days off. Thanks to these documents, we were able to piece together fairly well the things that happened to him. Gradually, step by step, Bobby came closer to his rendezvous with destiny. It was necessary to reach a certain parallel and to confront a wave of yellow-skinned soldiers who descended from the northern hills like kernels of corn. For this, the volunteers, the unconquerable watchmen of the West, were there to lend a hand.

José María was saved by a miracle and proudly showed off the stump of his right arm when he returned to Lima months later. His squad had been sent to scout a rice field, where supposedly the Korean advance guard was waiting to ambush them. Bobby didn't suffer, José María said; the first blast blew his helmet off and his head rolled into a trench, all of its dyed, tangled hair hanging down. Now he had only lost an arm, but he was there, alive, telling his story, drinking cold beer, powder gone now and more zambo than ever, living comfortably off what he received as compensation for having been mutilated.

By then Roberto's mother had suffered her second attack, one which erased her from the world. She never read the official letter informing her that Bob López had died in action and was entitled to an honorable citation and remuneration for his family. No one could collect it.

Footnote

And Queca? Perhaps if Bob had known her story maybe his life would have been different or maybe it wouldn't have; no one will ever know. Billy Mulligan took her to his country, as agreed, to a town in Kentucky where his father owned a pork-canning business. They spent several months in ecstasy in that pretty house with wide sidewalks, a fence, a garden, and all the electric appliances invented by technology: in short, it was a house like hundred thousand others in that country-continent. Gradually the Irish in him, which his Puritan upbringing had suppressed for so long, began to reveal itself; at the same time, Queca's eyes grew larger and acquired that sadness typical of the Limeños. Billy was coming home later each night; he became addicted to slot machines and car racing; his feet grew bigger and developed callouses; he discovered a malignant mole on his neck; on Saturdays he filled up on bourbon at the Kentucky Friends' Club; he had an affair with a woman employee at the firm; he wrecked the car twice; his look turned into a fixed, watery stare; and he ended up beating his wife, the pretty, unforgettable Queca, in the early hours of dawn on Sundays, while he smiled stupidly and called her a shitty half-breed.

You may do this with a partner also, as long as both of you are engaged in the observations and the writing.

1   Go over to a local shopping center or marketplace or downtown area. Depending on your location, you can choose anything from a department or clothing store like Macy's, Sears, Marks & Spencer, Saks Fifth Avenue, Nordstrom's, Gap, or a local establishment. If represented in the store of your choice, visit all of the following departments: baby–infant, girls, boys, teens, women's, and men's. What are the different classifications? Are they by age, size, gender, lifestyle, occasion? Note as many differentiations as you can. What kind of marketing and production niches have been created? Can you see any openings for new niches? If so, what are they?

2   Choose a particular event/outing. It could be anything from a date for dinner or a movie, a night out at a pub, a party, a wedding, to a holiday celebration. What would you wear to this event/outing? Describe both the event and the outfit in detail and why this is the appropriate attire for the event.

9

VIPs: Very Important People, Places, and Performances

Certain people, places, events, and cultural practices become iconic; they embody cultural myths or epitomize cultural values. Jesse Owens. Princess Diana. Why are certain people described as "larger than life"? The Statue of Liberty. The Beatles. The global circulation of such icons.

VIPs: Very Important People, Places, and Performances

When you visit a different country or a different region in your own country, there are certain sites you are told you simply must see, people you need to know about, and activities you must participate in if you are to get a feel for that culture. This is because the people who live in that country or region or village feel they represent something important about their area. For example, when I was first in Turkey I was told I simply had to see Atatürk's Mausoleum, a huge structure that dominates Ankara's skyline; in so doing, of course, I also had to learn something about Atatürk, the founder of the Republic. Often these very important places are spectacular – highly visible and well known – such as the Houses of Parliament in Britain, the Eiffel Tower in France, the Taj Mahal in India, the Pyramids in Egypt, or the Statue of Liberty in the United States.

Additionally, there are certain people, including folk heroes/heroines, one must know about if one is to understand a given society. These are figures that have become cultural icons because they epitomize personal attributes and qualities that are culturally valued. In the United States these could be traditional American folk heroes like Horatio Alger, Paul Bunyan, and, today, might even include figures from films such as *The Matrix*, *Star Trek*, or the *James Bond* series.[1] But they can also be important political figures like George Washington, Abraham Lincoln, John F. Kennedy, or Martin Luther King, Jr. These would be typical choices for Americans, but so, too, might Madonna or Oprah. The British might single out Queen Elizabeth (I and II), Churchill, the Beatles, or the late Princess Diana.

Very important performances might include the celebration of the Fourth of July in the United States, Bastille Day in France, the Changing of the Guard at Buckingham Palace, or the celebration of Mardi Gras in Rio de Janeiro. But another

Figure 9.1   The Taj Mahal, Agra, India. © Alamy Images.

type of important cultural performance could be a baseball game in the United States or the very mundane ritual of making and taking tea in England or Japan or Turkey.

To begin to understand what it is to be British, for example, it might help to know something about the traditional daily ritual of "tea." It might also help you get the rhythm of an English day and a sense of their culinary predilections. It would certainly help you to begin to understand aspects of British history: their relationship to India, perhaps, or the symbolism of the American Tea Party in Boston Harbor. What is it about baseball, for instance, that made it the "national pastime" of the Americans, while cricket might say something important about being British, and the passion for soccer or tango is thought to characterize Brazilians (Archetti 1994, 1999)? Life-cycle events, like births or weddings or the rituals surrounding death, are also very important cultural performances; the very different ways that such events are marked incorporate cultural meanings and values.[2]

In this chapter I have chosen to discuss the Grand Canyon, the British (and Turkish) tea ceremony, Princess Diana, the Beatles, the Statue of Liberty, American football, and the Olympics. These are my choices; they would probably not be yours. As I discuss at greater length on page 373, to a large extent these choices reflect not only my individual preferences but also my ethnicity, socioeconomic class, age, gender – a wide range of factors. It would be foolish to claim that they are the only

Figure 9.2   Martin Luther King, Jr. Photo Rex Features.

– or even the most important – VIPs; I offer them as a way to get you to think about what makes these people, places, and practices cultural icons or archetypal practices; I hope that you will look anew at those VIPs that you and your fellow students admire. Whom might you choose? What about Mahatma Gandhi? Rosa Parks? Amelia Earhart? Martin Luther King, Jr. or Malcolm X? Albert Einstein? Cesar Chavez? Bob Marley?

I found this chapter was a particularly difficult one to write for several reasons. First, it demanded research into a range of topics that, perhaps because they are

Figure 9.3 Bob Marley in 1981. Photo Sheila Rock/Rex Features.

familiar and popular ones, are also difficult ones on which to get perspective. Second, because this chapter does not have a single theme like space or language – which could run like a thread throughout the whole and provide coherence – there was no easy way for me to gracefully string my examples together. What's more, as you will see, cultural icons that appear to represent a particular culture cannot be confined within national boundaries; the very things that I found most representative of a certain culture were, I recognized, also global phenomena. That realization might seem to undermine the whole project! And in important ways it does, but I think you will find that this understanding makes us more aware of how porous the boundaries are, how much the so-called individual cultures of various people and countries overlap, and – perhaps most important – how the very idea of culture as a static contained object or condition is artificial and misleading. Culture is not and cannot be isomorphic with the nation conceived as a territory with specific boundaries, but, as a system of symbols, meanings, and myths, it can spread as far and as wide as the people who are its avatars.

> I want to remind readers again that while we often discuss culture as if it were a discrete entity, this can be misleading. It is more accurate, I believe, to think of culture as a system of symbols and meanings that clearly are porous and extensive. It might be worth referring back to my earlier discussion of the use of the word culture and the concepts of culture in chapter 1.

The spread of culture, or specific aspects of specific cultures, is enabled in large part by the media, but also by personal contact. Those of us who have access to a wide range of media learn more about people in other parts of the world more quickly than ever before. Songs sung in one part are carried over airwaves around the globe. The death of an important figure becomes known almost immediately, and through television one can be present, virtually, at the funeral. Travel and immigration also bring us into contact with people from very different cultural backgrounds than our own. Films bring us visual images of spectacular cultural sites. Satellites allow millions of spectators around the world to watch sporting events as they occur. Such technological innovations that permit the spread of culture are symbolic of the changing social world we inhabit. It is becoming more and more difficult to say that *this* epitomizes British culture or *that* says something important about what it means to be an American. The people, places, and performances that I have chosen to discuss in this chapter both are and are not representative of their specific cultures. At the same time, I do not believe that we are moving toward a world culture, since each person, place, or performance that we look at is meaningfully incorporated in different ways in different cultural/national contexts. They represent different things not only to people living in different cultures but also to people differently located within the same culture. Nevertheless, there is overlap. Attending to the "conjuncture," as Marshall Sahlins calls it – where these overlaps occur and how they are variously incorporated – provides yet another way to investigate the things that matter to people and why.

If VIPs generally seem larger than life, it is because they are symbolically significant. In other words, they are more than just individual people, places, or performances. They embody, or are able to tap into, cultural myths that express qualities, beliefs, and values that, even if not consciously understood, nevertheless touch our emotions and make us feel that we, too, belong. We are enlarged because of their presence. The choice of who or what is a VIP will undoubtedly vary depending on race, class, gender, religion, and region. My choices in this chapter, for example, do indicate something about my own gender, race, and class position. At the same time, I do feel that there are some things that tend to override "region, class, formal religious affiliation, political sentiments, gender, ethnic group, and place of residence" (Kottak 1982: 74) even though they may be experienced slightly differently depending on those variables. There are plenty of studies that focus on differences but rather few that attend to the things that help to unify and bind a diverse people into a social whole. It is the broad mythic frameworks that help to accomplish this task.

Rather than assuming that we know what the important underlying cultural myths are, it is more instructive to begin with the people, places, and performances that simply attract our attention. Anthropologists should always begin with what is obvious and tangible – with what is right in front of them – and only after intensive analysis dig to the deeper symbolic and systemic level. If, as I noted at the beginning, everything is interrelated, you can begin the investigation of culture anywhere.

A Place

As I was thinking about the structure of this chapter I was sitting at the rim of the Grand Canyon. Not only is this my favorite place, but it is also the place that I tell everyone – friends, relatives, colleagues, and visitors – that they simply must see, at least once in a lifetime. It is awesome in the true meaning of the word. Being in the presence of the Grand Canyon is a humbling experience – your life and your problems are measured against the depth of its temporal perspective – and even the loudest and most rowdy of souls are subdued.

After driving through woods and meadows you come upon it so suddenly it takes your breath away. As one brochure says, "There is no warning . . . no time to prepare for the visual impact of the Grand Canyon." Even though I have been there several times, including a two-week rafting trip through it, I cry when I first catch a glimpse; I cannot help it, the impact is so overwhelming.[3] Although the Grand Canyon is not normally considered to be a pilgrimage destination, the fact that 5 million people every year make the journey indicates otherwise. Most people who visit feel it is a sacred place.

But what can such a *natural* wonder say about American *culture*? It is only accidental that it exists in the United States. Its vastness, majesty, and indomitability perhaps express something Americans would like to believe about their country. On a more mundane level, the protection, maintenance, and presentation of the Grand Canyon do say something about American beliefs and character. The dedication of it as a National Park in 1919, as a treasure to be preserved for future generations, reveals a foresight that many people would argue is in contrast to the generally shortsighted, short-term interests of American politics. More important, although it is probably my love for the place that makes me view things this way, I believe that many Americans display a less frequently celebrated aspect of the national character when they are at the Grand Canyon – a quieter, more contemplative, and less acquisitive side – a side that reveres nature rather than sees it as an exploitable commodity. Perhaps the grandeur of this site taps into an undercurrent in the so-called American psyche. This is what Catherine Albanese calls "nature religion" (1990) – a belief that nature can be a means to the divine or something through which we are healed – and such a current unites the early Puritans, the Transcendentalists such as Emerson and Thoreau, and a variety of New Age thinkers.

Figure 9.4   Grand Canyon, Arizona. © CORBIS.

In 1979 UNESCO named the Grand Canyon a World Heritage Site, thereby transforming it – at least in name – from an American national treasure to an international site. Today, many of the visitors as well as service personnel at the Grand Canyon are not American. Not only do such individuals have an opportunity to view this extraordinary physical site, they also have an interesting opportunity to observe Americans: to view Americans in a distinct cultural setting and to consider why Americans value this place.

A Ritual Performance

Turning now to a performance that depends on a specific commodity – tea – let us attend to the ways it is ritualized in different cultural contexts. "Taking tea" can be an elaborate ceremony, as in Japan, or a very ordinary, daily ritual, as in Britain and Turkey (although each has its own more formal tea ritual). Since much has been written about Japanese tea ceremony, I will not reiterate that literature here;[4] instead I will briefly discuss British and Turkish tea rituals.

British tea

This expression is borrowed from the title of Robert A. Heinlein's classic 1961 novel *Stranger in a Strange Land*. I am using the phrase literally in my text, but this is a slight misrepresentation of Heinlein. I include the phrase because the allusion to Heinlein's work is significant. His novel is a social satire that is, as well, a meditation on cultural inquiry or investigation, for the "strange land" of the novel is, in fact, the protagonist's home culture. Heinlein tells the story of Valentine Michael Smith, an orphan of the first manned expedition to Mars, who was raised by Martians and then brought back to Earth by a second human expedition to Mars. Upon returning to his home, Earth, Smith ironically finds himself a stranger in a strange land, because everything he encounters is foreign to him and he must take on the job of learning how to be a human being.

Teatime, from my outsider's point of view, seems to represent something quintessential about being British – tea is the national beverage, as, I suppose, beer is represented as the national beverage in Germany or wine in France. The British drink about 185 million cups a day according to one report (Beck, *Wall Street Journal*, October 30, 1998) and tea drinkers down an average of three a day.[5] Ironically, I came to appreciate the custom when I was outside Britain – at the British Institute of Archaeology in Ankara, Turkey. Perhaps it is in such outposts that certain customs are observed most strictly because it is often when we are "strangers in a strange land" that we cling most firmly to patterns that remind us of our home(land).

In any case, it was in Ankara that I became much more aware of teatime as significant not just to British well-being and as a means of marking time (cf. Hazan 1987), but also as a means of performing their identity. The course of the day's meals followed a very strict pattern. The day commenced with breakfast (which began with tea) and was followed by elevenses, lunch, tea, and, finally, supper. *Elevenses* was mid-morning tea and was not as significant or elaborate as afternoon tea. Afternoon tea was and is *de rigueur*; the people at the British Institute were adamant about preserving the ritual of afternoon tea as a cultural institution in an "alien" land. It was, clearly, a way to maintain their distinct identity in Turkey.

"Tea," as one American in London commented,

is a word used not only to describe the leaves of some Oriental plant that yield an almost-tasteless brownish infusion when you pour water on them, but also to designate the entire feast of scones and biscuits and cakes, jams and honey and clotted cream, even those silly little cucumber-and-butter sandwiches, for which the sipping of the liquid is an excuse. (Wallberg, *Wall Street Journal*, March 13, 1990)

Words, obviously, of a confirmed coffee drinker! Nevertheless, as a good traveler (nascent anthropologist), he admitted, "I couldn't really experience English culture unless I began to enjoy their national drink." A proper tea, however, is not just the tea itself or even the food but also the service. Proper tea is made in a china teapot (or – in elite circles – in a silver teapot), warmed by swirling boiling water around its interior. Then one places the tea leaves in the pot and pours boiling water over them. The tea should steep for 5–10 minutes before being poured into fine, thin, china cups. Teacups and tea sets are prized possessions, heirlooms handed down over the generations; even those people with little material wealth would manage to procure a proper tea cup.[6]

So what, you might ask, does all this have to do with being British? Although the Dutch East India Company first imported tea into Europe in 1610, it took another 50 years or so before English people began to develop a taste for it. "It is the years around 1700 which mark its establishment as a major force in British social life. 20,000 pounds weight of tea a year was being imported by 1700, but in 1721 the figure exceeded a million pounds weight" (Emmerson 1992: 5).

Tea, first enjoyed by the upper class, was an expression of hospitality – a sign of civility and refinement – a meaning that eventually "trickled down" to the working class so that participation in the ritual of tea has come to be one way that binds all the people into one, seemingly unified, seemingly genteel, nation. By drinking tea you demonstrate that you are British. Teatime is longer than a "coffee break"; taking time for tea conveys a message that time with friends and family is important, that leisure is, or should be, an integral component of daily life, and that work time has to accommodate teatime.

Curiously, this stereotype of tea's cultural significance is just the opposite of tea's perceived meanings and uses during the industrial revolution in Britain. Then, its stimulant qualities, in conjunction with the energy supplied by the sugar that was customarily used to sweeten it, were valued and deployed as a means of keeping workers productive over the long workday. As the workers of that era became habituated to increased consumption of tea and sugar, their eating and spending patterns shifted. In order to afford the quantities of tea and sugar to which they were accustomed, workers started to spend less money on nutritious food and thus, in the long run, their health suffered. People found that tea, especially when consumed with just a bit of food, was quite filling and could replace a meal – especially if followed, later in the evening, by a light supper. Although the typically starchy or sugary food served to accompany tea was less expensive than the protein and vegetables that might comprise a typical dinner, it was also less nutritious. In a cynical mood, one might characterize teatime as an institution whereby Britain managed to power the industrial revolution at lower cost by feeding its population less nutritious food. In *Sweetness and Power: The Place of Sugar in Modern History* (1985), anthropologist Sidney Mintz claims that while "[t]here was no conspiracy at work to wreck the nutrition of the British working class, to turn them into addicts, or to ruin their teeth" (p. 186), there were clearly very different class interests at work.

Although tea, as well as coffee and chocolate, was introduced into England in the seventeenth century, Mintz suggests that tea was pushed harder primarily because of capitalist interests in the production of sugar in the West Indies and the

East India Company's interest in tea in China and India. At the end of the eighteenth century, a rural English minister lamented how odd it was "that the common people of any European nation should be obliged to use, as part of their daily diet, two articles imported from the opposite sides of the earth" (cited in Mintz 1985: 116). Indeed, "[s]o vital had sugar and tea become in the daily lives of the people that the maintenance of their supply had by then become a political, as well as economic, matter" (p. 116). Indeed, the greater the demand for these products among the British populace, the greater the potential for profit for the capitalists and, in turn, the greater the enslavement of native populations who produced these commodities.

One might also understand the institution of teatime to represent England's (former) world dominance, since the tea itself is imported from the countries that were its colonies, especially India, and, thus, the very act of drinking tea is a symbolic reminder of that domination – each sip consuming (the product of) its subordinates. It should hardly be surprising that Americans, in general, have eschewed tea – after all, it was over tea that Americans first staged a demonstration of their independence from Britain. When Americans did resume consumption of tea it was in a wholly new form – as iced tea with lemon and mint and honey. Today in the United States, drinking hot tea is being promoted again, as one can see in the proliferation of upscale teashops and the popularity of so-called exotic blends such as *chai*. Even so, the Boston Tea Party is a revolutionary icon that still resonates with symbolic significance in the American myth.

> Chai, of course, is not exotic – except in the Orientalist imagination – but the motivation in marketing blends of tea under this banner is to evoke ideas of The Exotic. Generally, chai refers to the tea traditionally brewed with milk and spices and served in India for thousands of years. The word *chai* is, however, simply the word for tea. One finds variations of the words in many different languages. For example, the Turkish word for tea is *çay* and is pronounced like chai, it is *chá* in Portuguese, *chai* in Swahili, and in Chinese the sound of the symbol for tea when pronounced sounds very much like chai.

Turkish tea

While many people associate *coffee* with the Turks, tea drinking is actually more widespread and more representative. Coffee must be imported, is more expensive, and, until recently, was a relative luxury, so the majority of the population consumed coffee infrequently. Excellent tea, however, has been grown in Turkey along the Black Sea coast for some time.

Turkish tea was traditionally made in a samovar but is rarely made that way any more except, perhaps, in specialty teahouses for tourists. Most everywhere – in teahouses, in restaurants, at home in both the city and the village – tea is made by putting two teapots one on top of the other. Tea is placed in the smaller pot on top; it is warmed as the water boils in the lower pot. When the water has boiled some of it is poured into the pot containing the tea leaves. More water is added to the lower pot and the whole apparatus then simmers for about half an hour or more – or until all of the tea leaves have settled to the bottom of the top pot. One would think that brewing the leaves for so long would produce a tea that was bitter and very strong but, instead, it produces a silky, soft tea that seems to have less caffeine than the typical British tea. A small amount of the concentrated tea is poured into tiny tulip-shaped glasses, boiling water is added to dilute it to the appropriate strength, and sugar is passed. Turks typically take 2–3 cubes of sugar with each tiny glass! And it is considered rude if one does not drink at least 3 glasses. During my fieldwork I would often consume at least 10 glasses of tea a day and yet never had

Figure 9.5   A Turkish tea set. Photo by author.

any adverse reaction and was able to sleep well. When I drink any kind of tea made in the normal Anglo-American fashion I get very jittery – much more so than from coffee.

When villagers noticed I drank my tea without sugar they wondered if I was trying to save money, because skimping on sugar is a sign of stinginess. Sugar, as a former luxury commodity, acquired social significance; it became a symbol of generosity and hospitality.

As is obvious from the above, the making of tea is a lengthy procedure; one does not just "drop in" for a cup of tea expecting to leave soon afterward to get on with one's work. Once tea has been put on to brew, you are expected to settle in for a social visit that will last at least an hour and typically more. Even when villagers went to the fields to work they brought along all of the tea-making paraphernalia and took leisurely tea breaks.

British anthropologist Chris Hann argues that the development of the tea industry and the habit of drinking tea in Turkey parallels "the domestication of the Turkish state" (Hann 1990), that is, as it was transformed from the Ottoman Empire into a modern democracy. He claims that the impact of tea – both its indigenous production and the adoption of it by the population – has had an egalitarian effect. "It has helped foster among Turks everywhere (including migrant workers in West Germany and Saudi Arabia as well as all the regional cultures of Anatolia, including the Laz) the sense of belonging to a democratic national society" (p. 79). What he did not say, however, is that the democratic society is not *yet* egalitarian: tea drinking is still an activity that is often segregated by gender. Men gather in the *çayhane* (lit. tea house) from which women are excluded. In villages there is usually only a *çayodası*– a room set aside where men gather for tea. Middle- and upper-class women in the cities can drink tea in *pastahanes* – establishments that basically serve pastry such as baklava, cakes, and tea. Today, upper- and middle-class young men and women can be seen having tea and cakes together in fancy, and expensive, pastry shops in Istanbul or Ankara, but this is not yet an option for people of lower income or women in rural areas; furthermore, such activity (i.e., unmarried men and women meeting together) is frowned upon by conservative Muslims. So, as we saw in chapter 7, the rituals surrounding the preparation of even the simplest foods or drinks have symbolic import; by looking at such seemingly mundane activities, we can uncover powerful non-verbal messages.

Sports

Ironically, soccer is called football in many parts of the world while the American game of that name is referred to as American football.

Soccer is probably the most widely played sport around the world; baseball and basketball are catching on elsewhere, but American "football is an almost uniquely American pastime" and one that "unites Americans regardless of ethnic group, region, state, urban, suburban, or rural residence, religion, political party, job, status, wealth, gender, or sexual preference" (Kottak 1982: 46)! Americans travel on weekends to high school or college football games or watch college or major league games on television and "more than half of the adult population of the United States regularly watches the annual Super Bowl" (Kottak 1982: 46). Such impressive cultural facts ought to make anthropologists take note. Yet for a long time sports were not considered a worthy focus of anthropological attention. Serious scholars exhibited "a contempt from which those of us who were having our most important experiences in sport felt ourselves daily to suffer." So confessed a collegiate runner, Olympic hopeful turned anthropologist (MacAloon 1981: xi). Although studies of popular culture and the media have altered this somewhat, the serious anthropological study of sport remains in the minor league.[7]

Cricket might be considered a very English game, though it is also played in other countries and even in the Trobriand Islands. A classic anthropological film, *Trobriand Cricket*, shows what happened when the game was transferred (translated) to a different culture. The Trobrianders changed not only the size and material of the ball, but also the wicket and the bat. More important, the goal of the game was not to win but to tie in order to foster a friendly relationship with a potentially warring neighbor! Their cheers, costumes, commentary, and the game itself could be seen as a parody of the way it is played in the West.

If football, especially the Super Bowl, has, as many argue, displaced baseball as the "All-American" sport, then perhaps we can read something about American cultural values in this shift. But what? Today, baseball seems nostalgic, harking back to a more innocent age; it was, and is, generally played in the summer and culminates at summer's end in what is called "the World Series," even though the only teams playing are American. In comparison with football, baseball is a slower and more desultory sport, though nowhere near as slow and desultory as cricket. Football is a contact sport and generally more violent, its players are more anonymous than in baseball, where home-run hitters and strike-out pitchers are eulogized and enshrined in the "Baseball Hall of Fame."[8] Baseball is played throughout the summer, a season that most Americans associate with a more relaxed pace of life, outdoor pleasures, and vacation time.

Kottak interprets football as expressing one facet of American society (what he calls the "technical side") that concerns industrial organizations and business values. He sees this aspect as contrasting with the "creative side" of American society, which he believes is represented in popular music such as rock (1982: 47–8). Through his structural analysis, he explores these opposite sides of American cultural life: the value of teamwork versus individual accomplishment (as in the iconoclastic achievement of a rock musician), and the emphasis on traditional notions of gender (e.g., hypermasculinity among football players) versus the blurring of traditional gender roles (e.g., the celebrated androgyny of many rock stars). Football is quintessentially a team sport, and "the values associated with football: discipline, teamwork, coordination, dedication, and submission to authority" are those, according to Kottak, traditionally appreciated in the business world (1982: 52).

The qualities traditionally valued in football players are also those that are valued in the military. It is therefore not surprising that sports, especially football, became an integral part of American military training at the end of the nineteenth century under the motto "the better the athlete, the better the soldier." Military personnel believed that sports would help build stronger bodies and prepare men psychologically for warfare. In military training, as in much sports training, instructors emphasize the importance of *team* spirit and individual acts of courage are evaluated in light of how they reinforce or undermine the group's sense of solidarity. All for one and one for all. These qualities were so integral to the traditional American sense of manhood that even school curricula were adjusted to reflect these values. Male students were expected to participate in sports as a patriotic duty, for the training they received was expected to prepare them for service to the country if they should be called upon to serve (Pope 1997: 147).[9] It is therefore culturally consistent that one of the more important football games in the United States each year is the Army–Navy game, instituted in 1890 – inspiring perhaps a bit of competition between two branches of the armed forces – a rivalry that continues today. Returning to my earlier discussion about what constitutes the most "American" of sports, perhaps the shift in emphasis from the more bucolic baseball to the more aggressive football reflects a similar shift in the way warfare is now conducted: in under a century warfare has grown more destructive, more violent, and much more anonymous. In a humorous paper, modeled after the famous "Body Ritual among the Nacirema," one of my students, a former football player and aficionado of the game, made that point:

> The Super Bowl is the culmination of all the football ritual battles that are enacted in the months of autumn and winter. Mock-warriors are divided into thirty-two separate warrior-clans at the beginning of the ritual season. These clans are assigned to battle groups based on geographical location and traditional rivalries. The clans then combat one another on a rotating schedule. The most successful clans are then allowed to battle for the right to participate in the Super Bowl. Only the two best clans make it this far. The Super Bowl is the final battle of the ritual season, and determines which clan will be celebrated as the most dominant and ultimately triumphant.[10]

He also noted that the leaders of each clan (coaches) "who command the attack, defense, and specific actions of the warriors . . . are much like the leaders of the real armies of the Nacirema." In battle, the warrior is in a genuinely life-threatening position whereas the football player's risks are minor by comparison and his potential rewards enormous: superstar status and multi-million dollar contracts. Despite those very real differences, it would be interesting to consider whether it is merely a coincidence that the majority of football players, like the rank-and-file soldiers in the military, are black, while the individuals with the authority to give them orders – the coaches and commanders – are usually white.

Just as men have traditionally fought to protect the nation, so too have they been traditionally the combatants in ritual battles of sport.[11] Susan Brownmiller, who has written extensively on the gendered nature of war, has pointed out in her writings that the age-old idea that "to the victor belong the spoils"[12] often included access to women. "Down through the ages," Brownmiller writes, "triumph over women by rape became a way to measure victory, part of a soldier's proof of masculinity and success, a tangible reward for services rendered" (1975: 35). In one of the more sinister enactments of this principle, rape of the enemies' women has often served as a means of humiliating defeated soldiers. It was not until recently that such behavior was criminalized as a war crime.[13] So, let's apply these ideas to our examination of sports culture in the United States. What can we learn? If women were imagined as the spoils of battle in actual wars, and if we recognize that sports competitions are constructed as mock battles, is it then possible that male athletes might consider sex their due after winning a competition?

While we all know that women can make formidable athletes and competitors, regrettably they were traditionally confined to the role of spectators (or cheerleaders). As we have seen, in many competitive displays of male prowess, women represented – and in many cases still represent – the prize won. More than that, however, the very field on which the game is played is, I believe, symbolically female. The earth is personified as a woman and there is a long history in literature that identifies woman as fertile (or barren) ground, land, and soil of the nation. This analogy derives from a theory of procreation discussed earlier in which men are thought to plant the "seed," thus configuring women as the soil in which it is planted. In war, men are fighting to protect the land of the nation, to keep it from being violated or penetrated by the enemy. This was clearly appreciated by Mustafa Kemal (later to become Atatürk, founder of the Turkish Republic), who used gendered rhetoric to rally men to come to the defense of the *motherland* that had been prostituted under "capitulations" to foreign powers and was about to be mutilated by partition. His appeal was made to the sense of male honor to rise up against the intruders and eject them from their soil (see Delaney 1995: 186).

Such sentiments, I believe, also provoked the ire of many Muslims during the US's Gulf War in 1991 where the use of gendered language and imagery was prevalent.[14] While the government of Saudi Arabia, somewhat reluctantly (see Clark 1992), permitted American soldiers (symbolically and overwhelmingly male) on their soil, many Muslims saw the presence of the infidels as defiling the land and as potentially defiling the purity of "their" women. The anger of Osama bin Laden against the United States has deep roots in the Gulf War: "The deployment of US troops to Saudi Arabia – land considered sacred by Muslims – not only has infuriated groups like bin Laden's but has also inflamed popular opinion" (*Boston Globe*, September 13, 2003; see also CNN.com posting January 2001). The Americans, meanwhile, talked of *penetrating* the enemy and kept score of the bombs dropped and targets hit in a way that many felt was profanely and uncomfortably close to a football scoreboard.

Sports, even the Super Bowl, are *intra*-national, that is, different teams, perhaps originally symbolizing different regional affiliations, are like rival clans *within* the nation. They enact a ritual – not a real – battle, although real battles are also ritualized. In any case, the ritual battle is taken to an entirely different level at the Olympics. There the competition is *inter*-national where the contest is among (representatives of) nations. While the Olympics does not symbolize any particular nation, participation in the Games has become an issue of national pride and honor for individual nations.

The Olympics

The Olympic Games, first organized in 776 BC in ancient Greece, were revived at the end of the nineteenth century after a hiatus of more than 1,500 years. The inspiration for the Games came from Baron Pierre de Coubertin (1863–1937), a French educator commissioned by the French government to form a universal sports association. His interest in the original Olympics was spurred, in part, by the archaeological discoveries of ancient Olympia that were being displayed in the capitals of Europe at that time. The first modern Olympics were held, appropriately, in Athens in 1896 not far from the ancient site. Although the idea was to bring nations together in unity and friendship, the Games promote competition.[15] The modern Olympics continue to be an arena in which each nation competes against others: to win the privilege of hosting the Games, to best others in terms of the size of the national team and the number of sports in which the nation competes – even to have the most impressive uniforms or the most fantastic stories of achievement by individual athletes – and, above all else, to win the greatest number of (gold) medals. The athletes who are selected to participate are intended as representatives of their nation; they are theoretically the best each nation has to offer inasmuch as their success or failure reflects on the honor of their nation as a whole. Interestingly, while the American team, for example, represents the United States, the team is actually composed of a series of sub-teams since there are different teams organized, and individuals selected, to compete on behalf of the national team in the various events. The language of "national teams" belies the heterogeneous composition of each individual team as well as the heterogeneity of an individual nation – despite the popular rhetoric of a homogeneous united social body.

The Games recognize only three kinds or levels of identities – the individual, the nation-state, and humankind (MacAloon 1984: 252) – but it is the nation-state that seems to be the most salient. When a team or individual receives the gold medal, their national anthem is played and their own pride and honor appear to merge with that of the nation. But such symbolism stops there. While the individuals represent the nation at the Olympics, the Games are not like the Miss World contest, for example, in which the winner is meant to represent the world.

Such claims to universality almost always generate conflict. For example, before the 2002 Miss World Pageant began in Nigeria, thousands of Muslims protested, claiming, among other things, that this public display of near-naked women was sinful. Any claim to representing the world that the pageant might have made was pushed aside; devout Muslims certainly did not see their values represented therein. As a result of violent protests that caused the death of over 100 people in the northern part of the country, organizers announced that they would move the pageant from the Nigerian capital of Abuja to London.

The winners in games at the Olympics represent their own nation, not a generic humankind. That seems to reflect the beliefs of Pierre de Coubertin. For him, according to Olympic scholar John MacAloon, humankind "exists . . . not in spite of, but because of social and cultural diversity . . . true internationalism understands cultural differences as an enduring and marvelous feature of the human landscape and . . . world peace depends upon the celebration of human diversity and not the eradication of it" (MacAloon 1984: 252). To be human is not to be "everyman."

The human body – its techniques and capabilities – is, not surprisingly, the primary focus of the Games. And yet it is not the generic human body but the specific bodies that come to symbolize the nation. This was made clear during the Olympics that were hosted by Germany in Berlin in the summer of 1936. The basic story is familiar to us all. Since coming to power Adolf Hitler had been promoting sport and "physical culture" among German youth (see Mosse 1985) and proclaiming the superiority of the Aryan body. It was his fundamental belief that history was the record of struggles among races and he prophesied that the Aryan race, centered in Germany, would be the final victor of these struggles because of its superiority. Because of Hitler's policies there had been discussion by a number of countries of boycotting the 1936 Games. That was rejected, but mindful of this opportunity to put a humane face on their regime, during the Olympics, the Nazis took care to try to minimize the racist and militaristic character of their government and to court foreign spectators and journalists. But all did not go as planned. Enter Jesse Owens: an African American born in Alabama, educated at Ohio State, and a member of the US Olympic track team. In a single week in Berlin he won four gold medals – tying one Olympic record, setting three new Olympic records, and breaking a world record. Despite Owens's outstanding performance, Hitler refused to congratulate him because of his race. As sportswriter Larry Schwartz recalled with gleeful journalistic bravado: "When Owens finished competing, the African-American son of a sharecropper and the grandson of slaves had single-handedly crushed Hitler's myth of Aryan supremacy" (Larry Schwartz for ESPN.com: http://msn.espn.go.com/sportscentury/features/00016393.html). In an interesting postscript to this dramatic cultural tableau, it is moving to see how gracefully Owens deflected the inclination by Americans and others to vilify Hitler's racism without recognizing the cultures from whence they came. As Schwartz wrote:

> Owens never rubbed it in. Just as sure as he knew fascism was evil, he also knew his country had a ways to go too in improving life for African-Americans. "When I came back to my native country, after all the stories about Hitler, I [still] couldn't ride in the front of the bus," Owens said. "I had to go to the back door. I couldn't live where I wanted. I wasn't invited to shake hands with Hitler, but I wasn't invited to the White House to shake hands with the President, either."

As students of anthropology, in considering the Olympics, it is important to look to the work of John MacAloon, the athlete-turned-scholar to whom I referred

Figure 9.6 Jesse Owens at the Olympic Games, Berlin, 1936. Photo Rex Features.

earlier. MacAloon received training in anthropology from Victor Turner at the University of Chicago in the 1970s and made the Olympics the special focus of his research. He looked at the Games from various angles. He considered their frequency. Because the Olympics occur every four years, MacAloon observed that "for many people the routines of daily life grind to a halt for two weeks every four years. Weddings are postponed, crops go untended, work is interrupted, and the Olympics crowd most other topics out of conversation" (MacAloon 1984: 242). He considered the site chosen for the Games and its impact: the "faces of entire cities have been permanently altered by the Games, and their impact on regional and national economies is considerable" (p. 241). If we thought the number of spectators at Super Bowl was enormous, it pales in comparison to the Olympics. As MacAloon wrote of the 1976 Games: "According to reasonable estimates, 1.5 billion people – approximately one out of every three persons then alive on the earth – watched or listened to at least a part of the proceedings" (p. 241). Since that time the number of spectators both attending the Games and watching them on television has increased. The Games bring together athletes from around the world – as well as a diverse group of spectators. People of different nationalities, from a wide range of cultures, and speaking a plurality of languages all attend – jostling together, dining together, and getting to know each other in a way different from other interactions because there is no other venue quite like the Olympics. Not only are those who journey to the host country on display, but also the nation that sponsors the Olympics has a rare opportunity to present an image of itself through various cultural performances, food, native dress, and important cultural sites and icons. Indeed, looking at MacAloon's work, it is interesting to realize that he employs most of the strategies that we have discussed in each chapter of this book to investigate the phenomenon of the Olympics: space, time, language, social relations, body, food, clothes.

But what is it about the Olympics – about moments such as Jesse Owens's victories – that has so captivated the imaginations of so many people? What does it represent about our contemporary world? MacAloon has come up with a theory about certain kinds of performance genres: spectacle, festival, ritual, and game. While the Olympics incorporates and displays all of them, it is primarily a spectacle, and it is this aspect, he believes, that expresses changes in the world situation, namely, the movement toward globalization and interconnection expressed by such metaphors as the "Global Village" or "Spaceship Earth," and the growth of multinational institutions like the UN (1964: 267). MacAloon notes that while more nations are represented at the UN, the world audience of the Games is much larger. This he attributes to

> the felt need for living, dramatic images of the "others" with whom we are increasingly conscious of sharing a biosphere and sets of political economies and ways of living. . . . From a subjective standpoint, the world has not shrunk, as we like to say, it has immeasurably expanded. Spectacle may be the genre which most reflects and refracts this social expansion. . . . If in our daily lives, we must increasingly take account of the "size" of the earth, then our performances must surely take account of it too. Spectacle may be society in action, groping on the level of expressive culture, toward a new order in a changing world. (pp. 267–8)

Durkheim long ago felt that new social forms are created during periods of "collective effervescence" when groups of people are gathered in celebration. At the Olympic Games there surely are such moments, and there is always the possibility that they might create more widespread feelings of what Victor Turner called *communitas* – where we might get a glimpse of what it would be like to break down the barriers dividing rich and poor, white and black, male and female, nation and nation.

That, I believe, was the hope of Coubertin. The Games, for him, were meant to be just such a peaceful and joyful celebration.[16] Whatever *communitas* was achieved during the Games was not meant to gloss over the social and political inequities and injustices but rather make attendees more compassionately aware of, and committed to, doing something about them. Regardless of their celebratory nature, the Games have never been insulated from political eruptions; one need only recall the slight of Owens at the Berlin Games (1936), the killing of Jews in Munich (1972), the American boycott of the Moscow Games (1980), and a bomb at the Atlanta Games (1996). Indeed, rather than insulating the public from the political, the Games have become a vehicle for broadcasting political messages to an international audience.

There is yet another way that the Games are political. According to Nigerian scholar and cultural critic Chinweizu, it is questionable whether the Games are really even international or global. He contends "that the Olympic Games are neither in fact nor name the World Games they pretend to be – that is, they are not games organized by all nations, governed by all nations, and free from political domination by a parochial minority of nations" (1987: 201). African nations have, of course, sent teams to the Olympics but the Games have never been held in an African nation. Nor are representatives from African nations included on the governing board. Chinweizu writes:

> When shall we [Africans] stop tolerating our being treated as guests in international institutions? . . . We have integrated the U.N. and the Olympics: we have even collected some Nobel Prizes. But the owners and managers of these institutions repeatedly make it clear that we are barely tolerated guests. (pp. 206–7)

"The point," he says, "is not to put black nations on the map as it exists, but rather to remake the map." This sounds like Mazrui's views about the map of the world discussed in chapter 1. Chinweizu suggests several options for resisting the current state of Olympic administration: (1) hold the Games in a city in a predominantly black nation; (2) boycott or withdraw from the Games; or (3) withdraw and then initiate a World Games Organization, and "invite all the world to join on non-racist, non-hegemonist terms" (p. 208).

Chinweizu is a compelling spokesperson and his cultural critique is part of a much larger intellectual and political tradition. I turn now to a discussion of a group of musicians that emerged from another country and other traditions, but also came to be associated with ideas of transglobal, pan-human, resistance and celebration.

The Beatles

George Bernard Shaw said that the United States and Great Britain were two nations divided by a common language. What language could not do, the music of the

It should be noted that Beatles' fans, like the Beatles themselves, were overwhelmingly white. The Beatles were also nominally, at least, Protestant, though like many youth in the US, they soon discovered Hindu thought and became devotees of an Indian guru. During the same period of time there was also a proliferation of "black" music in the US which was one of the influences on the Beatles. An especially important figure was the Rastafarian Bob Marley, who made the distinctive sound of reggae music known around the world. Recall, also, the discussion (chapter 8) by Hebdige about how British youth came to define themselves by the music they listened to and the clothes they wore.

Beatles accomplished, for they captured the minds and hearts of the better part of a generation on both sides of the Atlantic. According to one analyst, they were "the Pied Pipers who led the Western world absent-mindedly from a moribund Modern Age into the Age to come. . . . [T]hey composed the main musical soundtrack accompanying this transition" (Sullivan 1995: xi). Those of us who lived through the 1960s – whether those of us who came of age during that time or our parents – can all agree that a major social transformation was taking place. And it happened very fast – from the parietals of my college days to the removal of them, from formal dates to the "be-ins" of the "flower children," from alcohol to mind-altering drugs, from a fear of sex to the sexual revolution, from a relative lack of political consciousness among the young to the civil rights movement, free-speech movement, and anti-Vietnam protests. Not only did the social transformation happen fast, all these different changes were happening simultaneously.

It is important to point out that when I discuss the 1960s in relation to the music of the Beatles, I necessarily obscure other enormously signifi-cant figures of that time, like Martin Luther King, Jr., who came to sym-bolize the civil rights movement and whose eloquence continues to inspire. Despite the vivid memory of such individuals, for many of us, the Beatles and their music came to symbolize the 1960s. They both reflected that era and contributed to it. Like them, many of us really believed we could change the world – "All You Need is Love." Listening to their music as I write this, it all comes back. There was a brief window through which we glimpsed the possibility of a different kind of world. Regrettably, in retrospect, the hope that many felt, and the vision we tried to advance, provoked a virulent conservative backlash. Indeed, many of the leaders of that era – Martin Luther King, Jr., Medgar Evers, John F. Kennedy, and Robert Kennedy – were assassinated.

How to explain the meteoric success of the Beatles? Was there some astral con-junction between their music and the times? The "mass reaction to the Beatles is without social precedent. No religious leader, politician, general or any other public figure has ever been lionized to such an extent or for so long a period" (Davies 1969: 273). If the Beatles were the most significant musical phenomenon of the twenti-eth century, as so many claim, what do they signify?

I, like most Americans, first saw them on the Ed Sullivan show on February 9, 1964 – generally a stodgy program with a stodgy host. It was my sister's twenty-first birthday, I was two years older and, as a young married person, soon to become pregnant, I was initially not as taken with them as were all the screaming teenagers from whom I wanted to distance myself. Despite early resistance, I was soon a convert and by the next year had a poster of them prominently displayed in my living room. Their music seemed to beat the pulse of our lives and because they were such cultural icons, their lives, both public and private – including their beliefs, problems, marriages, children, and divorces – became a means of gauging our own lives and the changes we were undergoing. Since my contemporaries and I are the same age as the remaining Beatles, the widely publicized deaths of John Lennon,

Figure 9.7   The Beatles in 1964. Photo David Magnus/Rex Features.

(1980) Paul McCartney's wife Linda (1998), and, most recently, George Harrison (2001) have been painful reminders of our mortality. Accustomed as I have grown to having their music as a part of my life, I cannot help but wish they had left a song that would help guide us through that transition.

Several commentators have attributed the success of the Beatles to "their magnificent, original music" (Sullivan 1995: 34). For Davies, the Beatles were modern-day bards not unlike the ancient Celtic order of singing poets whose instruments were traditionally the guitar, lute, and harp.

> Those of us who had grown up with the Beatles can remember exactly where we were when we heard of Lennon's death, just as we can remember where we were when we heard of JFK's death. Both of these violent deaths defined a culture and an age.

> The most striking aspect of their music is the archaic aspect. . . . The melodic simplicity, limited range, simplicity of rhythmic content, modal tonality, elements of fourteenth-century style, clarity of diction, are all elements of bardic style. (Davies 1969: 275)

Although born in Liverpool, several of the Beatles claimed Irish ancestry, and Paul and John each had a musical parent, thus it is not unlikely that they were familiar with Celtic poetic and musical styles.

> The most misleading part of their myth is the idea that Liverpool is 'nowhere,' for nowhere else in Britain – and probably the world – was beat music as alive as it was

in the Merseyside scene when the Beatles cut their chops. Over three hundred bands worked the area . . . [making for] a competitive edge between groups that challenged them all to greater heights. (Sullivan 1995: 39)

Although the seaport was declining, there was a different kind of transatlantic traffic as US sailors and the Liverpudlians exchanged music in the seamy city clubs. The Beatles "quickly outdid their peers with a talent and ambition that left all the others behind" (Riley 1987, cited in Sullivan 1995: 39). The Beatles never remained in one musical mode but continued to transform it as they transformed their clothes and hairstyles – from the styles of the rough Teddy Boys to psychedelics to the styles of Eastern mysticism.

From Sullivan's perspective, the 1950s in England and the United States were drab. "The clothes people wore were dull: black, gray, dark blue or brown. Automobiles were basic black. Most movies were still shown in black and white. TV was still a black and white medium" (Sullivan 1995: 37). The Beatles brought a range of color into this milieu and in so doing they broke apart the class-based social styles in both Britain and the United States.

In Britain in the 1950s class was still very much an important social indicator and was signified primarily by three things: accent, schooling, and pedigree. Sullivan asserts that a person in the UK "situates himself socially for others the minute he opens his mouth" and instantly places him/herself by region and by class (Sullivan 1995: 32). It is amazing, then, how these lower-middle and working-class lads with nasal Liverpudlian accents and little education beyond what Americans would call "public school" rose so far as to be invited to Buckingham Palace in 1965 for an audience with the queen during which she bestowed on them the MBE – the medal of Member of the British Empire. (Much later, in 1997, Paul McCartney would be knighted and become Sir Paul McCartney.) Given their humble origins, Sullivan wonders how "all classes of British society – including royalty and aristocracy . . . embraced the Beatles with a frenzy of acceptance and bedazzlement little different from the intoxication felt by their teenybopper fans" (p. 32).

In the US at the same time, the signifying markers of social identity were race, religion, and money, although class was indicated by "old money," appropriate accent, schooling, and being listed in the *Social Register*. Nevertheless, it was somewhat easier to understand the Beatles' success in America because in many ways they embodied the American myth of Horatio Alger: that celebration of the "rags to riches" transformation, that anyone with enough drive and fortitude, and some talent, can make their fortune. This myth, like all myths, promotes a partial truth as it obscures others – the socially ascribed impediments of race and gender as well as class.

We may never be able to explain the success of the Beatles, but part of the answer has to do with the extraordinarily fortuitous conjunction of talent, personality, and timing. Many people, especially young people, were ready for a change; they were ready to slough off the shackles in which they felt enchained. The Beatles did provide the sounds, the words, and the sentiments that ushered in a new age for those individuals. It was a heady period well characterized by Durkheim's notion of "effervescence" that Sullivan also uses to describe the early period of their achievement. During periods of "collective effervescence" when people come together and merge their individual wills for the collective good, new creative elements are released which, in turn, help bring about social change. The Beatles embodied "collective effervescence" and it was contagious; they helped pass it along to others. That time has passed but not their music; passed down from parents and even grandparents, their music continues to resonate. While it certainly dates to and characterizes a particular period, it does not seem out-of-date. For many of us, their music lives on even as they separated and two have died.

Princess Diana: She Did Not Live Happily Ever After

For many, news of the death of Princess Diana in a car crash in Paris on August 31, 1997 was shocking. Somehow one tends to think royalty is immune from such all-too-ordinary but gruesome events. The announcement went around the world in a flash. But the terrible descriptions of her death along with that of her companion Dodi Al-Fayed cannot explain the extraordinary international outpouring of grief.[17] Such a reaction cannot be attributed simply to the fact that she was a princess, although that had something to do with it; nor was it entirely because of her good deeds or her lovely smile even as they, too, had something to do with it. Why and how are we to understand that phenomenon? Many have tried but perhaps it is never possible to completely comprehend such events. Carol Gilligan, a psychologist at New York University, wrote in the *New York Times*:

> I was surprised by my response to the death of Diana, Princess of Wales. I had not expected to feel such a raw edge of grief for this woman I did not know and whose life I had not particularly followed. (*New York Times*, September 9, 1997, C4)

I confess I felt the same way and I, too, had not paid too much attention to her life. Many people – especially many women – seem to have responded in similar ways. Why did she affect us like this? Famous people die all the time; why did her death, in particular, strike so many people so hard?

I think one could say that the death of Diana had greater cultural implications. In other words, a princess was killed but a myth was shattered. She was the archetype of a very powerful myth that resides, subliminally perhaps, in the imaginations of many women. The myth, in essence, is of the young woman who, because of her sweet nature, will one day marry the handsome prince and live happily ever after. In the US, UK, and Europe, children read, or are read, such stories from an early age and fantasize about them. They insert themselves into the myth so that "each individual story draws on a common culture" (Samuel and Thompson 1990: 2). By assimilating our own private myth to larger cultural patterns, or even by placing our own in opposition to them, we find meaning in our lives. Despite the reality that ought to dissuade them and that diminishes their own sense of agency, millions of girls still grow up dreaming that they, too, will one day marry the charming prince and live happily ever after. In their imagination, any man can be transformed into a prince.

Diana's wedding at St. Paul's Cathedral on July 29, 1981 had millions of people around the world glued to the television. She symbolized that dream come true; it was real, it did happen. People were entranced by her looks, her demeanor, her clothes, her hair, and sought to emulate her. When she gave birth to William and then Harry, she not only fulfilled her duty as a princess by providing an heir to the throne, she became, in the eyes of her public, a loving and attentive mother. She was admired because she fulfilled the role of the "good mother" seemingly to perfection. Many lauded her as a role model. The fact that she had begun her career as a kindergarten teacher enlarged her mystique: she was enhanced in the eyes of many because her career took a back seat to her role as wife and mother and her virtue as wife and mother was simultaneously enhanced by her affiliation with a career that underscored the image of the nurturing "good woman." Her later work only solidified such perceptions for she championed causes (e.g., ending the use of landmines and helping people with AIDS) that further enhanced her stereotypes of nurturing womanliness.

Then cracks began to appear in the image. "What drew women to Diana," continued Gilligan, "was that she failed publicly and, in doing that, shattered an *icon* that imprisons all women" (Gilligan 1997; emphasis mine).

> Things that happen to ordinary women happened to her. Her husband rejected her for another woman; she developed an eating disorder; she felt that she was all alone; she tried to kill herself. And then she broke the spell. She aired in the full public eye of the media humiliations that, for centuries, have silenced women because women feel that they reflect failures on their part and because speaking out carried the risk of further rejection and shame. . . . Like Eve she had come to know both good and evil and shared that knowledge. Unlike Eve she resisted shame and refused to hide. (Gilligan 1997)

When so public a figure does this it opens a window and brings light to other women who suffer similar problems; it empowers them. Yet, until the cracks began to appear, Diana was a conventional woman trying to play the conventional role; she had little interest in feminism. Only after her revelations did she attract feminist attention and become an icon.

> In Diana, the fairy-tale princess who was cruelly awakened to the world of hurt, betrayal, and humiliation, women of all ages found a mirror image of themselves, however magnified and glamorized. (Joyce Carol Oates, *Time*, September 15, 1997: 58)

Diana fulfilled, challenged, and ultimately succumbed to the myths about women we all share. For there is another, more sinister myth that collided with the one about the princess who marries the prince and lives happily ever after. That is the myth of what happens to independent women who seek their own happiness outside of conventional boundaries. Quite often they are killed, die a tragic death, or are left to die alone. Go to almost any opera (except for the comedies that end with a wedding) and you will see this theme played out over and over.

Diana's death fulfilled *exactly* that mythological scheme. Thus the reaction to her death is, I think, quite complicated. It is not only that women identified with the

Figure 9.8 Princess Diana's grave at Althorp, showing the lake and island. Photo Rex Features.

flawed "people's princess," as prime minister Tony Blair labeled her, but also because her tragic death personified the specter created by the double standard that many women fear. Her pleasure was obvious, and was displayed across the media; she was, at the time of her death, an unmarried mother and was enjoying the company of a man but without her children in tow. It is not difficult to see how the conflation of the image of the good and devoted mother and of the sexually active woman created problems for the royal family (and no doubt for others). According to the mythology, she would, or should, be punished. The question of whether or not Diana's death was truly an accident has been raised. Although the question cannot be answered with absolute certainty, the doubts surrounding her death were in large part evoked because of the mythic scenario.

After a long discussion about the nature of royalty, its meaning for Britain, and its importance "in order to warrant the degree of national sentiment her death elicited," British anthropologist C. W. Watson concluded that "Diana is for British society the royal sacrificial victim" (1997: 6). Her death allowed the nation to undergo "a cathartic rite of communal purification: the dross of their lives, the mistakes, the false starts, the failings, are sublimated in the dead person of Diana" (p. 7). It was not just a metamorphosis of Diana into sacrificial victim but her apotheosis into a saint that was the most popular image. This was evidenced by the most publicized reference that accompanied "one of the floral tributes laid by the roadside which . . . read: 'Born a Lady, Became a Princess, Died a Saint'" (p. 7).

Even Diana's final resting place evokes the many myths she embodied and debunked. She is buried on a tiny island in the middle of a pond on the family estate at Althorp – in a setting that many would willingly characterize as fairy-tale-like.

Blood and Nation

When I was a Fulbright scholar in Belgium, my hosts thought it was very important that I be taken to see all the World War I and II cemeteries where many Americans are buried.

Watson went on to note how the blood of martyrs serves to regenerate the nation. Whether Diana can really be considered a "social martyr," as he calls her, is an open question; nevertheless, it is important to consider the way in which the blood of innocent victims has often called forth a unification of a nation. While happy events such as a royal wedding or coronation are also unifying social forces wherein "the values of the community are celebrated and affirmed" (Watson 1997: 4), it is more often the dead who perform this function. I am thinking here especially of those who die in war, eulogized as those who *sacrificed* their lives for the nation.

A classic anthropological article, "An American Sacred Ceremony" (1953) by Lloyd Warner, describes Memorial Day and the commemoration of the war dead (World War I and II) in a New England town. It was an early attempt to analyze the way in which sacrifice for the nation performs a unifying function. What is it, asked Benedict Anderson in *Imagined Communities* (1983), about the concept of the imagination – the nation – that millions of people have been willing to die for it? While the sacrificial rhetoric used to legitimate war continues, it has been less compelling since Vietnam divided rather than unified the American nation.

They have also created deep divisions – especially about the restitutions (often those with the most insurance and money got the most in the settlements while the families of the lowest-paid workers got the least amount of money). And the event spawned anti-Islamic sentiment and acts of violence and destruction.

However, the deaths of all the people at the World Trade Center, the Pentagon, and on Flight 93 that crashed in Pennsylvania on September 11, 2001 have, in many ways, served the unifying function. The wealth of analysis and interpretation of this extraordinary event is well beyond the scope of this chapter (I am still unable to look at the stack of news clippings and articles piled on a chair in my living room), yet a few words are in order. President Bush immediately labeled the September 11 event as "an attack on America," thus rendering the dead as victims of war. Images of the destruction, which did look like a war zone, dominated the media for weeks and months after the event, and the victims were publicly mourned and eulogized; the *New York Times*, for example, printed short biographies of each of the dead – a series that was still running almost a year later.

Meanwhile, the terrible space left by the destruction of the Trade Center became hallowed ground. Ground Zero, as it is called, became a sacred place to which millions have made pilgrimage (see *New York Times*, January 17, 2002 and *San Francisco Chronicle* June 23, 2002). Debates rage over what is an appropriate memorial: the two beams of light reaching to the heavens for a month in April–May 2002 were a spectacular and moving memorial, but alas impermanent. Some people wanted the World Trade Center to be built again exactly as before, others thought that would be sacrilege and wanted to see a public park there. Still others thought it should be left as is – a devastating reminder of the event. But almost everyone seems to feel that the ground is sacred; it is, after all, a burial ground, and burial grounds are, by their very nature, sacred.

The Statue of Liberty

Out of the ashes, like a phoenix, the Statue of Liberty rose to new life, to become, once again, the quintessential symbol of the nation. Of course, the Statue of Liberty has long been a symbol representing America and a very popular destination for visitors and natives alike, but she was mostly taken for granted. I use the feminine pronoun since she is often referred to as "Lady Liberty." During the bicentennial celebrations of 1976 she had a brief period of prominence before receding into the background. At that time, she was seen in the company of the tall ships as they sailed into New York harbor, and her distinctive, goddess-like headdress was copied (in aqua foam) and donned by millions throughout the nation during the celebrations.

After a number of designs were submitted and many months of deliberation including public discussions in the media, the architect chosen to rebuild the site was Daniel Libeskind, who also designed Berlin's Jewish Museum. One extraordinary aspect of the design is the "Wedge of Light," whereby every September 11 a special space will be filled with light during the times that the towers were first hit until the second tower collapsed (from 8:46 a.m. to 10:48 a.m).

The events of 9/11 catapulted her back into the forefront of everyone's mind. There were photographs and drawings of her in the news and on television. The *New York Times* made reproductions of their Statue of Liberty photo collection available for purchase. One photograph, "Liberty Framed by World Trade Center," became a poignant reminder of what had been and was no more. The flag also symbolizes the nation but the Statue of Liberty personifies it. Not surprisingly, after 9/11 media images depicted her expressing the national emotions: one depicted her weeping and another defiant with both arms raised. Also, not surprising, she, too, became sacred and protected. She was cordoned off for months and no visitors were allowed. Rumors spread that she was also a target and to protect her the president ordered planes to circle around to keep watch.

Compared to Britain with its long history and its real crowned queen, the United States is a young country; nevertheless, it has its own crowned figure standing as a benevolent, protective deity at the entrance to our land. Why and how did she become this potent symbol?

A symbol doesn't just happen; there is a process of construction and an accumulation of meaning. Many Americans are unaware that the Statue of Liberty was a gift from France. Not only was she not made in the United States, but the very *idea* for her construction was French. Story has it that at a dinner party in Paris in 1865, a discussion of democracy in America arose. The host, Edouard René Lefebvre de Laboulaye, commented to his guests:

> Wouldn't it be wonderful if people in France gave the United States a great monument as a lasting memorial to independence and thereby showed that the French government was also dedicated to the idea of human liberty? (From http://www.americanparknetwork.com/parkinfo/sl/history/liberty.html)

Frédéric-Auguste Bartholdi, a sculptor, was a guest at the dinner; the idea took hold and he began to design the statue. Later he sailed to the United States at the

Figure 9.9   The Statue of Liberty and the Twin Towers of the World Trade Center. Photo by Fred R. Conrad, 1983/New York Times Photo Archive.

suggestion of Laboulaye to discuss the possibility with the government. It was also he who determined where the eventual statue would be placed – at his first sight of the New World – Bedloe's Island. The steel skeleton to support Bartholdi's design was made by none other than Alexandre-Gustave Eiffel!

Americans were not initially enthusiastic – it was too expensive (they were to pay for the pedestal while France paid for the statue) and, anyway, many thought it was a New York thing;[18] why should they help pay for it? Finally, when it looked as if the project might languish in an *atelier* in France, Joseph Pulitzer used his newspaper, *The World*, to appeal to the people by promising that the names of all donors, regardless of the amount of their contribution, would be published. The money was raised, the statue set sail, dismantled and shipped in 214 packing crates, was installed on its pedestal on Bedloe's Island, and was finally unveiled on October 28, 1886 to a crowd of more than a million.

The words that have come to symbolize the statue – and which give the meaning that most Americans attribute to her – were not inscribed until much later. The last five lines taken from a poem by Emma Lazarus, written as part of the campaign to raise money, were engraved on a plaque and attached in 1903. Emma Lazarus never knew what role her poem was to play, since it was found among her belongings after her death. Later the lines were included in the Broadway musical *Miss Liberty*, by Irving Berlin, and in 1945 the entire poem was placed over the main entrance to the statue.

The New Colossus

Not like the brazen giant of Greek fame
With conquering limbs astride from land to land;
Here at our sea-washed, sunset gates shall stand
A mighty woman with a torch, whose flame
Is the imprisoned lightning, and her name
Mother of Exiles. From her beacon-hand
Glows world-wide welcome; her mild eyes command
The air-bridged harbor that twin cities frame,
"Keep, ancient lands, your storied pomp!" cries she
With silent lips. "**Give me your tired, your poor,
Your huddled masses yearning to breathe free,**
The wretched refuse of your teeming shore,
Send these, the homeless, tempest-tost to me,
I lift my lamp beside the golden door!"

These words have helped create the myth that many of the downtrodden and oppressed around the world respond to as they set forth for America hoping to start a new and better life. The reality, when they arrive, is often quite different.

Although a woman symbolizes both liberty and America, indeed, female figures, for example Britannia, are often symbols of the nation, men traditionally represent it. Ironically, at the time these lines were written and the statue installed, neither American nor French women could vote, a point made by suffragettes who protested at the installation. Nevertheless, the Statue of Liberty *has* been a beacon to all people, not just Americans, a major symbol of freedom, and a magnet for immigrants.[19] For many it is undoubtedly a pilgrimage site.

Concluding Section: Pilgrimage, Myth, Religion

In the discussions of some of the VIPs above, a few of the same words have surfaced repeatedly and in quite different contexts – words like myth, pilgrimage, and sacrifice. I would like to explore this a little further for I think they take us to a deeper level of meaning and understanding of why some things, but not others, become cultural icons. As noted on p. 373, I believe they perform this function because they are able to tap into widespread beliefs or cultural myths. A relatively simple example was tea – which is obviously not just a commodity but a potent symbol – one that symbolizes a British way of life and their former world dominance, but also American rebellion.

Some of the most powerful VIPs, however, cannot be confined to national boundaries even as they may symbolize the nation; they have spread far and wide and become globally recognized phenomena that are saturated with meaning, for example the Statue of Liberty or Princess Diana. They have become larger than life, and people in different places have felt connected to them in some way and view them as beacons or lodestars providing light and guidance, or a point of reference by which to chart their own lives. Some people want contact and feel compelled to make pilgrimages to the sites connected to them as if their magic will rub off.

Pilgrimage

Pilgrimage is most often associated with religion, and since religion is felt to be transnational, it is not tied to any specific nation. For example, Christians from many different countries make a pilgrimage to Lourdes to be cured, or walk the El Camino to Santiago de Compostela (Hoinacki 1996), or go to the house of the Virgin Mary near Ephesus in Turkey. Victor Turner, whose work we discussed in chapter 1, was very interested in pilgrimage because of its "liminal" character – one is neither here nor there but "betwixt and between" – which can have transformative effects. However, because pilgrimage is undertaken voluntarily, unlike other age-specific rites of passage, he described it as "liminoid" (Turner and Turner 1978: 1–39). The studies he and his wife made of pilgrimages, primarily to shrines of the Virgin in both Ireland and Mexico, are classic readings on the topic (see also Turner 1972–3).

These pilgrimages are not just Christian, they are Catholic. Protestants have, in general, not made a practice of pilgrimage. In the English-speaking world, at least, Protestants tend to view life itself as a pilgrimage – an idea influenced, perhaps, by Bunyan's *Pilgrim's Progress*. One is always "on the road," a phrase immortalized by Jack Kerouac and secularized by the beats of the 1950s.

Figure 9.10   Circumambulation of the Kaa'ba – an important ritual during the *hajj* to Mecca. Photo Rex Features.

A very different meaning is conveyed by the Muslim pilgrimage, or *hajj*, to Mecca. For most Muslims, unlike Catholics, there is one "canonical" or predominant destination – Mecca. (Shiite Muslims also make pilgrimages to the holy cities of Najaf and Kerbala, both in Iraq.) Muslims from all over the world make the pilgrimage to Mecca, which is considered the one, true, original home – the first place dry earth appeared upon the waters. It is the place closest to heaven. In some Muslim traditions, it is the place Abraham is thought to have been asked to sacrifice his son;[20] Mecca is also the place Muhammad is thought to have cleansed of its idols and recalled the people back to the one true religion given in the beginning to Abraham. It is felt to be auspicious to die there.

While there are resemblances between Christian and Muslim pilgrimages, they are quite distinct. Buddhists and Hindus (e.g. Gold 1988) also have specific sites of pilgrimage, but it would be a mistake to think that they are all undertaken for the same purposes or to accomplish the same goals. As anthropologist Clifford Geertz noted some time ago, "we need to look for systematic relationships among diverse phenomena, not for substantive identities among similar ones" (1973: 44).

That statement enabled me to think about comparing the annual journey back to their village made by Turks in Europe with the *hajj* to Mecca made by the Turkish villagers with whom I had lived (Delaney 1990). By loosening the rigid classifications whereby pilgrimage can only be thought of in conventional religious terms, I was able to see more clearly the secular aspects of religious pilgrimage and spiritual or religious aspects of secular journeys. In a similar fashion, one might then be able to think of visits not only to Princess Diana's grave, Ground Zero, the Statue of Liberty, and the Grand Canyon as pilgrimages, but also those to Graceland, Elvis Presley's home, or to Bob Marley's mausoleum in Jamaica and the grave of Jim Morrison in Paris, as well as to Disneyland as Kottak (1982) suggested. It is, after all, the place that many dying children wish to visit. Even though these are all secular sites, they also have religious overtones or underpinnings for, at least in relation to Disneyland, as Kottak notes, "there is a quasi-religious aspect to our relationship to Disney and his works; this emerges most clearly in Americans' behavior at the two Disney amusement parks," which is not unlike that during pilgrimages made to more obvious religious sites. Such a study might seem frivolous to some readers, but the analyses uncover compelling aspects of national mythology.

Myth

Earlier I noted that cultural icons and archetypal practices partake of and express cultural myths whether personal, family, national, or religious, or some combination. When I use the word myth, I do not mean ancient or false stories, but instead use it in its meaning as "a real or fictional story, recurring theme, or character type that appeals to the consciousness of a people by embodying its cultural ideals or by giving expression to deep, commonly felt emotions" (*American Heritage Dictionary*, 2nd edition, 1991).

This is also the sense in which Malinowski meant it when he said: "Myth is not merely a story told, but a reality lived" (1954: 100). So, by mythic framework I mean the underlying stories we tell ourselves about who we are, where we came from, and where we are going – how we make sense of the world and our place in it. This has not been the traditional approach; instead numerous theorists have tried to plumb them for what they might reveal about human psychology.

Perhaps the most famous example is Freud's interpretation of the Oedipus myth. He felt it reflected universal psychological dynamics as they developed within the family. The story moves us, he said, because it is ours: "it is the fate of all of us, perhaps, to direct our first sexual impulse towards our mother and our first hatred and our first murderous wish against our father" (Freud 1900, 4: 262). While he may have captured something about Western, especially Victorian, family forms and values, he was unaware of very different kinds of kinship structures, gender meanings, and their implications (see Delaney 1998 and the discussion in chapter 5 about kinship).

In a somewhat similar way, French anthropologist Claude Lévi-Strauss believed that myths expressed something universal about the human condition – "myths get thought in man unbeknownst to him" (1979: 3). He believed they represented the unacceptable contradictions that all humans confront – and the underlying structure of the human mind rather than the generative beliefs of any particular culture; thus regardless of the extraordinary detail he documented, the cultural specificity in myth was less important to him than the logical relations between the different elements, the "mythemes."[21] While his method has been productive and cannot be dispensed with, I would argue strongly that the cultural specificity is important, that people's psychology and identity are affected by the very myths they listen to and pass on. As Mary Douglas noted: "Psychological explanations cannot of their nature account for what is culturally distinctive" (1966: 121).

A number of students of Franz Boas, for example Paul Radin and Zora Neale Hurston, were interested in psychology and myth but, in contrast to Freud and Lévi-Strauss, they were not trying to uncover universal psychological structures and themes. In his now classic study, *The Trickster: A Study in American Indian Mythology* (1955), Paul Radin focused on the "trickster" – a prominent figure in Native American myths – to explore its *particular* psychological and cultural significance. He also gave space in his work for informants to speak, a move that foreshadowed some contemporary work. So, too, did Zora Neale Hurston, who traveled throughout the American South recording folktales of African Americans and capturing some of the mythic structures, values, and worldview in a much more intimate way, perhaps because she also inserted her own voice and her own responses. "Departing from standard ethnographic conventions that demand the use of a distant voice, Hurston readily admits she is part of the cultural scene she observes" (Hernandez 1995: 156). Her insistence on such positionality was extremely unusual for the time, which may be why her work languished until relatively recently; now it is fairly well accepted as standard practice. The specificity in her ethnography, short stories, and novels brings readers closer to the meanings and motivations of the people she studied, not unlike the way that Elenore Smith Bowen did in *Return to Laughter* that we discussed in chapter 1.[22]

We live by myths and we cannot live without them; they are active forces in society. Even history – what we normally take to be a scientific description of past events – is, according to famous historian William McNeill, constructed within a narrative framework that is, at base, mythic. This is the import of his short but incisive book, *Mythistory* (1986). The title, as one word, shows that he thinks myth and history are two aspects of the same thing. I quote a passage at length because it sums up very well what I am trying to convey.

> Myth and history are close kin inasmuch as both explain how things got to be the way they are by telling some sort of story. But our common parlance reckons myth to be false while history is, or aspires to be true. Accordingly, a historian who rejects someone else's conclusions calls them mythical, while claiming that his own views are true.
>
> A century or more ago, when history was first established as an academic discipline [so too were comparative religion and anthropology], our predecessors recognized this dilemma, and believed they had a remedy. Scientific source criticism would get the facts straight. Whereupon a conscientious and careful historian needed only to arrange the facts into a readable narrative to produce genuinely scientific history. And science of course . . . was true and eternal.
>
> Yet in practice something quite different occurred. Early in this century, thoughtful historians began to realize that the arrangement of facts to make a history involved subjective judgments and intellectual choices that had little to do with source criticism, scientific or otherwise. . . .

Facts that could be established beyond all reasonable doubt remained trivial in the sense that they did not, in and of themselves, give meaning or intelligibility to the record of the past. A catalogue of undoubted and indubitable information, even if arranged chronologically, remains a catalogue.

To become history, facts have to be put together into a pattern that is understandable and credible; and when that has been achieved, the resulting portrait of the past may become useful as well – a font of practical wisdom upon which people may draw when making decisions and taking action. (1986: 3–5)

The patterns that organize facts are the myths we live by. There are different kinds, and perhaps different levels, of myths which, in any one culture, are often interrelated. I mention only three: (1) personal/family myths, (2) national or ethnic myths, and (3) myths of origin (of the world, humans etc.).

(1) Stories you cherish about your personal life give it meaning and seem to explain how you came to be the way you are. Family myths are those stories told by parents and relatives about your ancestors, your other relatives, and about you. They give you a sense of your place and belonging but they often tap into myths of national or ethnic origin – how your group came to be as a people.

(2) For example, there are two popular myths of national origin told by and to Americans; namely, the stories about Columbus and his "discovery" of America in 1492 and the landing of the Pilgrims at Plymouth Rock in 1620 in search of freedom to practice their beliefs. Until fairly recently we heard little about the betrayal of the native populations, the signing of treaties that were not kept, the raping of women, the spread of disease, and the massacres. If we did, they were rationalized in terms of the bravery of the conquerors and the perfidy of the Indians.

All myths of national origin gloss over other stories. For example, the Turkish myth of origin taught to children for generations is that they are descended from the Ur Turks who migrated from Central Asia. This myth obliterates the numerous peoples and cultures that occupied the land since ancient times and with whom ethnic Turks intermarried over the centuries. National myths can also be intertwined with origin myths that have wider significance.

(3) Genesis, the first book of the Hebrew Bible, is the predominant origin myth of the West. It purports to be about the origin of the universe, of humans, of plants and animals, of language and agriculture, etc. But it is also the origin story of a particular people – the people of Abraham. Europeans who first came to America often interpreted the country as the new Israel, that is, they placed the country within biblical myth. This was woven into the myth of "Manifest Destiny" that had significant implications for the way the native people were treated and their land appropriated. Myths of origin are extremely important; people fight over them and have been willing to die for them. After all, Navajos might not accept Genesis instead of their own origin story, nor would Christians easily accept an Australian aboriginal myth as equivalent to their own. Clearly, some of the most powerful myths are religious myths.

Religion

Although the study of religion was prominent among early anthropologists, many in the late twentieth century shied away from it, perhaps under the influence of modernization theory which projected that the growth of science and rationality would lessen the hold of religion on society. Nothing could have shocked those who belittled the influence of religion more than to see how religion flourished at the end of the twentieth and now into the twenty-first century. Intellectuals heralded the collapse of "master-narratives" (explanatory frameworks such as Marxism, the Enlightenment, modernization theory, evolution, or progress and secularism, etc.), but the one thing they forgot to consider was religion, which encompasses not only peoples' notions of origin and destiny but also identity. I think it is extremely important not just for anthropologists but for all people to have some knowledge and understanding of the world's religious beliefs and practices.[23]

For those who believe their religion is the whole truth and nothing but the truth, this section will be difficult.[24] From my personal experience at Divinity School and among religious leaders, however, I came to realize that many of those most involved with religion and theology have a far more nuanced view of religion than do lay people. Part of the problem may be that in the United States, at least, religion is not taught in public schools, and thus students do not learn other approaches to thinking about it.

My interest in this section, and in general, is not on liturgy, ritual practices, prayers, or clergy but on religious myths or stories that are told to us and that we internalize. For many people, they form the most basic and pervasive notions of the way the world simply is. Since they are generally told in childhood, children are enveloped by the religious worldview long before they have the ability to see it differently. Parents who may not even be that religious often find themselves unwittingly perpetuating religious myths precisely because they have become so much a part of the culture. On the other hand, fundamentalists understand very well why it is important to begin religious instruction early. Because religious myths are so pervasive, they are the most difficult to dislodge. They are part of what the person takes for granted, part of what the person is. Threats to his or her worldview can be felt as threats to his or her being. Thus, it should not be surprising that people will defend them with all their strength and unfortunately too often with violence.

Because I feel that religious concepts and worldview are an integral part of culture that both reflect and contribute to its construction, my own work has focused on the religious traditions that have had the greatest effect on Western culture, namely the monotheistic traditions – Judaism, Christianity, and Islam. While many Westerners would not include Islam, it is a branch of the same tree. Despite the revelations given to Moses, Jesus, and Muhammad, all three trace their origins to the story of Abraham, which is why they are called the Abrahamic religions (see figure 9.11). Although they share a common "father"[25] and many of the same stories, practices, and beliefs, they are construed in three mutually exclusive worldviews – you cannot be both a Muslim and a Jew, or a Jew and a Christian, or a Christian and a Muslim – which is also why I believe the fighting is interminable. I view them as three sibling faiths fighting over the patrimony – the promises given in the beginning to Abraham – promises, primarily, to be *the* proper interpreter of God's word, although land, the afterlife, and the number of adherents are also important.

Since I have written a whole book on this topic (Delaney 1998), I will give only the briefest summary of it. The story of Abraham has troubled me ever since I was a child; it led to my study of religion at Harvard Divinity School and then to anthropology at

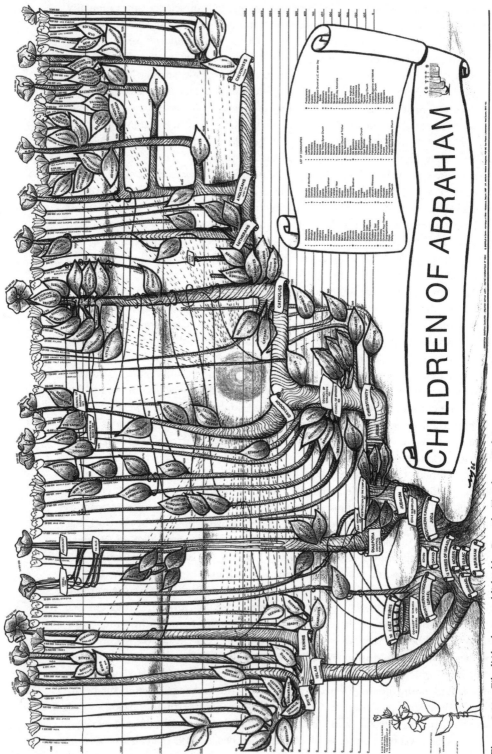

Figure 9.11 Fils d'Abraham, published by Brepols, Turnhout, Belgium.

Let's Send All Our Missiles to the Sun

To the Editor:

"Nuclear Designers From East and West Plan Bomb Disposal" (Science Times, Dec. 17), on a meeting of scientists to discuss disposal of nuclear weapons, prompts me to offer a suggestion I've been thinking about for some time. Let us mark the year 2000 with a worldwide celebration as we send all nuclear weapons to the sun, itself a nuclear entity.

I call it a potlatch – a feast traditionally practiced by Indian groups of the Northwest Coast and Alaska, in which the chiefs of warring groups tried to outdo one another in disposing of their wealth. Let them guide the leaders of the superpowers in planning the ceremony.

Ridding the planet of these weapons would be a priceless gift and a brilliant message to ourselves – "the human race has overcome the arms race and has chosen life instead of destruction."

Everyone could get involved, from governments to schoolchildren. Scientists could handle the technical side, and the rest of us could plan a party on a scale never seen before. Something of this magnitude would capture the imagination and just possibly might help to unite us to a peaceful world community.

It's just a thought, but we have eight years to try and make it a reality.

CAROL DELANEY
Stanford, Calif., Dec. 17, 1991

the University of Chicago. The story that troubled me and is foundational for the three faiths is the story told in Genesis 22 of the Bible or Sura 37 of the Qur'an where God asks Abraham to sacrifice his son. There have been innumerable commentaries attempting to explain this story but none of them has raised the question that motivated my research and my book: Why is the willingness to sacrifice, rather than protect, the child *the* model of faith at the foundation of these religions? Furthermore, what has been the social legacy of this model? Abraham was asked (by God) to sacrifice his child – that is, to take the life of another person – and he is the "father of faith" for his *willingness* to obey. The act required was not self-sacrifice and surely not just giving up something – meanings that are too often conflated and distort and diminish what was and is at stake. While the story, the interpretations, and the traditions are complex, I nevertheless believe that the moral tradition stemming from the story of Abraham and the values, social structures and institutions, and theories that support it – such as the patriarchal family, the virtue of obedience, and the power to interpret the sacred that is vested in the few – has produced cultures in which sacrifice and death instead of celebration and life have been the major social unifying theme. But, as with the nation, it is unifying only for those who belong. We are witnessing the boundaries between nations being broken down and new, more inclusive, entities coming into being. Is it possible something similar might happen with religious boundaries, beliefs, and the hatreds that keep people at each other's throats? It would be a wondrous world if *celebration* in recognition of our common *human* life were the worldwide unifying theme at the center of our spiritual values. There was a brief glimpse during the 1960s, and the turn of the millennium was a possibility too quickly lost. But I do believe it is possible. My hope is that young people today can transform the stories, the metaphors, and the symbols as well as the economics and politics to bring this about. To do so, however, demands that you challenge taken-for-granted ideas and structures, look behind cultural myths, and imagine that things might be otherwise; the task ahead demands a very intensive investigation of culture, for which I hope this book is just the beginning.

Notes

1   See "The Story of Bond," where anthropologist Lee Drummond analyzes the deeper cultural significance of the films (Drummond 1988).
2   See chapter 3 for a discussion of weddings.
3   It was also the response of my daughter when she saw it for the first time in the summer of 2003.
4   For those interested, a classic is Kakuzo Okakura's *The Book of Tea* (Charles E. Tuttle 1956). See also anthropologist Dorine Kondo's article, "The Way of Tea: A Symbolic Analysis," *Man*, 20 (1985): 287–306, and Jennifer Anderson's "Japanese Tea Ritual: Religion in Practice" (1987).
5   It is interesting to compare coffee consumption by Americans which, according to www.coffeeresearch.com, is 1.9 cups per day for American men and 1.4 for women. Clearly, I am over the top with 4 cups a day; however, I drink all my coffee half decaf.
6   For a brief history of tea drinking in Britain and an interesting look at tea "equipage" – the equipment deemed necessary for a proper tea ceremony – see Robin Emmerson's illustrated *British Teapots and Tea Drinking: 1700–1850* (1992).
7   See Jeremy MacClancy, ed., *Sport, Identity, and Ethnicity* (Oxford: Oxford University Press, 1996), who claims that although sport is now a major industry, it has received very little serious attention from anthropologists (perhaps more from sociologists).
8   A character in Richard Greenberg's play *Take Me Out* thinks "that baseball is a perfect metaphor for hope in a democratic society. . . . Equality, that is, of opportunity. Everyone is given exactly the same chance. And the opportunity to exercise that chance at his own pace" (*New York Times*, April 5, 2003).
9   See also Cynthia Enloe's *Bananas, Beaches, and Bases: Making Feminist Sense of International Politics* (Berkeley: University of California Press, 1990).
10   "Ritual Battle among the Nacirema" by Brian Goodman. In this section I have also drawn on a paper by Becky Meldrum.
11   Two films that play with these stereotypes are *A League of Their Own*, about a very popular all-women's baseball league created during World War II, and *Private Benjamin*, about a pampered, "dumb blonde" who joins the army when her husband dies and then gets tough, outsmarts all the men including a general, and becomes part of an elite corps and eventually a top military advisor at NATO.
12   This phrase is attributed to William Learned Marcy, American politician and former US Secretary of War from 1845 to 1849.
13   See Susan Brownmiller's *Against Our Will* (1975) and Cynthia Enloe's *The Morning After: Sexual Politics at the End of the Cold War* (1993).
14   The language and imagery of war should not be surprising since war has always been a gendered affair. For important analyses of this see Brownmiller (1975) and Enloe (1993).

15   The five interlocking rings on the Olympic flag are meant to symbolize the five regions of the world joined together in the Olympic movement: Africa, the Americas, Europe, Asia, and Oceania (from www.enchantedlearning.com/olympics/printouts/Flag.shtm, accessed December 22, 2002). Two students (Jessica Mendoza and Chad Fore) in two different courses during the fall of 2002 wrote papers on the Olympics. I hereby wish to acknowledge their insights, which added to and helped confirm my own research.

16   "If anyone were to ask me the formula for 'Olympizing' oneself, I should say to him, 'the first condition is to be joyful'" (MacAloon 1984: 248). This was the view of Pierre de Coubertin, a French aristocrat, who was the primary instigator of the modern Games.

17   According to one reporter Diana's death "drew an emotional response from the British that contradicted all stereotypes of the English as cold and unemotional" (Lennon 1998: 38), though this judgment depends, of course, on that stereotype.

18   I have heard from a New Jersey resident that it is actually within the boundaries of that state, but most people associate it with New York. In my opinion, as most would agree, she is bigger than any state, even bigger than the nation, so the debate seems puerile. Costs for her upkeep ought to be part of a national budget; however, retired auto executive Lee Iaoccoa took on the job of raising the money as chair of the Statue of Liberty-Ellis Island Foundation (*Parade Magazine*, *San Francisco Chronicle*, December 15, 2002). Ellis Island is, of course, the place through which new immigrants passed and were registered. At the new immigration museum displaying its history, descendants of immigrants can trace their ancestry.

19   The symbol has endured despite the difficulties many immigrants face as they struggle to survive in the United States. It will be interesting to see how it fares as America squanders its moral standing among nations in the aftermath of the war against Iraq.

20   Other Muslim traditions have the spot in Jerusalem, as Jews and Christians also believe (see Firestone 1990). The Dome of the Rock, also called the Temple Mount, is now the site of a Muslim mosque. It is perhaps the most volatile place in the world, fought over by the sibling faiths. There have been plots by radical fundamentalist Jews to blow it up, an action that could very easily be the spark for World War III (see Gorenberg 2000).

21   See the bibliography at the end of the chapter for references to Lévi-Strauss's approach to myth. Note the wealth of detail in the 4-volume set of *Mythologiques*, where each volume is over 500 pages! Another mythologist, perhaps more familiar to some of you, is Joseph Campbell, whose *Hero of a Thousand Faces* became very popular during the 1980s and 1990s. It is a delightful read but it, too, is reductive, that is, he believes that all stories of heroes are at base one and the same. On the other hand, Marshall Sahlins's *Historical Metaphors, Mythical Realities* (1981) uses a structural approach to a very different end.

22   See the bibliography at the end of the chapter for references to Hurston's work, and to the excellent review of it by Hernandez.

23   One of the best courses I ever took as an undergraduate was a year-long course on the world's religious traditions. It made me aware of different worldviews, different ways of approaching the world, and some of the motivations behind historical events in a way that history courses never did. For interested students, there are at least three different kinds of texts to begin such a study. The first category includes books that discuss each different religious tradition noting the important beliefs, sacred texts, practices, and institutional structure (e.g., Oxtoby 2002; Smith [1958] 1991); the second category are often "readers" in the anthropology of religion that focus on particular themes such as sacrifice, or include classical articles by theorists of religion (e.g., Bowen 1998; Lambek 2002); the third, and arguably the most important, are the sacred texts themselves. Such study should always, however, be complemented by a study of the history and culture of the

societies influenced by the religious traditions, and where possible speaking with those who believe and practice it.

24   I highly recommend the now classic *The True Believer* by Eric Hoffer (1951).

25   In the 1970s many feminists began to question the patriarchal nature, language, and structure of institutionalized religions and the impact of these on social life and definitions of gender. (As noted earlier on p. 155, these issues had been raised also by nineteenth-century feminists.) Mary Daly's *Beyond God the Father* (1973) was the first arrow launched in this new endeavor; now they are myriad. My own work has been part of this intellectual trend.

Bibliography

Albanese, Catherine (1990) *Nature Religion in America: From the Algonkian Indians to the New Age*. Chicago: University of Chicago Press.

Anderson, Benedict (1983) *Imagined Communities*. London: Verso.

Anderson, Jennifer L. (1987) "Japanese Tea Ritual: Religion in Practice." *American Ethnologist*, 22: 475–98.

Anderson, Jennifer L. (1991) *An Introduction to Japanese Tea Ritual*. Albany: State University of New York Press.

Archetti, Eduardo (1994) "Masculinity and Football: The Formation of National Identity in Argentina." In *Game Without Frontier: Football, Identity and Modernity*, ed. Richard Giulianotti and John Williams. Aldershot, Hampshire: Gower House, pp. 225–44.

Archetti, Eduardo (1999) *Masculinities: Football, Polo and the Tango in Argentina*. Oxford: Berg.

Bowen, John R. (1998) *Religions in Practice: An Approach to the Anthropology of Religion*. Boston: Allyn & Bacon.

Bromell, Nick (2000) *Tomorrow Never Knows: Rock and Psychedelics in the 1960s*. Chicago: University of Chicago Press.

Brownmiller, Susan (1975) *Against Our Will: Men, Women, and Rape*. New York: Simon and Schuster.

Campbell, Joseph ([1949] 1968) *The Hero With a Thousand Faces*. Princeton: Princeton University Press.

Caplow, Theodore and Williamson, Margaret Holmes (1980) "Decoding Middletown's Easter Bunny: A Study in American Iconography." *Semiotica*, 32 (3/4): 221–32.

Chinweizu (1987) *Decolonizing the African Mind*. Lagos, Nigeria: Pero Press.

Clark, Ramsey (1992) *The Fire Next Time: U.S. War Crimes in the Gulf*. New York: Thunder's Mouth Press.

Daly, Mary (1973) *Beyond God the Father: Toward a Philosophy of Women's Liberation*. Boston: Beacon Press.

Davies, Evan (1969) "Psychological Characteristics of Beatle Mania." *Journal of the History of Ideas*, 30 (2): 273–80.

Delaney, Carol (1990) "The *Hajj*: Sacred and Secular." *American Ethnologist*, 17 (3): 513–30.

Delaney, Carol (1995) "Father-State, Motherland, and the Birth of Modern Turkey." In *Naturalizing Power: Essays in Feminist Cultural Analysis*, ed. Sylvia Yanagisako and Carol Delaney. New York: Routledge.

Delaney, Carol (1998) *Abraham on Trial: The Social Legacy of Biblical Myth*. Princeton: Princeton University Press.

Douglas, Mary (1966) *Purity and Danger: An Analysis of the Concepts of Pollution and Taboo*. London: Routledge & Kegan Paul.

Drummond, Lee (1988) "The Story of Bond." In *Symbolizing America*, ed. Hervé Varenne. Lincoln: University of Nebraska Press.

Emmerson, Robin (1992) *British Teapots and Tea Drinking: 1700–1850*. London: HMSO.

Enloe, Cynthia (1993) *The Morning After: Sexual Politics at the End of the Cold War*. Berkeley: University of California Press.

Firestone, Reuven (1990) *Journeys in Holy Lands: The Evolution of the Abraham-Ishmael Legends in Islamic Exegesis*. Albany: State University of New York Press.

Freud, Sigmund (1900) *Interpretation of Dreams*. Vol. 4. In *The Standard Edition of the Complete Psychological Works of Sigmund Freud*, ed. James Strachey. London: Hogarth Press.

Geertz, Clifford (1973) *Interpretation of Cultures*. New York: Basic Books.

Gold, Ann (1988) *Fruitful Journeys: The Ways of Rajasthani Pilgrims*. Berkeley: University of California Press.

Gorenberg, Gershom (2000) *The End of Days: Fundamentalism and the Struggle for the Temple Mount*. Oxford: Oxford University Press.

Hann, Chris (1990) *Tea and the Domestication of the Turkish State* (SOAS, Modern Turkish Studies Programme, Occasional Papers, 1). Huntingdon, Cambridgeshire: Eothen Press.

Hazan, Haim (1987) "Holding Time Still With Cups Of Tea." In *Constructive Drinking: Perspectives on Drink from Anthropology*, ed. Mary Douglas. Cambridge: Cambridge University Press.

Hernandez, Graciela (1995) "Multiple Subjectivities and Strategic Positionality: Zora Neale Hurston's Experimental Ethnographies." In *Women Writing Culture*, ed. Ruth Behar and Deborah A. Gordon. Berkeley: University of California Press.

Hoffer, Eric (1951) *The True Believer*. New York: Harper & Row.

Hoinacki, Lee (1996) *El Camino: Walking to Santiago de Compostela*. University Park, PA: Pennsylvania State University Press.

Hurston, Zora Neale ([1935] 1978) *Mules and Men*. Preface by Franz Boas. Bloomington: Indiana University Press.

Hurston, Zora Neale ([1937] 1991) *Their Eyes Were Watching God*. Urbana: University of Illinois Press.

Kottak, Conrad, ed. (1982) *Researching American Culture*. Ann Arbor: University of Michigan Press.

Lambek, Michael, ed. (2002) *A Reader in the Anthropology of Religion*. Malden, MA: Blackwell.

Lennon, David (1998) "London: Diana – One Year After." *Europe*, 380 (October): 38–40.

Lévi-Strauss, Claude (1963) "The Structural Study of Myth." In *Structural Anthropology*. New York: Basic Books.

Lévi-Strauss, Claude (1969) *Mythologiques*, vol. 1: *The Raw and the Cooked*. New York: Harper & Row.

Lévi-Strauss, Claude (1973) *Mythologiques*, vol. 2: *From Honey to Ashes*. London: Cape.

Lévi-Strauss, Claude (1978) *Mythologiques*, vol. 3: *The Origin of Table Manners*. Trans. J. and D. Weightman. New York: Harper & Row.

Lévi-Strauss, Claude (1979) *Myth and Meaning*. New York: Shocken Books.

Lévi-Strauss, Claude (1981) *Mythologiques*, vol. 4: *The Naked Man*. New York: Harper & Row.

MacAloon, John (1981) *This Great Symbol: Pierre de Coubertin and the Origins of the Modern Olympic Games*. Chicago: University of Chicago Press.

MacAloon, John (1984) "Olympic Games and the Theory of Spectacle in Modern Societies." In *Rite, Drama, Festival, Spectacle: Rehearsals Toward a Theory of Cultural Performance*, ed. John MacAloon. Philadelphia: Institute for the Study of Human Issues.

McGuigan, Jim (2000) "British Identity and the 'People's Princess.'" *Sociological Review*, 48 (1): 1–18.

McNeill, William (1986) *Mythistory and Other Essays*. Chicago: University of Chicago Press.

Malinowski, Bronislaw (1954) *Magic, Science, and Religion, and Other Essays*, with an introduction by Robert Redfield. Garden City: Doubleday.

Marty, Martin and Appleby, Scott (1992) *The Glory and the Power: The Fundamentalist Challenge to the Modern World*. Boston: Beacon Press.

Merck, Mandy, ed. (1998) *After Diana: Irreverent Elegies*. London: Verso.

Mosse, George (1985) *Nationalism and Sexuality*. New York: Howard Fertig.

Mintz, Sidney (1985) *Sweetness and Power: The Place of Sugar in Modern History*. New York: Viking Press.

Oxtoby, Willard (2002) *World Religions: Eastern Traditions*. Don Mills: Oxford University Press.

Pope, S. W. (1997) *Patriotic Games: Sporting Tradition in the American Imagination, 1876–1926*. New York: Oxford University Press.

Riley, Tim (1987) "For the Beatles: Notes on their Achievement." *Popular Music*, 6 (3): 257–71.

Sahlins, Marshall (1981) *Historical Metaphors, Mythical Realities: Structure in the Early History of the Sandwich Islands Kingdom*. Ann Arbor: University of Michigan Press.

Samuel, Raphael and Thompson, Paul, eds. (1990) *Myths We Live By*. London: Routledge.

Smart, Ninian (1983) *Worldviews: Crosscultural Explorations of Human Beliefs*. New York: Charles Scribner's Sons.

Smith, Huston ([1958] 1991) *The World's Religions*. San Francisco: Harper.

Stokes, Geoffrey (1980) *The Beatles*. New York: Times Books.

Sullivan, Henry W. (1995) *The Beatles with Lacan: Rock & Roll as Requiem for the Modern Age*. New York: Peter Lang.

Turner, Victor (1972–3) "The Center Out There: Pilgrim's Goal." *History of Religions*, 12: 191–230.

Turner, Victor and Turner, Edith (1978) *Image and Pilgrimage in Christian Culture: Anthropological Perspectives*. New York: Columbia University Press.

Turnock, Robert (2000) *Interpreting Diana: Television Audiences and the Death of a Princess*. London: British Film Institute.

Warner, Lloyd (1953) "An American Sacred Ceremony." In *American Life*. Chicago: University of Chicago Press, pp. 1–26.

Watson, C. W. (1997) "Born a Lady, Became a Princess, Died a Saint." *Anthropology Today*, 13: 3–7.

R
E
A
D
I
N
G
S

The Impact of the Concept of Culture on the Concept of Man
Clifford Geertz

I

Toward the end of his recent study of the ideas used by tribal peoples, *La Pensée Sauvage*, the French anthropologist Lévi-Strauss remarks that scientific explanation does not consist, as we have been led to imagine, in the reduction of the complex to the simple. Rather, it consists, he says, in a substitution of a complexity more intelligible for one which is less. So far as the study of man is concerned, one may go even further, I think, and argue that explanation often consists of substituting complex pictures for simple ones while striving somehow to retain the persuasive clarity that went with the simple ones.

Elegance remains, I suppose, a general scientific ideal; but in the social sciences, it is very often in departures from that ideal that truly creative developments occur. Scientific advancement commonly consists in a progressive complication of what once seemed a beautifully simple set of notions but now seems an unbearably simplistic one. It is after this sort of disenchantment occurs that intelligibility, and thus explanatory power, comes to rest on the possibility of substituting the involved but comprehensible for the involved but incomprehensible to which Lévi-Strauss refers. Whitehead once offered to the natural sciences the maxim "Seek simplicity and distrust it"; to the social sciences he might well have offered "Seek complexity and order it."

Certainly the study of culture has developed as though this maxim were being followed. The rise of a scientific concept of culture amounted to, or at least was connected with, the overthrow of the view of human nature dominant in the Enlightenment – a view that, whatever else may be said for or against it, was both clear and simple – and its replacement by a view not only more complicated but enormously less clear. The attempt to clarify it, to reconstruct an intelligible account of what man is, has underlain scientific thinking about culture ever since. Having sought complexity and, on a scale grander than they ever imagined, found it, anthropologists became entangled in a tortuous effort to order it. And the end is not yet in sight.

The Enlightenment view of man was, of course, that he was wholly of a piece with nature and shared in the general uniformity of composition which natural science, under Bacon's urging and Newton's guidance, had discovered there. There is, in brief, a human nature as regularly organized, as thoroughly invariant, and as marvelously simple as Newton's universe. Perhaps some of its laws are different, but there *are* laws; perhaps some of its immutability is obscured by the trappings of local fashion, but it *is* immutable.

A quotation that Lovejoy (whose magisterial analysis I am following here) gives from an Enlightenment historian, Mascou, presents the position with the useful bluntness one often finds in a minor writer:

> The stage setting [in different times and places] is, indeed, altered, the actors change their garb and their appearance; but their inward motions arise from the same desires and passions of men, and produce their effects in the vicissitudes of kingdoms and peoples.[1]

Now, this view is hardly one to be despised; nor, despite my easy references a moment ago to "overthrow," can it be said to have disappeared from contemporary anthropological thought. The notion that men are men under whatever guise and against whatever backdrop has not been replaced by "other mores, other beasts."

Yet, cast as it was, the Enlightenment concept of the nature of human nature had some much less acceptable implications, the main one being that, to quote Lovejoy himself this time, "anything of which the intelligibility, verifiability, or actual affirmation is limited to men of a special age, race, temperament, tradition or condition is [in and of itself] without truth or value, or at all events without importance to a reasonable man."[2] The great, vast variety of differences among men, in beliefs and values, in customs and institutions, both over time and from place to place, is essentially without significance in defining his nature. It consists of mere accretions, distortions even, overlaying and obscuring what is truly human – the constant, the general, the universal – in man.

Thus, in a passage now notorious, Dr. Johnson saw Shakespeare's genius to lie in the fact that "his characters are not modified by the customs of particular places, unpractised by the rest of the world; by the peculiarities of studies or professions, which can operate upon but small numbers; or by the accidents of transient fashions or temporary opinions."[3] And Racine regarded the success of his plays on classical themes as proof that "the taste of Paris . . . conforms to that of Athens; my spectators have been moved by the same things which, in other times, brought tears to the eyes of the most cultivated classes of Greece."[4]

The trouble with this kind of view, aside from the fact that it sounds comic coming from someone as profoundly English as Johnson or as French as Racine, is that the image of a constant human nature independent of time, place, and circumstance, of studies and professions, transient fashions and temporary opinions, may be an illusion, that what man is may be so entangled with where he is, who he is, and what he believes that it is inseparable from them. It is precisely the consideration of such a possibility that led to the rise of the concept of culture and the decline of the uniformitarian view of man. Whatever else modern anthropology asserts – and it seems to have asserted almost everything at one time or another – it is firm in the conviction that men unmodified by the customs of particular places do not in fact exist, have never existed, and most important, could not in the very nature of the case exist. There is, there can be, no backstage where we can go to catch a glimpse of Mascou's actors as "real persons" lounging about in street clothes, disengaged from their profession, displaying with artless candor their spontaneous desires and unprompted passions. They may change their roles, their styles of acting, even the dramas in which they play; but – as Shakespeare himself of course remarked – they are always performing.

This circumstance makes the drawing of a line between what is natural, universal, and constant in man and what is conventional, local, and variable extraordinarily difficult. In fact, it suggests that to draw such a line is to falsify the human situation, or at least to misrender it seriously.

Consider Balinese trance. The Balinese fall into extreme dissociated states in which they perform all sorts of spectacular activities – biting off the heads of living chickens, stabbing themselves with daggers, throwing themselves wildly about, speaking with tongues, performing miraculous feats of equilibration, mimicking sexual intercourse, eating feces, and so on – rather more easily and much more suddenly than most of us fall asleep. Trance states are a crucial part of every ceremony. In some, fifty or sixty people may fall, one after the other ("like a string of firecrackers going off," as one observer puts it), emerging anywhere from five minutes to several hours later, totally unaware of what they have been doing and convinced, despite the amnesia, that they have had the most extraordinary and deeply satisfying experience a man can have. What does one learn about human nature from this sort of thing and from the thousand similarly peculiar things anthropologists discover, investigate, and describe? That the Balinese are peculiar sorts of beings, South Sea Martians? That they are just the same as we at base, but with some peculiar, but really incidental, customs we do not happen to have gone in for? That they are innately gifted or even instinctively driven in certain directions rather than others? Or that human nature does not exist and men are pure and simply what their culture makes them?

It is among such interpretations as these, all unsatisfactory, that anthropology has attempted to find its way to a more viable concept of man, one in which culture, and the variability of culture, would be taken into account rather than written off as caprice and prejudice, and yet, at the same time, one in which the governing principle of the field, "the basic unity of mankind," would not be turned into an empty phrase. To take the giant step away from the uniformitarian view of human nature is, so far as the study of man is concerned, to leave the Garden. To entertain the idea that the diversity of custom across time and over space is not a mere matter of garb and appearance, of stage settings and comedic masques, is to entertain also the idea that humanity is as various in its essence as it is in its expression. And with that reflection some well-fastened philosophical moorings are loosed and an uneasy drifting into perilous waters begins.

Perilous, because if one discards the notion that Man with a capital "M," is to be looked for "behind," "under," or "beyond" his customs and replaces it with the notion that man, uncapitalized, is to be looked for "in" them, one is in some danger of losing sight of him altogether. Either he dissolves, without residue, into his time and place, a child and a perfect captive of his age, or he becomes a conscripted soldier in a vast Tolstoian army, engulfed in one or another of the terrible historical determinisms with which we have been plagued from Hegel forward. We have had, and to some extent still have, both of these aberrations in the social sciences – one marching under the banner of cultural relativism, the other under that of cultural evolution. But we also have had, and more commonly, attempts to avoid them by seeking in culture patterns themselves the defining elements of a human existence which, although not constant in expression, are yet distinctive in character.

II

Attempts to locate man amid the body of his customs have taken several directions, adopted diverse tactics; but they have all, or virtually all, proceeded in terms of a single overall intellectual strategy: what I will call, so as to have a stick to beat it with, the "stratigraphic" conception of the relations between biological, psychological, social, and cultural factors in human life. In this conception, man is a composite of "levels," each superimposed upon those beneath it and underpinning those above it. As one analyzes man, one peels off layer after layer, each such layer being complete and irreducible in itself, revealing another, quite different sort of layer underneath. Strip off the motley forms of culture and one finds the structural and functional regularities of social organization. Peel off these in turn and one finds the underlying psychological factors – "basic needs" or what-have-you – that support and make them possible. Peel off psychological factors and one is left with the biological foundations – anatomical, physiological, neurological – of the whole edifice of human life.

The attraction of this sort of conceptualization, aside from the fact that it guaranteed the established academic disciplines their independence and sovereignty, was that it seemed to make it possible to have one's cake and eat it. One did not have to assert that man's culture was all there was to him in order to claim that it was, nonetheless, an essential and irreducible, even a paramount ingredient in his nature. Cultural facts could be interpreted against the background of noncultural facts without dissolving them into that background or dissolving that background into them. Man was a hierarchically stratified animal, a sort of evolutionary deposit, in whose definition each level – organic, psychological, social, and cultural – had an assigned and incontestable place. To see what he really was, we had to superimpose findings from the various relevant sciences – anthropology, sociology, psychology, biology – upon one another like so many patterns in a *moiré*; and when that was done, the cardinal importance of the

cultural level, the only one distinctive to man, would naturally appear, as would what it had to tell us, in its own right, about what he really was. For the eighteenth century image of man as the naked reasoner that appeared when he took his cultural costumes off, the anthropology of the late nineteenth and early twentieth centuries substituted the image of man as the transfigured animal that appeared when he put them on.

At the level of concrete research and specific analysis, this grand strategy came down, first, to a hunt for universals in culture, for empirical uniformities that, in the face of the diversity of customs around the world and over time, could be found everywhere in about the same form, and, second, to an effort to relate such universals, once found, to the established constants of human biology, psychology, and social organization. If some customs could be ferreted out of the cluttered catalogue of world culture as common to all local variants of it, and if these could then be connected in a determinate manner with certain invariant points of reference on the subcultural levels, then at least some progress might be made toward specifying which cultural traits are essential to human existence and which merely adventitious, peripheral, or ornamental. In such a way, anthropology could determine cultural dimensions of a concept of man commensurate with the dimensions provided, in a similar way, by biology, psychology, or sociology.

In essence, this is not altogether a new idea. The notion of a *consensus gentium* (a consensus of all mankind) – the notion that there are some things that all men will be found to agree upon as right, real, just, or attractive and that these things are, therefore, in fact right, real, just, or attractive – was present in the Enlightenment and probably has been present in some form or another in all ages and climes. It is one of those ideas that occur to almost anyone sooner or later. Its development in modern anthropology, however – beginning with Clark Wissler's elaboration in the 1920s of what he called "the universal cultural pattern," through Bronislaw Malinowski's presentation of a list of "universal institutional types" in the early forties, up to G. P. Murdock's elaboration of a set of "common-denominators of culture" during and since World War II – added something new. It added the notion that, to quote Clyde Kluckhohn, perhaps the most persuasive of the *consensus gentium* theorists, "some aspects of culture take their specific forms solely as a result of historical accidents; others are tailored by forces which can properly be designated as universal."[5] With this, man's cultural life is split in two: part of it is, like Mascou's actors' garb, independent of men's Newtonian "inward motions"; part is an emanation of those motions themselves. The question that then arises is: Can this halfway house between the eighteenth and twentieth centuries really stand?

Whether it can or not depends on whether the dualism between empirically universal aspects of culture rooted in subcultural realities and empirically variable aspects not so rooted can be established and sustained. And this, in turn, demands (1) that the universals proposed be substantial ones and not empty categories; (2) that they be specifically grounded in particular biological, psychological, or sociological processes, not just vaguely associated with "underlying realities"; and (3) that they can convincingly be defended as core elements in a definition of humanity in comparison with which the much more numerous cultural particularities are of clearly secondary importance. On all three of these counts it seems to me that the *consensus gentium* approach fails; rather than moving toward the essentials of the human situation it moves away from them.

The reason the first of these requirements – that the proposed universals be substantial ones and not empty or near-empty categories – has not been met is that it cannot be. There is a logical conflict between asserting that, say, "religion," "marriage," or "property" are empirical universals and giving them very much in the way of specific content, for to say that they are empirical universals is to say that they have the same content, and to say they have the same content is to fly in the face of the undeniable fact that they do not. If one defines religion generally and indeterminately – as man's most fundamental orientation to reality, for example – then one cannot at the same time assign to that orientation a highly circumstantial content; for clearly what composes the most fundamental orientation to reality among the transported Aztecs, lifting pulsing hearts torn live from the chests of human sacrifices toward the heavens, is not what comprises it among the stolid Zuñi, dancing their great mass supplications

to the benevolent gods of rain. The obsessive ritualism and unbuttoned polytheism of the Hindus express a rather different view of what the "really real" is really like from the uncompromising monotheism and austere legalism of Sunni Islam. Even if one does try to get down to less abstract levels and assert, as Kluckhohn did, that a concept of the afterlife is universal, or as Malinowski did, that a sense of Providence is universal, the same contradiction haunts one. To make the generalization about an afterlife stand up alike for the Confucians and the Calvinists, the Zen Buddhists and the Tibetan Buddhists, one has to define it in most general terms, indeed – so general, in fact, that whatever force it seems to have virtually evaporates. So, too, with any notion of a sense of Providence, which can include under its wing both Navajo notions about the relations of gods to men and Trobriand ones. And as with religion, so with "marriage," "trade," and all the rest of what A. L. Kroeber aptly called "fake universals," down to so seemingly tangible a matter as "shelter." That everywhere people mate and produce children, have some sense of mine and thine, and protect themselves in one fashion or another from rain and sun are neither false nor, from some points of view, unimportant; but they are hardly very much help in drawing a portrait of man that will be a true and honest likeness and not an unteneted "John Q. Public" sort of cartoon.

My point, which should be clear and I hope will become even clearer in a moment, is not that there are no generalizations that can be made about man as man, save that he is a most various animal, or that the study of culture has nothing to contribute toward the uncovering of such generalizations. My point is that such generalizations are not to be discovered through a Baconian search for cultural universals, a kind of public-opinion polling of the world's peoples in search of a *consensus gentium* that does not in fact exist, and, further, that the attempt to do so leads to precisely the sort of relativism the whole approach was expressly designed to avoid. "Zuñi culture prizes restraint," Kluckhohn writes; "Kwakiutl culture encourages exhibitionism on the part of the individual. These are contrasting values, but in adhering to them the Zuñi and Kwakiutl show their allegiance to a universal value; the prizing of the distinctive norms of one's culture."[6] This is sheer evasion, but it is only more apparent, not more evasive, than discussions of cultural universals in general. What, after all, does it avail us to say, with Herskovits, that "morality is a universal, and so is enjoyment of beauty, and some standard for truth," if we are forced in the very next sentence, as he is, to add that "the many forms these concepts take are but products of the particular historical experience of the societies that manifest them"?[7] Once one abandons uniformitarianism, even if, like the *consensus gentium* theorists, only partially and uncertainly, relativism is a genuine danger; but it can be warded off only by facing directly and fully the diversities of human culture, the Zuñi's restraint and the Kwakiutl's exhibitionism, and embracing them within the body of one's concept of man, not by gliding past them with vague tautologies and forceless banalities.

Of course, the difficulty of stating cultural universals which are at the same time substantial also hinders fulfillment of the second requirement facing the *consensus gentium* approach, that of grounding such universals in particular biological, psychological, or sociological processes. But there is more to it than that: the "stratigraphic" conceptualization of the relationships between cultural and noncultural factors hinders such a grounding even more effectively. Once culture, psyche, society, and organism have been converted into separate scientific "levels," complete and autonomous in themselves, it is very hard to bring them back together again.

The most common way of trying to do so is through the utilization of what are called "invariant points of reference." These points are to be found, to quote one of the most famous statements of this strategy – the "Toward a Common Language for the Areas of the Social Sciences" memorandum produced by Talcott Parsons, Kluckhohn, O. H. Taylor, and others in the early forties –

in the nature of social systems, in the biological and psychological nature of the component individuals, in the external situations in which they live and act, in the necessity of coordination in social systems. In [culture] . . . these "foci" of structure are never ignored. They must in some way be "adapted to" or "taken account of."

Cultural universals are conceived to be crystallized responses to these unevadable realities, institutionalized ways of coming to terms with them.

Analysis consists, then, of matching assumed universals to postulated underlying necessities, attempting to show there is some goodness of fit between the two. On the social level, reference is made to such irrefragable facts as that all societies, in order to persist, must reproduce their membership or allocate goods and services, hence the universality of some form of family or some form of trade. On the psychological level, recourse is had to basic needs like personal growth – hence the ubiquity of educational institutions – or to panhuman problems, like the Oedipal predicament – hence the ubiquity of punishing gods and nurturant goddesses. Biologically, there is metabolism and health; culturally, dining customs and curing procedures. And so on. The tack is to look at underlying human requirements of some sort or other and then to try to show that those aspects of culture that are universal are, to use Kluckhohn's figure again, "tailored" by these requirements.

The problem here is, again, not so much whether in a general way this sort of congruence exists, but whether it is more than a loose and indeterminate one. It is not difficult to relate some human institutions to what science (or common sense) tells us are requirements for human existence, but it is very much more difficult to state this relationship in an unequivocal form. Not only does almost any institution serve a multiplicity of social, psychological, and organic needs (so that to say marriage is a mere reflex of the social need to reproduce, or that dining customs are a reflex of metabolic necessities, is to court parody), but there is no way to state in any precise and testable way the interlevel relationships that are conceived to hold. Despite first appearances, there is no serious attempt here to apply the concepts and theories of biology, psychology, or even sociology to the analysis of culture (and, or course, not even a suggestion of the reverse exchange) but merely a placing of supposed facts from the cultural and subcultural levels side by side so as to induce a vague sense that some kind of relationship between them – an obscure sort of "tailoring" – obtains. There is no theoretical integration here at all but a mere correlation, and that intuitive, of separate findings. With the levels approach, we can never, even by invoking invariant points of reference," construct genuine functional interconnections between cultural and noncultural factors, only more or less persuasive analogies, parallelisms, suggestions, and affinities.

However, even if I am wrong (as, admittedly, many anthropologists would hold) in claiming that *consensus gentium* approach can produce neither substantial universals nor specific connections between cultural and noncultural phenomena to explain them, the question still remains whether such universals should be taken as the central elements in the definition of man, whether a lowest-common-denominator view of humanity is what we want anyway. This is, of course, now a philosophical question, not as such a scientific one; but the notion that the essence of what it means to be human is most clearly revealed in those features of human culture that are universal rather than in those that are distinctive to this people or that is a prejudice we are not necessarily obliged to share. Is it in grasping such general facts – that man has everywhere some sort of "religion" – or in grasping the richness of this religious phenomenon or that – Balinese trance or Indian ritualism, Aztec human sacrifice or Zuñi raindancing – that we grasp him? Is the fact that "marriage" is universal (if it is) as penetrating a comment on what we are as the facts concerning Himalayan polyandry, or those fantastic Australian marriage rules, or the elaborate bride-price systems of Bantu Africa? The comment that Cromwell was the most typical Englishman of his time precisely in that he was the oddest may be relevant in this connection, too: it may be in the cultural particularities of people – in their oddities – that some of the most instructive revelations of what it is to be generically human are to be found; and the main contribution of the science of anthropology to the construction – or reconstruction – of a concept of man may then lie in showing us how to find them.

III

The major reason why anthropologists have shied away from cultural particularities when it came to a question of defining man and have taken refuge instead in bloodless universals is that, faced as they are with the enormous variation in human behavior, they are haunted by a fear of historicism, of becoming lost in a whirl of cultural relativism so convulsive as to deprive them of any fixed bearings at all. Nor has there not been some occasion for such a fear: Ruth Benedict's *Patterns of Culture*, probably the most popular book in anthropology ever published in this country, with its strange conclusion that anything one group of people is inclined toward doing is worthy of respect by another, is perhaps only the most outstanding example of the awkward positions one can get into by giving oneself over rather too completely to what Marc Bloch called "the thrill of learning singular things." Yet the fear is a bogey. The notion that unless a cultural phenomenon is empirically universal it cannot reflect anything about the nature of man is about as logical as the notion that because sickle-cell anemia is, fortunately, not universal, it cannot tell us anything about human genetic processes. It is not whether phenomena are empirically common that is critical in science – else why should Becquerel have been so interested in the peculiar behavior of uranium? – but whether they can be made to reveal the enduring natural processes that underlie them. Seeing heaven in a grain of sand is not a trick only poets can accomplish.

In short, we need to look for systematic relationships among diverse phenomena, not for substantive identities among similar ones. And to do that with any effectiveness, we need to replace the "stratigraphic" conception of the relations between the various aspects of human existence with a synthetic one; that is, one in which biological, psychological, sociological, and cultural factors can be treated as variables within unitary systems of analysis. The establishment of a common language in the social sciences is not a matter of mere coordination of terminologies or, worse yet, of coining artificial new ones; nor is it a matter of imposing a single set of categories upon the area as a whole. It is a matter of integrating different types of theories and concepts in such a way that one can formulate meaningful propositions embodying findings now sequestered in separate fields of study.

In attempting to launch such an integration from the anthropological side and to reach, thereby, a more exact image of man, I want to propose two ideas. The first of these is that culture is best seen not as complexes of concrete behavior patterns –

customs, usages, traditions, habit clusters – as has, by and large, been the case up to now, but as a set of control mechanisms – plans, recipes, rules, instructions (what computer engineers call "programs") – for the governing of behavior. The second idea is that man is precisely the animal most desperately dependent upon such extragenetic, outside-the-skin control mechanisms, such cultural programs, for ordering his behavior.

Neither of these ideas is entirely new, but a number of recent developments, both within anthropology and in other sciences (cybernetics, information theory, neurology, molecular genetics) have made them susceptible of more precise statement as well as lending them a degree of empirical support they did not previously have. And out of such reformulations of the concept of culture and of the role of culture in human life comes, in turn, a definition of man stressing not so much the empirical commonalities in his behavior, from place to place and time to time, but rather the mechanisms by whose agency the breadth and indeterminateness of his inherent capacities are reduced to the narrowness and specificity of his actual accomplishments. One of the most significant facts about us may finally be that we all begin with the natural equipment to live a thousand kinds of life but end in the end having lived only one.

The "control mechanism" view of culture begins with the assumption that human thought is basically both social and public – that its natural habitat is the house yard, the marketplace, and the town square. Thinking consists not of "happenings in the head" (though happenings there and elsewhere are necessary for it to occur) but of a traffic in what have been called, by G. H. Mead and others, significant symbols – words for the most part but also gestures, drawings, musical sounds, mechanical devices like clocks, or natural objects like jewels – anything, in fact, that is disengaged from its mere actuality and used to impose meaning upon experience. From the point of view of any particular individual, such symbols are largely given. He finds them already current in the community when he is born, and they remain, with some additions, subtractions, and partial alterations he may or may not have had a hand in, in circulation after he dies. While he lives he uses them, or some of them, sometimes deliberately and with care, most often spontaneously and with ease, but always with the same end in view: to put a construction upon the events through which he lives, to orient himself within "the ongoing course of experienced things," to adopt a vivid phrase of John Dewey's.

Man is so in need of such symbolic sources of illumination to find his bearings in the world because the nonsymbolic sort that are constitutionally ingrained in his body cast so diffused a light. The behavior patterns of lower animals are, at least to a much greater extent, given to them with their physical structure; genetic sources of information order their actions within much narrower ranges of variation, the narrower and more thoroughgoing the lower the animal. For man, what are innately given are extremely general response capacities, which, although they make possible far greater plasticity, complexity, and, on the scattered occasions when everything works as it should, effectiveness of behavior, leave it much less precisely regulated. This, then, is the second face of our argument: Undirected by culture patterns – organized systems of significant symbols – man's behavior would be virtually ungovernable, a mere chaos of pointless acts and exploding emotions, his experience virtually shapeless. Culture, the accumulated totality of such patterns, is not just an ornament of human existence but – the principal basis of its specificity – an essential condition for it.

Within anthropology some of the most telling evidence in support of such a position comes from recent advances in our understanding of what used to be called the descent of man: the emergence of *Homo sapiens* out of his general primate background. Of these advances three are of critical importance: (1) the discarding of a sequential view of the relations between the physical evolution and the cultural development of man in favor of an overlap or interactive view; (2) the discovery that the bulk of the biological changes that produced modern man out of his most immediate progenitors took place in the central nervous system and most especially in the brain; (3) the realization that man is, in physical terms, an incomplete, an unfinished, animal; that what sets him off most graphically from nonmen is less his sheer ability to learn (great as that is) than how much and what particular sorts of things he *has* to learn before he is able to function at all. Let me take each of these points in turn.

The traditional view of the relations between the biological and the cultural advance of man was that the former, the biological, was for all intents and purposes completed before the latter, the cultural, began. That is to say, it was again stratigraphic: Man's physical being evolved, through the usual mechanisms of genetic variation and natural selection, up to the point where his anatomical structure had arrived at more or less the status at which we find it today; then cultural development got under way. At some particular stage in his phylogenetic history, a marginal genetic change of some sort rendered him capable of producing and carrying culture, and thenceforth his form of adaptive response to environmental pressures was almost exclusively cultural rather than genetic. As he spread over the globe, he wore furs in cold climates and loin cloths (or nothing at all) in warm ones; he didn't alter his innate mode of response to environmental temperature. He made weapons to extend his inherited predatory powers and cooked foods to render a wider range of them digestible. Man became man, the story continues, when, having crossed some mental Rubicon, he became able to transmit "knowledge, belief, law, morals, custom" (to quote the items of Sir Edward Tylor's classical definition of culture) to his descendants and his neighbors through teaching and to acquire them from his ancestors and his neighbors through learning. After that magical moment, the advance of the hominids depended almost entirely on cultural accumulation, on the slow growth of conventional practices, rather than, as it had for ages past, on physical organic change.

The only trouble is that such a moment does not seem to have existed. By the most recent estimates the transition to the cultural mode of life took the genus *Homo* several million years to accomplish; and stretched out in such a manner, it involved not one or a handful of marginal genetic changes but a long, complex, and closely ordered sequence of them.

In the current view, the evolution of *Homo sapiens* – modern man – out of his immediate pre*sapiens* background got definitely under way nearly four million years ago with the appearance of the now famous Australopithecines – the so-called ape men

of southern and eastern Africa – and culminated with the emergence of *sapiens* himself only some one to two or three hundred thousand years ago. Thus, as at least elemental forms of cultural, or if you wish protocultural, activity (simple toolmaking, hunting, and so on) seem to have been present among some of the Australopithecines, there was an overlap of, as I say, well over a million years between the beginning of culture and the appearance of man as we know him today. The precise dates – which are tentative and which further research may later alter in one direction or another – are not critical; what is critical is that there was an overlap and that it was a very extended one. The final phases (final to date, at any rate) of the phylogenetic history of man took place in the same grand geological era – the so-called Ice Age – as the initial phases of his cultural history. Men have birthdays, but man does not.

What this means is that culture, rather than being added on, so to speak, to a finished or virtually finished animal, was ingredient, and centrally ingredient, in the production of that animal itself. The slow, steady, almost glacial growth of culture through the Ice Age altered the balance of selection pressures for the evolving *Homo* in such a way as to play a major directive role in his evolution. The perfection of tools, the adoption of organized hunting and gathering practices, the beginnings of true family organization, the discovery of fire, and, most critically, though it is as yet extremely difficult to trace it out in any detail, the increasing reliance upon systems of significant symbols (language, art, myth, ritual) for orientation, communication, and self-control all created for man a new environment to which he was then obliged to adapt. As culture, step by infinitesimal step, accumulated and developed, a selective advantage was given to those individuals in the population most able to take advantage of it – the effective hunter, the persistent gatherer, the adept toolmaker, the resourceful leader – until what had been a small-brained, protohuman *Australopithecus* became the large-brained fully human *Homo sapiens*. Between the cultural pattern, the body, and the brain, a positive feedback system was created in which each shaped the progress of the other, a system in which the interaction among increasing tool use, the changing anatomy of the hand, and the expanding representation of the thumb on the cortex is only one of the more graphic examples. By submitting himself to governance by symbolically mediated programs for producing artifacts, organizing social life, or expressing emotions, man determined, if unwittingly, the culminating stages of his own biological destiny. Quite literally, though quite inadvertently, he created himself.

Though, as I mentioned, there were a number of important changes in the gross anatomy of genus *Homo* during this period of his crystallization – in skull shape, dentition, thumb size, and so on – by far the most important and dramatic were those that evidently took place in the central nervous system; for this was the period when the human brain, and most particularly the forebrain, ballooned into its present top-heavy proportions. The technical problems are complicated and controversial here; but the main point is that though the Australopithecines had a torso and arm configuration not drastically different from our own, and a pelvis and leg formation at least well-launched toward our own, they had cranial capacities hardly larger than those of the living apes – that is to say, about a third to a half of our own. What sets true men off most distinctly from protomen is apparently not overall bodily form but complexity of nervous organization. The overlap period of cultural and biological change seems to have consisted in an intense concentration on neural development and perhaps associated refinements of various behaviors – of the hands, bipedal locomotion, and so on – for which the basic anatomical foundations – mobile shoulders and wrists, a broadened ilium, and so on – had already been securely laid. In itself, this is perhaps not altogether startling; but, combined with what I have already said, it suggests some conclusions about what sort of animal man is that are, I think, rather far not only from those of the eighteenth century but from those of the anthropology of only ten or fifteen years ago.

Most bluntly, it suggests that there is no such thing as a human nature independent of culture. Men without culture would not be the clever savages of Golding's *Lord of the Flies* thrown back upon the cruel wisdom of their animal instincts; nor would they be the nature's noblemen of Enlightenment primitivism or even, as classical anthropological theory would imply, intrinsically talented apes who

had somehow failed to find themselves. They would be unworkable monstrosities with very few useful instincts, fewer recognizable sentiments, and no intellect: mental basket cases. As our central nervous system – and most particularly its crowning curse and glory, the neocortex – grew up in great part in interaction with culture, it is incapable of directing our behavior or organizing our experience without the guidance provided by systems of significant symbols. What happened to us in the Ice Age is that we were obliged to abandon the regularity and precision of detailed genetic control over our conduct for the flexibility and adaptability of a more generalized, though of course no less real, genetic control over it. To supply the additional information necessary to be able to act, we were forced, in turn, to rely more and more heavily on cultural sources – the accumulated fund of significant symbols. Such symbols are thus not mere expressions, instrumentalities, or correlates of our biological, psychological, and social existence; they are prerequisites of it. Without men, no culture, certainly; but equally, and more significantly, without culture, no men.

We are, in sum, incomplete or unfinished animals who complete or finish ourselves through culture – and not through culture in general but through highly particular forms of it: Dobuan and Javanese, Hopi and Italian, upper-class and lower-class, academic and commercial. Man's great capacity for learning, his plasticity, has often been remarked, but what is even more critical is his extreme dependence upon a certain sort of learning: the attainment of concepts, the apprehension and application of specific systems of symbolic meaning. Beavers build dams, birds build nests, bees locate food, baboons organize social groups, and mice mate on the basis of forms of learning that rest predominantly on the instructions encoded in their genes and evoked by appropriate patterns of external stimuli: physical keys inserted into organic locks. But men build dams or shelters, locate food, organize their social groups, or find sexual partners under the guidance of instructions encoded in flow charts and blueprints, hunting lore, moral systems and aesthetic judgments: conceptual structures molding formless talents.

We live, as one writer has neatly put it, in an "information gap." Between what our body tells us and what we have to know in order to function, there is a vacuum we must fill ourselves, and we fill it with information (or misinformation) provided by our culture. The boundary between what is innately controlled and what is culturally controlled in human behavior is an ill-defined and wavering one. Some things are, for all intents and purposes, entirely controlled intrinsically: we need no more cultural guidance to learn how to breathe than a fish needs to learn how to swim. Others are almost certainly largely cultural; we do not attempt to explain on a genetic basis why some men put their trust in centralized planning and others in the free market, though it might be an amusing exercise. Almost all complex human behavior is, of course, the interactive, nonadditive outcome of the two. Our capacity to speak is surely innate; our capacity to speak English is surely cultural. Smiling at pleasing stimuli and frowning at unpleasing ones are surely in some degree genetically determined (even apes screw up their faces at noxious odors); but sardonic smiling and burlesque frowning are equally surely predominantly cultural, as is perhaps demonstrated by the Balinese definition of a madman as someone who, like an American, smiles when there is nothing to laugh at. Between the basic ground plans for our life that our genes lay down – the capacity to speak or to smile – and the precise behavior we in fact execute – speaking English in a certain tone of voice, smiling enigmatically in a delicate social situation – lies a complex set of significant symbols under whose direction we transform the first into the second, the ground plans into the activity.

Our ideas, our values, our acts, even our emotions, are, like our nervous system itself, cultural products – products manufactured, indeed, out of tendencies, capacities, and dispositions with which we were born, but manufactured nonetheless. Chartres is made of stone and glass. But it is not just stone and glass; it is a cathedral, and not only a cathedral, but a particular cathedral built at a particular time by certain members of a particular society. To understand what it means, to perceive it for what it is, you need to know rather more than the generic properties of stone and glass and rather more than what is common to all cathedrals. You need to understand also – and, in my opinion, most critically – the specific concepts of the relations

among God, man, and architecture that, since they have governed its creation, it consequently embodies. It is no different with men: they, too, every last one of them, are cultural artifacts.

IV

Whatever differences they may show, the approaches to the definition of human nature adopted by the Enlightenment and by classical anthropology have one thing in common: they are both basically typological. They endeavor to construct an image of man as a model, an archetype, a Platonic idea or an Aristotelian form, with respect to which actual men – you, me, Churchill, Hitler, and the Bornean headhunter – are but reflections, distortions, approximations. In the Enlightenment case, the elements of this essential type were to be uncovered by stripping the trappings of culture away from actual men and seeing what then was left – natural man. In classical anthropology, it was to be uncovered by factoring out the commonalities in culture and seeing what then appeared – consensual man. In either case, the result is the same as that which tends to emerge in all typological approaches to scientific problems generally: the differences among individuals and among groups of individuals are rendered secondary. Individuality comes to be seen as eccentricity, distinctiveness as accidental deviation from the only legitimate object of study for the true scientist: the underlying, unchanging, normative type. In such an approach, however elaborately formulated and resourcefully defended, living detail is drowned in dead stereotype: we are in quest of a metaphysical entity, Man with a capital "M," in the interests of which we sacrifice the empirical entity we in fact encounter, man with a small "m."

The sacrifice is, however, as unnecessary as it is unavailing. There is no opposition between general theoretical understanding and circumstantial understanding, between synoptic vision and a fine eye for detail. It is, in fact, by its power to draw general propositions out of particular phenomena that a scientific theory – indeed, science itself – is to be judged. If we want to discover what man amounts to, we can only find it in what men are: and what men are, above all other things, is various. It is in understanding that variousness – its range, its nature, its basis, and its implications – that we shall come to construct a concept of human nature that, more than a statistical shadow and less than a primitivist dream, has both substance and truth.

It is here, to come round finally to my title, that the concept of culture has its impact on the concept of man. When seen as a set of symbolic devices for controlling behavior, extrasomatic sources of information, culture provides the link between what men are intrinsically capable of becoming and what they actually, one by one, in fact become. Becoming human is becoming individual, and we become individual under the guidance of cultural patterns, historically created systems of meaning in terms of which we give form, order, point, and direction to our lives. And the cultural patterns involved are not general but specific – not just "marriage" but a particular set of notions about what men and women are like, how spouses should treat one another, or who should properly marry whom; not just "religion" but belief in the wheel of karma, the observance of a month of fasting, or the practice of cattle sacrifice. Man is to be defined neither by his innate capacities alone, as the Enlightenment sought to do, nor by his actual behaviors alone, as much of contemporary social science seeks to do, but rather by the link between them, by the way in which the first is transformed into the second, his generic potentialities focused into his specific performances. It is in man's *career*, in its characteristic course, that we can discern, however dimly, his nature, and though culture is but one element in determining that course, it is hardly the least important. As culture shaped us as a single species – and is no doubt still shaping us – so too it shapes us as separate individuals. This, neither an unchanging subcultural self nor an established cross-cultural consensus, is what we really have in common.

Oddly enough – though on second thought, perhaps not so oddly – many of our subjects seem to realize this more clearly than we anthropologists ourselves. In Java, for example, where I have done much of my work, the people quite flatly say, "To be human is to be Javanese." Small children, boors, simpletons,

the insane, the flagrantly immoral, are said to be *ndurung djawa*, "not yet Javanese." A "normal" adult capable of acting in terms of the highly elaborate system of etiquette, possessed of the delicate aesthetic perceptions associated with music, dance, drama, and textile design, responsive to the subtle promptings of the divine residing in the stillnesses of each individual's inward-turning consciousness, is *sampun djawa*, "already Javanese," that is, already human. To be human is not just to breathe; it is to control one's breathing, by yogalike techniques, so as to hear in inhalation and exhalation the literal voice of God pronouncing His own name – "hu Allah." It is not just to talk, it is to utter the appropriate words and phrases in the appropriate social situations in the appropriate tone of voice and with the appropriate evasive indirection. It is not just to eat; it is to prefer certain foods cooked in certain ways and to follow a rigid table etiquette in consuming them. It is not even just to feel but to feel certain quite distinctively Javanese (and essentially untranslatable) emotions – "patience," "detachment," "resignation," "respect."

To be human here is thus not to be Everyman; it is to be a particular kind of man, and of course men differ: "Other fields," the Javanese say, "other grasshoppers." Within the society, differences are recognized, too – the way a rice peasant becomes human and Javanese differs from the way a civil servant does. This is not a matter of tolerance and ethical relativism, for not all ways of being human are regarded as equally admirable by far; the way the local Chinese go about it is, for example, intensely dispraised. The point is that there are different ways; and to shift to the anthropologist's perspective now, it is in a systematic review and analysis of these – of the Plains Indian's bravura, the Hindu's obsessiveness, the Frenchman's rationalism, the Berber's anarchism, the American's optimism (to list a series of tags I should not like to have to defend as such) – that we shall find out what it is, or can be, to be a man.

We must, in short, descend into detail, past the misleading tags, past the metaphysical types, past the empty similarities to grasp firmly the essential character of not only the various cultures but the various sorts of individuals within each culture, if we wish to encounter humanity face to face. In this area, the road to the general, to the revelatory simplicities of science, lies through a concern with the particular, the circumstantial, the concrete, but a concern organized and directed in terms of the sort of theoretical analyses that I have touched upon – analyses of physical evolution, of the functioning of the nervous system, of social organization, of psychological process, of cultural patterning, and so on – and, most especially, in terms of the interplay among them. That is to say, the road lies, like any genuine Quest, through a terrifying complexity.

"Leave him alone for a moment or two," Robert Lowell writes, not as one might suspect of the anthropologist but of that other eccentric inquirer into the nature of man, Nathaniel Hawthorne.

> Leave him alone for a moment or two,
> and you'll see him with his head
> bent down, brooding, brooding,
> eyes fixed on some chip,
> some stone, some common plant,
> the commonest thing,
> as if it were the clue.
> The disturbed eyes rise,
> furtive, foiled, dissatisfied
> from meditation on the true
> and insignificant.[8]

Bent over his own chips, stones, and common plants, the anthropologist broods, too, upon the true and insignificant, glimpsing in it, or so he thinks, fleetingly and insecurely, the disturbing, changeful image of himself.

Notes

1 A. O. Lovejoy, *Essays in the History of Ideas* (New York, 1960), p. 173.
2 Ibid., p. 80.
3 "Preface to Shakespeare," *Johnson on Shakespeare* (London, 1931), pp. 11–12.
4 From the Preface to *Iphigénie*.
5 A. L. Kroeber, ed., *Anthropology Today* (Chicago, 1953), p. 516.
6 C. Kluckhohn, *Culture and Behavior* (New York, 1962), p. 280.
7 M. J. Herskovits, *Cultural Anthropology* (New York, 1955), p. 364.
8 Reprinted with permission of Farrar, Straus & Giroux, Inc., and Faber & Faber, Ltd., from "Hawthorne," in *For the Union Dead*, p. 39. Copyright © 1964 by Robert Lowell.

E
X
E
R
C
I
S
E
S

1 If you had written this chapter from your perspective (rather than mine), what VIPs would you have chosen from your life and culture? People? Places? Performances? For each one, write a bit about why your choices are meaningful to you personally.

2 Then, for each, try to think about why your choices reflect larger groups to which you belong or with which you identify. (Hint: Are your choices typical or atypical of men/women? Students? People who have grown up in the region in which you grew up?)

Index